FORMS OF SPEECHES

24 The Informative Speech
25 The Persuasive Speech
26 Developing Arguments for the Persuasive Speech
27 Organizing the Persuasive Speech
28 Special Occasion Speeches

pages 317–422

SPEAKING BEYOND THE SPEECH CLASSROOM

29 Preparing Online Presentations
30 Collaborating and Presenting in Groups
31 Speaking in Other College Courses
32 Business and Professional Presentations

pages 423–480

SAMPLE SPEECHES

Sample Informative Speech
Sample Persuasive Speech
Sample Special Occasion Speech

pages 481–502

REFERENCE AND RESEARCH APPENDICES

A. Handling Question-and-Answer Sessions
B. Preparing for Mediated Communication
C. Public Discussions: Panels, Symposiums, and Forums
D. Commonly Mispronounced Words
E–I. Documentation Styles: *Chicago*, APA, MLA, CBE/CSE, IEEE
J. Glossary

pages 503–551

P9-CPZ-575

Quick Access Menu

Using *A Speaker's Guidebook*

The menu to the left briefly displays the book's content. Each menu box corresponds to a tabbed divider in the text. The dividers contain more detailed lists of contents in each section and are followed by "Speaker's Reference" pages that offer executive-like summaries of the subsequent chapters. At the back of the book, you will find other reference aids:

- The index
- A list of feature boxes and checklists
- A list of sample speeches
- A list of visual guides

WEB Using *A Speaker's Guidebook* Online Tools

Icons throughout the book refer the reader to the *Speaker's Guidebook* companion Web site, where a wealth of online learning tools are available to support and extend concepts in the book and help with the speech-building process—chapter quizzes, sample speeches, more than 100 video clips including short examples and full speeches, suggested speech topics, outlining and biography tools, and more.
bedfordstmartins.com/speakersguide

To Find Out More

For more on using the book's reference aids and online tools, turn to "How to Use This Book" (p. v), which includes tutorials that show you how to get quick answers to your questions.

A SPEAKER'S GUIDEBOOK

Text and Reference

FIFTH EDITION

A SPEAKER'S GUIDEBOOK
Text and Reference

Dan O'Hair
University of Kentucky

Rob Stewart
Texas Tech University

Hannah Rubenstein

Bedford/St. Martin's
Boston • New York

For Bedford/St. Martin's

Publisher for Communication: Erika Gutierrez
Developmental Editor: Stephanie Ventura
Associate Editor: Mae Klinger
Senior Production Editor: Harold Chester
Production Supervisor: Andrew Ensor
Senior Marketing Manager: Adrienne Petsick
Editorial Assistant: Mollie Laffin-Rose
Copy Editor: Denise Quirk
Indexer: Melanie Belkin
Photo Researcher: Julie Tesser
Permissions Manager: Kalina Ingham Hintz
Art Director: Lucy Krikorian
Text Design: Jerilyn Bockorick
Cover Design: Marine Miller
Composition: Nesbitt Graphics, Inc.
Printing and Binding: Quad/Graphics Taunton

President: Joan E. Feinberg
Editorial Director: Denise B. Wydra
Director of Development: Erica T. Appel
Director of Marketing: Karen R. Soeltz
Director of Production: Susan W. Brown
Associate Director, Editorial Production: Elise S. Kaiser
Managing Editor: Shuli Traub

Library of Congress Control Number: 2011924032

Manufactured in the United States of America.

6   5   4

f   e

For information, write: Bedford/St. Martin's, 75 Arlington Street,
Boston, MA 02116   (617-399-4000)

ISBN: 978-0-312-64286-0 (Student Edition)
ISBN: 978-0-312-67886-9 (Student Edition with *The Essential Guide to Rhetoric*)

Acknowledgments

How to Use This Book

A *Speaker's Guidebook: Text and Reference* has been carefully designed to help you easily and quickly access the information you need to prepare speeches and presentations. The text may be used not only in a public speaking course but also in other college courses, in your working life after college, and in your civic activities in your community.

The Main Menu and Table of Contents

The twelve tab dividers (discussed in more detail on the next page) allow the book to flip open easily, and the book's binding lets it lie flat. On the inside front cover you will find the **Main Menu** that offers a listing of the thirty-two chapters in the text and a visual link to help you find each one. For even more information or to find a specific topic, simply turn to the full **table of contents** on p. xxvii.

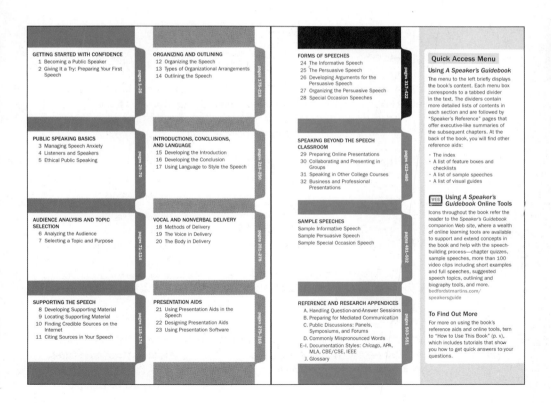

GETTING STARTED WITH CONFIDENCE
1 Becoming a Public Speaker
2 Giving It a Try: Preparing Your First Speech

pages 1–28

PUBLIC SPEAKING BASICS
3 Managing Speech Anxiety
4 Listeners and Speakers
5 Ethical Public Speaking

pages 29–70

AUDIENCE ANALYSIS AND TOPIC SELECTION
6 Analyzing the Audience
7 Selecting a Topic and Purpose

pages 71–114

SUPPORTING THE SPEECH
8 Developing Supporting Material
9 Locating Supporting Material
10 Finding Credible Sources on the Internet
11 Citing Sources in Your Speech

pages 115–174

ORGANIZING AND OUTLINING
12 Organizing the Speech
13 Types of Organizational Arrangements
14 Outlining the Speech

pages 175–218

INTRODUCTIONS, CONCLUSIONS, AND LANGUAGE
15 Developing the Introduction
16 Developing the Conclusion
17 Using Language to Style the Speech

pages 219–260

VOCAL AND NONVERBAL DELIVERY
18 Methods of Delivery
19 The Voice in Delivery
20 The Body in Delivery

pages 261–278

PRESENTATION AIDS
21 Using Presentation Aids in the Speech
22 Designing Presentation Aids
23 Using Presentation Software

pages 279–316

FORMS OF SPEECHES
24 The Informative Speech
25 The Persuasive Speech
26 Developing Arguments for the Persuasive Speech
27 Organizing the Persuasive Speech
28 Special Occasion Speeches

pages 317–422

SPEAKING BEYOND THE SPEECH CLASSROOM
29 Preparing Online Presentations
30 Collaborating and Presenting in Groups
31 Speaking in Other College Courses
32 Business and Professional Presentations

pages 423–480

SAMPLE SPEECHES
Sample Informative Speech
Sample Persuasive Speech
Sample Special Occasion Speech

pages 481–502

REFERENCE AND RESEARCH APPENDICES
A. Handling Question-and-Answer Sessions
B. Preparing for Mediated Communication
C. Public Discussions: Panels, Symposiums, and Forums
D. Commonly Mispronounced Words
E–I. Documentation Styles: *Chicago*, APA, MLA, CBE/CSE, IEEE
J. Glossary

pages 503–551

Quick Access Menu

Using *A Speaker's Guidebook*

The menu to the left briefly displays the book's content. Each menu box corresponds to a tabbed divider in the text. The dividers contain more detailed lists of contents in each section and are followed by "Speaker's Reference" pages that offer executive-like summaries of the subsequent chapters. At the back of the book, you will find other reference aids:

- The index
- A list of feature boxes and checklists
- A list of sample speeches
- A list of visual guides

Using *A Speaker's Guidebook* Online Tools

Icons throughout the book refer the reader to the *Speaker's Guidebook* companion Web site, where a wealth of online learning tools are available to support and extend concepts in the book and help with the speech-building process—chapter quizzes, sample speeches, more than 100 video clips including short examples and full speeches, suggested speech topics, outlining and biography tools, and more. bedfordstmartins.com/speakersguide

To Find Out More

For more on using the book's reference aids and online tools, turn to "How to Use This Book" (p. v), which includes tutorials that show you how to get quick answers to your questions.

The Tabs

A Speaker's Guidebook is divided into twelve tabbed sections that are arranged into four color banks—blue, orange, purple, and green. Each section opens with a tab divider; the front of the tab divider identifies the tab name and the chapters contained in that section. The back indicates chapter titles and detailed information about major topics covered. To find the specific information you want, look for the appropriate tab and open the book to it.

The back of each tab divider offers a table of contents for the chapters within that tabbed section. The **Speaker's Reference** pages for the chapters within the section follow each tab divider.

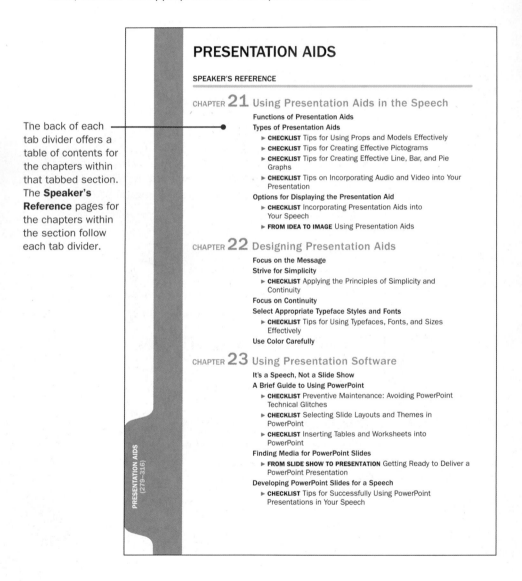

PRESENTATION AIDS

SPEAKER'S REFERENCE

CHAPTER 21 Using Presentation Aids in the Speech

Functions of Presentation Aids
Types of Presentation Aids
▶ **CHECKLIST** Tips for Using Props and Models Effectively
▶ **CHECKLIST** Tips for Creating Effective Pictograms
▶ **CHECKLIST** Tips for Creating Effective Line, Bar, and Pie Graphs
▶ **CHECKLIST** Tips on Incorporating Audio and Video into Your Presentation
Options for Displaying the Presentation Aid
▶ **CHECKLIST** Incorporating Presentation Aids into Your Speech
▶ **FROM IDEA TO IMAGE** Using Presentation Aids

CHAPTER 22 Designing Presentation Aids

Focus on the Message
Strive for Simplicity
▶ **CHECKLIST** Applying the Principles of Simplicity and Continuity
Focus on Continuity
Select Appropriate Typeface Styles and Fonts
▶ **CHECKLIST** Tips for Using Typefaces, Fonts, and Sizes Effectively
Use Color Carefully

CHAPTER 23 Using Presentation Software

It's a Speech, Not a Slide Show
A Brief Guide to Using PowerPoint
▶ **CHECKLIST** Preventive Maintenance: Avoiding PowerPoint Technical Glitches
▶ **CHECKLIST** Selecting Slide Layouts and Themes in PowerPoint
▶ **CHECKLIST** Inserting Tables and Worksheets into PowerPoint
Finding Media for PowerPoint Slides
▶ **FROM SLIDE SHOW TO PRESENTATION** Getting Ready to Deliver a PowerPoint Presentation
Developing PowerPoint Slides for a Speech
▶ **CHECKLIST** Tips for Successfully Using PowerPoint Presentations in Your Speech

PRESENTATION AIDS
(279–316)

Speaker's Reference Sections

You may well find one of the most useful features of *A Speaker's Guidebook* to be its **Speaker's Reference** pages that immediately follow each tab divider. These pages provide executive-like summaries of the material covered within the subsequent chapters. A list of key terms in the chapters appears at the end of the Speaker's Reference pages, just before the opening of the first chapter within that tabbed section.

Speaker's Reference pages offer a quick review of the most important information in subsequent chapters through summaries and key terms.

To refer to the full in-text coverage of a topic, simply flip to the page indicated in parentheses.

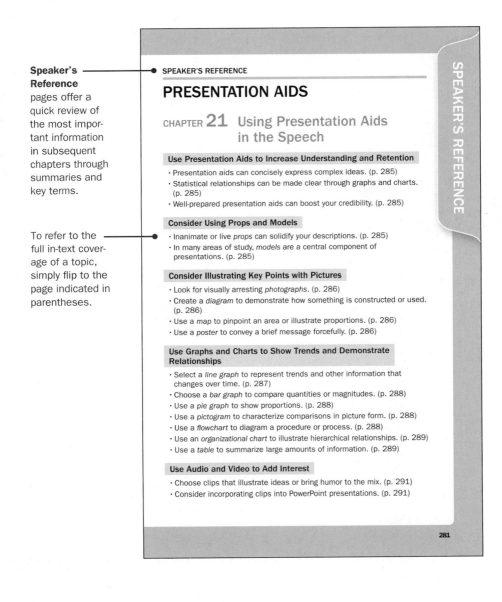

SPEAKER'S REFERENCE

PRESENTATION AIDS

CHAPTER **21** Using Presentation Aids in the Speech

Use Presentation Aids to Increase Understanding and Retention

· Presentation aids can concisely express complex ideas. (p. 285)
· Statistical relationships can be made clear through graphs and charts. (p. 285)
· Well-prepared presentation aids can boost your credibility. (p. 285)

Consider Using Props and Models

· Inanimate or live *props* can solidify your descriptions. (p. 285)
· In many areas of study, *models* are a central component of presentations. (p. 285)

Consider Illustrating Key Points with Pictures

· Look for visually arresting *photographs*. (p. 286)
· Create a *diagram* to demonstrate how something is constructed or used. (p. 286)
· Use a *map* to pinpoint an area or illustrate proportions. (p. 286)
· Use a *poster* to convey a brief message forcefully. (p. 286)

Use Graphs and Charts to Show Trends and Demonstrate Relationships

· Select a *line graph* to represent trends and other information that changes over time. (p. 287)
· Choose a *bar graph* to compare quantities or magnitudes. (p. 288)
· Use a *pie graph* to show proportions. (p. 288)
· Use a *pictogram* to characterize comparisons in picture form. (p. 288)
· Use a *flowchart* to diagram a procedure or process. (p. 288)
· Use an *organizational chart* to illustrate hierarchical relationships. (p. 289)
· Use a *table* to summarize large amounts of information. (p. 289)

Use Audio and Video to Add Interest

· Choose clips that illustrate ideas or bring humor to the mix. (p. 291)
· Consider incorporating clips into PowerPoint presentations. (p. 291)

SPEAKER'S REFERENCE

281

A Speaker's Guidebook New Media

WEB Icons throughout the book refer the reader to the book's companion Web site, **bedfordstmartins.com/speakersguide**, where a wealth of online learning tools are available to support and extend concepts in the book and help you with the speech-building process. Some assets require premium access, which is *free* when packaged with the book or an affordable option available directly through the book's companion Web site.

WEB Chapter quizzes

The Selective Nature of Listening   **WEB** Chapter quizzes

Most of us understand that giving a speech involves preparation and practice, but fewer recognize the hard work that listening requires. Rather than being a passive activity that simply "happens" to us, listening is a complex behavior. In contrast to hearing, which is the physiological process of perceiving sound and largely reflexive or automatic in nature, **listening** is the conscious act of recognizing, understanding, and accurately interpreting the messages communicated by others.

Visual Guides

Visual Guides (ten total) walk you through the most challenging aspects of the speechmaking process—from research and organization through creating presentation aids. A complete list of visual guides is available on the inside back cover.

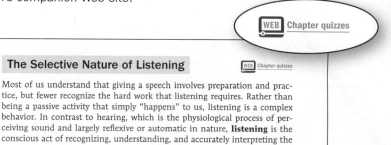

The Checklists

Useful general checklists located throughout the text are another hallmark of *A Speaker's Guidebook*. These checklists offer step-by-step directions, assessment exercises, and content reviews. Consult one of the ninety checklists to review key concepts and to get tips on applying those concepts to your own presentations. For a full list of *Checklists,* see p. 595.

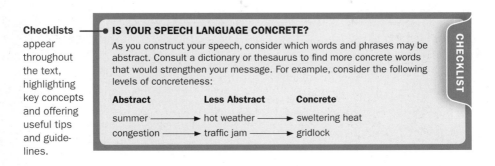

Checklists appear throughout the text, highlighting key concepts and offering useful tips and guidelines.

IS YOUR SPEECH LANGUAGE CONCRETE?

As you construct your speech, consider which words and phrases may be abstract. Consult a dictionary or thesaurus to find more concrete words that would strengthen your message. For example, consider the following levels of concreteness:

Abstract	Less Abstract	Concrete
summer ⟶	hot weather ⟶	sweltering heat
congestion ⟶	traffic jam ⟶	gridlock

CHECKLIST

The Glossary

When you wish to verify the meaning of a key term, refer to the glossary that begins on p. 530. There you will find explanations of the many terms associated with the fields of rhetoric and communication. These important terms are vital to your understanding of the book's content and are likely to appear on tests.

List of Boxed Features and Full-Text Speeches

Throughout *A Speaker's Guidebook* you will find three types of special boxed features. "A Cultural Perspective" explores the many ways that culture informs public speaking; "ESL Speaker's Notes" offer detailed guidance for non-native speakers; and "Ethically Speaking" boxes offer students ways to ensure an ethical stance when speaking. Throughout, you also will find twelve full-text sample speeches that can serve as models to help you learn the art and craft of creating your own speeches. For a full list of the boxes and sample speeches, refer to pp. 594 and 596.

Preface

A Speaker's Guidebook: Text and Reference is a groundbreaking public speaking text that offers better solutions to the wide range of challenges that students face. Adopted at more than eight hundred schools since the first edition was published in 2001, the book grew out of the realization that public speaking courses are not ends in themselves. The principles and skills taught in this book are meant to be of lasting use to students and to help them beyond merely meeting the requirements of the course—in their other college courses, in their working lives after college, and in the vital roles they may play in their communities. The book functions not only as a brief yet comprehensive classroom text but also as a unique and useful post-classroom reference, one that will prove an invaluable resource in any public speaking situation.

The key goal of *A Speaker's Guidebook* has always been to effectively address the fundamental challenges of public speaking, both inside and outside the speech classroom. And we recognize that as times have changed—especially due to advances in technology—the fundamental challenges of presentational speaking have evolved as well. Thus, with the support of hundreds of instructors nationwide, we have developed a book that students use and keep, that reinforces basic skills while providing cutting-edge coverage, and that helps students apply what they've learned to their own speeches.

The Story of the New Edition

In preparing this new edition, we turned to more than one hundred instructors and experts from across the United States to learn about the course challenges they face and to unearth new developments in the field. These instructors told us that students keep bumping up against the same obstacles that have derailed them for years, such as competency in basic skills like organizing and outlining, overcoming speech anxiety, and applying lessons from the course to their own speeches. We also learned about newer obstacles stemming largely from developments in technology: for example, the fact that today, many students conduct research for their speeches online and that students often are unsure how to prepare and present presentations across a wide range of *mediated* venues—synchronous video conferences, vlogs, YouTube postings, and beyond.

Based on this knowledge, in this new edition we've aimed at the perennial problems *and* at today's new challenges by creating a book that offers even better solutions:

- Stronger coverage of public speaking fundamentals
- Cutting-edge guidance for preparing and presenting speeches in the *digital world*
- Improved learning tools that help students apply what they learn to their own speeches
- A new design and streamlined coverage that make the book more engaging and even easier to use

In developing this edition, we have also harnessed the power of digital media to offer powerful new learning tools that will help students overcome fundamental course challenges in ways impossible even a few years ago.

Stronger Coverage of Public Speaking Fundamentals

Because many students struggle throughout the speech preparation process—from choosing and narrowing a topic and researching the speech to organizing, outlining, and overcoming speech anxiety—we offer more help than ever before on these fundamental skills.

- **More coverage of managing speech anxiety**—one of the greatest challenges students continue to face—explains the causes of speech apprehension, the body's reaction to it, and provides even more classroom-tested strategies and suggestions for preparation and practice.
- **A new chapter on orally citing sources** helps students move from the research stage of speech preparation to verbally establishing and proving their argument to listeners.
- **A revised chapter on outlining** takes students step by step through the various stages of outlining—from a working draft to a speaking outline.

Cutting-Edge Coverage of the New Realities

We live in a digital age in which the realties of preparing and delivering presentations continue to evolve. A growing number of instructors are teaching an online public speaking course for the first time, and more and more students (and even professionals) are expected to prepare and deliver mediated presentations, creating new challenges across the board. Therefore, in this edition, we bring *A Speaker's Guidebook* into the present and future by addressing these challenges directly.

- **Expanded section on supporting the speech.** In speaking with instructors across the country, and in our own teaching, we have found that the vast majority of students are doing research online—and that many are doing their research *exclusively* online. As a result, finding credible sources has become more of an issue than ever before. Thus, we have expanded the entire section on supporting the speech, especially Chapter 10, "Finding Credible Sources on the Internet," by providing even more coverage of source credibility and by including new tips and guidance for finding and citing credible online sources.

- **A new chapter on online presentations.** We also realize that more and more students are preparing mediated presentations—whether for online courses, virtual meetings, recorded presentations, or other contexts. The new Chapter 29, "Preparing Online Presentations," provides students with comprehensive, accessible, and easy-to-use advice designed to help students create and deliver their own presentations online: It explains the key differences between live (real-time) and recorded presentations, highlights the unique characteristics of online speaking, discusses a variety of formats and technologies to choose from, and offers guidance throughout on structuring and delivering mediated presentations. And all the while, we emphasize the importance of applying time-tested techniques for preparing and presenting a speech while adapting to the specific requirements of presenting online.

- **More on presenting in groups and teams.** To meet the needs of instructors and businesses alike who increasingly emphasize group participation, we have expanded Chapter 30, "Collaborating and Presenting in Groups," to provide students with useful guidance for preparing and delivering team presentations. Revised coverage encourages students to set goals, assign roles and tasks, establish transitions between speakers, and be mindful of nonverbal behavior.

Improved Tools That Help Students Apply What They Learn to Their Own Speeches

Because we understand that students learn more when they see visual illustrations of specific concepts in action, the fifth edition includes a host of visual learning tools that have worked in hundreds of classrooms.

- **New and updated visual guides.** Throughout the text, unique visual guides combine words and images to walk students through the most challenging stages in the speechmaking process. Each guide gives students an overview of a key skill or process in a single glance, such as incorporating and citing sources, assessing source credibility, or incorporating effective transitions. This edition features two new visual guides (making a total of ten): the first on selecting and narrowing a topic to fit the audience and the second on getting ready to deliver a PowerPoint presentation.

- **Three new "visually annotated" sample speeches (seven total).** Each of these full-text model speeches offers traditional textual annotations (that help students understand the language, organization, and arguments used in a speech) alongside innovative "visual annotations"—photographs that show action shots of speakers delivering their presentations. These visual annotations go beyond the traditional printed page by bringing the elements and analysis of speech delivery into clear focus.

New speeches include student Zachary Dominque's engaging informative speech on mountain biking, student Una Chua's persuasive speech on cyberbullying, and a special occasion speech by Yael Averbuch titled " 'Love the Process': A Soccer Star's Philosophy of Life."

- ***VideoCentral: Public Speaking* offers over 100 speech videos online.** *A Speaker's Guidebook* now offers more video online than any competing college-level public speaking text. This online speech video library is available as a premium resource that can be packaged *free* with each new copy of *A Speaker's Guidebook*. Not only does *VideoCentral: Public Speaking* include some student speeches from the main text, it also includes hundreds of additional speech clips that bring virtually every concept in the book to life. These excellent models are searchable by chapter and integrated directly into the premium *A Speaker's Guidebook e-Book*. Students can read about a specific concept in the text and then watch that concept come to life by watching an associated video clip.

New Design and Streamlined Coverage

A revised design, including a brighter, friendlier palette, and streamlined coverage make the book more engaging and even easier to use. The text feels modern and clean at the same time as it highlights key content and features.

Enduring Features

The following features have made *A Speaker's Guidebook: Text and Reference* extremely successful in its first four editions:

A Comprehensive Classroom Text

A Speaker's Guidebook covers all the topics included in the standard public speaking texts—and much more. Although we designed the coverage to be accessible, we didn't lose sight of the need for comprehensiveness. *A Speaker's Guidebook* covers all the traditional topics, including listening, speaking ethically, managing speech anxiety, analyzing the audience, selecting a topic and purpose, locating and using supporting materials, organizing and outlining ideas, using language, creating presentation aids, delivering the speech, and constructing various speech types. But *A Speaker's Guidebook* offers much more than traditional texts, including chapters on using the Internet to support the speech, using presentation software, preparing business and professional presentations, and speaking in other courses.

To give students advice that is grounded in the theory of speech communication, we have included references to current communication research and classical rhetorical theory throughout the book, using them as the basis for concrete suggestions in real-world speaking situations. Examples range from coverage of individual contemporary theorists and their work to discussions of rhetorical proofs and the classical canons of rhetoric.

Because persuasive speaking is a major aspect of most speech courses, the text offers three full chapters on persuasion, more than any other text. The unique Chapter 27, "Organizing the Persuasive Speech," demonstrates how to organize persuasive speeches using Monroe's motivated sequence, cause-effect, comparative-advantage, and refutative patterns.

A Speaker's Guidebook also offers students a wealth of resources to help them adapt their speeches to the cultural requirements of the speech situation. Along with extensive coverage within chapters, **A Cultural Perspective** boxes feature such topics as comparing cultural values, vocal delivery and culture, and variations in nonverbal communication.

Special consideration has also been given to the non-native speaker. **ESL Speaker's Notes** boxes focus on critical areas of concern to speakers whose first language is not English and offer practical ways to address those concerns. Sample features include "Avoiding the Pitfalls of Manuscript Delivery" and "Vocal Variety and the Non-Native Speaker." Another characteristic that defines *A Speaker's Guidebook* is its strong focus on ethics. Chapter 5, "Ethical Public Speaking," is devoted to this topic and includes an in-depth consideration of the role that values play in the ethical quality of speeches. **Ethically Speaking** boxes appear throughout the text, continually reminding students that ethical conduct should apply to all aspects of the speechmaking process.

Finally, *A Speaker's Guidebook* recognizes the importance of solid sample speeches, and it provides twelve total. Speeches include two speeches of introduction, one speech of demonstration, three informative speeches, four persuasive speeches, and two special occasion speeches. All of the sample speeches are excellent models for student study and analysis, and seven of them include innovative visual annotations.

An Invaluable Reference beyond the Speech Classroom

A Speaker's Guidebook features a unique, user-friendly design, convenient and accessible reference features throughout, and extensive reference and research appendices. The information in *A Speaker's Guidebook* is designed for quick and easy retrieval. Twelve tabbed dividers allow the book to flip open easily, and a comb binding lets it lie flat. A **Main Menu** on the inside front cover listing all tabs and chapters, paired with a full table of contents beginning on p. xxvii, quickly directs students to the sections they need.

Speaker's Reference pages at the beginning of each tabbed section allow students to quickly access and review the most important information in each chapter; convenient cross-references enable readers to flip quickly to a full discussion of the material, should they so choose.

Every chapter in *A Speaker's Guidebook* contains **checklists**, offering step-by-step directions, self-assessments, and content review checks. Widely praised by reviewers for their precision and conciseness, these checklists help students and professionals both plan their speeches and assess their efforts.

The **Sample Speeches** appendix and a wealth of **Reference** appendices— including "Commonly Mispronounced Words" and a useful glossary of key terms—allow students to easily access practical information.

A Superior Resource in Any Public Speaking Situation

Along with providing students with an accessible, up-to-date classroom guide, *A Speaker's Guidebook* contains many features that will make it an invaluable resource in other college courses and *after* the public speaking course.

"Speaking in Other College Courses." Chapter 31 provides guidance for creating the kinds of oral presentations students are likely to deliver in other college courses, from the social sciences and humanities to science and engineering. Separate sections describe sample presentations in technical, scientific and mathematical, arts and humanities, social science, and education courses, along with a section on speaking in nursing and allied health courses.

More about public speaking on the job. *A Speaker's Guidebook* gives students more in-depth preparation than any other text for the kinds of speaking situations they are likely to encounter on the job. Chapter 32 covers business and professional speeches, sales presentations, status reports, and staff reports.

Extensive help with the research process. In addition to three full chapters dedicated to finding and developing supporting material (Chapters 8–10), *A Speaker's Guidebook* includes unique appendices showing students how to use the *Chicago,* APA, MLA, CBE/CSE, and IEEE documentation styles.

Microsoft PowerPoint tutorial. Generating presentation aids in a presentation software program has become one of the key challenges for the contemporary public speaker and presenter. Chapter 23, "Using Presentation Software," includes a tutorial on using Microsoft's PowerPoint that teaches readers how to enter and edit text, insert objects into slides, and use PowerPoint's text animation and transition effects.

Resources for Students and Instructors

Online Resources for Students

For more information on the Student Resources or to learn about package options, please visit the online catalog at **bedfordstmartins.com/speakersguide/catalog**.

SpeechClass for A Speaker's Guidebook at **yourspeechclass.com.** *SpeechClass* is designed to support students in all aspects of the public speaking course. It's fully loaded with an e-book, hundreds of speech clips and full sample speeches, outlining and relaxation tools, and opportunities for students to assess their learning. Even better, video uploading and annotating tools make working with speech video even easier than before—from assignments to peer review and collaboration. Get into *SpeechClass* and get all our premium content and tools in one fully customizable course space; then assign, rearrange, and mix our resources with yours.

Free and open book companion site at bedfordstmartins.com/speakers guide offers access to a host of useful tools and resources including: multiple-choice self-assessment quizzes for each chapter in the book; suggested speech topics plus speech topics research links to help students develop their own ideas; a how-to guide for using Microsoft PowerPoint; tutorials for evaluating online sources and avoiding plagiarism; additional full-text sample speeches; and much more. In addition, students can access other premium online resources such as *VideoCentral: Public Speaking* and the *A Speaker's Guidebook e-Book*.

A Speaker's Guidebook e-Book at bedfordstmartins.com/speakersguide, available free when packaged with a new copy of the main text or priced affordably as a stand-alone. The e-book includes all the content in the print book and enables students to add notes, highlight, and assess their understanding through quizzing. Instructors can customize the e-book by adding their own content and deleting or reordering chapters. In addition, accessing the e-book allows students seamless access to a host of premium resources integrated with the e-book itself including:

- *VideoCentral: Public Speaking.* This powerful resource offers access to more video than any competing speech text and includes over 100 speech clips along with several sample student speeches in the book. These videos help students learn best public speaking practices as well as master the skills described in the book. Clips are organized alphabetically and by chapter and are integrated directly onto each page of *A Speaker's Guidebook e-Book*. Video clips are also linked with every key concept in the text, allowing students to read about a specific concept onscreen and then immediately see that concept come to life.
- *The Bedford Speech Outliner* walks the student through the outline-building process with targeted feedback.
- *Video Quizzes* help students review fundamental speech concepts in a fun and interactive way.
- *Relaxation Audio Download* aids students in overcoming their own communication apprehension.
- **All materials from the book companion site** are integrated as well, including chapter quizzes, learning tools, and links, enabling students to study and review as they read.

Other popular e-book formats. Students can purchase *A Speaker's Guidebook* in a variety of digital options for computer, tablet, and e-reader formats.

Print Resources for Students

The Essential Guide to Rhetoric by William M. Keith, University of Wisconsin, Milwaukee, and Christian O. Lundberg, University of North Carolina,

Chapel Hill. This guide—available as a *free* package with any new copy of *A Speaker's Guidebook*—is a powerful addition to the public speaking class, providing an accessible and balanced overview of key historical and contemporary rhetorical theories. Written by two leaders in the field, this brief guide uses concrete, relevant examples and jargon-free language to bring these concepts to life.

The Essential Guide to Presentation Software by Allison Ainsworth, Gainesville State College, and Rob Patterson, James Madison University. This completely revised guide shows students how presentation software can be used to support, not overtake, their speeches. Sample screens and practical advice make this an indispensable resource for students preparing electronic visual aids.

The Essential Guide to Interpersonal Communication and ***The Essential Guide to Group Communication,*** both by Dan O'Hair and Mary Wiemann, and *The Essential Guide to Intercultural Communication* by Jennifer Willis-Rivera. These brief and readable guides offer succinct yet comprehensive coverage of key aspects of interpersonal, group, and intercultural communication, covering basic concepts and theories backed by current scholarship.

Outlining and Organizing Your Speech by Merry Buchanan, University of Central Oklahoma. This student workbook provides step-by-step guidance for preparing informative, persuasive, and professional presentations and gives students the opportunity to practice the critical skills of conducting audience analysis, dealing with communication apprehension, selecting a speech topic and purpose, researching support materials, organizing and outlining, developing introductions and conclusions, enhancing language and delivery, and preparing and using presentation aids.

Media Career Guide: Preparing for Jobs in the 21st Century, **Eighth Edition,** by Sherri Hope Culver, Temple University, and James Seguin, Robert Morris University. Practical, student-friendly, and revised with recent trends in the job market, like the role of social media in a job search, this guide includes a comprehensive directory of media jobs, practical tips, and career guidance for students considering a major in communication studies and mass media.

Research and Documentation in the Electronic Age, **Fifth Edition,** by Diana Hacker, late of Prince George's Community College, and Barbara Fister, Gustavus Adolphus College. This handy booklet covers everything students need for college research assignments at the library and on the Internet, including advice for finding and evaluating Internet sources.

Resources for Instructors

For more information or to order or download the Instructor Resources, please visit the online catalog at **bedfordstmartins.com/speakersguide/catalog**.

Instructor's Resource Manual by LeAnne Lagasse, Texas Tech University; Jennifer Emerling Bone, State University of New York, Oneonta; Elaine Wittenberg-Lyles, University of Texas at San Antonio; and Melinda Villagran, George Mason University. Available in print and downloadable online, this revised comprehensive manual is a valuable resource for new and experienced instructors alike. It offers extensive advice on topics such as helping students use their public speaking skills to become more engaged citizens; ideas for preparation and practice to reduce speech anxiety; setting and achieving student learning goals; managing the classroom; facilitating group discussion; understanding culture and gender considerations; dealing with ESL students; evaluating speeches (for both instructors and students); and evaluating Internet resources. In addition, each chapter of the main text is broken down into chapter challenges, detailed outlines, suggestions for facilitating class discussion from topics covered in feature boxes, additional activities and exercises, and recommended supplementary resources. The new edition includes more guidelines for first-time instructors, advice for integrating technology into the speech class, and expanded suggestions for videos and other classroom resources.

ESL Students in the Public Speaking Classroom: A Guide for Teachers by Robbin Crabtree, Fairfield University, and Robert Weissberg, New Mexico State University. As the United States increasingly becomes a nation of non-native speakers, instructors must find new pedagogical tools to aid students for whom English is a second language. This guide specifically addresses the needs of ESL students in the public speaking course and offers instructors valuable advice for helping students deal successfully with the challenges they face.

Teaching Public Speaking: A Guide for New Instructors by Paula Youra, Lynchburg College, provides adaptable advice on cultivating credibility and comfort in the classroom, and on succeeding during the first day, week, and semester of the course.

Coordinating the Communication Course: A Guidebook by Deanna L. Fassett, San José State University, and John T. Warren, Southern Illinois University, Carbondale, offers practical advice on every topic central to the coordinator/director role.

Print and Electronic Test Bank by LeAnne Lagasse, Texas Tech University; Jennifer Emerling Bone, State University of New York, Oneonta; and Merry Buchanan, University of Central Oklahoma. A Speaker's Guidebook offers a complete testing program, available both in print and for Windows and Macintosh environments. Each chapter includes multiple-choice, true-false, and fill-in-the-blank exercises, as well as essay questions. Sample midterm and final examinations are also included in the testing program.

Instructor's materials at bedfordstmartins.com/speakersguide. The companion Web site to A Speaker's Guidebook, Fifth Edition, offers rich teaching resources for new and experienced instructors, including a downloadable version of the *Instructor's Resource Manual,* completely revised PowerPoint slides for each chapter in the text, speech assignment suggestions, discussion questions for sample speeches, and an electronic gradebook for online quizzing.

Content for course management systems. Instructors can access content specifically designed for *A Speaker's Guidebook* for course management systems such as WebCT and Blackboard. Visit **bedfordstmartins.com/cms** for more information.

Custom solutions. Qualified adopters can customize *A Speaker's Guidebook* and make it their own by adding their own content or mixing it with ours. To learn more, visit **bedfordstmartins.com/custom**.

VideoCentral: Public Speaking **DVD.** The instructor DVD for *VideoCentral: Public Speaking* gives you another convenient way to access the collection of over 100 speech clips and speech samples from the book. The DVD is available upon adoption of *VideoCentral: Public Speaking*; please contact your local sales representative.

Professional Speeches. Available in DVD and VHS formats, Volume 19 of the esteemed *Great Speeches* series offers dynamic contemporary speeches for today's classroom. This video features compelling speeches including President Clinton's 1998 State of the Union Address, Madeleine Albright's first speech as secretary of state, Christopher Reeve's address to the 1996 Democratic National Convention, and a speech on spirituality by the Dalai Lama. Additional videos are available from the Bedford/St. Martin's Video Library.

Student Speeches. A three-video set of student speeches provides students with attainable models for study, analysis, and inspiration. Included are a variety of speeches that fulfill the most common assignments in public speaking—informative and persuasive speeches—by students of varying ability from Texas Tech and the University of Oklahoma.

Acknowledgments

We are especially thankful for the contributions of several individuals who helped us develop this edition of *A Speaker's Guidebook*. We would like to thank Teri Varner of St. Edward's University and her students for new speeches. We are also grateful to Jennifer Keohane, Business Outreach Librarian, Simsbury, Connecticut Public Library, and Kelley Cowden from University of Kentucky for their helpful suggestions. We would like to thank LeAnne Lagasse of Texas Tech University for her excellent work revising the *Instructor's Resource Manual* (originally created by Elaine Wittenberg-Lyles of the University of Texas at San Antonio and Melinda Villagran of George Mason University, and revised for the third edition by Jennifer Emerling Bone of the State University of New York, Oneonta) and Test Bank (originally created by Tom Howard of the University of Oklahoma and Merry Buchanan of the University of Central Oklahoma, and updated by Jennifer Emerling Bone). Thank you also to Bruce Sherwin and Publishers Solutions for their work on Web content and PowerPoint slides to accompany *A Speaker's Guidebook,* Fifth Edition.

We very much appreciate the assistance of the hundreds of reviewers whose feedback and advice allowed us to make *A Speaker's Guidebook: Text and Reference,* Fifth Edition, better. Please see the following pages for a list of each of these reviewers.

It has been a privilege to work with the pioneering editors and publishers of Bedford/St. Martin's, whose innovative ideas led to the format of this text. President Joan Feinberg, Editorial Director Denise Wydra, Publisher Erika Gutierrez, Director of Development Erica T. Appel, and Executive Editor Simon Glick understand how to deliver information to readers in ways that are most useful and also most compelling, and we are grateful to them for sharing their expertise with us. A special thanks to Developmental Editor Stephanie Ventura for sharing her insight, creativity, and truly superior management and interpersonal skills, and for expertly shepherding this edition from its earliest stages. We also thank Associate Editor Mae Klinger and Editorial Assistant Mollie Laffin-Rose for their always swift and efficient help, hard work, and good instincts. Managing Editor Shuli Traub and Senior Project Editor Harold Chester expertly guided the text through a complicated production process, while Production Supervisor Andrew Ensor helped turn the book from a manuscript into a beautiful publication. Finally, for their work in developing the Web site and other technology products, we are grateful to Tom Kane, Sarah O'Connor, Harriet Wald, and Nick Carbone.

Reviewers and Survey Respondents, Fifth Edition

Diane Auten, *Allan Hancock College*

Diane M. Badzinski, *Colorado Christian University*

Raymond Bell, *Calhoun Community College*

Jeffrey D. Brand, *Millikin University*

Lacinda Brese, *Southeastern Oklahoma State University*

Jennifer L. Chakroff, *Lasell College*

Jeannette Duarte, *Rio Hondo College*

Richard E. Edwards, *Baylor University*

Donna Elkins, *Jefferson Community and Technical College*

Nancy M. Fisher, *Ohio State University*

David S. Fusani, *Erie Community College*

Jeffery Gentry, *Rogers State University*

Kim Gerhardt, *San Diego Mesa College*

Steven Grant, *Florida State College at Jacksonville*

Carla Harrell, *Old Dominion University*

Constance G. Hudspeth, *Rollins College* and *Valencia Community College*

Carie Kapellusch, *Texas Christian University*

Carol Koris, *Johnson & Wales University*

Steve Madden, *Coastal Carolina University*

Brian R. McGee, *College of Charleston*

Teresa Metzger, *California State University San Marcos*

Alexa G. Naramore, *University of Cincinnati*

Clayton Coke Newell, *University of Saint Francis*

Nikki Poppen-Eagan, *Pierce College*

Mark Ristroph, *Augusta Technical College*

Gary E. Russell, *Quincy University*

Jeffrey VanCleave, *University of Kentucky*

Teri Lynn Varner, *St. Edward's University*

John T. Warren, *Southern Illinois University, Carbondale*

Allyson Zadeh, *Front Range Community College*

Reviewers and Survey Respondents, Fourth Edition

Stephanie Ahfeldt, Concordia College; Allison Ainsworth, Gainesville State College; Timothy Anderson, Elgin Community College; Dencil K. Backus, California University of Pennsylvania; Robert Betts, Rock Valley College; Thomas Bovino, Suffolk County Community College; Amanda Brown, University of Wisconsin, Stout; Christa Brown, Minnesota State University; Edward Clift, Woodbury University; Michael D. Crum, Coastal Carolina Community College; Kevin Cummings, Mercer University; Julie Davis, College of Charleston; Gary Deaton, University of Transylvania; Cynthia Dewar, City College of San Francisco; Thomas F. Downard, Northeastern University; Fred Fitch, Kean University; James J. Floyd, University of Central Missouri; Sonia Margarita Gangotena, Blinn College; Ron Gephart, Southwest Tennessee Community College; Valerie Manno Giroux, University of Miami; Keith H. Griffin, University of South Carolina; Diane Gruber, Arizona State University; Deborah Hefferin, Broward Community College; Emily Holler, Kennesaw State University; Brendan B. Kelly, University of West Florida; Carol Koris, Johnson & Wales University, North Miami; Lynn Kuechle, Minnesota State University, Mankato; Victoria Leonard, College of the Canyons; Nancy Levin, Palm Beach Community College; Natabhona Mabachi, University of Kansas; Anne McIntosh, Central Piedmont Community College; Marjorie Keeshan Nadler, Miami University; Phyllis Ngai, The University of Montana, Missoula; Kekeli Nuviadenu, Bethune-Cookman College; Keith Perry, Abraham Baldwin Agricultural College; Brian Pilling, Westminster College; Roger D. Priest, Ivy Tech Community College; Paul Raptis, Gainesville State College; Kenna J. Reeves, Emporia State University; John Reffue, Hillsborough Community College; Rebecca Robideaux, Boise State University; Karin Russell, Keiser University; John Saunders, Columbus State University; James M. Schnoebelen, Washburn University; Karen Michelle Scott, Savannah College of Art & Design; Pam Speights, Wharton County Junior College; Erik Stroner, Iowa Central Community College; Bonnye Stuart, Winthrop University; Sarah Elizabeth Symonds, Coastal Carolina Community College; Laura R. Umphrey, Northern Arizona University; Steve Vrooman, Texas Lutheran University; Marta Walz, Elgin Community College; Stephanie Webster, University of Florida; Kristopher Robert Weeks, Montclair State University; David E. Williams, Texas Tech University; and Jim Wilson, Shelton State Community College.

Reviewers and Survey Respondents, Third Edition

Helen Acosta, Bakersfield College; Nedra Adams-Soller, College of Lake County; Sue Aiello, New York Institute of Technology–Main Campus; Robert Alexander, Bucks County Community College; Jason Ames, Chabot College; James Anderson, Johnson & Wales University; Robert Arend, San Diego Miramar College; Mike Armstrong, Tallahassee Community College; Jay Baglia, San Jose State University; Kaylene Barbe, Oklahoma Baptist University; Cameron Basquiat, Community College of Southern Nevada; Kimberly Batty-Herbert, Broward Community College North; Elizabeth Bell, University of South Florida; Ray Bell, John C. Calhoun State Community College; Christina Benac, Ball State University; Mary Jane Berger, College of Saint Benedict; Kathy Berggren, Cornell University; Mark Bergmooser, Monroe County Community College; Sandra Berkowitz, University of Maine; Constance Berman, Berkshire Community College; Bob Betts, Rock Valley College; Pete Bicak, Rockhurst University; Rochelle Bird, Utah Valley State College; T. Black, Shepherd College; Marian Blue, Skagit Valley Community College–Oak Harbor; Jennifer Emerling Bone, University of Colorado–Boulder; Robert Bookwalter, Marshall University; Jennifer Boyenga, Indian Hills Community College; Chris Braden, Alverno College; Linda Brigance, SUNY College at Fredonia; Joel Brouwer, Montcalm Community College; Jin Brown, University of Alaska–Fairbanks; Nate Brown, Santa Monica College; Ferald Bryan, Northern Illinois University; Glenn Byrne, Stonehill College; Lisa Callihan, Florence Darlington Technical College; Diana Cameron, North Iowa Area Community College; Amy Capwell-Burns, University of Toledo; Harry Carrell, Missouri Valley College; Karishma Chatterjee, Ohio State University–Main Campus; Susan Childress, Santa Rosa Junior College; Sally Cissna, Milwaukee School of Engineering; Carolyn Clark, Salt Lake Community College; Annie Clement, Winona State University; Robert Cohen, Ohio State University–Mansfield; Jennifer Cohen-Rosenberg, Los Angeles Pierce College; Linda Combs, Daytona Beach Community College; Melanie Conrad, Midwestern State University; John Cook, University of Texas at Brownsville; Diana Cooley, North Harris College; Kimberly Corey, McIntosh College; Ed Coursey, Palm Beach Community College Glades Center; Ken Cox, Florence Darlington Technical College; Sandra Coyner, Southern Oregon University; Christine Cranford, East Carolina University; Rita Crockett, Howard College; Billye Currie, Samford University; Daniel Dahlquist, University of Wisconsin at Platteville; Phillip Dalton, Stetson University; William Davidson, University of Wisconsin–Stevens Point; Dale Davis, University of Texas at San Antonio; Thomas DelVecchio, Iona College; Andrew Denhart, Stetson University; Ron Dluger, North Park University; Paul Duax, American River College; Betty Dvorsen, City College of San Francisco; Jarvis Elena, Daytona Beach Community College; Dennis Elkins, Savannah College of Art and Design; Scott Ellis, San Jacinto College–Central Campus; Valerie Endress, Rhode Island College; Carolyn Engdahl, Fitchburg State University; David Engel, Marshalltown Community College; Kathleen M. Farrell, St. Louis University; Judy Ferrand, Wor-Wic Community College; William Ferreira, Houston Community College Southwest; Nilo Figur, Concordia University; Sondra Fishinger, Union County

College; Peter Fjeld, Berkeley College; Charles Fleischman, Hofstra University; James J. Floyd, Central Missouri State University; Marjorie Ford, Stanford University; Christine Foster, Ramapo College of New Jersey; James Friauf, Milwaukee School of Engineering; William Furnell, Santa Monica College; James Gallagher, New Mexico State University at Alamogordo; Pat Gehrke, University of South Carolina; John Gillette, Lake City Community College; Susan Gilpin, Marshall University; Valerie Giroux, University of Miami; Curt Gilstrap, Drury University; Louis Giuliana, Holy Family College; Susan Giusto, Francis Marion University; Eric Gnezda, Ohio Wesleyan University; Robert Gobetz, University of Indianapolis; William "Bubba" Godsey, John C. Calhoun State Community College; Janna Goodwin, Regis University; Luke Gordon, Portland State University; Michelle Gorthy, City College of San Francisco; Frank Gray, Ball State University; Neil Gregersen, University of Wisconsin at Waukesha; Laura Gregg, Saginaw Chippewa Tribal College; Jean Groshek, Alverno College; Diane Gruber, Arizona State University–West; Phil Hamilton, San Bernardino Valley College; Greg Hammond, New Mexico Junior College; Reeze Hanson, Haskell Indian Nations University; Eric Harlan, Mississippi University for Women; John Hatch, University of Dubuque; Linda Heil, Harford Community College; Mark Henderson, Jackson State University; Andrew Herman, State University of New York at Genesee; Dan Higgins, Heidelberg College; Rick Hogrefe, Crafton Hills College; Angela Holland, Community College of Southern Nevada; Emily Holler, Kennesaw State University; Victoria Howitt, Grossmont College; Kevin Howley, DePauw University; Karen Huck, Central Oregon Community College; W. A. Kelly Huff, Truett-McConnell–Watkinsville; Lynette Jachowicz, Maple Woods Community College; Dale Jenkins, Virginia Technical College; Ronald C. Jones, Norfolk State University; Linda Karch, Norwich University; Susan Katz, University of Bridgeport; Bill Keith, University of Wisconsin–Milwaukee; Tim Kelley, Northwest-Shoals Community College; Helen Kingkade, Midlands Technical College–Airport; David Kosloski, Clark College; Jeffrey Kotz, University of Connecticut; Mary Lahman, Manchester College; Jon Larson, Inver Hills Community College; Betty Jane Lawrence, Bradley University; Peter Lee, Golden West College; Diana Leonard, University of Arizona; Victoria Leonard, College of the Canyons; Douglas Lepter, Trevecca Nazarene University; Wendy Leslie, Missouri Valley College; Jason Lind, Skagit Valley College; Linda Linn, Western Wyoming College; Steven Long, Wayland Baptist University; Bob Loss, Barton County Community College; Louis Lucca, La Guardia Community College, CUNY; Thomas Marshall, Robert Morris University; Ben Martin, Santa Monica College; Michael McFarland, Stetson University; Lee McGavin, University of Texas–Permian Basin; Libby McGlone, Columbus State Community College; Annie McKinlay, North Idaho College; Gordon McLean, Arizona Western College; Scott McLean, Arizona Western College; Miriam McMullen-Pastrick, Pennsylvania State University at Erie, Behrend; Rebecca Meisnebach, Concord College; Deborah Meltsner, Old Dominion University; Andrew Merolla, Ohio State University; John Morrison, Rollins College; Alfred Mueller, Pennsylvania State University at Mont Alto; Lisa Mueller, Northeast Iowa Community College; Donna Munde, Mercer County Community College; Diana Karol Nagy, University of Florida; Helen

Nelson, Spalding University; Kathleen Norris, Loyola Marymount University; Linda Norris, Indiana University of Pennsylvania; Karen O'Donnell, Finger Lakes Community College; Jennifer O'Dorisio, Pomona High School; Richard Olsen, University of North Carolina at Wilmington; Susan Ondercin, Carroll Community College; Elenie Opffer, Regis University; Donald Painter Jr., University of South Florida; Teresa Palmitessa, Pennsylvania State University at Erie, Behrend; Emily Paramonova, Cogswell Polytechnical College; Daniel Paulnock, Saint Paul College; Holly Payne, Western Kentucky University; Karl Payton, Le Tourneau University; Kimberly Pearce, De Anza College; Sheila Peebles, Baldwin-Wallace College; Ray Penn, Lincoln Memorial University; Pamela Perkins, San Diego City College; Jean Perry, Glendale Community College; William Petkanas, Western Connecticut State University; Chuck Pierce, Central Carolina Technical College; Dann Pierce, University of Portland; Michael Pitts, Los Angeles Southwest College; Dwight Podgurski, Colorado Christian University; Linda Powers, Wofford College; Joyce Puls, Baker College; Kathleen Quimby, Messiah University; Susan Rabideau, University of Wisconsin–Fox Valley; Alan Ragains, Windward Community College; Gail Reid, State University of West Georgia; Pamela Reid, Copiah-Lincoln Community College; Paula Reif, Carl Albert State College; Larry Reynolds, Johnson City Community College; William Richter, Lenoir-Rhyne College; Lisa Riede, Lockhaven University of Pennsylvania; Nita Ritzke, University of Mary; Rick Roberts, University of San Francisco; Patricia Rockwell, University of Louisiana at Lafayette; Rita Rosenthal, Boston College and Stonehill College; Susan Sanders, Northern Essex Community College; Carol Saunders, Chipola Junior College; Kimberly Schwartz, University of Dubuque; Steve Schwarze, University of Montana; Marlene Sebeck, Wheeling Jesuit University; Lois Self, Northern Illinois University; Susan Selk, El Paso Community College; Colleen Shaughnessy-Zeena, Salem State College; Charla Markham Shaw, University of Texas at Arlington; Alisa Shubb, American River College; Elizabeth Simas, California State University at Northridge; Jacqueline Simon, Palomar College; John Kares Smith, SUNY Oswego State University; Andrew Snyder, Saint Gregory's University; Jay Soldner, Western Wisconsin Technical College; Rick Soller, College of Lake County; Pam Speights, Wharton County Junior College; Ebba Stedillie, Casper College; Susan Stehlik, Rutgers University–Newark Campus; Lesa Stern, Southern Illinois University–Edwardsville; James Stewart, Tennessee Technical University; Pamela Stovall, University of New Mexico–Gallup; Anthony Stubbs, Iowa Lakes Community College South; Pat Sutherland, Tennessee Wesleyan College; Michael Swinford, Shorter College; Sarah Symonds, Coastal Carolina Community College; Kelly Tait, University of Nevada–Reno; Georgia Talsma, Mount Marty College; April Dupree Taylor, University of South Alabama; Katherine Taylor, University of Louisville; Donna Thomsen, Johnson & Wales University; Ray Tipton, Walters State Community College; Hank Tkachuk, Concordia College–Moorehead; Candice Todd, Lynchburg College; Michael Tomaschyk, Cuyahoga Community College–Western; Amy Trombley, Western Michigan University; Anita Turpin, Roanoke College; Clint Uhrich, Luther College; Joseph Valcourt, Central Carolina Technical College; Marilyn Valentino, Lorain County Community College; Jay VerLinden, Humboldt State University; Valerie

Vlahakis, John Wood Community College; Steve Vrooman, Texas Lutheran University; Chris Wagner, Cosumnes River College; Anthony Wainwright, Onondaga Community College; Lisa Waite, Kent State University–Stark Campus; Bill Wallace, Northeastern State University; Dennis Waller, Northwest Nazarene University; David Weinandy, Aquinas College; Nancy Wendt, Oregon State University; Estelle Wenson, Stonehill College; Beverly West-Dorny, San Joaquin Delta College; Steven Wiegenstein, Culver-Stockton College; Thomas Wilkinson, Rowan University; David Williams, Texas Technical University; Frances Winsor, Pennsylvania State University at Altoona; Marianne Worthington, Cumberland College; Miriam Zimmerman, Notre Dame de Namur University; and Joe Zubrick, University of Maine–Fort Kent.

Reviewers and Survey Respondents, Second Edition

Cameron Basquiat, Community College of Southern Nevada; Carolyn Clark, Salt Lake Community College; Letitia Dace, University of Massachusetts–Dartmouth; Francis Dance, University of Denver; Layne Dearden, Brigham Young University–Idaho; Rebecca Faery, Massachusetts Institute of Technology; Joyce Fernandes, Bristol Community College; John Giertz, Bakersfield College; Heather Grace, University of Pittsburgh–Bradford; Marc Martin, San Francisco State University; Charles McMahan, Vincennes University; Deborah Meltsner, Old Dominion University; Andrea Morgan, Georgia Perimeter College; Dann Pierce, University of Portland; Patricia Rockwell, University of Louisiana–Lafayette; Robert Sadowski, University of Michigan–Flint; Michael Searcy, University of Iowa, Scott Community College; Lisa Stefani, Grossmont College; Elena Strauman, Auburn University; Jeremy Teitelbaum, California Polytechnic State University; Gregory Thomas, Morgan Community College; and Robert Witkowski, Midlands Technical College.

Reviewers and Survey Respondents, First Edition

Linda Brown, El Paso Community College; Tamara Burk, Columbia College; Lawrence J. Chase, California State University–Sacramento; Helen Chester, Milwaukee Area Technical College; Jeanine Congalton, Fullerton College; Lauren Sewell Coulter, University of Tennessee–Chattanooga; Karen D. Covey, New River Community College; Michal Dale, Southwest Missouri State; William F. Ferreira, Houston Community College, Southwest; Eric Fife, College of Charleston; William Fustield, University of Pittsburgh; Kathleen M. Galvin, Northwestern University; Kelby Halone, Clemson University; William J. Jordan, North Carolina State University; Ruth Ann Kinzey, University of North Carolina–Charlotte; Lt. Col. George Luker, USAF Academy; Joseph Martinez, El Paso Community College; Virgil Moberg, Flagler College; Carlos Perez, Maple Woods Community College; Jean Perry, Glendale Community College; Tina Pieraccini, State University of New York–Oswego; Lora Sager, Greenville Technical College; Dr. Roy Schwartzmann, Northwest Missouri State University; John Kares Smith, State University of New York–Oswego; Kimberly Terrill, Francis Marion University; and Glenda Treadaway, Appalachian State University.

Contents

How to Use This Book v

Preface xi

GETTING STARTED WITH CONFIDENCE

SPEAKER'S REFERENCE 3

CHAPTER **1**   **Becoming a Public Speaker** 6

Why Study Public Speaking? 6

  Gain Real-Life Skills 6

  Advance Your Professional Goals 7

  Enhance Your Career as a Student 7

  Become an Engaged Citizen 8

The Classical Roots of Public Speaking 8

  Classical Terms and the Canons of Rhetoric 9

  A Rich and Relevant Heritage 10

Public Speaking and Other Forms of Communication 11

  Similarities between Public Speaking and Other Forms of
    Communication 11

  Differences between Public Speaking and Other Forms of
    Communication 12

Public Speaking as an Interactive Communication Process 13

Learning to Speak in Public 15

  Draw on Conversational Skills 15

  Draw on Skills in Composition 15

  Develop an Effective Oral Style 16

  Become an Inclusive Speaker 16

CHAPTER **2**   **Giving It a Try: Preparing Your First Speech** 17

A Brief Overview of the Speechmaking Process 17

  Select a Topic 17

  Analyze the Audience 17

  Determine the Speech Purpose 18

  Compose a Thesis Statement 18

Develop the Main Points 19

Gather Supporting Material 19

Separate the Speech into Its Major Parts 19

Outline the Speech 20

Consider Presentation Aids 21

Practice Delivering the Speech 22

▶ **CHECKLIST:** Record the Speech to Bolster Confidence 22

▶ **ESL SPEAKER'S NOTES:** Identifying Linguistic Issues as You Practice Your Speech 22

Take the Plunge 23

▶ **SELF-ASSESSMENT CHECKLIST:** My First Speech 23

▶ **SAMPLE VISUALLY ANNOTATED INTRODUCTORY SPEECH:** The Dance of Life, Ashley White 24

▶ **SAMPLE INTRODUCTORY SPEECH:** Past, Present, and Future, Lisa Tran 26

PUBLIC SPEAKING BASICS

SPEAKER'S REFERENCE 31

CHAPTER **3**   Managing Speech Anxiety 36

What Makes Us Anxious about Public Speaking? 36

Lack of Positive Experience 36

Feeling Different 37

Being the Center of Attention 37

Pinpoint the Onset of Public Speaking Anxiety 37

▶ **CHECKLIST:** Recognizing and Overcoming Your Underlying Fears about Public Speaking 38

Pre-Preparation Anxiety 38

Preparation Anxiety 39

Pre-Performance Anxiety 39

Performance Anxiety 39

Use Proven Strategies to Build Your Confidence 40

Prepare and Practice 40

Modify Thoughts and Attitudes 41

▶ **ESL SPEAKER'S NOTES:** Confidence and Culture: When English Isn't Your First Language 41

Visualize Success 42

Activate the Relaxation Response 43

Use Movement to Minimize Anxiety 44

Learn from Feedback 44

Enjoy the Occasion 45

▶ **CHECKLIST:** Preparing to Speak with Confidence 45

CHAPTER **4**   Listeners and Speakers 46

The Selective Nature of Listening 46
▶ **ESL SPEAKER'S NOTES:** Learning by Listening 47

Listening and Speaking as Dialogic Communication 48

Barriers to Active Listening 48
Minimize External and Internal Distractions 48
▶ **CHECKLIST:** Dealing with Distractions during Delivery of a Speech 49
Guard against Scriptwriting and Defensive Listening 49
Beware of Laziness and Overconfidence 49
▶ **ETHICALLY SPEAKING:** The Responsibilities of Listening in the Public Arena 49
Work to Overcome Cultural Barriers 50

Becoming a More Active Listener 50
▶ **A CULTURAL PERSPECTIVE:** Helping Diverse Audiences Understand You 51
Set Listening Goals 51
Listen for Main Ideas 51
Watch for Nonverbal Clues 52

Active Listening and Critical Thinking 53
▶ **CHECKLIST:** Use the Thought/Speech Differential to Listen Critically 54

Guidelines for Evaluating Speeches and Presentations 54
Be Honest and Fair in Your Evaluation 54
Adjust to the Speaker's Style 54
Be Compassionate in Your Criticism 55

CHAPTER **5**   Ethical Public Speaking 57

Take Responsibility for Your Words 57
Earn Your Listeners' Trust 57
Respect Your Listeners' Values 58
Bring Your Own Values into Focus 58

Use Your Rights of Free Speech Responsibly 59
▶ **SELF-ASSESSMENT CHECKLIST:** Identifying Values 60
Make a Positive Contribution to Public Discourse 61
▶ **A CULTURAL PERSPECTIVE:** Comparing Cultural Values 62

Observe the Ground Rules for Ethical Speaking 62
Be Trustworthy 63
Demonstrate Respect 63
▶ **ETHICALLY SPEAKING:** Speech Codes on Campus: Protection or Censorship? 64
Make Responsible Choices 65
Demonstrate Fairness 65

Avoid Plagiarism 66

    Rules for Avoiding Plagiarism 66

    Avoid Plagiarism on the Internet 68

    ▶ **CHECKLIST:** Steps to Avoid Plagiarism 68

Respect the Laws of Copyright and Fair Use 68

    ▶ **SELF-ASSESSMENT CHECKLIST:** An Ethical Inventory 69

AUDIENCE ANALYSIS AND TOPIC SELECTION

SPEAKER'S REFERENCE 73

CHAPTER **6**   Analyzing the Audience 77

Adapt to Audience Psychology: Who Are Your Listeners? 77

    Appeal to Audience Members' Attitudes, Beliefs, and Values 78

    "If the Value Fits, Use It" 78

    Gauge Listeners' Feelings toward the Topic, Speaker, and Occasion 79

    ▶ **CHECKLIST:** Respond to the Audience as You Speak 81

Adapt to Audience Demographics 82

    Appeal to Your Target Audience 82

    Age 82

    Ethnic or Cultural Background 83

    Socioeconomic Status 83

    Religion 84

    Political Affiliation 84

    Gender 84

    Disability 85

Adapt to Cultural Values 85

    Hofstede's Value-Dimensions Model 86

    Lewis's Cultural Types Model 88

    ▶ **A CULTURAL PERSPECTIVE:** Cross-National Surveys 88

    Consult Cross-Cultural and Cross-National Polls 89

    Focus on Universal Values 89

    ▶ **ESL SPEAKER'S NOTES:** Comparing Cultural Values 89

Techniques for Learning about Your Audience 90

    Interview Audience Members 90

    Survey the Audience 90

    Consult Published Sources 92

Analyze the Speech Setting 93
    Size of Audience and Physical Setting 93
    Time and Length of Speech 93
    The Speech Context (Rhetorical Situation) 94
    ▶ **CHECKLIST:** Analyzing the Speech Situation 94
    ▶ **CHECKLIST:** Reviewing Your Speech in Light of Audience
    Demographics 95

CHAPTER **7** Selecting a Topic and Purpose 96

Assigned versus Self-Selected Topics 96
Identify the General Speech Purpose 97
    When the General Speech Purpose Is to Inform 97
    When the General Speech Purpose Is to
      Persuade 98
    When the General Speech Purpose Is to Mark a
      Special Occasion 99
    ▶ **CHECKLIST:** Identifying Your General Speech Purpose 99
Choosing a Topic for Your Speech 99
    Identify Personal Interests 99
    Consider Current Events and Controversial
      Issues 101
    Survey Grassroots Issues: Engage the
      Community 101
    Steer Clear of Overused and Trivial Topics 101
    Try Brainstorming to Generate Ideas 101
    ▶ **CHECKLIST:** Criteria for Selecting a Topic 103
    ▶ **FROM SOURCE TO SPEECH:** Narrowing Your Topic to Fit Your
    Audience 104
    ▶ **FROM SOURCE TO SPEECH:** Narrowing Your Topic Using a
    Library Portal 106
Refine the Topic and Purpose 108
    Narrow the Topic 108
    ▶ **CHECKLIST:** Narrowing Your Topic 108
    Form a Specific Speech Purpose 108
From Topic and Purpose to Thesis Statement 109
    Use the Thesis Statement to Convey the
      Central Idea 109
    ▶ **ETHICALLY SPEAKING:** Ethical Considerations in Selecting
    a Topic and Purpose 110
    Use the Thesis Statement to Guide Your Speech
      Preparation 111
    ▶ **CHECKLIST:** Formulating the Thesis Statement 112
**Make the Thesis Statement Relevant and
Motivating** 113

SUPPORTING THE SPEECH

SPEAKER'S REFERENCE 119

CHAPTER **8** Developing Supporting Material 124

Use a Variety of Supporting Materials 124
Consider the Target Audience 124
Offer Examples 125
   Brief Examples 125
   Extended Examples 126
   Hypothetical Examples 126
Share Stories 127
   ▶ **CHECKLIST:** Selecting the Right Example or Story 128
Draw on Testimony 128
   ▶ **ESL SPEAKER'S NOTES:** Broaden Your Listeners'
   Perspectives 128
   ▶ **CHECKLIST:** Evaluating the Credibility of Testimony 129
Provide Facts and Statistics 129
   Use Statistics Selectively 129
   Use Statistics Accurately 129
   Present Your Statistics Ethically 131
   ▶ **ETHICALLY SPEAKING:** Evaluating the Validity of the
   Statistics You Cite 132
   ▶ **SELF-ASSESSMENT CHECKLIST:** Using Statistics in Your
   Speech: An Ethical Inventory 133
   Use Visual Aids Whenever Possible 133
Win Acceptance of Your Supporting Materials 133

CHAPTER **9** Locating Supporting Material 134

Before You Begin: Assess Your Research Needs 134
Locating Secondary Sources 135
   ▶ **CHECKLIST:** Making an Inventory of Your Research
   Needs 135
   Books 136
   Newspapers and Periodicals 136
   Weblogs and Social News Sites 136
   Government Publications 137
   Digital Collections 138
   Reference Works 138
   ▶ **A CULTURAL PERSPECTIVE:** Discovering Diversity in
   Reference Works 139

▶ **CHECKLIST:** Finding Speeches Online 140

Generating Primary Sources: Interviews and Surveys 141

Interviews 141

▶ **CHECKLIST:** Preparing for the Interview 143

Surveys 143

Evaluate and Document Your Sources 144

Critically Evaluate Your Sources 144

Record References as You Go 145

▶ **CHECKLIST:** Creating a Bibliography 145

Choose Helpful Tools 145

Identify Quoted, Paraphrased, and Summarized
Material 146

▶ **ETHICALLY SPEAKING:** Researching Your Speech in an
Ethical Manner 147

▶ **FROM SOURCE TO SPEECH:** Recording and Citing
Books 148

▶ **FROM SOURCE TO SPEECH:** Recording and Citing Articles
from Periodicals 150

CHAPTER **10** **Finding Credible Sources on the
Internet** 152

Begin Your Search at a Library Portal 152

Access the Invisible ("Deep") Web 153

Be a Critical Consumer of Information 153

Distinguish among Information, Propaganda,
Misinformation, and Disinformation 154

Make the Most of Internet Search Tools 155

▶ **FROM SOURCE TO SPEECH:** Evaluating Web Sources 156

▶ **CHECKLIST:** Is My Online Research Effective? 158

Distinguish among Types of Search Engines 158

Consult Subject (Web) Directories 159

Know When to Use Search Engines and Subject (Web)
Directories 160

▶ **CHECKLIST:** Choosing between a Subject (Web) Directory
and a Search Engine 160

Beware of Commercial Factors Affecting Search
Results 161

▶ **CHECKLIST:** Identifying Paid Listings in Search Results 161

Conduct Advanced Searches 161

Record and Cite Internet Sources 163

▶ **CHECKLIST:** Documenting Internet Sources 163

▶ **FROM SOURCE TO SPEECH:** Recording and Citing Web
Sources 164

CHAPTER **11**   Citing Sources in Your Speech   166

Alert Listeners to Key Source Information   166
> ▶ **CHECKLIST:** Offering Key Source Information   167

Establish the Source's Trustworthiness   167

Avoid a Mechanical Delivery   168
> Vary the Wording   168
> Preview the Source   168

Overview of Source Types with Sample Oral Citations   169
> Book   169
> Print Article   169
> Online-Only Magazine   169
> Web Site   169
> ▶ **FROM SOURCE TO SPEECH:** Demonstrating Your Sources' Reliability and Credibility   170
> Weblog   172
> Television or Radio Program   172
> Online Video   172
> Testimony (Lay or Expert)   172
> Personal Interview   172

Properly Citing Facts and Statistics   172

Properly Citing Summarized, Paraphrased, and Quoted Information   174

ORGANIZING AND OUTLINING

SPEAKER'S REFERENCE   177

CHAPTER **12**   Organizing the Speech   181

Beyond the Speech: Organizing as a Life Skill   181

Parts of a Speech   182

Use Main Points to Express Key Ideas   182
> Let the Speech Thesis and Purpose Guide You   183
> ▶ **SELF-ASSESSMENT CHECKLIST:** Do the Speech Points Illustrate or Prove the Thesis?   183
> Restrict the Number of Main Points   183
> Restrict Each Main Point to a Single Idea   184

Use Supporting Points to Substantiate Your Claims   185

Pay Close Attention to Coordination and Subordination   187

Strive for a Unified, Coherent, and Balanced Outline   188
> Unity   188

Coherence 188

Balance 188

▶ **CHECKLIST:** Do the Speech Points Reflect Unity, Coherence, and Balance? 189

Use Transitions to Give Direction to the Speech 189

Use Transitions between Main Points 190

Use Transitions between Supporting Points 190

Use Previews and Summaries as Transitions 191

▶ **SELF-ASSESSMENT CHECKLIST:** Using Transitions 191

▶ **FROM POINT TO POINT:** Using Transitions to Guide Your Listeners 192

CHAPTER **13** Types of Organizational Arrangements 194

▶ **CHECKLIST:** Choosing an Organizational Pattern 194

Arranging Speech Points Chronologically 195

Arranging Speech Points Using a Spatial Pattern 195

Arranging Speech Points Using a Causal (Cause-Effect) Pattern 196

Arranging Speech Points Using a Problem-Solution Pattern 197

Arranging Speech Points Topically 198

Arranging Speech Points Using a Narrative Pattern 199

Arranging Speech Points Using a Circular Pattern 200

Subpoints Need Not Match the Pattern of Main Points 200

▶ **CHECKLIST:** Evaluating Organizational Patterns 201

▶ **A CULTURAL PERSPECTIVE:** Arrangement Formats and Audience Diversity 201

CHAPTER **14** Outlining the Speech 202

Plan on Creating Two Outlines 202

Use Sentences, Phrases, or Key Words 202

Use a Key-Word Outline for Optimal Eye Contact 204

Create a Working Outline First 204

Separate the Introduction and Conclusion from the Body 205

List Your Sources 205

Create a Title 205

▶ **CHECKLIST:** Steps in Creating a Working Outline 206

Sample Working Outline 206

Preparing the Speaking Outline 211

Indicate Delivery Cues 211

Practice the Speech 211

▶ **CHECKLIST:** Tips on Using Notecards or Sheets of Paper 212

▶ **CHECKLIST:** Steps in Creating a Speaking Outline 212

Sample Speaking Outline 212

Full-Text Speech: Staying Ahead of Spyware, John Coulter 215

INTRODUCTIONS, CONCLUSIONS, AND LANGUAGE

SPEAKER'S REFERENCE 221

CHAPTER **15** Developing the Introduction 225

Functions of the Introduction 225

▶ **CHECKLIST:** Guidelines for Preparing the Introduction 226

Gain Audience Attention 226

▶ **SELF-ASSESSMENT CHECKLIST:** Using Humor Appropriately 228

Preview the Purpose and Topic 229

Establish Credibility as a Speaker 230

Preview the Main Points 230

▶ **A CULTURAL PERSPECTIVE:** Humor and Culture: When the Jokes Fall Flat 231

Motivate the Audience to Accept Your Goals 231

▶ **SELF-ASSESSMENT CHECKLIST:** How Effective Is Your Introduction? 232

CHAPTER **16** Developing the Conclusion 233

Functions of Conclusions 233

▶ **CHECKLIST:** Guidelines for Preparing the Conclusion 233

Signal the Close of a Speech and Provide Closure 234

Summarize the Key Points and Goals 234

Reiterate the Topic and Speech Purpose 234

Challenge the Audience to Respond 235

Make the Conclusion Memorable 235

Use Quotations 236

Tell a Story 236

Pose a Rhetorical Question 237

▶ **SELF-ASSESSMENT CHECKLIST:** How Effective Is Your Conclusion? 237

CHAPTER 17 Using Language to Style the Speech 238

Prepare Your Speeches for the Ear 238
Strive for Simplicity 239
Be Concise 239
Experiment with Phrases and Sentence Fragments 240
Make Frequent Use of Repetition 240
Use Personal Pronouns 240
▶ CHECKLIST: Personalizing Your Speech with Personal Pronouns 241
▶ SELF-ASSESSMENT CHECKLIST: Does Your Speech Incorporate Effective Oral Style? 241
Use Concrete Language and Vivid Imagery 241
▶ CHECKLIST: Is Your Speech Language Concrete? 242
Use Descriptive Adjectives and Strong Verbs 242
Use Figures of Speech 242
Choose Language That Builds Credibility 244
Use Words Appropriately 244
Use Language Accurately 245
Use the Active Voice 245
Use "I" Language 246
Avoid Powerless Speech 246
Use Culturally Sensitive and Gender-Neutral Language 246
▶ A CULTURAL PERSPECTIVE: Adapting Your Language to Diverse Audiences 247
▶ SELF-ASSESSMENT CHECKLIST: Does Your Language Build Trust and Credibility? 248
Choose Language That Creates a Lasting Impression 249
Use Repetition for Rhythm and Reinforcement 249
Use Alliteration for a Poetic Quality 250
Experiment with Parallelism 250

VOCAL AND NONVERBAL DELIVERY

SPEAKER'S REFERENCE 253

CHAPTER 18 Methods of Delivery 257

Qualities of Effective Delivery 257
Strive for Naturalness 257
Show Enthusiasm 258

Project a Sense of Confidence 258
Be Direct 258

Select a Method of Delivery 259
Speaking from Manuscript 259
Speaking from Memory 260
▶ **ESL SPEAKER'S NOTES:** Avoiding the Pitfalls of Manuscript Delivery 260
Speaking Impromptu 261
▶ **CHECKLIST:** Speaking Off-the-Cuff: Preparing for the Impromptu Speech 261
▶ **ETHICALLY SPEAKING:** A Tool for Good and Evil 262
Speaking Extemporaneously 263
▶ **CHECKLIST:** Ready for the Call: Preparing for the Extemporaneous Speech 263

CHAPTER **19** The Voice in Delivery 264
Adjust Your Speaking Volume 264
Vary Your Intonation 264
▶ **CHECKLIST:** Tips on Using a Microphone 265
Adjust Your Speaking Rate 266
Use Strategic Pauses 266
Strive for Vocal Variety 266
▶ **ESL SPEAKER'S NOTES:** Vocal Variety and the Non-Native Speaker 267
▶ **SELF-ASSESSMENT CHECKLIST:** Practice Check for Vocal Effectiveness 268
Carefully Pronounce and Articulate Words 268
▶ **A CULTURAL PERSPECTIVE:** Using Dialect (Language Variation) with Care 269

CHAPTER **20** The Body in Delivery 271
Functions of Nonverbal Communication in Delivery 271
Clarify Verbal Messages 271
Facilitate Feedback 272
Establish Relationships between Speaker and Audience 272
Establish Speaker Credibility 272
Pay Attention to Body Movement 272
Animate Your Facial Expressions 273
▶ **SELF-ASSESSMENT CHECKLIST:** Tips for Using Effective Facial Expressions 273
Maintain Eye Contact 273
Use Gestures That Feel Natural 274

▶ **CHECKLIST:** Tips for Effective Gesturing 274

Be Aware of General Body Movement 274

▶ **CHECKLIST:** Broad Dress Code Guidelines 274

Dress Appropriately 275

▶ **A CULTURAL PERSPECTIVE:** Nonverbal Communication
Patterns in Different Cultures 275

Practice the Delivery 276

Focus on the Message 276

Record the Speech 276

Be Prepared to Revise Your Speaking Notes 277

Practice under Realistic Conditions 277

Time Your Speech 277

Plan Ahead and Practice Often 277

▶ **CHECKLIST:** Practicing Your Speech 278

PRESENTATION AIDS

SPEAKER'S REFERENCE 281

CHAPTER **21**   Using Presentation Aids in the
Speech 284

Functions of Presentation Aids 284

Help Listeners Process and Retain Information 284

Promote Interest and Motivation 285

Convey Information Concisely 285

Lend a Professional Image 285

Types of Presentation Aids 285

Props and Models 285

Pictures 286

▶ **CHECKLIST:** Tips for Using Props and Models
Effectively 287

Graphs and Charts 287

▶ **CHECKLIST:** Tips for Creating Effective Pictograms 290

▶ **CHECKLIST:** Tips for Creating Effective Line, Bar, and Pie
Graphs 291

Audio and Video 291

▶ **CHECKLIST:** Tips on Incorporating Audio and Video into
Your Presentation 292

Multimedia 292

Options for Displaying the Presentation Aid 292

Computer-Generated Graphics and Displays 292

▶ **CHECKLIST:** Incorporating Presentation Aids into Your Speech 293

Overhead Transparencies 293

▶ **FROM IDEA TO IMAGE:** Using Presentation Aids 294

Flip Charts 297

Chalkboards and Whiteboards 297

Handouts 297

CHAPTER **22** Designing Presentation Aids 298

Focus on the Message 298

Strive for Simplicity 298

Assign Each Point a Separate Slide 298

Use Active Construction 298

Avoid Clutter 299

Focus on Continuity 299

▶ **CHECKLIST:** Applying the Principles of Simplicity and Continuity 300

Select Appropriate Typeface Styles and Fonts 300

▶ **CHECKLIST:** Tips for Using Typefaces, Fonts, and Sizes Effectively 301

Use Color Carefully 302

CHAPTER **23** Using Presentation Software 304

It's a Speech, Not a Slide Show 304

A Brief Guide to Using PowerPoint 305

▶ **CHECKLIST:** Preventive Maintenance: Avoiding PowerPoint Technical Glitches 305

Become Familiar with the Presentation Options 305

▶ **CHECKLIST:** Selecting Slide Layouts and Themes in PowerPoint 307

Become Familiar with View Options and Slide Masters 308

Entering and Editing Text 310

Using Slide Inserts 310

▶ **CHECKLIST:** Inserting Tables and Worksheets into PowerPoint 312

Finding Media for PowerPoint Slides 313

▶ **FROM SLIDE SHOW TO PRESENTATION:** Getting Ready to Deliver a PowerPoint Presentation 314

Using Transitions and Animation Effects 316

Developing PowerPoint Slides for a Speech 316

▶ **CHECKLIST:** Tips for Successfully Using PowerPoint Presentations in Your Speech 316

FORMS OF SPEECHES

SPEAKER'S REFERENCE   321

CHAPTER **24**   **The Informative Speech**   329

   Focus on Sharing Knowledge   329

      Enlighten Rather Than Advocate   329

      Use Audience Analysis   330

      Present New and Interesting Information   330

      Look for Ways to Increase Understanding   330

      ▶ **CHECKLIST:** Help Listeners Follow Along   331

   Categories of Informative Speeches   331

      Speeches about Objects or Phenomena   331

      Speeches about People   332

      Speeches about Events   332

      Speeches about Processes   332

      Speeches about Issues   333

      Speeches about Concepts   333

   Decide How to Convey the Information   333

      Definition   333

      Description   335

      Demonstration   335

      Explanation   335

   Take Steps to Reduce Confusion   336

      Use Analogies to Build on Prior Knowledge   336

      Demonstrate Underlying Causes   337

      ▶ **CHECKLIST:** Strategies for Explaining Complex Information   337

      Appeal to Different Learning Styles   337

   Arrange Speech Points in a Pattern   338

      ▶ **CHECKLIST:** Guidelines for Clearly Communicating Your Informative Message   339

      ▶ **SAMPLE SPEECH OF DEMONSTRATION:** An Ounce of Prevention Keeps the Germs Away, Christie Collins   340

      ▶ **SAMPLE VISUALLY ANNOTATED INFORMATIVE SPEECH:** John Kanzius and the Quest to Cure Cancer, David Kruckenberg   344

CHAPTER **25**   **The Persuasive Speech**   350

   What Is a Persuasive Speech?   350

      ▶ **CHECKLIST:** Conditions for Choosing a Persuasive Purpose   350

Persuasive Speeches Attempt to Influence Audience Choices 351

Persuasive Speeches Limit Alternatives 351

Persuasive Speeches Seek a Response 351

▶ **ETHICALLY SPEAKING:** Persuasive Speeches Respect Audience Choices 351

The Process of Persuasion 352

Classical Persuasive Appeals: Using Proofs 353

Logos: Proof by Reason 353

Pathos: Proof by Emotion 355

▶ **ETHICALLY SPEAKING:** Using Emotions Ethically 356

Ethos: Proof through Speaker Character 357

▶ **CHECKLIST:** Displaying Ethos in the Persuasive Speech 358

Contemporary Persuasive Appeals: Needs and Motivations 358

Persuading Listeners by Appealing to Their Needs 358

Persuading Listeners by Appealing to the Reasons for Their Behavior 359

Persuading Listeners by Focusing on What's Most Relevant to Them 361

Persuading Listeners through Speaker Credibility 362

▶ **SELF-ASSESSMENT CHECKLIST:** Tips for Increasing Speaker Credibility 363

CHAPTER **26** **Developing Arguments for the Persuasive Speech** 365

What Is an Argument? 365

Stating a Claim 365

Providing Evidence 366

Warrants: Justifying the Link between the Claim and Evidence 366

▶ **ETHICALLY SPEAKING:** Engaging in Arguments in the Public Arena 366

Types of Claims, Evidence, and Warrants 368

Claims Used in Persuasive Speeches: Fact, Value, and Policy 368

▶ **A CULTURAL PERSPECTIVE:** Addressing Culture in the Persuasive Speech 369

Using Evidence to Support Your Claims 370

▶ **CHECKLIST:** Testing the Strength of Your Evidence 372

Types of Warrants Used to Link Claims with Evidence 372

▶ **CHECKLIST:** Making Effective Use of Reasoning by Cause 375

Addressing the Other Side of the Argument 376

▶ **CHECKLIST:** Techniques for Addressing Competing Arguments 376

Fallacies in Reasoning 376

    Begging the Question 377

    Bandwagoning 377

    Either-Or Fallacy 377

    Ad Hominem Argument 377

    Red Herring 377

    Hasty Generalization 378

    Non Sequitur 378

    Slippery Slope 378

    Appeal to Tradition 378

CHAPTER **27** **Organizing the Persuasive Speech** 379

Factors to Consider When Choosing an Organizational Pattern 379

    Do the Arguments and Evidence Suggest a Specific Pattern? 379

    What Is the Disposition of the Audience? 380

    What Response Do You Seek? 381

Problem-Solution Pattern of Arrangement 381

    ▶ **CHECKLIST:** Organizing a Claim of Policy 383

Monroe's Motivated Sequence 383

    Step 1: Attention 384

    Step 2: Need 384

    Step 3: Satisfaction 385

    ▶ **CHECKLIST:** Steps in the Motivated Sequence 385

    Step 4: Visualization 385

    Step 5: Action 386

Comparative Advantage Pattern of Arrangement 386

Refutation Pattern of Arrangement 387

    ▶ **SAMPLE VISUALLY ANNOTATED PERSUASIVE SPEECH:** Emergency in the Emergency Room, Lisa Roth 388

    ▶ **SAMPLE VISUALLY ANNOTATED PERSUASIVE SPEECH:** Preventing Cyberbullying, Una Chua 393

    ▶ **SAMPLE VISUALLY ANNOTATED PERSUASIVE SPEECH:** The Importance of Community Engagement and Volunteerism, Stephanie Poplin 401

CHAPTER **28** **Special Occasion Speeches** 406

Functions of Special Occasion Speeches 406

    Entertainment 406

    Celebration 406

    Commemoration 407

    Inspiration 407

    Social Agenda-Setting 407

Types of Special Occasion Speeches 407

Speeches of Introduction 407

▶ **CHECKLIST:** Guidelines for Introducing Other Speakers 409

Speeches of Acceptance 409

Speeches of Presentation 410

▶ **CHECKLIST:** Guidelines for Delivering Speeches of
Acceptance 410

Roasts and Toasts 411

Eulogies and Other Tributes 412

▶ **CHECKLIST:** Tips for Delivering Effective Eulogies 413

After-Dinner Speeches 413

Speeches of Inspiration 414

▶ **CHECKLIST:** Delivering a Successful Speech of
Inspiration 416

▶ **ETHICALLY SPEAKING:** Tailor Your Message to the Audience
and Occasion 416

▶ **SAMPLE VISUALLY ANNOTATED SPECIAL OCCASION SPEECH:**
"Love the Process": A Soccer Star's Philosophy of Life,
Yael Averbuch 417

SPEAKING BEYOND THE SPEECH CLASSROOM

SPEAKER'S REFERENCE 427

CHAPTER **29** Preparing Online Presentations 435

Online and Face-to-Face Speaking: How Do They Compare? 435

Recognize Shared Features 435

Anticipate and Plan for Differences 436

▶ **CHECKLIST:** Tools for Developing Online Presentations 437

Real-Time versus Recorded: Plan for the Delivery Mode 438

Advantages of Real-Time Presentations 438

Limitations of Real-Time Presentations 438

Advantages of Recorded Presentations 439

Limitations of Recorded Presentations 440

Online Presentation Formats: From Single Speaker to Panel 440

Single-Speaker Presentations 440

Speaker-Audience Interactive Presentations 440

Interview-Style Presentations 441

Moderated Panel Presentations 441

Online Presentation Platforms: From Podcast to Webinar 442

Video 442

Podcast 442

▶ **CHECKLIST:** Creating a Podcast 443

Webinar 444

Graphical/Multimedia-Intensive Presentation 444

Online Presentations Checklist: Planning Ahead 444

▶ **CHECKLIST:** Steps in Preparing an Online Presentation 445

CHAPTER **30 Collaborating and Presenting in Groups** 446

Becoming an Effective Group Participant 446

Plan on Assuming Dual Roles 446

Center Disagreement around Issues 447

Resist Groupthink 448

Adopting an Effective Leadership Style 448

Set Goals 448

▶ **CHECKLIST:** Guidelines for Setting Group Goals 449

Encourage Active Participation 449

Use Reflective Thinking 449

Making Presentations in Teams 450

Analyze the Audience and Set Goals 451

Assign Roles and Tasks 451

Establish Transitions between Speakers 451

Be Mindful of Your Nonverbal Behavior 451

For Maximum Impact, Consider the Presenters' Strengths 451

Coordinate the Presentation Aids 451

Rehearse the Presentation Several Times 452

▶ **CHECKLIST:** Team Presentation Tips 452

CHAPTER **31 Speaking in Other College Courses** 453

Presentational versus Public Speaking 453

Typical Speaking Assignments across the Curriculum 454

Review of Academic Articles 454

Team Presentations 454

Debates 454

▶ **CHECKLIST:** Tips for Winning a Debate 456

Poster Sessions 456

Presenting to Different Audiences 457

▶ **CHECKLIST:** Tips on Presenting to a Mixed Audience 458

Speaking in Science and Mathematics Courses 458

Research (Oral Scientific) Presentation 458

Methods/Procedure Presentation 459

Research Overview Presentation 460

▶ **SELF-ASSESSMENT CHECKLIST:** Evaluating Your Original
    Research Presentation 460

    Field Study Presentation 460

▶ **CHECKLIST:** Tips for Preparing Successful Scientific
    Presentations 461

    Preparing Successful Presentations in Science and
      Mathematics 461

Speaking in Technical Courses 462

    Engineering Design Review 462

    Architecture Design Review 462

    Request for Funding 463

    Preparing Successful Technical Presentations 463

Speaking in Social Science Courses 464

    Debate Controversial Topics 464

    Review the Literature 464

    Explain Social Phenomena 464

    Evaluate Policies and Programs 465

    Recommend Policies 465

    Preparing Successful Presentations in the Social
      Sciences 465

Speaking in Arts and Humanities Courses 466

    Informative Talks of Description and Analysis 466

    Presentations That Compare and Contrast 466

    Debates 467

    Classroom Discussions 467

    Preparing Successful Arts and Humanities
      Presentations 467

Speaking in Education Courses 468

    Delivering a Lecture 468

    Facilitating a Group Activity 468

    Facilitating a Classroom Discussion 468

    Preparing Successful Presentations in Education 469

Speaking in Nursing and Allied Health Courses 469

    Community Service Learning Project 470

    Treatment Plan Report 470

    Policy Recommendation Report 470

    Preparing Successful Presentations in Nursing and Allied
      Health 471

CHAPTER **32** **Business and Professional
Presentations** 472

The Case Study 472

Sales Presentations 472

    Audience Considerations 473

▶ **ESL SPEAKER'S NOTES:** Steps to Counteract Problems in Being Understood 473

Organizing the Sales Presentation 474

▶ **CHECKLIST:** Applying Monroe's Motivated Sequence in a Sales Presentation 474

Proposals 474

Audience Considerations 475

▶ **CHECKLIST:** Preparing a Proposal 475

Organizing the Proposal 475

Staff Reports 475

Audience Considerations 476

Organizing the Staff Report 476

Progress Reports 476

Audience Considerations 476

Organizing the Progress Report 477

Crisis-Response Presentations 477

Audience Considerations 477

Organizing the Crisis-Response Presentation 478

▶ **ETHICALLY SPEAKING:** Code of Ethics for Professional Communicators 478

SAMPLE SPEECHES

Sample Visually Annotated Informative Speech 483

The History and Sport of Mountain Biking, Zachary Dominque

Sample Persuasive Speech 489

Remarks at a Human Trafficking Symposium, Washington, D.C., W. Ralph Basham

Sample Special Occasion Speech 495

2008 Harvard University Commencement Address, J. K. Rowling

REFERENCE AND RESEARCH APPENDICES

A **Handling Question-and-Answer Sessions** 505

B **Preparing for Mediated Communication** 507

C **Public Discussions: Panels, Symposiums, and Forums** 509

D **Commonly Mispronounced Words** 511

E **Chicago Documentation** 513

F **APA Documentation** 517

G **MLA Documentation** 521

H **CBE/CSE Documentation** 526

I **IEEE Documentation** 529

J **Glossary** 530

Notes 552
Acknowledgments 567
Index 569

A SPEAKER'S GUIDEBOOK

Text and Reference

GETTING STARTED WITH CONFIDENCE

GETTING STARTED WITH CONFIDENCE

SPEAKER'S REFERENCE

CHAPTER **1** **Becoming a Public Speaker** 6

Why Study Public Speaking? 6
The Classical Roots of Public Speaking 8
Public Speaking and Other Forms of Communication 11
Public Speaking as an Interactive Communication Process 13
Learning to Speak in Public 15

CHAPTER **2** **Giving It a Try: Preparing Your First Speech** 17

A Brief Overview of the Speechmaking Process 17
- ▶ **CHECKLIST** Record the Speech to Bolster Confidence 22
- ▶ **ESL SPEAKER'S NOTES** Identifying Linguistic Issues as You Practice Your Speech 22

Take the Plunge 23
- ▶ **SELF-ASSESSMENT CHECKLIST** My First Speech 23
- ▶ **SAMPLE VISUALLY ANNOTATED INTRODUCTORY SPEECH** The Dance of Life, Ashley White 24
- ▶ **SAMPLE INTRODUCTORY SPEECH** Past, Present, and Future, Lisa Tran 26

GETTING STARTED WITH CONFIDENCE

CHAPTER 1 Becoming a Public Speaker

Recognize the Many Benefits of Public Speaking

- Gain real-life skills that lead to greater confidence and satisfaction. (p. 6)
- Advance your professional goals. (p. 7)
- Enhance your career as a student, and deliver better oral presentations in other courses. (p. 7)
- Hone your researching, writing and outlining, reasoning, critical thinking, and listening skills. (p. 7)

Become an Engaged Citizen

- Use public speaking to become more involved in addressing social problems. (p. 8)
- Learn the rules of engagement for effective and ethical public discourse. (p. 8)

Recognize the Enduring Nature of the Study of Public Speaking

- The *canons of rhetoric,* a five-part speechmaking process developed in ancient Greece, remain relevant for today's public speaker. (p. 9)

Recognize the Similarities between Public Speaking and the Other Forms of Communication

- As in *conversation (dyadic communication),* you attempt to make yourself understood, involve and respond to your conversational partner, and take responsibility for what you say. (p. 11)
- As in *small group communication,* you address a group of people who are focused on you and expect you to clearly discuss issues that are relevant to the topic and to the occasion. (p. 11)
- As in *mass communication,* you must understand and appeal to audience members' interests, attitudes, and values. (p. 11)

Recognize the Differences between Public Speaking and the Other Forms of Communication

- Opportunities for feedback are fewer than in conversation or in small group communication, and greater than in mass communication. (p. 12)

- Preparation required is greater than in other forms of communication. (p. 12)
- The degree of formality tends to be greater than in other forms of communication. (p. 12)

Recognize the Elements of the Communication Process

- Understand the nature of source, receiver, message, and channel. (p. 13)
- Understand and plan for the rhetorical situation—the circumstance that calls for a public response (the speech). (p. 14)

Set Clearly Defined Goals for Your Speeches

- Establish a set of goals early in the speechmaking process. (p. 14)
- Keep a clear focus in mind. (p. 14)
- Assess the outcome of the speech. (p. 15)
- Use constructive feedback for self-evaluation and improvement. (p. 15)

Draw on the Familiar Skills of Conversation and Writing

- Consider that in both conversation and writing, you try to uncover the audience's interests and needs before speaking. (p. 15)
- Consider that in both conversation and writing, you check to make certain that you are understood, and adjust your speech to the listeners and to the occasion. (p. 15)
- Much of what you've learned about organizing written papers can be applied to organizing your speeches. (p. 15)

Foster a Sense of Inclusion in All of Your Speeches

- Try to identify and respectfully address the diversity of values and viewpoints held by audience members. (p. 16)
- Work toward making every member of the audience feel recognized and included in your message. (p. 16)

CHAPTER 2 Giving It a Try: Preparing Your First Speech

To Gain Confidence, Deliver a Brief First Speech

Use This Overview to Construct and Deliver the First Speech

- Select a topic. (p. 17)
- Analyze the audience. (p. 17)

- Determine the speech purpose. (p. 18)
- Compose a thesis statement. (p. 18)
- Develop the main points. (p. 19)
- Gather supporting material. (p. 19)
- Separate the speech into its major parts: introduction, body, and conclusion. (p. 19)
- Outline the speech using coordinate and subordinate points. (p. 20)
- Consider presentation aids. (p. 21)
- Practice delivering the speech. (p. 22)

KEY TERMS

Chapter 1

rhetoric

oratory

agora

forum

public forum

forensic oratory

deliberative oratory

epideictic oratory

canons of rhetoric

invention

arrangement

style

memory

delivery

dyadic communication

small group communication

mass communication

public speaking

source

encoding

receiver

decoding

feedback

message

channel

noise

shared meaning

rhetorical situation

audience-centered approach

culture

cultural intelligence

Chapter 2

topic

audience analysis

general speech purpose

specific speech purpose

thesis statement

main points

supporting material

introduction

body

conclusion

coordinate points

subordinate points

organizational pattern

presentation aids

CHAPTER 1

Becoming a Public Speaker

As a student of public speaking, you are joining a very large and venerable club. People have studied public speaking in one form or another for well over two thousand years. Indeed, public speaking may be the single most studied skill in history! Since before the time of the great Greek thinker Aristotle (384–322 B.C.E.) and the Roman statesman and orator Cicero (106–43 B.C.E.), practitioners of this ancient art have penned countless volumes bearing advice on how to address an audience. Our own frenzied era of electronic communication has not in any way diminished the need for this singularly effective form of communication, and public speaking remains an indispensable vehicle for the expression of ideas. Whatever people care deeply about, public speaking offers a way to communicate their concerns with others. Indeed, few other activities offer quite the same opportunity to make one's voice heard.

This guidebook offers the tools you need to create and deliver effective speeches, from presentations made to fellow students, co-workers, or fellow citizens to major addresses given to large audiences. Here you will discover the basic building blocks of any good speech and acquire the skills to deliver presentations in a variety of specialized contexts—from the college psychology class to the business and professional arena. You'll also find proven techniques to build your confidence by overcoming the anxiety associated with public speaking.

Why Study Public Speaking?

WEB Other college courses

The ability to speak confidently and convincingly in public is an asset to anyone who wants to take an active role in the classroom, workplace, and community. As you master the skills of public speaking, you'll find that it is a powerful vehicle for professional and personal growth.

Gain Real-Life Skills

Skill in public speaking will give you an unmistakable edge in life, leading to greater confidence and satisfaction. Whether you want to do well in an interview, stand up with poise in front of classmates or in other group situations, or parlay your skills in the public arena, public speaking offers you a way to fulfill your goals.

Advance Your Professional Goals

Now, more than ever, public speaking has become both a vital life skill and a secret weapon in career development.[1] As a report entitled "What Students Must Know to Succeed in the Twenty-First Century" states:

> Clear communication is critical to success. In the marketplace of ideas, the person who communicates clearly is also the person who is seen as thinking clearly. Oral and written communication are not only job-securing, but job-holding skills.[2]

Recruiters of top graduate school students report that what distinguishes the most sought-after candidates is not their "hard" knowledge of finance or physics, but the "soft skills" of communication.[3] Further, dozens of surveys of managers and executives reveal that ability in oral and written communication is the most important skill they look for in a college graduate. In a recent survey of employers, oral communication skills ranked first among such critical areas as teamwork, work ethic, and analytical skills (see Table 1.1).

Enhance Your Career as a Student

Preparing speeches calls upon numerous skills that you can apply in other courses, including those of researching, writing and outlining, listening, and reasoning and critical analysis. As in public speaking, courses in writing and composition, history, sociology, and many more also require that you research topics, outline and organize ideas, construct claims, and logically support them.

These and other skill sets covered in this text, such as working with visual aids and controlling voice and body during delivery, are valuable in any course that includes an oral-presentation component, from engineering to art history to nursing. Students in technical disciplines and the sciences are often called upon to explain complex information clearly and accessibly, and visual aids are often an important part of such presentations (Chapters 21–23). Identifying target audiences (Chapter 6) and selecting appropriate modes of delivery

---

TABLE 1.1   Top Five Skills Employers Seek

1. Oral communication skills
2. Strong work ethic
3. Teamwork skills
4. Analytical skills
5. Initiative

Source: "Top Skills for Job Candidates." *Job Outlook 2011 Survey,* November 2010. National Association of Colleges and Employers, www.naceweb.org.

(Chapters 18–20) are critical skills for anyone speaking to an audience, from the business student to the health sciences major. Guidelines for speaking across the curriculum, including speaking in science and mathematics, technical, social science, arts and humanities, education, nursing and allied health, and business courses are the focus of Chapter 31, "Speaking in Other College Courses."

Become an Engaged Citizen

While public speaking skills will help you in your courses and contribute to both career advancement and personal enrichment, they also offer you ways to enter the public conversation about social concerns and become a more engaged citizen.

Climate change, energy, health care, immigration reform—such large public issues require our considered judgment and action. Yet too many of us leave it up to politicians, journalists, and other "experts" to make decisions about critical issues such as these. Not including presidential elections, only about 35 percent of people in the United States regularly vote. Of these, only 22 percent are 18 to 29 years old.[4] When citizens speak up in sufficient numbers, change occurs. Leaving problems such as pollution and global warming to others, on the other hand, is an invitation to special interest groups who may or may not act with our best interests in mind. As Rebecca Rimel, president of the Pew Charitable Trusts, noted in a speech about civic engagement:

> Imagine, for a moment, our nation in 20 years' time if our citizenry remains as disengaged—and special interests remain as engaged—as they are now. We'd have a democracy that responds to the particular interests of the few over the pressing demands of the many . . . a society increasingly alienated from its government and each other.[5]

As you study public speaking, you will have the opportunity to address topics that are meaningful to you, consider alternate viewpoints, and if appropriate, choose a course of action.[6] You will learn to distinguish between argument that advances constructive goals and uncivil speech that serves merely to inflame and demean others. You will learn, in short, the "rules of engagement" for effective public discourse.[7] As you do, you will gain confidence in your ability to join your voice with others in pursuit of issues you care about.

Table 1.2, "Civic Engagement on the Web," lists Web sites devoted to education about key policy debates and engagement in them through online conversations, petitions to policymakers, and participation in polls.

The Classical Roots of Public Speaking

WEB Links

Originally the practice of giving speeches was known as **rhetoric** (also called **oratory**). Rhetoric flourished in the Greek city-state of Athens in the fifth century B.C.E. and referred to making effective speeches, particularly those of a persuasive nature.

TABLE 1.2   Civic Engagement on the Web

Public Agenda www.publicagenda.org	**Public Agenda** aims to provide nonbiased research that explains public attitudes about complex policy issues. The Web site contains Issues Guides on topics ranging from abortion to terrorism.
The Public Forum Institute www.publicforuminstitute.org	**The Public Forum Institute** Similar to Public Agenda, the Public Forum Institute offers unbiased research on a variety of important public issues, such as oceans under stress and health care.
Project Vote Smart www.vote-smart.org	**Project Vote Smart** offers a wealth of information about political candidates and elected officials, including their voting records, campaign contributions, public statements, biographical data, and evaluations of them generated by over one hundred competing special interest groups.
e.thePeople www.e-thepeople.org	**e.thePeople** explores political issues and allows you to publish "conversations" for the *e.thePeople* community to read and respond to. You may also express your opinion by taking polls and circulating petitions to policymakers.

Athens was governed by some forty thousand free, property-holding males (neither women nor slaves had the rights of citizens) who established the Western world's first system of direct democracy. Meeting in a public square called the **agora**, the Athenians routinely spoke with great skill on the issues of public policy, and their belief that citizenship demanded active participation in public affairs endures to this day. As Greece fell and Rome rose (ca. 200 B.C.E.), citizens in the Roman republic (the Western world's first known representative democracy) plied their public speaking skills in a public space called a **forum**. Today, the term **public forum** denotes a variety of venues for the discussion of issues of public interest, including traditional physical spaces such as town halls as well as virtual forums streamed to listeners online.

Classical Terms and the Canons of Rhetoric

For the Greeks, oratory was the means by which they settled civil disputes, determined public policy, and established laws. In cases involving major crimes, for example, juries usually included five hundred members.[8] People served as their own advocates, so their chances of persuading jurors to vote in their favor depended on the quality of their speaking skills. The Greeks called this kind of advocating or legal speech **forensic oratory**; speech given in legislative or political contexts, **deliberative**; and speech delivered in special ceremonies, such as celebrations and funerals, **epideictic**. The great Athenian leader-general Pericles, for example, used his considerable powers of political persuasion, or *deliberative oratory,* to convince Athenians to rebuild the Acropolis and erect other great temples, such as the Parthenon, that would endure and amaze the world for centuries to come.

From the beginning, public speakers, notably the great classical rhetorician and teacher Aristotle (384–322 B.C.E.), divided the process of preparing a speech into five parts—*invention, arrangement, style, memory,* and *delivery*—called the **canons of rhetoric**. **Invention** refers to adapting speech information to the audience in order to make your case. **Arrangement** is organizing the speech in ways that are best suited to the topic and the audience. **Style** is the way the speaker uses language to express the speech ideas. **Memory** is the practice of the speech until it can be artfully delivered. Finally, **delivery** is the vocal and nonverbal behavior you use when speaking. The Romans later renamed these canons *inventio* (discovering the speech material), *dispositio* (arranging the material), *elocutio* (styling the speech), *memoria* (remembering all the various lines of argument to prove a case), and *pronuntiatio* (vocal and nonverbal delivery).

Table 1.3, "Classical Rhetoric on the Web," lists several sites on the Web devoted to classical rhetoric.

A Rich and Relevant Heritage

Although such a founding scholar as Aristotle surely didn't anticipate the omnipresent PowerPoint slide show that accompanies so many contemporary speeches, the speechmaking structure he bequeathed to us as the canons of rhetoric remains remarkably intact. Often identified by terms other than the original ones, these canons nonetheless continue to be taught in current books on public speaking, including this one. For example, Chapters 6–10, on audience analysis and selection and research of topics, and Chapters 25–26, on composing arguments, correspond to *invention*. Chapters 12–14 and 27, on outlining and organizing the speech, represent *arrangement*. Chapter 17 (on language) focuses on *style*. Finally, Chapters 18–20 describe the process of *practice* (*memory*) and *delivery* (see Table 1.4).

TABLE 1.3 Classical Rhetoric on the Web	
Silva Rhetoricae humanities.byu.edu/rhetoric/silva.htm	Sponsored by Brigham Young University, this site offers detailed descriptions of the canons of rhetoric, along with entries of thousands of rhetorical terms.
Virtual Salt: A Handbook of Rhetorical Devices www.virtualsalt.com/rhetoric.htm	Virtual Salt contains definitions and examples of more than sixty traditional rhetorical devices useful for improving your speeches.
A Glossary of Rhetorical Terms with Examples (University of Kentucky, Division of Classics) www.uky.edu/AS/Classics/rhetoric.html	From the University of Kentucky Classics Department, this site offers brief definitions of rhetorical strategies and a number of examples to illustrate each concept.

TABLE 1.4   The Classic Canons of Rhetoric and Speechmaking Today

The Canons of Rhetoric	Addressed in *A Speaker's Guidebook*
1. *Invention* (Selecting and adapting speech material to the audience; constructing arguments)	Chapter 6: Analyzing the Audience Chapter 7: Selecting a Topic and Purpose Chapter 8: Developing Supporting Material Chapter 9: Locating Supporting Material Chapter 10: Finding Credible Sources on the Internet Chapter 25: The Persuasive Speech Chapter 26: Developing Arguments for the Persuasive Speech
2. *Arrangement* (Ordering the speech)	Chapter 12: Organizing the Speech Chapter 13: Types of Organizational Arrangements Chapter 14: Outlining the Speech Chapter 27: Organizing the Persuasive Speech
3. *Style* (Use of language, including figures of speech)	Chapter 17: Using Language to Style the Speech
4. *Memory* (Practice of the speech)	Chapter 18: Methods of Delivery Chapter 19: The Voice in Delivery
5. *Delivery* (Vocal and nonverbal delivery)	Chapter 20: The Body in Delivery

Public Speaking and Other Forms of Communication

Public speaking is one of four categories of human communication: dyadic, small group, mass, and public speaking. **Dyadic communication** happens between two people, as in a conversation. **Small group communication** involves a small number of people who can see and speak directly with one another. **Mass communication** occurs between a speaker and a large audience of unknown people. In mass communication the receivers of the message are not present with the speaker, or are part of such an immense crowd that there can be little or no interaction between speaker and listener. Mass public rallies and television and radio news broadcasts are examples of mass communication.

In **public speaking**, a speaker delivers a message with a specific purpose to an audience of people who are present during the delivery of the speech. Public speaking always includes a speaker who has a reason for speaking, an audience that gives the speaker its attention, and a message that is meant to accomplish a specific purpose. Public speakers address audiences largely without interruption and take responsibility for the words and ideas being expressed.

Similarities between Public Speaking and Other Forms of Communication

Like small group communication, public speaking requires that you address a group of people who are focused on you and expect you to clearly discuss issues that are relevant to the topic and to the occasion. As in mass communication, public speaking requires that you understand and appeal to the audience members' interests, attitudes, and values. And like dyadic communication, or conversation, public speaking requires that you attempt to make yourself understood, involve and respond to your conversational partners, and take responsibility for what you say.

A key feature of any type of communication is sensitivity to the listeners. Whether you are talking to one person in a coffee shop or giving a speech to a hundred people, your listeners want to feel that you care about their interests, desires, and goals. Skilled conversationalists do this, and so do successful public speakers. Similarly, skilled conversationalists are in command of their material and present it in a way that is organized and easy to follow, believable, relevant, and interesting. Public speaking is no different. Moreover, the audience will expect you to be knowledgeable and unbiased about your topic and to express your ideas clearly.

Differences between Public Speaking and Other Forms of Communication

Although public speaking shares many characteristics of other types of communication, several factors distinguish public speaking from these other forms. These include (1) opportunities for feedback, (2) level of preparation, and (3) degree of formality.

Public speaking presents different opportunities for *feedback,* or listener response to a message, than does dyadic, small group, or mass communication. Opportunities for feedback are high both in conversation and in small group interactions. Partners in conversation continually respond to one another in back-and-forth fashion; in small groups, participants expect interruptions for purposes of clarification or redirection. However, because the receiver of the message in mass communication is physically removed from the messenger, feedback is delayed until after the event, as in TV ratings.

Public speaking offers a middle ground between low and high levels of feedback. Public speaking does not permit the constant exchange of information between listener and speaker that happens in conversation, but audiences can and do provide ample verbal and nonverbal cues to what they are thinking and feeling. Facial expressions, vocalizations (including laughter or disapproving noises), gestures, applause, and a range of body movements all signal the audience's response to the speaker. The perceptive speaker reads these cues and tries to adjust his or her remarks accordingly. Feedback is more restricted in public speaking situations than in dyadic and small group communication, and *preparation* must be more careful and extensive. In dyadic and small group communication, you can always shift the burden to your conversational partner or to other group members. Public speaking offers no such shelter, and lack of preparation stands out starkly.

Public speaking also differs from other forms of communication in terms of its *degree of formality.* In general, speeches tend to occur in more formal settings than do other forms of communication. Formal gatherings such as graduations lend themselves to speeches; they provide a focus and give form—a "voice"—to the event. In contrast, with the exception of formal interviews, dyadic communication (or conversation) is largely informal. Small group communication also tends to be less formal than public speaking, even in business meetings.

Thus public speaking shares many features of everyday conversation, but because the speaker is the focal point of attention in what is usually a formal setting, listeners expect a more systematic presentation than they do in conversation or small group communication. As such, public speaking requires more preparation and practice than the other forms of communication.

Public Speaking as an Interactive Communication Process

In any communication event, including public speaking, several elements are present and interact with one another. These include the source, the receiver, the message, the channel, and shared meaning, as well as context, goals, and outcome (see Figure 1.1).[9]

The **source**, or sender, is the person who creates a message. The speaker transforms ideas and thoughts into messages and sends them to a receiver, or an audience. Creating, organizing, and producing the message is called **encoding**—the process of converting thoughts into words.

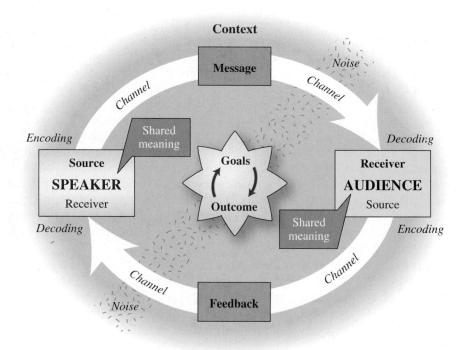

FIGURE 1.1 The Communication Process

The recipient of the source's message is the **receiver**, or audience. The process of interpreting the message is called **decoding**. Audience members decode the meaning of the message selectively, based on their own experiences and attitudes. **Feedback**, the audience's response to a message, can be conveyed both verbally and nonverbally. For example, an audience member may yell out "You lie" (as Rep. Joe Wilson [R-SC] did during President Barack Obama's 2009 State of the Union speech), or may smile and nod. Feedback from the audience often indicates whether a speaker's message has been understood, or, in the case of Congressman Wilson, accepted. Note that here, the original receiver is now in the role of source, and the original source is in the role of receiver. This change in roles between speaker and audience represents the interactive nature of public speaking.

The **message** is the content of the communication process: thoughts and ideas put into meaningful expressions. Content can be expressed verbally (through the sentences and points of a speech) and nonverbally (through eye contact and gestures). Miscommunication can happen when audience members misinterpret the speaker's intended message, or when the speaker misreads audience feedback.

The medium through which the speaker sends a message is the **channel**. If a speaker is delivering a message in front of a live audience, the channel is the air through which sound waves travel. Other channels include telephones, televisions, computers, and written communication. **Noise** is any interference with the message. Noise can disrupt the communication process through physical sounds such as cell phones ringing and people talking or heckling the speaker, through psychological distractions such as heated emotions, or through environmental interference such as a frigid room or the presence of unexpected people.

Shared meaning is the mutual understanding of a message between speaker and audience. Shared meaning occurs in varying degrees, with the lowest level occurring when the speaker has merely caught the audience's attention. As the message develops, a higher degree of shared meaning is possible. Thus listener and speaker together truly make a speech a speech—they co-create its meaning.

Context includes anything that influences the speaker, the audience, the occasion, and thus, ultimately, the speech. In classroom speeches, context would include (among other things) recent events on campus or in the outside world, the physical setting (e.g., a small classroom or large auditorium), the order and timing of speeches, and the cultural orientations of audience members. Successful communication can never be divorced from the concerns and expectations of others.

Part of the context of any speech is the situation that created the need for it in the first place. All speeches are delivered in response to a specific **rhetorical situation**, or a circumstance calling for a public response.[10] Bearing the rhetorical situation in mind ensures that you keep an **audience-centered approach**—that is, that you keep the needs, values, attitudes, and wants of your listeners firmly in focus.

A clearly defined goal is a prerequisite for an effective speech. What is it that you want the audience to learn or do or believe as a result of your speech?

Establishing a *speech purpose* early on will help you proceed through speech preparation and delivery with a clear focus in mind. (See Chapter 7 for guidelines on formulating the speech goal.)

Finally, a speech is not truly complete until you have assessed its effects and decided whether you have accomplished what you set out to do. Usually this assessment is informal, as in listening to audience reactions. Sometimes it is more formal, as in receiving an evaluation from an instructor or from the audience itself. Constructive feedback is an invaluable tool for self-evaluation and improvement. (See Chapter 5 for further discussion and tips on giving and receiving constructive criticism.)

Learning to Speak in Public   WEB Other college courses

None of us is born knowing how to speak in public. Even seemingly effortless communicators such as the late Professor Randy Pausch, whose inspirational "Last Lecture" continues to capture the attention of tens of millions of viewers (on YouTube and other sites), have worked hard—perhaps hardest of all—to achieve good results.

As with anything else, public speaking is an acquired skill that improves with practice. It is also a skill that shares much in common with other, more familiar activities, such as conversing and writing, and it can be much less daunting when you realize that you can draw on expertise you already possess.

Draw on Conversational Skills

In several respects, planning and delivering a speech resemble engaging in a particularly important conversation. When speaking to a friend, you automatically check to make certain you are understood and adjust your meaning accordingly. You also tend to discuss issues that are appropriate to the circumstances. When a relative stranger is involved, however, you try to get to know his or her interests and attitudes before revealing any strong opinions. These instinctive adjustments to your audience, topic, and occasion represent critical steps in creating a speech. Although public speaking requires more planning, both the conversationalist and the public speaker try to uncover the audience's interests and needs before speaking.

Draw on Skills in Composition

Preparing a speech also has much in common with writing. Both depend on having a focused sense of who the audience is.[11] Both speaking and writing require that you research a topic, offer credible evidence, employ effective transitions to signal the logical flow of ideas, and devise persuasive appeals. You'll also find that the principles of organizing a speech parallel those of organizing an essay, including offering a compelling introduction, a clear thesis statement, supporting ideas, and a thoughtful conclusion.

Develop an Effective Oral Style

Although public speaking has much in common with everyday conversation and with writing, it is, obviously, "its own thing." More so than writers, successful speakers generally use familiar words, easy-to-follow sentences, straightforward syntax (subject-verb-object agreement), and transitional words and phrases. Speakers also routinely repeat key words and phrases to emphasize ideas and help listeners follow along, and even the briefest speeches make frequent use of repetition (see Chapter 17).

Spoken language is often more interactive and inclusive of the audience than written language. Audience members want to know what the speaker thinks and feels, and that he or she recognizes them and relates them to the message. Speakers accomplish this by making specific references to themselves and to the audience. Yet because public speaking usually occurs in more formal settings than does everyday conversation, listeners expect a somewhat more formal style of communication from the speaker. When you give a speech, listeners expect you to speak in a clear, recognizable, and organized fashion. Thus, in contrast to conversation, in order to develop an effective oral style you must practice the words you will say and the way you will say them.

Good conversationalists, captivating writers, and engaging public speakers share an important quality: They keep their focus on offering something of value for the audience.

Become an Inclusive Speaker

Every audience member wants to feel that the speaker has his or her particular needs and interests at heart, and to feel recognized and included in the speaker's message. To create this sense of inclusion, a public speaker must be able to address diverse audiences with sensitivity, demonstrating respect for differences in **culture**—the language, beliefs, values, norms, behaviors, and even material objects that are passed from one generation to the next. More than ever, public speakers must cultivate their cultural intelligence.[12] As David C. Thomas and Kerr Inkson explain, **cultural intelligence** means being skilled and flexible about understanding a culture, learning more about it from your ongoing interactions with it, and gradually reshaping your thinking to be more sympathetic to the culture and to be more skilled and appropriate when interacting with others from the culture.[13]

When you adopt an inclusive, audience-centered perspective, you keep your audience's interests, needs, and values foremost in your mind as you envision your speech. Striving for inclusion and being audience centered throughout the speechmaking process will bring you closer to the goal of every public speaker—establishing a genuine connection with the audience.

Giving It a Try: Preparing Your First Speech

Novice speakers in any circumstance—at school, at work, or in the community—will benefit from preparing and delivering a first short speech of between two and five minutes. An audience of as few as two other people will suffice to test the waters and help you gain confidence in your ability to "stand up and deliver." Experts will tell you that the best way to overcome nervousness about speaking in public is to get up and deliver a speech. After all, you can't learn how to swim if you don't get wet.

A Brief Overview of the Speechmaking Process

WEB Chapter quizzes

If you are a beginning speaker, you are not expected to know all the conventions of speechmaking described in subsequent chapters. If you have had some experience as a speaker, some of the conventions are more familiar to you than others. In either case, it is helpful to have a general sense of the various steps involved in putting together and delivering a speech or a presentation (see Figure 2.1).

Select a Topic

The first step is to decide what you want to speak about. Let your interests and passions guide you. What really excites or concerns you? What recent local, national, or world events have drawn your attention? What are your areas of expertise? Your hobbies? Be aware, however, that it's equally important that your **topic** will be of interest to the audience. Whatever you settle on, make sure to consider your audience members and their interests.

Analyze the Audience

Audiences have personalities, interests, and opinions all their own that affect how receptive they will be toward a given topic. Thus it is imperative that you learn as much as you can about the similarities and differences among the members of your audience through **audience analysis**, a process of getting to know your listeners relative to the topic and the speech occasion. The process involves the use of techniques such as interviews and questionnaires (see Chapter 6). For this first speech assignment it should be sufficient to ask three or four prospective members of your audience a few questions about your topic. For example, What do they already know about it? Does it interest them?

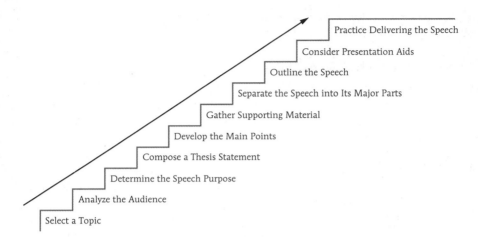

FIGURE 2.1 Steps in the Speechmaking Process

Determine the Speech Purpose

Once you have a topic, you will need to decide what you wish to convey about it. As you will learn in Chapter 7, you can direct your speech toward one of three **general speech purposes**: *to inform, to persuade,* or *to mark a special occasion.* Thus you need to decide whether your goal is to inform your audience about an issue or event, to persuade them to accept one position to the exclusion of other positions, or to mark a special occasion such as a wedding, a funeral, or a dinner event. Your speech should also have a **specific purpose**. This is a single phrase stating what you expect the speech to accomplish. For example, if your general purpose is to inform, your specific purpose might be "to inform my audience about three key qualities of distance courses." Write your specific purpose on a sheet of paper or on a Post-it note placed on the edge of your computer monitor. It will be an important guide in developing the rest of the speech.

Compose a Thesis Statement

Once you've identified the general and specific speech purposes, you need to compose a **thesis statement** that clearly expresses the central idea of your speech. While the specific purpose describes what *you* want to achieve with the speech, the thesis statement concisely identifies for your audience, in a single sentence, what the speech is about:

GENERAL PURPOSE: To inform

SPECIFIC PURPOSE: To inform my audience about the popularity and growth of Facebook.

THESIS STATEMENT: The growth of the social networking site Facebook has made it one of the top most visited Web sites daily.

Wherever you are in the planning stage, always refer to the thesis statement to make sure that you are on track to illustrate or prove your thesis.

Develop the Main Points

Organize your speech around two or three **main points**. These are the primary pieces of knowledge (in an informative speech) or the key arguments in favor of your position (in a persuasive speech) (see Chapter 12). If you create a clear, specific purpose statement for your speech, the main points will be easily identifiable (if not explicit).

SPECIFIC PURPOSE: To inform my audience about the popularity and growth of Facebook.

    I.   Facebook began with slow growth compared to its primary competitor, MySpace.

    II.   Facebook's popularity grew beyond teens and young adults to middle and older adults.

    III.   Facebook is now one of the top five most visited Web sites daily.

Gather Supporting Material

Supporting material illustrates the main points by clarifying, elaborating, and verifying the speaker's ideas. Supporting material includes the entire world of information available to you—from personal experiences to statistics from outside sources. Unless your speech is about yourself or a compelling personal experience, plan to research your topic for supporting material to provide evidence for your assertions and lend credibility to your message. Chapters 8–10 describe developing, locating, and using many kinds of supporting material.

Separate the Speech into Its Major Parts

WEB Video quizzes

Every speech will have an introduction, a body, and a conclusion (see Table 2.1). Develop each part separately, then bring them together using transition statements (see Chapters 12 and 14).

The **introduction** serves to introduce the topic and the speaker, to alert audience members to your specific speech purpose, and to catch the audience's attention and interest. Making a startling statement, telling a story, or using humor are some of the ways to grab audience attention (see Chapter 15). Just like the body of a written essay, the speech **body** contains the speech's main points and subpoints, all of which support the speech's thesis. It is here that you should illustrate or argue each of your main ideas, using the supporting material you have gathered to clarify, elaborate, or substantiate your points. The **conclusion** restates the speech purpose and reiterates how the main points confirm it. Because the conclusion represents your last opportunity to motivate your listeners and to state your theme in a memorable manner, make sure to end on a strong note (see Chapter 16).

TABLE 2.1 Major Speech Parts		
Introduction	**Body**	**Conclusion**
• Welcome your audience. • Introduce yourself, your topic, and your speech thesis. • Catch the audience's attention and interest with the use of a quote, a short story, or an example. • Provide a clear transition statement to the body of the speech.	• State the main ideas of the speech and illustrate each one with relevant supporting material. • Organize your ideas and evidence in a structure that suits your topic, audience, and speech occasion. • Use transition statements and phrases to move between main points and to the conclusion.	• Restate the speech thesis and reiterate how the main points confirm it. • Leave your audience with something to think about.

Outline the Speech

WEB Outliner

An outline is the framework upon which to arrange the elements of your speech in support of your thesis. Outlines are based on the principle of *coordination* and *subordination*—the logical placement of ideas relative to their importance to one another. **Coordinate points**, more often referred to as main points, are of equal importance and are indicated by their parallel alignment. **Subordinate points**, also called sub-points, comprise the substance of the main points and are identified in outlines by their placement below and to the right of the points they support. (For a full discussion of outlining, see Chapter 14.)

As your speeches become more detailed you will need to select an appropriate **organizational pattern** (see Chapters 13 and 27). You will also need to familiarize yourself with developing both *working* and *speaking* outlines (see Chapter 14). To allow for the full development of your ideas, *working outlines* generally contain points stated in complete sentences. As a rule, *speaking outlines* (also called presentation outlines) are far briefer than working outlines and are usually prepared using either short phrases or key words.

Following is a working full-sentence outline created by a beginning public speaking student for a speech of introduction (see speech below):

TOPIC:	Speech of Introduction for Lisa Tran
SPEECH PURPOSE:	To inform
SPECIFIC SPEECH PURPOSE:	To inform my audience about my odyssey as a refugee from war-torn Vietnam to a person fulfilling her potential and realizing her dreams in America

Introduction

(*Captures audience attention—in this case, with a startling statement and select dramatic details of her story.*) My story begins in Saigon, where my father was imprisoned. We fled the country without taking any belongings. The boat ride was horrific, and we arrived to harsh media attention. We first settled in Kansas, where we were finally reunited with Dad.

(States thesis statement and previews main points. In a brief speech, the preview can act as a transition.) We set forth on American soil some years ago, but my journey has just begun. Little did I dream then of what was in store for me. Little do I know of what my future will bring.

Body

I.   We become American citizens, and I achieve things I never dreamed of.

   A.   I become the first Asian pom captain at the University of Oklahoma.

   B.   I become a member of Kappa Kappa Gamma and the 1999 Miss Greek OU.

II.   My achievements could not have occurred if I did not have some knowledge of the difficulties and hardships of life.

   A.   Though I could not afford lessons in Vietnam, as a child I trained myself to dance.

   1.   Nine years later, I earned honors as a dancer and today I teach dance.

   2.   In 1999, I was crowned the first Asian Miss Greek OU.

   B.   Thanks to the love and support of my sorority, my friends, and my family, I have come far.

   C.   The journey is not over.

Conclusion

(Restates the thesis in a memorable way.) As an anonymous poet once wrote, "Dream what you want to dream, go where you want to go, be what you want to be, because you have only one life and one chance to do all the things you want to do." Rather than proving my self-worth, my accomplishments merely symbolize the true passion and drive we have for living and succeeding.

(Leaves the audience with a motivating message.) We are what we learn and take with us during this journey we call life. I am the past because I have appreciation; I am the present because I have learned humbleness; I am the future because I have so much more to learn.

Consider Presentation Aids

As you prepare your speech, consider whether using visual, audio, or a combination of different **presentation aids** will help your audience understand your points. A presentation aid can be as simple as writing the definition of a word on a blackboard or manipulating a physical object while describing it or as involved as a multimedia slide show. Presentation aids that summarize and highlight data, such as charts and graphs, can often help the audience to retain ideas and understand difficult concepts (see Chapter 21).

Practice Delivering the Speech

Preparation and practice are necessary for the success of even your first speech in class. You will want to feel and appear "natural" to your listeners, an effect best achieved by rehearsing both the verbal and nonverbal delivery of your speech (see Chapters 19 and 20). So, practice your speech often. It has been suggested that a good speech is practiced at least five times. For a four- to six-minute speech, that's only twenty to thirty minutes (figuring in re-starts and pauses) of actual practice time.

CHECKLIST

RECORD THE SPEECH TO BOLSTER CONFIDENCE

Many public speaking experts agree that of the vast array of high-tech audiovisual devices available, the audio recorder, along with the video camera (see Chapter 21), are among some of the truly indispensable aids to building confidence in public speaking. Listening to and watching your speech help make it real and, therefore, less scary.

Use an audio recorder as you practice so you can assess your verbal delivery:

✔ Identify awkward words and phrases to avoid.

✔ Reduce your use of fillers such as "uhm" and "I mean."

✔ Check the clarity of your pronunciations.

✔ Time your speech.

Use a video recorder to consider your nonverbal delivery:

✔ Assess appropriate use of gestures.

✔ See that you are smiling when you should.

✔ Check for unwanted body movements, such as swaying or fidgeting.

✔ Determine the quality of your eye contact.

✔ Handle presentation aids effectively.[1]

1. Andrew Dlugan, "Speech Preparation #8: How to Practice Your Presentation," *Six Minutes* (blog), Mar. 9, 2008, http://sixminutes.dlugan.com/speech-preparation-8-practice-presentation/.

ESL SPEAKER'S NOTES

Identifying Linguistic Issues as You Practice Your Speech

As noted in the preceding checklist, most experts recommend that you prepare for delivering your speech by practicing with an audio or video recorder. Non-native speakers may wish to pay added attention to pronunciation and articulation as they listen. *Pronunciation* is the correct formation of word sounds. *Articulation* is the clarity or forcefulness with which the sounds are made, regardless of whether they are pronounced correctly. If possible, try to arrange an appointment with an instructor or fellow student to help you identify key linguistic issues in your speech practice tape.

Each of us will speak a non-native language a bit differently from native speakers. That is, we will have some sort of accent. This should not concern you in and of itself. What is important is identifying which specific features of your pronunciation, if any, seriously interfere with your ability to make yourself understandable. Once you have listened to your speech tape and identified which words you tend to mispronounce, you can work to correct the problem.

As you listen to your recording, watch as well for your articulation of words. ESL students whose first languages don't differentiate between the /sh/ sound and its close cousin /ch/, for example, may say "share" when they mean "chair" or "shoes" when they mean "choose."[1] It is therefore important that you also check to make sure that you are using the correct meaning of the words you have selected for your speech.

1. Based on Robbin Crabtree and Robert Weissberg, *ESL Students in the Public Speaking Classroom* (Boston: Bedford/St. Martin's, 2000), 23.

Take the Plunge

WEB Sample speeches

As you prepare for your first speech, it is very important to follow each step in the speechmaking process described in the previous section. Keep track of your progress and stay aware of your feelings about the whole process—from the time the assignment is given to the few minutes immediately following the speech. Remember, the first speech is usually simple and fun, so try not to focus all your energies on how nervous or anxious you're feeling—even the most experienced speakers go through some degree of anxiety. But by taking as many opportunities as come their way to speak in public, and by practicing extensively, they learn to control their fear—you can, too.

MY FIRST SPEECH

Consider each item in the following checklist in two ways—as something to accomplish during preparation, and as something to consider after you have presented your speech. Use this self-assessment tool to improve future speeches by isolating areas where you need improvement.

Introduction

_____ 1. How will/did I capture attention?

_____ 2. What is/was my thesis statement?

_____ 3. What will/did I say to relate the topic to the audience?

_____ 4. What will/did I say to preview the main points of the speech?

_____ 5. What will/did I say to make the transition from my introduction to my first main point?

(continued on next page)

SELF-ASSESSMENT CHECKLIST

Body

_____ 1. Is/was the arrangement of my main points clear and logical?

_____ 2. What transition statements will/did I use between main points?

_____ 3. Do I have/did I use appropriate support material for each point?

Conclusion

_____ 1. How will/did I restate the thesis/purpose of my speech?

_____ 2. What will/did I say to summarize the main points?

_____ 3. What memorable thought will/did I end the speech with?

Delivery

_____ 1. What will/did I do to assure consistent eye contact?

_____ 2. What will/did I do to project appropriate vocal qualities (rate and volume, clear articulation)?

_____ 3. What will/did I do to ensure proper posture, gestures, and general movement?

My overall assessment of this speech is: _____

What I consider strengths in this speech: _____

Elements I need to improve on: _____

Goals for my next speech: _____

SAMPLE VISUALLY ANNOTATED INTRODUCTORY SPEECH

 WEB Video

The Dance of Life
ASHLEY WHITE

Warm smile connects with audience

We are on a lifelong journey to find our identity. On this journey, we look for those things that make us unique, that bring us success, and that hold us back, and we discover how they define our personality. We set standards for ourselves and observe our boundaries. We take so many extraordinary measures, but when exactly are we supposed to discover who we are? Is there a specific moment? Is there an initiation age? Is it ever certain? What happens if what defines us must suddenly be let go? How do we find new purpose with what is left? •

• Even though the speaker's topic is herself, she draws the audience in with the personal pronoun "We." This captures the audience's attention and makes listeners feel included. The speaker's use of a series of rhetorical questions is a dramatic way to introduce her thesis—the search for identity and purpose in life—and to preview the main points.

I have always identified myself as a dancer. Since age three I have been in dance classes, but since birth I have danced. It is not a path for the faint of heart, and yet seldom are dancers taken very seriously. Few people outside of the discipline understand the commitment, the scrutiny, the self-sacrifice, the physical and emotional pain—and the unspeakable joy—that dance affords its chosen ones. Dance truly does offer an inexpressible enjoyment, whether performed in the classroom, in rehearsal, or on stage. It becomes more than a hobby. It is self-defining. •

• The speaker's first main point introduces dance as her passion.

Quick pause to glance at notecard

My dance teacher was the first to notice the curve, and then I was formally diagnosed with scoliosis at the age of ten. Scoliosis is a lateral curvature of the spine ranging from slight to severe. It often gets worse during adolescent growth and stops worsening when growth stops. It affects girls and boys, but it is not life threatening. •

• The speaker introduces her second main point, that she developed scoliosis. She adds drama by signaling, in story form, that something has gone wrong with her chosen path.

At eleven, I was wearing a back brace at night, and at twelve, both day and night. Adolescence is a difficult time to deal with any anomaly. During a time when everyone was trying to fit the norm, the brace made me feel different. This caused me much anxiety and depression. Dance class was my only time of liberation, which made my desire to dance even stronger.

Effective gestures underscore emotion

I stopped wearing the brace once I got to high school because I had stopped growing; but during my second semester of college I received troubling news. My curve had worsened by fifteen degrees in four years, and it was time to consider surgery. The doctor informed me from the start that, with the surgery, dancing professionally would not be likely, although I would be able to dance recreationally. He also advised that without the surgery, my spine would continue to curve, leaving me with lifelong discomfort and misshapenness. I went through with the surgery in July 2007. The doctors placed two titanium rods on either side of my spine, held in place by hooks. Two months later, I am still recovering and have little pain.

Ashley turns to address audience members in all corners of the room

I am thankful for my overall health, for the success of the surgery, that one day soon I will dance again, and that amongst all this emotional turmoil, I have found a new passion. This art is expressed in the kitchen, not in the dance studio, and my training begins here at Johnson and Wales University. Cooking and dancing require many of the same skills: discipline, artistry, technique. •

However, knowledge of food can also provide me with endless career opportunities, where as a dancer I might never have worked steadily. This transition of redefining myself has been a difficult one, and I have learned that it is actually an ongoing one. Being in touch with oneself requires constant learning, redefining, and reapplying, and not just being dedicated to a single interest. This lifelong journey I am on? I know now that this is just the beginning of finding my own identity. •

• In a surprise twist, the speaker tells us that she has found a new passion. This is her third main point.

• The speaker concludes by returning to the theme she introduced in her introduction: the quest for identity.

SAMPLE INTRODUCTORY SPEECH

Past, Present, and Future
LISA TRAN

Introduction

Everybody has a history; some, perhaps, more interesting than others. • Mine began nearly twenty-one years ago in Saigon, Vietnam. My father, who was an affluent businessman, was taken captive along with many other men by the Vietnamese communist government and imprisoned because of his Chinese descent. All of our

• The speaker captures the audience's attention with a short but dramatically phrased introductory statement.

money, property, and rights were stripped away from us. My mother, three sisters, brother, and I escaped with thousands of other Vietnamese and Chinese refugees in search of safety and freedom.

For six long months, my family and I survived the most horrific boat ride to the United States. Hundreds of people died due to the grotesque conditions and diseases prevalent on the boat. Nevertheless, we landed on the coast of California only to find harsh media attention focused on us upon our arrival.

A program was implemented by placing each refugee family with an American caretaker. For three years, my family and I resided in Caney, Kansas, with Father Mike. •

In 1981, my family and I were finally reunited with my father, who was released by the strict communist government. Due to the untimely death of Father Mike, we moved south to Tulsa, Oklahoma, where my family and I have lived for almost twenty years. Although my journey seemed to begin in Vietnam, it has only just begun. •

Body

Through the trials and tribulations my family and I have undergone, we are lucky and fortunate to have become American citizens. I never dreamed that I would be the first Asian pom captain at the University of Oklahoma, a member of Kappa Kappa Gamma, and the 1999 Miss Greek OU. • I could not have accomplished these honors without knowing the difficulties and hardships of life. •

As a young child, I would mimic the choreography performed by the dancers on the television show *Star Search*. However, because we were poor, I could not afford dance lessons each week. Through hard work and perseverance, I trained myself to dance. Nine years later, I have earned individual honors as a dancer and have been teaching dance for a national company.

Because of my ability to dance, my sorority encouraged me to enter a pageant. I had never been in a pageant before, and was apprehensive from the moment my sorority voted me in. The house was confident in me, though, and offered support throughout the weeks I was training.

• Even in a short speech like this, the speaker probably should offer a little information about Father Mike.

• This preview—that the speaker's journey "has only just begun"—also acts as a transition statement.

• In just one sentence the speaker sets up three main, coordinate points— becoming pom captain, a sorority member, and a pageant winner.

• A series of subordinate points shows how the speaker overcame several personal trials and attained several noteworthy accomplishments.

On April 23, 1999, I was crowned Miss Greek OU. This title has allowed me to be a role model for young women in my community. • Most important, I have also been given the opportunity to represent my culture as one of the first Asian women to be voted Miss Greek OU. I could not have achieved this honor without the love and support of my sorority, my friends, and my family. These three accomplishments have shown me how far my life has come. My story does not end here, because the journey is not over.

• Rather than merely reciting a list of her accomplishments, the speaker frames them within the larger context of support from family, friends, and community.

Conclusion

"Dream what you want to dream, go where you want to go, be what you want to be, because you have only one life and one chance to do all the things you want to do." • I do not let the achievements that I have accomplished prove my self-worth. They merely symbolize the true passion and drive we have for living and succeeding. We are what we learn and take with us during this journey we call life. I am the past because I have appreciation; I am the present because I have learned humbleness; I am the future because I have so much more to learn. •

• This quotation reinforces the inspirational nature of the speech. Using her own life as an example, the speaker exhorts others to use their time wisely.

• The speaker's strong conclusion leaves the audience with something to think about as we ponder the precise meaning of her near-poetic statement, "I am the past because. . . ."

PUBLIC SPEAKING BASICS

PUBLIC SPEAKING BASICS

CHAPTER **3** Managing Speech Anxiety 36

What Makes Us Anxious about Public Speaking? 36

Pinpoint the Onset of Public Speaking Anxiety 37

▶ **CHECKLIST** Recognizing and Overcoming Your Underlying Fears about Public Speaking 38

Use Proven Strategies to Build Your Confidence 40

▶ **ESL SPEAKER'S NOTES** Confidence and Culture: When English Isn't Your First Language 41

▶ **CHECKLIST** Preparing to Speak with Confidence 45

CHAPTER **4** Listeners and Speakers 46

The Selective Nature of Listening 46

▶ **ESL SPEAKER'S NOTES** Learning by Listening 47

Listening and Speaking as Dialogic Communication 48

Barriers to Active Listening 48

▶ **CHECKLIST** Dealing with Distractions during Delivery of a Speech 49

▶ **ETHICALLY SPEAKING** The Responsibilities of Listening in the Public Arena 49

▶ **A CULTURAL PERSPECTIVE** Helping Diverse Audiences Understand You 51

Becoming a More Active Listener 51

Active Listening and Critical Thinking 53

▶ **CHECKLIST** Use the Thought/Speech Differential to Listen Critically 54

Guidelines for Evaluating Speeches and Presentations 54

▶ **PEER EVALUATION FORM** 56

CHAPTER **5** Ethical Public Speaking 57

Take Responsibility for Your Words 57

Use Your Rights of Free Speech Responsibly 59

▶ **SELF-ASSESSMENT CHECKLIST** Identifying Values 60

▶ **A CULTURAL PERSPECTIVE** Comparing Cultural Values 62

Observe the Ground Rules for Ethical Speaking 62

▶ **ETHICALLY SPEAKING** Speech Codes on Campus: Protection or Censorship? 64

Avoid Plagiarism 66

▶ **CHECKLIST** Steps to Avoid Plagiarism 68

Respect the Laws of Copyright and Fair Use 68

▶ **SELF-ASSESSMENT CHECKLIST** An Ethical Inventory 69

PUBLIC SPEAKING BASICS

CHAPTER **3** Managing Speech Anxiety

Recognize What Underlies the Fear of Public Speaking

- A lack of public speaking experience: It can be difficult to put the anxiety that often precedes new experiences into perspective. (p. 36)
- Feeling different: Everyone is different from everyone else, and even seasoned speakers experience anxiety. (p. 37)
- Being the center of attention: The audience won't notice things about you that you don't want to reveal. (p. 37)

Pinpoint the Onset of Your Anxiety and Plan to Overcome It

- Some people become anxious upon hearing that they must give a speech (pre-preparation anxiety). (p. 38)

    Don't allow your anxiety to deter you from planning your speech.
- For some, the onset of anxiety occurs as they begin to prepare the speech (preparation anxiety). (p. 39)

    Beware of avoidance and procrastination.
- Some people don't feel anxious until it's time to rehearse the speech (pre-performance anxiety). (p. 39)

    Practice your speech to build confidence.
- Many people don't experience public speaking anxiety until they actually begin to deliver the speech (performance anxiety). (p. 39)

    Practice stress-control breathing and other relaxation techniques.

To Build Confidence, Prepare and Practice

- Manage your time wisely during the preparation phase. (p. 40)
- Rehearse until you know how you want to express yourself. (p. 40)

View Giving a Speech as a Positive Opportunity

- Lessen anxiety by using positive thoughts prior to delivery. (p. 41)
- Picture the speech as an extension of an ordinary conversation. (p. 41)

Use Visualization and Relaxation Techniques to Gain a Sense of Control

- Visualize a positive outcome. (p. 42)
- Consider meditation, stress-control breathing, natural gestures, and movement. (p. 43)

Try to Lessen Your Fear of Being Judged

- Rather than thinking of your speech as a formal performance, try thinking of it as an ordinary conversation. (p. 41)

Focus on the Enjoyable and Empowering Aspects of Speaking

- You have the chance to influence others. (p. 45)
- Preparation and practice, attitude, stress management, and visualization all make public speaking challenging and exciting. (p. 45)

CHAPTER 4 Listeners and Speakers

As You Prepare, Consider Factors That Influence Listening

- People pay attention to what they hold to be important. (p. 47)
- People pay attention to information that touches their experiences and backgrounds. (p. 47)
- People filter new information based on what they already know. (p. 47)

Incorporate the Factors That Influence Listening into Your Speech

- Try to uncover what is important to your listeners. (p. 47)
- When explaining unfamiliar concepts, consider using analogies, metaphors, and other figures of speech. (p. 47)
- When introducing new information, associate it with something with which your listeners are already familiar. (p. 47)
- Appeal to your listeners' experiences and backgrounds. (p. 47)
- Use dialogic communication to balance speaking and listening. (p. 48)

Anticipate and Cope with Common Obstacles to Listening

- Plan ahead in order to minimize the impact of external distractions such as noise, movement, light, darkness, heat or cold, and so forth. (p. 48)
- Channel your energy into truly listening. (p. 48)
- As a speaker be sensitive to any distractions your audience may face. (p. 48)
- Internal distractions such as daydreaming, time pressures, emotional turmoil, or fatigue due to illness or lack of sleep can disrupt concentration. (p. 48)
- Don't assume that you already know what the speaker will say. (p. 49)
- Beware of listening defensively: Wait for the speaker to finish before devising your own mental arguments. (p. 49)

- Don't judge the speaker on the basis of his or her accent, appearance, or demeanor. Focus instead on what is actually being said. (p. 50)
- Reveal your needs to the speaker, try to gain clarification, and ask questions. (p. 50)

Use Strategies to Become a More Active Listener

- Set listening goals that encourage action. (p. 51)
- Listen for main ideas, take notes, and focus on the organizational pattern. (p. 52)
- Watch for nonverbal cues: eye contact, body language, facial expressions, and gestures. (p. 53)

Listen Critically to the Speaker's Evidence and Arguments

- Evaluate the speaker's evidence for accuracy and credibility. (p. 53)
- Analyze the speaker's assumptions and biases. (p. 53)
- Assess the speaker's reasoning: Look for faulty logic or inappropriate causal relationships. (p. 53)
- Resist false assumptions, overgeneralizations, and either-or thinking. (p. 53)
- Consider multiple perspectives. (p. 53)
- Summarize and assess the relevant facts and evidence before deciding how you will act on the speaker's information or argument. (p. 53)

Offer Constructive Feedback When Evaluating Speeches and Presentations

- Be honest and fair in your evaluation. (p. 54)
- Do not judge the message's content on the basis of the speaker's communication style. (p. 54)
- Be compassionate in your criticism: Start with something positive; focus on the speech, not on the speaker; and be selective in your criticism. (p. 55)

CHAPTER 5   Ethical Public Speaking

Take Responsibility for Your Power to Influence Others

- Be morally accountable for your message. (p. 57)
- Accept responsibility for the stands you take. (p. 57)

Earn the Audience's Trust

- Display good character (ethos). (p. 57)
- Develop a solid grasp of your subject (competence). (p. 57)

- Display sound reasoning skills. (p. 57)
- Present information honestly and without manipulation. (p. 57)
- Be genuinely interested in the welfare of your listeners. (p. 57)

Recognize and Respect Audience Values

- Consider what your audience's core values might be, and address them with sensitivity. (p. 58)
- When your topic is controversial, consider both sides of an issue and look for common ground. (p. 58)
- To get a better sense of your own and others' values, analyze them using the instruments in the text. (p. 58)

Recognize That Legal Speech Is Not Always Ethical Speech

- The First Amendment provides protection both to truthful speakers and to speakers whose words are inflammatory and offensive. (p. 60)
- Codes of ethical speech are built on moral rather than legal principles: Though often legally protected, racist, sexist, homophobic, and pornographic speech are clearly unethical. (p. 60)

Be Aware That Certain Types of Speech Are Illegal

- Speech that provokes people to violence ("fighting words") (p. 60)
- Speech that can be proved to harm an individual's reputation (slander or defamatory statements) (p. 61)
- Words spoken with a reckless disregard for the truth (p. 61)

Contribute to Positive Public Discourse

- Advance constructive goals. (p. 61)
- Avoid introducing conversation stoppers into public discourse. (p. 61)
- Follow the rules of engagement for civil public discourse. (p. 61)

Exhibit Trustworthiness, Respect, Responsibility, and Fairness

- Tell the truth, don't distort information, and acknowledge sources. (p. 63)
- Avoid ethnocentrism, stereotyping, and any hint of hate speech. (p. 63)
- Focus on issues, not on personalities. (p. 63)
- Make sure that your topic is socially constructive. (p. 65)
- Strive hard for accuracy. (p. 65)
- Acknowledge alternative and opposing views so that the audience can make informed decisions. (p. 65)

Avoid Plagiarism

· Orally acknowledge any source that requires credit in written form: other people's ideas, opinions, theories, evidence, and research; direct quotations; paraphrased information; facts and statistics. (p. 66)

Know the Copyright Law

· Facts and statistics that are common knowledge cannot be copyrighted but must be orally credited in your speech. (p. 66)
· Copyright law protects *intellectual property* (original authorship or expression). (p. 68)
· The fair use doctrine permits limited use of copyrighted materials without permission; such material must be orally credited in your speech. (p. 69)

KEY TERMS

Chapter 3

public speaking anxiety (PSA)
pre-preparation anxiety
preparation anxiety

pre-performance anxiety
anxiety stop-time
performance anxiety
trait anxiety

visualization
"fight or flight response"

Chapter 4

feedback loop
listening
selective perception
dialogic communication

active listening
listening distraction
external listening distraction
internal listening distraction

defensive listening
critical thinking
valid generalization
overgeneralization

Chapter 5

responsibility
ethics
ethos
speaker credibility
values
First Amendment
free speech
"fighting words"
slander
reckless disregard
for the truth
public discourse

invective
conversation stopper
rules of engagement
dignity
integrity
trustworthiness
respect
heckler's veto
ethnocentrism
stereotypes
hate speech
fairness

plagiarism
wholesale plagiarism
patchwrite plagiarism
direct quotation
paraphrase
common knowledge
copyright
public domain
intellectual property
fair use

CHAPTER 3

Managing Speech Anxiety

Anxiety is the handmaiden of creativity.

— Chuck Jones, animator

Everyone, even accomplished speakers, can feel jittery before they give a speech. It turns out that feeling nervous is not only normal but desirable. Channeled properly, nervousness can boost performance. Sometimes, as singer Stevie Nicks of Fleetwood Mac testifies, those butterflies we feel before facing a crowd can actually be the "key to that magical performance."

The difference between seasoned public speakers and the rest of us is not that seasoned speakers don't feel nervous or anxious. It's just that they're more practiced at making nervousness work *for* rather than *against* them. They use specific techniques, described in this chapter, to help them cope with and minimize their tension.

> I focus on the information. I try not to think about being graded. I also practice my speech a ton to really make sure I do not speak too quickly. I time myself so that I can develop an average time. This makes me more confident [in dealing] with time requirements. And, because I know that I am well prepared, I really try to just relax. — *Kristen Obracay, student*

What Makes Us Anxious about Public Speaking?

Researchers have identified several factors that underlie the fear of public speaking.[1] These factors include lack of public speaking experience (or having had a negative experience), feeling different from members of the audience, and uneasiness about being the center of attention. Each factor can lead to the onset of **public speaking anxiety (PSA)**—that is, fear or anxiety associated with either actual or anticipated communication to an audience as a speaker.[2] Anxiety is simply a state of increased fear or arousal. Some of us tend to be more anxious than others in the face of public speaking, depending on our psychological traits, life experiences, and even genetic factors.[3] Fortunately, regardless of where we begin, we can learn techniques to tame this anxiety and make it work for us.

Lack of Positive Experience

If you have had no exposure to public speaking or have had unpleasant experiences, anxiety about what to expect when you give a speech is only natural, and is hard to put into perspective. It's a bit of a vicious circle. Some people react by deciding to avoid making speeches altogether. But gaining more experience is a key to overcoming speech anxiety. Each time we give a speech, we learn more about meeting various challenges, from keeping track of our thoughts to feeling confident about facing different types of audiences and occasions.

Feeling Different

Novice speakers often feel alone—as if they were the only person ever to experience the dread of public speaking. The prospect of getting up in front of an audience makes them extra-sensitive to their personal idiosyncrasies, such as a less-than-perfect haircut, a slight lisp, or an accent. They may believe that no one could possibly be interested in anything they have to say.

As inexperienced speakers, we become anxious because we assume that being different somehow means being inferior. Actually, everyone is different from everyone else in many ways. Just as true, nearly everyone experiences nervousness about giving a speech.

> I control my anxiety by mentally viewing myself as being 100 percent equal to my classmates.
> — *Lee Morris, student*

Being the Center of Attention

Certain audience behaviors—such as lack of eye contact with the speaker, pointing, or conversing with a neighbor—can be disconcerting. Our tendency in these situations is to think that we must be doing something wrong; we wonder what it is and whether the entire audience has noticed it.

Left unchecked, this kind of thinking can distract us from the speech itself, with all our attention now focused on "me." As a result, we become all the more sensitive to things that might be wrong with what we're doing—and that makes us feel even more conspicuous, which in turn increases our anxiety! In fact, an audience generally notices very little about us that we don't want to reveal, especially if the speech is well developed and effectively delivered. Remind yourself that you see yourself more critically than the audience does, so relax and focus on delivering your message.

> It's always scary to speak in front of others, but you just have to remember that everyone is human. . . . Nobody wants you to fail; they're not waiting on you to mess up. If I keep that in mind, I can survive giving a speech.
> — *Mary Parrish, student*

Pinpoint the Onset of Public Speaking Anxiety

Different people become anxious at different times during the speechmaking process. For some people PSA arises as soon as they learn that they will have to give a speech at some point in the future. For others it arises as they approach the podium. By pinpointing where you might initially experience speech anxiety, you can address it promptly with specific anxiety-reducing techniques (see Figure 3.1).

RECOGNIZING AND OVERCOMING YOUR UNDERLYING FEARS ABOUT PUBLIC SPEAKING

Problem	Solution
✔ Are you intimidated by a lack of experience?	Prepare well for your speech and practice it several times. Rehearse in front of at least one other person. This will give you actual experience with your speech and build your confidence.
✔ Are you worried about appearing different from others?	Remember that everyone is different from everyone else in many ways. Dress well, be well groomed, and trust that you will make a good impression.
✔ Are you uncomfortable about being the center of attention?	Put the focus on the speech instead of on yourself, and remind yourself that the audience won't notice anything about you that you don't want to reveal.

Pre-Preparation Anxiety

Some people feel anxious the minute they know they will be giving a speech. **Pre-preparation anxiety** can be a problem for two reasons. First, a highly anxious person may be reluctant to begin planning for the speech. Second, anxiety

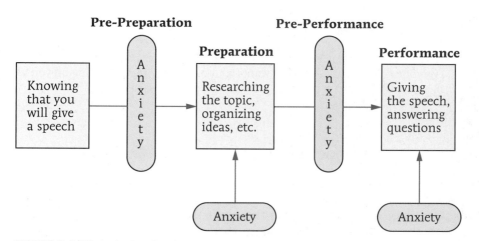

FIGURE 3.1 Where Anxiety Can Occur in the Speechmaking Process

can preoccupy the person to such an extent that he or she misses vital information that is required to fulfill the speech assignment. If you feel particularly nervous when presented with a speech assignment, start very early using the techniques for managing speech anxiety described later in this chapter.

Preparation Anxiety

For some people, anxiety arises only when they actually begin to prepare for the speech. They might feel overwhelmed at the amount of time and planning required. They might hit a roadblock that puts them behind schedule, or be unable to locate adequate support for a critical point. These kinds of pressures produce a cycle of stress, procrastination, and outright avoidance. All contribute to **preparation anxiety**. Research has shown, however, that for the great majority of people, anxiety is lowest during the preparation phase.[4] If you find yourself feeling anxious during this point in the preparation process, take short, relaxing breaks to regain your confidence and focus.

Pre-Performance Anxiety

Some people experience anxiety as they rehearse their speech. This is when the reality of the situation sets in: Soon they will face an audience that will be watching and listening only to them. Or they may feel that their ideas don't sound as focused or as interesting as they should. Or they sense that time is short. If this **pre-performance anxiety** is strong enough, and is interpreted negatively, they may even decide to stop rehearsing. If you experience heightened anxiety at this point in preparing a speech, consider using **anxiety stop-time**, a technique recommended by entertainer and life coach Christine Kane. With this technique, you allow your anxiety to present itself for up to a few minutes until you declare time for confidence to step in so you can proceed to complete your practice.[5]

> I experience anxiety before, during, and after the speech. My "before speech" anxiety begins the night before my speech, but then I begin to look over my notecards, and I start to realize that I am ready for this speech. I practice one more time and I tell myself I am going to be fine.   — *Paige Mease, student*

Performance Anxiety

[WEB] Relaxation audio

For most people, anxiety tends to be highest just before speaking begins.[6] This is true even of actors who report that their worst stage fright occurs just as they walk on stage to begin their performances. **Performance anxiety** is probably most pronounced during the introduction of the speech, when we utter the first words of the speech and are most aware of the audience's attention. As might be expected, audiences we perceive to be hostile or negative usually cause us to feel more anxious than those we sense are positive or neutral.[7] However, experienced speakers agree that if they control their nervousness during the introduction, the rest of the speech comes relatively easily.

Each of us will experience more or less speech anxiety at these four different points in the process depending mainly on our level of **trait anxiety**. People with high trait anxiety are naturally anxious much of the time, whereas people with low trait anxiety will experience nervousness usually only in novel situations. Public speaking situations tend to make both kinds of people nervous, for the reasons outlined earlier (lack of experience, feeling different, being the center of attention). But high trait-anxious individuals can have a more challenging time overall than low trait-anxious persons. In particular, researchers have shown that low trait-anxious people get nervous when starting a speech but gain confidence throughout the speech. High trait-anxious people, by contrast, start out nervous and continue getting more nervous throughout the speech. After their speeches, low trait-anxious speakers often comment positively about the experience and look forward to the next opportunity. But high trait-anxious speakers tend to focus on what they felt went wrong and how they didn't enjoy making the speech.[8] Regardless of when anxiety about a speech strikes, and whether you are high or low in trait anxiety, the important thing to remember is to manage your anxiety and not let it manage you.

Use Proven Strategies to Build Your Confidence

A number of proven strategies can help you rein in your fears about public speaking, from meditation and visualization to other forms of relaxation techniques. The first step in effective management of speech anxiety involves planning and practicing your speech. Professional speaker Lenny Laskowski sums it up pithily in the 9Ps: "Prior Proper Preparation Prevents Poor Performance of the Person Putting on the Presentation."[9]

Prepare and Practice

Preparation should begin as soon as possible after a speech is assigned. If you are confident that you know your material and have adequately rehearsed your delivery, you're far more likely to feel confident at the podium. Once you have prepared the speech, you should rehearse it several times. Recent research points to the advantages of practicing your speech in front of a small audience of, say, seven or eight people.[10] Students who practiced this way received significantly higher evaluations of their classroom speeches than students who didn't practice or practiced in different ways. And whereas practicing didn't correlate directly with reduced speech anxiety, the overall greater performance outcomes for those who did practice suggests that even the students who were more anxious were better able to control their anxiety. Speech coach John Robert Colombo asserts that the best way to work out your fear of speaking is to *overwork* it.[11] That is, take every opportunity you can to confront what scares you—practice as often as you can, and, in the future, accept as many speaking engagements as appropriate.

Knowing your material is crucial! The worst anxiety comes when you feel un-prepared. You just can't help but be nervous, at least a little. If you are confi-dent about what you're speaking the anxiety fades and you'll feel more comfortable.   — *Shea Michelle Allen, student*

Modify Thoughts and Attitudes

Negative thoughts increase speech anxiety.[12] A positive attitude, by contrast, results in lowered heart rate and reduced anxiety during delivery of the speech.[13] From start to finish, regard your speech as a valuable, worthwhile, and chal-lenging activity. Remind yourself of all the reasons that public speaking is help-ful personally, socially, and professionally. Rather than thinking of your speech as a formal performance where you will be judged and critiqued, try thinking of it as a kind of ordinary conversation. By doing so, you will feel less threatened and more relaxed about the process.[14] And with each successive speech experi-ence, your attitude about public speaking will grow more positive.

ESL SPEAKER'S NOTES

Confidence and Culture: When English Isn't Your First Language

For native English speakers, the fear of being at center stage is normal. If you are a non-native speaker, anxiety about delivering a speech in a non-native language is equally normal. It is important to know that you are not alone.

Try to think about public speaking as an opportunity to learn more about the English language and how to use it. Following are some tips that all novice speakers, regardless of whether English is their first language, will find helpful:

1. Take your time and speak slowly as you introduce the purpose and the main points of your speech. This will give your listeners time to get used to your voice and to focus on your message.

2. Practice saying any English words that may be troublesome for you five times. Then say the words again, five times. Progress slowly until each word becomes clearer and easier to pronounce. This type of practice will give you time to work on any accent features you might want to improve. [1]

3. Avoid using jargon (see Chapter 17 and the Glossary). Learn to use a the-saurus to find *synonyms,* or words that mean the same thing, that are sim-pler and easier to pronounce.

4. Offer words from your native language as a way of drawing attention to a point you're making. This helps the audience appreciate your native lan-guage and your accent. For example, the Spanish word *corazón* has a more lyrical quality than its English counterpart, *heart.* Capitalize on the beauty of your native tongue.

1. J. E. Flege, J. M. Munro, and I. R. A. MacKay, "Factors Affecting Strength of Perceived Foreign Accent in a Second Language," *Journal of the Acoustical Society of America* 97 (1995): 3125ff.

Just before a speech those feelings of anxiety undoubtedly try to sneak in. The way I keep them from taking over is to not let my mind become negative! As long as I keep positive thoughts of confidence in my head, anxiety doesn't stand a chance!   — *Morgan Verdery, student*

Visualize Success

Visualization is a highly successful way to reduce nervousness and help you prepare effectively for your speech.[15] Popular among athletes, the technique is used to summon feelings and actions consistent with effective performance.[16] Speech communication researchers have developed visualization techniques for increasing positive expectations associated with speechmaking. The following is their script for visualizing success on a public speaking occasion. The exercise requires you, the speaker, to close your eyes and visualize a series of positive feelings and actions that will occur on the day of your speech.

Close your eyes and allow your body to get comfortable in the chair in which you are sitting. Move around until you feel that you are in a position that will continue to be relaxing for you for the next ten to fifteen minutes. Take a deep, comfortable breath and hold it . . . now slowly release it through your nose. Now take another deep breath and make certain that you are breathing from the diaphragm . . . hold it . . . now slowly release it and note how you feel while doing this. Now one more deep breath . . . hold it . . . and release it slowly . . . and begin your normal breathing pattern. Shift around if you need to get comfortable again.

Now begin to visualize the beginning of a day in which you are going to give an informative speech. See yourself getting up in the morning, full of energy, full of confidence, looking forward to the day's challenges. You are putting on just the right clothes for the task at hand that day. Dressing well makes you look and feel good about yourself, so you have on just what you want to wear, which clearly expresses your sense of inner well-being. As you are driving, riding, or walking to the speech setting, note how clear and confident you feel, and how others around you, as you arrive, comment positively regarding your fine appearance and general demeanor. You feel thoroughly prepared for the target issue you will be presenting today.

Now you see yourself standing or sitting in the room where you will present your speech, talking very comfortably and confidently with others in the room. The people to whom you will be presenting your speech appear to be quite friendly and are very cordial in their greetings and conversations prior to the presentation. You feel absolutely sure of your material and of your ability to present the information in a forceful, convincing, positive manner.

Now you see yourself approaching the area from which you will present. You are feeling very good about this presentation and see yourself move eagerly forward. All of your audiovisual materials are well organized, well planned, and clearly aid your presentation.[17]

Practicing the mental exercise of seeing yourself give a successful speech will help you prepare with confidence and strengthen your positive attitudes and expectations for speechmaking.

Activate the Relaxation Response

Before, during, and sometimes after a speech you may experience rapid heart rate and breathing, dry mouth, faintness, freezing-up, or other uncomfortable sensations. These are automatic physiological reactions that result from the **"fight or flight response"**—the body's automatic response to a threatening or fear-inducing event. The sensations associated with this response indicate the body is preparing to confront a threat head-on ("fight") or to make a hasty escape from the threat ("flight").[18] Research shows that you can reduce these sensations by activating the relaxation response using techniques such as meditation and controlled breathing.[19] Just as you would warm up before taking a lengthy jog, plan on practicing the following relaxation techniques before—and even during—your speech. They can improve how you respond to stress by slowing your heart rate, lowering your blood pressure, slowing your breathing rate, increasing blood flow to major muscles, and reducing muscle tension, all of which help you feel better about public speaking[20] and result in better concentration and sharper performance as a speaker.

Briefly Meditate

You can calm yourself considerably with this brief meditation exercise:

1. Sit comfortably in a quiet place.
2. Relax your muscles, moving from neck to shoulders to arms to back to legs.
3. Choose a word, phrase, or prayer that is associated with your belief system (e.g., "Namaste," "Om," "Hail Mary, full of grace"). Breathe slowly and say it until you become calm (about ten to twenty minutes).

Use Stress-Control Breathing

When you feel stressed, the center of your breathing tends to move from the abdomen to the upper chest, leaving you with a reduced supply of air. The chest and shoulders rise, and you feel out of breath. With *stress-control breathing,* you will feel more movement in the stomach than in the chest. Try stress-control breathing in two stages.

Stage One.   Inhale air and let your abdomen go out. Exhale air and let your abdomen go in. Do this for a while until you get into the rhythm of it.

Stage Two.   As you inhale, use a soothing word such as *calm* or *relax,* or a personal mantra, as follows: "Inhale *calm,* abdomen out, exhale *calm,* abdomen in." Go slowly. Each inhalation and exhalation of stress-control breathing takes about three to five seconds.

Begin practicing stress-control breathing several days before you're scheduled to speak. Then, once the speaking event arrives, begin stress-control breathing while awaiting your turn at the podium. (You can even place your hand on your abdomen unobtrusively to check how you're doing.) After you've been called to the podium, you can focus on breathing once more while you're arranging your notes and getting ready to begin.

> I get very anxious before I'm about to speak, so I have two ways to cope with my nervousness. I take a couple deep breaths through my stomach; I breathe in through my nose and out of my mouth. This allows more oxygen to the brain so you can think clearly. I also calm myself down by saying, "Everything will be okay, and the world is not going to crumble before me if I mess up." — *Jenna Sanford, student*

Use Movement to Minimize Anxiety

While delivering your speech, you can use controlled movements with your hands and body to release nervousness.

Practice Natural Gestures

Practice some controlled, natural gestures that might be useful in enhancing your speech, such as holding up your index finger when stating your first main point. Think about what you want to say as you do this, instead of thinking about how you look or feel. (See Chapter 20 for tips on practicing natural gestures.)

Move as You Speak

You don't have to stand perfectly still behind the podium when you deliver a speech. Walk around as you make some of your points. Movement relieves tension and helps hold the audience's attention. One way to prepare for more fluid but controlled movement is to exercise early on the day of your speech. Exercise can sharpen your mental focus and leave you more limber and better able to manage your movements.[21]

Learn from Feedback

Speech evaluations help to identify ways to improve what you do. Evaluation allows you to compare what you were assigned to do and what you planned to do with what you actually do, and thus indicates ways to deliver a more effective speech. You can learn a lot through self-evaluation, but objective evaluations by others often are more helpful because self-evaluations tend to be distorted.[22] Although no one likes to feel evaluated, it is a necessary part of a speech class; inevitably, your speech assignments will be evaluated by your instructors (a more formal evaluation that is written and graded) and probably by your classmates (an informal evaluation) as well. Your classmates and instructor will provide practical feedback to help you do better in your next speech. Using their evaluations is part of learning to be an effective speaker.

Enjoy the Occasion

WEB Chapter quizzes

Tara's course schedule for the new semester included a speech course. She says that she dreaded it all summer long. On her way to class on the first day she seriously considered bypassing it and going straight to her adviser's office to drop it. But she went to class anyway, perhaps realizing that she would have to take the course or one very much like it before she could graduate. "I was surprised after the first day of class to feel optimistic about it," she says. "The instructor was friendly and seemed to understand the students with concerns like mine." Hearing some of her classmates comment about how they looked forward to the challenge of giving speeches gave Tara a sense that the course could be worthwhile. But the clincher came after the instructor had students stand and say a few words about themselves and their ambitions. "It was obvious that some of my classmates were nervous about this activity, but it was also easy to see that, really, all of them enjoyed talking to the class." It made her feel that she had something meaningful in common with them. She left the class feeling much better than when she walked in; not fully confident yet, but at least wanting to see what she could do.

Most people ultimately find that giving speeches can indeed be fun. It's satisfying and empowering to influence people, and a good speech is a sure way to accomplish that goal. Preparing and practicing, maintaining a positive attitude, managing the inevitable stress of public speaking by making it work for you, and visualizing success—all of this makes public speaking both challenging and exciting. Think of it in these terms, and chances are it will come out that way.

PREPARING TO SPEAK WITH CONFIDENCE

Upon each successful completion of a speech assignment, your confidence will grow, but you need to work conscientiously at building confidence. As you prepare for each speech assignment, follow these general steps as outlined in more detail in this chapter.

1. *Prepare and practice.* As soon as you have been given an assignment to speak, start planning not only your topic but also when and where you will practice your speech.

2. *Modify thoughts and attitudes.* Keep your thoughts positive, concentrating on what works and makes good sense as you develop your topic, and on the positive outcomes that will result from your speech.

3. *Visualize success.* Use the visualization exercise to practice seeing yourself in an optimistic frame of mind with well-developed speech points that you deliver enthusiastically and effectively.

4. *Utilize relaxation techniques.* Use the techniques of stress-control breathing, natural gesturing, and general movement while speaking to help yourself relax.

5. *Learn from the task and enjoy it.* Think of your speech assignment as a learning opportunity rather than just another hurdle to jump for your degree.

CHECKLIST

CHAPTER 4

Listeners and Speakers

As a student of public speaking, you wear two hats—those of speaker and listener. Listeners and speakers are interdependent: Listeners need someone to whom they will listen, and speakers need someone to whom they will address their remarks. Thus it is listener and speaker together who truly make a speech a speech—who co-create its meaning. Successful speakers adjust their message based on their listeners' reactions, and vice versa. Communication scholars call this continual flow, or *circular response* between speaker and listener, the **feedback loop**.[1]

Listening is a communication activity that you do more than any other. On average, you listen 40 percent of the time, but speak only 35 percent. Because listening research reveals that most people retain only half of what they hear immediately and only 35 percent of what they heard after twenty-four hours, it is essential to hone your listening skills.[2] This course is the perfect place to do so.

The more skilled you are at listening to speeches, the more you will learn about what will and won't work for your speech. Focusing on the art of listening will also serve you well in many arenas other than public speaking. Numerous studies show that competent listeners tend to be efficient and successful in both their personal and professional lives and tend to be better problem solvers and more engaged citizens. In fact, recent research indicates that listening skills are the most highly valued skills among new hires.[3]

The Selective Nature of Listening

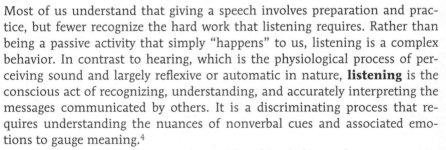 WEB Chapter quizzes

Most of us understand that giving a speech involves preparation and practice, but fewer recognize the hard work that listening requires. Rather than being a passive activity that simply "happens" to us, listening is a complex behavior. In contrast to hearing, which is the physiological process of perceiving sound and largely reflexive or automatic in nature, **listening** is the conscious act of recognizing, understanding, and accurately interpreting the messages communicated by others. It is a discriminating process that requires understanding the nuances of nonverbal cues and associated emotions to gauge meaning.[4]

Can you recall sharing reactions with a friend about a lecture, a movie, or another event and noticing that even though you both attended the same affair, you formed quite different impressions? In any given situation, no two listeners will process information in exactly the same way. The reason lies in

selective perception—people pay attention selectively to certain messages while ignoring others. Several factors influence what we listen to and what we ignore:

1. *We pay attention to what we hold to be important.* We are most motivated to listen to others if we think that what is being said affects us or reflects our interests, needs, values, attitudes, and beliefs.

2. *We pay attention to information that touches our experiences and backgrounds.* If we listen to something that is foreign to us, chances are we'll just zone out. To catch and sustain listeners' attention, a speaker must in some way touch upon audience members' experiences and backgrounds.

3. *We sort and filter new information on the basis of what we already know.* According to learning theory, all new concepts are understood as analogies to previous concepts.[5]

As a speaker, in line with these principles, try to uncover what is important to your audience. To capture listeners' attention, appeal to their experiences and backgrounds. When introducing new information, make it relevant by associating it with something with which your listeners are already familiar. Consider clarifying your meaning through analogies, similes, metaphors, and other figures of speech, and help listeners visualize your ideas with presentation aids (see Chapters 17 and 21–23).

ESL SPEAKER'S NOTES

Learning by Listening

As every student of a foreign language knows, listening is the key to learning a language. Using textbooks to study usage and grammar is important, but it is through the spoken language—hearing it and speaking it—that we gain fluency.

Listening to the speeches of colleagues or classmates, as well as those broadcast over the air or on podcasts, can help you hone the skills you need to become a better speaker. Nearly all college libraries own many recorded and online materials made specifically for ESL speakers such as yourself, and the reference librarian will be happy to locate them for you. The Internet also offers many helpful listening resources. Among the many sites you will find is the *Merriam-Webster Online Dictionary* (www.merriam-webster.com), which includes an audio feature that allows you to hear the correct pronunciation of words. You can also download and listen to speeches directly on the Internet.

As you listen to these resources, you can:

· Build your vocabulary.

· Improve pronunciation through guided repetition.

· Learn new idioms, or informal expressions, used by native speakers of English.

· Observe body posture, gestures, intonation, and other nonverbal aspects of delivery.

Listening and Speaking as Dialogic Communication

Dialogic communication is the open sharing of ideas in an atmosphere of respect.[6] In contrast to *monologue,* in which we try merely to impose what we think on another person or group of people, true dialogue encourages both speaker and listener to reach conclusions together. For the speaker, this means approaching a speech not as an argument that must be "won," but as an opportunity to achieve understanding with audience members. For listeners, it means maintaining an open mind and listening with empathy.

In the public sphere, where so many people of diverse backgrounds and opinions converge in the attempt to solve problems, dialogic communication offers us a better chance of avoiding conflict and discord and achieving workable compromises.[7]

Barriers to Active Listening

Active listening—listening that is focused and purposeful—isn't possible under conditions that distract us.[8] As you listen to speeches, try to identify and overcome some common obstacles.

Minimize External and Internal Distractions

A **listening distraction** is anything that competes for attention we are trying to give to something else. You may have every intention of listening to someone's presentation but instead find yourself thinking about an upcoming exam. Or perhaps you're hungry, tired, or angry about a recent incident. Distractions can originate outside of us, in the environment (external distractions), or within us, in our thoughts and feelings (internal distractions).

External listening distractions—anything from the din of jackhammers to competing conversations to poor lighting—can significantly reduce listening rates and interfere with the active listening process.[9] To minimize these distractions, try to anticipate and plan for them. For example, if you struggle to see or hear at a distance, arrive early and sit in the front.

So often we attend an event, whether it be a class lecture or a major speech, and fail to follow the speaker's words. We might be tired or upset about something that occurred prior to the event. To reduce these kinds of **internal listening distractions**, make some intentions for yourself. Consciously focus on listening. Avoid daydreaming and monitor yourself for lapses in attention. Plan on being well rested for any important speaking event you attend.

In your role as speaker, you can help listeners stay focused by addressing promptly any distractions they may face. For example, rather than ignore intruding noise, you can close windows and doors or ask audience members to move closer to you.

DEALING WITH DISTRACTIONS DURING DELIVERY OF A SPEECH

✓ *Problem:* **Passing distractions** (chatting, entry of latecomers)
   Solution: Pause until distraction recedes.

✓ *Problem:* **Ongoing noise** (construction)
   Solution: Raise speaking volume.

✓ *Problem:* **Sudden distraction** (collapsing chair, falling object)
   Solution: Minimize response and proceed.

✓ *Problem:* **Audience interruption** (raised hand, prolonged comment)
   Solution: Acknowledge audience reaction and either follow up or defer response to conclusion of speech.

Guard against Scriptwriting and Defensive Listening

When we engage in scriptwriting, we focus on what we, rather than the speaker, will say next.[10] Similarly, people who engage in **defensive listening** decide either that they won't like what the speaker is going to say or that they know better.

When you find yourself scriptwriting or listening with a defensive posture, hear the speaker out. Try to focus on the speaker's motives for the remarks that offend you. Remember, by being open to the speaker you demonstrate respect, a first step in creating dialogue.[11] You may still end up disagreeing with the speaker, but at least you'll do so from a position of actually having heard what he or she has said. Remind yourself that effective listening precedes successful rebuttal.[12]

Beware of Laziness and Overconfidence

Laziness and overconfidence can manifest themselves in several ways: We may expect too little from speakers, ignore important information, or display an arrogant attitude. Later, we discover that we missed important information. Never assume that you already know what a speaker will say. You'll very seldom be right.

ETHICALLY SPEAKING

The Responsibilities of Listening in the Public Arena

As a speaker you have the power of the podium, but as a listener you also have considerable power that you can wield constructively or destructively. An example of the latter includes rude listening behaviors such as heckling, name-calling, interrupting out of turn, and other breaches in civility. Beyond short-circuiting communication, these acts can easily

(continued on next page)

lead to explosive results—from menacing clashes among activists on opposite sides of a cause to eruptions at town hall meetings and other civic venues.

Perhaps you have witnessed the fallout of such clashes. In one such instance, at a school board meeting in Connecticut, an audience member who took exception to a board member's proposal threw a pitcher of ice water in his face. Visibly shaken, the board member had to be escorted out of the room by the police. The meeting was adjourned abruptly, some on the board considered resigning, and many parents were fearful of attending other meetings.

The ability to dissent from prevailing opinion is one of the hallmarks of a free society. As listeners, we are ethically bound to refrain from disruptive and intimidating tactics that are meant to silence those with whom we disagree. If we find the arguments of others morally offensive, we are equally bound to speak up in refutation. Only in this manner can we preserve the freedom to express our ideas. Clearly, the power to listen can translate into being socially responsible or socially destructive.

Work to Overcome Cultural Barriers

Differences in dialects or accents, nonverbal cues, word choice, and even physical appearance can serve as barriers to listening, but they need not do so if you focus on the message rather than the messenger and follow these strategies:

- Refrain from judging a speaker on the basis of his or her accent, appearance, or demeanor, and focus instead on what is actually being said. Put yourself in the speaker's shoes, and imagine what it would be like if you were addressing an audience in a new language.

- Reveal your needs to the speaker whenever possible. Try to gain clarification by asking questions. Turn confusion into curiosity and an opportunity to learn about other people's experiences.[13]

Overcoming cultural barriers to listening is important in all contexts of communication, including public discourse. When listening to (and delivering) speeches on such culturally laden public policy issues as border security and immigration reform, do your part to help diverse members of your audience actively listen to and understand your message. Whether as a speaker or an audience member, grappling with conflicts rooted in cultural differences demands empathetic listening and the suspension of disbelief characteristic of dialogic communication.

Becoming a More Active Listener

WEB Links

Active listeners use their eyes as well as their ears to decode a speaker's nonverbal and verbal cues. They listen for the speaker's main points and critically evaluate evidence used to support claims. Active listeners:

A CULTURAL PERSPECTIVE

Helping Diverse Audiences Understand You

When speaking to diverse audiences, the following steps will minimize barriers to understanding:

- Watch for *idioms,* or colloquial expressions such as "under the weather," "apple of his eye," and "bad-mouth," that non-native speakers might not know. Either eliminate or define them. (See Chapter 17 for additional tips on using language in a culturally sensitive manner.)

- Speak at a rate that is neither too fast nor too slow. Pay particular attention to pronunciation and articulation. (See Chapter 19.)

- Be alert to nonverbal cues that suggest that listeners may not comprehend you, and clarify points when indicated.

- Set listening goals.
- Listen for main ideas.
- Watch for the speaker's nonverbal cues and communicate their own.

Set Listening Goals

Setting listening goals helps you prepare to get the most from a listening situation. What do you need and expect from the listening situation? Keep these goals in mind as you listen. Try to state your listening goals in a way that encourages action. Table 4.1 illustrates the steps in setting listening goals.

Listen for Main Ideas

No one has perfect retention. To ensure that you hear and retain the speaker's most important points, try these strategies:

- *Listen for the speaker's organizational pattern* (see Chapters 13 and 27). Knowing the sequence and structure of a speech makes it easy for you to understand and remember the content.

- *Listen for introductions, transitions, and conclusions to alert you to the main points.* Most speakers will introduce their main points in their *introductory remarks.* This gives the listener the chance to identify these points and focus on their discussion later: "I have three points I want to make tonight. First, . . ."

    Transitions can also alert the listener to the fact that a main point is about to be discussed: "My next major point is. . . ." Speakers often use many of the following transitions to preview a main idea: "One, two, three, . . ."; "First, second, third, . . ."; "Most important, . . ."; "Another

TABLE 4.1 Steps in Setting Listening Goals
Identify Need: "I must know Suzanne's speech thesis, purpose, main points, and type of organization in order to complete and hand in a written evaluation."
Indicate Performance Standard: "I will get a better grade on the evaluation if I am able to identify and evaluate the major components of Suzanne's speech."
Make Action Statement (Goal): "I will minimize distractions and practice the active listening steps during Suzanne's speech. I will take careful notes during her speech and ask questions about anything I do not understand."
Assess Goal Achievement: "Before I leave the classroom, I will review my notes carefully to make sure that I covered everything."

point (issue) I would raise. . . ." *Conclusions* are a valuable place to re-check your memory of the main points: "Let me recap those three rules for living overseas. One, . . ."

- *Watch for a more direct eye gaze.* Speakers are more likely to look at you when they are trying to make an important point. In addition, they are likely to shift their gaze to a different part of the audience when moving from one main point to another.
- *Take notes on the speaker's main points.* Several different methods of note taking—bullet, column, and outline—can be helpful when listening to public speeches (see Table 4.2).

Watch for Nonverbal Cues

Much of a message's meaning is communicated nonverbally; visual cues can increase listening rates up to 40 percent.[14] You can use this information as

TABLE 4.2 Methods of Note Taking		
Method	Description	Example
Bullet	Notes list the main points and/or supporting material in bullet form.	• Bipolar disorder is actually a spectrum of disorders. • Adults suffer more classical patterns of mood swings.
Column	Notes are taken in two columns. One column is used for verbatim notes, and the other is used for interpretations or notes to yourself.	"Make sure your hands are dry." Grip the ball with the thumb and first two fingers.
Outline	Notes are taken according to the organizational format or outline that the speaker is using (see Chapters 13 and 27).	

you listen to speeches. *Body language* is an excellent source of information. Watch the speaker's stance and posture. Do they seem rigid and wooden? If so, the speaker may be nervous and may not feel comfortable with the material he or she is presenting. *Facial expressions* also provide cues to help you listen better. Speakers who are committed to their material are more likely to display facial expressions that are consistent with their commitment to the message. Smiling, frowning, raising eyebrows, and other expressions of emotion are useful cues in determining the speaker's sincerity and enthusiasm for the message.[15] The same cues can betray the speaker's real feelings. If verbal and nonverbal messages do not correspond, the nonverbal cues are usually the more honest ones.

Active Listening and Critical Thinking

Active listening and critical thinking go hand in hand. The use of one skill builds the other. **Critical thinking** is the ability to evaluate claims on the basis of well-supported reasons. Critical thinkers are able to look for flaws in arguments and resist claims that have no supporting evidence.[16] They don't take things at face value.

As you listen to speeches, use your critical faculties to:

- *Evaluate the speaker's evidence.* Is it accurate? Are the sources credible?
- *Analyze the speaker's assumptions and biases.* What lies behind the speaker's assertions? Does the evidence support these assertions?
- *Assess the speaker's reasoning.* Does it betray faulty logic? Does it rely on false assumptions, overgeneralizations, either-or thinking, or other fallacies in reasoning? A **valid generalization** is supported by different types of evidence from different sources, but it does not make claims beyond a reasonable point. **Overgeneralizations** are unsupported conclusions (e.g., "All welfare recipients are lazy"). Test the validity of a generalization by determining if the basis of support is biased in any way. *Either-or thinking* is dominated by just two choices and creates false dilemmas that do not in fact exist. (See Chapter 26 for additional fallacies of reasoning.)
- *Consider multiple perspectives.* Is there another way to view the argument? How do other perspectives compare with the speaker's?
- *Summarize and assess the relevant facts and evidence.* If the speaker asks for an action on the part of listeners (as is often the case in persuasive speeches; see Chapter 25), decide how you will act on the basis of the evidence. Will you be more apt to act on the evidence itself, or in line with what you think most people will do?

CHECKLIST

USE THE THOUGHT/SPEECH DIFFERENTIAL TO LISTEN CRITICALLY

Did you know that we think at a much faster rate than we speak? We speak at ninety to two hundred words per minute, but we think at five hundred to six hundred words per minute. This differential between "thought speed" and "speech speed" is one reason we can be so easily distracted. But you can use the differential to your advantage. When you find yourself "thinking ahead" of the speaker, use the time to focus on questions that foster critical thinking:

✔ What does the speaker really mean?

✔ Why is he or she presenting this material?

✔ Is the speaker leaving anything out?

✔ How can I use what the speaker is telling me?[1]

1. Thomas E. Anastasi Jr., *Listen! Techniques for Improving Communication Skills* (Boston: CBI Publishing, 1982), 35.

Guidelines for Evaluating Speeches and Presentations

As public speakers, we want to know the results of our efforts. While audience members' reactions during the speech provide clues to their feelings about it, more specific feedback is needed if we are to gain insight into our strengths and weaknesses. By critically evaluating the speeches of others, you'll be better able to assess your own strengths and weaknesses as a speaker.

Be Honest and Fair in Your Evaluation

Keep in mind the need to be honest and fair in your evaluation. Sometimes we have a tendency to focus on certain aspects of a speech and, as a result, minimize some of the most important elements. Focusing on a topic that you really like or dislike, for example, may cause you to place undue importance on that speech element. It is also important to remain open to ideas and beliefs that differ from your own. This openness will help your ideas, as well as your role as a citizen engaged with public issues, prosper. You can always learn something from differing viewpoints, and, likewise, honest and fair listeners will learn from your viewpoints.

Adjust to the Speaker's Style

Each of us has a unique communication style, a way of presenting ourselves through a mix of verbal and nonverbal signals. As listeners, we form impressions of speakers based on this communication style. Depending on our own preferences, we may find some speakers dull, others dynamic, still others off-putting, and so on. Adjusting to a speaker means not judging the content of that speaker's message based on his or her communication style. As listeners, it's up to us to identify which impressions create the most difficulty and then develop techniques for overcoming any listening problems. Accents, awkward grammatical phrases, and word choice are not good reasons to "tune out" a speaker. Maintaining respect for all types of speakers is a sign of good listening.

Be Compassionate in Your Criticism

How can you critically evaluate a presentation in a way that's constructive rather than cruel? In keeping with the biblical injunction to "do unto others," consider the following approach:[17]

1. *Start by saying something positive.* The benefits of this are twofold: You'll boost the speaker's self-confidence, and he or she will probably be more receptive to the criticism you do offer.

2. *Focus on the speech, not on the speaker.* One of the most challenging aspects of giving a speech is the feeling of being exposed to others. Don't confirm the speaker's fears of being ripped apart. When a speaker's ideas conflict with your own, concentrate on what you find disagreeable with his or her arguments, rather than judging the speaker as a person. People are more similar than we think, even when our viewpoints differ. Address your remarks to the characteristics of the speech, not to the speaker.

3. *Target your criticism.* Global statements such as "I just couldn't get into your topic" or "That was a great speech" don't give the speaker any information that he or she can use. If something fell short, be as specific as possible in describing it: "I wanted to hear more about the importance of such and such as it related to. . . ."

Peer Evaluation Form

In the space below, offer your evaluation of the speaker. Make your evaluation honest but constructive, providing the sort of feedback that you would find helpful if you were the speaker.

Did the speaker seem confident?   Yes   Somewhat   No
Suggestions: _____

Did the speaker use appropriate volume?   Yes   Somewhat   No
Suggestions: _____

Did the speaker use good eye contact?   Yes   Somewhat   No
Suggestions: _____

Did the speaker use effective vocal expression? Yes   Somewhat   No
Suggestions: _____

Did the speaker use appropriate gestures
and facial expressions?   Yes   Somewhat   No
Suggestions: _____

Was the speaker's introduction effective?   Yes   Somewhat   No
Suggestions: _____

Was the speaker's conclusion effective?   Yes   Somewhat   No
Suggestions: _____

Could you easily identify and remember
the speaker's main points?   Yes   Somewhat   No
Suggestions: _____

Did the speaker's organizational patterns
make sense to you?   Yes   Somewhat   No
Suggestions: _____

Did the speaker use effective supporting
evidence?   Yes   Somewhat   No
Suggestions: _____

The best thing about the speaker was: _____

The best thing about the speech was: _____

Recommendations for improvement: _____

CHAPTER 5

Ethical Public Speaking

One of the most consistent expectations that we as listeners bring to any speech situation is that the speaker will be honest and straightforward with us. Why else give our attention to someone unless we believe that he or she is sincere? Yet, while we assume an attitude of trust, we instinctively remain alert to hints that might signal dishonesty. As we listen to the actual words the speaker utters, for example, we are simultaneously evaluating his or her posture, tone of voice, gaze, and other potential markers of sincerity or lack thereof.

How can you ensure that your listeners will find you worthy of their trust? As ethicist Michael Josephson has noted, there are both practical and moral reasons for maintaining an ethical stance in public speaking.[1] At the practical level, you must establish credibility with listeners before they will accept your message. Credibility is based on trust, honesty, and believability. You also have a moral obligation to treat your listeners with respect—to behave ethically toward them. Central to ethical public speaking is responsibility to oneself and others.

Take Responsibility for Your Words

WEB Chapter quizzes

Public speakers are in the unusual position of being able to influence or persuade people and, at times, move them to act—for better or for worse. With this power to affect the minds and hearts of others comes **responsibility**—the heart of ethics. One definition of *responsibility* is "a charge, trust, or duty for which one is accountable."[2] **Ethics** is the study of moral conduct—how people should act toward one another. In terms of public speaking, ethics refers to the responsibilities we have toward our audience and ourselves. It also encompasses the responsibilities listeners have toward speakers.

Earn Your Listeners' Trust

Ethics is derived from the Greek word ***ethos***, meaning "character." According to the ancient Greek rhetorician Aristotle, audiences listen to and trust speakers who demonstrate positive ethos (positive character). Positive ethos includes *competence* (as demonstrated by the speaker's grasp of the subject matter), *good moral character* (as reflected in the speaker's trustworthiness, straightforwardness, and honest presentation of the message), and *goodwill* (as demonstrated by the speaker's knowledge and attitude of respect toward the audience and the particular speech occasion).

For Aristotle, speakers were regarded positively only when they were well prepared, honest, and respectful toward their audience. Some 2,500 years after Aristotle, surprisingly little has changed. Modern research on **speaker credibility** reveals that people place their greatest trust in speakers who

- have a solid grasp of the subject,
- display sound reasoning skills,
- are honest and straightforward, and
- are genuinely interested in the welfare of their listeners.[3]

Listeners tend to distrust speakers who deviate even slightly from these qualities. However, merely being an expert is not enough to inspire listeners' trust. Studies reveal that we trust only those speakers who we believe have our best interests in mind.[4]

Respect Your Listeners' Values

Our ethical conduct is a reflection of our **values**—our most enduring judgments or standards of what's good and bad in life, of what's important to us. Values shape our worldview, drive our behavior, and form the basis on which we judge the actions of others. Our ethical choices—including those we make in our speeches—are our values in action.

Like the individuals who hold them, values can conflict and clash. The larger and more diverse the society, the greater these clashes will tend to be. One only has to think of the so-called values divide in the United States between "red states" (representing conservative values) and "blue states" (representing liberal values).

Conflicting values lie at the heart of many controversies that public speakers might address, making it difficult to speak about certain topics without challenging cherished beliefs. The United States is a country of immigrants, for example, but half of the population with only a high-school education believes that immigrants threaten traditional U.S. values, while only a quarter of college-educated Americans agree.[5] Some of us support same-sex marriage while others firmly oppose it. As you plan your speech, anticipate that audience members will hold a range of values that will differ not only from your own, but from each other's, and proceed with sensitivity. Audience analysis is key to discovering these differences (see Chapter 6 on values and how to identify them in audience members).

Bring Your Own Values into Focus

Analyzing the underlying values that lead you to your position on an issue can help you do the same for audience members. What basic values underlie your support of or opposition to the death penalty? Are they religious in nature or more broadly humanistic? What personal characteristics might lead others to take a different position?

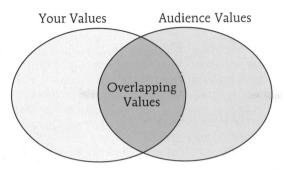

FIGURE 5.1 Comparing Values

Through extensive research, psychologist Milton Rokeach identified thirty-six values important to a large cross section of people, distinguishing between two kinds of values: instrumental and terminal. *Instrumental values* are socially desirable behavioral characteristics, such as being courageous. *Terminal values* are desirable states of being, such as living a comfortable life.

To bring some of your personal values into focus, complete the self-assessment exercise in the accompanying checklist. To identify which values mean the most to you, rank both terminal and instrumental values from least to most important. Then compare what you care about with what your audience analysis indicates that your listeners might value (see Figure 5.1). Where your values overlap those of your audience, you may be able to identify some common ground from which to present your topic.

Use Your Rights of Free Speech Responsibly

As a public speaker, you must balance the rights of free speech with the responsibilities that accompany it. Perhaps no other nation in the world has as many built-in safeguards for its citizens' right to free expression as the United States. The **First Amendment** of the U.S. Constitution plays a pivotal role in enforcing these safeguards by guaranteeing freedom of speech ("Congress shall make no law . . . abridging the freedom of speech . . ."). However, it is often difficult for our state and federal judges (who are charged with interpreting the Constitution) to find a satisfactory balance between our right to express ourselves (our *civil liberties*) and our right to be protected from speech that harms us (our *civil rights*). Whose rights, for example, should be protected? Should a "shock jock's" right to spew racist remarks be upheld over the objections of the victims of those remarks?

As today's judges interpret the Constitution, it would appear that profane radio announcers, along with the rest of us, are largely free to disparage groups and individuals on the basis of their race, gender, weight, or other characteristics. The United States vigorously protects **free speech**—defined as the right to be free from unreasonable constraints on expression[6]—even when the targets of that speech claim that it infringes on their civil rights to be protected from discrimination.

IDENTIFYING VALUES

As a way of uncovering where your values lie, rank each item from 1 to 10 (from least to most important). From these, select your top five values and write them down in the circle labeled "Your Values" in Figure 5.1. Repeat the exercise, but this time rank each value in terms of how important you think it is to your audience. Select the top five of these values and place them in the circle labeled "Audience Values." Finally, draw arrows to the overlapping area to indicate where your highest values (of those listed) coincide with those you think are most important to your listeners.

Terminal Values (states of being you consider important)	Instrumental Values (characteristics you value in yourself and others)
A comfortable life	Ambitious
An exciting life	Broadminded
A sense of accomplishment	Capable
A world at peace	Cheerful
A world of beauty	Clean
Equality	Courageous
Family security	Forgiving
Freedom	Helpful
Happiness	Honest
Inner harmony	Imaginative
Mature love	Independent
National security	Intellectual
Pleasure	Logical
Salvation	Loving
Self-respect	Obedient
Social recognition	Polite
True friendship	Responsible
Wisdom	Self-controlled

Source: Milton Rokeach, *Value Survey* (Sunnydale, Calif.: Halgren Tests, 1967).

Nevertheless, there remain important limits on our right to speak freely, and as a public speaker you should be aware of these limitations. For example, certain types of speech are actually illegal, including the following:

- Speech that provokes people to violence (incitement or "**fighting words**") and is, in the words of First Amendment expert David L. Hudson, "of such slight social value as a step to the truth that any benefit that may be derived from [the speech] is clearly outweighed by the social interest in order and morality."[7]

- Speech that can be proved to be defamatory (termed **slander**), or potentially harmful to an individual's reputation at work or in the community.

- Speech that invades a person's privacy, such as disclosing personal information about an individual that is not in the public record.

The law makes a distinction between whether the issues or individuals you are talking about are public or private. If you are talking about a public figure or a matter of public concern, you have much more latitude to say what you think, and you will not be legally liable unless it can be shown that you spoke with a **reckless disregard for the truth**. That is, you can be legally liable if it can be shown that you knew that what you were saying was false but said it anyway. If, on the other hand, in your speech you talk about a private person or private matters involving that person, it will be easier for that person to successfully assert a claim for defamation. You will then have the burden of proving that what you said was true.

While a limited range of speech is not legal, speakers who seek to distort the truth about events often can do so and not suffer any consequences. You may express an opinion questioning the existence of the Holocaust or the suffering of African Americans under slavery and not be arrested. The fact that this sort of offensive speech is *legal,* however, does not necessarily mean that it is ethical. While there are various approaches to evaluating ethical behavior, common to all of them are the fundamental moral precepts of not harming others and telling the truth.

Make a Positive Contribution to Public Discourse

One way to evaluate whether your speech is ethical is to consider whether it contributes something positive to **public discourse**—speech involving issues of importance to the larger community, such as debates on campus about U.S. involvement in the Middle East or on the need to take action to slow climate change.

What might constitute a positive contribution to public debates of this nature? Perhaps most important is the *advancement of constructive goals.* An ethical speech appeals to the greater good rather than to narrow self-interest. Speaking merely to inflame and demean others, on the other hand, degrades the quality of public discourse. Consider the case of the right-wing commentator Ann Coulter, who once harshly criticized a group of activist widows of victims of the 9/11 attack for their role in establishing the bipartisan 9/11 Commission. Disliking the commission's conclusions that U.S. intelligence failed to anticipate the attacks, Coulter charged, "These broads are millionaires, lionized on TV and in articles about them, reveling in their status as celebrities and stalked by grief-arazzies. I have never seen people enjoying their husbands' death so much."[8]

Coulter's **invective**, or verbal attack, served as a **conversation stopper**—speech designed to discredit, demean, and belittle those with whom one disagrees. Conversation stoppers and other forms of attack breach the acceptable "rules of engagement" for public conversations. As communication scholar W. Barnett Pearce explains, the concept of the **rules of engagement**, originally

A CULTURAL PERSPECTIVE

Comparing Cultural Values

Do the criteria for an ethical speaker outlined in this chapter—that is, displaying the qualities of trustworthiness, respect, responsibility, and fairness—apply equally in every culture? For example, does telling the truth always take precedence over other qualities, such as protecting the interests of your clan or group, or simply being eloquent? Are ethical standards for speeches merely a product of a particular culture? What about the concept of plagiarism? In the United States, speakers who fail to acknowledge their sources meet with harsh criticism and often suffer severe consequences, even if, as in the case of several recent college presidents, the speakers are otherwise highly respected.[1] Is this universally true?[2] Can you think of examples in which ideas of ethical speech expressed in this chapter are not necessarily shared by other cultures? Do you personally hold values for ethical speech that are different from those cited here?

1. See for example, "President Tobin to Step Down," Hamilton College Web site, October 2, 2002, www.hamilton.edu/news.
2. For an instructive article about plagiarism in China, in which the author disputes the notion of cultural relativity regarding plagiarism in that country, see Dilin Liu, "Plagiarism in ESOL Students: Is Cultural Conditioning Truly the Major Culprit?" *ELT* 59 (2005): 234–41.

used as a military term, can also be applied to the ways we relate to one another in the public arena: "Comparable to the orders about the circumstances in which soldiers may use their weapons are the rights and responsibilities to speak, to speak the truth, to disclose one's purposes, to respond to others, to respond coherently, to listen, and to understand. . . ."[9]

Observe the Ground Rules for Ethical Speaking

To ensure that your speech fulfills the rights and responsibilities—the "rules of engagement"—of ethical speaking, consider the following guidelines.

The qualities of dignity and integrity should infuse every aspect of a speech. **Dignity** refers to ensuring that your listeners feel worthy, honored, or respected as individuals.[10] Each of us wants to be accorded dignity. **Integrity** signals the speaker's incorruptibility—that he or she will avoid compromising the truth for the sake of personal expediency.[11] For example, slanting facts in your favor during a speech to persuade others to take your side demonstrates a lack of integrity. Speakers who demonstrate dignity and integrity care about themselves and their listeners. They exhibit a hallmark of ethical speaking: concern for the greater good.

Speaking ethically also requires that we adhere to certain "pillars of character,"[12] including being trustworthy, respectful, responsible, and fair in our presentations.

Be Trustworthy

We find speakers trustworthy when we sense that they are honest about their intentions and don't sacrifice the truth to achieve their aims. **Trustworthiness** is a combination of honesty and dependability. At the broadest level, being a trustworthy speaker is essential to the democratic process because democracy depends on an informed citizenry.[13]

Ethically, you are required to support your points truthfully and accurately. Manipulating data to achieve a particular purpose is untrustworthy, as are any attempts to deceive an audience by misrepresentation, omission, or making up of information (see Chapter 8 on the ethical use of statistics).

Truth telling can be an especially difficult issue in persuasive speeches (see Chapters 25–27). When the goal is to try to persuade others, the temptation is to fashion the information in a way that fits the goal, even if it means omitting a fact here or there that would convince the audience otherwise. But all kinds of speeches, not just persuasive ones, should be built on the truth. Acknowledging sources is also an essential aspect of being a trustworthy speaker (see rules for avoiding plagiarism later in this chapter).

Demonstrate Respect

Speakers demonstrate **respect** by addressing audience members as unique human beings and refraining from any form of personal attack. The respectful speaker focuses on issues rather than personalities and allows the audience the power of rational choice. Sensationalist or lurid appeals rob people of this power. In most cases, it's not necessary to use graphic pictures or upsetting verbal descriptions just to make a point. More drastically, drowning out a speaker's message with which you disagree—called a **heckler's veto**—robs us of the ability to make up our own minds about an issue and silences the free expression of ideas.

A serious ethical breach and sign of disrespect is the expression of ethnocentrism, stereotypes, or outright prejudice in a speech. Speakers who exhibit **ethnocentrism** act as though everyone shares their point of view and points of reference. They may tell jokes that require a certain context or refer only to their own customs. Ethical speakers, by contrast, assume differences and address them respectfully.

Generalizing about an apparent characteristic of a group and applying that generalization to all of its members is another serious affront to people's dignity. When such racial, ethnic, gender, or other **stereotypes** roll off the speaker's tongue, they pack a wallop of indignation and pain for the people to whom they refer. In addition, making in-group and out-group distinctions, with respect shown only to those in the "in group," can make listeners feel excluded or, worse, victimized. Speaking as though all audience members share the same religious and political beliefs, for instance, and treating those beliefs as superior to those held by others, is but one example of making in-group and out-group distinctions. Hate speech is the ultimate vehicle for promoting in-group and out-group distinctions.

Hate speech is any offensive communication—verbal or nonverbal—that is directed against people's racial, ethnic, religious, gender, or other characteristics. Racist, sexist, or ageist slurs, gay bashing, and cross burnings are all forms of hate speech. Ethically, you are bound to scrupulously avoid any hint of ethnocentrism, stereotyping, and hate speech.

ETHICALLY SPEAKING

Speech Codes on Campus: Protection or Censorship?

U.S. colleges and universities have long been at the center of the debate over free speech versus censorship. On the one side are those who resist restrictions of any kind, often in support of the constitutional rights of the First Amendment. On the other side are advocates of speech codes and other policies that limit what students and faculty can and cannot say and do; these advocates argue that such codes are necessary to ensure a tolerant and safe environment.

Since the 1980s, thousands of schools, both public and private, have instituted speech codes prohibiting certain forms of offensive speech and acts deemed intimidating or hostile to individuals or groups. Many of these early codes were found to be unconstitutional, but new codes have also come under fire. In 2010, for example, the Foundation for Individual Rights in Education (FIRE) found that 70 percent of 375 of the nation's largest and most prestigious colleges and universities unconstitutionally restricted free speech.[1]

Many colleges and universities limit student protests and demonstrations to designated areas on campus called "free speech zones"; and these, too, are subject to ongoing legal challenges. Colleges have even tried to collect fees from student groups who sponsor speakers that require campus security. In October of 2009, for example, Dutch politician Geert Wilders spoke about the dangers of Islamic extremism at Temple University. A month later, the student group Temple University Purpose (TUP) received a bill for $800 for charges needed to "secure the room." The university later dropped the fee when it was shown to be unconstitutional to financially burden students for speech "simply because it might offend a hostile mob."[2]

And what about that speech topic you might have in mind? In 2008, Central Connecticut State University student John Wahlberg was asked to prepare a speech on a topic covered by the mainstream media. Wahlberg chose to argue that had students at Virginia Tech been allowed to carry concealed weapons on campus during the 2007 shootings at that campus, the shooter might have been killed before killing as many students as he did. Believing that Wahlberg's opinions made the class "uncomfortable," his professor reported him to campus police, who ordered him to explain his beliefs.[3]

Restrictions on speech on campus raise important ethical questions. Supporters of speech codes claim that they are necessary to protect students from intimidation, to ensure equal opportunity, and to enforce the norms of a civil society.[4] Detractors argue that limits on free speech prevent students with unpopular or politically incorrect views from freely expressing themselves. What do you think?

1. "Spotlight on Speech Codes, 2010: The State of Free Speech on Our Nation's Campuses," Foundation for Individual Rights in Education (FIRE), accessed April 14, 2010, www.thefire.org.
2. "Temple University Charges Unconstitutional 'Security' Fee for Geert Wilders Event; Dutch Trial Begins Today over Controversial Expression," Foundation for Individual Rights in Education (FIRE), January 20, 2010, http://www.thefire.org/article/11493.html.
3. Jay Bergman, "Free Speech under Fire at Universities," *Hartford Courant*, March 17, 2009.
4. Jon B. Gould, "Returning Fire," *Chronicle of Higher Education*, April 20, 2007, chronicle.com/weekly/v53/i33/33b01301.htm.

Make Responsible Choices

Communication is a strong tool for influencing people, and even one message has the potential to change people's lives. When preparing a speech, consider the following:

Topic and purpose. Will learning about your topic in some way benefit listeners? Are your overall speech aims socially constructive? What effect will your speech have on your listeners? (See Chapter 7 for more on selecting an ethical topic and purpose.)

Evidence and reasoning. Are your arguments sound? Sloppy evidence and reasoning distort the truth. (See Chapter 26 on developing arguments.)

Accuracy. Is the content of your message accurate? Are the facts correct? Accuracy is a hallmark of ethical speaking.

Honest use of emotional appeals. Using emotional appeals supported by facts is a legitimate way to achieve your goal (see Chapter 25). However, using them as a crutch when your argument is weak on evidence or facts is a breach of ethics.

Demonstrate Fairness

Few subjects are black and white; rarely is there only one right or wrong way to view a topic. **Fairness** is ensured when you make a genuine effort to see all sides of an issue and to be open-minded. Using only information that helps your case is unfair to listeners because it prevents them from making informed decisions. Speakers who do so also betray a lack of sensitivity to other people's values and moral stances.

Avoid Plagiarism

WEB Tutorial

Crediting sources is a crucial aspect of any speech. **Plagiarism**—the passing off of another person's information as one's own—is unethical. To plagiarize is to use other people's ideas or words without acknowledging the source. **Wholesale plagiarism** occurs when you simply "cut-and-paste" material from sources into your speech and represent it as your own. **Patchwrite plagiarism** is copying material into your speech draft from a source and then changing or rearranging words and sentence structures here and there to make the material appear as if it were your own.[14] For example, one form of plagiarism in a public speaking course is taking a written essay and turning it into a speaking outline.[15] A student might read an article in the *Atlantic Monthly* on problems faced by refugees fleeing from a war-torn country. The student bases the entire presentation on this one article, outlining it point-by-point and turning it into a speech. Even if he or she acknowledges the source of the information, this is an act of plagiarism because the student copied *the organization and structure* of another person's work. As much if not more an essential feature of the article than the facts and ideas is the unique manner in which the author expresses them.

Whether it's done intentionally or not, plagiarism in any form is stealing and is a serious breach of ethics. When you present plagiarized material as your own speech material, you abuse the trust that an audience places in you. More than any other single action, acknowledging sources lets listeners know that you are trustworthy and will represent both fact and opinion fairly and responsibly.

Rules for Avoiding Plagiarism

The basic rule for avoiding plagiarism as a public speaker is straightforward: *Any sources that require credit in written form should be acknowledged in oral form.* These include direct quotations, paraphrases, and summarized information— any facts and statistics, ideas, opinions, and theories gathered and reported by others. For each source that requires citation, you need to include the *type of source* (magazine, book, personal interview, Web site, etc.), the *author or origin of the source,* the *title or a description of the source,* and the *date of the source.*

Oral presentations need not include full bibliographic references (including full names, dates, titles, and volume and page numbers) in the speech itself. However, you should include complete references in a bibliography page or at the end of the speech outline. (For guidelines on creating a bibliography for your speeches, see Chapter 14 and Appendices E–I.)

Orally Credit Direct Quotations

Direct quotations are statements quoted verbatim, or word for word, from a source. Direct quotes should always be acknowledged in a speech. Although it is not a requirement, you can call attention to a source's exact wording with phrases such as "As [the source] put it" and "As [the source] observes." For example:

> As my esteemed colleague Dr. Vance Brown told an audience of ALS researchers at the International ALS Convention last year, "The cure may be near or it may be far, but the human suffering is very much in the present."

Orally Credit Paraphrased Information

A **paraphrase** is a restatement of someone else's ideas, opinions, or theories in your own words. Because paraphrases alter the form but not the substance of another person's ideas, you must acknowledge the original source. After all, the ideas are not your ideas.

When you paraphrase in a speech, restate the idea from the original source, making sure to use your own words and sentence structure:

Original Version

> It was in the 1980s that food began disappearing from the American supermarket, gradually to be replaced by "nutrients," which are not the same thing. Where once the familiar name of recognizable comestibles—things like eggs or breakfast cereal or cookies—claimed pride of place on the brightly colored packages crowding the aisles, now new terms like "fiber" and "cholesterol" and "saturated fat" rose to large-type prominence. More important than mere foods, the presence or absence of these invisible substances was now generally believed to confer health benefits on their eaters.   — Nir Rosen

Oral Paraphrase

> In an essay on "The Age of Nutritionism" published in the January 28, 2007, issue of the *New York Times Magazine,* Nir Rosen says that we have taken our focus off real food and put it on its chemical composition—on the nutrients in it. Thus we no longer eat apples and oranges, but "an important source of soluble and insoluble fiber" and "80 fat-free calories containing a healthy dose of vitamin C." Nir says that rather than the actual food we eat, we now believe it is the unseen substances such as cholesterol, saturated fat, and fiber, that make us healthy or sick.

Orally Credit Facts and Statistics

The source for any data that was not gathered by you should be cited in your speech. You don't have to cite **common knowledge**—information that is likely to be known by many people—but such information must truly be widely disseminated. For example, it is common knowledge that Haiti suffered a massive earthquake in January 2010, but it is not common knowledge that the last time the fault segment that caused the Haiti earthquake broke was in 1770. These facts require acknowledgment of a source: in this case, MIT geophysicist Bradford Hager, in an interview published in the *MIT News* on January 28, 2010.[16] (For detailed guidelines on how to orally cite sources in your speech, see Chapter 11, "Citing Sources in Your Speech.")

Avoid Plagiarism on the Internet

Just as with print sources, information found on the Internet, including direct quotations, paraphrased information, facts, statistics, or other content that was gathered and reported by someone other than yourself, must be accurately credited. This includes information obtained from Web sites, blogs, electronic publications, mailing lists, newsgroups, and online databases. (For specific guidelines on acknowledging Internet sources, see Chapter 10 and Appendices E–I. For additional direction on orally crediting sources of various types, see Chapter 11.)

STEPS TO AVOID PLAGIARISM

1. Keep track of your sources as you collect them.
2. Create a system for tracking sources (using notecards, Microsoft Word, EndNote, or another note-tracking program).
3. Be especially careful to keep track of and cite Internet sources (see Chapter 10).
4. Review your speech to ensure that you've credited any quoted, paraphrased, and summarized information drawn from others' work.

CHECKLIST

Respect the Laws of Copyright and Fair Use

Copyright is a legal protection afforded original creators of literary and artistic works.[17] When including copyrighted materials in your speeches—such as reproductions of graphs or photographs, a video or sound clip, and so forth—you must determine when and if you need permission to use such works.

When a work is copyrighted, you may not reproduce, distribute, or display it without permission from the copyright holder or you will be liable for copyright infringement. For any work created from 1978 to the present, the copyright is good for the author's lifetime, plus fifty years. After that time, unless extended, the work falls into the **public domain**, which means that anyone may reproduce it. Not subject to copyright are federal (but *not* state or local) government publications, common knowledge, and select other categories.

Copyright laws are designed to protect **intellectual property**—the ownership of an individual's creative expression. As publishing attorney Steve Gillen explains:

> Copyright law concerns authorship or expression, i.e., words and images, not the underlying facts or ideas. . . . Facts, statistics, and concepts can be recited without permission [though failure to cite the source for them constitutes plagiarism unless they are common knowledge]. What you cannot do is copy or plagiarize the original or creative manner in which the original data was expressed.[18]

An exception to the prohibitions of copyright restrictions is the doctrine of **fair use**, which permits the limited use of copyrighted works without permission for the purposes of scholarship, criticism, comment, news reporting, teaching, and research.[19] This means that when preparing speeches for the classroom, you have much more latitude to use other people's creative work (with credit in all cases) without seeking their permission. For example, as long as you acknowledged your source, you could use a song from Katy Perry's CD as part of an in-class presentation. Different rules apply to the professional speaker, whose use of copyrighted materials is considered part of a for-profit "performance." In this event, you would need to obtain a performance license from a performing rights society such as ASCAP (American Society of Composers, Authors, and Publishers).

The same principles of fair use that apply to music apply to any graphics you might have decided to project during your presentation. Bear in mind, however, that while the *data* within a table or chart may not be copyrighted, its particular visual arrangement usually is.[20] Thus, you must accurately credit both the *source of the data* as well as the *creator of its graphic display*. For example, suppose that for a speech on women in the sciences you locate a graph in *Time* magazine that visually illustrates the percentage of men versus women who receive PhDs in the sciences and engineering. The source of the data is a federal government agency, which falls within the public domain. However, as the creator of the graph, *Time* magazine owns the copyright for this particular display of the data.

The long and short of it? If you are a professional public speaker who makes use of copyrighted materials in your speeches, you must obtain copyright clearance. For speeches created for onetime use in the classroom or for other nonprofit, educational purposes, accurately crediting your sources will often suffice. (For more on copyright, visit the U.S. Copyright Office online at www.copyright.gov.)

AN ETHICAL INVENTORY

_____ 1. Do I distort any information to make my point?

_____ 2. Does my speech focus on issues rather than on personalities?

_____ 3. Do I try to foster a sense of inclusion?

_____ 4. Is my topic socially constructive?

_____ 5. Is the content of my message as accurate as I can make it?

_____ 6. Whenever appropriate, do I acknowledge alternative and opposing views so that my audience can make informed decisions?

_____ 7. Do I acknowledge each of my sources?

_____ Direct quotations

_____ Paraphrased information

_____ Facts and statistics gathered from any source other than your own research

SELF-ASSESSMENT CHECKLIST

AUDIENCE ANALYSIS AND TOPIC SELECTION

AUDIENCE ANALYSIS
AND TOPIC SELECTION

SPEAKER'S REFERENCE

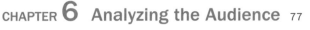

CHAPTER **6** Analyzing the Audience 77

Adapt to Audience Psychology: Who Are Your Listeners? 77
   ▶ **CHECKLIST** Respond to the Audience as You Speak 81
Adapt to Audience Demographics 82
Adapt to Cultural Values 85
   ▶ **A CULTURAL PERSPECTIVE** Cross-National Surveys 88
   ▶ **ESL SPEAKER'S NOTES** Comparing Cultural Values 89
Techniques for Learning about Your Audience 90
Analyze the Speech Setting 93
   ▶ **CHECKLIST** Analyzing the Speech Situation 94
   ▶ **CHECKLIST** Reviewing Your Speech in Light of Audience
   Demographics 95

CHAPTER **7** Selecting a Topic and Purpose 96

Assigned versus Self-Selected Topics 96
Identify the General Speech Purpose 97
   ▶ **CHECKLIST** Identifying Your General Speech Purpose 99
Choosing a Topic for Your Speech 99
   ▶ **CHECKLIST** Criteria for Selecting a Topic 103
   ▶ **FROM SOURCE TO SPEECH** Narrowing Your Topic to Fit Your
   Audience 104
   ▶ **FROM SOURCE TO SPEECH** Narrowing Your Topic Using a Library
   Portal 106
Refine the Topic and Purpose 108
   ▶ **CHECKLIST** Narrowing Your Topic 108
From Topic and Purpose to Thesis Statement 109
   ▶ **ETHICALLY SPEAKING** Ethical Considerations in Selecting a Topic
   and Purpose 110
   ▶ **CHECKLIST** Formulating the Thesis Statement 112
Make the Thesis Statement Relevant and Motivating 113

AUDIENCE ANALYSIS AND TOPIC SELECTION

CHAPTER 6 Analyzing the Audience

Learn about Your Audience and Adapt Your Message Accordingly

- Identify what your audience needs and wants to know. (p. 77)
- Maintain an audience-centered approach. (p. 77)

Investigate Audience Psychology

- Seek information on relevant attitudes, beliefs, and values. (p. 78)
- Adjust your approach depending on whether listeners are positively, negatively, or neutrally disposed toward the topic. (p. 79)

Establish Common Bonds between Yourself and the Audience

- Stress shared experiences. (p. 79)
- Emphasize common goals and values. (p. 79)
- Focus on areas of agreement. (p. 79)

Anticipate Audience Expectations of the Speech Occasion

- Adjust content and timing accordingly. (p. 79)

Investigate Your Target Audience

- Identify whom in the audience you are most likely to influence. (p. 82)

Address the Age Range of Your Audience

- Offer examples they will recognize and identify with. (p. 82)

Consider the Ethnic and Cultural Background of Audience Members

- Learn about and demonstrate respect for differences. (p. 83)

Consider the Socioeconomic Status of Your Audience

- Consider that listeners' attitudes may be closely tied to occupational status. (p. 83)
- Use examples that are appropriate to the audience's level of sophistication and education. (p. 84)

Consider Religious and Political Affiliations

- Identify potential religious sensitivities and tread carefully. (p. 84)
- To the extent possible, gauge the audience's degree of political involvement and tread sensitively. (p. 84)

Avoid Judgments Based on Gender Stereotypes and Avoid Sexist Language

- Treat gender-related issues evenly. (p. 84)
- Anticipate listeners' attitudes with respect to gender. (p. 84)

Consider How Disability May Affect Audience Members

- Review both your topic and your delivery in light of the potential disabilities of audience members. (p. 85)
- Use language and examples that are respectful of persons with disabilities. (p. 85)

Adapt to Cultural Values

- Identify listeners' major values and cultural orientation related to your topic and adapt your speech accordingly. (p. 85)
- Consult cross-cultural polls to further identify audience attitudes. (p. 89)
- Focus on universal values. (p. 89)

Gather Information about Your Audience from a Variety of Sources

- Consider interviewing one or more representatives of the audience. (p. 90)
- For classroom speeches, consider questionnaires or instant polls. (p. 90)
- Look for information about the audience in published sources, such as company Web sites, brochures, articles, and other related materials. (p. 92)

Investigate the Logistics of the Speech Setting

- Find out in advance what the physical setting will be like. (p. 93)
- Plan appropriately for the length of your speech. (p. 93)
- Learn about the seating arrangement and where you will be placed. (p. 94)
- Consider the rhetorical situation. (p. 94)

CHAPTER 7 Selecting a Topic and Purpose

Be Aware That Speech Topics May or May Not Be Assigned

Select from the Three General Speech Purposes

- Use an informative speech to increase audience understanding and awareness. (p. 97)
- Use a persuasive speech to effect change in audience attitudes, beliefs, values, or behavior. (p. 98)
- Use a special occasion speech when the specific event calls for entertainment, celebration, commemoration, inspiration, or setting a social agenda. (p. 99)

Consider Various Approaches to Selecting Your Topic

- Rely on your own interests. (p. 99)
- Survey current events. (p. 101)
- Consider controversial and community issues. (p. 101)
- Avoid overused topics. (p. 101)
- Brainstorm with word association, topic mapping, and Internet tools to generate ideas. (p. 101)

Narrow Your Topic and Purpose

- Narrow your topic to align with time constraints, audience expectations, and the occasion. (p. 108)
- Use action terms to develop your specific purpose. (p. 108)

Formulate the Thesis Statement

- State the thesis as a single, declarative sentence that poses the central idea of your speech. (p. 109)
- Use the thesis to help you develop main points. (p. 110)
- Make the thesis statement relevant and motivating by adding key words or phrases and considering audience interests. (p. 113)

KEY TERMS

Chapter 6

audience analysis
audience-centered approach
pandering
attitudes
beliefs
values
identification
captive audience
demographics
target audience
audience segmentation
generational identity
co-culture

socioeconomic status (SES)
gender
sexist language
gender stereotypes
persons with disabilities (PWD)
individualistic culture
collectivist culture
uncertainty avoidance
high-uncertainty avoidance culture
low-uncertainty avoidance culture

power distance
linear-active cultures
multi-active cultures
reactive cultures
interview
questionnaire
closed-ended question
fixed alternative question
scale question
open-ended question

Chapter 7

general speech purpose
informative speech
persuasive speech

special occasion speech
brainstorming
word association

topic map
specific speech purpose
thesis statement

CHAPTER 6

Analyzing the Audience

Advertisers are shrewd analysts when it comes to reading people's needs and wants. They extensively research our buying habits and lifestyle choices to identify what motivates us; then, they craft messages that will convince us to want what they are selling. In at least one sense, to make a successful speech or presentation you, too, must function like an advertiser. To spark interest and sustain the audience's involvement in your message, you also must investigate and appeal to your audience.

Audience analysis is the process of gathering and analyzing information about audience members' attributes and motivations *with the explicit aim of preparing your speech in ways that will be meaningful to them.* This is the single most critical aspect of preparing for any speech. What are your listeners' attitudes with respect to your topic? What might they need or want to know? How will their values influence their response to your presentation? How much do audience members have in common with one another?

Maintaining an **audience-centered approach** throughout the entire speech preparation process—from selection and treatment of the speech topic to making decisions about how you will organize, word, and deliver it—will help you prepare a presentation that your audience will want to hear.

Adapt to Audience Psychology: Who Are Your Listeners?

WEB Chapter quizzes

One of the most important psychological principles you can learn as a speaker is that audience members, and people in general, tend to evaluate information in terms of their own—rather than the speaker's—point of view. Establishing a connection with your listeners thus starts with seeking to understand *their* outlook and motivations and letting this information guide you in constructing your speech. You may want to convince your classmates to support a four-day school week, but unless you know how they feel and what they know about the proposal, you won't know how to adapt your presentation accordingly.

Being audience-centered does not mean that you must abandon your own convictions or cater to the audience's whims. This practice, called **pandering**, will only undermine your credibility in the eyes of the audience. Think of audience analysis as an opportunity to get to know and establish common ground with audience members, just as you might do with a new acquaintance. The more you find out about someone, the more you can discover what you share in common and how you differ.

Appeal to Audience Members' Attitudes, Beliefs, and Values

The audience members' attitudes, beliefs, and values provide crucial clues to how receptive they will be toward your topic and your position on it. While intertwined, attitudes, beliefs, and values reflect distinct mental states that reveal a great deal about us.

Attitudes are our general evaluations of people, ideas, objects, or events.[1] To evaluate something is to judge it as relatively good or bad, useful or useless, desirable or undesirable, and so on. People generally act in accordance with their attitudes (although the degree to which they do so depends on many factors).[2] If your listeners have a positive attitude toward reading, for example, they're likely to read and to want to listen to you discuss books. If they have a negative attitude toward religion, chances are they'll avoid attending religious services—as well as your speech praising the value of religion.

Attitudes are based on **beliefs**—the ways in which people perceive reality.[3] They are our feelings about what is true. Whereas attitudes deal with how we feel about some activity or entity ("Reading is good" or "God is good"), beliefs refer to our level of confidence about the very existence or validity of something ("I believe God exists" or "I'm not so sure that God exists"). The less faith listeners have that something exists—UFOs, for instance—the less open they are to hearing about it.

Both attitudes and beliefs are shaped by **values**—our most enduring judgments about what's good and bad in life, as shaped by our culture and our unique experiences within it. We have fewer values than either attitudes or beliefs, but they are more deeply felt and resistant to change. For some of us, the sanctity of marriage between a man and a woman is a core value. For others, the value of social justice supersedes that of material comfort. Whatever the nature of our values, they are central to our sense of who we are.

In one classic study, researchers identified a set of core values prevalent in the United States, including achievement and success, equal opportunity, material comfort, hard work, practicality and efficiency, change and progress, science, democracy, and freedom.[4] A survey of several Asian societies revealed such core values as the spirit of harmony, humility toward one's superiors, awe of nature, and a desire for prosperity.[5] People in every culture also possess values related to their personal relationships, religion, occupation, and so forth. Note that rather than indicating that everyone in these societies shares in them, these values paint a broad picture of national tendencies. Table 6.1 illustrates some prevalent values in China, India, Mexico, and Iraq.

"If the Value Fits, Use It"

Evoking some combination of the audience's values, attitudes, and beliefs in the speeches you deliver will make them more personally relevant and motivating. Recognizing this, the Biodiversity Project, a communications group that

TABLE 6.1 Core Values in China, India, Mexico, and Iraq			
China	India	Mexico	Iraq
• Modesty	• Family orientation	• Group loyalty	• Devoutness
• Tolerance	• Material success	• Mañana (cyclical	• Hospitality
• Filial piety	and creativity	time)	• Gender inequality
• Stoicism	• Fatalism	• Machismo	• Values rhetoric
• Respect for	• Do-it-yourself	• Family closeness	• Pride in ancient
hierarchy	mentality	• Saving face at all	heritage
• Pride (not losing	• Honor of family	costs	• Moralistic
face)	and group	• Deference to age	
• Wisdom	• Problem-solving	• Mysticism, fatalism	

Source: Adapted from material in Richard D. Lewis, *When Cultures Collide: Leading across Cultures,* 3rd ed. (Boston, MA: Intercultural Press-Nicholas Brealey International, 2005).

designs campaigns to raise public awareness about the environment, advises its clients: "If the value fits, use it."[6] The project asked a representative sample of Americans to choose their most important personal reason for protecting the environment.[7] The three values most widely cited included: (1) wanting one's family to enjoy healthy surroundings; (2) feeling responsible for future generations ("stewardship"); and (3) believing that nature is God's creation and, as such, sacred. Based on this information, the organization counseled its speakers to touch directly upon these values in their presentations, offering the following as an example of how to do this:

> You care about your family's health (value #1), and you feel a responsibility to protect your loved ones' quality of life (value #2). The local wetland provides a sanctuary to many plants and animals. It helps to clean our air and water and provides a space of beauty and serenity (value #3). All of this is about to be destroyed by irresponsible development.[8]

Gauge Listeners' Feelings toward the Topic, Speaker, and Occasion

With any speech, it's important to assess the audience's feelings and expectations toward (1) the topic of your speech, (2) you as the speaker, and (3) the speech occasion. This perspective taking will help you anticipate listeners' reactions and develop the speech accordingly.

Gauge Listeners' Feelings toward the Topic

Knowing where your audience stands in relation to your topic can provide you with important information for planning your speech. Is your topic one with which the audience is familiar, or is it new to them? Do your listeners hold positive, negative, or neutral attitudes toward the topic? As a general rule, people pay more attention to and feel more positively about topics that are in keeping with their values and beliefs. The less we know about something, the more indifferent we tend to be. Once you gauge the audience's knowledge level and attitudes toward the topic, these guidelines can help you appeal to the different types of audiences:

If the topic is *new to listeners*

- Start by showing why the topic is relevant to them.
- Relate the topic to familiar issues and ideas about which they already hold positive attitudes.

If listeners know *relatively little* about the topic

- Stick to the basics and include background information.
- Steer clear of jargon, and define unclear terms.
- Repeat important points, summarizing information often.

If listeners are *negatively disposed* toward the topic

- Focus on establishing rapport and credibility.
- Don't directly challenge listeners' attitudes; instead begin with areas of agreement.
- Discover if they have a negative bias in order to tactfully introduce the other side of the argument.
- Offer solid evidence from sources they are likely to accept.
- Give good reasons for developing a positive attitude toward the topic.[9]

If listeners hold *positive attitudes* toward the topic

- Stimulate the audience to feel even more strongly by emphasizing the side of the argument with which they already agree.
- Tell stories with vivid language that reinforces listeners' attitudes.[10]

If listeners are a *captive audience*

- Motivate listeners to pay attention by focusing as much as possible on what is most relevant to them.
- Pay close attention to the length of your speech.

Gauge Listeners' Feelings toward the Speaker

How audience members feel about you will also have considerable bearing on their attentiveness and responsiveness to your message. A speaker who is well liked can gain at least an initial hearing by an audience even if listeners are unsure of what to expect from the message itself. Conversely, an audience that feels negatively toward the speaker will disregard even the most important or interesting message. We tend to put up barriers against people whom we hold in low regard.

Listeners have a natural need to identify with the speaker and to feel that he or she shares their perceptions,[11] so look for ways to establish a common bond, or feeling of **identification**, between you and the audience. Many times, especially when the topic is controversial, a speaker will do this by emphasizing those aspects of the topic about which the audience members are likely to agree. When speaking to an audience of abortion rights activists, for example, then-Senator Hillary Clinton called on opposing sides in the debate to find "common ground" by focusing on education and abstinence:

> We should all be able to agree that we want every child born in this country and around the world to be wanted, cherished, and loved. The best way to get there is to do more to educate the public about reproductive health, about how to prevent unsafe and unwanted pregnancies.[12]

Clinton clearly was attempting to reach out beyond her core constituency and achieve some measure of identification with those who oppose abortion.

Sharing a personal story, emphasizing a shared role, and otherwise stressing mutual bonds all help to create identification. So, too, does the strategic use of inclusive language such as *we, you, I,* and *me.* Notice, for example, how Clinton uses the personal pronoun *we* to encourage identification with the speech goal (see Chapter 17 for more on the power of inclusive language) and to build a sense of community within the audience. Even your physical presentation can foster identification. We're more apt to identify with the speaker who dresses like us (or in a manner we aspire to) than with someone whose style and grooming seems strange or displeasing.

CHECKLIST

RESPOND TO THE AUDIENCE AS YOU SPEAK

As you deliver your speech, monitor the audience for signs of how they are receiving your message. Look for bodily clues as signs of interest or disengagement:

✓ Large smiles and eye contact suggest a liking for and agreement with the speaker.

✓ Arms closed across the chest may signal disagreement.

✓ Averted glances, slumped posture, and squirming usually indicate disengagement.

Engage with the audience if it appears they aren't with you:

✓ Invite one or two listeners to briefly relate their own experiences on the topic.[1]

✓ Share a story linked to the topic to increase identification.

1. Nick Morgan, *Working the Room: How to Move People to Action through Audience-Centered Speaking* (Cambridge, Mass.: Harvard Business School Press, 2003), 181–97; 2.

Gauge Listeners' Feelings toward the Occasion

Part of any audience analysis is anticipating audience reactions to the rhetorical situation—the circumstance calling for the speech. Depending on the speech occasion, people bring different sets of expectations and emotions to it. Imagine being a businessperson attending a conference—it's your third night away from home, you're tired from daylong meetings, and now you're expected to listen to company executives explain routine production charges for the coming fiscal year. In contrast, imagine attending a speech of your own free will to listen to a speaker you've long admired. Obviously, a **captive audience** will tend to present greater challenges than one that is voluntary.

Adapt to Audience Demographics
WEB Links

Collecting psychological data about audience members takes you halfway through an audience analysis. Equally important is to learn demographic information about them. **Demographics** are the statistical characteristics of a given population. At least six characteristics are typically considered when analyzing speech audiences: *age, ethnic and cultural background, socioeconomic status* (including *income, occupation,* and *education*), *religious and political affiliations, gender,* and *disability.* Keep in mind that any number of other traits—for example, social group membership (online and off), sexual orientation, or place of residence—may be important to investigate as well.

Appeal to Your Target Audience

Knowing audience demographics lets you identify your **target audience**—those individuals with similar characteristics, wants, and needs whom you are most likely to influence in your direction. Mass communicators rely upon **audience segmentation**—dividing a general audience into smaller groups to identify target audiences with similar characteristics, wants, and needs. Whether used by advertisers selling Apple computers, advocacy groups selling cleaner air, or you, as a public speaker, segmentation is a crucial tool for those attempting to reach an audience.

Consider a speech delivered to your classmates about lowering fees for campus parking violations. Your target audience will be those persons in the class who drive, rather than bicycle or walk, to campus. Whenever you appeal to a target audience, however, aim to make the topic relevant to other audience members, lest they feel excluded. Here, you might mention that lower fees will benefit non-drivers in the future, should they bring cars to campus.

Age

Age can be a very important factor in determining how listeners will react to a topic. Each age group brings with it its own concerns and psychological drives and motivations. The quest for identity in adolescence (around the ages of 12–20), for example, differs markedly from the need to establish stable careers and relationships in early adulthood (ages 20–40). Similarly, adults in their middle years (40–65) tend to grapple with a full plate of issues related to career, children, aging parents, and an increased awareness of mortality. And as we age (65 and older), physical changes and changes in lifestyle (from work to retirement) assume greater prominence.

In addition to sharing the concerns associated with a given life stage, people of the same generation often share a familiarity with significant individuals, local and world events, noteworthy popular culture, and so forth. Being aware of the age range and **generational identity** of your audience, such as the millennials (those born between 1977 and 1995) or baby boomers (those born between 1946 and 1964) allows you to develop points that are relevant to the experiences and interests of the widest possible cross section of your listeners.

Ethnic or Cultural Background

An understanding of and sensitivity to the ethnic and cultural composition of your audience are key factors in delivering a successful (and ethical) speech. As a speaker in a multicultural and multiethnic society, you are all but certain to encounter audience members of different national origins (or first-generation Americans). Some audience members may have a great deal in common with you. Others may be fluent in a language other than yours and must struggle to understand you. Some members of the audience may belong to a distinct **co-culture**, a social community whose values and style of communicating may or may not mesh with your own. (For guidelines on adapting to diverse audiences, see p. 85, "Adapt to Cultural Values.")

Socioeconomic Status

Socioeconomic status (SES) includes income, occupation, and education. Knowing roughly where an audience falls in terms of these key variables can be critical in effectively targeting your message.

Income

Income determines people's experiences on many levels. It directly affects how they are housed, clothed, and fed, and determines what they can afford. Beyond this, income has a ripple effect, influencing many other aspects of life. For example, depending on income, home ownership is either a taken-for-granted budget item or an out-of-reach dream. The same is true for any activity dependent on income. Given how pervasively income affects people's life experiences, insight into this aspect of an audience's makeup can be quite important.

Occupation

In most speech situations, the occupation of audience members is an important and easily identifiable demographic characteristic that you as a speaker should try to determine in advance. The nature of people's work has a lot to do with what interests them. Occupational interests are tied to several other areas of social concern, such as politics, the economy, education, and social reform. Personal attitudes, beliefs, and goals are also closely tied to occupational standing.

Education

Level of education strongly influences people's ideas, perspectives, and range of abilities. A higher level of education appears to be associated with greater fluctuation in personal values, beliefs, and goals. In other words, people with higher levels of education may be more open to changing their minds.

If the audience is generally well educated, your speech may need to be quite sophisticated. When speaking to a less-educated audience, you may choose to clarify your points with more examples and illustrations.

Religion

The *Encyclopedia of American Religions* identifies more than 2,300 different religious groups in the United States,[13] from Seventh-Day Adventists to Zen Buddhists, so don't assume that everyone in your audience shares a common religious heritage. Furthermore, don't assume that all members of the same spiritual tradition agree on all issues. People who identify themselves as Catholic disagree on birth control and divorce, Jews disagree on whether to recognize same-sex unions, and so forth. Awareness of an audience's general religious orientation can be especially helpful when your speech addresses a topic as potentially controversial as religion. Capital punishment, same-sex marriage, and teaching about the origins of humankind—all are rife with religious overtones and implications.

Political Affiliation

As with religion, beware of making unwarranted assumptions about an audience's political values and beliefs. Some people like nothing better than a lively debate about public-policy issues. Others avoid anything that smacks of politics. And many people are very touchy about their views on political issues. Unless you have prior information about the audience's political values and beliefs, you won't know where your listeners stand.

Gender

Gender is another important factor in audience analysis, if only as a reminder to avoid the minefield of gender stereotyping. Distinct from the fixed physical characteristics of biological sex, **gender** is our social and psychological sense of ourselves as males or females.[14] Making assumptions about the preferences, abilities, and behaviors of your audience members based on their presumed gender can seriously undermine their receptivity to your message. Using **sexist language**, language that casts males or females into roles on the basis of sex alone, will also swiftly alienate many listeners. Equally damaging to credibility is the inclusion of overt **gender stereotypes**—oversimplified and often severely distorted ideas about the innate nature of what it means to be male or female.

Beyond ensuring that you treat issues of gender evenly, try to anticipate the audience members' attitudes with respect to gender and plan accordingly. For example, if you are speaking about the significant role of women in U.S. military frontline capacities (as combat medics, members of support deployment battalions, and pilots of attack helicopters and fighter jets), keep in mind that age might play a role in audience members' attitudes toward your topic. Some members of your audience, for instance—perhaps Korean-, Vietnam-, and Gulf-war-era veterans—might find your topic controversial. Depending on audience composition, ethnic and cultural background could also come into play. In certain cultures, for example, it is unthinkable that women would take any role in the military.

Disability

According to the U.S. Census Bureau, more than 19 percent of the population, or about fifty million people, five years and older (excluding persons who are institutionalized) has some sort of mental, physical, emotional, or employment disability; some two-thirds of these have a severe disability. Over 14 percent of those enrolled in college and graduate school are counted as disabled.[15] Problems range from sight and hearing impairments to constraints on physical mobility and employment. Thus disability is another demographic variable to consider when analyzing an audience. Keep **persons with disabilities (PWD)** in mind when you speak, and use language and examples that afford them respect and dignity.

Adapt to Cultural Values

In the United States, at least 34 percent of the population belongs to a racial or ethnic minority group, or one designated by the U.S. Census Bureau as other than "Non-Hispanic White." Today, in states such as California and Texas, groups that were formerly in the minority, such as Hispanic or Latino Americans, now increasingly comprise the majority.[16] Additionally, thirty-eight million people, or 12.5 percent of the U.S. population, are foreign-born (see Figure 6.1). California leads the nation, with 27 percent of its residents foreign-born; New York, New Jersey, and Hawaii follow close behind. Nationwide, nearly 20 percent of the population speaks a language other than English in the home.[17] Worldwide, there are more than two hundred recognized countries, and many more distinct cultures within these countries.[18]

With figures such as these, chances are that you will find yourself facing listeners who hold different cultural perspectives that may or may not mesh with your own. How might you prepare to speak in front of an ethnically and culturally diverse audience, including that of your classroom? In any speaking situation, your foremost concern should be to treat your listeners with dignity and to act with integrity. You do this by infusing your speech with the pillars of character described in Chapter 5: trustworthiness, respect, responsibility, and fairness. Since values are central to who we are, familiarizing yourself with those of your listeners can help you to communicate with sensitivity.

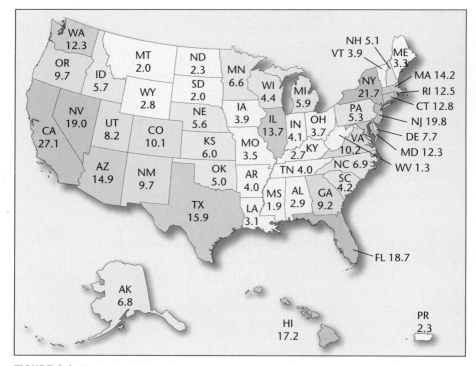

FIGURE 6.1 Percentage of People Who Are Foreign-Born, State by State   *Note:* Data are limited to the household population and exclude the population living in institutions, college dormitories, and other group quarters.   *Source:* U.S. Census Bureau, 2006–2008 American Community Survey.

Cross-cultural scholars offer numerous models that compare and contrast differing values and associated behavioral patterns among various cultures. Two that have been particularly helpful to public speakers include Geert Hofstede's *value dimensions* and Richard D. Lewis's *cultural types*.

Hofstede's Value-Dimensions Model

Researchers have shown that as with individuals, nations differ in the values held by the majority of their members. For example, cross-cultural scholar Geert Hofstede has identified five major "value dimensions," or "broad preferences for one state of affairs over another, usually held unconsciously," as being significant across all cultures, but in widely varying degrees; he then ranks forty countries in terms of how they compare on these dimensions.[19]

Individualism versus Collectivism

Individualistic cultures tend to emphasize the needs of the individual rather than those of the group, upholding such values as individual achievement and decision making. In **collectivist cultures**, by contrast, personal identity, needs, and desires are viewed as secondary to those of the larger group. Audience members who share collectivist values may believe that the wishes of parents and the family group must come before their own. In Hofstede's analysis, the United States, Australia, Great Britain, and Canada rank highest on individualism. Venezuela, Peru, Taiwan, and Pakistan rank highest in collectivist characteristics.

Uncertainty Avoidance

Uncertainty avoidance refers to the extent to which people feel threatened by ambiguity. **High-uncertainty avoidance cultures** tend to structure life more rigidly and formally for their members, while **low-uncertainty avoidance cultures** are more accepting of uncertainty in life and therefore allow more variation in individual behavior. Among the nations Hofstede investigated, Portugal, Greece, Peru, Belgium, and Japan rank highest in uncertainty avoidance; the United States, Sweden, Denmark, Ireland, and Norway rank lowest.

Power Distance

Power distance is the extent to which a culture values social equality versus tradition and authority. Cultures with *high levels of power distance* tend to be organized along more rigidly hierarchical lines, with greater emphasis placed on honoring authority. Those with *low levels of power distance* place a higher value on social equality. High power distance countries include India, Brazil, Singapore, Greece, Venezuela, and Mexico. Austria, Finland, Denmark, Norway, New Zealand, and Israel rank lowest on this dimension. The United States ranks somewhat above the midpoint range among the nations in Hofstede's survey.

Masculinity versus Femininity

The *masculinity and femininity dimension* refers to the degree to which a culture values traits that it associates with masculinity and with femininity. Traditional masculine traits include ambition, assertiveness, performance, and overt displays of manliness. Feminine traits stress nurturance and cooperation. In Hofstede's analysis, Ireland, the Philippines, Greece, and South Africa ranked highest in masculinity, while Sweden, Norway, Finland, and Denmark ranked highest in femininity. The dominant values in the United States were weighted toward masculinity.

Long- versus Short-Term Time Orientation

The *time orientation* dimension refers to the degree to which a culture values behavior that is directed to future rewards, such as perseverance and thrift, versus behavior that is directed toward the present, such as expecting quick results. China, Hong Kong, Taiwan, and South Korea ranked highest in long-term orientation, while Great Britain, Canada, the Philippines, Germany, and Australia ranked highest in short-term orientation.

To find out individual country rankings and compare your home culture with another culture, see www.geert-hofstede.com/hofstede_dimensions.php.

Lewis's Cultural Types Model

In place of value dimensions, Richard D. Lewis offers a model that classifies cultures according to whether they are linear-active, multi-active, or reactive.[20]

Linear-Active Cultures

People in **linear-active cultures** approach tasks systematically, preferring to do one thing at a time and in an organized fashion. They tend to be cool, factual, decisive planners. In Lewis's model, Germany, Switzerland, the United States, and Great Britain rank highest in linear-active traits; Argentina, Brazil, Mexico, Sub-Saharan Africa, and the Arab Middle East rank lowest.

Multi-Active Cultures

Persons in **multi-active cultures** tend to do many things at once, are people-oriented, and extroverted. They tend to be warm, emotional, talkative, and impulsive. Argentina, Mexico, Brazil, Chile, and the Arab Middle East rank highest in multi-active traits.

Reactive Cultures

In **reactive cultures**, people rarely initiate discussions or actions, preferring to listen to what others have to say first. They tend to be courteous, accommodating, and good listeners. Japan, China, Vietnam, Korea, and Thailand rank highest in reactive traits.

A CULTURAL PERSPECTIVE

Cross-National Surveys

Cross-national surveys can be extremely useful for learning about how values vary across cultures. Globally, the largest-scale cross-national surveys are the World Values Survey (www.worldvaluessurvey.org) and those conducted by the International Social Survey Programme (ISSP) (www.issp.org/data.shtml). Using representative national samples of at least one thousand individuals, the World Values Survey offers a fascinating look at the values and beliefs of people in 97 countries in all six continents, while the International Social Survey Programme surveys 43 nations. Through these resources you can discover how people of other nations feel about work, family, religion, and even who should do the housework.

The Pew Global Attitudes Project (http://pewglobal.org/) is a series of worldwide opinion surveys conducted in 57 countries, on issues ranging from how people see their own lives to reactions to world events. Gallup World View (worldview.gallup.com) surveys 150 countries on attitudes related to issues ranging from well-being to the environment. For a helpful overview of international polls, see Yale University's Social Science Library Web page on opinion polls (http://guides.library.yale.edu/content.php?pid=14700&sid=809599).

Bear in mind that the value dimensions and cultural patterns identified by Hofstede and Lewis reflect those of the *dominant culture;* they do not necessarily reflect the behaviors of all the groups living within a society. Although individualism characterizes the dominant culture of the United States, for example, various co-cultures, such as Hispanic Americans, Native Americans, and, to varying degrees, African Americans, have been described as collectivist in nature.

Consult Cross-Cultural and Cross-National Polls

To hone in on how persons from other cultures might view specific issues, consult cross-cultural polls, such as those conducted by the International Social Survey Programme. The Cultural Perspective box on cross-national surveys on p. 88 offers suggestions on investigating attitudes, beliefs, and values across cultures; see also "Consult Published Sources" on p. 92 for a list of U.S.-based national opinion surveys.

Focus on Universal Values

Becoming familiar with the range of cultural values among audience members can be helpful in preparing speeches that make audience members feel included in the message. At the same time, if you have trouble discovering this information, you can focus on certain values that are widely or even universally shared. In terms of the environment, for example, researchers have identified stewardship, or feeling a responsibility to care for the planet, as a core value shared by most Americans.[21] Further, you can always focus on certain values that, if not universally shared, are probably universally aspired to in the human heart. These include love, truthfulness, fairness, unity, tolerance, responsibility, and respect for life.[22]

ESL SPEAKER'S NOTES

Comparing Cultural Values

As you consider your own values, think about the influence of culture. Can you identify values that you hold but that your listeners probably will not share? What role does culture play in these values? Are there certain values your listeners are likely to hold that you do not share? What are these? Have you experienced clashes of values between yourself and others regarding what you believe to be good and bad, important and unimportant? As you think about your own values, the role culture plays in them, and the values of those around you, consider how you can use this information to develop a speech that will best express what you want to say.

Techniques for Learning about Your Audience

Now that you know the kind of information to look for when analyzing an audience, how do you actually uncover it? Unlike a professional pollster, you cannot survey thousands of people and apply sophisticated statistical techniques to analyze your results. On a smaller scale, however, you can use the same techniques. These include interviewing, surveying, and consulting published sources.

Interview Audience Members

An **interview** is a face-to-face communication for the purpose of gathering information. Interviews, even brief ones, can reveal a lot about the audience's interests and needs. You can conduct interviews one-on-one or in a group, in person, or by telephone or e-mail, depending on the time and the feasibility of making such arrangements. Rather than interviewing everyone in an audience, which often would be impractical, consider interviewing a smaller sampling or even just *one* knowledgeable representative of the group that you will address. As in questionnaires (see "Survey the Audience," which follows), interviews usually consist of a mix of open- and closed-ended questions. (See Chapter 9 for more on conducting interviews.)

Survey the Audience

Written surveys, or **questionnaires**, are designed to gather information from a pool of respondents. Because you can distribute them simultaneously to large groups, questionnaires offer a more efficient means of gathering information from a pool of people than do interviews.

A questionnaire consists of a series of questions containing a mix of open- and closed-ended questions. **Closed-ended questions** supplied by the interviewer are designed to elicit a small range of specific answers:

"Do you or did you ever smoke cigarettes?"
Yes _____ No _____ Sometimes _____

Answers will be "Yes," "No," or "I smoked for *x* number of years." Closed-ended questions are especially helpful in uncovering shared attitudes, experiences, and knowledge of audience members.

Closed-ended questions may be either fixed alternative or scale questions. **Fixed alternative questions** contain a limited choice of answers, such as "Yes," "No," or "Sometimes" (as in the preceding example). **Scale questions**— also called *attitude scales*—measure the respondent's level of agreement or disagreement with specific issues:

"Flag burning should be outlawed."
Strongly agree _____ Agree _____ Undecided _____ Disagree _____
Strongly disagree _____

In addition to agreement, scale questions can be used to measure how important listeners judge something to be and how frequently they engage in a particular behavior:

"How important is religion in your life?"
Very important _____   Important _____   Moderately important _____
Of minor importance _____   Unimportant _____

"How frequently do you attend religious services?"
Very frequently _____   Frequently _____   Occasionally _____   Never _____

Open-ended questions are designed to allow respondents to elaborate as much as they wish:

"How do you feel about using the results of DNA testing to prove innocence or guilt in criminal proceedings?"

Open-ended questions are particularly useful for probing beliefs and opinions. They elicit more individual or personal information about the audience members' thoughts and feelings. They are also more time-intensive than closed-ended questions.

Often, it takes just a few questions to get some idea of where audience members stand on each of the demographic factors. By using a mix of open- and closed-ended questions, you can draw a fairly clear picture of the backgrounds and attitudes of the members of your audience.

Sample Audience Analysis Questionnaire

Part I: Demographic Analysis

1. What is your age?   _____ years

2. What is your sex?   _____ Male   _____ Female

3. Please indicate your primary heritage:

   _____ Native American   _____ African American

   _____ Asian American   _____ European

   _____ Latino   _____ Middle Eastern   _____ Other

4. Please indicate your level of formal education:

   _____ High school   _____ Some college

   _____ College degree   _____ Other (please specify)

5. What is your approximate annual income range?

   _____ less than $10,000   _____ $10,000–$25,000

   _____ $25,000–$50,000   _____ $50,000–$75,000

   _____ $75,000–$100,000   _____ over $100,000

(continued on next page)

6. With which political party are your views most closely aligned?

_____ Democratic _____ Republican _____ Neither (Independent)

7. Please check the box below that most closely matches your religious affiliation:

_____ Buddhist _____ Christian

_____ Hindu _____ Jewish

_____ Muslim _____ Not religious _____ Other (please specify)

8. How would you characterize your religious involvement?

_____ Very religious _____ Somewhat religious _____ Not very religious

9. How would you characterize your political position?

_____ Liberal _____ Conservative _____ Moderate

Part II: Analysis of Attitudes, Values, and Beliefs on a Specific Topic

Indicate your answers to the following questions about stem cell research by checking the appropriate blank.

10. It is unethical and immoral to permit any use of stem cells for medical research.

_____ Strongly agree _____ Agree _____ Undecided

_____ Disagree _____ Strongly disagree

11. Do you think the government should or should not fund stem cell research?

_____ Should _____ Should not _____ Neutral

12. Rather than destroy stem cells left over from *in vitro* fertilization, medical researchers should be allowed to use them to develop treatments for diseases.

_____ Strongly agree _____ Agree _____ Undecided

_____ Disagree _____ Strongly disagree

13. What kind of cells come to mind when you think of stem cell therapy?

_____

14. Which of the following has had the biggest influence on your thinking about stem cell research?

_____ Media reports _____ Opinions of friends and family

_____ Your religious beliefs _____ Personal experience

Consult Published Sources

Another avenue to explore when analyzing your audience is published sources. Organizations of all kinds publish information describing their missions, goals, operations, and achievements. Sources include Web sites and related online articles, print brochures, newspaper and magazine articles, annual reports, and industry guides. These materials often contain a wealth of information that you can use to identify salient information about your listeners.

Also consider consulting published opinion polls, such as the following:

- Pew Research Center for the People & the Press: people-press.org
- National Opinion Research Center (NORC): www.norc.uchicago.edu
- Roper Center for Public Opinion Research: ropercenter.uconn.edu
- The Gallup Organization: www.gallup.com

Polls offer excellent insight into the range of attitudes that exist about a given issue as well as how representative state, national, or international samples responded to questions about your issue. You may also wish to use the published data as supporting material for your speeches (see Chapter 8).

Analyze the Speech Setting

As important as analyzing the audience is assessing (and then preparing for) the setting in which you will give your speech—size of audience; location, time, and length of speech; and rhetorical situation. Planning for these factors will help you further adjust your speech to the actual circumstances in which it will occur.

Size of Audience and Physical Setting

The size of the audience and the physical setting in which a speech occurs can have a significant impact on the outcome of the speech. Some settings are formal, others less so. The atmosphere of a classroom is different from that of a banquet room, an outdoor amphitheater, or a large auditorium. The larger the group, the less you are likely to interact with the audience—an important factor to consider when planning your delivery (see Chapters 18–20). You will also need to plan how to position yourself and adjust your voice, with or without a microphone.

Time and Length of Speech

Both the time at which your speech is scheduled and its length will affect listeners' receptivity to it. People gathered at breakfast, lunch, or dinner meetings, for example, come to the speech occasion with more than one agenda. They may wish to hear you, but they will also want time to eat and converse with other people. Your boss or fellow employees may expect to receive information quickly so that they can proceed to other business.

In any speaking situation, always find out how long you are expected to speak. Bear in mind that few matters of speech etiquette are as annoying to an

TABLE 6.2 Typical Length of Presentations	
Kind of Presentation	**Length**
In-depth speech	15–20 minutes
Presentation to boss	1–10 minutes
Toast	1–2 minutes
Award acceptance speech	3–5 minutes

audience as a speaker's apparent disregard for time. Start on time and end well within the time allotted to you. Table 6.2 includes typical lengths for various presentations.

The Speech Context (Rhetorical Situation)

Any speech or presentation you deliver will always occur in a particular context. You may be the third of six speakers on a panel, for instance. You might precede or follow a speaker who is more dynamic or well known than you are. Your listeners may be preoccupied with unusual circumstances—a local sports team just won a championship, extreme weather conditions have disrupted everyday life, the president of the company just resigned, and so forth. By being alert to any of these contingencies, you can address them in your speech.

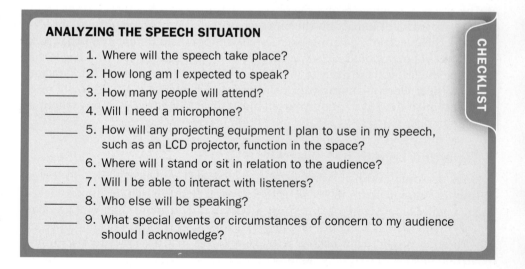

ANALYZING THE SPEECH SITUATION

_____ 1. Where will the speech take place?

_____ 2. How long am I expected to speak?

_____ 3. How many people will attend?

_____ 4. Will I need a microphone?

_____ 5. How will any projecting equipment I plan to use in my speech, such as an LCD projector, function in the space?

_____ 6. Where will I stand or sit in relation to the audience?

_____ 7. Will I be able to interact with listeners?

_____ 8. Who else will be speaking?

_____ 9. What special events or circumstances of concern to my audience should I acknowledge?

CHECKLIST

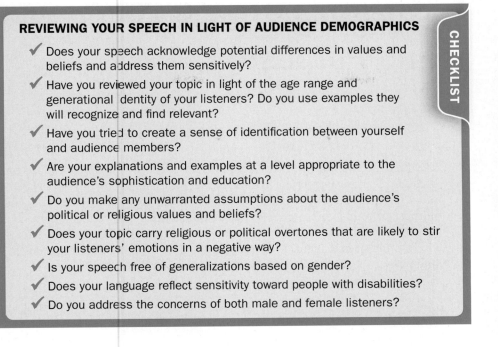

REVIEWING YOUR SPEECH IN LIGHT OF AUDIENCE DEMOGRAPHICS

✓ Does your speech acknowledge potential differences in values and beliefs and address them sensitively?

✓ Have you reviewed your topic in light of the age range and generational identity of your listeners? Do you use examples they will recognize and find relevant?

✓ Have you tried to create a sense of identification between yourself and audience members?

✓ Are your explanations and examples at a level appropriate to the audience's sophistication and education?

✓ Do you make any unwarranted assumptions about the audience's political or religious values and beliefs?

✓ Does your topic carry religious or political overtones that are likely to stir your listeners' emotions in a negative way?

✓ Is your speech free of generalizations based on gender?

✓ Does your language reflect sensitivity toward people with disabilities?

✓ Do you address the concerns of both male and female listeners?

CHECKLIST

CHAPTER 7

Selecting a Topic and Purpose

The first task in preparing any speech is to select a topic and purpose for speaking that are *appropriate to the audience, occasion, and overall speech situation* (i.e., the *rhetorical situation*). Choosing the topic and identifying the purpose of your speech addresses three key questions that you should be able to answer with total confidence before delivering any speech: "What precisely is my speech about?" "What is my goal in speaking to the audience?" and "What specifically do I want my listeners to know or do?"

Assigned versus Self-Selected Topics

In your speech course and other courses you will probably be assigned various kinds of speeches, some of which might have a prescribed topic. In work, civic, and other speech contexts, you may or may not select your own speech topic. Your boss might ask you to prepare a talk explaining how your team developed its latest project. The local Chamber of Commerce might request that you address "businesses that grow a town's tax base." Often speakers are invited because of their expertise in a subject area, so they cover the same general topic in every speech.

Whether a specific topic is assigned to you, or you speak on the same topic over and over, you must adapt to the rhetorical situation. Even when the choice of topic is your decision, you are usually given some direction as to how your talk should be presented. For example:

- You may be given a *purpose*. The adviser for the youth group you volunteer for asks you to speak at the next meeting to "boost morale." The topic you select for this is yours to decide.

- You are given *time constraints*. Your boss informs you that you are on the agenda to talk to a group of foreign visitors for three to five minutes next Monday. How you fill this time is up to you.

- You are given a *challenge*. The master of ceremonies for a roast to honor the retiring basketball coach asks you to "make the audience laugh."

Identify the General Speech Purpose

 WEB Chapter quizzes

As the speaker, you are accountable for both selecting a relevant topic and accomplishing a desired purpose. Public speeches typically address one of three general purposes: to *inform,* to *persuade,* or to *mark a special occasion.* The **general speech purpose** for any speech answers the question, "Why am I speaking on this topic to this particular audience on this occasion?"

The speech occasion often determines the general speech purpose, or at least suggests what might be most appropriate. For example, a town activist, invited to address a civic group about installing solar panels in town buildings, may choose a persuasive purpose to encourage the group to get behind the effort. If invited to describe the initiative to the town finance committee, the activist may choose an informative purpose, in which the main goal is to help the finance members understand project costs. Addressing the same topic, the speaker selects a different general speech purpose to suit the audience and occasion.

When the General Speech Purpose Is to Inform

Your purpose in an informative speech is to share your knowledge or point of view about a subject with others by defining, describing, explaining, or demonstrating this knowledge. Thus the general purpose of an **informative speech** is *to increase the audience's understanding and awareness of a topic.*

When selecting a topic for an informative speech, try to gauge how much the audience already knows about it. There's no surer way to lose audience members' attention than to speak over—or under—their heads. Everyone knows about taxes, for instance, and we're interested to learn new ways to reduce the amount we owe. Just about any topic is appropriate for an informative speech (see Tables 7.1 and 7.2), as long as you present it with the goal of giving the audience something new to expand their understanding and awareness.

TABLE 7.1	Some General Categories of Informative Topics				
Objects	**People**	**Events**	**Concepts**	**Processes**	**Issues**
Their origin, construction, function, symbolic, or concrete meaning. For example, how wind turbines work; what's behind Native American cliff dwellings.	Their biographies, noteworthy achievements, anecdotes about them. For example, Barack Obama's childhood; Facebook founder Mark Zuckerberg.	Noteworthy or unusual occurrences, both past and present. For example, rebuilding of New Orleans; criminality in professional sports.	Abstract and difficult ideas or theories. For example, the nature of love; the definition of peace; the theory of intelligent design.	A series of steps leading to an end result. For example, how one becomes an astronaut; how to succeed in a college internship.	Problems or matters of dispute. For example, U.S. border security; whether reality television is really real.

> **TABLE 7.2   Sample Informative Speech Topics**
>
> • The Effectiveness of Nutritional Supplements
> • Service Vacations
> • Violence on College Campuses
> • The Booming Business of Wine
> • Careers We Didn't Have Ten Years Ago
> • Community Service Options for Busy College Students
> • Lesser Known Uses of the iPhone and Droid
> • The Increasing Prevalence of Autism

When the General Speech Purpose Is to Persuade

As with informative speeches, persuasive speeches also increase listeners' knowledge of a topic. But rather than primarily seeking this goal, the general purpose of a **persuasive speech** is to *effect some degree of change in the audience's attitudes, beliefs, or even specific behaviors* (e.g., "Only eat wild salmon").

Topics or issues on which there are competing perspectives are particularly suitable for persuasive speeches. Issues such as immigration reform, stem cell research, and binge drinking naturally lend themselves to a persuasive purpose because people hold strongly contrasting opinions about them. Most any topic is suitable for a persuasive speech as long as the speaker can fashion it into a message that is intended to effect some degree of change in the audience (see Table 7.3).

Consider the topic of binge drinking. A persuasive purpose (e.g., "To persuade my audience to avoid binge drinking") would be appropriate if:

- The audience feels considerably different about the topic than you do (e.g., members of the audience engage in binge drinking).

- The audience holds similar attitudes and beliefs about the topic as you do but needs direction in taking action (e.g., the audience consists of people who want to help friends avoid binge drinking and are seeking strategies to do so).

> **TABLE 7.3   Sample Persuasive Speech Topics**
>
> • Take Nutritional Supplements for Better Health
> • Use Spring Break for a Service Vacation
> • Attend Campus Emergency Preparedness Workshops
> • Consider a Career in the Wine Industry
> • Use Your Major to Develop a New Career Area
> • Spend One Weekend Each Quarter in Community Service
> • Admit and Break Your iPhone Addiction
> • Assist in the Care of a Special Needs Child

- The audience agrees with your position but is likely to encounter opposing information or circumstances in the near future (e.g., beer will be readily available at an upcoming annual celebration of college students).

When the General Speech Purpose Is to Mark a Special Occasion

Some speeches are prepared for a purpose dictated by a special occasion. **Special occasion speeches** *entertain, celebrate, commemorate, inspire, or set a social agenda* and include speeches of introduction, speeches of acceptance, speeches of presentation, roasts and toasts, eulogies, and after-dinner speeches, among others. Special occasion speeches sometimes have secondary specific purposes to inform or to persuade. For example, a speech to mark the occasion of Veterans Day might include a message to devote more time to volunteering with the local Veterans Hospital.

IDENTIFYING YOUR GENERAL SPEECH PURPOSE

✓ If your goal in speaking is primarily to increase the audience's knowledge of a topic or to share your point of view, your general purpose is to inform.

✓ If it is primarily to effect some degree of change in the way your listeners view things, your general purpose is to persuade.

✓ If it is primarily to mark a special occasion, your general purpose will be variously to entertain, celebrate, commemorate, inspire, or set a social agenda.

CHECKLIST

Choosing a Topic for Your Speech

 WEB Topics

A good speech topic must pique not only your own curiosity but the audience's, too. As you explore topics, consider each one's potential appeal to the audience, as well as its appropriateness for the occasion. Will the topic be relevant to your listeners' specific attributes and motivations? Will it meet listeners' expectations for the speech?

Identify Personal Interests

Selecting a topic you are familiar with and enthusiastic about offers many advantages. You'll enjoy researching and learning more about it. You'll bring a sense of genuine enthusiasm to your presentation, which will help convey your competence and encourage the audience to see you as a highly credible speaker.

As seen in Table 7.4, personal interests run the gamut from favorite activities and hobbies to deeply held goals and values. Personal experiences

TABLE 7.4 Identifying Topics

Favorite Hobbies	Personal Experiences	Values	Goals
• Sports • Building computers • Cars • Fashion • Reading • Video games • Music • Travel • Outdoor life	• Exotic travel destinations • Service in the armed forces • Volunteer work in a foreign country* • Immigration • Life-threatening disease • Surviving cancer	• Building a greater sense of community* • Spirituality • Philanthropy* • Political activism*	• Being a high-tech entrepreneur • Attending graduate or professional school • Starting a family • Being fit* • Learning more about my religion
Specific Subject Interests	**Social Problems**	**Health and Nutrition**	**Current Events**
• Local history* • Ancient history • Politics* • Art* • Religion • Science	• Road rage* • Violence in the schools • Unemployment • Environmental issues* • Lack of affordable childcare	• Diets • Circle contact lenses • Exercise regimens • HMOs • Health insurance* • Assisted living • Herbal and vitamin supplements	• Pending legislation— crime bills, property taxes, land use* • Political races • Climate and biodiversity • Race relations • Foreign aid • National security
Grassroots Issues	**New or Unusual Angles**	**Issues of Controversy**	
• Land development versus conservation* • Local organizations* • School issues	• Unsolved crimes* • Unexplained disappearances • Scandals	• Creationism versus evolution • Airport security • Stem cell research	

*Note: Topics marked with an asterisk are good possibilities for speeches on civic responsibility.

provide powerful topics, especially if, by your sharing them, the audience in some way benefits from your experience. "What it's like" stories also yield interesting topics. For example, what is it like to go hang gliding in the Rocky Mountains or to be part of a medical mission's team working in Uganda?

Some personal interest topics are particularly amenable for speeches encouraging civic responsibility. For example, the purpose of a speech based on your experience in taking a service vacation (e.g., building homes in a Mexican village) could be to generate interest in establishing a local organization for promoting and structuring service vacations, or for encouraging the development of a local chapter of Habitat for Humanity, an organization that builds homes for low-income families.

Consider Current Events and Controversial Issues

People are constantly barraged with newsworthy topics, but few of us have the time to delve into them. Thus, many of us appreciate and even hunger for information that broadens our understanding of these topics. As an interested and responsible citizen of your community, you are surrounded by issues that beg for attention and action. Select the ones that are most important to you and your audience, and see if you can make a difference. But a word of warning: Steer clear of highly charged topics for which people have deeply held beliefs, such as abortion or prayer in schools. People rarely respond to persuasion directed at their core values, so speeches on such topics are likely to accomplish little except to raise tensions in your classroom.

Survey Grassroots Issues: Engage the Community

Most people respond with interest to issues that affect them directly, especially those of a local nature. Parents want to know about quality day care in the area; town residents need information about upcoming referendums. People are also interested in what other people in their communities are doing. Are you involved in a club on campus, or do you volunteer for a local charity? Consider giving a speech about the organization's mission, membership, or upcoming event. Review your community's newspapers and news blogs for the local headlines.

   Matching community-related topics to an appropriate purpose for your speech will not be as difficult as it may seem, especially if you are focusing on issues that are relevant and meaningful to your audience. And, because such topics are in the news, you should be able to find ample materials to develop your speech.

Steer Clear of Overused and Trivial Topics

To avoid boring your classmates and instructor, stay away from tired issues, such as drunk driving and gun control, as well as trite topics such as "how to change a tire." These and other overused topics appear far too frequently in student classroom speeches across the country. Instead, seek out subject matter that yields new or refreshing insight. As one source of ideas, consider searching your favorite print or online publications. Or consider how you can use personal experience, backed by relevant secondary research, as a topic. Fresh ideas based on firsthand knowledge are more intriguing and provide an opportunity for others to get to know you better.

Try Brainstorming to Generate Ideas

Brainstorming is a problem-solving process that involves the spontaneous generation of ideas through word association, topic mapping, or Internet browsing using search engines and Web (subject) directories. It is a structured and effective way to identify topic ideas in a relatively brief period of time.

Word Association

To brainstorm by **word association**, write down *one* topic that might interest you and your listeners. Then jot down the first thing that comes to mind related to it. Repeat the process until you have a list of fifteen to twenty items. Narrow the list to two or three, and then select a final topic.

- health ⇒ alternative medicine ⇒ naturopathy ⇒ fraud
- children ⇒ parenting ⇒ working ⇒ day care ⇒ living expenses
- diving ⇒ snorkeling ⇒ Bahamas ⇒ conch shells ⇒ deep-sea fishing
- Internet ⇒ Web sites ⇒ blogging ⇒ Facebook
- exercise ⇒ StairMaster ⇒ weight lifting ⇒ swimming

Topic Mapping

A **topic map** is a brainstorming technique in which you lay out words in diagram form to show categorical relationships among them (see Figure 7.1). Put a potential topic in the middle of a piece of paper and draw a circle around it. As related ideas come to you, write them down as shown in Figure 7.1. Keep going until you hit upon an idea that appeals most to you.

Internet Tools

The ability to move instantaneously from one link to another makes the Web an excellent brainstorming tool. Popular Internet search engines such as Google (www.google.com), Yahoo! (www.yahoo.com), and Bing (www.bing .com) offer a wealth of resources both to discover topics and to narrow them. For example, the "More" Menu, located at the top of Google's main page, leads you to additional search tools, including "Directory" and "Trends" search.

- "Directory" search contains alphabetized general topics you can use to brainstorm word associations for your topic. Clicking highlighted words leads to category subtopics.

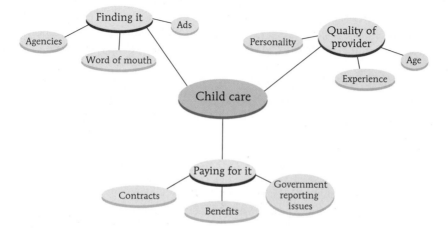

FIGURE 7.1 A Topic Map

- The "Trends" search page displays the day's "Hot Topics" and "Hot Searches," based on the highest volume of searches occurring on Google at the time. This function can help identify topics of current interest that your classmates might share.

You can also consult Google's Wonder Wheel for help finding a topic. For example, start at the Google main page (www.google.com) and type in a potential topic, such as "oil spill recovery." Click on the "Wonder wheel" link on the left-hand side of the search results page. A page produces a topic map for the search topic. You can then choose from among the associated search topics one of further interest. Each successive link narrows the topic further (see Figure 7.2).

Another online tool you can use to find (and narrow) a topic is a library's portal, or its home page (see "From Source to Speech: Narrowing Your Topic Using a Library Portal," on p. 106). If you've already chosen a topic, consult the library's online databases, such as Academic OneFile, to locate credible sources (see Chapter 10, "Finding Credible Sources on the Internet").

CRITERIA FOR SELECTING A TOPIC

1. Is the topic appropriate to the occasion?
2. Will the topic appeal to my listeners' interests and needs?
3. Is the topic something I can speak about with enthusiasm and insight?
4. Can I research and report on the topic in the time allotted?
5. Will I be able to offer a fresh perspective on the topic?

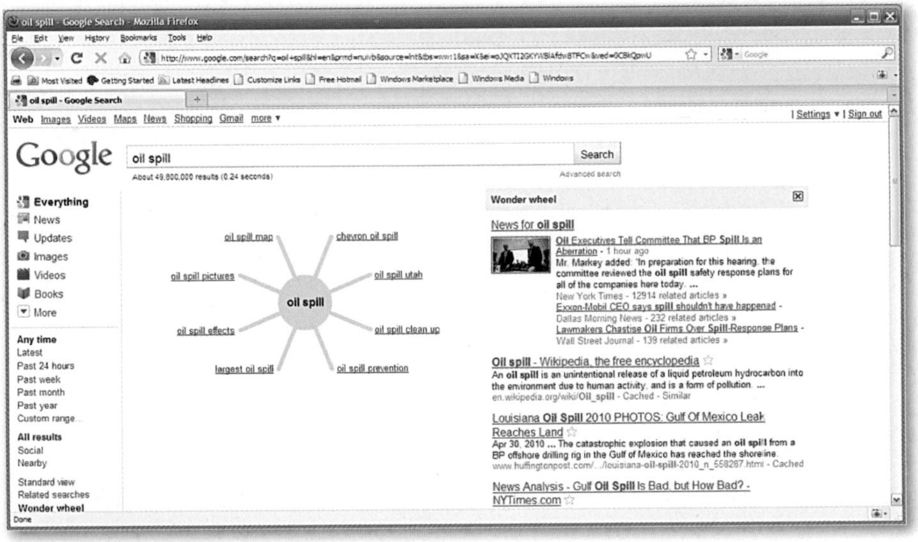

CHECKLIST

FIGURE 7.2 Google Wonder Wheel

Narrowing Your Topic to Fit Your Audience

Why Narrow Your Topic?

Choosing a topic that interests you is only the beginning. A vital step in moving from topic to speech is narrowing your topic and tailoring it to fit your audience and the speech occasion.

A Case Study

Jenny is a member of the campus animal rights club and a student in a public speaking class. She is giving several persuasive speeches this semester: one to her public speaking class, one to the student council, and one in an online video for the Web page of the animal rights club. For all three presentations, Jenny plans to speak on the broad topic of animal rights and welfare. But she must narrow this topic considerably to fit each audience and the speech occasion, and this means different narrowed topics.

First, Jenny draws a topic map to generate ideas.

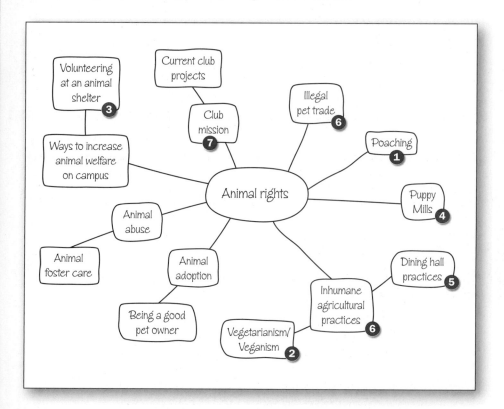

For each presentation, Jenny narrows her topic after considering her audience and the speech occasion.

Public speaking class (25–30 people):

- Mixed ages, races, and ethnicities, and an even mix of males and females
- Busy with classes, jobs, sports, and clubs
- Half live in campus housing, where pets are not allowed

1 Jenny eliminates poaching because it's not an everyday concern for students.

2 She eliminates vegetarianism because she will be unlikely to change listeners' minds in a six-minute speech.

3 Volunteering at an animal shelter may appeal to animal lovers who are not allowed to have pets on campus. Jenny argues that students should donate an hour a week to a nearby shelter, so that busy students can still participate.

Student Council (8–10 people):

- Mixed demographic characteristics
- Similar interests: government, maintaining a rich campus life, an investment in ethics and the honor code, and an interest in keeping student affairs within budget

4 Jenny can eliminate puppy mills—though the student council may agree that they are harmful, it's not likely that they'll be able to do anything about the problem.

5 Jenny zeros in on dining hall practices because it is directly tied to campus life. A resolution to use free-range eggs in the campus dining hall benefits all students and requires the support of the council—an ideal topic for this audience.

Animal rights club Web site (open to all searchers of the Internet):

- Most diverse audience—unknown mix of demographic characteristics
- Likely interest in animal rights

6 Jenny can easily eliminate many topics, such as illegal pet trade and inhumane agricultural practices, because they are too complicated for a brief video clip.

7 She opts for the club's mission as a topic. A very brief welcome message that states the club's mission and invites Web visitors to attend a longer information session will likely capture the most interest and appeal to both the curious passerby and the dedicated animal rights activist.

Narrowing Your Topic Using a Library Portal

One of several ways to research your topic is to use a library's online portal. This is an especially good approach because using such a tool to generate narrower ideas also guarantees that the new ideas are supported by *credible* sources. For example, to narrow down the topic of smoking in movies, you could use a library portal to locate relevant books and access online periodical databases that offer full-text articles evaluated for reliability by librarians and other content experts.

Navigating the Library Portal through Basic Searches

To search the portal of the Brooklyn Public Library, you could find sources through links on the home page: "Library Catalog" to find books, and "Articles and Databases" to find full-text articles.

A basic search within "Articles and Databases" results in multiple hits, all with numerous articles from various databases.

This psychology journal article reveals a level of results that general search engines do not find—an article that has undergone peer review and can be viewed in full-text, PDF form.

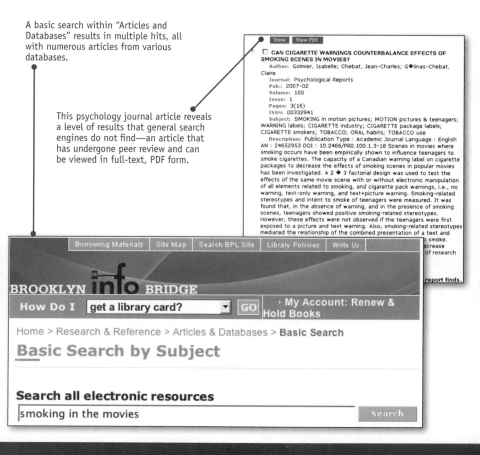

Using Advanced Library Portal Searches

An advanced search allows you to hone in on credible sources that are even more likely to help you. This function will allow you to better distill the specific purpose of your speech and to develop your thesis statement.

1. Linking search terms *cigarettes* and *movies* by Boolean operator "AND" results in hits containing both these terms.

2. Limiting the search from 2000 to 2008 ensures that only articles in this period appear.

3. Limiting the resource categories yields results that cover only the areas on which you want to focus your thesis.

Refine the Topic and Purpose

WEB Topics research links

Once you have an idea of what you'd like to speak about and have established the general speech purpose, you need to narrow your focus so that it's in line with time constraints, audience expectations, and the nature of the occasion.

Narrow the Topic

As you narrow your topic, you must carefully evaluate it in light of audience interests, knowledge, and needs. Consider the following questions: What is the purpose of your speech? How long is the speech to be? How much time do you have to do research? How much information can you responsibly review so that you avoid distorting or falsifying the material? Imagine, for example, how your approach to the topic "The Worldwide Popularity of Smartphones" may change as you consider the following factors:

- The speech is for an informative speaking assignment.
- The time limit is five to seven minutes.
- The library does not have a copy of a recent telecommunications industry report on smartphone use, and your computer is down.

Just as brainstorming can be used to discover a general topic, it can also be helpful in narrowing one. One way of doing this is to brainstorm by category. What sorts of categories can you break your general topic into? Do a Google or Bing search as described on p. 102 to generate some categories. For the general topic of smartphones, some related categories are models, manufacturers, and calling plans. As you brainstorm by category, ask yourself, "What questions do I have about the topic? Am I more interested in how smartphones work or in how much they cost? What aspect of smartphones is my audience most likely to want to hear about?" You can also use topic mapping, trend searching, or Google's Wonder Wheel (see p. 103) to narrow your topic).

NARROWING YOUR TOPIC

CHECKLIST

✔ What is my audience most likely to know about the subject?

✔ What are my listeners most likely to want to learn?

✔ What aspects of the topic are most relevant to the occasion?

✔ Can I develop the topic using just two or three main points?

✔ How much can I competently research and report on in the time I am given to speak?

Form a Specific Speech Purpose

The **specific speech purpose** lays out precisely what you want the audience to get from the speech. To determine the specific purpose, ask yourself, "What is it about my topic that I want the audience to learn/do/reconsider/agree with?" Be specific about your aim, and then state this aim in action form, as in the following, written for an informative speech:

GENERAL TOPIC:	Consolidating Student Loans
NARROWED TOPIC:	Understanding when and why consolidating student loans makes sense
GENERAL PURPOSE:	To inform
SPECIFIC PURPOSE:	To inform my audience about the factors to consider when deciding whether to consolidate student loans

The specific purpose statement is seldom articulated in the speech itself. Still, it is important to formulate it for yourself in order to implant in your mind exactly what you want your speech to accomplish.

From Topic and Purpose to Thesis Statement

Once you have narrowed your topic and devised your general and specific purposes, your next step is to formulate a thesis statement. The **thesis statement** is the theme or central idea of the speech stated in the form of a single declarative sentence. It concisely expresses what the speech will attempt to support from the speaker's point of view. It is a single line that serves to connect all the parts of the speech, much like a backbone. The main points, the supporting material, and the conclusion all emanate from and relate to the thesis.

The thesis statement and the specific purpose are closely linked. Both state the speech topic, but in different forms. The specific purpose describes in action form what outcome you want to achieve with the speech. The thesis statement concisely declares, in a single idea, what the speech is about. By clearly stating what your speech is about, you set in your mind exactly what outcome you want to accomplish.

Use the Thesis Statement to Convey the Central Idea

The thesis statement conveys the central idea or core assumption about the topic (see Figure 7.3). Whether the speech is informative or persuasive, the thesis offers your comment on the topic. For instance, the thesis statement "Three major events caused the United States to go to war in 1941" expresses your view that three factors played a part in the U.S. entry into World War II. The speech is then developed from this thesis, presenting facts and evidence to support it.

The thesis statement aids you in developing a coherent, understandable arrangement of information so that the audience can easily follow the ideas that make up the body of the speech. Thus, you should postpone the development of main points and supporting material until you have correctly formulated the specific purpose and thesis statement (see Chapter 12).

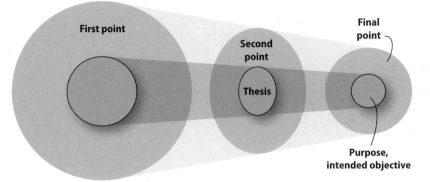

FIGURE 7.3 Main points should relate to and bolster the thesis, and ultimately lead to the specific speech purpose.

ETHICALLY SPEAKING

Ethical Considerations in Selecting a Topic and Purpose

Respect for your audience members and adaptation to their needs and interests should always guide your topic choices. What makes a speech ethical or unethical depends on how it empowers the audience to think or act. In other words, ethical considerations begin with your goal or purpose. Speakers who select persuasive purposes should be particularly careful; under pressure to sway an audience, some speakers may be tempted to tamper with the truth. As you review your speech goal, consider the following:

- Have you deliberately distorted information to achieve a desired result?
- Is it your intent to deceive?
- Do you try to coerce the audience into thinking or acting in a certain way?
- Have you knowingly tried to appeal to harmful biases?

Although few hard-and-fast rules exist when it comes to ethical guidelines for selecting topics, some areas are clearly off-limits—at least in U.S. culture:

- The topic shows an audience how to perform actions prohibited by law.
- The topic provides audience members with information that may result in their physical or psychological harm.
- The topic humiliates or degrades the fundamental values of an audience's culture, religion, or political system.

The nature of the thesis statement varies according to the speech purpose. In a persuasive speech, your comment on the speech as stated in the thesis represents what you are going to prove in the address. All the main points in the speech are arguments that develop this position.

Example 1

GENERAL PURPOSE: To persuade

SPECIFIC PURPOSE: To persuade the audience to raise money on behalf of green charities

THESIS: A donation to a member organization of green charities is an investment in a sustainable environment.

Example 2

SPECIFIC PURPOSE: To persuade the audience that abstinence is the way to avoid the harm alcohol can cause

THESIS: Abstinence is the best way to avoid the harm alcohol can cause.

Notice that in each case, after you read the thesis you find yourself asking "Why?" or thinking "Prove it!" This will be accomplished by the evidence you give in the main points (see Chapter 12).

The thesis statement in an informative speech conveys the scope of the topic, the steps associated with the topic, or the underlying elements of the topic. It describes what the audience will learn.

Example 1

GENERAL PURPOSE: To inform

SPECIFIC PURPOSE: To educate the audience about how the U.S. government is structured

THESIS: The three branches of the U.S. government form our unique representative democracy.

Example 2

SPECIFIC PURPOSE: To enable audience members to invest their money properly

THESIS: Consider six steps to investing in the stock market.

Use the Thesis Statement to Guide Your Speech Preparation

The point of creating a thesis statement is to help you identify precisely what your speech is about. As you develop the speech, use the thesis to keep yourself on track. Depicted as the inner core of a cylinder, as in Figure 7.3, the thesis is a straight and narrow path to follow from when you first state it to when you reach your last point and fulfill the speech purpose. As you research materials, review them in the light of whether they contribute to the thesis or stray from it. When you actually draft your speech, work your thesis statement into it and restate it where appropriate. Doing so will encourage your audience to understand and accept your message.

Following are some examples of student speech topics and the corresponding general and specific speech purposes and thesis statements:

Example 1

SPEECH TOPIC:	Blogs
GENERAL SPEECH PURPOSE:	To inform
SPECIFIC SPEECH PURPOSE:	To inform my audience of three benefits of keeping a blog
THESIS STATEMENT:	Maintaining a blog provides the opportunity to practice writing, a means of networking with others who share similar interests, and the chance to develop basic Web site management skills.

Example 2

SPEECH TOPIC:	Student Internships
GENERAL SPEECH PURPOSE:	To persuade
SPECIFIC SPEECH PURPOSE:	To persuade my audience that internships are beneficial
THESIS STATEMENT:	To prepare for a difficult job market and enhance your résumé, you should get a student internship to help link your academic studies to specific job skills.

FORMULATING THE THESIS STATEMENT

✔ Does my thesis statement sum up in a single sentence what my speech is about?

✔ Is it restricted to a single idea?

✔ Is it in the form of a complete declarative sentence?

✔ Is it stated in a way that is relevant to the audience?

CHECKLIST

Make the Thesis Statement Relevant and Motivating

As you refine the draft of your speech, try to express the thesis statement in a way that will motivate the audience to listen. In many cases, creating a relevant thesis can be accomplished quite easily by adding a few key words or phrases. You can preface an informative thesis statement with a phrase such as "Few of us know" or "Contrary to popular belief" or "Have you ever." A persuasive thesis statement can also be adapted to establish relevance for the audience. Phrases such as "As most of you know" or "As informed members of the community" or "As concerned adults" can attract listeners' attention and interest and help them see the topic's relevance.

The exact phrasing or rewording of your thesis statement depends on the type of audience to which you are speaking. Once you gain some information about your audience members, you won't have trouble making the topic relevant for them.

SUPPORTING
THE SPEECH

SUPPORTING THE SPEECH

SPEAKER'S REFERENCE

CHAPTER **8** Developing Supporting Material 124

Use a Variety of Supporting Materials 124
Consider the Target Audience 124
Offer Examples 125
Share Stories 127
▶ **CHECKLIST** Selecting the Right Example or Story 128
Draw on Testimony 128
▶ **ESL SPEAKER'S NOTES** Broaden Your Listeners' Perspectives 128
▶ **CHECKLIST** Evaluating the Credibility of Testimony 129
Provide Facts and Statistics 129
▶ **ETHICALLY SPEAKING** Evaluating the Validity of the Statistics You Cite 132
▶ **SELF-ASSESSMENT CHECKLIST** Using Statistics in Your Speech: An Ethical Inventory 133
Win Acceptance of Your Supporting Materials 133

CHAPTER **9** Locating Supporting Material 134

Before You Begin: Assess Your Research Needs 134
Locating Secondary Sources 135
▶ **CHECKLIST** Making an Inventory of Your Research Needs 135
▶ **A CULTURAL PERSPECTIVE** Discovering Diversity in Reference Works 139
▶ **CHECKLIST** Finding Speeches Online 140
Generating Primary Sources: Interviews and Surveys 141
▶ **CHECKLIST** Preparing for the Interview 143
Evaluate and Document Your Sources 144
▶ **CHECKLIST** Creating a Bibliography 145
▶ **ETHICALLY SPEAKING** Researching Your Speech in an Ethical Manner 147
▶ **FROM SOURCE TO SPEECH** Recording and Citing Books 148
▶ **FROM SOURCE TO SPEECH** Recording and Citing Articles from Periodicals 150

CHAPTER **10** Finding Credible Sources on the Internet 152

    Begin Your Search at a Library Portal 152

    Make the Most of Internet Search Tools 155

        ▶ **FROM SOURCE TO SPEECH** Evaluating Web Sources 156

        ▶ **CHECKLIST** Is My Online Research Effective? 158

        ▶ **CHECKLIST** Choosing between a Subject (Web) Directory and a Search Engine 160

        ▶ **CHECKLIST** Identifying Paid Listings in Search Results 161

    Record and Cite Internet Sources 163

        ▶ **CHECKLIST** Documenting Internet Sources 163

        ▶ **FROM SOURCE TO SPEECH** Recording and Citing Web Sources 164

CHAPTER **11** Citing Sources in Your Speech 166

    Alert Listeners to Key Source Information 166

        ▶ **CHECKLIST** Offering Key Source Information 167

    Establish the Source's Trustworthiness 167

    Avoid a Mechanical Delivery 168

    Overview of Source Types with Sample Oral Citations 169

        ▶ **FROM SOURCE TO SPEECH** Demonstrating Your Sources' Reliability and Credibility 170

    Properly Citing Facts and Statistics 172

    Properly Citing Summarized, Paraphrased, and Quoted Information 174

SUPPORTING THE SPEECH

CHAPTER 8 Developing Supporting Material

Offer a Variety of Supporting Materials

- Provide more than your own personal opinions or experiences. (p. 125)
- Illustrate each main point with several different types of supporting material. (p. 125)

Keep the Audience in Mind When Selecting Sources

- Choose evidence and sources based on audience factors. (p. 125)
- Remember that not every source is appropriate for every audience. (p. 125)

Choose Accurate, Relevant, Motivating, and Audience-Centered Supporting Material

- Seek out compelling *examples* to illustrate or describe your ideas. (p. 125)
- Share *stories,* either real or hypothetical, to drive your point home. (p. 127)
- Use firsthand findings in the form of *testimony*. (p. 128)
- Hunt for relevant *facts* or documented occurrences. (p. 129)
- Consider whether you need *statistics,* or quantified evidence. (p. 129)
- Draw your statistics from reliable sources and present them in context. (p. 131)
- Beware of cherry-picking and other unethical ways of presenting data. (p. 131)

Convince Listeners to Accept Your Supporting Material as Credible

- Make it a priority to establish your source's trustworthiness and reliability. (p. 133)
- Emphasize your source's qualifications. (p. 133)

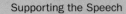

SPEAKER'S REFERENCE

CHAPTER 9 Locating Supporting Material

Plan a Research Strategy

- Keep in mind your goal of substantiating your thesis. (p. 134)
- Consider a mix of credible primary and secondary sources. (p. 134)
- Use sources appropriate to the rhetorical situation. (p. 134)

Consider Various Secondary Sources

- Books (p. 136)
- Newspapers and periodicals (p. 136)
- Weblogs and social news sites (p. 136)
- Government publications (p. 137)
- Digital collections (p. 138)
- Reference works (e.g., encyclopedias, almanacs, books of quotations, poetry collections, and atlases) (p. 138)

Create Your Own Sources with Interviews and Surveys

- Plan your questions well in advance. (p. 141)
- Avoid vague, leading, and loaded questions. (p. 141)
- Use active listening strategies such as paraphrasing. (p. 141)

Offer Only Credible Sources

Document Your Sources

- Record appropriate bibliographic information for each piece of evidence. (p. 145)
- Select a method to organize your sources, and follow it systematically. (p. 145)

CHAPTER 10 Finding Credible Sources on the Internet

Start Your Search at Your Library's Home Page

- Library portals provide an entry point for sources that have been vetted for quality. (p. 152)
- Portals and virtual libraries can help you access the invisible Web. (p. 153)

Critically Evaluate All Information Found Online

- Distinguish information from misinformation, propaganda, and disinformation. (p. 154)
- Understand the nature of propaganda and approach advisedly. (p. 154)
- Avoid sources based on misinformation or disinformation. (p. 154)
- Check the most authoritative Web sites first. (p. 156)
- Evaluate authorship and sponsorship. (p. 156)
- Check for currency. (p. 156)
- Check that the site credits its sources and that sources are credible. (p. 156)

Make the Most of Internet Search Tools

- Use *general search engines* as a way to find information on a well-defined topic. (p. 158)
- Use *meta-search engines* to search several search engines simultaneously. (p. 158)
- Use *specialized search engines* to delve into specific topics. (p. 158)
- Use *subject (Web) directories* to progressively narrow your topic. (p. 159)

Know That Commercial Influences Can Taint Search Results

- For a fee, some search tools guarantee a higher ranking ("paid placement"). (p. 161)
- For a fee, some search tools guarantee inclusion, without guaranteeing higher ranking ("paid inclusion"). (p. 161)

Use Advance Search Commands to Enhance Results

- Use advance search fields, such as language, country, domain, and date-range to narrow returns. (p. 161)

Record Your Sources Systematically

- Orally reveal the source of your ideas located online. (p. 163)

CHAPTER 11 Citing Sources in Your Speech

Cite Your Sources to Enhance Your Own Authority and Demonstrate Solid Support for Your Reasoning

- Credit information drawn from other people's ideas. (p. 166)
- Information that is common knowledge need not be credited. (p. 166)

Offer Key Source Information

- Cite author or origin of source. (p. 166)
- Cite type (format) of source. (p. 166)
- Cite title or description. (p. 166)
- Cite date of creation or publication. (p. 166)

Demonstrate the Source's Trustworthiness

- If the source is affiliated with a respected institution, identify it. (p. 167)
- If citing a study linked to a reputable institution, identify it. (p. 167)
- If a source has relevant credentials, note them. (p. 168)
- If the source has relevant real-life experience, mention it. (p. 168)

Avoid a Mechanical Delivery of Sources

- Be sure to acknowledge the different source types correctly—whether books, periodicals, or Web sites. (p. 169)
- Put facts and statistics in context. (p. 172)
- Provide sources for summarized and paraphrased material. (p. 174)
- Identify and credit quoted material. (p. 174)

KEY TERMS

Chapter 8

supporting material	anecdote	percentage
example	testimony	average
brief example	expert testimony	mean
extended example	lay testimony	median
hypothetical example	facts	mode
story	statistics	cherry-picking
narrative	frequency	

Chapter 9

invention	periodical	almanac
primary sources	blog	fact book
secondary sources	social news site	atlas
database	U.S. Government Printing Office (GPO)	interview
reference librarian		working bibliography
Library of Congress call number	encyclopedia	fabrication
Dewey decimal number	general encyclopedia	
	specialized encyclopedia	

Chapter 10

library portal
virtual library
invisible (the deep) Web
information
propaganda
misinformation

disinformation
domain
tilde (~)
search engine
individual search engine
meta-search engine

specialized search engine
subject (Web) directory
paid placement
paid inclusion
advanced searching (field searching)

Chapter 11

oral citation
source reliability
source qualifier

CHAPTER 8

Developing Supporting Material

Often, the key to a good speech is not the topic itself, but how it is developed and supported. You can easily see this in speeches on the same theme prepared by different speakers. Good speeches contain accurate, relevant, motivating, and audience-centered **supporting material** in the form of memorable examples, narratives, testimony, facts, and statistics (see Table 8.1).

Broadly speaking, supporting material performs three functions: (1) It illustrates and elaborates on the meaning of your ideas; (2) it substantiates or proves your statements, adding evidence to your assertions; (3) it arouses interest and encourages engagement with the message. As you gather supporting material, consider how you can use it to fulfill these functions.

Use a Variety of Supporting Materials

WEB Research room

Virtually any speech you deliver will require a variety of supporting material other than your own personal opinion or experience. This holds true whether or not you possess expert knowledge on a topic. People want to know the truth about a given matter, and, unless they view you as a true authority on the subject, they will not merely accept your word for it. In general, listeners respond most favorably to a variety of supporting materials derived from multiple sources to illustrate each main point.[1] Alternating among different types of supporting material—moving from a story to a statistic, for example—will make the presentation more interesting and credible while simultaneously appealing to your audience members' different learning styles.

Consider the Target Audience

Bear in mind your target audience as you decide upon your particular mix of supporting materials. Depending on audience factors, it may be wise to weight your evidence in favor of facts and expert testimony, or, conversely, personal stories and examples. Think as well about your choice of sources. Even if reputable, not every source is appropriate for every audience. A politically conservative audience may reject testimony you quote from a liberal politician, and a devoutly religious audience may resist examples drawn from certain secular

TABLE 8.1   Types and Functions of Supporting Material

Type of Supporting Material	Definition	Purpose
Example	Illustrates, describes, or represents things; it can be brief or extended, and real or hypothetical.	Aids understanding by making ideas, items, or events more concrete; creates interest.
Narrative	A story, either real or imaginary, and short or drawn-out in length. Can constitute a small part of the presentation or serve as a basis for the speech itself.	Generates interest and identification.
Testimony	Firsthand findings, eyewitness accounts, and opinions by people, both lay (nonexpert) and expert.	Provides evidence and aids credibility.
Facts	Actual events, dates, times, and places that can be independently verified.	Provides evidence (including people involved) and demonstrates points.
Statistics	Data that demonstrate relationships.	Summarizes information, demonstrates proof, makes points memorable.

sources, such as *Time* or *Newsweek*. Keeping the audience in mind as you develop supporting materials will help avoid potential mismatches such as these between audience and support for your speech.

Offer Examples

"We learn by example" became a popular saying because it is indeed true. **Examples** illustrate, describe, or represent things. Their purpose is to aid understanding by making ideas, items, or events more concrete.

Study the text of any winning speech and you will see that it is liberally sprinkled with good examples that clarify and enliven the speaker's message. Examples are particularly helpful when they are used to describe or explain things with which the audience may not be familiar. Examples can be *brief* or *extended* and may be either *factual* or *hypothetical*.

Brief Examples

Brief examples offer a single illustration of a point. Barrington D. Parker, in a speech about visa problems among foreign-born graduate students, uses the following single illustration to show that compared to students in many other countries, relatively fewer U.S. students pursue degrees in science and engineering:

> Your children and mine gravitate towards humanities and social science majors as opposed to the quantitative ones such as mathematics, natural science, or engineering. . . . This aspect of our culture is radically different from many other places in the world. For example, a member of the Yale Corporation originally from Bombay told us that if you were at a social gathering of professionals there, and a son or daughter was going to college, you would be positively embarrassed to admit that he or she was studying humanities or liberal arts. This meant you had somehow failed. The ablest, hardest-working students there are expected to become scientists, physicians, or engineers.[2]

Extended Examples

Sometimes it takes more than a brief example to effectively illustrate a point. **Extended examples** offer multifaceted illustrations of the idea, item, or event being described, thereby allowing the speaker to create a more detailed picture for the audience. Here, Jonathan Drori uses an extended example to illustrate how pollen (the fertilizing element of plants) can provide strong circumstantial evidence linking criminals to their crimes:

> Pollen forensics can be very subtle. It's being used now to track where counterfeit drugs have been made, where banknotes have come from, to look at the provenance of antiques to see that they really did come from the place the seller said they did. And murder suspects have been tracked using their clothing. . . . Some of the people were brought to trial [in Bosnia] because of the evidence of pollen, which showed that bodies had been buried, exhumed, and then reburied somewhere else.[3]

Hypothetical Examples

In some speeches you may need to make a point about something that could happen in the future if certain things occurred. For example, if you argue the thesis "We should eliminate summer vacations for all school-age children," you automatically raise the question of what will happen if this comes to pass. Since it hasn't happened yet, you'll need a **hypothetical example** of what you believe the outcome will be. Republican Representative Vernon Ehlers of Michigan offered the following hypothetical example when he spoke at a congressional hearing in support of a bill to ban human cloning:

> What if in the cloning process you produce someone with two heads and three arms? Are you simply going to euthanize and dispose of that person? The answer is no. We're talking about human life.[4]

Share Stories

Often, one of the most powerful means of conveying a message is through a **story**, or **narrative**. Narratives tell tales, both real and imaginary, about practically anything under the sun. They can relate personal experiences, folk wisdom, parables, myths, and so forth. Scholars of narratives have commented that all human history consists of stories. "Most of our experience, our knowledge, and our thinking is organized as stories," notes language scholar Mark Turner. "One story helps us make sense of another."[5] A growing body of neuroscientific evidence also suggests that it is through stories that we organize our thinking.[6] The universal appeal of stories explains why speakers often use stories when addressing diverse audiences, particularly those whose members represent a variety of national cultures.

Personal narratives (also called *first-person narratives*) are stories that we tell about ourselves. *Third-person narratives* are stories that we tell about others. Common to all narratives are the essential storytelling elements of plot, character, setting, and some sort of time line. Stories can be brief and simple descriptions of short incidents worked into the body of the speech, or relatively drawn-out accounts that constitute most of the presentation and serve as the organizing framework for it (see narrative pattern of organization, p. 199). In either case, a successful story will strike a chord and create an emotional connection between speaker and audience members. For example, in a speech on helping more Americans earn post-secondary degrees, Melinda French Gates offered the following brief story to illustrate that although some community college students encounter many barriers to completing their degrees, they persevere:

> Last year, we met a young man named Cornell at Central Piedmont Community College in Charlotte, North Carolina. We asked him to describe his typical day. He clocks into work at 11 P.M. When he gets off at 7 the next morning, he sleeps for an hour. In his car. Then he goes to class until 2 o'clock. "After that," Cornell said, "I just crash."[7]

Many speakers, whether they're ministers at the Sunday morning pulpit or high-tech entrepreneurs rallying the troops, liberally sprinkle their speeches with **anecdotes**—brief stories of interesting and often humorous incidents based on real life. Obviously, the most effective anecdotes are those that the audience hasn't heard before and that link back to the speaker's theme. In a speech about the need to preserve our national parks, Brock Evans, the director of the Endangered Species Coalition, does this artfully:

> One of the leaders of the fight was a fifth-generation rancher, Carroll Noble. . . . [H]e had a spread over near Pinedale. I'll never forget how he loved this Wyoming land, and how he expressed his feelings about it. One day, we were having dinner at his place. He had a big picture window there, framing that whole magnificent vista of the Wind River Range, its snowcapped jagged peaks, and the great tumbling mass of green forest spilling down its flank to the lake. At one point, he gestured out there, and turned to me with the greatest sadness: "You see that?" he said. "If they start cutting that, I'll never look out that window again."[8]

CHECKLIST

SELECTING THE RIGHT EXAMPLE OR STORY

_____ 1. Does the example or story truly illustrate or prove the point I need to make?

_____ 2. Is it credible?

_____ 3. Is it compelling enough?

_____ 4. Is it suitable for my audience's background and experiences?

Draw on Testimony

When looking for supporting material, consider quoting or paraphrasing people who have an intimate knowledge of your topic. **Testimony** (from the Latin word for "witness") is firsthand findings, eyewitness accounts, and people's opinions. **Expert testimony** includes findings, eyewitness accounts, or opinions by professionals trained to evaluate a given topic. For example, a medical doctor may provide cutting-edge information on the threat of cholesterol. **Lay testimony**, or testimony by nonexperts such as eyewitnesses, can reveal compelling firsthand information that may be unavailable to others, such as that given by volunteers who traveled to Japan in the wake of the March 2011 earthquake.

Credibility plays a key role in the effectiveness of testimony, since a source is only as credible as an audience believes it to be. When selecting testimony, consider whether the audience will assign credibility to the source, and then take steps to establish the source's reputation. Briefly establish the person's qualifications and inform listeners of when and where the testimony was offered. It isn't always necessary to cite the exact date (though do keep a written record of this); in the oral presentation, terms such as "recently" and "last year" are fine:

> In testimony before the U.S. House Subcommittee on Human Rights and Wellness last week, Derek Ellerman, co-executive director of the Polaris Project said, "Many people have little understanding of the enormity and the brutality of the sex trafficking industry in the United States. When they think of sex slavery,

ESL SPEAKER'S NOTES

Broaden Your Listeners' Perspectives

As a non-native speaker of English, consider sharing a personal experience with the audience. Stories from other lands and other ways of life often fascinate listeners. Unique cultural traditions, eyewitness accounts of newsworthy events, or tales passed down orally from one generation to the next are just some of the possibilities. Depending on the goal of your speech, you can use your experiences as supporting material for a related topic or as the topic itself.

they think of Thailand or Nepal—not a suburban house in the DC area, with $400,000 homes and manicured lawns. . . ."[9]

EVALUATING THE CREDIBILITY OF TESTIMONY

✔ Are the experts I've cited proven in their fields?

✔ Is the lay testimony reliable?

✔ Do the sources have any obvious biases?

✔ Is their testimony timely? Is it relevant?

✔ Do their views effectively support my thesis?

✔ Are there reasons that the audience may not react favorably to the testimony?[1] Testimony that does not meet these standards is likely to do more harm to your speech than good.

CHECKLIST

1. The idea for these questions was prompted by O. M. Walter and R. L. Scott, *Thinking and Speaking: A Guide to Intelligent Oral Communication*, 3rd ed. (New York: Macmillan, 1973), 52.

Provide Facts and Statistics

WEB Links

Most people, especially in Western societies,[10] require some type of evidence, usually in the form of facts and statistics, before they will accept someone else's claims or position.[11] **Facts** represent documented occurrences, including actual events, dates, times, people, and places. Facts are truly facts only when they have been independently verified by people other than the source. For example, we accept as true that Abraham Lincoln was the sixteenth president of the United States because this fact has been independently verified by eyewitnesses, journalists, historians, and so forth. Listeners are not likely to accept your statements as factual unless you back them up with credible evidence. **Statistics** are quantified evidence that summarizes, compares, and predicts things, from batting averages to birthrates. Statistics can clarify complex information and help make abstract concepts or ideas concrete for listeners.

Use Statistics Selectively

Although audience members may want you to offer some statistics in support of your assertions, they don't want an endless parade of them. Rather than overwhelm the audience with numbers, choose a few statistics that will make your message most compelling. For example, to avoid bombarding the audience with sales figures, Steve Jobs, CEO of Apple Computer, Inc., described iTune's early success this way: "We're selling over five million songs a day now. Isn't that unbelievable? That's 58 songs every second of every minute of every hour of every day."[12]

Use Statistics Accurately

Statistics add precision to speech claims, *if* you know what the numbers actually mean and use the terms that describe them accurately.

Use Frequencies to Indicate Counts

A common type of statistic used in speeches, a **frequency** is simply a count of the number of times something occurs:

"On the midterm exam there were 8 As, 15 Bs, 7 Cs, 2 Ds, and 1 F."

Frequencies can help listeners understand comparisons between two or more categories, indicate size, or describe trends:

- According to *Census 2000,* the total population of the State of Colorado comprised 2,165,983 males and 2,135,278 females.[13] *(compares two categories)*
- Inside the cabin, the Airbus A380 has room for at least 550 passengers— and as many as 1,000.[14] *(shows size)*
- According to the CDC, the birth rate among young adolescents in the United States aged 10 to 14 has declined steadily from a peak of 12,901 in 1994, to the current low of 7,315.[15] *(describes a trend)*

Use Percentages to Express Proportion

As informative as frequencies can be, the similarity or difference in magnitude between things may be more meaningfully indicated in percentages. A **percentage** is the quantified portion of a whole. Describing the frequencies of males and females in the Colorado population in percentages shows even more clearly how similar the two amounts are: 50.36 percent male and 49.64 percent female. (Common practice in speeches permits us to round off the figures, using such terms as "roughly.")

Percentages are especially useful when comparing categories or classes of something, as, for example, in the reasons for delays of domestic flights:

Nearly 4.45 percent of April 2010 flights were delayed by aviation system delays, over 4.70 percent by late-arriving aircraft; over 4.30 percent by factors within the airline's control, such as maintenance or crew problems; 0.33 percent by extreme weather; and 0.04 percent for security reasons.[16]

Because audience members cannot take the time to pause and reflect on the figures as they would with written text, speakers must help listeners interpret the numbers, as in this example:

As you can see, late-arriving flights caused far more delays than did security measures, which accounted for just about one half of a percentage point.

(See Chapter 17 for more on the differences between oral and written language.)

Use Averages to Describe Typical Characteristics

An **average** describes information according to its typical characteristics. Usually we think of the average as the sum of the scores divided by the number of scores. This is the *mean,* the arithmetic (or computed) average. But there are two other kinds of averages—the *median* and the *mode.* As a matter of accuracy, in your speeches you should distinguish among these three kinds of averages.

Consider a teacher whose nine students scored 5, 19, 22, 23, 24, 26, 28, 28, and 30, with 30 points being the highest possible grade. The following illustrates how she would calculate the three types of averages:

- The **mean** score is 22.8, the *arithmetic average,* the sum of the scores divided by nine.
- The **median** score is 24, the *center-most score in a distribution* or the point above and below which 50 percent of the nine scores fall.
- The **mode** score is 28, the *most frequently occurring score* in the distribution.

The following speaker, claiming that a rival organization misrepresented the "average" tax rate, illustrates how the inaccurate use of the different types of averages can distort reality:

> The Tax Foundation determines an *average* [*mean*] tax rate for American families simply by dividing all taxes paid by the total of everyone's income. . . . For example, if four middle-income families pay $3,000, $4,000, $5,000, and $6,000, respectively, in taxes, and one very wealthy family pays $82,000 in taxes, the *average* [*mean*] tax paid by these five families is $20,000 ($100,000 in total taxes divided by five families). But four of the five families have a tax bill equaling $6,000 or less. . . . Many analysts would define a *median* income family—a family for whom half of all families have higher income and half have lower income—to be the "typical family" and describe the taxes paid by such a median-income family as the taxes that typical middle-class families owe.[17]

Present Your Statistics Ethically

Whether done inadvertently or intentionally, offering listeners inaccurate statistics is unethical. Following are some steps you can take to reduce the likelihood of using false or misleading statistics in your speeches:

Use Only Reliable Sources

Include statistics from the most authoritative source you can locate, and evaluate the methods used to generate the data. The more information that is available about the methods used to generate the data, including how and why it was collected and what researchers hoped to learn from it, the more reliable the source of the information is likely to be.

Present Statistics in Context

Statistics are meaningful only within a proper context. To help audience members accurately interpret statistical information, indicate why the statistics were collected, who or what they are intended to represent, what methods were used to collect them, and what period of time they refer to. The best and maybe only sure way to answer these questions is to know the sources of your statistical information.

Note how this speaker describes when the data were collected (2009), the method used to collect the data (survey), and the scope of the research (national):

> According to a report posted on the Centers for Disease Control and Prevention Website, 33 million adults ages 18 and over (15%) engage in binge drinking, defined as consuming four or more alcoholic drinks per occasion for women and five or more for men during the past 30 days. Binge drinking is more common among men ages 18–24 (25%), whites (16%), and persons with annual incomes of over $75,000 (19%). The data was gathered in a phone survey from nearly 412,000 U.S. adults from the 2009 Behavioral Risk Factor Surveillance System (BRFSS) and 16,000 high school students from the 2009 National Youth Risk Behavior Survey (YRBS) who all self-reported their binge drinking activity within the past 30 days.[18]

Avoid Confusing Statistics with "Absolute Truth"

Rather than the absolute or only truth, statistics represent a quantification of something at a given point in time. Thus, statistics are rarely definitive. Even the most recent data available on a subject will change the next time the data are collected. Nor are statistics necessarily any more perfect than the people who collect them. Offer the data as they appropriately represent your point or claim, but refrain from declaring that these data are absolute.

ETHICALLY SPEAKING

Evaluating the Validity of the Statistics You Cite

Researchers use many different statistical tools to analyze their data. Unfortunately, it's extremely easy to misuse any of these methods. If misuse does occur, whether intentionally to advance an agenda or accidentally, through error, the conclusion may misrepresent an important relationship or effect.[1] The flawed data that result from such misinterpretations often evolve into widespread misconceptions.

Before using statistics in your speeches, take the time to assess whether the data were collected scientifically and interpreted objectively. Ask yourself "What is the sample size? Are the results statistically relevant? Was the experiment well designed?"

If you are reporting on a poll, ask yourself "Who took the poll, and when was it conducted? Who paid for the poll, and why was it taken? How many people were interviewed for the survey, and how were they chosen? What area (nation, state, or region) or group (teachers, lawyers, Democratic voters, etc.) were these people chosen from? Are the results based on the answers of all the people interviewed? Who should have been interviewed and was not? What is the sampling error for the poll results? What other kinds of factors could have skewed the poll results?"[2]

1. John S. Gardenier and David B. Resnik, "The Misuse of Statistics: Concepts, Tools, and a Research Agenda" (proceedings of 2001 conference, "Investigating Research Integrity," U.S. Department of Health and Human Services, Office of Research Integrity), ori.dhhs.gov/multimedia/acrobat/papers/gardenier.pdf (accessed July 2, 2002).
2. Excerpted from Sheldon R. Gawiser and G. Evans Witt, "Twenty Questions a Journalist Should Ask about Poll Results"; Earl Babbie, *The Practice of Social Research,* 12th ed. (Belmont, CA: Wadsworth, 2010).

Avoid Cherry-Picking

To **cherry-pick** is to selectively present only those statistics that buttress your point of view while ignoring competing data.[19] Cherry-picking is a popular tool of politicians and policymakers, who are often accused of selectively referring to only those statistics that boost their arguments and policies.

When you find yourself searching for statistics to confirm an opinion or a belief you already hold, you are probably engaging in cherry-picking.[20] Choosing from among the mean, median, and mode of a distribution the one average that makes the best case for your point, when in fact one of the other averages is the better indicator of what your data represent, is an instance of cherry-picking. Researching statistical support material is not a trip through a buffet line to select what looks good and discard what doesn't. You must locate as much information as possible that is pertinent to your particular point, and then present it in context or not at all.

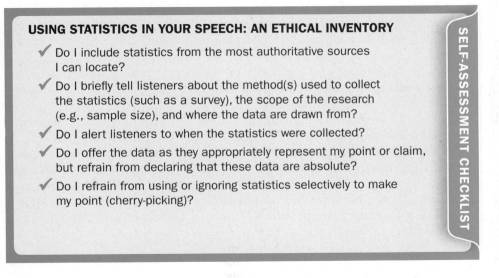

USING STATISTICS IN YOUR SPEECH: AN ETHICAL INVENTORY

✔ Do I include statistics from the most authoritative sources I can locate?

✔ Do I briefly tell listeners about the method(s) used to collect the statistics (such as a survey), the scope of the research (e.g., sample size), and where the data are drawn from?

✔ Do I alert listeners to when the statistics were collected?

✔ Do I offer the data as they appropriately represent my point or claim, but refrain from declaring that these data are absolute?

✔ Do I refrain from using or ignoring statistics selectively to make my point (cherry-picking)?

SELF-ASSESSMENT CHECKLIST

Use Visual Aids Whenever Possible

When your speech relies heavily on statistical information, use appropriate tables, graphs, and charts to display the statistics (see Chapters 21–23).

Win Acceptance of Your Supporting Materials

Audience members will accept your examples, narratives, testimony, facts, and statistics as legitimate only if they believe that they are derived from sources that are credible. It is up to you to establish your sources' trustworthiness and reliability. You can do this by alerting listeners to the sources' qualifications to report on the information. For detailed guidelines on how to win audience acceptance of supporting material, see Chapter 11, "Citing Sources in Your Speech."

CHAPTER 9

Locating Supporting Material

The search for supporting material—for the examples, facts and statistics, opinions, stories, and testimony described in Chapter 8—can be one of the most enjoyable parts of putting together a speech. It is at this stage that you can delve into your subject, sift through sources, and select material that best conveys and supports your message. Classical rhetoricians termed this research process **invention**. According to Aristotle, one of the speaker's most important tasks is to select from among the many different types of evidence available those materials that are most likely to lead listeners to accept the speaker's point of view.[1]

Speech sources may be primary or secondary. **Primary sources** provide firsthand accounts or direct evidence of events.[2] Examples of primary sources include eyewitness testimony, letters and diary entries, oral histories, interviews and surveys (including those conducted by you), newspaper accounts, vital records, and any form of original research. **Secondary sources** provide analysis or commentary about phenomena produced by others (e.g., by primary sources); these include the vast world of "secondhand" information found in books, articles, biographies, and a myriad of sources other than the original. As you look for these materials, consider how you can use the information you find to generate interest, illustrate and clarify your meaning, and add solid evidence to your assertions.

Before You Begin: Assess Your Research Needs

 WEB Research room

Before beginning your search, take a few moments to review your thesis statement and speech goal. Consider what you need to support them. What do you need to elaborate upon, explain, demonstrate, or prove? How can you best substantiate your thesis with material that is most likely to be accepted by your audience? What kinds of sources will help you accomplish this?

A speech that contains both primary and secondary sources can be more compelling than one that relies on one or another source type alone. The firsthand nature of a credible primary source can build trust and engage audience members emotionally. At the same time, credible secondary sources can help listeners put the topic in perspective. A speech on the disastrous 2010 oil spill in the Gulf of Mexico, for example, can be made more compelling if it includes testimony by oil riggers and other eyewitnesses (primary sources) along with descriptions and analyses of the consequences of the spill in a general interest magazine such as the *Atlantic Monthly* (a secondary source).

Different topics, audiences, purposes, and occasions will suggest a different balance of sources, so reflect on what might work best for your particular rhetorical situation. Bear in mind that nearly all speeches can benefit from examples, statistics, stories, and testimony from a mix of both primary and secondary sources.

Locating Secondary Sources

WEB Bibliographer

The most likely sources of secondary research include books, newspapers, periodicals, blogs, government publications, digital collections, and reference works such as encyclopedias, almanacs, books of quotations, and atlases. In the past, most of these sources appeared only in print. Increasingly, the information they contain can be located on an online **database**—a searchable place, or "base," in which information is stored and from which it can be retrieved. Every library contains a unique mix of print works and online database subscription services. At the reference desk you can find out what this mix is and, with the help of a **reference librarian**, learn how to use these resources to research your topic. You can find out what your library owns directly by consulting the online library catalog, which is searchable by author, title, and subject. Libraries organize books and other holdings according to the **Library of Congress call number** or the **Dewey decimal number**. Every database has its own way of conducting searches, so to avoid wasting time, consult the "Search Tips" section.

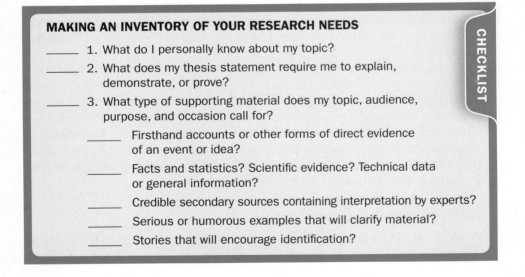

MAKING AN INVENTORY OF YOUR RESEARCH NEEDS

_____ 1. What do I personally know about my topic?

_____ 2. What does my thesis statement require me to explain, demonstrate, or prove?

_____ 3. What type of supporting material does my topic, audience, purpose, and occasion call for?

_____ Firsthand accounts or other forms of direct evidence of an event or idea?

_____ Facts and statistics? Scientific evidence? Technical data or general information?

_____ Credible secondary sources containing interpretation by experts?

_____ Serious or humorous examples that will clarify material?

_____ Stories that will encourage identification?

CHECKLIST

Books

Books explore topics in depth. A well-written book provides detail and perspective and can serve as an excellent source of supporting examples, stories, facts, and statistics. To locate a book in your library's holdings, refer to the library's online catalog. To search the titles of all books currently in print in the United States, refer to *Books in Print* at www.booksinprint.com. Alternatively, log on to an online bookseller such as Amazon.com or BarnesandNoble.com and key in your topic.[3]

Newspapers and Periodicals

Newspapers can be a rich source of support material, containing a mix of eyewitness accounts, in-depth analyses of local and world events, and human-interest feature stories of all kinds. Three comprehensive databases for searching newspaper articles include: *LexisNexis Academic, InfoTrac Newspapers,* and *ProQuest Newsstand.* To research historical newspapers from 1753 to the present, go to Newspaper Archive (www.newspaperarchive.com). To search U.S. newspapers by state, try NewsVoyager (www.newsvoyager .com). World newspapers may be found at world-newspapers.com. Indexes to individual newspapers such as the *New York Times* and *Wall Street Journal* are also available online as well as on microfiche. News reported on television and radio may be accessed on sites such as NPR.org, CNN.com, and BBC .co.uk.

A **periodical** is a regularly published magazine or journal. Periodicals can be excellent sources because they often include the various types of supporting material discussed in Chapter 8 (examples, narratives, testimony, facts, and statistics). Periodicals include general-interest magazines such as *Time* and *Newsweek,* as well as the thousands of specialized academic, business, and technical magazines, newsletters, and refereed journals in circulation. Articles in *refereed journals* are evaluated by experts before being published and supply sources for the information they contain. Articles in *general-interest magazines,* by contrast, rarely contain citations and may or may not be written by experts on the topic.

Most general-interest magazines are available in InfoTrac's *GeneralOne File;* to locate both general periodicals and more specialized scholarly journals, see *Academic Search Premier* and *Academic Search Elite.* There is also an ever-increasing number of periodical databases devoted to individual disciplines. For business-related topics, consider using *ABI/INFORM, LexisNexis Academic,* and *Business Source Complete.* If you plan to talk about a health or medical topic, examine *Health & Wellness Resource Center* or *PubMed.* See Table 9.1 for a list of specialized databases available in many college libraries.

Weblogs and Social News Sites

Weblogs (or simply *blogs*) and social news sites can provide up-to-the-minute information and opinions on certain speech topics, *if the source is reputable.*

TABLE 9.1	Specialized Databases Found in Many Libraries
Database	**Description**
WorldCat	WorldCat is the world's largest library catalog, allowing you to search many libraries at once to find the resource at a library nearest to you.
ABI/INFORM	Covers the foremost journals and news in business, management, economics, and a wide range of related fields. Contains abstracts and full text.
Alt HealthWatch	Focuses on the many perspectives of complementary, holistic, and integrated approaches to health care and wellness; offers full-text articles from international journals, periodicals, booklets, and book excerpts.
ERIC	(Education Resources Information Center) The world's largest digital library of educational information, with more than 1.3 million citations of education-related documents and journal articles; 1966–present.
Ethnic NewsWatch	ENW presents a comprehensive, full-text collection of hundreds of publications (dating from 1990) offering both national and regional coverage from a multiethnic perspective.
Scirus	Searches millions of science-specific Web pages, allowing you to find the latest scientific, scholarly, technical, and medical data on the Web.
PsycINFO	Includes indexes and summaries of journal articles, book chapters, books, and reports—all in the field of psychology, psychiatry, and related disciplines.
PubMed	The U.S. National Library of Medicine's database of citations for biomedical literature from MEDLINE, life science journals, and online books.
CINAHL	(Nursing and Allied Health) A comprehensive resource for nursing and allied health literature, including biomedicine, alternative/complementary medicine, consumer health, and seventeen allied health disciplines.

A **blog** is a site containing journal-type entries maintained by individuals or groups. Newest entries appear first. A **social news site** allows users to submit news stories, articles, and videos to share with other users of the site. The most popular items win more visibility.

Use these sources of supporting material with extreme care, referencing only those that are affiliated with reputable (local, regional, or national) news agencies and media outlets, or by well-known bloggers. See Chapter 10, "Finding Credible Sources on the Internet," for information on locating blogs and news sites.

Government Publications

Part of every tax dollar supports the constant production of publications by the **U.S. Government Printing Office (GPO)**, and the result is a resource that every citizen should enjoy—and every speaker should know about. The GPO is responsible for publishing and distributing all information collected and produced by federal agencies, from the U.S. Census Bureau to the Department of Education and the Environmental Protection Agency. GPO publications also include all congressional reports and hearings. Most federal, state, and local government agencies provide statistics and other information freely and in a timely manner.

Nearly all the information contained in government documents comes from highly credible primary sources, so it's well worth the effort to consult them. Get started by logging on to USA.gov, the official portal to all government information and services. USA.gov contains links to millions of Web pages from federal, local, and tribal governments as well as nations around the world. You may also wish to access GobiernoUSA.gov, which offers resources in Spanish. Translations in many other languages are also available.

Digital Collections

Digital collections include oral histories, letters, newspapers, photographs, and audio and video recordings. Libraries have become increasingly active in building these collections, and they provide a rich source of primary materials. At the federal level, the Library of Congress offers a gateway to a treasury of digitized images, recordings, and documents, and the New York Public Library Digital Gallery contains millions of rare images. Other digital collections are more specialized. Middle Tennessee State University Library, for instance, hosts *The American Women's History* digital collection of primary sources. Most state and local libraries continue to build their own collections. Digital collections are generally organized by subject, time period, or geographic area.

Reference Works

Reference works include, but are not limited to, encyclopedias, almanacs, biographical reference works, books of quotations, poetry collections, and atlases.

Encyclopedias

Encyclopedias summarize knowledge that is found in original form elsewhere. Their usefulness lies in providing a broad overview of subjects and highlighting important terms, people, and concepts to build a search upon. **General encyclopedias** attempt to cover all important subject areas of knowledge; **specialized encyclopedias** delve deeply into one subject area, such as religion, science, art, sports, or engineering. The most comprehensive of the general encyclopedias is the *Encyclopaedia Britannica*.

For a more in-depth look at a topic, consult specialized encyclopedias of all types, from the *McGraw-Hill Encyclopedia of Science and Technology* to the *Encyclopedia of Religion* and the *Oxford Encyclopedia of Latinos and Latinas in the United States*. To discover encyclopedias in your subject area, go to your library home page and key in encyclopedias: [your subject].

Almanacs

Almanacs and **fact books**, published annually, contain interesting facts and statistics on many subjects, from notable Supreme Court decisions to a complete listing of vital statistics for all nations of the world. As with encyclopedias, there are both general and specialized almanacs. In the general category, one of the most comprehensive sources is the *World Almanac and Book of Facts*. Other helpful almanacs include the *Information Please Almanac, People's Almanac,* and *Guinness World Records* (see also the Web site at www.guinnessworldrecords.com).

Biographical Resources

For information about famous or noteworthy people, the *Biography and Genealogy Master Index* is an excellent starting point, indexing thousands of biographical sources on both living and deceased persons worldwide. For analyses and criticism of the published works of individuals you may be speaking about, consider such biographical resources as *Current Biography, Dictionary of American Biography, Famous Hispanics in the World and in History* (access is free at coloquio.com/famosos/), and *The African American Biographical Database (AABD)*.

Books of Quotations

Public speakers often use quotations in the introductions and conclusions of speeches; quotations are also liberally sprinkled throughout examples, narratives,

A CULTURAL PERSPECTIVE

Discovering Diversity in Reference Works

In addition to the rich cultural resources to be found in digital collections (see "Digital Collections," p. 138), a wealth of reference works exists for speakers who seek information on the accomplishments of the many ethnic, cultural, and religious communities that make up the United States. Gale alone publishes more than six hundred encyclopedias, including  many related to specific groups and religions. Macmillan publishes the *Encyclopedia of African-American Culture and History,* while Grolier publishes *Encyclopedia Latina*. Routledge publishes the *Encyclopedia of Modern Jewish Culture*.

Among biographical resources, Gale publishes *African American Biography, Contemporary Black Biography, Hispanic American Biography, Asian American Biography, Arab American Biography,* and *Native American Biography*. All are multivolume sets that contain portraits, quotes, interviews, and articles about prominent men and women.

Among specialized almanacs, available now are the *Asian American Almanac, Muslim Almanac, St. James Press Gay and Lesbian Almanac, Native North American Almanac, African American Almanac,* and *Hispanic American Almanac* (all published by Gale), along with a host of similar publications. Each reference work contains essays that focus on all major aspects of group life and culture. One way to see what's available is to search a database such as WorldCat.

and, of course, testimony. First published in 1855, *Bartlett's Familiar Quotations* contains a collection of passages, phrases, and proverbs traced to their sources in ancient and modern literature. Many collections are targeted specifically at public speakers, including *Quotations for Public Speakers: A Historical, Literary, and Political Anthology,* by Robert G. Torricelli,[4] and *Nelson's Complete Book of Stories, Illustrations, and Quotes: The Ultimate Contemporary Resource for Speakers,* by Robert J. Morgan.[5]

Poetry Collections

Lines of poetry, if not entire poems, are often used by speakers both to introduce and conclude speeches and to illustrate points in the speech body. Every library has a collection of poetry anthologies as well as the collected works of individual poets. Based on the print version of *The Columbia Granger's Index to Poetry,* which indexes poems by author, title, and first line, *The Columbia Granger's World of Poetry* Web site includes the full text of 250,000 poems. The Library of Congress Poetry Resources Web Guide offers links to poetry resources. Poets.org is the Web site of the Academy of American Poets. To search for classic works, see Bartleby .com and the *American Verse Project* (quod.lib.umich.edu/a/amverse).

Atlases

An **atlas** is a collection of maps, text, and accompanying charts and tables. As well as serving to locate a particular locale (and to learn about its terrain, demographic information, and proximity to other places), many atlases use maps to explore art history, human anatomy, and other subjects. For straightforward geographic atlases, consult *National Geographic Atlas of the World* and *Rand McNally Commercial Atlas and Guide*. Online, go to the *National Geographic* Web site. To learn about what atlases offer beyond geography, conduct a search of atlases related to your topic, and key in, for example, *art* AND *atlas*.

CHECKLIST

FINDING SPEECHES ONLINE

You can find numerous videos and audiofiles of speeches online. These can be useful both as supporting material and as models of good speeches.

✔ *American Rhetoric (*www.americanrhetoric.com/) contains 5000+ speeches

✔ *Gifts of Speech* (http://gos.sbc.edu/) features speeches by women from 1848

✔ The Wake Forest University's Political Speeches gateway (www.wfu .edu/~louden/Political%20Communication/Class%20Information/ SPEECHES.html) offers links to collections of political speeches

✔ The United States Senate (www.senate.gov) includes speeches by U.S. senators

✔ Vital Speeches of the Day (vsotd.com) features current speeches delivered in the United States and is published monthly

Generating Primary Sources: Interviews and Surveys

 WEB Bibliographer

As described earlier, a *primary source* provides firsthand accounts or direct evidence of events. To support your speech on a given topic, you may wish to produce your own primary sources by conducting interviews and surveys. These tools can provide valuable information to support and enliven a speech.

Interviews

Even with all the information available today, oftentimes you can gain considerably more insight into a topic, and obtain more interesting material, by speaking personally to someone who has expertise on the subject. An **interview** is a face-to-face communication for the purpose of gathering information.

Preparing for the Interview

Many people make the mistake of treating an interview as they would a conversation, assuming that things will "just flow." In fact, getting the information you need from a subject requires advance planning:

- Prepare questions for the interview. Plan the questions you will ask in advance of the actual interview and word them carefully.
- Avoid *vague questions,* those that don't give the person being interviewed enough to go on. Vague questions waste the interviewee's time and reflect the interviewer's lack of preparation.
- Avoid *leading questions,* those that encourage, if not force, a certain response and reflect the interviewer's bias (e.g., "Like most intelligent people, are you going to support candidate X?").
- Avoid *loaded questions,* those that are phrased to reinforce the interviewer's agenda or that have a hostile intent (e.g., "Isn't it true that you've never supported school programs?").
- Aim to create *neutral questions,* those that don't lead the interviewee to a desired response. Usually, this will consist of a mix of open, closed, primary, and secondary questions (see Table 9.2).

Structuring the Interview

Think about an interview as having the same broad structure as a speech, with an introduction (the opening), a body, and a conclusion (the closing).

The Opening: Getting Off to a Good Start.   A spirit of collaboration is crucial in the interview setting, so focus on creating a positive first impression.

TABLE 9.2 Forms of Interview Questions	
Question Form	**Description/Purpose in the Interview**
Open/closed	• **Open questions:** Allow the interviewee to elaborate as he or she desires. • **Closed questions:** Permit only "Yes," "No," or other limited responses (see Chapter 6; section on questionnaires).
Primary/secondary	• **Primary questions:** Introduce new topics or areas of questioning (e.g., "What made you want to become a veterinarian?"). • **Secondary questions:** Expand upon topics introduced in primary questions (e.g., "Did you go to veterinary school right after college?" and "Was it difficult to get student loans?").
Types of Secondary Questions	• **Questions seeking clarification:** Designed to clarify the interviewee's statements (e.g., "By 'older mothers,' do you mean over 30, over 40, or over 50?"). • **Questions seeking elaboration:** Designed to elicit additional information (e.g., "Were there other reasons that you chose your profession?"). • **"Clearinghouse" questions:** Designed to check that all important information has been discussed (e.g., "Have we covered all the important points?").

H. Dan O'Hair, Gustave W. Friedrich, and Linda D. Dixon, *Strategic Communication in Business and the Professions,* 6th ed. (Boston: Allyn & Bacon, 2007), 216.

It is at this stage that your interviewee will decide whether you are credible and trustworthy:

- Acknowledge the interviewee and express respect for his or her expertise.
- Briefly summarize your topic and informational needs.
- State a (reasonable) goal—what you would like to accomplish in the interview—and reach agreement on it.
- Establish a time limit for the interview and stick to it.

The Body: Posing the Questions. It is in the body of the interview that you will pose your substantive questions. Using your prepared questions as a guide, permit the interviewee to introduce new topics and elaborate as he or she sees fit. Don't be afraid to ask for clarification or to repeat your questions if they remain unanswered.

It is vital to listen well as your subject answers your questions. As journalist Jim Short counsels, "Listen to what the subject is saying, not just to what you want to hear." Strive to use the active listening strategies described in Chapter 4 (e.g., set goals, listen for main ideas, and watch for nonverbal cues). Don't break in when the subject is speaking or interject with leading comments. *Paraphrase* the interviewee's answers where appropriate in order to establish understanding. Ask for *clarification* and *elaboration* when necessary.

The Closing: Recheck and Confirm. Too often, people who conduct interviews end them in haste. Before ending the interview, recheck your notes and, if necessary, confirm them:

- Check to see that your notes have been properly recorded and are legible.
- Briefly offer a positive summary of important things you learned in the interview.
- Offer to send the interviewee the results of the interview, as in a printed speech.
- Send a written note of thanks.

Recording the Interview

More than one interview has gone splendidly—and entirely—unrecorded. As a result, the interviewer had to reconstruct from memory what was said, with the result usually being a slew of inaccuracies. Avoid this pitfall by taking detailed notes, recording the interview, or using a combination of note taking, recording, and videotaping. To establish an air of authenticity, you might even decide to replay short excerpts during your speech.

PREPARING FOR THE INTERVIEW

_____ 1. Do I have a written set of questions?

_____ 2. Can the questions be answered within a reasonable time frame?

_____ 3. Are my questions relevant to the purpose of my speech?

_____ 4. Are my questions posed in a well-thought-out sequence?

_____ 5. Are my questions free of bias or hostile intent?

_____ 6. Are controversial questions reserved until the end of the interview?

_____ 7. Have I obtained advance permission to record the interview?

_____ 8. Do I have a working writing implement and ample notepaper (or a working laptop)?

_____ 9. Am I comfortable operating any recording equipment I plan to use?

CHECKLIST

Surveys

Like interviews, a *survey* is useful both as a tool to investigate audience attitudes (see Chapter 6) and as supporting material. Surveys are an especially effective source of support for topics related to the attitudes, values, and beliefs of people in your immediate environment. (For information on creating surveys, refer to Chapter 6.)

Remember, however, that any informal survey you conduct is unlikely to be statistically sound enough to be taken as actual proof of your claims. Present your findings to the audience in a manner that acknowledges this, and consider shoring up any informal survey research you conduct with other forms of support. (See Chapter 8 for a discussion of using statistics in speeches.)

Evaluate and Document Your Sources

Doing research can be fascinating, but organizing it can be frustrating. Fortunately, a few simple steps can help you. (For visual guidelines on citing print sources and incorporating source material in your speech, see "From Source to Speech" on citing books, pp. 148–49, and on citing periodical articles, pp. 150–51).

Critically Evaluate Your Sources

In an age of endless information, it is now easier than ever for both the honest and the dishonest, the expert and the uninformed, to get into print—or its electronic equivalent online. (See Chapter 10 for more on evaluating Internet sources.) Thus it is vital to critically evaluate sources before using them. Whether you are reviewing a book, a newspaper article, or any other source, consider the following:

- What is the author's background—experience, training, and reputation—in the field of study?

- How credible is the publication? Who is the publisher? Is the person or organization reputable? What other publications has the author or organization published?

- How reliable are the data, especially the statistical information? Generally, statistics drawn from government documents and scientific and academic journals are more reliable than those reported in the popular press (e.g., general-interest magazines). The reason for this is that the former kinds of publications print primary data officially collected by the government or by researchers who are subject to peer review. (See also "Use Statistics Accurately" in Chapter 8.)

- How recent is the reference? As a rule, it is best to be familiar with the most recent source you can find, even when the topic is historical. (See also "From Source to Speech: Evaluating Web Sources," pp. 156–57, and "Distinguish among Information, Propaganda, Misinformation, and Disinformation," p. 154, in Chapter 10.)

Record References as You Go

To avoid losing track of sources, maintain a **working bibliography** as you conduct your research. Whether you are photocopying an article, downloading it from the Internet, or copying a passage by hand, make sure to record the information outlined in the accompanying checklist for each source. (See Chapter 10 for more on how to organize Internet sources.)

Of course, you won't cite all of this information in the speech itself. You will need a complete record of your references, however, for an end-of-speech bibliography. For your written bibliography, the most commonly used documentation systems are those of the *Chicago Manual of Style,* the APA (American Psychological Association), the MLA (Modern Language Association), the CSE (Council of Science Editors, formerly Council of Biology Editors), and the IEEE (Institute of Electrical and Electronic Engineers). (See Appendices E through I for a description of each of these documentation styles.)

CREATING A BIBLIOGRAPHY

For each relevant source, be sure to record the following elements:

_____ 1. Names of author(s) or editor(s) as cited

_____ 2. Title of publication

_____ 3. Volume or edition number, if applicable

_____ 4. Name of publisher

_____ 5. Place of publication (city and state); if published only online, give Internet address

_____ 6. Date and year of publication

_____ 7. Page number on which the material appears

_____ 8. All relevant information for any direct quotations, paraphrases, or specific ideas or theories put forth by others

_____ 9. The source of the facts and statistics used in the speech

_____ 10. All relevant bibliographic information for any examples and stories supplied by someone else

_____ 11. The source of any testimony presented in the speech

_____ 12. Any relevant information related to any presentation aids you plan to use

CHECKLIST

Choose Helpful Tools

Rather than jotting down your notes helter-skelter, develop a system for organizing your research. Use notecards, spiral notebooks, and computer bookmarks and file folders to store your research. Insert the reference for each source directly onto the applicable note. Use Microsoft Word's footnote function, or consider software programs such as NoodleBib or EndNote to organize your bibliography.

Identify Quoted, Paraphrased, and Summarized Material

To avoid plagiarism (see Chapter 5), insert quotation marks around directly quoted material. When paraphrasing someone else's words or summarizing passages in articles, books, or other sources, record the page number on which the original quotation or passage appears (see Figures 9.1, 9.2, and 9.3).

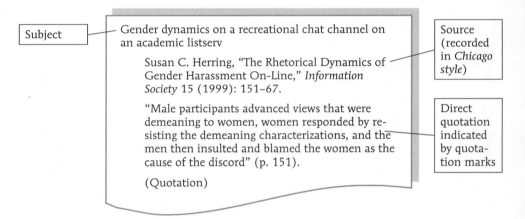

Subject

Gender dynamics on a recreational chat channel on an academic listserv

Susan C. Herring, "The Rhetorical Dynamics of Gender Harassment On-Line," *Information Society* 15 (1999): 151–67.

"Male participants advanced views that were demeaning to women, women responded by resisting the demeaning characterizations, and the men then insulted and blamed the women as the cause of the discord" (p. 151).

(Quotation)

Source (recorded in *Chicago style*)

Direct quotation indicated by quotation marks

FIGURE 9.1 Sample Note for a Direct Quotation

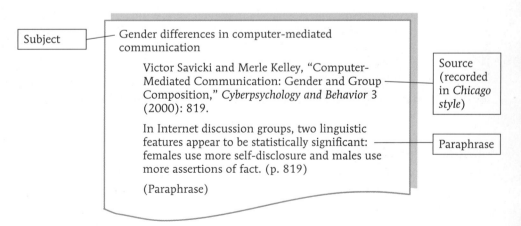

Subject

Gender differences in computer-mediated communication

Victor Savicki and Merle Kelley, "Computer-Mediated Communication: Gender and Group Composition," *Cyberpsychology and Behavior* 3 (2000): 819.

In Internet discussion groups, two linguistic features appear to be statistically significant: females use more self-disclosure and males use more assertions of fact. (p. 819)

(Paraphrase)

Source (recorded in *Chicago style*)

Paraphrase

FIGURE 9.2 Sample Note for a Paraphrase

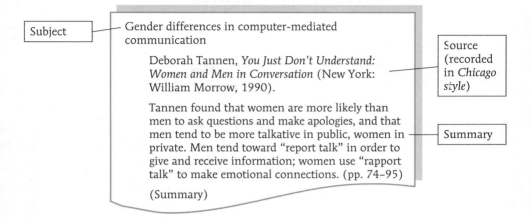

| Subject | Gender differences in computer-mediated communication |

Deborah Tannen, *You Just Don't Understand: Women and Men in Conversation* (New York: William Morrow, 1990).

Tannen found that women are more likely than men to ask questions and make apologies, and that men tend to be more talkative in public, women in private. Men tend toward "report talk" in order to give and receive information; women use "rapport talk" to make emotional connections. (pp. 74–95)

(Summary)

Source (recorded in *Chicago style*)

Summary

FIGURE 9.3 Sample Note for a Summary

ETHICALLY SPEAKING

Researching Your Speech in an Ethical Manner

As you research your speech topic, it's helpful to remind yourself of your ethical responsibilities. As discussed in Chapter 5, central to conducting ethical research is avoiding plagiarism by using your own organization and ideas and properly citing sources when using the work of others. In addition to plagiarism, fabricating information, deceiving research subjects about your real purposes, and breaching confidentiality are equally unethical. **Fabrication** is the making up of information, such as falsifying data or experiments or claiming a source when none exists. Perhaps the most widely publicized case of fabrication in recent times was that of former *New York Times* reporter Jayson Blair, who invented stories outright, wrote "eyewitness" accounts of events he never actually witnessed, and otherwise lied his way through his reporting career at the *Times*.[1]

Fabrication can also include altering quotes to "fit" a point; claiming credentials or expertise for yourself that you don't possess, in an effort to boost your credibility; inflating figures to promote your point; and so forth. Each of these examples represents an act of deception.

Conducting research ethically extends to any interviews or surveys that you undertake. In some cases, for example, people will not talk with you or provide information unless you agree to maintain their anonymity. Ethically, it is the speaker's responsibility to protect his or her source's confidentiality when requested.

Ethical conduct in public speaking goes beyond doing no harm. The goal of any speech should be to in some way serve the audience well. For example, by investigating whether a certain food ingredient can harm the body, a speaker may help audience members live healthier and longer lives. By conducting research into the pros and cons of different savings options, a speaker may assist audience members in better preparing for retirement. Use your research to advance the knowledge of others or to show them a new way of viewing a problem or an issue.

1. Dan Barry, David Barstow, Jonathan D. Glater, Adam Liptak, and Jacques Steinberg, "Correcting the Record: *Times* Reporter Who Resigned Leaves Long Trail of Deception," *New York Times*, May 11, 2003.

Recording and Citing Books

When using a book as a source, locate and record the following citation elements:

1. Book Title
2. Author
3. Publisher
4. City and State of Publication
5. Year of Publication
6. Page Number

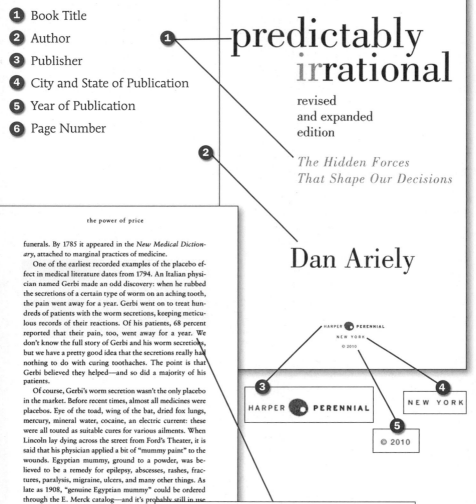

predictably irrational

revised and expanded edition

The Hidden Forces That Shape Our Decisions

Dan Ariely

HARPER ● PERENNIAL

NEW YORK

© 2010

the power of price

funerals. By 1785 it appeared in the *New Medical Dictionary*, attached to marginal practices of medicine.

One of the earliest recorded examples of the placebo effect in medical literature dates from 1794. An Italian physician named Gerbi made an odd discovery: when he rubbed the secretions of a certain type of worm on an aching tooth, the pain went away for a year. Gerbi went on to treat hundreds of patients with the worm secretions, keeping meticulous records of their reactions. Of his patients, 68 percent reported that their pain, too, went away for a year. We don't know the full story of Gerbi and his worm secretions, but we have a pretty good idea that the secretions really had nothing to do with curing toothaches. The point is that Gerbi believed they helped—and so did a majority of his patients.

Of course, Gerbi's worm secretion wasn't the only placebo in the market. Before recent times, almost all medicines were placebos. Eye of the toad, wing of the bat, dried fox lungs, mercury, mineral water, cocaine, an electric current: these were all touted as suitable cures for various ailments. When Lincoln lay dying across the street from Ford's Theater, it is said that his physician applied a bit of "mummy paint" to the wounds. Egyptian mummy, ground to a powder, was believed to be a remedy for epilepsy, abscesses, rashes, fractures, paralysis, migraine, ulcers, and many other things. As late as 1908, "genuine Egyptian mummy" could be ordered through the E. Merck catalog—and it's probably still in use somewhere today.[14]

Mummy powder wasn't the most macabre, though. One seventeenth-century recipe medication advised: "Take the fresh corpse

229

229

One of the earliest recorded examples of the placebo effect in medical literature dates from 1794. An Italian physician named Gerbi made an odd discovery: when he rubbed the secretions of a certain type of worm on an aching tooth, the pain went away for a year. Gerbi went on to treat hundreds of patients with the worm secretions, keeping meticulous records of their reactions. Of his patients, 68 percent reported that their pain, too, went away for a year.

Record Notes

When taking notes, create a separate heading for each idea and record each of the citation elements (author, title, and so forth). Indicate whether the material is a direct quotation, a paraphrase, or a summary of the information.

Following are sample notes for a direct quotation and a paraphrase.

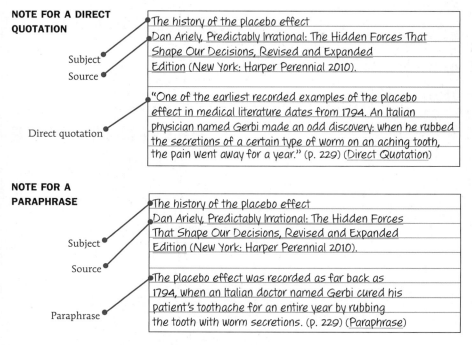

NOTE FOR A DIRECT QUOTATION

Subject
Source

The history of the placebo effect
Dan Ariely, Predictably Irrational: The Hidden Forces That
Shape Our Decisions, Revised and Expanded
Edition (New York: Harper Perennial 2010).

Direct quotation

"One of the earliest recorded examples of the placebo
effect in medical literature dates from 1794. An Italian
physician named Gerbi made an odd discovery: when he rubbed
the secretions of a certain type of worm on an aching tooth,
the pain went away for a year." (p. 229) (Direct Quotation)

NOTE FOR A PARAPHRASE

Subject
Source

The history of the placebo effect
Dan Ariely, Predictably Irrational: The Hidden Forces
That Shape Our Decisions, Revised and Expanded
Edition (New York: Harper Perennial 2010).

Paraphrase

The placebo effect was recorded as far back as
1794, when an Italian doctor named Gerbi cured his
patient's toothache for an entire year by rubbing
the tooth with worm secretions. (p. 229) (Paraphrase)

Orally Cite Sources in Your Speech

In your speech, alert the audience to the source of any ideas not your own. You can find more information on oral citations in Chapter 11. For guidelines on various citation styles, including *Chicago,* APA, MLA, CSE, and IEEE, see Appendices E–I.

SPEECH EXCERPT INDICATING A DIRECT QUOTATION

The placebo effect is no new phenomenon, with various episodes documented throughout history. **According to Dan Ariely's book *Predictably Irrational*, published in 2010**, about how hidden forces shape our decisions, this phenomenon dates as far back as the 1790s. In 1794, an Italian doctor named Gerbi made, and I quote Ariely, "An odd discovery: when he rubbed the secretions of a certain type of worm on an aching tooth, the pain went away for a year."

SPEECH EXCERPT INDICATING A PARAPHRASE

As documented in Dan Ariely's 2010 book *Predictably Irrational*, about hidden factors that influence our decision making process, the placebo effect was recorded as far back as 1794, when an Italian doctor named Gerbi cured his patient's toothache for an entire year by rubbing the tooth with, of all things, worm secretions.

Recording and Citing Articles from Periodicals

When using an article as a source, locate and record the following citation elements:

1 Author

2 Article Title

3 Periodical Title

4 Date of Publication

5 Page Number

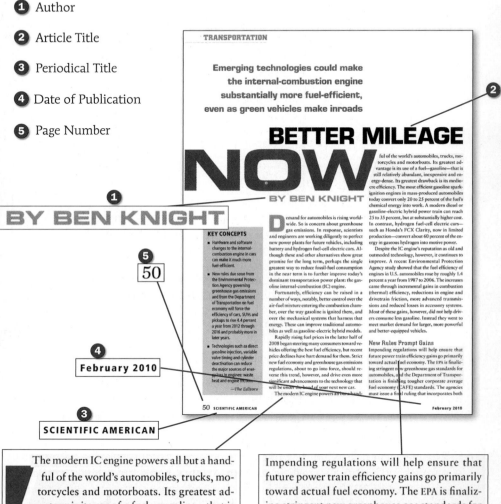

TRANSPORTATION

Emerging technologies could make the internal-combustion engine substantially more fuel-efficient, even as green vehicles make inroads

BETTER MILEAGE
NOW

BY BEN KNIGHT

1 BY BEN KNIGHT

5 50

4 February 2010

3 SCIENTIFIC AMERICAN

2

The modern IC engine powers all but a handful of the world's automobiles, trucks, motorcycles and motorboats. Its greatest advantage is its use of a fuel—gasoline—that is still relatively abundant, inexpensive and energy-dense. Its greatest drawback is its mediocre efficiency. The most efficient gasoline spark-ignition engines in mass-produced automobiles today convert only 20 to 25 percent of the fuel's chemical energy into work.

Impending regulations will help ensure that future power train efficiency gains go primarily toward actual fuel economy. The EPA is finalizing stringent new greenhouse gas standards for automobiles, and the Department of Transportation is finishing tougher corporate average fuel economy (CAFE) standards.

Record Notes

When taking notes, create a separate heading for each idea and record each of the citation elements (author, title, and so forth). Indicate whether the material is a direct quotation, a paraphrase, or a summary of the information.

Following are sample notes for a paraphrase and a summary.

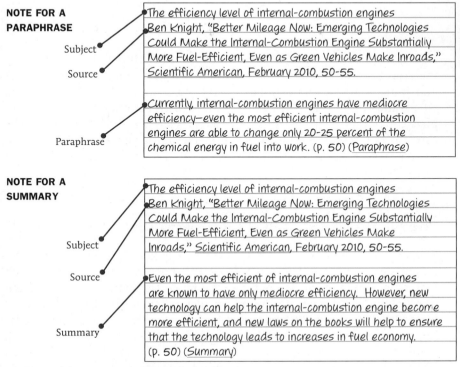

NOTE FOR A PARAPHRASE

Subject
Source

Paraphrase

The efficiency level of internal-combustion engines
Ben Knight, "Better Mileage Now: Emerging Technologies Could Make the Internal-Combustion Engine Substantially More Fuel-Efficient, Even as Green Vehicles Make Inroads," Scientific American, February 2010, 50-55.

Currently, internal-combustion engines have mediocre efficiency—even the most efficient internal-combustion engines are able to change only 20-25 percent of the chemical energy in fuel into work. (p. 50) (Paraphrase)

NOTE FOR A SUMMARY

Subject

Source

Summary

The efficiency level of internal-combustion engines
Ben Knight, "Better Mileage Now: Emerging Technologies Could Make the Internal-Combustion Engine Substantially More Fuel-Efficient, Even as Green Vehicles Make Inroads," Scientific American, February 2010, 50-55.

Even the most efficient of internal-combustion engines are known to have only mediocre efficiency. However, new technology can help the internal-combustion engine become more efficient, and new laws on the books will help to ensure that the technology leads to increases in fuel economy. (p. 50) (Summary)

Orally Cite Sources in Your Speech

In your speech, alert the audience to the source of any ideas not your own. You can find more information on oral citations in Chapter 11. For guidelines on various citation styles, including *Chicago,* APA, MLA, CSE, and IEEE, see Appendices E–I.

SPEECH EXCERPT INDICATING A PARAPHRASE

In his article "Better Mileage Now," from the February 2010 issue of *Scientific American*, Ben Knight characterizes the efficiency of internal-combustion engines as mediocre—even the most efficient internal-combustion engines on the road today are able to change only about 20 to 25 percent of the chemical energy in fuel into work.

SPEECH EXCERPT INDICATING A SUMMARY

According to Ben Knight's article "Better Mileage Now," in the February 2010 issue of *Scientific American*, even the most efficient of internal-combustion engines are known for having mediocre efficiency. However, there is still a future for the internal-combustion engine: new technology can help the internal-combustion engine become more efficient, and new laws on the books will help to ensure that these innovations lead to increases in fuel economy.

CHAPTER 10

Finding Credible Sources on the Internet

The Internet represents a vast world of possibilities for discovering material for your speech. You can access primary sources, consult news and journal articles, peruse books and blogs, and gather data, images, video, and sound for presentation aids. As with conducting research in a physical library, the key to a productive search online lies in a well-thought-out research strategy, an understanding of how to locate and verify trustworthy sources, and a grasp of how to use Internet search tools effectively.

Begin Your Search at a Library Portal

`[WEB]` Research link

Easy access to the Internet may lead you to rely heavily or even exclusively on popular search engines such as Google, Yahoo!, or Bing to locate speech materials. Doing so, however, presents a host of potential problems, from overlooking key sources not found on these sites, to finding false and/or biased information, to becoming lost in a sea of information and still coming up empty-handed. For these reasons, when searching for supporting material online, in general it is helpful to begin your search at your school's **library portal**, or electronic entry point into its holdings (e.g., the library's home page). The databases and other resources you will find on a library's portal are as much a part of its holdings as are its shelved materials. (For details on how to narrow your speech topic using a library portal, see "From Source to Speech: Narrowing Your Topic Using a Library Portal" in Chapter 7, p. 106.)

All library holdings are built through careful and deliberate selection processes by trained professionals.[1] Libraries classify and order resources, both print and electronic, according to well-defined standards and in consultation with the faculty at your school. When you select speech material from a library's resources, be it a quotation from an e-journal article, a statistic from a government publication, or an example from a nonfiction book, you can be assured that an information specialist has vetted that source for reliability and credibility. No such standards exist for popular Web search engines. Table 10.1 lists the types of online resources available at most college libraries.

TABLE 10.1   Typical Resources Found on Library Portals

- Full-text databases (newspapers, periodicals, journals)
- General reference works (dictionaries, encyclopedias, quotation resources, fact books, directories)
- Books and monographs
- Statistical resources (e.g., FedStats.gov and *Statistical Abstract*)
- Academic journals
- Digitized texts (primary documents; ebooks)
- Digitized image collections
- Video collections

Access the Invisible ("Deep") Web

In addition to the online collections of actual libraries, a host of **virtual libraries** can be found on the Internet. The oldest of these is the WWW Virtual Library (www.vlib.org) founded by Tim Berners-Lee, who also founded the World Wide Web. A list of virtual libraries appears in Table 10.2.

Because library portals and virtual libraries often take you to links that do not readily appear in general search engines and subject directories, they are sometimes considered part of the **invisible Web** (also called the **deep Web**)— the large portion of the Web that general search engines often fail to find. Countless documents and Web sites form part of the invisible Web, most featuring higher quality information produced by scholars and vetted by information specialists; this is yet another reason why you should not rely solely on popular search engines for your speech sources.

Be a Critical Consumer of Information

Apart from a library's electronic resources section, how can you distinguish between information on the Internet that is reputable and credible and information that is untrustworthy? Search engines such as Google cannot discern the quality of information; only a human editor can do this. Each time you examine a document or Web site, especially one that has not been evaluated

TABLE 10.2   Selected Virtual Libraries

- **WWW Virtual Library:** vlib.org
- **ipl2: Information You Can Trust:** www.ipl.org
- **The Library of Congress:** www.loc.gov/rr/index.html
- **Infomine:** infomine.ucr.edu
- **Academic Info:** www.academicinfo.net
- **Digital Librarian:** www.digital-librarian.com

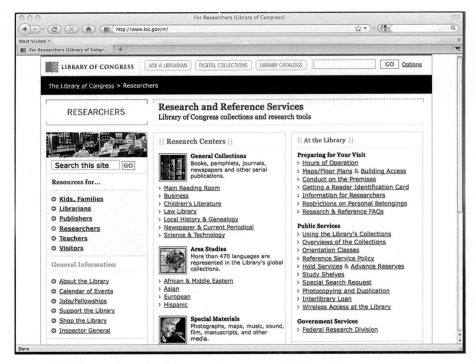

FIGURE 10.1 Virtual Research Library from the Library of Congress

and rated by credible editors, ask yourself, "Who put this information here, and why did they do so? What are the source's qualifications? Where is similar information found? When was the information posted, and is it timely? Are there links to primary sources?" Each time you examine a source, consider these questions and check it against the criteria set forth in "From Source to Speech: Evaluating Web Sources" on p. 156.

Distinguish among Information, Propaganda, Misinformation, and Disinformation

Anyone can post material on the Web, and with a little bit of design savvy, make it look professional. Discerning the accuracy of the content, however, is not always easy. One way to evaluate the nature of the information you find, both online and in print, is to ask yourself: Is it reliable *information,* or is it *propaganda, misinformation,* or *disinformation?*[2] (See Figure 10.2.)

- **Information** is data presented in an understandable context. *Data* are raw and unprocessed facts; information makes sense of data. For example, a patient's vital signs (temperature, blood pressure, pulse, etc.) are data. Interpreting the vital signs in the context of health status is information.

Information ⟶	Propaganda ⟶	Misinformation ⟶	Disinformation
Data set in a context for relevance. *Example:* A fact	Information represented in such a way as to provoke a desired response. *Example:* An advertisement to conserve energy	Something that is not true. *Example:* An urban legend	Deliberate falsification of information. *Example:* A falsified profit-and-loss statement

FIGURE 10.2 Information, Propaganda, Misinformation, and Disinformation

- **Propaganda** is information represented in such a way as to provoke a desired response. Many people believe that propaganda is based on false information, but this is not necessarily so. Instead, propaganda may well be based in fact, but its purpose is to instill a particular attitude or emotion in order to gain public support for a cause or issue. Usually presented as advertising or publicity, propaganda encourages you to think or act according to the ideological, political, or commercial perspective of the message source.[3] World War II military posters that encouraged enlistment are an example of propaganda.

- **Misinformation** always refers to something that is not true. While propaganda may include factual information, misinformation does not. One common form of misinformation on the Internet is the *urban legend*—a fabricated story passed along by unsuspecting people.

- **Disinformation** is deliberately falsified information; it purposely misleads. For example, doctored photographs and falsified profit-and-loss statements are examples of disinformation in action. Unfortunately, disinformation thrives on the Internet.

Ethical speeches are based on sound information rather than on misinformation, propaganda, or disinformation. Being alert to these distinctions is therefore an important aspect of being both a speaker and a consumer of speeches.

Make the Most of Internet Search Tools

Rather than simply logging on to the Internet and expecting to stumble upon the information you need, take a moment to consider what will help you meet your speech goals. Jot down a research plan, as described in the "Checklist: Is My Online Research Effective?" (p. 158). Your search will be most effective if you familiarize yourself with the capabilities of various Internet search engines and subject (Web) directories.

FROM SOURCE TO SPEECH

Evaluating Web Sources

Check the Most Authoritative Web Sites First

Seek out the most authoritative Web sites on your topic. If your speech explores the NBA draft, investigate the NBA's official Web site first. For information on legislation, government statistics, health, the environment, and other relevant topics, check government-sponsored sites at the official U.S. Government portal, www.usa.gov. Government-sponsored sites are free of commercial influence and contain highly credible primary materials.

Evaluate Authorship and Sponsorship

1 *Examine the **domain** in the Web address*—the suffix at the end of the address that tells you the nature of the site: educational (.edu), government (.gov), military (.mil), nonprofit organization (.org), business/commercial (.com), and network (.net). A **tilde** (~) in the address usually indicates that it is a personal page rather than part of an institutional Web site. Make sure to assess the credibility of each site, whether it is operated by an individual, a company, a government agency, or a nonprofit group.

2 *Look for an "About" link that describes the organization or a link to a page that gives more information.* These sections can tell a great deal about the nature of the site's content. Be wary of sites that do not include such a link.

3 *Identify the creator of the information.* If an individual operates the site—and such sites are now prolific in the form of blogs and professional profile pages—does the document provide relevant biographical information, such as links to a résumé or a listing of the author's credentials? Look for contact information. A source that doesn't want to be found, at least by e-mail, is not a good source to cite.

Check for Currency

4 *Check for a date that indicates when the page was placed on the Web and when it was last updated.* Is the date current? Web sites that do not have this information may contain outdated or inaccurate material.

Check That the Site Credits Trustworthy Sources

5 *Check that the Web site documents its sources.* Reputable Web sites document the sources they use. Follow any links to these sources, and apply the same criteria to them that you did to the original source document. Verify the information you find with at least two other independent, reputable sources.

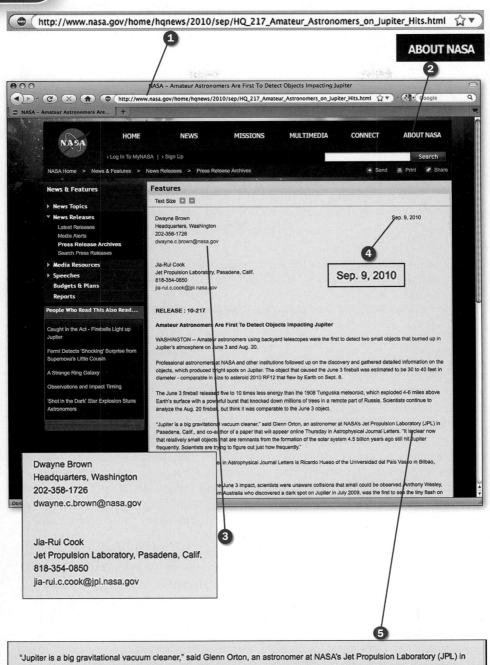

http://www.nasa.gov/home/hqnews/2010/sep/HQ_217_Amateur_Astronomers_on_Jupiter_Hits.html

1

ABOUT NASA

2

NASA – Amateur Astronomers Are First To Detect Objects Impacting Jupiter

http://www.nasa.gov/home/hqnews/2010/sep/HQ_217_Amateur_Astronomers_on_Jupiter_Hits.html · Google

NASA – Amateur Astronomers Are...

HOME   NEWS   MISSIONS   MULTIMEDIA   CONNECT   ABOUT NASA

› Log In To MyNASA | › Sign Up

Search

NASA Home > News & Features > News Releases > Press Release Archives

➔ Send   ⬛ Print   ➤ Share

News & Features

▸ News Topics
▾ News Releases
    Latest Releases
    Media Alerts
    Press Release Archives
    Search Press Releases
▸ Media Resources
▸ Speeches
    Budgets & Plans
    Reports

People Who Read This Also Read...

Caught in the Act - Fireballs Light up Jupiter

Fermi Detects 'Shocking' Surprise from Supernova's Little Cousin

A Strange Ring Galaxy

Observations and Impact Timing

'Shot in the Dark' Star Explosion Stuns Astronomers

Features

Text Size ⊞ ⊟

Dwayne Brown
Headquarters, Washington
202-358-1726
dwayne.c.brown@nasa.gov

Jia-Rui Cook
Jet Propulsion Laboratory, Pasadena, Calif.
818-354-0850
jia-rui.c.cook@jpl.nasa.gov

Sep. 9, 2010

4

Sep. 9, 2010

RELEASE : 10-217

Amateur Astronomers Are First To Detect Objects Impacting Jupiter

WASHINGTON -- Amateur astronomers using backyard telescopes were the first to detect two small objects that burned up in Jupiter's atmosphere on June 3 and Aug. 20.

Professional astronomers at NASA and other institutions followed up on the discovery and gathered detailed information on the objects, which produced bright spots on Jupiter. The object that caused the June 3 fireball was estimated to be 30 to 40 feet in diameter - comparable in size to asteroid 2010 RF12 that flew by Earth on Sept. 8.

The June 3 fireball released five to 10 times less energy than the 1908 Tunguska meteorid, which exploded 4-6 miles above Earth's surface with a powerful burst that knocked down millions of trees in a remote part of Russia. Scientists continue to analyze the Aug. 20 fireball, but think it was comparable to the June 3 object.

"Jupiter is a big gravitational vacuum cleaner," said Glenn Orton, an astronomer at NASA's Jet Propulsion Laboratory (JPL) in Pasadena, Calif., and co-author of a paper that will appear online Thursday in Astrophysical Journal Letters. "It is clear now that relatively small objects that are remnants from the formation of the solar system 4.5 billion years ago still hit Jupiter frequently. Scientists are trying to figure out just how frequently."

in Astrophysical Journal Letters is Ricardo Hueso of the Universidad del País Vasco in Bilbao,

the June 3 impact, scientists were unaware collisions that small could be observed. Anthony Wesley, from Australia who discovered a dark spot on Jupiter in July 2009, was the first to see the tiny flash on

Dwayne Brown
Headquarters, Washington
202-358-1726
dwayne.c.brown@nasa.gov

Jia-Rui Cook
Jet Propulsion Laboratory, Pasadena, Calif.
818-354-0850
jia-rui.c.cook@jpl.nasa.gov

3

5

"Jupiter is a big gravitational vacuum cleaner," said Glenn Orton, an astronomer at NASA's Jet Propulsion Laboratory (JPL) in Pasadena, Calif., and co-author of a paper that will appear online Thursday in Astrophysical Journal Letters. "It is clear now that relatively small objects that are remnants from the formation of the solar system 4.5 billion years ago still hit Jupiter frequently. Scientists are trying to figure out just how frequently."

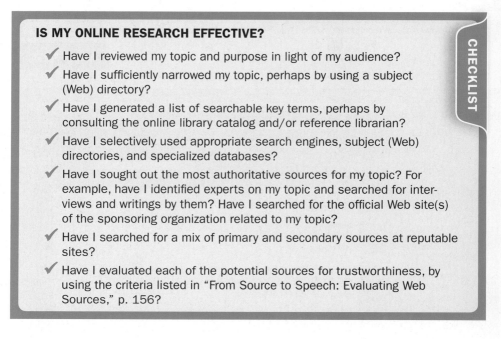

IS MY ONLINE RESEARCH EFFECTIVE?

✓ Have I reviewed my topic and purpose in light of my audience?

✓ Have I sufficiently narrowed my topic, perhaps by using a subject (Web) directory?

✓ Have I generated a list of searchable key terms, perhaps by consulting the online library catalog and/or reference librarian?

✓ Have I selectively used appropriate search engines, subject (Web) directories, and specialized databases?

✓ Have I sought out the most authoritative sources for my topic? For example, have I identified experts on my topic and searched for interviews and writings by them? Have I searched for the official Web site(s) of the sponsoring organization related to my topic?

✓ Have I searched for a mix of primary and secondary sources at reputable sites?

✓ Have I evaluated each of the potential sources for trustworthiness, by using the criteria listed in "From Source to Speech: Evaluating Web Sources," p. 156?

Distinguish among Types of Search Engines

Search engines index the contents of the Web. These engines use powerful software programs that automatically scan up to billions of documents that contain the keywords and phrases you command them to search. Results are generally ranked from most to least relevant, though criteria for relevance vary by engine. Some search engines search only the Web. Others also scan the files of publicly accessible personal journals ("blogs"), worldwide public discussion forums or newsgroups, and discussion groups that occur via mass e-mail distribution, such as Google Groups (http://groups.google.com). Some engines index more Web pages than others or index pages more often than others.

Search engines are distinguished by whether or not they compile their own databases. **Individual search engines** (such as Google, Yahoo! and Bing, the three largest) compile their own databases of Web pages. **Meta-search engines** (such as Ixquick, Qrobe, Dogpile, and Metacrawler) scan a variety of individual search engines simultaneously. Meta-search engines run wide but not necessarily deep and can produce disappointing results that include only the top listings from each search engine and far too many paid listings.[4] As a result, many librarians no longer recommend using them.[5] With that disclaimer, new meta-search engines continue to appear and will perhaps improve. Qrobe, for example, which compiles results from Google and Bing, may be one of them.

Specialized search engines let you conduct narrower but deeper searches into a particular field. **Specialized search engines** are databases created by researchers, government agencies, businesses, or other parties with a deep interest in a topic. Examples of specialized search engines include:

- USA.gov (allows you to search government sites)
- Scirus.gov (the foremost scientific-only, peer-reviewed search engine)
- GoogleScholar.com (lets you search specifically for scholarly literature, including peer-reviewed papers, theses, books, preprints, abstracts, and technical reports from all broad areas of research)
- BestoftheWebBlogs.org (searches for blogs)

To find a search engine geared specifically to your topic, type in the topic term with the keywords *search engine*. For example, a search for *climate change* AND *search engine* will lead you to various specialized search sites devoted to climate change.

Consult Subject (Web) Directories

Unlike search engines, which rely on automated crawlers to retrieve documents matching your keywords, people create and manage subject directories. A **subject (Web) directory** (also called "subject guide") is a searchable catalog of Web sites organized into subject categories such as "Science," "Reference," or "Arts and Humanities" (see Figure 10.3). Four of the most reliable subject (Web) directories include Open Directory Project or DMOZ (www.dmoz.org), Infomine (infomine.ucr.edu), ipl2: Information You Can Trust (www.ipl.org), and Yahoo! Directory (dir.yahoo.com).

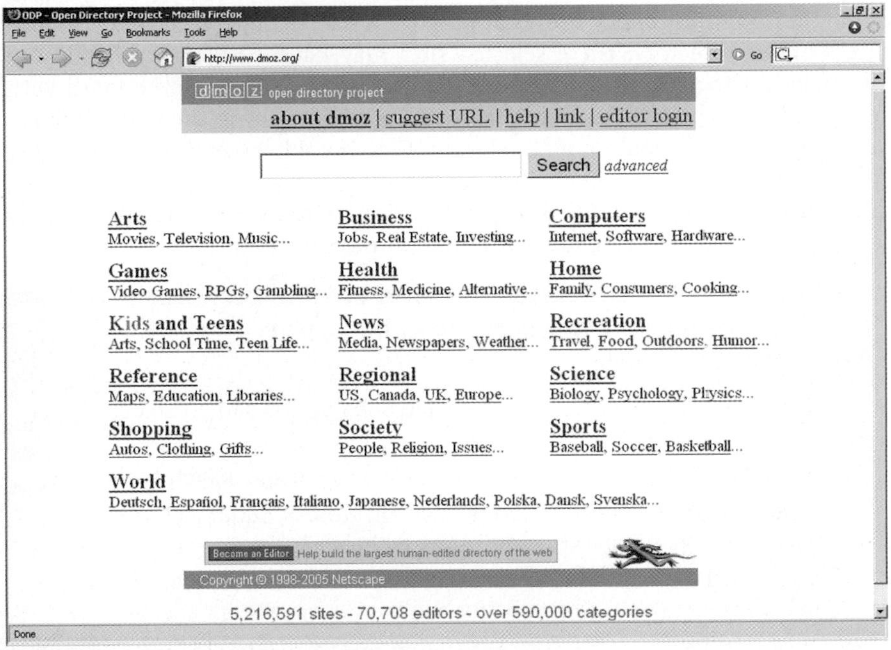

FIGURE 10.3 Home Page for the Open Directory Project (DMOZ)

Subject (Web) directories allow you to progressively narrow your search, or "drill down" into your topic, until you find what you are looking for. If your speech is on some aspect of baseball teams, for example, you would follow these links, continuing until you find what you want:

sports $\Rightarrow$ baseball $\Rightarrow$ amateur $\Rightarrow$ leagues $\Rightarrow$ teams

If you attempt to search in a manner other than by subject (e.g., by proper name), the directory will not return results.

Know When to Use Search Engines and Subject (Web) Directories

Both search engines and subject (Web) directories offer valuable help in locating supporting material for your speech, but each is best used for a somewhat different purpose. Because search engines index so many documents, they often find information that isn't listed in subject (Web) directories, making them extremely useful when your topic is already very defined. You will locate a wide variety of materials, though, because the information has not been vetted by an editor, so you will need to play that role yourself. In addition, since they scan the full text of a document rather than just its title, first few pages, or URL address, search engines are also the tool of choice when you need to find very defined information (such as specific terms, facts, figures, or quotations) that may be buried within documents.

In contrast, subject (Web) directories are more useful in both finding and narrowing a topic (see Chapter 7). When you are looking for information on a general topic such as automobiles, for instance, subject (Web) directories offer a far easier and less time-consuming way of surveying information. In this case, you might find links to fifty sites that have been selected by the editors or maintainers of the directory; these selected sites may have a higher probability of being relevant to your search. With a search engine, you would be faced with the task of sifting through countless documents containing the word *automobile,* many of which would not be relevant. One notable exception to the utility of search engines for narrowing a topic, however, is Google's Wonder Wheel, which produces very helpful topic maps. Similar tools are offered by other search engine sites. See Chapter 7 for more information on these tools.

CHOOSING BETWEEN A SUBJECT (WEB) DIRECTORY AND A SEARCH ENGINE

✓ If you are looking for a list of reputable sites on the same subject, use a subject (Web) directory.

✓ If you are looking for a specific page within a site, use a search engine.

✓ If you need to find specific terms, facts, figures, or quotations that may be buried within documents, use a search engine.

✓ If you want to locate a wide variety of materials related to your search, use a subject (Web) directory first and then use a search engine.

CHECKLIST

Beware of Commercial Factors Affecting Search Results

When researching your topic outside of a library portal or virtual library, be alert to unwanted commercial influence on your search results—specifically, whether a particular listing appears in your search results merely because an advertiser has paid to put it there.

Some engines and directories accept fees from companies in exchange for higher rankings within results (called **paid placement**). Others accept fees to include companies in the full index of possible results, without a guarantee of ranking (called **paid inclusion**).[6] When you are looking to purchase something, finding links that advertisers have paid to include is not necessarily a bad thing. But when you need unbiased information of a factual nature, it clearly is a problem.

Identifying paid-placement listings is relatively easy: Look for a heading labeled "Sponsored Links" or "Sponsored Results" at the top, side, or bottom of the main page. Be aware that these headings are in an inconspicuous color or small typeface and may be hard to read. Identifying paid-inclusion listings is much more difficult because they are mixed in with the main results. Sometimes they may be grouped under headings such as "Web Results" or "Web Pages," but most often there is no way to identify whether or not someone paid to include the listing in the search engine's index (recall that paid inclusion does not guarantee any particular ranking in the listings).

IDENTIFYING PAID LISTINGS IN SEARCH RESULTS

✓ Look for a heading labeled "Sponsored Links" or "Sponsored Results" at the top, side, or bottom of the main page. This indicates a paid placement listing.

✓ Use multiple search engines and compare the results.

✓ Beware of meta-search engines, which often include many paid-inclusion listings.

✓ Click beyond the first page of your search results to find relevant sites.

✓ Read the fine print on a search engine's disclosure pages to find its policy on paid inclusion.

CHECKLIST

Conduct Advanced Searches

WEB Chapter quizzes

To maximize the odds of finding the materials you need, familiarize yourself with the features of the search tools you select. Go to the "Help" command located near the search window to find tips on entering your search terms efficiently. Most search tools are programmed to respond to such basic commands as *quotation marks* (" ")—used to find exact phrases (e.g., *"white wine"*)—and *Boolean operators*—words placed between keywords in a search to specify how keywords are related (e.g., AND, OR, NOT, and +/−). They act as filters to help you eliminate potential items that are unrelated to your search.

Advanced searching (also called **field searching**) goes beyond the basic search commands to narrow results even further (see Figure 10.4). Search engines sort results according to several attributes or "fields" common to all pages on the Web. An advanced search option includes (at least) the following fields:

- *Keywords:* "All," "exact phrase," "at least one," and "without" filter results for keywords in much the same way as the basic search commands. Keyword field searches allow you the option of limiting your search to a Web site's title or URL.
- *Language* includes search results with pages written in the specified language.
- *Country* searches result in documents originating in the specified country.
- *File format* returns results with links to particular document formats, such as Microsoft Word (.doc or .docx), Adobe Acrobat (.pdf), PowerPoint (.ppt), and Excel (.xls).
- *Domain* limits results to specified Internet domains (e.g., .com, .edu, .gov, .org). Specifying the domain can be extremely helpful in locating credible sources. For example, by only searching for sources within the education or government domain, you will avoid links to commercial sources that may be less than reliable.

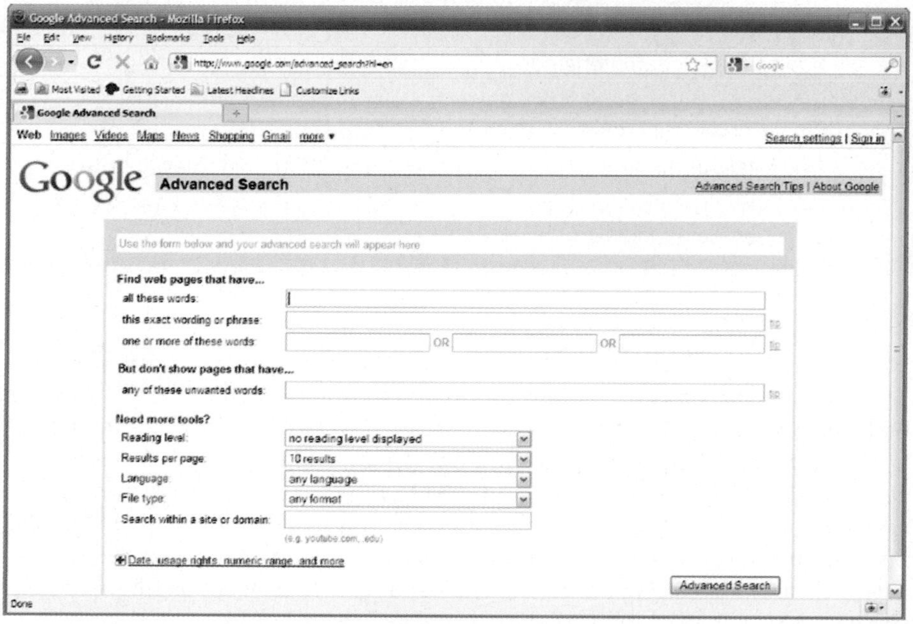

FIGURE 10.4 Google's Advanced Search Page for Conducting Field Searches

- *Date* searches focus on a specified range of time.
- *Page-specific* searches attempt to obtain a very limited set of results by seeking pages that contain the same basic information as a known page does or that link to the known page.

Record and Cite Internet Sources

Because Internet sites often change, take special care to record sources as you use them, either by creating footnotes with your word processing program or with dedicated citation software such as Noodlebib or Endnote. For detailed guidelines, refer to the "From Source to Speech" visual guides on citing Web sources (this chapter, p. 164), books (p. 148), and periodicals (p. 150). Additionally, as with print sources, consider how to orally cite Web sources effectively as you deliver your speeches. Check that you provide credit for any direct quotations, paraphrased information, facts, opinions, and statistics that are not your own and are outside the pool of common knowledge. For guidance, see Chapter 11, "Citing Sources in Your Speech."

DOCUMENTING INTERNET SOURCES

As in documentation of print sources, styles of documenting Internet sources for a written bibliography vary according to discipline. Three of the most widely used formats are the American Psychological Association (APA) style, the Modern Language Association (MLA) style, and the *Chicago* style. (See Appendices E through I for specific documentation guidelines.) Each referencing style varies in the precise ordering and formatting of information, but all generally require that you provide as much of the following information as possible:

✓ Name of the author, editor, or site maintainer (if applicable). (Some sources may be identified only by a login name.)

✓ Publication information of any print version

✓ Date of electronic publication or last revision (if known)

✓ Title of document, whether it's a scholarly project, database, periodical, or, for a professional or personal site with no title, a description such as "home page"

✓ Title of complete work of which it is a part (if relevant)

✓ Other relevant information (volume number, page numbers, etc.)

✓ Retrieval date statement (e.g., "Retrieved March 16, 2011" or "Accessed March 16, 2011"). Some citation styles do not require this date, but it is good for you to record it to keep track of your research process.

✓ URL

Source: Andrew Hamack and Eugene Kleppinger, *Online! A Reference Guide to Using Internet Sources* (Boston: Bedford/St. Martin's, 2002).

CHECKLIST

Recording and Citing Web Sources

When using a Web document as a source, locate and record the following citation elements:

1 Author of the Work

4 Date of Publication/Last Update

2 Title of the Work

5 Site Address (URL)

3 Title of the Web Site

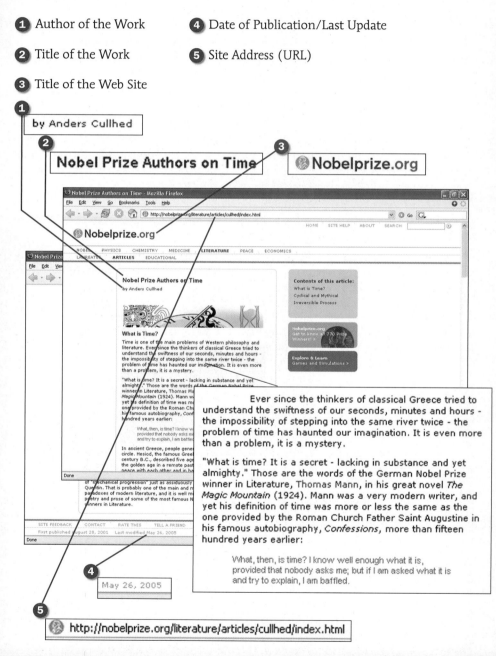

Record Notes

When taking notes, create a separate heading for each idea and record the citation elements from your source. Indicate whether the material is a direct quotation, a paraphrase, or a summary of the information.

Following are sample notes for a quotation and a paraphrase.

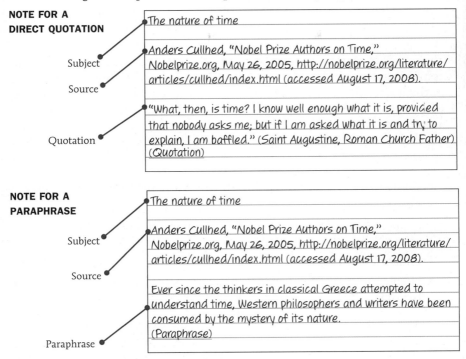

NOTE FOR A DIRECT QUOTATION

Subject

Source

Quotation

The nature of time

Anders Cullhed, "Nobel Prize Authors on Time," Nobelprize.org, May 26, 2005, http://nobelprize.org/literature/articles/cullhed/index.html (accessed August 17, 2008).

"What, then, is time? I know well enough what it is, provided that nobody asks me; but if I am asked what it is and try to explain, I am baffled." (Saint Augustine, Roman Church Father) (Quotation)

NOTE FOR A PARAPHRASE

Subject

Source

Paraphrase

The nature of time

Anders Cullhed, "Nobel Prize Authors on Time," Nobelprize.org, May 26, 2005, http://nobelprize.org/literature/articles/cullhed/index.html (accessed August 17, 2008).

Ever since the thinkers in classical Greece attempted to understand time, Western philosophers and writers have been consumed by the mystery of its nature. (Paraphrase)

Orally Cite Sources in Your Speech

In your speech, alert the audience to the source of any ideas not your own. You can find more information on oral citations in Chapter 11. For guidelines on various citation styles including *Chicago,* APA, MLA, CBE/CSE, and IEEE, see Appendices E–I.

SPEECH EXCERPT INDICATING A DIRECT QUOTATION

Many famous thinkers have grappled with the concept of time. For example, Saint Augustine wrote in his biography, *Confessions,* "What, then, is time? I know well enough what it is, provided that nobody asks me; but if I am asked what it is and try to explain, I am baffled."

SPEECH EXCERPT INDICATING A PARAPHRASE

In an article on the nature of time posted on the Web site Nobleprize.org, professor of comparative literature Anders Cullhed notes that beginning with thinkers in ancient Greece, Western philosophers and writers have tried to understand the nature of time.

CHAPTER 11

Citing Sources in Your Speech

Thousands of years ago, Aristotle counseled speakers to use expert opinion to convince an audience of their reasoning. In this regard, nothing has changed in the intervening centuries. We continue to be most persuaded by speakers who support their positions with sources we find trustworthy. Alerting the audience to the sources you use, as well as offering ones that they will find authoritative, is a critical aspect of delivering a speech or presentation. When you credit speech sources, you:

- Demonstrate the quality and range of your research to audience members.
- Demonstrate that reliable sources support your position.
- Avoid plagiarism and gain credibility as an ethical speaker who acknowledges the work of others.
- Enhance your own authority and win more support for your point of view.
- Enable listeners to locate your sources and pursue their own research on the topic.

As described in Chapter 5 (p. 66), ethically you are bound to attribute any information drawn from other people's ideas, opinions, and theories, as well as any facts and statistics gathered by others, to their original sources. Remember, you need not credit sources for ideas that are *common knowledge*—established information likely to be known by many people and described in multiple places (see p. 67).

Alert Listeners to Key Source Information

An **oral citation** credits the source of speech material that is derived from other people's ideas. During your speech, always cite your sources at the same time as you present the information derived from them, rather than waiting until the end of the speech to disclose them to the audience. For each source, plan on briefly alerting the audience to the following:

1. The *author* or *origin of the source* ("documentary filmmaker *Ken Burns* . . ."; or "On the *National Science Foundation Web site* . . .")

2. The *type of source* (magazine, book, personal interview, Web site, blog, online video, etc.)

3. The *title* or a *description of the source* ("In the book *Endangered Minds* . . .";
   or "In *an article on sharks* . . .")

4. The *date of the source (exact or approximate, depending on importance in the
   speech)*: ("The article, published in the *October 10th, 2010*, issue . . ."; or
   "On their Web page, *last updated March 8, 2010* . . .")

Spoken citations need not include a complete bibliographic reference (exact
titles, volume, page numbers); indeed, doing so will interrupt the flow of your
presentation and unnecessarily divert listeners' attention. However, keep a running list of source details for a bibliography to appear at the end of your speech
draft or outline. (For guidelines on creating a written bibliography for your
speeches, see Appendices E–I.)

In place of bibliographic details, focus on presenting your sources in a
rhetorically effective manner. Bear in mind that not every source is appropriate
for every audience, though never omit mention of a source once you have
included the material in your speech (see Chapter 8, "Developing Supporting
Material").

OFFERING KEY SOURCE INFORMATION

_____ 1. Have I identified the author or origin of the source?

_____ 2. Have I indicated the type of source?

_____ 3. Have I offered the title or description of the source?

_____ 4. Have I noted the date of the source?

_____ 5. Have I qualified the source to establish its reliability and
credibility?

CHECKLIST

Establish the Source's Trustworthiness

Too often, inexperienced speakers credit their sources in bare-bones fashion,
offering a rote recitation of citation elements. For example, they might cite
the publication name and date but leave out key details that could convince
the audience to accept the source as reliable and its conclusions as true. But
discerning listeners will accept as legitimate the supporting materials you
offer for your claims—examples, stories, testimony, facts, and statistics (see
Chapter 8)—only if they believe that the sources are reliable and accurate, or
credible.

Source reliability refers to our level of trust in a source's credentials and
track record for providing accurate information. If you support a scientific
claim by crediting it to an unknown 14-year-old's personal blog, for example,
most listeners won't find it as reliable as if you credited it to a scientist affiliated
with a reputable institution.

While a source that is reliable is usually accurate, this is not always so.[1] Sometimes we have information that contradicts what we are told by a reliable source. For example, a soldier based in Iraq might read a news article in the *Wall Street Journal* about a battle in which he or she participated. The soldier knows the story contains inaccuracies because the soldier was there. In general, however, the soldier finds the *Wall Street Journal* a reliable source. Since even the most reliable source can sometimes be wrong, it is always better to offer a variety of sources, rather than a single source, to support a major point. This is especially the case when your claims are controversial.

To demonstrate a source's trustworthiness, offer a **source qualifier**, or brief description of the source's qualifications to address the topic. Briefly mention any relevant affiliations and credentials that will help the audience put the source in perspective and establish credibility (e.g., "researcher at the Mayo Clinic," "Pulitzer-Prize–winning author"). And when offering your own insights or experience, don't forget to mention your own qualifications. Including a source qualifier in your presentation can make the difference between winning or losing acceptance for your supporting material. The "From Source to Speech" guide on p. 170 illustrates how you can orally cite your sources in a way that listeners will accept them.

Avoid a Mechanical Delivery

Acknowledging sources need not interrupt the flow of your speech. On the contrary, audience members will welcome information that adds backing to your assertions. The key is to avoid a formulaic, or mechanical, delivery. Audience members expect a natural style of delivery of your speech, and this includes delivery of speech sources.

Vary the Wording

One way to avoid a rote delivery of sources is to vary your wording. For example, if you introduce one source with the phrase, "According to . . . ," switch to another construction, "As reported by . . ." for the next. Alternating introductory phrases, such as "In the words of . . . "; "*Wall Street Journal* reporter Jonathan X writes that . . . "; and so forth contributes to a natural delivery and provides the necessary aural variety.

Preview the Source

Another means of introducing variety is occasionally to summarize or preview a claim first, for example, "Caffeine can cause actual intoxication," before elaborating on and acknowledging the source of it, for example, "a report in the July 5th, 2010, issue of the *New England Journal of Medicine* has found . . ." Much as transitions help listeners follow, summarizing and previewing evidence can help listeners process it better.

Overview of Source Types with Sample Oral Citations

When you reveal your sources to the audience, be sure to alert them to the type—whether it is a book, article, Web site, and so forth. This will ensure that they will be able to locate the source at a later time should they wish to. Following is an overview of common types of sources cited in a speech, the specific citation elements to mention, and examples of how you might refer to these elements in a presentation. Note that each example includes a source qualifier.

Book

When orally citing elements from a book with *two* or *fewer* authors, state first and last names, source qualifier, title, and date of publication. If *three* or *more* *authors,* state first and last name of first author, and state the word "coauthors."

> *Example:* In the book *1948: The First Arab-Israeli War,* published in 2008, noted *Israeli historian* Benny Morris claims that . . .

> *Example:* In *The Civic Potential of Video Games,* published in 2009, Joseph Kahne, *noted professor of education and director of the Civic Education Research Group at Mills College,* and his *two coauthors, both educators,* wrote that . . .

Print Article

When citing from a print article, use the same guidelines as you do for a book.

> *Example:* In an article published in the May 2010 edition of *Atlantic Monthly* magazine, Marc Ambider, a journalist and political editor of the *Atlantic Monthly,* outlines the epidemic of obesity in the United States and describes his own decision to have bariatric surgery . . .

Online-Only Magazine

If you are citing an online magazine, follow the same guidelines you would for a book and identify the publication as an "online magazine."

> *Example: Environmental columnist* Nina Shen Rastogi, writing on the socioeconomic arguments against genetically modified crops in the *May 18, 2010,* edition of the online magazine *Slate* . . .

Web Site

For a Web site, you should name the Web site, source qualifier, section of Web site cited (if applicable), and the last update.

> *Example:* On its Web site, *last updated July 8, 2010,* the *Society of Interventional Radiology* explains that radio waves are harmless to healthy cells . . .

Demonstrating Your Sources' Reliability and Credibility

How Can I Lead the Audience to Accept My Sources as Reliable and Credible?

- If the source is affiliated with a respected institution, identify that affiliation.
- If citing a study linked to a reputable institution, identify the institution.
- If a source has relevant credentials, note the credentials.
- If the source has relevant real-life experience, mention that experience.

In the following excerpt from a speech about emergency room care in the United States, the speaker omits information about her key sources that would help convince the audience that her evidence and sources are trustworthy:

> According to a series of three reports by the Institute of Medicine on the breakdown of our emergency room system, the need for emergency rooms has increased by 26 percent since 1993. Today, we'll uncover the catastrophic conditions existing in America's emergency rooms, discover what is causing these conditions, and look at how to restore faith in a system that has—to quote from a New York editorial—"reached a breaking point."

Below we see a much more convincing use of the same sources.

1   **2**

> According to a **landmark** series of three reports on the breakdown of our emergency room system conducted by the **Institute of Medicine, a unit of the National Academy of Sciences**, the need for emergency rooms has increased by 26 percent since 1993.   **3**
>
> . . . Today, we'll uncover the catastrophic conditions existing in America's emergency rooms, discover what is causing these conditions, and look at how to restore our faith in a system that has — to quote from an editorial in the **June 21st, 2006,**   **4**
> **edition of the *New York Times*** — "reached a breaking point."

1 The speaker wisely includes the adjective "landmark" to signal credibility for her evidence.

2 The speaker communicates relevant affiliations, connecting the source to an entity that raises the audience's confidence level.

CONTACT

Institute of Medicine
500 Fifth Street NW
Washington DC 20001

iomwww@nas.edu

tel: 202.334.2352
fax: 202.334.1412

Staff Directory

>> LATEST WEBCASTS & PRESENTATIONS

> Agenda. 2006 IOM Annual Meeting: Ste
> Agenda. 2007 IOM Annual Meeting: Evi
> Agenda. 2005 IOM Annual Meeting: Pha

■ more webcasts & presentations

> RSS

Home | About | Topics | Projects| Memberships| Boards | Events | Reports | Sitemap
Copyright © 2008 National Academy of Sciences. All rights reserved.

3 The speaker identifies the source as a respected government agency. Listeners are more likely to trust the source if it is connected to a trusted entity.

4 The speaker supports her thesis that a crisis exists with a quotation from a notable source: the *New York Times*, a well-known, well-respected national paper.

Crisis of care in ERs

Editorial, "Emergency in the Emergency Rooms,"
NYTimes.com, June 21, 2006,
http://www.nytimes.com/2006/06/21.opinion/21Wed4.html?_
r=1 (accessed June 26, 2006).

"The nation's emergency rooms have been stretched thin
for at least a decade or more, but a new analysis suggests
that they have reached a breaking point."
(New York Times Editorial, Quotation)

Weblog

When orally citing a Weblog, name the blogger, source qualifier, affiliated Web site (if applicable), and date of posting.

> *Example:* In a *July 8, 2010*, posting on *Talking Points Memo, a news blog that specializes in original reporting on government and politics*, editor *Josh Marshall* notes that . . .

Television or Radio Program

If you are citing a television or radio program, name the program, segment, reporter, source qualifier, and date aired.

> *Example:* Jim Lehrer, *National Public Television's Newshour* host, described in a segment on the auto industry *aired on November 2, 2010* . . .

Online Video

For online videos, name the online video source, program, segment, source qualifier, and date aired (if applicable).

> *Example:* In a session on "What's Next for Mindfulness" delivered at the *University of California, Berkeley's Greater Good Science Center* on *April 20, 2010,* and *broadcast on YouTube,* Jon Kabat-Zinn, *scientist, author, and founding director of the Stress Reduction Clinic* . . .

Testimony (Lay or Expert)

If you are citing testimony, name the person, source qualifier, context in which information was offered, and the date information was offered.

> *Example:* On *March 25, 2010,* in congressional testimony before the *Tom Lantos Human Rights Commission of the U.S. House of Representatives, Luis CdeBaca,* the Obama Administration's *top advisor in the global fight against contemporary forms of slavery* revealed that . . .

Personal Interview

For a personal interview, name the person, source qualifier, and the date of interview.

> *Example:* In an interview I conducted *last week, Tim Zeutenhorst, chairman of the Orange City Area Health System Board*, at Orange City Hospital in Iowa, said . . .

Properly Citing Facts and Statistics

Acknowledging your sources when credit is due is a necessary aspect of delivering a speech. However, some facts (documented occurrences, including actual events, dates, times, people, and places) are common knowledge—for example, that the earth revolves around the sun. Facts that are widely disseminated and commonly known require no attribution (see Chapter 5). Otherwise, credit the source of the fact in your speech:

> *According to the Galileo Project Web site* (name), *a project supported by Rice University* (source qualifier), *Galileo was appointed professor of mathematics at the University of Padua in 1592* (fact).

Used sparingly, statistics (quantified evidence) add credibility to speech claims, *if* you tell listeners what the numbers actually mean, use terms that describe them accurately, and reveal the methods and scope of the research:

> *According to a landmark series of three reports* (methods and scope of research) on the breakdown of our emergency room system *conducted by the Institute of Medicine* (source qualifier), *the need for emergency rooms has increased by 26 percent since 1993; during the same period, 425 emergency departments closed their doors* (what the numbers actually mean).

Data changes over time, so rather than using phrases such as "this number proves," which represents the statistics as absolute truth, use conditional language such as "these numbers suggest/imply. . . ." For more detailed guidelines on citing statistics see Chapter 8, p. 129. See also Table 11.1 for more information on how to credit facts and statistics in your speech as well as other types of supporting materials.

TABLE 11.1	Types of Supporting Materials and Sample Oral Citation
Type of Supporting Material	**Sample Oral Citation**
Examples (real or hypothetical)	"One example of a fiscally effective charity is Lance Armstrong's Livestrong Foundation. According to the Foundation's Annual Report, in 2011 the Livestrong Challenge events raised . . ."
Stories (extended or anecdotal)	"In J.R.R. Tolkien's classic trilogy, *The Lord of the Rings,* a young Hobbit boy named Frodo . . ."
Testimony (expert or lay)	"Dr. Mary Klein, a stem-cell researcher from the Brown University School of Medicine, echoed this sentiment when she spoke last Monday at the Public Health Committee meeting . . ."
Facts	"According to the *Farmer's Almanac,* published every year since 1818, originally the phrase 'blue moon' referred to the second of two full moons appearing in a single month."
Statistics	"Data from the *U.S. Census Bureau,* which produces national population estimates annually using the latest available data on births, deaths, and international migration, indicates that in 2009, there was one birth every eight seconds and one death every twelve seconds in the United States."

Properly Citing Summarized, Paraphrased, and Quoted Information

As discussed in Chapter 5, information not your own may be cited in the form of a *summary* (a brief overview of someone else's ideas, opinions, or theories), *paraphrase* (a restatement of someone else's ideas, opinions, or theories in the speaker's own words), or *direct quotation* (statements made verbatim by someone else).

For examples of how to cite quotations, paraphrases, and summaries, see Chapter 9, p. 145, and "From Source to Speech" on pp. 148–51.

ORGANIZING
AND OUTLINING

ORGANIZING AND OUTLINING

SPEAKER'S REFERENCE

CHAPTER **12** Organizing the Speech 181

Beyond the Speech: Organizing as a Life Skill 181

Parts of a Speech 182

Use Main Points to Express Key Ideas 182

▶ **SELF-ASSESSMENT CHECKLIST** Do the Speech Points Illustrate or Prove the Thesis? 183

Use Supporting Points to Substantiate Your Claims 185

Pay Close Attention to Coordination and Subordination 187

Strive for a Unified, Coherent, and Balanced Outline 188

▶ **CHECKLIST** Do the Speech Points Reflect Unity, Coherence, and Balance? 189

Use Transitions to Give Direction to the Speech 189

▶ **SELF-ASSESSMENT CHECKLIST** Using Transitions 191

▶ **FROM POINT TO POINT** Using Transitions to Guide Your Listeners 192

CHAPTER **13** Types of Organizational Arrangements 194

▶ **CHECKLIST** Choosing an Organizational Pattern 194

Arranging Speech Points Chronologically 195

Arranging Speech Points Using a Spatial Pattern 195

Arranging Speech Points Using a Causal (Cause-Effect) Pattern 196

Arranging Speech Points Using a Problem-Solution Pattern 197

Arranging Speech Points Topically 198

Arranging Speech Points Using a Narrative Pattern 199

Arranging Speech Points Using a Circular Pattern 200

Subpoints Need Not Match the Pattern of Main Points 200

▶ **CHECKLIST** Evaluating Organizational Patterns 201

▶ **A CULTURAL PERSPECTIVE** Arrangement Formats and Audience Diversity 201

CHAPTER **14** Outlining the Speech 202

Plan on Creating Two Outlines 202

Create a Working Outline First 204

▶ **CHECKLIST** Steps in Creating a Working Outline 206

Preparing the Speaking Outline 211

▶ **CHECKLIST** Tips on Using Notecards or Sheets of Paper 212

▶ **CHECKLIST** Steps in Creating a Speaking Outline 212

▶ **SAMPLE INFORMATIVE SPEECH** Staying Ahead of Spyware, John Coulter 215

ORGANIZING AND OUTLINING

CHAPTER 12 Organizing the Speech

Create Main Points That Express Your Key Ideas and Major Claims

- Use the specific purpose and thesis statements as guides. (p. 183)
- Check that each main point flows directly from these statements. (p. 183)
- Restrict the number of main points to between two and five. (p. 183)
- Focus each main point on a single idea. (p. 183)
- Present each main point as a declarative sentence. (p. 183)
- State main points in parallel form. (p. 183)

Use Supporting Points to Substantiate or Prove Your Main Points

- Create supporting points with your research materials. (p. 184)
- Ensure that supporting points follow logically from main points. (p. 185)
- Check that supporting points are in fact subordinate in weight to main points. (p. 187)

Pay Attention to Coordination and Subordination

- Make ideas of equal weight coordinate to one another. (p. 187)
- Make an idea that has less weight than another idea subordinate to it. (p. 187)

Create Speech Points That Are Unified, Coherent, and Balanced

- Focus each point, whether main or subordinate, on a single idea. (p. 188)
- Review the logical connections between points. (p. 188)
- Dedicate roughly the same amount of time to each main point. (p. 188)
- Ensure that the introduction and the conclusion are approximately of the same length and that the body is the longest part of the speech. (p. 188)
- Substantiate each main point with at least two supporting points. (p. 188)

Use Transitions to Signal Movement from One Point to Another

- Use clear transitions to move from point to point. (p. 189)
- Use full-sentence transitions to move from one main point to another. (p. 190)

Use Signal Phrases or Words to Indicate Transitions

- Use internal previews to help listeners anticipate what is ahead. (p. 191)
- Use internal summaries to help listeners review what has been said. (p. 191)

CHAPTER 13 Types of Organizational Arrangements

Be Audience Centered When Arranging Main Points

- Select a pattern that listeners can easily follow. (p. 194)
- Select a pattern that helps you achieve your speech goals. (p. 194)

Choose from a Variety of Organizational Patterns

- To motivate listeners to adopt a course of action, consider *Monroe's motivated sequence*. (p. 194 and Chapter 27)
- To demonstrate the superiority of one viewpoint or proposal over another, consider the *comparative advantage pattern*. (p. 194 and Chapter 27)
- To disprove an opposing claim to your position, consider the *refutation pattern*. (p. 194 and Chapter 27)
- To describe a series of developments in time or a set of actions occurring sequentially, consider a *chronological pattern*. (p. 195)
- To emphasize physical arrangement, consider a *spatial pattern*. (p. 195)
- To demonstrate a topic in terms of its underlying causes (or its effects), consider a *causal (cause-effect) pattern*. (p. 196)
- To demonstrate a problem and then provide justification for a solution, consider a *problem-solution pattern*. (p. 197)
- To stress natural divisions or categories in a topic, consider a *topical pattern*. (p. 198)
- To convey speech ideas through a story, consider a *narrative pattern*. (p. 199)
- To demonstrate how each speech idea builds on the previous idea and in turn supports the thesis, consider a *circular pattern*. (p. 200)
- Subpoints need not always follow the pattern selected for main points. (p. 200)

CHAPTER 14   Outlining the Speech

Plan on Developing Two Outlines before Delivering Your Speech

- Begin by creating a working outline in sentence format. (p. 202)
- Transfer your ideas to a speaking outline in phrase or key-word format. (p. 202)

Become Familiar with Sentence, Phrase, and Key-Word Outlines

- Sentence outlines express speech points in full sentences. (p. 202)
- Phrase outlines use shortened versions of the sentence form. (p. 203)
- Key-word outlines use just a few words associated with the specific point. (p. 203)

Know the Benefits and Drawbacks of the Three Outline Formats

- Sentence outlines offer the most protection against memory lapses but sacrifice eye contact. (p. 204)
- The less you rely on your outline notes, the more eye contact you can have with the audience. (p. 204)
- Key-word outlines promote eye contact and natural delivery, *if* you are well rehearsed. (p. 204)

Plan Your Speech with a Working Outline

- Treat the working outline as a document to be revised and rearranged. (p. 204)
- Include everything you want to say in your working outline. (p. 204)

Create a Speaking Outline to Deliver the Speech

- Condense the working outline into a phrase or key-word outline. (p. 211)
- Clearly indicate delivery cues. (p. 211)

KEY TERMS

Chapter 12

arrangement	conclusion	parallel form
outlining	main points	supporting points
introduction	primacy effect	indentation
body	recency effect	roman numeral outline

SPEAKER'S REFERENCE

coordination and subordination

transitions (connectives)

full-sentence transitions

"restate-forecast" transition

rhetorical question

signposts

preview statement

internal preview

internal summary

Chapter 13

chronological pattern of arrangement

spatial pattern of arrangement

causal (cause-effect) pattern of arrangement

problem-solution pattern of arrangement

topical pattern of arrangement

narrative pattern of arrangement

circular pattern of arrangement

Chapter 14

working outline

speaking outline

sentence outline

phrase outline

key-word outline

delivery cues

Organizing the Speech

Audience members quickly note the difference between a well-organized speech and one that has been put together haphazardly, with decidedly negative results when the speech is disorganized. Listeners' understanding of a speech, for example, is directly linked to how well it is organized.[1] Apparently, a little bit of disorganization won't ruin a speech if the speaker is otherwise engaging, but audience attitudes plummet when the speech is very disorganized.[2] Listeners also find speakers whose speeches are well organized more credible than those who present poorly organized ones.[3] Given all this, you won't want to skip the crucial steps of arranging and outlining speech points.

Organizing the speech (also called **arrangement** by classical rhetoricians) is the strategic process of deciding how to order speech points into a coherent and convincing pattern for your topic and audience. **Outlining** is the physical process of plotting those speech points on the page in hierarchical order of importance. An *outline* is an essential tool that lets you check for logical inconsistencies in the placement of speech points and pinpoint weaknesses in the amount and kind of support for them. Rather than making the job of drafting a speech harder, outlining your speech provides a vivid snapshot of its strengths and weaknesses and clearly points to how you can fix the flaws. Although a few famous speakers have managed to deliver successful speeches without first arranging and outlining them, for the vast majority of us, the success or failure of a speech will depend on doing so.

Beyond the Speech: Organizing as a Life Skill

As well as being of immense practical value in fashioning better speeches, skill in arranging and outlining information can have far-reaching positive effects on many aspects of your academic and professional life. As noted in Chapter 1, written and verbal skill in communication rank first in employers' "wish list" for employees.[4] Employers seek workers who can communicate ideas logically and convincingly. Nearly all professional-level jobs, for example, require you to prepare well-organized written and oral reports, PowerPoint presentations, and so forth. Similarly, written assignments in the classroom depend upon how convincingly and logically you present your viewpoint. Learning how to arrange ideas into a coherent pattern and gaining proficiency with outlining—a skill that depends on the logical coordination and subordination of ideas (see p. 187)—will serve you well as a public speaker and in these other arenas (see Tables 12.1 and 12.2).

TABLE 12.1 Sample Outline Format

Extended Outline Format

I. Main point
    A. Subordinate to main point I
    B. Coordinate with subpoint A
        1. Subordinate to subpoint B
        2. Coordinate with sub-subpoint 1
            a. Subordinate to sub-subpoint 2
            b. Coordinate with sub-sub-subpoint a
                (1) Subordinate to sub-sub-subpoint b
                (2) Coordinate with sub-sub-sub-subpoint (1)
II. Main point: Coordinate with main point I

Parts of a Speech

WEB Chapter quizzes

A speech structure is simple, composed of just three general parts: an introduction, a body, and a conclusion. The **introduction** establishes the purpose of the speech and shows its relevance to the audience. It lets listeners know where the speaker is taking them. The **body** of the speech presents main points that are intended to fulfill the speech purpose. Main points are developed with various kinds of supporting material to fulfill this purpose. The **conclusion** ties the purpose and the main points together. It brings closure to the speech by restating the purpose and reiterating why it is relevant to the audience, and by leaving audience members with something to think about. In essence, the introduction tells listeners where they are going, the body takes them there, and the conclusion lets them know that they have arrived.

Chapter 13 describes organizational patterns you can use to order speech points to greatest effect, and Chapter 14 illustrates the three types of outline formats—sentence, phrase, and key word. Chapters 15 and 16 focus on how to create effective introductions and conclusions. In this chapter we explore the body of the speech. It consists of three elements: main points, supporting points, and transitions.

Use Main Points to Express Key Ideas

Main points express the key ideas and major themes of the speech. Their function is to represent each of the main elements or claims being made in support of the speech thesis. The first step in creating main points is to identify the central ideas and themes of the speech. What are the most important ideas you want to convey? What is the thesis? What central ideas emerge from your research? What ideas can you substantiate with supporting material? Each of these ideas or claims should be expressed as a main point.

Let the Speech Thesis and Purpose Guide You

You can use the specific purpose and thesis statements as reference points to help generate main points. As discussed in Chapter 7, the *specific purpose statement* expresses the goal of the speech. Formulating it in your mind allows you to articulate precisely what you want the speech to accomplish (without stating it directly in the speech itself). The *thesis statement* (which *is* stated in the speech) expresses the speech's theme or central idea. It concisely lays out what the speech is about. The main points should flow directly from these two statements expressing the speech goal and the central idea, as seen in the following example:

SPECIFIC PURPOSE: (what you want your audience to get from the speech; not stated in speech itself): To show my audience, through a series of easy steps, how to perform meditation.

THESIS: (the central idea of the speech; thesis is expressed in speech): When performed correctly, meditation is an effective and easy way to reduce stress.

Main Points

I. The first step of meditation is "positioning."

II. The second step of meditation is "breathing."

III. The third step of meditation is "relaxation."

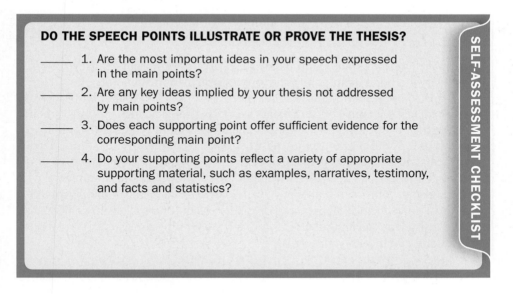

DO THE SPEECH POINTS ILLUSTRATE OR PROVE THE THESIS?

_____ 1. Are the most important ideas in your speech expressed in the main points?

_____ 2. Are any key ideas implied by your thesis not addressed by main points?

_____ 3. Does each supporting point offer sufficient evidence for the corresponding main point?

_____ 4. Do your supporting points reflect a variety of appropriate supporting material, such as examples, narratives, testimony, and facts and statistics?

SELF-ASSESSMENT CHECKLIST

Restrict the Number of Main Points

Research has shown that many audiences can comfortably take in only between two and seven main points. For most speeches, and especially those delivered in the classroom, between two and five main points should be sufficient.[5] As a rule, the fewer main points in a speech, the greater are the odds that you will keep your listeners' attention. Listeners have a better recall of the main points made at the beginning of a speech, a phenomenon termed the **primacy effect**, and at the end of a speech (the **recency effect**) than of those made in between (unless the ideas made in between are far more striking than the others).[6] Thus, if it is especially important that listeners remember certain ideas, introduce those ideas near the beginning of the speech and reiterate them at the conclusion.

If you find you have too many main points while organizing your speech, consider whether your topic is sufficiently narrow (see Chapter 7). If the problem does not lie in an overly broad topic, review your main and supporting points for proper subordination (see p. 187 for a discussion on these topics).

Restrict Each Main Point to a Single Idea

A main point should not introduce more than one idea. If it does, split it into two (or more) main points:

Incorrect

    I.   West Texas has its own Grand Canyon, and South Texas has its own desert.

Correct

    I.   West Texas boasts its own Grand Canyon.

    II. South Texas boasts its own desert.

The main points should be mutually exclusive of one another. If they are not, consider whether a main point more properly serves as a subpoint.

Express each main point as a *declarative sentence* (one that states a fact or argument). This emphasizes the point and alerts audience members to the main thrusts of your speech. For example, if one of your main points is that children need more vitamin D, you should clearly state, "According to the nation's leading pediatricians, children from infants to teens should double the recommended amount of vitamin D." In addition, as shown in the example below, strive to state your main points in **parallel form**—that is, in similar grammatical form and style. (See Chapter 17 for a discussion of parallelism.) This helps listeners understand and retain the points (by providing consistency) and lends power and elegance to your words:

THESIS STATEMENT: The Group of Eight (G8) of the world's leading industrial nations should take stronger steps at its next summit to reduce carbon dioxide emissions linked to global warming.

Incorrect

1.   The United States must adopt new stricter policies to reduce carbon dioxide emissions.

2. Canada failed to adopt a sound global-warming policy.

3. Switzerland didn't do anything either.

Correct

I. The United States must adopt stricter policies to reduce carbon dioxide emissions.

II. Canada must readdress the question of carbon dioxide emissions in its next session of parliament.

III. Switzerland must reevaluate its position on carbon dioxide emissions in its next plenary session.

Use Supporting Points to Substantiate Your Claims

Supporting points represent the supporting material or evidence you have gathered to explain (in an informative speech) or justify (in a persuasive speech) the main points. It is here that you substantiate or prove your thesis with examples, narratives, testimony, and facts and statistics.

Listeners respond most favorably to a variety of supporting materials derived from multiple sources to illustrate each main point.[7] Alternating among different types of supporting material—such as beginning with a short story, followed by examples, statistics, and perhaps credible testimony—sparks interest and builds credibility while simultaneously appealing to listeners' different learning styles. For example, to support the claim that Michael Jordan was the most dominant player in the history of basketball, you could relate a story about how he won the final game of the 1998 NBA championship against the Utah Jazz team, quote from journalist David Halberstam's biography of Jordan, and then provide some of Jordan's lifetime stats.

To determine whether they have the right amount and kind of supporting points, some speakers check them against a series of questions used by journalists: *who* (did it), *what* (did they do), *when* (did they do it), *where* (did it occur), *why* (did it happen), and *how* (did it happen)? This formula dictates that every news story should answer these questions, usually in descending order of importance in case the story has to be shortened. While these particular questions may not reflect the most relevant criteria for your selection of supporting materials, the idea is to carefully evaluate whether your subpoints satisfactorily flesh out your main claims and that they do so with a mix that is likely to appeal to listeners.

In an outline, supporting points appear in a subordinate position to main points. This is indicated by **indentation** (see the following section on coordination and subordination). As with main points, supporting points should be ordered in a logical fashion—that is, arranged in order of their importance or relevance to the main point. The most common format is the **roman numeral outline** (used thus far in this chapter). Main points are enumerated with uppercase roman numerals (I, II, III . . .), supporting points are enumerated with capital letters (A, B, C . . .), third-level points are enumerated with Arabic numerals (1, 2, 3 . . .), and fourth-level points are enumerated with lowercase letters (a, b, c . . .), as seen in the format shown on p. 186 (see also Table 12.2):

TABLE 12.2 **Principles of Coordination and Subordination**

- Assign ideas that are coordinate equal weight.
- Assign ideas that are subordinate relatively less weight.
- Indicate coordinate points by their parallel alignment.
- Indicate subordinate points by their indentation below the more important points.
- Every point must be supported by at least two points or none at all (consider how to address one "dangling" point in the point above it).

I. Main point
  A. Supporting point
    1. Sub-supporting point
      a. Sub-sub-supporting point
      b. Sub-sub-supporting point
    2. Sub-supporting point
      a. Sub-sub-supporting point
      b. Sub-sub-supporting point
  B. Supporting point
II. Main point

Here is an example (in phrase outline form; see p. 203) from a speech about using effective subject lines in business-related e-mails:

I. Subject line most important, yet neglected, part of e-mail.
  A. Determines if recipient reads message
    1. Needs to specify point of message
    2. Needs to distinguish from spam
  B. Determines if recipient ignores message
    1. May ignore e-mail with missing subject line
    2. May ignore e-mail with unclear subject line
II. Use proven techniques for effective subject lines
  A. Make them informative
    1. Give specific details
    2. Match central idea of e-mail
    3. Be current
  B. Check for sense
    1. Convey correct meaning
    2. Reflect content of message
  C. Avoid continuing subject line in text
    1. May annoy the reader
    2. May be unclear
      a. Could be confused with spam
      b. Could be misinterpreted

Note that different levels of points are also distinguished by different levels of indentation. These differences clearly indicate the direction of your speech. They also enhance your recollection of points and make it easy for you to follow the outline as you speak.

Pay Close Attention to Coordination and Subordination

Outlines are based on the principles of **coordination and subordination**. These principles refer to the logical placement of ideas relative to their importance to one another. Ideas that are *coordinate* are given equal weight; coordinate points are indicated by their parallel alignment. An idea that is *subordinate* to another is given relatively less weight; as mentioned earlier, subordinate points are indicated by their indentation below the more important points.

As you review your outline, evaluate whether any of your main points more properly belong as subpoints to other main points. In a speech draft about interviewing and etiquette training, University of Oklahoma student Amber Pointer found this to be the case when she saw that she had created six main points:

I.   Interviewing is competitive and requires preparation.

II. As in sports, interviewing requires training to compete well against others.

III. When you sell yourself in an interview, you want to make your best impression.

IV. When you take a course on interviewing, you become more competitive.

V.   Dressing appropriately is critical to making a good impression.

VI. Proper table manners are key to making a positive impression during a luncheon interview.

Upon examination, Amber realized that main points II and IV are actually subpoints of point I:

I.   Interviewing is competitive and requires preparation.

~~II.~~ A. As in sports, interviewing requires training to compete well against others.

~~IV.~~ B. When you take a course on interviewing, you become more competitive.

Similarly, points V and VI are subpoints of point III (which now becomes main point II):

II. When you sell yourself in an interview, you want to make your best impression.

~~V.~~ A. Dressing appropriately is critical to making a good impression.

~~VI.~~ B. Proper table manners are key to making a positive impression during a luncheon interview.

As she examined her outline, Amber realized that she had introduced ideas toward the end of her speech that properly supported the first main point and presented material early on that was actually subordinate to her second main point. Rather than six main points, Amber's speech in fact consists of just two.

Strive for a Unified, Coherent, and Balanced Outline

 WEB Outliner

A well-organized speech is characterized by unity, coherence, and balance. Try to adhere to these principles as you arrange your speech points.

Unity

There is a type of skilled speaker—often a preacher—who routinely seems to meander off point, only to surprise the audience at the end by artfully tying each idea to the speech theme. Such speeches retain the quality of unity, if only at the last minute. A speech exhibits *unity* when it contains only those points that are implied by the purpose and thesis statements. Nothing is extraneous or tangential. Each main point supports the thesis, and each supporting point provides evidence for the main points. Each subpoint supports each supporting point. Each point focuses on a single idea.

Coherence

A speech exhibits *coherence* when it is organized clearly and logically, using the principles of coordination and subordination. The speech body should follow logically from the introduction, and the conclusion should follow logically from the body. Within the body of the speech itself, main points should follow logically from the thesis statement, and supporting points should follow logically from the main points. Transitions serve as logical bridges that help establish coherence.

Balance

One common mistake on the part of many inexperienced public speakers is to give overly lengthy coverage to one point and insufficient attention to others. Another mistake is to give scanty evidence in the body of the speech after presenting an impressive introduction. Yet another error is jumping right into the speech without properly introducing the topic. The principle of *balance* suggests that appropriate emphasis or weight be given to each part of the speech relative to the other parts and to the theme.

The body of a speech should always be the longest part, and the introduction and the conclusion should be roughly the same length. Stating the main points in parallel form is one aspect of balance. *Assigning each main point at least two supporting points is another.* Students often forget this and assign a main point only one subpoint. If you have only one subpoint, consider how you might incorporate it into the superior point. Think of a main point as a tabletop and supporting points as table legs; without at least two legs, the table cannot stand.

DO THE SPEECH POINTS REFLECT UNITY, COHERENCE, AND BALANCE?

_____ 1. Does each main point refer directly to your specific purpose or thesis statement?

_____ 2. Does each point focus on a single idea?

_____ 3. Do your main points follow logically from your thesis statement?

_____ 4. Do your supporting points follow logically from the main points?

_____ 5. Do you spend roughly the same amount of time on each main point?

_____ 6. Is each main point substantiated by at least two supporting points?

_____ 7. Are the speech points stated in parallel form?

Use Transitions to Give Direction to the Speech

WEB Links

Transitions are words, phrases, or sentences that tie the speech ideas together and enable the speaker to move smoothly from one point to the next. Considered the "neurosystem" of speeches, transitions (also called **connectives**) provide consistency of movement from one point to the next and cue the audience that a new point will be made. (See Table 12.3 for a list of common transitions.)

TABLE 12.3   Transitional Words and Phrases

Function	Example
To show comparisons	similarly, in the same way, likewise, in comparison, just as
To contrast ideas	on the other hand, and yet, at the same time, in spite of, however, in contrast
To illustrate cause and effect	as a result, therefore, hence, because, thus, consequently, so the evidence shows, for this reason
To illustrate sequence of time or events	first, second, third, following this, before, after, later, earlier, at present, in the past, until now, tomorrow, next week, eventually
To indicate explanation	for example, to illustrate, in other words, to simplify, to clarify
To indicate additional examples	not only, in addition to, let's look at
To emphasize significance	most important, above all, remember, keep in mind
To summarize	as we have seen, altogether, in summary, finally, in conclusion, let me conclude by saying

As you develop your speech, think about creating transitions to move listeners from one main point to the next, from main points to supporting points, and from one supporting point to another supporting point. Transitions are also used to move from the introduction to the body of the speech, and from the body to the conclusion. Transitions can take the form of full sentences, phrases, or single words.

Use Transitions between Main Points

When moving from one main point to another, **full-sentence transitions** are especially effective. For example, to move from main point I in a speech about sales contests ("Top management should sponsor sales contests to halt the decline in sales over the past two years") to main point II ("Sales contests will lead to better sales presentations"), the speaker might use the following transition:

> Next, let's look at exactly what sales contests can do for us.

Very often, a speaker will transition from one point to the next by first restating the points just covered and then previewing the material to be covered next in what's called a **"restate-forecast" transition**:

> Now that we've established a need for sales contests (*restatement*), let's look at what sales contests can do for us (*forecast*).

Another frequently used full-sentence transition is the **rhetorical question**. Rather than inviting actual responses, rhetorical questions make the audience think (see Chapter 15):

> Will contests be too expensive? Well, actually . . .

> How do the costs of contests stack up against the expense of training new people?

Use Transitions between Supporting Points

Transitions between supporting points can also be handled with full sentences, or with phrases or single words. For example, to move from supporting point A ("Sales personnel will be motivated by competition") to supporting point B ("Contests are relatively inexpensive") the speaker might use the following transition:

> Another way that sales competitions will benefit us is by their relative cost effectiveness.

Likewise, the speaker could state the transition from supporting point B1 ("Contests cost less than losses in sales revenues") to supporting point B2 ("Contests cost less than training new sales staff") as follows:

> In addition, sales competitions are less expensive than training new people.

Conjunctions or phrases or single words (also called **signposts**) such as the following can be just as effective:

Next, . . .

First, . . . (second, third, and so forth)

We now turn . . .

Finally, let's consider . . .

If you think that's shocking, . . .

Similarly, . . .

Use Previews and Summaries as Transitions

Previews are transitions that tell the audience what to expect next. In a speech introduction, the **preview statement** briefly describes what will be covered in the body of the speech (see Chapter 15). Within the body itself, **internal previews** can be used to alert audience members to a shift from one main point or idea to another:

> Victoria Woodhull was a pioneer in many respects. Not only was she the first woman to run her own brokerage firm, but she was also the first to run for the presidency of the United States, though few people know this. Let's see how she accomplished these feats. . . .

Similar to the internal preview, the **internal summary** draws together ideas before the speaker proceeds to another speech point. Internal summaries help listeners review and evaluate the thread of the theme thus far:

> It should be clear that the kind of violence we've witnessed in the schools and in our communities has a deeper root cause than the availability of handguns. Our young children are crying out for a sense of community, of relatedness and meaning, that they just aren't finding in the institutions that are meant to serve them.

(See Chapter 14, "Outlining the Speech," to learn how to include transitions in the outline of your speech.)

USING TRANSITIONS

_____ 1. Do you include enough transitions to adequately guide your listeners through your speech?

_____ 2. Do you use transitions to signal comparisons, cause and effect, sequences in time, contrasting ideas, summaries, and so forth?

_____ 3. Do you use transitions when moving from one main point to the next?

_____ 4. Do you use internal previews and summaries where appropriate?

_____ 5. Do you use transitions between the introduction and the body and between the body and the conclusion of the speech?

SELF-ASSESSMENT CHECKLIST

Using Transitions to Guide Your Listeners

Transitions direct your listeners from one point to another in your speech, leading them forward along a logical path while reinforcing key ideas along the way. At a bare minimum, plan on using transitions to move between:

- The introduction and the body of the speech
- The main points
- The subpoints, whenever appropriate
- The body of the speech and the conclusion

Introduction

I.   Today I'll explore the steps you can take to create a greener campus . . .

(**Transition:** Let's begin by considering what "going green" actually means.)

Body

I.   "Going green" means taking action to promote and maintain a healthy environment.

(**Transition:** So how do you go green?)

A.   Get informed—understand what is physically happening to your planet

(**Transition:** Understanding the issues is only part of going green, however. Perhaps most important, . . .)

B.   Recognize that change starts here, on campus, with you. . . .

While transitions help guide your listeners from point to point, they can also do a lot more, including:

 Introduce propositions (major speech points)

❷ Illustrate cause and effect

❸ Signal explanations and examples

❹ Emphasize, repeat, compare, or contrast ideas

❺ Summarize and preview information

❻ Suggest conclusions from evidence

Following is an excerpt from a working outline on a speech about campuses going green. Note how the student edits himself to ensure that he (1) uses transitions to help listeners follow along and retain his speech points and (2) uses transitions strategically to achieve his goal of persuading the audience.

1 Student inserts a transition (**rhetorical question**) to introduce a new proposition (e.g., main point).

2 Student realizes he needs to insert this transitional phrase to signal a **cause-effect relationship**.

1 Student uses a transition to **move to the next proposition**.

3 This transitional phrase **introduces additional examples**.

4 **5** Student inserts an **internal summary** to help listeners retain information and transition to the next main point.

5 Student inserts an **internal preview** to move to the next main point.

6 Student inserts a transition to signal a **shift to his concluding point**.

(Transition: Why are environmentalists targeting college campuses?)

I. College campuses generate the waste equivalent of many large towns . . .

(Transition: As a result. . .)

   A. Colleges face disposal issues, especially of electronics . . .

   B. Administrators face decisions about mounting energy costs . . .

(**Transition:** Following are some ideas to create a greener campus. First . . .)

II. Promote a campus-wide recycling program

(**Transition:** For example . . .)

   A. Decrease the availability of bottled water and disposable . . .

   B. Insist on recycling bins at all residence halls . . .

   C. Encourage computer centers to recycle . . .

(Transition: Recycling is a critical part of going green. Decreasing the consumption of plastic and paper, installing recycling bins, and responsibly disposing of print cartridges will make a huge difference. Another aspect of going green is using sustainable energy . . .)

III. Lobby administrators to investigate solar, wind, and geothermal . . .

   A. Make an argument for "eco-dorms . . ."

   B. Explore alternative heating . . .

(Transition: So far, we've talked about practical actions we can take to encourage a greener lifestyle on campus, but what about beyond the campus?)

IV. Get involved at the town government level

   A. Town-grown committees . . .

   B. Speak up and voice your concerns . . .

(Transition: As you can see, we have work to do . . .)

Conclusion

I. If we want our children and our children's children to live to see a healthy earth, we must take action now . . .

CHAPTER 13

Types of Organizational Arrangements

Once you have selected the main points for your speech, you must decide on a type of organizational arrangement (or combination of arrangements) for them. Speeches make use of at least a dozen different organizational arrangements of main and supporting points. Here we look at seven commonly used patterns for all forms of speeches: chronological, spatial, causal (cause-effect), problem-solution, topical, narrative, and circular. These patterns offer an organized way to link points together to maximum effect. In Chapter 27, you will find three additional patterns designed specifically for persuasive speeches: *Monroe's motivated sequence, refutation,* and *comparative advantage.*

As you review these organizational designs, bear in mind that there are multiple ways to organize a speech. Each method communicates something different, even if the topic is the same. Regardless of the specific pattern, studies confirm that the way you organize your ideas affects your audience's understanding of them, so you'll want to make use of a pattern.[1] Your goal should be to choose one that your audience can easily follow and that will best achieve your speech purpose.

CHOOSING AN ORGANIZATIONAL PATTERN

Does your speech . . .

✓ Describe a series of developments in time or a set of actions that occur sequentially? Use the *chronological pattern of arrangement.*

✓ Describe or explain the physical arrangement of a place, a scene, or an object? Use the *spatial pattern of arrangement.*

✓ Explain or demonstrate a topic in terms of its underlying causes or effects? Use the *causal (cause-effect) pattern of arrangement.*

✓ Demonstrate the nature and significance of a problem and justify a proposed solution? Use the *problem-solution pattern of arrangement.*

✓ Stress natural divisions in a topic, in which points can be moved to emphasize audience needs and interests? Use a *topical pattern of arrangement.*

✓ Convey ideas through a story, using character, plot, and settings? Use a *narrative pattern of arrangement,* perhaps in combination with another pattern.

✓ Stress a particular line of reasoning that leads from one point to another, and then back to the thesis? Use a *circular pattern of arrangement.*

Arranging Speech Points Chronologically

Some speech topics lend themselves well to the arrangement of main points according to their occurrence in time relative to each other. The **chronological pattern of arrangement** (also called the *temporal pattern*) follows the natural sequential order of the main points. To switch points around would make the arrangement appear unnatural and might confuse the audience. Topics that describe a series of events in time (such as events leading to the adoption of a peace treaty) or develop in line with a set pattern of actions or tasks (such as plans for building a model car, procedures for admitting patients to a hospital) call out to be organized according to a chronological pattern of arrangement. A speech describing the development of the World Wide Web, for example, calls for a chronological, or time-ordered, sequence of main points:

THESIS STATEMENT: The Internet evolved from a small network designed for military and academic scientists into a vast system of networks used by billions of people around the globe.

    I.   The Internet was first conceived in 1962 as the ARPANET to promote the sharing of research among scientists in the United States.

    II.   In the 1980s a team created TCP/IP, a language that could link networks, and the Internet as we know it was born.

    III. At the end of the cold war, the ARPANET was decommissioned, and the World Wide Web made up the bulk of Internet traffic.[2]

In addition to topics that involve timelines, the chronological arrangement is appropriate for any topic that involves a series of sequential steps. A speaker might describe the steps in a research project on fruit flies, for example, or explain the steps in a recipe.

Arranging Speech Points Using a Spatial Pattern

When describing the physical arrangement of a place, a scene, or an object, logic suggests that the main points be arranged in order of their physical proximity or direction relative to each other. This calls for the **spatial pattern of arrangement**. For example, you can select a spatial arrangement when your speech provides the audience with a "tour" of a particular place:

THESIS STATEMENT: El Morro National Monument in New Mexico is captivating for its variety of natural and historical landmarks.

    I.   Visitors first encounter an abundant variety of plant life native to the high-country desert.

    II. Soon visitors come upon an age-old watering hole that has receded beneath the 200-foot cliffs.

    III. Beyond are the famous cliff carvings made by hundreds of travelers over several centuries of exploration in the Southwest.

    IV. At the farthest reaches of the magnificent park are the ancient ruins of a pueblo dwelling secured high atop "the Rock."

In a speech describing the spread of geothermal heating and cooling systems across various regions of the country, a student speaker uses the following spatial arrangement:

THESIS STATEMENT: Sales of geothermal systems have grown in every region of the country.

    I. Sales are strongest in the Eastern Zone.

    II. Sales are growing at a rate of 10 percent quarterly in the Central Zone.

    III. Sales are up slightly in the Mountain Zone.

    IV. Sales in the Western Zone are lagging behind the other regions.

Arranging Speech Points Using a Causal (Cause-Effect) Pattern

Some speech topics represent cause-effect relationships. Examples might include events leading to higher interest rates, reasons students drop out of college, or causes of spousal abuse. In speeches on topics such as these, the speaker relates something known to be a "cause" to its "effects." The main points in a **causal (cause-effect) pattern of arrangement** usually take the following form:

    I. Cause

    II. Effect

Sometimes a topic can be discussed in terms of multiple causes for a single effect, or a single cause for multiple effects:

Multiple Causes for a Single Effect (Reasons Students Drop Out of College)	**Single Cause for Multiple Effects (Reasons Students Drop Out of College)**
I. Cause 1 (lack of funds)	I. Cause (lack of funds)
II. Cause 2 (unsatisfactory social life)	II. Effect 1 (lowered earnings over lifetime)

III. Cause 3 (unsatisfactory academic performance)

IV. Effect (drop out of college)

III. Effect 2 (decreased job satisfaction over lifetime)

IV. Effect 3 (increased stress level over lifetime)

Some topics are best understood by presenting listeners with the effect(s) first and the cause(s) subsequently. In an informative speech on the 1988 explosion of Pan Am flight 103 over Lockerbie, Scotland, for instance, a student speaker arranges his main points in this manner:

THESIS STATEMENT: The explosion of Pan Am flight 103 over Lockerbie, Scotland, killed 270 people and resulted in the longest-running aviation investigation in history.

I.   (Effect) Two hundred and fifty-nine passengers and crew members died; an additional eleven people on the ground perished.

II. (Effect) Longest-running aviation investigation in history.

III. (Cause) Court found cause of explosion was a terrorist act, a bomb planted by Libyan citizen Al Megrahi.

IV. (Cause) Many people believe that Megrahi did not act alone, if he acted at all.

In this case, the speaker presents the effects of the airplane explosion as the first two main points. He subsequently addresses the causes of the explosion in the ensuing main points.

Arranging Speech Points Using a Problem-Solution Pattern

The **problem-solution pattern of arrangement** organizes main points both to demonstrate the nature and significance of a problem and to provide justification for a proposed solution. This type of arrangement can be as general as two main points:

I.   Problem (define what it is)

II. Solution (offer a way to overcome the problem)

But many problem-solution speeches require more than two points to adequately explain the problem and to substantiate the recommended solution:

I.   The nature of the problem (identify its causes, incidence, etc.)

II. Effects of the problem (explain why it's a problem, for whom, etc.)

III. Unsatisfactory solutions (discuss those that have not worked)

IV. Proposed solution (explain why it's expected to work)

Following is a partial outline of a persuasive speech about cyber-bullying arranged in a problem-solution format (for more on the problem-solution pattern, see Chapter 27):

THESIS STATEMENT: To combat cyber-bullying on the Internet, we need to educate the public about it, report it when it happens, and punish the offenders.

MAIN POINT: I. Nature of online bullying
   A. Types of activities involved
      1. Name-calling, insults
      2. Circulation of embarrassing pictures
      3. Sharing of private information
      4. Threats
   B. Incidence of bullying
   C. Profile of offenders

MAIN POINT: II. Effects of online bullying on victims
   A. Acting out in school
   B. Feeling unsafe in school
   C. Skipping school
   D. Experiencing depression

MAIN POINT: III. Unsuccessful attempts at solving online bullying
   A. Let offenders and victims work it out on their own
   B. Ignore problem, assuming it will go away

MAIN POINT: IV. Ways to solve online bullying
   A. Educate in schools
   B. Report incidences to authorities
   C. Suspend or expel offenders

Arranging Speech Points Topically

 Chapter quizzes

When each of the main points is a subtopic or category of the speech topic, the **topical pattern of arrangement** (also called the *categorical pattern*) may be most appropriate. Consider preparing an informative speech about choosing Chicago as a place to establish a career. You plan to emphasize three reasons for choosing Chicago: the strong economic climate of the city, its cultural variety, and its accessible public transportation. Since these three points are of relatively equal importance, they can be arranged in any order without negatively affecting one another. For example:

THESIS STATEMENT: Chicago is an excellent place to establish a career.

   I.   Accessible transportation

   II.   Cultural variety

   III.   Economic stability

This is not to say that, when using a topical arrangement, you should arrange the main points without careful consideration. You may decide to arrange the points in ascending or descending order according to their relative importance, complexity, or timeliness. Perhaps you have determined that listeners' main concern is the city's economic stability, followed by an interest in its cultural variety and accessible transportation. You may then decide to arrange the points in the order of the audience's most immediate needs and interests:

   I.   Economic stability

   II.   Cultural variety

   III.   Accessible transportation

Topical arrangements give you the greatest freedom to structure main points according to how you wish to present your topic. You can approach a topic by dividing it into two or more categories, for example. You can lead with the strongest evidence or leave your most compelling points until you near the conclusion. If your topic does not call out for one of the other patterns described in this chapter, be sure to experiment with the topical pattern.

Arranging Speech Points Using a Narrative Pattern

Storytelling is often a natural and effective way to get your message across. In the **narrative pattern of arrangement**, the speech consists of a story or a series of short stories, replete with characters, settings, plot, and vivid imagery.

In practice, a speech built largely upon a story (or series of stories) is likely to incorporate elements of other designs described in this chapter. For example, you might organize the main points of the story in an effect-cause design, in which you first reveal why something happened (such as a drunken driving accident) and then describe the events that led up to the accident (the causes).

Whatever the structure, simply telling a story is no guarantee of giving a good speech. Any speech should include a clear thesis, a preview, well-organized main points, and effective transitions. For example, in a speech entitled "Tales of the Grandmothers,"[3] Anita Taylor uses the real-life history of her grand-mothers to illustrate how women in the United States have always worked, even if they were unpaid. Although the story dominates the speech, Taylor frequently leaves off and picks up the story's thread in order to orient her listeners and drive home her theme. For example, in addition to explicitly stating her thesis, Taylor pauses to preview main points:

> My grandmothers illustrate the points I want to make. . . .

Taylor also makes frequent use of transitions, including internal previews, summaries, and simple signposts, to help her listeners stay on track:

> But, let's go on with Luna Puffer Squire Nairn's story.

Taylor also pauses in her story to signal the conclusion:

> So here we are today. . . . And finally . . .

Arranging Speech Points Using a Circular Pattern

A pattern that is particularly useful when you want listeners to follow a particular line of reasoning is the **circular pattern of arrangement**. Here, you develop one idea, which leads to another, which leads to a third, and so forth, until you arrive back at the speech thesis.[4] In a speech on the role that friendship plays in physical and mental well-being, a student speaker showed how acts of consideration and kindness lead to more friendships, which in turn lead to more social support, which then results in improved mental and physical health. Each main point leads directly into another main point, with the final main point leading back to the thesis.

Subpoints Need Not Match the Pattern of Main Points

Once you select an organizational arrangement, you can proceed to flesh out the main points with subordinate ideas. The pattern of organization you select for your subpoints need not always follow the pattern you select for your main points. Do keep your main points in one pattern, but feel free to use other patterns for subpoints when it makes sense to do so. For instance, for a speech about the recent history of tattooing in the United States, you might choose a chronological pattern to organize the main points but switch to a cause-effect arrangement for some of your subpoints about why tattooing is on the rise today. (See the Checklist on p. 194 for descriptions of patterns.) Organization, whether of main points or subpoints, should be driven by what's most effective for the particular rhetorical situation.

EVALUATING ORGANIZATIONAL PATTERNS

_____ 1 Does the arrangement move the speech along in a logical and convincing fashion?

_____ 2. Do my ideas flow naturally from one point to another, leading to a satisfying conclusion?

_____ 3. Does the organizational pattern lend my speech momentum?

_____ 4. Does the organizational plan convey the information listeners expect or need in a way that they will be able to grasp?

A CULTURAL PERSPECTIVE

Arrangement Formats and Audience Diversity

Studies confirm that the way you organize your ideas affects your audience's understanding of them.[1] Another factor that may affect how we organize relationships among ideas is culture.[2] Are certain organizational formats better suited to certain cultures? Consider the chronological arrangement format. It assumes a largely North American and Western European orientation to time, because these cultures generally view time as a linear (or chronological) progression in which one event follows another along a continuum, with events strictly segmented. In contrast, some Asian, African, and Latin American cultures view time more fluidly, with events occurring simultaneously or cyclically.[3] When a speaker uses a chronological arrangement of the typical linear fashion, audience members from cultures with different time orientations may have difficulty making the connections among the main points. For these audiences, an alternative arrangement, such as the narrative or circular pattern, may be a more appropriate form in which to express speech ideas.

1. R. G. Smith, "Effects of Speech Organization upon Attitudes of College Students," _Speech Monographs_ 18 (1951): 547–49; E. Thompson, "An Experimental Investigation of the Relative Effectiveness of Organizational Structure in Oral Communication," _Southern Speech Journal_ 26 (1960): 59–69.

2. Devorah A. Lieberman, _Public Speaking in the Multicultural Environment_, 2nd ed. (Englewood Cliffs, N.J.: Prentice Hall, 1997).

3. Edward T. Hall, _The Dance of Life: Other Dimensions of Time_ (New York: Doubleday, 1983); J. K. Burgoon, D. B. Buller, and W. G. Woodall, _Nonverbal Communication: The Unspoken Dialogue_ (New York: Harper & Row, 1989).

CHAPTER 14

Outlining the Speech

Outlines are enormously helpful in putting together a speech, providing a framework within which to organize your research and a blueprint for your presentation. By plotting ideas in hierarchical fashion (such that coordinate ideas receive relatively equal weight and subordinate ideas relatively less so), and by using indentation to visually represent this hierarchy, you can't help but examine the underlying logic of the speech and the relationship of ideas to one another.[1] (For a review of the principles of coordination and subordination and the mechanics of outlining, see Chapter 12.)

Plan on Creating Two Outlines

WEB Chapter quizzes

As you develop a speech, you will actually create two outlines: a working outline (also called a *preparation* or *rough* outline), and a speaking, or delivery, outline. The purpose of the **working outline** is to organize and firm up main points and, using the evidence you've collected, develop supporting points to substantiate them. It is at this point that you decide what supporting material you want to keep or need to add, and how it can best demonstrate your central idea. Completed, the working outline will contain your entire speech, organized and supported to your satisfaction.

The **speaking outline** (also called a *delivery outline*) is the one you will use when you are practicing and actually presenting the speech. Speaking outlines, which contain your ideas in condensed form, are much briefer than working outlines. Table 14.1 provides an overview of the steps involved in outlining a speech.

Before we look at the working outline, let's consider the three types of wording formats speakers use to outline speeches.

Use Sentences, Phrases, or Key Words

Speeches can be outlined in complete sentences, phrases, or key words.

The Sentence Outline Format

Sentence outlines represent the full "script," or text, of the speech. In a **sentence outline**, each main and supporting point is stated in sentence form as a declarative sentence (one that makes an assertion about a subject). Often, these sentences are stated in much the same way the speaker wants to express the idea during delivery.

TABLE 14.1 Steps in Organizing and Outlining the Speech

1. Create the Main Speech Points
2. Note Any Obvious Subpoints
3. Select an Organizational Pattern
4. Create a Working Outline
   - Finalize Main Points to Express the Key Speech Ideas
   - Use Research to Support the Main Ideas with Subpoints and, if Needed, Sub-subpoints
   - Review the Final Outline for Coordination and Subordination of Main and Supporting Points
5. Transfer the Working Outline to a Speaking Outline Using Phrases or Key Words

Generally, sentence outlines are used for working outlines, reflecting much of the text of the speech, but not for speaking outlines, which use phrases or key words. The following is an excerpt in sentence format from a speech by Mark B. McClellan on keeping prescription drugs safe:[2]

I. The prescription drug supply is under unprecedented attack from a variety of increasingly sophisticated threats.

   A. Technologies for counterfeiting—ranging from pill molding to dyes—have improved across the board.

   B. Inadequately regulated Internet sites have become major portals for unsafe and illegal drugs.

The Phrase Outline Format

A **phrase outline** uses partial construction of the sentence form of each point. The idea is that the speaker is so familiar with the speech that a glance at a few words associated with each point will serve as a reminder of exactly what to say. A section of McClellan's sentence outline would appear as follows in phrase outline form:

I. Drug supply under attack

   A. Counterfeiting technologies more sophisticated

   B. Unregulated Internet sites

The Key-Word Outline Format

The **key-word outline** uses the smallest possible units of understanding to outline the main and supporting points. In this format, each speech point contains just a few cue words to spur your memory.

A section of McClellan's outline would appear as follows in key-word outline form:

I. Threats

   A. Counterfeiting

   B. Internet

Use a Key-Word Outline for Optimal Eye Contact

The type of outline you select will affect how well you deliver the speech. Of the three outline formats, sentence outlines permit the least amount of eye contact, which is why they aren't recommended for use during delivery. Eye contact is essential to the successful delivery of a speech. While sentence outlines offer the most protection against memory lapses, they may prompt you to look at the outline rather than at the audience, thereby cutting down on eye contact. The less you rely on your outline notes, the more eye contact you can have with audience members. For this reason, key-word or phrase outlines are recommended over sentence outlines in delivering most speeches, with the key-word outline often being the preferred format. Key-word outlines permit the greatest degree of eye contact, greater freedom of movement, and better control of your thoughts and actions than either sentence or phrase outlines. They are also less conspicuous to the audience.

If there are points in your speech where you want to note exact quotations or precisely state complicated facts or figures, you can write those out in full sentences within the key-word outline. Sentences may help under the following conditions:

1. When the issue is highly controversial or emotion-laden for listeners and precise wording is needed to make the point as clear as possible
2. When the material is highly technical and exact sentence structure is critical to an accurate representation of the material
3. When a good deal of material relies on quotations and facts from another source that must be conveyed precisely as worded

Even with the inclusion of an occasional sentence, if at any time during the speech you experience stage fright or a lapse in memory, a key-word outline may not be of much help. This is why preparation is essential when using one. You must be confident in knowing the topic and the speech arrangement well enough to deliver the speech extemporaneously. An extemporaneous speech is carefully planned and practiced in advance and then delivered from a key-word or phrase outline (see Chapter 18).

Create a Working Outline First

 WEB Outliner

Begin drafting your speech with a working outline. Working outlines are meant to be changed as you work through the mass of information you've collected. As you progress, you will no doubt rearrange points and add or omit material before you are satisfied that you have adequately demonstrated your speech thesis.

The completed working outline will give you confidence that you've satisfactorily fleshed out your ideas. Instead of worrying about whether you will have enough to say, or whether your speech will be well organized, you'll have an accurate picture of what you'll be able to communicate. Rather than writing out the speech word for word, your instructor may prefer that you use full sentences for the main points and phrases for subpoints. The key is to focus on charting a well-supported document containing all of your claims and research.

Separate the Introduction and Conclusion from the Body

Whether you are drafting a working or speaking outline, prepare the body of the speech before the introduction and the conclusion, and keep the introduction and conclusion *separate from* the main points. The introduction is the preface; the conclusion is the epilogue. The actual main points—or body—of the speech come between the preface and the epilogue, or the head and the feet.

In outlines, treatments of the introduction can vary. You can use such labels as *Attention Getter, Thesis, Credibility Statement,* and *Preview* to indicate how you will gain the audience's attention, introduce the thesis, establish your credibility, and preview the speech topic and main points (see Chapter 15 for more on developing the introduction). Alternatively, your instructor may prefer that you assign the introduction its own numbering system or simply write it out in paragraph format.

Similarly, in the conclusion you can indicate where you signal the close of the speech, summarize main points, reiterate the thesis and purpose, and leave the audience with something to think about or offer a call to action—or, again, assign it its own numbering system or write it out. (See Chapter 16 for more on developing the conclusion.)

List Your Sources

As you work on the outline, clearly indicate to yourself where speech points require source credit. Directly after the point, either insert a footnote *or* enclose in parentheses enough of the reference to be able to retrieve it in full (see sample outlines in this chapter). Once you complete the outline, prepare a bibliography. Instructors may prefer that you order the references alphabetically and place them on a sheet titled "Works Cited"; or that you create a "Works Consulted" list, including all sources consulted rather than just those cited in the speech. For guidelines on what to include in a source note, see Chapters 9 and 10 (especially the From Source to Speech sections); see Appendices E–I for particular citation styles. For directions on what to include in an oral citation, see Chapter 11.

Create a Title

As the last step, assign the speech a title, one that informs the audience of the subject in a way that invites them to listen to or read it. Neatly crafted titles communicate the essence of a speech. At times, you might even refer to the title during your speech, as a means of previewing the topic or harkening back to the subject of the speech.

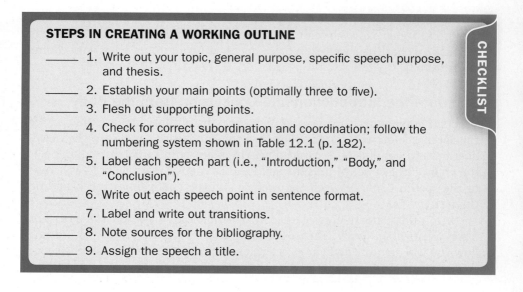

STEPS IN CREATING A WORKING OUTLINE

_____ 1. Write out your topic, general purpose, specific speech purpose, and thesis.

_____ 2. Establish your main points (optimally three to five).

_____ 3. Flesh out supporting points.

_____ 4. Check for correct subordination and coordination; follow the numbering system shown in Table 12.1 (p. 182).

_____ 5. Label each speech part (i.e., "Introduction," "Body," and "Conclusion").

_____ 6. Write out each speech point in sentence format.

_____ 7. Label and write out transitions.

_____ 8. Note sources for the bibliography.

_____ 9. Assign the speech a title.

Sample Working Outline

The following outline is from a speech delivered by John Coulter at Salt Lake Community College. It uses the sentence format and includes labeled transitions as well as the wording John will use to cite his sources. Brief source references appear in parentheses (e.g., FTC, March 2010) for ease in assembling a bibliography.

Staying Ahead of Spyware

JOHN COULTER
Salt Lake Community College

TOPIC: Problems and solutions associated with spyware

SPECIFIC PURPOSE: To inform my audience members of the dangers of spyware so that they may take appropriate steps to prevent infection

THESIS STATEMENT: Computer and smartphone users must understand the evolving nature of spyware and what it can do in order to take the necessary steps to protect themselves.

Introduction

  I.   Do you worry about identity theft online?

 II.   Are you anxious about the security of your passwords and credit card numbers? _(Attention getter)_

III. Many of you are aware of software known as spyware that can install itself on your computer and smartphone without your knowledge and harvest sensitive information, and many of you have taken steps to protect yourself.

IV. Spyware is constantly evolving, however, and to stay safe, we need to learn about and arm ourselves against the threats it poses. *(Thesis statement)*

V. Today, I'll talk about what forms spyware takes, how it gets into your computer, the harm it causes, and how to keep your computer and smartphone from becoming infected by it. *(Preview)*

TRANSITION: So, what is the state of spyware today?

Body

I. Spyware is a type of privacy invasion software known as *malware*.

A. According to a history of spyware published on the Federal Trade Commission's Web site, until the year 2000, *spyware* referred to monitoring devices on cameras. (FTC, OnGuardOnline.gov)

   1. The term first appeared in a software context in an ad for the security program *ZoneAlarm*.

   2. Today, *spyware* signifies any computer code that installs itself on your computer, gathers data from it, and sends it back to a remote computer *without your consent*.

B. Some types of spyware track your Web-browsing habits, selling this information to marketers.

C. Certain types of spyware capture your passwords and other sensitive information, potentially leading to identity theft.

D. Another type of spyware program can record everything you type or text.

TRANSITION: Many people are confused about the differences between spyware and other types of malware, such as viruses and adware.

E. According to a CNET video, spyware differs from viruses in a couple of ways. (CNET.com video)

   1. Individuals generally write viruses in order to brag about causing damage whereas spyware often is written by corporate teams to make money.

   2. Viruses have been around for decades and are illegal, whereas legislation outlawing spyware, such as the Internet Spyware Prevention Act (I-SPY), has thus far failed passage, according to GovTrack.us, a Web site that tracks the status of federal legislation. (govtrack.us)

    F.   *Adware* refers to programs that display ads on your computer. (*PC Magazine*)

       1.   Adware may be annoying, but it doesn't contain software that can track you.

       2.   On the other hand, spyware does what its name suggests—it spies on you, sending the stolen data to "the lair of the evil creator," as Neil Rubenking puts it. ("Nine Ways")

TRANSITION: You may be wondering how spyware gets into your computer.

II. Different forms of spyware take various routes into your computer, causing little harm or utter havoc, depending on the software and the sender's intent.

    A.   Spyware installs itself silently, often "piggybacking" onto downloadable programs, such as free file-sharing applications and games.

    B.   Links in pop-up ads and the "unsubscribe" button in spam are known sources.

    C.   One type of software, called "rogue" software or "scareware," appears as a legitimate-seeming antispyware protection program, but when downloaded, tricks the user into installing spyware.

    D.   A particularly harmful spyware—keystroke loggers—captures your keystrokes, enabling actual spying as well as identity theft.

       1.   People may deliberately install keystroke loggers to spy on their spouses, children, employees, or students.

       2.   Reporting in the June 29, 2010, edition of *Newsweek,* Jessica Ramirez writes that keystroke loggers can be attached to smartphone apps.

TRANSITION: We've seen how spyware can install itself on computers and smartphones, and how it can grab hold of personal data. This same malware lurks on social networking sites such as Facebook and Twitter.

    E.   Spyware represents a real threat on social media sites, as cyber criminals seek to send malicious code into a wide audience.

       1.   Clicking on pop-up ads and other links on your "Wall" may download the programs.

       2.   Invitations to take certain quizzes or join certain groups can activate spyware.

III. Users can learn to recognize the symptoms and problems associated with spyware.

A. One sign of infiltration, according to Google's Web search help page, is a constant stream of pop-up ads. (Google)

B. Strange toolbars may appear on the desktop.

C. Browser settings may be hijacked, forcing users to strange Web pages.

D. The computer may behave sluggishly, files may disappear, or the computer may crash.

TRANSITION: Now for the good news. You can protect yourself from spyware.

IV. Prevention is the best way to avoid spyware's harmful and potentially dangerous effects.

A. There are some good antispyware programs on the market.

1. For example, Microsoft now distributes *Windows Defender* (an antispyware product) with its operating systems and offers a free program called *Microsoft Security Essentials*.

2. *PC Magazine*'s Editor's Choice for stand-alone malware protection is *Spyware Doctor with Antivirus;* its choice for security suite is *Norton Internet Security*. (*PC Magazine,* "Free Virus and Spyware Protection")

3. Free antispyware software, according to *PC Magazine,* does not do as thorough a job as commercial software, and some free programs actually contain spyware.

TRANSITION: Along with the antispyware software you can install, what else can you do?

B. Keep your browser up-to-date to take advantage of security updates.

C. Don't install any software without reading the fine print, or first checking for reviews of it on a site such as CNET.

D. Download free software or any smartphone apps only from sites you know and trust.

E. Don't click on links in pop-up windows.

F. Don't reply to or even open spam or any e–mail that isn't from someone you know.

G. Don't hit the "unsubscribe" button in spam because spyware is known to lurk here.

H. Use the maximum security level settings on social media sites.

I. As suggested on the Web site Identity Theft 911, use strong passwords that can't be easily guessed and do not set up your smartphone to automatically remember them. (Identity Theft 911)

Conclusion

I.   The makers of spyware are in it for the money, so the problem is likely to be long lasting. *(Signals close of speech)*

II. Spyware appears in various guises in order to use personal information stored on computers or smartphones without your consent, but taking the right steps can help you avoid unwanted intrusions. *(Summarizes main points)*

III. One final suggestion is to stay abreast of developments related to spyware and malware by consulting reputable Web sites such as Stopbadware.org and StaySafeOnline.org. *(Leaves audience with something to think about)*

IV. Forewarned is forearmed. Good luck! *(Memorable close)*

Works Cited

Federal Trade Commission. "Spyware: Quick Facts." OnGuardOnline.gov Web site. February 2008. http://www.onguardonline.gov/topics/spyware .aspx.

"H.R. 1525: Internet Spyware (I-SPY) Prevention Act of 2007." GovTrack.us. http://www.govtrack.us/congress/bill.xpd?bill=h110-1525.

Identity Theft 911. "Get Wise about Smartphones." August 2010 Newsletter. http://identitytheft911.org/newsletters/newsletter.ext?sp=11291.

National Science Foundation. "Can Clever Hackers Target Smart Phones?" Accessed August 27, 2010. http://www.nsf.gov/news/news_summ .jsp?cntn_id=116723.

"National Survey: Online Safety Is a Personal Priority for Americans." StaySafe Online.org. Accessed August 30, 2010. http://staysafeonline.mediaroom .com/index.php?s=43&item=62.

Ramirez, Jessica. "Is Someone Spying on Your Cellphone Calls?" *Newsweek,* June 29, 2010, 16.

Rubenking, Neil. "Free Virus and Spyware Protection: What's Right for You?" *PC Magazine,* July 6, 2010. http://www.pcmag.com/article2/ 0,2817,2356509,00.asp.

---. "Nine Ways to Wipe Out Spyware." *PC Magazine,* February 5, 2008. http:// www.pcmag.com/article2/0,2817,2255854,00.asp.

"Suspicious Results and Strange Behavior: Strange Pop-Ups and Other Mal- ware." Google Web Search Help. Accessed August 30, 2010. http://www .google.com/support/websearch/bin/answer.py?hl=en&answer=809.

"Virus vs. Spyware." CNET.com. Videos section. September 1, 2010. http://cnettv .cnet.com/?tag=hdr;snav.

"Watch Out for Fake Virus Alerts." Microsoft Security Web site. Accessed Au- gust 25, 2010. www.microsoft.com/security/antivirus/rogue.aspx.

(TRANSITION: So, what is the state . . .?)

[PAUSE]

Body

   I. Type privacy invasion, *malware*

      A. History, FTC Web site, until 2000, cameras

         1. First software context, ad, *ZoneAlarm*

         2. Today, any code installs, gathers data, sends *without consent*

      B. Some, Web-browsing habits, marketers

      C. Capture passwords, potentially leading, identity theft

      D. Another type records type or text

(TRANSITION: Many people confused . . . differences spyware, malware, viruses, adware.)

      E. CNET video, differs from viruses

         1. Individuals write viruses, brag damage; spyware corporate, make money

         2. Viruses decades old; illegal, fewer laws spyware, federal legislation, I-SPY, failed passage, GovTrack.us

(TRANSITION: Adware, another type, also differs . . .)

      F. Neil Rubenking, *PC Magazine, adware* display ads computer

         1. Annoying, no software, track

         2. Spyware, name suggests—spies, stolen data "the lair of the evil creator"

(TRANSITION: May be wondering . . . into computer . . .)

   II. Different forms, routes, little harm, havoc, software, sender's intent.

      A. Installs silently, "piggybacking" downloadable, free file-sharing, games

      B. Links, pop-up ads, "unsubscribe" spam, known sources

      C. One type, "rogue/scareware," legitimate-seeming antispyware, downloaded, tricks

      D. Keystroke loggers, spying, identity theft [SHOW SLIDE]

         1. Deliberately

         2. June 29, 2010, *Newsweek,* Jessica Ramirez, smartphone apps

(TRANSITION: . . . Malware on social networking sites . . .)

    E. Criminals, malicious code, wide audience
        1. Clicking pop-up, links "Wall," download
        2. Invitations, quizzes, groups, activate spyware

III. Recognize symptoms and problems
    A. Sign infiltration, Google's Web search help page, stream, pop-up ads
    B. Strange toolbars [SHOW SLIDE]
    C. Browser settings hijacked, forcing
    D. Behave sluggishly, unstable
        1. Files, displaced, disappear
        2. Crash

(TRANSITION: Good news . . . protect . . .)

IV. Prevention, best way, harmful, potentially dangerous
    A. Companies advancements, protect users
        1. Microsoft, *Windows Defender* operating systems; free *Microsoft Security Essentials*
        2. *PC Editor's Choice* stand-alone malware *Spyware Doctor with Antivirus*; security suite *Norton Internet Security*
        3. Free antispyware, *PC Magazine:* doesn't do thorough job; contains spyware

(TRANSITION: So along with antispyware software . . .)

    B. Browser up-to-date, security updates
    C. Don't install, fine print, testing CNET
    D. Software, smartphone apps, know, trust
    E. Don't click links pop-up
    F. Reply, open spam, e-mail
    G. "Unsubscribe" spam, lurk here
    H. Maximum security, social media
    I. Strong passwords easily guessed; not smartphone automatically remember
  [PAUSE]

Conclusion

I. Money, problem long-lasting

II. Spyware guises use personal stored computers, smartphones without consent, right steps, unwanted intrusions

III. One final, abreast developments spyware, malware consulting reputable Stopbadware.org, StaySafeOnline.org

IV. Forewarned, forearmed, luck!

Full-Text Speech

Following is the full text of the speech outlined in this chapter. John's assignment was to deliver a ten-minute informative speech citing at least four authoritative sources, incorporating at least two presentation aids, and including a list of references in either APA or MLA style.[3]

Staying Ahead of Spyware
JOHN COULTER
Salt Lake Community College

Do you worry about identity theft online? Are you anxious about the security of your passwords and credit card numbers? • Many of you are aware of a type of software known as spyware that can install itself on your computer and smartphone without your knowledge and harvest sensitive information, and many of you have taken steps to protect yourself.

Spyware is constantly evolving, however, and to stay safe, we need to learn about and arm ourselves against the threats it poses. •

Today, I'll talk about what forms spyware takes, how it gets into your computer, the harm it causes, and how to keep your computer and smartphone from becoming infected by it. •

So, what is the state of spyware today? •

Spyware is a type of privacy invasion software known as *malware.* According to a history of spyware published on the Federal Trade Commission's Web site, until the year 2000, *spyware* referred to monitoring devices on cameras. The term first appeared in a software context

• John's rhetorical question serves as an attention getter.

• John states his thesis.

• John previews the main points.

• This transition signals that John is turning to the body of the speech.

in an ad for the security program *ZoneAlarm*. Today, *spyware* signifies any computer code that installs itself on your computer, gathers data from it, and sends it back to a remote computer *without your consent*.

Some types of spyware track your Web-browsing habits, selling this information to marketers. Certain types of spyware capture your passwords and other sensitive information, potentially leading to identity theft. Another type of spyware can record everything you type or text.

Many people are confused about the differences between spyware and other types of malware, such as viruses and adware. •

According to a CNET video, spyware differs from viruses in several ways. First, individuals generally write viruses in order to brag about causing damage, whereas spyware often is written by corporate teams to make money. Second, viruses have been around for decades and they are illegal, whereas legislation outlawing spyware, such as the Internet Spyware Prevention Act (I-SPY), has thus far failed passage, according to GovTrack.us, a Web site that tracks the status of federal legislation. •

Adware, another type of malware, also differs from spyware.

Adware refers to programs that display ads on your computer. Adware may be annoying, but it doesn't contain software that can track you. On the other hand, spyware does what its name suggests—it spies on you, sending the stolen data to "the lair of the evil creator," as Neil Rubenking of *PC Magazine* puts it. •

You may be wondering how spyware gets into your computer. •

Different forms of spyware take various routes into your computer, causing little harm or utter havoc, depending on the software and the sender's intent.

Spyware installs itself silently, often "piggybacking" onto downloadable programs, such as free file-sharing applications and games. Links in pop-up ads and the "unsubscribe" button in spam are known sources. One type of software, called "rogue" software or "scareware," appears as a legitimate-seeming antispyware protection program, but when downloaded, tricks the user into installing spyware.

A particularly harmful program, keystroke loggers, captures your keystrokes, enabling actual spying as well

• This is an effective lead-in to an explanation.

• Signal words—"first," "second"—move listeners from one point to another.

• This is an effective quotation to include, and John credits the source effectively.

• This transition alerts listeners to what is ahead.

as identity theft. As you've probably heard, people may deliberately install keystroke loggers to spy on their spouses, children, employees, or students. And reporting in the June 29, 2010, edition of *Newsweek*, Jessica Ramirez writes that keystroke loggers can be attached to smartphone apps.

We've seen how spyware can install itself on computers and smartphones, and how it can grab hold of personal data. This same malware lurks on social networking sites such as Facebook and Twitter. •

In fact, spyware represents a real threat on social media sites, as cyber criminals seek to send malicious code into a wide audience. Clicking on pop-up ads and other links on your "Wall" may download the programs. Invitations to take certain quizzes or join certain groups can activate spyware.

Users can learn to recognize the symptoms and problems associated with spyware.

One sign of infiltration, according to Google's Web search help page, is a constant stream of pop-up ads. Strange toolbars may appear on the desktop. Browser settings may be hijacked, forcing users to strange Web pages. The computer may behave sluggishly or become unstable, and files may become displaced or disappear. In the worst case, the computer may even crash.

Now for the good news. You can protect yourself from spyware!

There are some good antispyware programs on the market. For example, Microsoft now distributes *Windows Defender* (an antispyware product) with its operating systems and offers a free program called *Microsoft Security Essentials*.

PC Magazine's Editor's Choice for stand-alone malware protection is *Spyware Doctor with Antivirus;* its choice for security suite is *Norton Internet Security*. Free antispyware programs, according to *PC Magazine,* don't do as thorough a job as commercial software, and some free programs actually contain spyware. They are free, but they could hurt you.

So along with the antispyware software you can install, what else can you do? •

It's very important to keep your browser up-to-date to take advantage of security updates. Don't install any software without reading the fine print, or first checking

> • John internally summarizes what he has discussed thus far and previews what he will talk about next.

> • Transition stated as a rhetorical question.

its reputation on a site such as CNET. And make sure you download free software or any smartphone apps only from sites you know and trust.

Do *not* click on links in pop-up windows, and do *not* reply to, or even open, spam or any e-mail that isn't from someone you know. Additionally, don't hit the "unsubscribe" button in spam: spyware is known to lurk here. When you're on a social media site, use the maximum security level settings. And last but absolutely not least, use strong passwords that can't be easily guessed and do not—repeat *do not*—set up your smartphone to automatically remember them.

The makers of spyware are in it for the money, so the problem is likely to be long-lasting. •

- John signals the close of the speech.

Spyware appears in various guises in order to use personal information stored on computers or smartphones without your consent, but taking the right steps can help you avoid unwanted intrusions. •

- He summarizes main points.

One final suggestion is to stay abreast of developments related to spyware and malware by consulting reputable Web sites such as Stopbadware.org and StaySafeOnline.org. • Forewarned is forearmed. Good luck! •

- He leaves the audience with something to think about.

- This saying provides a memorable close.

INTRODUCTIONS, CONCLUSIONS, AND LANGUAGE

INTRODUCTIONS, CONCLUSIONS, AND LANGUAGE

SPEAKER'S REFERENCE

CHAPTER **15** Developing the Introduction 225

Functions of the Introduction 225
- ► **CHECKLIST** Guidelines for Preparing the Introduction 226
- ► **SELF-ASSESSMENT CHECKLIST** Using Humor Appropriately 228
- ► **A CULTURAL PERSPECTIVE** Humor and Culture: When the Jokes Fall Flat 231

Motivate the Audience to Accept Your Goals 231
- ► **SELF-ASSESSMENT CHECKLIST** How Effective Is Your Introduction? 232

CHAPTER **16** Developing the Conclusion 233

Functions of Conclusions 233
- ► **CHECKLIST** Guidelines for Preparing the Conclusion 233

Make the Conclusion Memorable 235
- ► **SELF-ASSESSMENT CHECKLIST** How Effective Is Your Conclusion? 237

CHAPTER **17** Using Language to Style the Speech 238

Prepare Your Speeches for the Ear 238
- ► **CHECKLIST** Personalizing Your Speech with Personal Pronouns 241
- ► **SELF-ASSESSMENT CHECKLIST** Does Your Speech Incorporate Effective Oral Style? 241

Use Concrete Language and Vivid Imagery 241
- ► **CHECKLIST** Is Your Speech Language Concrete? 242

Choose Language That Builds Credibility 244
- ► **A CULTURAL PERSPECTIVE** Adapting Your Language to Diverse Audiences 247
- ► **SELF-ASSESSMENT CHECKLIST** Does Your Language Build Trust and Credibility? 248

Choose Language That Creates a Lasting Impression 249

INTRODUCTIONS, CONCLUSIONS, AND LANGUAGE

CHAPTER 15 Developing the Introduction

Prepare the Introduction

- Prepare the introduction after you've completed the speech body. (p. 225)
- Keep the introduction brief: It should occupy no more than 10 to 15 percent of the overall speech. (p. 225)

Use the Introduction to Gain Audience Attention

- Use a quotation. (p. 226)
- Tell a story. (p. 226)
- Pose questions. (p. 227)
- Offer unusual information. (p. 227)
- Use humor. (p. 228)
- Establish common ground. (p. 229)
- Refer to the occasion. (p. 229)

Preview the Purpose and Topic

- Declare what your speech is about and what you hope to accomplish. (p. 229)

Establish Your Credibility

- Briefly state your qualifications for speaking on the topic. (p. 230)
- Emphasize some experience, knowledge, or perspective you have that is different from or more extensive than that of your audience. (p. 230)

Preview the Main Points

- Help listeners mentally organize the speech by introducing the main points and stating the order in which you will address them. (p. 230)

Motivate the Audience to Accept Your Goals

- Consider emphasizing the topic's practical implications. (p. 231)
- Consider specifying what the audience stands to gain by listening. (p. 231)

CHAPTER 16 Developing the Conclusion

Alert the Audience to the Conclusion of Your Speech

- Use transitional words or phrases. (p. 234)
- Indicate in the manner of your delivery that the speech is coming to an end. (p. 234)
- Once you've signaled the conclusion, finish the speech promptly. (p. 234)

Summarize the Key Speech Points

- Reiterate the main points of your speech, but don't do it in a rote way. (p. 234)
- Remind listeners of the topic and purpose of your speech. (p. 234)

Challenge the Audience to Respond to Your Ideas or Appeals

- If the goal is informative, challenge listeners to respond to the appeal of your message. (p. 235)
- If the goal is persuasive, challenge listeners to act in line with your message. (p. 235)

Employ Vivid Language and Attention-Getting Devices

- Use quotations. (p. 236)
- Tell a story. (p. 236)
- Pose rhetorical questions. (p. 237)

CHAPTER 17 Using Language to Style the Speech

Strive for Simplicity

- Try to say what you mean in short, clear sentences. (p. 239)
- Steer clear of unnecessary jargon. (p. 239)
- Avoid words unlikely to be understood by your audience. (p. 239)

Aim for Conciseness

- Use fewer words to express your thoughts. (p. 239)
- Experiment with phrases and sentence fragments. (p. 240)

Use Repetition

- Repeat key words and phrases to emphasize important ideas and to help listeners follow your logic. (p. 240)

Use Personal Pronouns

- Make specific references to yourself and to the audience. (p. 240)
- Foster a sense of inclusion by using the personal pronouns *I, you,* and *we.* (p. 240)

Choose Concrete Words and Vivid Imagery

- Use concrete vs. abstract language. (p. 241)
- Use colorful language that appeals to listeners' senses: smell, taste, sight, hearing, and touch. (p. 241)

Create Imagery with Descriptive Adjectives and Strong Verbs

- Use *similes, metaphors, analogies,* and other figures of speech. (p. 242)

Choose Language That Builds Credibility

- Use language that is appropriate to the audience, occasion, and subject. (p. 244)
- Choose words that are both denotatively (literally) and connotatively (subjectively) appropriate for the audience. (p. 245)
- Use the active voice. (p. 245)
- Use "I" language. (p. 246)
- Avoid powerless speech, such as hedges and tag questions. (p. 246)
- Use culturally sensitive and gender-neutral language. (p. 246)

Choose Language That Creates a Lasting Impression

- Repeat key words, phrases, or sentences at various intervals (anaphora). (p. 249)
- Choose words that repeat the same sounds in two or more neighboring words or syllables (alliteration). (p. 250)
- Arrange words, phrases, or sentences in similar form (parallelism). (p. 250)

KEY TERMS

Chapter 15

anecdote   rhetorical question   ethical appeal

Chapter 16

call to action

Chapter 17

style
rhetorical devices
jargon
concrete language
abstract language
imagery
figures of speech
simile
metaphor
cliché
mixed metaphor
analogy
faulty analogy

personification
understatement
irony
allusion
hyperbole
onomatopoeia
code-switching
malapropism
denotative meaning
connotative meaning
voice
hedges
tag questions

colloquial expressions
gender-neutral language
persons with disabilities
(PWD)
anaphora
epiphora
alliteration
hackneyed
parallelism
antithesis
triad

CHAPTER 15

Developing the Introduction

The introduction and conclusion, although not more important than the body of the speech, are essential to its overall success. Introductions set the tone and prepare the audience to hear the speech. A good opening previews what's to come in a way that engages audiences in the topic and establishes a tone of goodwill. An effective conclusion ensures that the audience remembers the speech and reacts in a way that the speaker intends.

This chapter describes the essential components of the speech introduction. Chapter 16 addresses the conclusion.

Functions of the Introduction

 Chapter quizzes

The choices you make about the introduction can affect the outcome of the entire speech. In the first several minutes (one speaker pegs it at ninety seconds[1]), audience members will decide whether they are interested in the topic of your speech, whether they will believe what you say, and whether they will give you their full attention. A good introduction serves to:

- Arouse your audience's attention and willingness to listen.
- Introduce the topic and purpose.
- Establish your credibility to address the topic.
- Preview the main points.
- Motivate the audience to accept your speech goals.

The introduction comes first in a speech, but it should be prepared after you've completed the speech body. This way, you will know exactly what your speech message is and what you need to preview. Keep the introduction brief—as a rule, it should occupy no more than 10 to 15 percent of the overall speech. Nothing will turn an audience off more quickly than waiting interminably for you to get to the main points.

GUIDELINES FOR PREPARING THE INTRODUCTION

✔ First complete the body of the speech.

✔ Review your research for material that you can use in the introduction.

✔ Keep the introduction brief. As a general rule, it should make up no more than 10 to 15 percent of the entire speech.

✔ Time your introduction before delivery.

✔ Revise the introduction freely until you're completely satisfied.

Gain Audience Attention

The first challenge faced by any speaker is to win the audience's attention. Some time-honored techniques for doing this include sharing a compelling quotation or story, posing a question, providing unusual information, using humor, referring to the occasion, and establishing a feeling of common ground with the audience.

Use a Quotation

A Czech proverb says, "Do not protect yourself by a fence but rather by your friends." A good quotation, one that elegantly and succinctly expresses an idea relevant to your topic, is a very effective way to draw the audience's attention. Quotations can be culled from literature, poetry, film, or directly from people. They need not be restricted to the famous. Clever sayings of any kind, whether spoken by a three-year-old child or by a wise friend, may express precisely the idea you are looking for.

Tell a Story

Noted speechwriter and language expert William Safire once remarked that stories are "surefire attention getters."[2] Speakers like to use stories, or *narratives,* to illustrate points, and audiences like to hear them, because they make ideas concrete and colorful.[3] Stories personalize issues by encouraging audience identification, and making ideas relevant. And they are, importantly, entertaining.

Recall from Chapter 8 that an **anecdote** is a brief story of interesting, humorous, or real-life incidents. As rhetorical scholar Edward Corbett notes, anecdotes are "one of the oldest and most effective gambits for seizing attention."[4] Corbett's assessment is supported by a 1998 study conducted by Dutch researchers, who found that speeches with anecdotal openers both motivate the audience to listen and promote greater understanding and retention of the speaker's message.[5] The key to successfully introducing a speech with an anecdote is choosing one that strikes a chord with the audience.

Like a joke, stories should be able to stand on their own. People want to be entertained. They don't want to listen to the speaker's explanation of what the story means. Of course, not all stories have to be real. Hypothetical stories can serve the same purpose as real ones. Just remember that the hypothetical story must be plausible and will seem more effective if you connect it to yourself.

Pose Questions

"Are you concerned about student loans?" Posing questions such as this can be an effective way to draw the audience's attention to what you are about to say. Questions can be real or rhetorical. **Rhetorical questions** do not invite actual responses. Instead, they make the audience think, as with, "Have you ever asked yourself, 'What is my real purpose in life?'"

Whenever you use a rhetorical question in an introduction, always let the audience know that your speech will attempt to answer it:

> Are you concerned about whether you'll be able to find a job when you graduate? Are you worried that unemployment will remain high? If so, we are in this together. Today I'm going to talk about some steps you can take in college that will help you enter the job market sooner once you graduate.

Posing questions that seek an actual response, either in a show of hands or by verbal reply, also sparks interest. Here is an example of how a speech about trends in technology usage might be introduced by using real, or "polling," questions:

> How many of you have gone without using any electronic device this year for at least three days in a row? *(Speaker waits for a show of hands.)* How many of you think you'd enjoy doing so? *(Speaker waits for show of hands.)* Do you think you'd be comfortable not using a cell phone, iPod, iTouch, Droid, laptop, or whatever other devices you own, for a week? *(Speaker waits for a show of hands.)* A month? *(Speaker waits for a show of hands.)* As you can see by looking around this room, not many of us can visualize being particularly comfortable without our electronic devices. Today I'm going to describe trends in technology usage and our dependence on these modern devices. . . .

Polling audience members is an effective way to gain their attention, if your questions are thought-provoking and novel, but it has drawbacks. Bear in mind when using this attention-gaining technique that it is possible that no one will respond, that the responses will be unexpected, or that you will be called on to answer in unanticipated ways. If you incorporate questions, make sure that you are prepared to adapt if things don't go according to plan.

Offer Unusual Information

WEB Links

"In the United States, a woman is physically abused every nine seconds." Surprising audience members with startling or unusual information is one of the surest ways to get their attention. Such statements stimulate your listeners' curiosity and make them want to hear more about your topic.

Speakers frequently base their startling statements on statistics, a powerful means of illustrating consequences and relationships—how one thing affects another. As you learned in Chapter 8, statistics can quickly bring things into focus. In the following example, a student addressing the issue of domestic violence uses statistics to drive home the main point:

> Crimes by intimate partners accounted for 23 percent of all violent crimes against females and 3 percent of all violent crimes against males. Of female murder victims, 35 percent were killed by an intimate partner; 2 percent of male murder victims were killed by an intimate partner.[6]

Use Humor—Perhaps

Few things build rapport and put people at ease as effectively as humor, used appropriately. Introducing a speech with a short joke or a funny story can set a positive tone for the theme of a speech and its key points. Humor can also enliven a speech about a topic that is dry, difficult, or complex.

Used ineffectively, however, humor can backfire. Include humor in your speech with caution. Simply telling a series of unrelated jokes without making a relevant point will likely detract from your purpose. And few things turn an audience off more quickly than tasteless or inappropriate humor. In any speech, you should strictly avoid humor or sarcasm that belittles others—whether on the basis of race, sex, ability, or otherwise. A good rule of thumb is that speech humor should always match the audience, topic, purpose, and occasion.

Self-deprecating humor often gets a chuckle, and it's usually safe. Former Vice President Al Gore famously began a speech this way:

> "Hello, my name is Al Gore, and I used to be the next president of the United States."[7]

USING HUMOR APPROPRIATELY

_____ 1. Is your humor appropriate to the occasion?

_____ 2. Does your humor help you make a point about your topic or the occasion?

_____ 3. Have you avoided any potentially offensive issues such as race or religion?

_____ 4. Is your humor likely to insult or demean anyone?

_____ 5. Will the audience understand your humor?

_____ 6. Have you given your humor a trial run?

_____ 7. Is your humor funny?

SELF-ASSESSMENT CHECKLIST

Refer to the Audience

Just as friendships are formed by showing interest in others, audiences are won over when speakers express interest in them and show that they share in the audiences' concerns and goals. This creates goodwill and a feeling of common ground (or *identification;* see Chapter 6).

When Nelson Mandela, an anti-apartheid leader in South Africa who later became the country's president, was first released from prison after twenty-seven years, he addressed a huge crowd of supporters beginning this way:

> Friends, comrades, and fellow South Africans. I greet you all in the name of peace, democracy, and freedom for all. I stand here before you not as a prophet but as a humble servant of you, the people. Your tireless and heroic sacrifices have made it possible for me to be here today. I therefore place the remaining years of my life in your hands.[8]

Although Mandela had just tasted his first hours of freedom after more than two decades in prison, he chose to express goodwill toward the audience rather than focus on himself. In response, Mandela's listeners could not help but hold him in even higher esteem.

Refer to the Occasion

Introductions that include references to the speech occasion and to any relevant facts about the audience make listeners feel recognized as individuals. People appreciate a direct reference to the event, and they are interested in the meaning the speaker assigns to it. In a speech on management, Vance Coffman began in this fashion:

> Let me say, right here at the beginning, that it is an honor—and a great personal pleasure—to be invited to participate in this Executive Forum of Mercer University. I understand that this is the 20th anniversary season of these innovative forums, so let me congratulate you and wish you every good fortune in continuing its success for at least another 20 years.[9]

Preview the Purpose and Topic

Once you've gained the audience's attention, perhaps using one or more of the techniques just described, use the introduction to alert listeners to the speech topic and purpose. You may already have alluded to your topic in the attention-getting phase of the introduction. If not, you now need to declare what your speech is about and what you hope to accomplish. Note an exception to this rule: When your purpose is to persuade, and the audience is not yet aware of this purpose, "forewarning" may predispose listeners in the opposite direction and thwart your persuasive goal. However, when the audience knows of your persuasive intent, previewing the topic and purpose can enhance understanding.[10]

Topic and purpose are clearly explained in this introduction to a speech by Marvin Runyon, postmaster general of the United States:

> This afternoon, I want to examine the truth of that statement—"Nothing moves people like the mail, and no one moves the mail like the U.S. Postal Service." I want to look at where we are today as a communications industry, and where we intend to be in the days and years ahead.[11]

Establish Credibility as a Speaker

Audience members want to know why they should listen to you and believe what you have to say. Thus another function of the introduction is to establish why you are qualified to address the topic.

Ethical appeals are particularly important when the audience does not know you well and when it is important to establish your professionalism.[12] To build your credibility, make a simple statement of your qualifications for speaking on the topic at the particular occasion and to the specific audience. Briefly emphasize some experience, knowledge, or perspective you have that is different from or more extensive than that of your audience. If your goal, for example, was to persuade your audience to be more conscientious about protecting city parks, you might state, "I have felt passionate about conservation issues ever since I started volunteering with the city's local chapter of the Nature Conservancy four summers ago."

Preview the Main Points

After indicating the topic and purpose and establishing your credibility, use the introduction to preview the main points of the speech. This helps audience members mentally organize the speech and helps you keep their attention. Introductory previews are straightforward. You simply tell the audience what the main points will be and in what order you will address them. For example, you might state, "First, I will address the issue of . . ." followed by "Second, I will provide information on. . . ."

In a speech titled "U.S. Roads and Bridges: Highway Funding at a Crossroads," the president of the American Automobile Association, Robert L. Darbelnet, effectively introduces his topic, purpose, and main points:

> Good morning. When I received this invitation, I didn't hesitate to accept. I realized that in this room I would find a powerful coalition: the American Automobile Association; the National Asphalt Pavement Association. Where our two groups come together, no pun intended, is where the rubber meets the road.
>
> Unfortunately, the road needs repair.
>
> My remarks today are intended to give you a sense of AAA's ongoing efforts to improve America's roads. Our hope is that you will join your voices to ours as we call on the federal government to do three things. Number one: Perhaps

A CULTURAL PERSPECTIVE

Humor and Culture: When the Jokes Fall Flat

While humor can be a highly effective tool for introducing speeches, it can also be the cause of communication breakdowns. As one scholar notes, "Humor goes beyond language; it takes us into the heart of cultural understanding."[1] Humor assumes shared understanding. When that understanding is absent, the jokes fall flat. Humor breakdowns can occur any time audience members do not share the same cultural assumptions as the speaker. These assumptions may be based on gender, social class, educational background, ethnicity, or nationality.[2] A new employee may not get a joke told by a presenter with a long history in the corporate culture. Or a non-native speaker may not be familiar with an idiom used to express humor or may not share the underlying belief on which the humor is based.

How can you avoid using humor that your audience won't understand? The obvious answer is to carefully consider your audience. Be as confident as possible that your material will make sense and be humorous to your listeners. Be particularly alert to nonverbal feedback. If you receive puzzled stares, consider clarifying your meaning. You might even acknowledge the cultural assumptions that your humor tacitly expresses.

1. William Lee, "Communication about Humor as Procedural Competence in Intercultural Encounters," n *Intercultural Communication: A Reader,* 7th ed., Larry A. Samovar and Richard E. Porter (Belmont, CA: Wadsworth, 1994), 373.
2. Ibid., 381.

the most important, provide adequate funding for highway maintenance and improvements.

Number two: Play a strong, responsible, yet flexible, role in transportation programs.

And number three: Invest in highway safety.

Let's see what our strengths are, what the issues are, and what we can do about them.[13]

When previewing your main points, simply mention those points, saving your in-depth discussion of each one for the body of your speech.

Motivate the Audience to Accept Your Goals

A final function of the introduction is to motivate the audience to care about your topic and believe that it is relevant to them. One way to do this is to address its practical implications and what the audience stands to gain by listening to you. Another is to convince audience members that your speech purpose is consistent with their motives and values. A student speech about the value of interview training shows how this can be accomplished:

> Let me start by telling you why you need interview training. It all boils down to competition. As in sports, when you're not training, someone else is out there training to beat you. All things being equal, the person who has the best interviewing skills has got the edge.

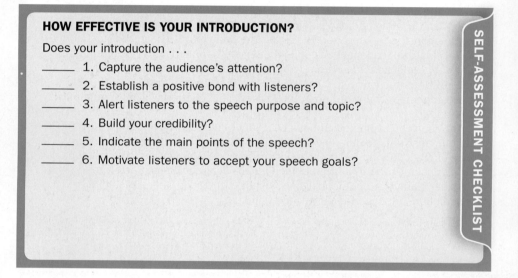

HOW EFFECTIVE IS YOUR INTRODUCTION?

Does your introduction . . .

_____ 1. Capture the audience's attention?

_____ 2. Establish a positive bond with listeners?

_____ 3. Alert listeners to the speech purpose and topic?

_____ 4. Build your credibility?

_____ 5. Indicate the main points of the speech?

_____ 6. Motivate listeners to accept your speech goals?

SELF-ASSESSMENT CHECKLIST

CHAPTER 16

Developing the Conclusion

Just as a well-crafted introduction gets your speech effectively out of the starting gate, a well-constructed conclusion ensures that you go out with a bang and not a whimper. Conclusions give you the opportunity to drive home your purpose, and they offer you a final chance to make the kind of impression that will accomplish the goals of your speech. Conclusions also provide the audience with a sense of logical and emotional closure, as well as further opportunity for you to build a relationship with your audience.

Functions of Conclusions

[WEB] Chapter quizzes

Like introductions, conclusions consist of several elements that work together to make the end of a speech as memorable as the beginning. Conclusions serve to:

- Signal to the audience that the speech is coming to an end and provide closure.
- Summarize the key points and goals.
- Reiterate the thesis or central idea of the speech.
- Challenge the audience to respond.

As with the introduction, prepare the conclusion after you've completed the speech body. Keep it brief—as a rule, no more than 10 to 15 percent, or about one-sixth, of the overall speech. And, just as you should outline the introduction in full-sentence and then key-word form, do so for the conclusion (see Chapter 14). Carefully consider your use of language in the conclusion. More than other parts of the speech, the conclusion can contain words that inspire and motivate (see Chapter 17).

GUIDELINES FOR PREPARING THE CONCLUSION

✓ During the research phase, be on the lookout for material that you can use in the conclusion.

✓ Do not leave the conclusion to chance. Prepare both a full sentence outline and a key-word outline.

✓ Keep the length of the conclusion to about one-sixth of the overall speech.

✓ Practice delivering the conclusion often, using your peers as sounding boards.

CHECKLIST

Signal the Close of a Speech and Provide Closure

People who listen to speeches are taking a journey of sorts, and they want and need the speaker to acknowledge the journey's end. The more emotional the journey, as in speeches designed to touch hearts and minds, the greater is the need for logical and emotional closure.

One way to alert the audience that a speech is about to end is by using a transitional word or phrase to signal closure: *finally, looking back, in conclusion, in summary, as I bring this to a close,* or *let me close by saying* (see Chapter 12). You can also signal closure by adjusting your manner of delivery; for example, you can vary your tone, pitch, rhythm, and rate of speech to indicate that the speech is winding down (see Chapter 19).

Few things annoy listeners more than hearing a speaker say "in conclusion," and then having to sit through another twenty minutes of the speech. Once you've signaled the end of your speech, conclude in short order (though not abruptly). Although there are no hard-and-fast rules about length, as a general rule about one-sixth of the speech can be spent on the introduction, one-sixth on the conclusion, and the remaining four-sixths on the body of the speech.[1]

Summarize the Key Points and Goals

One bit of age-old advice for giving a speech is "Tell them what you are going to tell them (in the introduction), tell them (in the body), and tell them what you told them (in the conclusion)." The idea is that emphasizing the main points three times will help the audience to remember them.

Summarizing the main points in the conclusion accomplishes the last step of "telling them what you've told them." However, the summary or review should be more than a rote recounting. Consider how Holger Kluge, in a speech titled "Reflections on Diversity," summarizes his main points:

> I have covered a lot of ground here today. But as I draw to a close, I'd like to stress three things.
> First, diversity is more than equity. . . .
> Second, weaving diversity into the very fabric of your organization takes time. . . .
> Third, diversity will deliver bottom line results to your businesses and those results will be substantial. . . .[2]

As the speaker reiterates each point, audience members are able to mentally check off what they've heard during the speech. Did they get all the key points? A restatement of points like the one above brings the speech full circle and helps give the audience a sense of completion.

Reiterate the Topic and Speech Purpose

Another function of the conclusion is to reiterate the topic and speech purpose—to imprint it in the audience's memory. In the conclusion to a persuasive speech about the U.S. immigration debate, Elpidio Villarreal reminds his listeners of his central idea:

Two paths are open to us. One path would keep us true to our fundamental values as a nation and a people. The other would lead us down a dark trail; one marked by 700-mile-long fences, emergency detention centers and vigilante border patrols. Because I really am an American, heart and soul, and because that means never being without hope, I still believe we will ultimately choose the right path. We have to.[3]

Reminding listeners of your speech purpose links their frame of reference to yours, thus allowing your audience to determine how well they've comprehended your central idea.

Challenge the Audience to Respond

A strong conclusion challenges audience members to put to use what the speaker has taught them. In an *informative speech,* the speaker challenges audience members to use what they've learned in a way that benefits them. In a *persuasive speech,* the challenge usually comes in the form of a **call to action**. Here the speaker challenges listeners to act in response to the speech, see the problem in a new way, change their beliefs about the problem, or change both their actions and their beliefs about the problem.

A concluding challenge is important because it shows audience members that the problem or issue being addressed is real and personally relevant to them. In the introduction, part of the goal is to show audience members how the topic is relevant to them; the call to action is a necessary part of completing that goal in the conclusion.

Note how Queen Gorga makes a specific call to action in her conclusion when addressing the Spartan Council in the film *300*:

> . . . We are at war, gentlemen. We must send the entire Spartan army to aid our king in the preservation of not just ourselves, but of our children. Send the army for the preservation of liberty. Send it for justice. Send it for law and order. Send it for reason. But most importantly, send our army for hope—hope that a king and his men have not been wasted to the pages of history—that their courage bonds us together, that we are made stronger by their actions, and that your choices today reflect their bravery.[4]

In this direct call to action, Queen Gorga appeals to her audience to save their nation. Her direct reference to the audience's core values—the welfare of children, reason, justice, liberty, and hope—strikes an emotional chord.

Make the Conclusion Memorable

Beyond summarizing and providing closure, a key function of the conclusion is to make the speech memorable—to increase the odds that the speaker's message will linger after the speech is over. A speech that makes a lasting impression is one that listeners are most likely to remember and act on.

Effective conclusions are crafted with vivid language that captures the audience's attention (see Chapter 17). Conclusions rely on (but are not limited to) the same devices for capturing attention as introductions—quotations, stories, startling statements, humor, rhetorical questions, and references to the audience and the occasion.

Use Quotations

As with introductions, using a quotation that captures the essence of the speech can be a very effective way to close a speech. Note how Sue Suter quotes a character in *Star Trek* to conclude her speech on discrimination and the disabled:

> That brings us to the final lesson from *Star Trek*. I'd like to leave you with two quotations from Captain Picard that define what it means to be human. In *The Next Generation,* Picard confronts discrimination by agreeing that, yes, we may be different in appearance. Then he adds, "But we are both living beings. We are born, we grow, we live, and we die. In all the ways that matter, we are alike."[5]

Quoting from poetry is also a highly effective way to conclude a speech, as seen in this commencement address given by Oprah Winfrey to graduates of Wellesley College:

> I want to leave you with a poem that I say to myself sometimes. . . . Maya Angelou wrote a poem and I don't know a poem more fitting than "Phenomenal Woman" for this crowd, because you are and these words are for you.
>
> She says, "Pretty women, honey, they wonder just where my secret lies 'cause I'm not cuter, built to suit a fashion model size, but when I start to tell them, they say, Girl, you're telling lies and I said, no, honey, it's in the reach of my arms, it's in the span of my hips, it's in the stride of my stepping, it's in the curl of my lips, 'cause I'm a woman, honey, phenomenally, phenomenal, phenomenal woman."[6]

Tell a Story

A short concluding story, or *anecdote,* can bring the entire speech into focus very effectively. It helps the audience to visualize the speech:

> I would conclude with a story that applies to all of us in this industry. In ancient times there was a philosopher who had many disciples. . . .

Another technique is to pick up on a story or an idea that you mentioned in the introduction, bringing the speech full circle. James May does this by reminding his audience of the story of Apollo 13 that started his speech:

> If I may draw one final lesson from the crippled spacecraft that made it back to earth on an empty fuel tank, it is that one should never underestimate the human capacity for doing "impossible" things. All through history, enterprising people have surprised themselves—and others around them—by finding ingenious solutions to the most complex problems. We can do that here.[7]

Pose a Rhetorical Question

Yet another effective way to make a speech memorable is to leave the audience with a *rhetorical question*. Just as such questions focus attention in the introduction, they can drive home the speech theme in the conclusion. A speech on groundwater contamination, for example, might end with a rhetorical question:

> Water has been cheap and plentiful, for most of us, for our entire lives. Easy access to our most necessary resource is now greatly threatened. Given this danger, we need to ask ourselves, "How long can we ignore the dangers of groundwater contamination?"

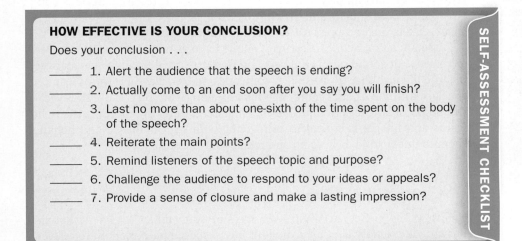

HOW EFFECTIVE IS YOUR CONCLUSION?

Does your conclusion . . .

_____ 1. Alert the audience that the speech is ending?

_____ 2. Actually come to an end soon after you say you will finish?

_____ 3. Last no more than about one-sixth of the time spent on the body of the speech?

_____ 4. Reiterate the main points?

_____ 5. Remind listeners of the speech topic and purpose?

_____ 6. Challenge the audience to respond to your ideas or appeals?

_____ 7. Provide a sense of closure and make a lasting impression?

SELF-ASSESSMENT CHECKLIST

CHAPTER 17

Using Language to Style the Speech

Words are the public speaker's tools of the trade, and the words you choose to style your speech will play a large role in how well it is received. **Style** is both the specific word choices and the **rhetorical devices** (techniques of language) that speakers use to express their ideas and achieve their speech purpose.

Used in all its richness, language allows us to visualize an image and even get a sense of sound or smell. Poets and novelists use descriptive language to breathe life into that something or someone and to make their words leap off the page into the reader's mind. In public speaking, you too can use the evocative power of language to captivate your audience. Carefully choosing the right words and images is crucial to connecting with your audience and helping them to understand, believe in, and retain your message.[1]

Prepare Your Speeches for the Ear

 WEB Chapter quizzes

In his memoir, George Shultz, secretary of state under President Ronald Reagan, tells a story about showing his boss a speech he was about to deliver. Reagan approved it, but then added, "Of course, if I were giving that speech, it would be different."

> The text, he opined to an abashed Shultz, had been written to be read in the *New York Times,* not to be spoken aloud. Flipping through the manuscript, Reagan penciled in a few changes and marked out the section that contained, or should contain, the "story." Nothing of substance was altered, but, writes Shultz, "I saw that he had changed the tone of my speech completely."[2]

A master of the spoken word, President Reagan was keenly aware that written language and oral language differ in several respects. Whereas readers who fail to understand something can reread a passage until they are satisfied that they understand what the writer means, listeners have only one chance to get the message.

The next time you listen to a speech or even a classroom lecture, consider how the speaker's language differs from that of this textbook. Here are some things you are likely to note:

- More so than written texts, effective speeches use familiar words, easy-to-follow sentences, and straightforward syntax (subject-verb-object agreement).

- Speeches make much more frequent use of repetition and transitions than do most forms of written communication.

- Because you cannot "rewind" a speaker's words, speeches must be more clearly organized than written language. A clear organizational pattern provides listeners with the necessary framework to follow spoken messages (see Chapter 13).

- Spoken communication is more interactive than written language. When you deliver a speech, you can adjust the content based on audience feedback. If listeners appear not to understand you, for example, you can supply additional examples or otherwise attempt to increase shared meaning.

Keeping these differences between oral and written language in mind, consider how you can use the following tips to write your speeches to be heard rather than read.

Strive for Simplicity

To make certain that your audience understands you, strive for simplicity of expression in your speeches. When selecting between two synonyms, choose the simpler term. Avoid pretentious and/or empty terms such as *extrapolate* for "guess" and *utilize* for "use." And unless the audience consists of the professionals who use it, translate **jargon**—the specialized, "insider" language of a given profession—into commonly understood terms. As former presidential speechwriter Peggy Noonan notes in her book *Simply Speaking:*

> Good hard simple words with good hard clear meanings are good things to use when you speak. They are like pickets in a fence, slim and unimpressive on their own but sturdy and effective when strung together.[3]

William Safire, another master speechwriter, puts it this way:

> Great speeches steer clear of forty-dollar words. Big words, or terms chosen for their strangeness—I almost said "unfamiliarity"—are a sign of pretension. What do you do when you have a delicious word, one with a little poetry in it, that is just the right word for the meaning—but you know it will sail over the head of your audience? You can use it, just as FDR used "infamy," and thereby stretch the vocabulary of your listeners. But it is best if you subtly define it in passing, as if you were adding emphasis.[4]

Be Concise

Concise wording is another feature of effective oral style. As a rule, use fewer rather than more words to express your thoughts. Edit any unnecessary words and phrases, bearing in mind that, in general, easy-to-pronounce words and shorter sentences are more readily understood. Because they reflect how the English language is actually spoken, use *contractions*—shortened forms of the verb *to be* and other auxiliary verbs in conjunction with pronouns (*I, he, she, you, we*) and proper nouns (*John, Juanita*). Thus, rather than

> I am so happy to be here today. I will first turn . . .

say,

> I'm happy to be here. I'll first turn . . .

Experiment with Phrases and Sentence Fragments

Although they are often avoided in written language, phrases and sentence fragments in place of full sentences can sometimes help to communicate an oral message. This speaker, a physician, demonstrates how they can add punch to a speech:

> I'm just a simple bone-and-joint guy. I can set your broken bones. Take away your bunions. Even give you a new hip. But I don't mess around with the stuff between the ears. . . . That's another specialty.[5]

Make Frequent Use of Repetition

Good speeches often repeat key words and phrases. Indeed, even very brief speeches make use of this extremely important linguistic device. Repetition adds emphasis to important ideas, helps listeners follow your logic, and imbues language with rhythm and drama. For examples of how to introduce repetition into your speeches, see p. 249 in this chapter ("Use Repetition for Rhythm and Reinforcement").

Use Personal Pronouns

Oral language is often more interactive and inclusive of the audience than is written language. The direct form of address, using the personal pronouns *we, us, I,* and *you,* occurs more frequently in spoken than in written text. Audience members want to know what the speaker thinks and feels, and to be assured that he or she recognizes them and relates them to the message. Note how the following speaker uses personal pronouns to accomplish this end:

> My talk today is about you. Each one of you personally. I know you hear many presentations. For the most part, they tend to be directed mostly to others with very little for you. My presentation today is different; the topic and the information will be important to every one of you, especially if you're at all interested in having a happy, successful, and important life. I'm going to show and tell each of you how to become a verbal visionary.[6]

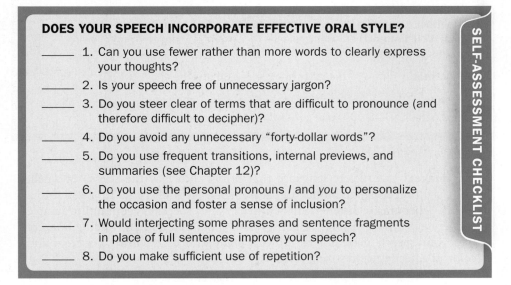

PERSONALIZING YOUR SPEECH WITH PERSONAL PRONOUNS

✓ "*I* am indebted to the ideas of . . ."

✓ "Those of *us* who have lived during a world war . . ."

✓ "*We* cannot opt out of this problem . . ."

✓ "To *me,* the truly great lessons . . ."

✓ "Some of *you* will recall . . ."

CHECKLIST

DOES YOUR SPEECH INCORPORATE EFFECTIVE ORAL STYLE?

_____ 1. Can you use fewer rather than more words to clearly express your thoughts?

_____ 2. Is your speech free of unnecessary jargon?

_____ 3. Do you steer clear of terms that are difficult to pronounce (and therefore difficult to decipher)?

_____ 4. Do you avoid any unnecessary "forty-dollar words"?

_____ 5. Do you use frequent transitions, internal previews, and summaries (see Chapter 12)?

_____ 6. Do you use the personal pronouns *I* and *you* to personalize the occasion and foster a sense of inclusion?

_____ 7. Would interjecting some phrases and sentence fragments in place of full sentences improve your speech?

_____ 8. Do you make sufficient use of repetition?

SELF-ASSESSMENT CHECKLIST

Use Concrete Language and Vivid Imagery

Concrete language and vivid imagery make a speech come alive for listeners, engaging their senses and encouraging involvement. Concrete language is specific, tangible, and definite. Concrete words, such as *mountain, spoon, dark,* and *heavy,* describe things we can physically sense (see, hear, taste, smell, and touch). In contrast, **abstract language** is general or nonspecific, leaving meaning open to interpretation. Abstract words, such as *peace, freedom,* and *love,* are purely conceptual; they have no physical reference. Politicians use abstract language to appeal to mass audiences, or to be noncommittal. ("We strive for peace.") In most speaking situations, however, listeners will appreciate concrete nouns and verbs, and they will retain more of your meaning if you use them and avoid abstractions.

Among the most overused abstract words in student speeches are these vague and imprecise adjectives:[7]

old	bad	a lot	short	good
thing	big	long	new	late

In the following example, note how concrete words add precision and color:

ABSTRACT: The old road was bad.

CONCRETE: The road was pitted with muddy craters and nearly
                         swallowed up by huge outcroppings of dark gray granite.

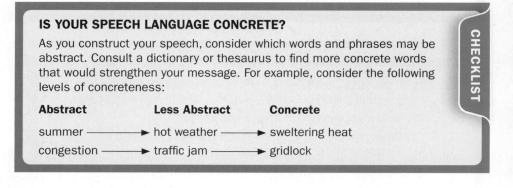

IS YOUR SPEECH LANGUAGE CONCRETE?

As you construct your speech, consider which words and phrases may be abstract. Consult a dictionary or thesaurus to find more concrete words that would strengthen your message. For example, consider the following levels of concreteness:

Abstract	Less Abstract	Concrete
summer ———►	hot weather ———►	sweltering heat
congestion ———►	traffic jam ———►	gridlock

CHECKLIST

Imagery is concrete language that brings into play the senses of smell, taste, sight, hearing, and touch to paint mental pictures. Imagery woven into a speech encourages listener involvement, and speeches containing ample imagery elicit more positive responses than those that do not.[8] Adding imagery into your speech need not be difficult; simply focus on using concrete and colorful adjectives and strong verbs.

Use Descriptive Adjectives and Strong Verbs

One easy but powerful means of creating imagery is to modify nouns with descriptive adjectives, such as describing the blue of a sky as "faint blue" or "sea blue." President Franklin D. Roosevelt used this technique when he portrayed the Japanese bombing of Pearl Harbor as "the dark hour,"[9] conveying with one simple adjective the gravity of the attack.

Another means of producing imagery is to trade weak and mundane verbs with those that are strong and colorful. Rather than "walk," you can say "saunter"; in place of "look," use "gaze." (See also the section on active vs. passive voice on p. 245 of this chapter.) Table 17.1 lists examples of mundane verb forms and more colorful alternatives.

Use Figures of Speech

Figures of speech, including similes, metaphors, and analogies, make striking comparisons that help listeners visualize, identify with, and understand the speaker's ideas. A **simile** explicitly compares one thing to another, using

TABLE 17.1 Choosing Strong Verbs	
Mundane Verb	**Colorful Alternative**
look	behold, gaze, glimpse, peek, stare
walk	stride, amble, stroll, skulk
throw	hurl, fling, pitch
sit	sink, plop, settle
eat	devour, inhale, gorge

like or *as:* "He works *like* a dog" and "The old woman's hands were *as* soft as a baby's." A **metaphor** also compares two things, but does so by describing one thing as actually *being* the other. Metaphors do not use *like* or *as:* "Time is a thief" and "All the world's a stage." Used properly, similes and metaphors express ideas compactly and cleverly. By comparing the unfamiliar to the known, they allow us to more quickly process information. However, try to avoid **clichés**, or predictable and stale comparisons (as in the above examples). Similarly, beware of **mixed metaphors**, or those that juxtapose or compare unlike images or expressions: for example, "Burning the midnight oil at both ends" incorrectly joins the expressions "burning the midnight oil" and "burning a candle at both ends."

An **analogy** is simply an extended simile or metaphor that compares an unfamiliar concept or process to a more familiar one to help listeners understand the unfamiliar one. For example, African American minister Phil Wilson used metaphoric language in a sermon to a Los Angeles congregation about the dangers of AIDS:

> Our house is on fire! The fire truck arrives, but we won't come out, because we're afraid the folks from next door will see that we're in that burning house. AIDS is a fire raging in our community and it's out of control![10]

As useful as analogies are, they can be misleading if used carelessly. A weak or **faulty analogy** is an inaccurate or misleading comparison suggesting that because two things are similar in some ways, they are necessarily similar in others. Some analogies are clearly faulty, as in suggesting that Israel is an "apartheid state" like the former South Africa because of its clash over territory with the Palestinians. Other analogies are less obviously so, requiring both speaker and listener to critically examine the limits of comparison and decide for themselves whether or not they agree with a particular analogy. (See Chapter 26 for a discussion of other logical fallacies.)

Table 17.2 lists other figures of speech that contribute to vivid imagery, including **personification**, **understatement**, **irony**, **allusion**, **hyperbole**, and **onomatopoeia**.

TABLE 17.2 Figures of Speech		
Figure of Speech	**Description**	**Example**
Personification	Endowing abstract ideas or inanimate objects with human qualities.	"Computers have become important members of our family."
Understatement	Drawing attention to an idea by minimizing, or lowering, its importance.	"Flunking out of college might be a problem."
Irony	Using humor, satire, or sarcasm to suggest a meaning other than the one that is actually being expressed.	"Our football players are great. They may not be big, but they sure are slow."
Allusion	Making vague or indirect reference to people, historical events, or concepts to give deeper meaning to the message.	"His meteoric rise to the top is an example for all of us."
Hyperbole	Using obvious exaggeration to drive home a point.	"Have you seen those students carrying backpacks the size of minivans filled with five-course dinners, cell phones, and an occasional textbook or two?"
Onomatopoeia	The imitation of natural sounds in word form; it adds vividness to the speech.	"The rain dripped a steady *plop plop plop* on the metal roof; the bees *buzzed* through the wood."

Source: Some examples taken from Andrea A. Lunsford, *The St. Martin's Handbook*, 6th ed. (Boston: Bedford/St. Martin's, 2008).

Choose Language That Builds Credibility

 Links

The way you handle language in your speech will have an immediate effect on how audience members perceive you. To demonstrate the competence and trustworthiness that audiences naturally look for in a speaker, and thereby gain their confidence, you'll want to use language that is appropriate, accurate, assertive, and respectful.

Use Words Appropriately

The language you use in a speech should be appropriate to the audience, the occasion, and the subject matter. As a rule, strive to uphold the conventional rules of grammar and usage associated with General American (GA) English, but as prepared for the ear. The more formal the occasion, the closer you will want to remain within these conventional bounds. Listeners view speakers who use General American English as more competent—though not necessarily more trustworthy or likable—than those who speak in a distinctive dialect (regional variation of speech).[11]

There are times, however, when it may be appropriate to mix casual language, dialects, or even slang in your speech. Done carefully, the selective use of dialect, sometimes called **code-switching**, can imbue your speech with friendliness, humor, earthiness, honesty, and nostalgia.[12] The key is to ensure that your meaning is clear and your use is appropriate for the audience. Consider the following excerpt:

> On the gulf where I was raised, *el valle del Rio Grande* in South Texas—that tri-angular piece of land wedged between the river *y el golfo* which serves as the Texas–U.S./Mexican border—is a Mexican *pueblito* called Hargill.[13]

Suggestive language, obscene references, or bathroom humor are never appropriate in a public speech event. Even those audience members who otherwise might not object to off-color material when delivered elsewhere, such as on a radio program hosted by a "shock jock," will react to it unfavorably in a speech.

Use Language Accurately

Audiences lose confidence in speakers who misuse words. Check that your words mean what you intend, and beware of the **malapropism**—the inadvertent use of a word or a phrase in place of one that sounds like it:[14] "It's a strange *receptacle*" for "It's a strange *spectacle*."

More broadly, choose words that are both denotatively and connotatively appropriate for the audience. The **denotative meaning** of a word is its literal, or dictionary, definition. Although some concrete words have mainly denotative meanings—*surgery* and *saline,* for example—through long use most words have acquired special associations that go beyond their dictionary definitions. The **connotative meaning** of a word is the special association that different people bring to bear on it. For instance, you may like to be called "slender" but not "skinny," or "thrifty" but not "cheap."

Ask yourself whether the words you have chosen carry connotative meanings to which the audience might react negatively. For example, depending on your audience, the terms "liberal" or "conservative" can generate either positive or negative connotations in listeners' minds.

Use the Active Voice

Voice is the feature of verbs that indicates the subject's relationship to the action. A verb is in the *active voice* when the subject performs the action and in the *passive voice* when the subject is acted upon or is the receiver of the action.[15] As in writing, speaking in the active rather than the passive voice will make your statements clear and assertive instead of indirect and weak:

PASSIVE: A test was announced by Ms. Carlos for Tuesday.

A president was elected by the voters every four years.

ACTIVE: Ms. Carlos announced a test for Tuesday.

The voters elect a president every four years.

Use "I" Language

As well as fostering a sense of inclusion, "I" language (as expressed through the personal pronouns *I, me*, and *my*) creates an impression of conviction. Instead of saying "This is a good idea for our university," it would be more convincing for you to say "I personally support this idea." If audience members are expected to accept your ideas and arguments, you must indicate convincingly that you accept them as well. Unless audience members believe you to be an expert on your topic, however, in most cases they will want you to back up your assertions with credible supporting material drawn from other sources (see Chapter 8 for more on supporting your speech).

Avoid Powerless Speech

Despite the great strides made toward gender equality in the United States, research shows that many women, and to a lesser extent men, tend to use weak language such as the passive voice, which undermines their message. Additionally, linguists Robin Lakoff and Deborah Tannen, among others, note that women are particularly prone to using weak language forms such as hedges and tag questions.[16] **Hedges** are unnecessary words and phrases that qualify or introduce doubt into statements that should be straightforward. Hedges make you sound as if you doubt your own words, thereby undermining your authority in the eyes of the audience. Examples include:

> I guess my question is . . .
>
> In my opinion . . .
>
> I may not be right, but . . .

Tag questions are unnecessary questions that are appended to statements or commands. Like hedges, tag questions undermine the speaker's authority by turning straightforward statements into questions that are left to the audience to resolve:

> The project was poorly managed, *or at least I thought so.*
>
> The proposal was too expensive, *wasn't it?*
>
> I will next address the issue of economics, *okay?*

Use Culturally Sensitive and Gender-Neutral Language

Perhaps more than any other aspect of human society, language defines and creates culture; it is through language that we are able to share meaning. As a public speaker, it is critical that you use language that reflects respect for your listeners' cultural beliefs, norms, and traditions. Review and eliminate from your speech any statements that reflect unfounded assumptions, negative descriptions, or stereotypes of a given group's age, class, gender, disability, geographic, ethnic, racial, or religious characteristics. Consider whether certain

TABLE 17.3 Gender-Neutral Terms	
Instead of	**Use**
mankind, early man, man	humankind, early peoples, humans
he, his	he or she, his or her, one, you, our, they
policeman, mailman, anchorman, chairman, middleman	police officer, mail carrier, news anchor, chair, intermediary

seemingly well-known names and terms may be foreign to some listeners, and include brief explanations for them. Sayings specific to a certain region or group of people (termed **colloquial expressions** or idioms), such as "back the wrong horse" and "ballpark figure," can add color and richness to your speech, but only if your listeners understand them. (See Chapter 4 for more on cultural barriers to understanding, and Chapter 6 for more on adapting to differing ethnic and cultural backgrounds.)

Word your speech with **gender-neutral language**: Avoid using third-person generic masculine pronouns (*his, he*) in favor of inclusive pronouns such as *his or her, he or she, we, ours, you, your,* or other gender-neutral terms (See Table 17.3).

Be sure to recognize the range of physical and mental disabilities that your listeners may experience. About one out of every five people in the United States has some sort of physical or mental disability.[17] Thus another way that you can demonstrate cultural sensitivity is to familiarize yourself with issues that are important to **persons with disabilities (PWD)**, and then ensure that your language accords them dignity, respect, and fairness.

A CULTURAL PERSPECTIVE

Adapting Your Language to Diverse Audiences

Using language that is appropriate to each of your listeners is one of the most important challenges facing you as a public speaker. Consider, for example, that many students at your school may be Arab, Jewish, Asian, African, or Hispanic American. Others may have families that come from Europe, Canada, Mexico, and elsewhere.

How do members of the co-cultures in your audience want you to refer to them? Are there important regional differences in languages you should address? Rather than being a monolithic group, Asian Americans and Pacific Islanders in the United States include those of Chinese, Samoan, Pakistani, Bangladeshi, Native Hawaiian, Vietnamese, Korean, Thai, and

(continued on next page)

Japanese descent, and this is merely a partial listing of countries of origin. Some Asian Americans have limited English proficiency (LEP) and live in linguistically isolated households in which all members fourteen years and older speak limited English,[1] while others excel at elite universities and in high-powered careers. Rather than treating any individual merely as a member of a broad category, audience members want to be addressed as individuals and to be recognized for their unique characteristics and life circumstances.

Similarly, a common misconception of Arab Americans is that they are a homogeneous group. For example, many people believe that all Arab Americans, who number about 3.5 million, are practicing Muslims. In fact, the largest portion are Catholics (35 percent); only 24 percent are Muslim, though numbers are rising.[2] Rather than sharing a religion, Arab Americans belong to many religions, including Islam, Christianity, Druze, Judaism, and others.[3] Using biased language based on these and other misconceptions can only alienate your listeners.

All people look to speakers to use language that is respectful and inclusive of them. As you prepare your speeches, consider whether you include terms that might leave your listeners feeling less than respected. For the long term, make learning about other cultures an ongoing endeavor. In this way, you will truly be able to address the sensitivities of diverse audiences.

1. "The Diverse Face of Asians and Pacific Islanders in California," National Asian Pacific American Legal Consortium, San Francisco, 2005, accessed June 8, 2010, www.napalc.org/?id=61&cid=4&pid=3&oid=1.
2. "Mapping the Global Muslim Population," The Pew Forum on Religion and Public Life Web site, accessed June 8, 2010, http://pewforum.org/Muslim/Mapping-the-Global-Muslim-Population(23).aspx.
3. Arab American Institute, "About Arab Americans," accessed June 8, 2010, www.aaiusa.org/definition.htm.

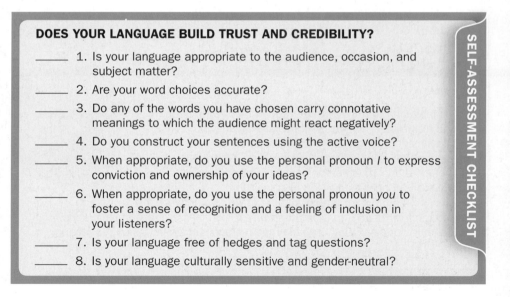

DOES YOUR LANGUAGE BUILD TRUST AND CREDIBILITY?

_____ 1. Is your language appropriate to the audience, occasion, and subject matter?

_____ 2. Are your word choices accurate?

_____ 3. Do any of the words you have chosen carry connotative meanings to which the audience might react negatively?

_____ 4. Do you construct your sentences using the active voice?

_____ 5. When appropriate, do you use the personal pronoun _I_ to express conviction and ownership of your ideas?

_____ 6. When appropriate, do you use the personal pronoun _you_ to foster a sense of recognition and a feeling of inclusion in your listeners?

_____ 7. Is your language free of hedges and tag questions?

_____ 8. Is your language culturally sensitive and gender-neutral?

SELF-ASSESSMENT CHECKLIST

Choose Language That Creates a Lasting Impression

Oral language that is artfully arranged and infused with rhythm draws listeners in and leaves a lasting impression on audience members. You can create the cadenced arrangement of language through rhetorical devices such as repetition, alliteration, and parallelism.

Use Repetition for Rhythm and Reinforcement

One of the most effective strategies for creating a lasting impression in a speech is *repetition*. Repeating key words, phrases, or even sentences at various intervals throughout a speech creates a distinctive rhythm and thereby implants important ideas in listeners' minds. Repetition works particularly well when delivered with the appropriate voice inflections and pauses. In a form of repetition called **anaphora**, the speaker repeats a word or phrase at the beginning of successive phrases, clauses, or sentences. For example, in his speech delivered in 1963 in Washington, DC, Dr. Martin Luther King Jr. repeated the phrase "I have a dream" numerous times, each with an upward inflection followed by a pause. In another example, President Barack Obama, in his November 4, 2008, election night speech repeated the phrase "It's the answer" (noted in italics below):

> If there is anyone out there who still doubts that America is a place where all things are possible . . . tonight is *your answer*. . . . *It's the answer* told by lines that stretched around schools. . . . *It's the answer* spoken by young and old. . . . *It's the answer.*[18]

Speakers have made use of anaphora since the earliest times. For example, Jesus preached:

> *Blessed are* the poor in spirit. . . . *Blessed are* the meek. . . . *Blessed are* the peacemakers. . . .[19]

In addition to reinforcing key ideas, repetition can help you create a thematic focus for your speech. Speakers often do this by using both anaphora (see above) and *epiphora* in the same speech. In anaphora you repeat words or phrases at the beginning of successive statements; in **epiphora** you repeat a word or phrase at the end of successive statements. In a speech to his New Hampshire supporters, note how Barack Obama used epiphora to establish a theme of empowerment:

> Some of them are illiterate and can't read the want-ad sections. And when they can, they can't find a job that matches their address. *They work hard every day.* I know. I'm one of them.
> I know they work. I'm a witness. They catch the early bus. *They work every day.* . . . They raise other people's children. *They work every day.* . . .[20]

Use Alliteration for a Poetic Quality

Alliteration is the repetition of the same sounds, usually initial consonants, in two or more neighboring words or syllables. Classic examples of alliteration in speeches include phrases such as Jesse Jackson's "Down with dope, up with hope" and former U.S. Vice President Spiro Agnew's disdainful reference to the U.S. press as "nattering nabobs of negativism."

Alliteration lends speech a poetic, musical rhythm. When used well, it drives home themes and leaves listeners with a lasting impression. When alliteration is poorly crafted or **hackneyed**, it can distract from a message. Use only those alliterative phrases that convey your point more concisely and colorfully than it can otherwise be conveyed.

Experiment with Parallelism

Another rhetorical device that is characteristic of memorable speeches is **parallelism**—the arrangement of words, phrases, or sentences in a similar form. Parallel structure can help the speaker emphasize important ideas in the speech, and can be as simple as orally numbering your points ("first, second, and third"). Like repetition, parallelism creates a sense of steady or building rhythm.

Parallelism in speeches often makes use of **antithesis**—setting off two ideas in balanced (parallel) opposition to each other to create a powerful effect:

> One small step for a man, one giant leap for mankind. —Neil Armstrong on the moon, 1969

> To err is human, to forgive divine. —Alexander Pope, 1711

> For many are called, but few are chosen. —Matthew 22:14

Speakers often make use of three parallel elements, or **triads**. There is something powerful about grouping concepts or ideas into threes. Consider the following examples:

> . . . of the people, by the people, and for the people. —Abraham Lincoln

> If 60 million Anglo-Saxons can have a place in the sun,
> If 60 million Japanese can have a place in the sun,
> If 7 million Belgians can have a place in the sun,
> I cannot see why 400 million black people cannot. —Marcus Garvey

As these examples indicate, when parallelism is used appropriately, it creates a powerful, poetic effect for the audience.

VOCAL AND NONVERBAL DELIVERY

VOCAL AND NONVERBAL DELIVERY

SPEAKER'S REFERENCE

CHAPTER **18** Methods of Delivery 257

Qualities of Effective Delivery 257
Select a Method of Delivery 259
▶ **ESL SPEAKER'S NOTES** Avoiding the Pitfalls of Manuscript Delivery 260
▶ **CHECKLIST** Speaking Off-the-Cuff: Preparing for the Impromptu Speech 261
▶ **ETHICALLY SPEAKING** A Tool for Good and Evil 262
▶ **CHECKLIST** Ready for the Call: Preparing for the Extemporaneous Speech 263

CHAPTER **19** The Voice in Delivery 264

Adjust Your Speaking Volume 264
Vary Your Intonation 264
▶ **CHECKLIST** Tips on Using a Microphone 265
Adjust Your Speaking Rate 266
Use Strategic Pauses 266
Strive for Vocal Variety 267
▶ **ESL SPEAKER'S NOTES** Vocal Variety and the Non-Native Speaker 267
▶ **SELF-ASSESSMENT CHECKLIST** Practice Check for Vocal Effectiveness 268
Carefully Pronounce and Articulate Words 268
▶ **A CULTURAL PERSPECTIVE** Using Dialect (Language Variation) with Care 269

CHAPTER **20** The Body in Delivery 271

Functions of Nonverbal Communication in Delivery 271
Pay Attention to Body Movement 272
▶ **SELF-ASSESSMENT CHECKLIST** Tips for Using Effective Facial Expressions 273
▶ **CHECKLIST** Tips for Effective Gesturing 274
▶ **CHECKLIST** Broad Dress Code Guidelines 274
▶ **A CULTURAL PERSPECTIVE** Nonverbal Communication Patterns in Different Cultures 275
Practice the Delivery 276
▶ **CHECKLIST** Practicing Your Speech 278

VOCAL AND NONVERBAL DELIVERY

CHAPTER 18 Methods of Delivery

Strive for Naturalness in Your Delivery

- Think of your speech as a particularly important conversation. (p. 257)
- Rather than behaving theatrically, strive for naturalness. (p. 257)

Show Enthusiasm

- Show enthusiasm for your topic and for the occasion. (p. 258)
- Speak about what excites you. (p. 258)

Project a Sense of Confidence and Composure

- Focus on the ideas you want to convey rather than on yourself. (p. 258)
- Inspire audience members' confidence in you by appearing confident. (p. 258)

Engage Your Audience by Being Direct

- Establish eye contact with your listeners. (p. 258)
- Use a friendly tone of voice. (p. 258)
- Smile whenever it is appropriate. (p. 258)
- Consider positioning yourself close to the audience. (p. 258)

If You Must Read from a Prepared Text, Do So Naturally

- Vary the rhythm of your words. (p. 259)
- Become familiar with the speech so you can establish some eye contact with the audience. (p. 259)
- Consider using compelling presentation aids. (p. 259)

In General, Don't Try to Memorize Entire Speeches

- Consider memorizing parts of your speech, such as quotations. (p. 260)
- Brief remarks, like toasts, can be well served by memorization. (p. 260)
- When delivering material from memory, know it well enough to do so with enthusiasm and directness. (p. 260)

When Speaking Impromptu, Maximize Any Preparation Time

- Anticipate situations that may require impromptu speaking. (p. 261)
- Consider what would best serve the audience. (p. 261)

- As you wait your turn to speak, take notes on what others are saying. (p. 261)
- Jot down a few key ideas in key-word form. (p. 261)
- Stay on topic. (p. 261)

In Most Situations, Select the Extemporaneous Method of Delivery

- Prepare and practice your speech in advance of delivery. (p. 263)
- Speak from an outline of key words and phrases. (p. 263)
- Use eye contact and body orientation and movement to maximize delivery. (p. 263)

CHAPTER 19 The Voice in Delivery

Adjust Your Speaking Volume

- The bigger the room and the larger the audience, the louder you need to speak. Yet the volume must not be too loud for those in front. (p. 264)
- Be alert to signals from the audience indicating problems in volume. (p. 264)

Beware of Speaking in a Monotone

- Vary your intonation to reflect meaning. (p. 264)
- Use pitch to animate your voice. (p. 264)

Adjust Your Speaking Rate for Comprehension and Expressiveness

- To ensure that your speaking rate is comfortable for your listeners (neither too fast nor too slow), be alert to their reactions. (p. 266)
- Vary your speaking rate to indicate different meanings. (p. 266)

Use Strategic Pauses and Avoid Meaningless Vocal Fillers

- Use pauses to emphasize points, to draw attention to key thoughts, or to allow listeners a moment to contemplate what you've said. (p. 266)
- Eliminate distracting vocal fillers, such as "uh," "hmm," "you know," "I mean," and "it's like." (p. 266)

Use Vocal Variety

- Use the various vocal elements—volume, pitch, rate, and pauses—to create an effective delivery. (p. 267)
- Use a mix of these elements throughout your speech. (p. 267)

Be Conscious of How You Pronounce and Articulate Words

- Learn to pronounce words correctly. (p. 268)
- If you use a dialect, make sure that your audience understands it. (p. 269)
- Don't mumble or slur your words. (p. 269)

CHAPTER 20 The Body in Delivery

Remember the Importance of Your Nonverbal Behavior

- Audiences are attuned to a speaker's vocal delivery (how you say something) and physical actions (facial expressions, gestures, body movement, and physical appearance). (p. 271)
- Audiences notice discrepancies between what you say and how you say it. (p. 271)
- Audiences do not so much listen to a speaker's words as they "read" the speaker who delivers them. (p. 272)

Animate Your Facial Expressions in Appropriate Ways

- Avoid a deadpan expression. (p. 273)
- Establish rapport with your audience with a smile. (p. 273)
- Avoid expressions that are out of character for you. (p. 273)

Maintain Eye Contact with Your Audience

- Establish eye contact to indicate that you recognize and respect listeners. (p. 273)
- Scan the room with your eyes, pausing to gaze at selected listeners. (p. 273)

Use Gestures That Feel Natural to Fill In Gaps in Meaning

- Use gestures to clarify your message. (p. 274)
- Avoid exaggerated gestures, but make them broad enough to be visible. (p. 274)
- Use appropriate gestures that arise from your feelings. (p. 274)

Avoid Standing Stiffly behind the Podium

- As space and time allow, try to get out from behind the podium. (p. 274)
- Move around at a comfortable, natural pace. (p. 274)
- Be aware of your posture. Stand erect, but not ramrod straight. (p. 274)

Pay Attention to Your Clothes and Grooming

- Dress appropriately for the occasion: dark-colored suits convey a sense of authority, while medium-blue or navy suits enhance credibility. (p. 274)
- Choices of clothing and grooming will probably be the first thing your listeners notice about you. (p. 275)
- Keep your hands free of distracting objects, such as pens and notecards. (p. 275)

Practice Your Speech Using a Speaking Outline

- Focus on your speech ideas rather than on yourself. (p. 276)
- After you've practiced several times, videorecord your delivery. Incorporate changes and record it again. (p. 276)
- Rework unsatisfactory parts of your speech as you practice. (p. 277)
- Practice under realistic conditions. (p. 277)
- Visualize the audience as you speak. (p. 277)
- Practice using your speaking notes unobtrusively. (p. 277)
- Ask at least one other person to serve as a constructive critic. (p. 277)
- Time each portion of your speech (introduction, body, conclusion). (p. 277)
- Evaluate and adjust your rate of speech. (p. 277)
- Don't wait until the last minute to begin practicing. (p. 277)
- For an extemporaneous speech, plan to practice five times. (p. 277)

KEY TERMS

Chapter 18

effective delivery	TelePrompTer	speaking impromptu
elocutionary movement	speaking from memory	speaking extemporaneously
speaking from manuscript	oratory	

Chapter 19

volume	speaking rate	mumbling
pitch	vocal fillers	lazy speech
intonation	pauses	dialects
lavalier microphone	vocal variety	
handheld or fixed microphone	pronunciation	
	articulation	

Chapter 20

aural channel	visual channel	talking head
paralanguage	scanning	

Methods of Delivery

I wish you to see that public speaking is a perfectly normal act, which calls for no strange, artificial methods, but only for an extension and development of that most familiar act, conversation.

—James Albert Winans, *Public Speaking*[1]

The process of putting together a speech may be challenging, but what often creates the bigger challenge for most of us is contemplating or actually getting up in front of an audience and speaking. Added to this uneasiness is the unfounded idea that speech delivery should be formulaic, mechanical, and exaggerated—that it is, in a way, unnatural or artificial. But as the early public speaking scholar James Albert Winans noted, a speech is really just an enlarged conversation, "quite the natural thing."

Natural, however, does not mean unplanned and unrehearsed. Each component of your speech "conversation," from the quality of your voice to your facial expressions, gestures, and manner of dress, affects how your listeners respond to you. As audience members listen to your words, they are simultaneously reacting to you on a nonverbal level—how you look, how you sound, and how you respond to them. If your verbal and nonverbal cues violate audience members' expectations, they will lose confidence in your credibility as a speaker.[2] Developing effective delivery skills is therefore a critical aspect of the speechmaking process.

Qualities of Effective Delivery

WEB Video quizzes

Effective delivery is the controlled use of voice and body to express the qualities of naturalness, enthusiasm, confidence, and directness. As Winans has noted, effective delivery is characterized by "a style at once simple and effective."[3] Thus an effective delivery style rests on the same natural foundation as everyday conversation, except that it is more rehearsed and purposeful.

Strive for Naturalness

Contemporary audiences expect naturalness from a speaker. Had you been a student in the early 1900s, during the heyday of the **elocutionary movement**, the opposite would have been true. The elocutionists regarded speechmaking as a type of performance, much like acting.[4] Students were given a rigid set of rules on how to use their eyes, faces, gestures, and voices to drive home certain points in the speech and to manipulate audience members' moods. Instructors emphasized delivery to such an extent that it often assumed more importance than the content of the speech.

Today, the content or message itself, rather than the delivery, is seen as being most important. Audience members expect speakers to be without artifice; to be genuine. Conveying these qualities, however, requires practice. Perhaps ironically, it is only by thoroughly rehearsing the message that you gain the confidence to deliver it in a natural manner.

Show Enthusiasm

Enthusiasm is contagious. When you talk about something that excites you, you talk more rapidly, use more gestures, look at your listeners more frequently, use more pronounced facial expressions, and probably stand closer to your listeners and perhaps even touch them more. Your enthusiasm spills over to your listeners, drawing them into your message. As their own enthusiasm grows, they listen more attentively because they want to know more about the thing that excites you. In turn, you sense their interest and responsiveness and realize that you are truly connecting with them. The value of enthusiastic delivery is thus accomplished: It focuses your audience's attention on the message.

Project a Sense of Confidence

Speeches delivered with confidence and composure inspire the audience's confidence in you and in your message. Your focus is on the ideas that you want to convey, not on memorized words and sentences and not on yourself. Instead of thinking about how you look and sound, think about the idea you're trying to convey and how well your listeners are grasping it. Confident delivery directs the audience's attention to the message and away from the speaker's behavior.

Be Direct

To truly communicate with an audience, you must build rapport with your listeners. You need to show that you care about them and their reasons for listening to you. This is generally done in two ways: by making your message relevant to the interests and attitudes of audience members, and by demonstrating your interest and concern for them in your delivery. The best way to do the latter is by being direct: Maintain eye contact; use a friendly tone of voice; animate your facial expressions, especially positive ones such as smiling; and position yourself so that you are physically close to the audience. Of course, you don't want to go overboard by becoming annoying or overly familiar with the audience. But neither do you want to appear distant, aloof, or uncaring. Both extremes draw audience attention away from the message. Chapters 19 and 20 focus on techniques for using your voice and body, respectively, to achieve a natural, enthusiastic, confident, and direct delivery. In the following section, we consider the major methods of delivery.

Select a Method of Delivery

For virtually any type of speech or presentation, you can choose from four basic methods of delivery: speaking from manuscript, speaking from memory, speaking impromptu, and speaking extemporaneously. Each method is distinguished by the expressive voice and body behaviors it uses or restricts, and by the qualities of delivery it promotes or impedes (see Table 18.1).

Speaking from Manuscript

When **speaking from manuscript**, you read a speech verbatim—that is, from prepared written text (either on paper or on a **TelePrompTer**) that contains the entire speech, word for word. As a rule, speaking from manuscript restricts eye contact and body movement, and may also limit expressiveness in vocal variety and quality. Watching a speaker read a speech can be monotonous and boring for the audience. Quite obviously, the natural, relaxed, enthusiastic, and direct qualities of delivery are all limited by this method. Commenting on the dangers of reading from a TelePrompTer, for instance, columnist and former speechwriter William Safire notes that it can make the speaker appear "shifty and untrustworthy."[5]

At certain times, however, it is advisable or necessary to read a speech, such as when you must convey a very precise message. As with politicians and business leaders, you may know that you will be quoted and must avoid misinterpretation. Or perhaps it is your responsibility to explain an emergency, so you will need to convey exact descriptions and directions (see Chapter 32 on crisis communication). In some speech circumstances, such as when an award is being presented, tradition may dictate that your remarks be read from a manuscript.

TABLE 18.1 Methods of Delivery and Their Probable Uses	
When	**Method of Delivery**
Precise wording is called for; for instance, when you want to avoid being misquoted or misconstrued, or you need to communicate exact descriptions and directions.	Consider *speaking from manuscript* (reading part or all of your speech from fully prepared text).
You must deliver a short special-occasion speech, such as a toast or introduction, or you plan on using direct quotations.	Consider *speaking from memory* (memorizing part or all of your speech).
You are called upon to speak without prior planning or preparation.	Consider *speaking impromptu* (organizing your thoughts with little or no lead time).
You have time to prepare and practice developing a speech or presentation that achieves a natural conversational style.	Consider *speaking extemporaneously* (developing your speech in working outline and then practicing and delivering it with a phrase or key-word outline).

If you must read from a prepared text, do what you can to deliver the speech naturally:

- Vary the rhythm of your words (see Chapter 19).
- Become familiar enough with the speech so that you can establish some eye contact.
- Use a large font and double- or triple-space the manuscript so that you can read without straining.
- Consider using some compelling presentation aids (see Chapter 21).

Speaking from Memory

The formal name for **speaking from memory** is **oratory**. In oratorical style, you put the entire speech, word for word, into writing and then commit it to memory. In the United States, speaking from memory rarely occurs anymore, though this form of delivery is common in other parts of the world.[6]

Memorization is not a natural way to present a message. True eye contact with the audience is unlikely, and memorization invites potential disaster during a speech because there is always the possibility of a mental lapse or block. When a mental block occurs, you are left with no or few options because you have focused practice on nothing else but the exact wording of the speech.

ESL SPEAKER'S NOTES

Avoiding the Pitfalls of Manuscript Delivery

Speaking from manuscript may be difficult and perhaps even ill-advised for some ESL speakers. Reading a speech aloud, word for word, is likely to exaggerate existing problems with pronunciation and *word stress,* or the emphasis given to words in a sentence. These emphasized words or syllables are pronounced more loudly and with a higher pitch. Robbin Crabtree and Robert Weissberg note:

One of the most characteristic features of spoken English is the tendency of native speakers to take one word in every sentence and give it a stronger push than the others. This feature is called *primary stress.* If you try out a couple of sample sentences, you'll note that the primary stress normally falls at the end, or very close to the end, of the sentence: "That was one of the best speeches I've ever heard." "Let me know if you have trouble; and I'll be glad to help."[1]

If you have difficulty with word and sentence stress and you find that you need to deliver a speech from manuscript, spend extra practice time reading your speech with the aim of ensuring that your word and sentence stress align with the meaning you intend.

1. Robbin Crabtree and Robert Weissberg, *ESL Students in the Public Speaking Classroom: A Guide for Teachers* (Boston: Bedford/St. Martin's, 2000), 24.

Some kinds of brief speeches, however, such as toasts and introductions, can be well served by memorization. Other times it's helpful to memorize a part of the speech, especially when you must present the same information many times in the same words, or when you use direct quotations as a form of support. If you do find an occasion to use the memorization strategy, be sure to learn your speech so completely that in actual delivery you can focus on conveying enthusiasm and directness.

Speaking Impromptu

Speaking impromptu, a type of delivery that is unpracticed, spontaneous, or improvised, involves speaking on relatively short notice with little time to prepare. It's not advisable to speak impromptu when you've been given adequate time to prepare and practice a speech (that's called procrastination). However, many occasions require that you make some remarks on the spur of the moment. For example, an instructor may ask you to summarize key points from an assignment, or a fellow employee who was scheduled to speak on a new project may be sick and your boss has invited you to take his or her place.

SPEAKING OFF-THE-CUFF: PREPARING FOR THE IMPROMPTU SPEECH

To succeed at giving impromptu speeches, follow these steps:

_____ 1. Find a pen and a piece of paper as quickly as possible.

_____ 2. Take a minute to reflect on how you can best address the audience's interests and needs. Take a deep breath, and focus on your expertise on the topic or on what you really want to say.

_____ 3. Jot down in key words or short phrases the ideas you may want to cover.

_____ 4. Stay on the topic. Don't wander off track.

_____ 5. If your speech follows someone else's, acknowledge that person's statements.

_____ 6. State your ideas, and then summarize them.

_____ 7. Use transitions such as _first, second,_ and _third,_ both to organize your points and to help listeners follow them.

CHECKLIST

To succeed in delivering impromptu remarks:

- _Follow the lead of Emmy and Academy Award nominees: Be prepared._ Try to anticipate situations that may require you to speak impromptu. If there is any chance that this might occur, prepare some remarks beforehand.

- _Think on your feet—and think first about your listeners._ Consider their likely needs and interests, and try to shape your remarks accordingly. For example, who are the people present, and what are their views on the issue?

- *As you wait your turn to speak, listen to what others around you are saying.* Take notes in a key-word or phrase format and arrange them into ideas or main points from which you can speak. Organizing a few thoughts beforehand will help you make your point and prevent you from talking aimlessly.
- *When you do speak, give a brief statement, if appropriate, summarizing what you've heard from others.* Then state your own position, make your points, and restate your position, referring as needed to your notes.

Taking steps like these will enhance your effectiveness because you will maintain the qualities of natural, enthusiastic, and direct delivery. And having even a hastily prepared plan can give you greater confidence than having no plan at all.

ETHICALLY SPEAKING

A Tool for Good and Evil

The philosopher Plato believed that the art of public speaking—or rhetoric, as the ancients referred to it—was too often corrupt.[1] Plato's cynicism toward public speaking was the result of unethical practices that he witnessed among his peers and other leaders in ancient Greece. From his perspective, rhetoric (at least as practiced) too often distorted the truth. Today, few people condemn public speaking per se as a dishonest form of communication. But many are aware of the power of delivery to corrupt. If history is any guide, these fears are well founded: one has only to think of such modern-day dictators as Mao Tse-tung, Joseph Stalin, Adolf Hitler, and Saddam Hussein, all of whom deliberately used delivery as a means of manipulation. Hitler's forceful delivery—a scorching stare, gestures, and a staccato voice—so mesmerized his listeners that millions accepted the horrific idea that an entire people should be annihilated. Historians note how Hitler spent countless hours practicing his vocal delivery and body language to achieve maximum hypnotic effect. As he did this, he would have himself photographed so that he could hone individual gestures to perfection.[2]

Like any tool, delivery can be used for both ethical and unethical purposes. Countless speakers, from Abraham Lincoln to Martin Luther King Jr., have used their flair for delivery to uplift and inspire people. Yet there will always be those who try to camouflage weak or false arguments with an overpowering delivery. You can ensure that your own delivery is ethical by reminding yourself of the ground rules for ethical speaking described in Chapter 5: trustworthiness, respect, responsibility, and fairness. Always reveal your true purpose to the audience, review your evidence and reasoning for soundness, and grant your audience the power of rational choice.

1. Thomas M. Conley, *Rhetoric in the European Tradition* (New York: Longman, 1990).
2. Ian Kershaw, "The Hitler Myth," *History Today* 35, no. 11 (1985): 23.

Speaking Extemporaneously

Speaking extemporaneously falls somewhere between impromptu and written or memorized deliveries. In an extemporaneous speech, you prepare well and practice in advance, giving full attention to all facets of the speech—content, arrangement, and delivery alike. Instead of memorizing or writing the speech word for word, you speak from an outline of key words and phrases (see Chapter 14), having concentrated throughout your preparation and practice on the ideas you want to communicate.

More speeches are delivered by extemporaneous delivery than by any other method. Because this technique is most conducive to achieving a natural, conversational quality of delivery, many speakers consider it to be the preferred method of the four types of delivery. Knowing your idea well enough to present it without memorization or manuscript gives you greater flexibility in adapting to the specific speaking situation. You can modify wording, rearrange your points, change examples, or omit information in keeping with the audience and the setting. You can have more eye contact, more direct body orientation, greater freedom of movement, and generally better control of your thoughts and actions than any of the other delivery methods allow.

Speaking extemporaneously does present several possible drawbacks. Because you aren't speaking from specifically written or memorized text, you may become repetitive and wordy. Fresh examples or points may come to mind that you want to share, so the speech may take longer than anticipated. Occasionally, even a glance at your speaking notes may fail to jog your memory on a point you wanted to cover, and you momentarily find yourself searching for what to say next. The remedy for these potential pitfalls is, of course, *practice*. If you practice delivering your speech using a speaking outline often enough, you will probably have no difficulty staying on target. In fact, you will be more likely to deliver a speech that is effectively natural, enthusiastic, confident, and direct.

READY FOR THE CALL: PREPARING FOR THE EXTEMPORANEOUS SPEECH

Follow these general steps below to prepare effective extemporaneous speeches:

_____ 1. Focus your topic as assigned or as appropriate to the audience and occasion.

_____ 2. Prepare a thesis statement that will serve as the central point or idea of your speech.

_____ 3. Research your topic in a variety of sources to gather support for your thesis and add credibility to your points.

_____ 4. Outline main and subordinate points.

_____ 5. Practice the speech at least six times.

(See Chapter 2 for more on speech preparation.)

CHECKLIST

CHAPTER 19

The Voice in Delivery

Used properly in the speaking situation, your voice is a powerful instrument of expression that should convey who you are and deliver your message in a way that engages listeners. Your voice also indicates your confidence and affects whether the audience perceives you to be in control of the situation.[1] If you have inadequate mastery of your voice, you may lose your audience's attention and fail to deliver a successful speech. Fortunately, as you practice your speech, you can learn to control each of the elements of vocal delivery. These include volume, pitch, rate, pauses, vocal variety, and pronunciation and articulation.

Adjust Your Speaking Volume

Volume, the relative loudness of a speaker's voice while giving a speech, is usually the most obvious and frequently cited vocal element in speechmaking, and with good reason. We need to hear the speaker at a comfortable level. *The proper volume for delivering a speech is somewhat louder than that of normal conversation.* Just how much louder depends on three factors: (1) the size of the room and the number of people in the audience, (2) whether or not you use a microphone, and (3) the level of background noise.

Speaking at the appropriate volume is critical to how credible your listeners will perceive you to be. Audience members view speakers whose volume is too low less positively than those who project their voices at a pleasing volume.

One expert suggests that if your tendency is to speak softly, initially you will need to project more than seems necessary. To do this, breathe deeply from your diaphragm rather than more shallowly from your vocal cords to gain the necessary force for effective vocal projection: "Start the breath with your diaphragm and let it propel your voice beyond the last row of the audience."[2]

The easiest way to judge whether you are speaking too loudly or too softly is to be alert to audience feedback. You need to increase volume if audience members appear to be straining to hear you.

Vary Your Intonation

Imagine the variation in sound between the left-most and the right-most keys of a piano. This variation represents the instrument's **pitch**, or range of sounds from high to low (or vice versa). Pitch is determined by the number of vibrations per unit of time; technically, the more vibrations per unit (also called *frequency*), the higher the pitch, and vice versa.[3] The classic warm-up singing exercise *"Do re mi fa so la ti do"* is an exercise in pitch.

Vocal pitch is important in speechmaking—indeed, in talk of any kind—because it powerfully affects the meaning associated with spoken words. For example, say "Stop." Now, say *"Stop!"* Hear the difference? The rising and falling of vocal pitch across phrases and sentences, termed **intonation**,[4] conveys two very distinct meanings. Intonation, or pitch, is what distinguishes a question from a statement:

> It's time to study already.
>
> It's time to study al*ready?*

As you speak, pitch conveys your mood, level of enthusiasm, concern for the audience, and overall commitment to the occasion. When there is no variety in pitch, speaking becomes monotonous. A monotone voice is the death knell to any speech. Speakers who are vocally monotone rapidly lose the audience's attention and goodwill. The famous comedian Ben Stein is just about the only speaker we know who uses monotone effectively—and that is because his content is so sharp. The best way to avoid speaking in monotone is to practice and listen to your speeches with a recording device. You will readily identify instances that require better intonation.

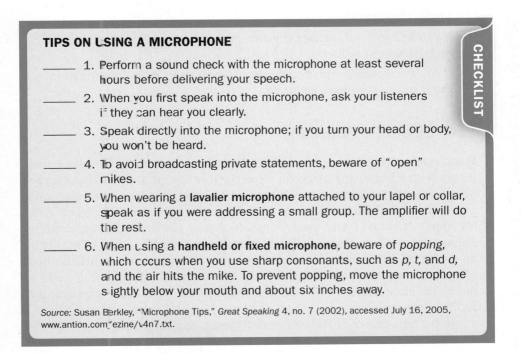

TIPS ON USING A MICROPHONE

CHECKLIST

_____ 1. Perform a sound check with the microphone at least several hours before delivering your speech.

_____ 2. When you first speak into the microphone, ask your listeners if they can hear you clearly.

_____ 3. Speak directly into the microphone; if you turn your head or body, you won't be heard.

_____ 4. To avoid broadcasting private statements, beware of "open" mikes.

_____ 5. When wearing a **lavalier microphone** attached to your lapel or collar, speak as if you were addressing a small group. The amplifier will do the rest.

_____ 6. When using a **handheld or fixed microphone**, beware of *popping*, which occurs when you use sharp consonants, such as *p, t,* and *d,* and the air hits the mike. To prevent popping, move the microphone slightly below your mouth and about six inches away.

Source: Susan Berkley, "Microphone Tips," *Great Speaking* 4, no. 7 (2002), accessed July 16, 2005, www.antion.com/ezine/v4n7.txt.

Adjust Your Speaking Rate

Successful speakers share a secret: The most effective way to hold an audience's attention, as well as to accurately convey meaning, is to vary your **speaking rate**, the pace at which you convey speech. A slow rate (at the right time) indicates thoughtfulness, seriousness, solemnity, reverence, concern, and the like. A lively pace indicates excitement, adventure, happiness, enthusiasm, and so on.

The normal rate of speech for adults is between 120 and 150 words per minute. A typical speech occurs at a rate slightly below 120 words per minute, but there is no standard, "ideal," or most effective rate. Being alert to the audience's reactions is the best way to know whether your rate of speech is too fast or too slow. An audience will get fidgety, bored, listless, perhaps even sleepy if you speak too slowly; if you speak too rapidly, listeners will appear irritated and confused, as though they can't catch what you're saying. One recent study suggests that speaking too fast will cause listeners to perceive you as tentative about your control of the situation.[5]

Learn to control your rate this way:

- Select a section of ten words from your speech.
- Write out a sentence or two if you don't already have a manuscript of your speech.
- Read the selection aloud over and over for thirty seconds. You should be able to repeat the selection seven or eight times in thirty seconds, or about fifteen times in one minute.
- If you find yourself stating the words more than eight times in thirty seconds, slow your rate.
- If you find yourself repeating the set of words fewer than seven times in thirty seconds, increase your rate.

Use Strategic Pauses

Many novice speakers are uncomfortable with pauses. It's as if some social stigma is attached to any silence in a speech. This tendency is probably a carry-over from everyday conversation, where we cover pauses with unnecessary and undesirable **vocal fillers**, such as "uh," "hmm," "you know," "I mean," "it's like," and "anyways." Like pitch, however, pauses can be important strategic elements of a speech. **Pauses** enhance meaning by providing a type of punctuation, emphasizing a point, drawing attention to a key thought, or just allowing listeners a moment to contemplate what is being said. In short, they make a speech far more effective than it might otherwise be. Both the speaker and the audience need pauses.

In his well-known "I Have a Dream" speech, Martin Luther King Jr. exhibits masterful use of strategic pauses. In what is now the most memorable segment of the speech, King pauses, just momentarily, to secure the audience's attention to the next words that are about to be spoken:

I have a dream [*pause*] that one day on the red hills of Georgia. . . .

I have a dream [*pause*] that one day even the great state of Mississippi. . . .[6]

Imagine how diminished the impact of this speech would have been if King had uttered "uh" or "you know" at each of these pauses!

Strive for Vocal Variety

WEB Chapter quizzes

Rather than operating separately, all the vocal elements described so far—volume, pitch, rate, and pauses—work together to create an effective delivery. Indeed, the real key to effective vocal delivery is to vary all these elements, thereby demonstrating **vocal variety**. For example, as King speaks the words "I have a dream," the pauses are immediately preceded by a combination of reduced speech rate and increased volume and pitch—a crescendo, you might say. The impact of this variety leaves an indelible impression on anyone who has heard his speech.

Enthusiasm is key to achieving effective vocal variety. Vocal variety comes quite naturally when you are excited about what you are saying to an audience, when you feel it is important and want to share it with them. However, be careful not to let your enthusiasm overwhelm your ability to control your vocal behavior. Talking too rapidly can lead to more filled pauses because you forget

ESL SPEAKER'S NOTES

Vocal Variety and the Non-Native Speaker

Learning to deliver a speech with the vocal variety that English-speaking people in the United States expect can be particularly challenging for non-native speakers. In addition to having concerns about pronunciation and articulation, the non-native speaker may also be accustomed to patterns of vocal variety—volume, pitch, rate, and pauses—that are different from those discussed in this chapter.

The pronunciation of English depends on learning how to combine a series of about forty basic sounds (fifteen vowels and twenty-five consonants) that together serve to distinguish English words from one another. Correct pronunciation also requires that the speaker learn proper word stress, rhythm, and intonation or pitch.[1] As you practice your speeches, pay particular attention to these facets of delivery. Seek feedback from others to ensure that your goal of shared meaning will be met whenever you deliver speeches.

1. Maryann Cunningham Florez, "Improving Adult ESL Learners' Pronunciation Skills," National Clearinghouse for ESL Literacy Education (1998), accessed July 16, 2005, www.cal.org/caela/digests/Pronun.htm.

what you want to say. Overexcitement can also result in a consistently high pitch that becomes monotonous. Hence, it is essential to practice your vocal delivery even when you are already enthusiastic about a speech.

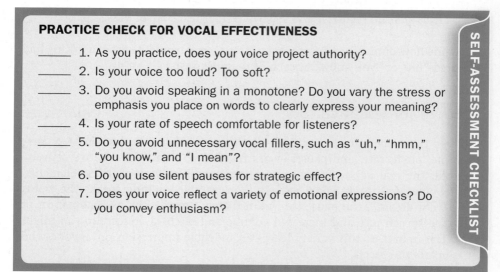

PRACTICE CHECK FOR VOCAL EFFECTIVENESS

_____ 1. As you practice, does your voice project authority?

_____ 2. Is your voice too loud? Too soft?

_____ 3. Do you avoid speaking in a monotone? Do you vary the stress or emphasis you place on words to clearly express your meaning?

_____ 4. Is your rate of speech comfortable for listeners?

_____ 5. Do you avoid unnecessary vocal fillers, such as "uh," "hmm," "you know," and "I mean"?

_____ 6. Do you use silent pauses for strategic effect?

_____ 7. Does your voice reflect a variety of emotional expressions? Do you convey enthusiasm?

SELF-ASSESSMENT CHECKLIST

Carefully Pronounce and Articulate Words

Another important element of vocal delivery involves correctly saying the words you speak. Few things distract an audience more than improper pronunciation or unclear articulation of words. **Pronunciation** is the correct formation of word sounds. **Articulation** is the clarity or forcefulness with which the sounds are made, regardless of whether they are pronounced correctly. In other words, you can be articulating clearly but pronouncing incorrectly. In this way, good articulation may betray poor pronunciation. It is important to pay attention to and work on both areas.

Consider these words that are routinely mispronounced:

- effect *(ee-fect)* is stated as *uh-fect.*
- anyway *(any-way)* is said as *any-ways.*
- mobile *(mo-bile)* is said as *mo-bull* or *mo-bill.*
- leaves *(leevz)* is stated as *leephs.*

Incorrect pronunciations are a matter of habit. Normally you may not know that you are mispronouncing a word because most people you talk with probably say the word much the same way you do. This habit may be associated with a regional accent or dialect. In that case, speaking to an audience of local origin may pose few problems if you pronounce words in regionally customary ways.

But if you are speaking to members of an audience for whom your accent and pronunciation patterns are not the norm, practice using correct pronunciation becomes especially important. In fact, the better your pronunciation all around, the more enhanced will be the audience's perceptions of your competence, and the greater will be the potential impact of your speech. (See Table 19.1 and Appendix D for lists of commonly mispronounced words.)

Articulation problems are also a matter of habit. A very common pattern of poor articulation is **mumbling**—slurring words together at a very low level of volume and pitch so that they are barely audible. Sometimes the problem is **lazy speech**. Common examples include saying "fer" instead of "far," "wanna" instead of "want to," "gonna" instead of "going to," and "theez 'er" instead of "these are." Like any habit, poor articulation can be overcome by practicing and by unlearning the problem behavior:

- If you mumble, practice speaking more loudly and with emphatic pronunciation.
- If you tend toward lazy speech, put more effort into your articulation.
- Consciously try to say each word clearly and correctly.
- Practice clear and precise enunciation of proper word sounds. Say *articulation* several times until it rolls off your tongue naturally.
- Do the same for these words: *want to, going to, Atlanta, chocolate, sophomore, California.*

A CULTURAL PERSPECTIVE

Using Dialect (Language Variation) with Care

Every culture has subcultural variations on the preferred pronunciation and articulation of its languages. These variations represent **dialects** of the language. In the United States, for example, there is so-called Standard English, Black English, Tex-Mex (a combination of Spanish and English spoken with a distinct Texas drawl or accent), and such regional variations as  those found in the South, New England, and along the border with Canada. In parts of Texas, for example, a common usage is to say "fixin' to" instead of "about to," as in "We're fixin' to go to a movie."

Your own dialect may be a factor in the effectiveness of your delivery when speaking to an audience of people whose dialect is different. At the least, your dialect might call attention to itself and be a distraction to the audience. One strategy that you can use is to determine which words in your usual vocabulary are spoken dialectically and then practice articulating them in General American (GA) English pronunciation.

TABLE 19.1   Thirteen Commonly Mispronounced Words

Correct Spelling	Wrong Pronunciation	Right Pronunciation
ac*ts*	*aks*	*ak*ts
a*sked*	*aks*	*askt*
et *c*etera	*ek set er uh*	*et set er uh*
fa*cts*	*faks*	*fakts*
fi*f*th	*fith or fif*	*fif th*
gen*ui*ne	*jen yu wine*	*jen yu in*
hund*red*	*hun dert*	*hun dred*
in*t*ernational	*innernashunal*	*in ter na shuh nal*
in*tro*duce	*innerdoos*	*in tro dyoos*
nu*c*lear	*nookyouluhr*	*nook klee uhr*
pi*c*ture	*pi chur*	*pik chur*
products	*prah duks*	*prah dukts*
re*cog*ni*zed*	*rekunized*	*re kug nized*

Source: Lilyan Wilder, *Seven Steps to Fearless Speaking* (New York: Wiley, 1999), 210–11. Reprinted with permission.

The Body in Delivery

Beyond the actual words that are spoken, audiences receive information from a speech through two nonverbal channels of communication: the aural and the visual. The **aural channel** is made up of the vocalizations that form and accompany spoken words. These vocalizations, or **paralanguage**, include the qualities of volume, pitch, rate, variety, and pronunciation and articulation described in Chapter 19. Paralanguage refers to *how* something is said, not to *what* is said.

The **visual channel** includes the speaker's physical actions and appearance—facial expressions, gestures, general body movement, physical appearance, dress, and objects held. These nonverbal elements have been called the *silent language*. Paralanguage and the visual elements of a speech are critical to an audience's full understanding of the message you wish to convey. According to one study, listeners derive only 7 percent of the meaning of any message about feelings and attitudes from the speaker's words, the verbal component, while 38 percent comes from the speaker's voice and 55 percent comes from the speaker's facial expressions and body movements, the nonverbal component.[1]

Functions of Nonverbal Communication in Delivery

Researchers have identified several ways in which nonverbal communication works together with the verbal component of a speech,[2] including (1) clarifying the meaning of verbal messages; (2) facilitating feedback between speaker and audience; (3) helping establish a relationship between speaker and audience; and (4) helping the speaker establish credibility.

Clarify Verbal Messages

The impact of the verbal component of your speech—what you say—depends largely on your vocal and bodily actions while saying it. The same words spoken with different body movements or different vocal emphasis convey different meanings. Similar shifts in meaning occur with gestures. If you say to the audience, "We'll miss him" while rolling your eyes and waving your hands dismissively, the meaning would be much different than if you said the same thing while giving a heartfelt sigh and perhaps opening your arms to indicate that the audience shares the feeling.

Facilitate Feedback

Listeners use a host of body cues—head shaking (either in agreement or in dis-agreement), smiles or frowns, arms rigidly folded across the chest, and friendly gazes or facing-away postures—to communicate their pleasure or displeasure with a speech. Being alert to such feedback and responding to it can mean the difference between an alienated audience and one that feels recognized and respected. Coughing and excessive shifting around, for example, may indicate difficulty in hearing and flagging interest. In response, you might increase your speaking volume and look in the direction of the affected listeners more fre-quently and for longer periods. If you receive negative cues such as frowns and head shaking, you might present some additional evidence or interject some relevant humor.

Establish Relationships between Speaker and Audience

Nonverbal behavior, such as how you position yourself vis-à-vis your listeners, allows you to adjust your relationship with them, establishing a level of famil-iarity and closeness that is suitable to the topic, purpose, and occasion. To stim-ulate a sense of informality and closeness, for example, you can move out from behind the podium and walk or stand among audience members. Talk-show host and comedian Jay Leno opens each of his nightly shows by walking to the front edge of the stage to greet and shake hands with members of the audience. His friendly, open behavior establishes a casual communicative atmosphere and a direct relationship with his audience. Conversely, remaining at a distance from the audience, such as behind the speaker's stand, using a more reserved vocal quality, and speaking at a somewhat slower and consistent rate establish a more formal relationship with listeners.

Establish Speaker Credibility

Nonverbal communication plays a key part in the audience's perception of your competence, trustworthiness, and character.[3] For example, audiences are more readily persuaded by speakers who emphasize vocal variety, eye contact, nod-ding at listeners, and standing with an open body position than by those who minimize these nonverbal cues.[4] Audience members also respond more posi-tively to speakers whom they perceive to be well dressed and attractive. They are apt to take them more seriously and are more objective in their responses than they are to speakers whom they do not find attractive.

Pay Attention to Body Movement

WEB Chapter quizzes

As audience members listen to you, they are simultaneously evaluating the cues sent by your facial expressions, eye behavior, gestures, and general body move-ments. Audiences do not so much listen to a speaker's words as they "read" the body language of the speaker who delivers them.[5]

Animate Your Facial Expressions

From our facial expressions, audiences can gauge whether we are excited about, disenchanted by, or indifferent to our speech—and the audience to whom we are presenting it.

Universally, few behaviors are more effective for building rapport with an audience than *smiling*.[6] A smile is a sign of mutual welcome at the start of a speech, of mutual comfort and interest during the speech, and of mutual good-will at the close of a speech. Smiling when you feel nervous or otherwise uncomfortable can help you relax and gain more composure. Of course, facial expressions need to correspond to the tenor of the speech. Doing what is natural and normal for the occasion should be the rule.

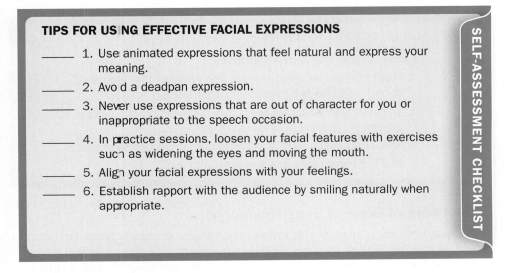

TIPS FOR USING EFFECTIVE FACIAL EXPRESSIONS

_____ 1. Use animated expressions that feel natural and express your meaning.

_____ 2. Avoid a deadpan expression.

_____ 3. Never use expressions that are out of character for you or inappropriate to the speech occasion.

_____ 4. In practice sessions, loosen your facial features with exercises such as widening the eyes and moving the mouth.

_____ 5. Align your facial expressions with your feelings.

_____ 6. Establish rapport with the audience by smiling naturally when appropriate.

SELF-ASSESSMENT CHECKLIST

Maintain Eye Contact

If smiling is an effective way to build rapport, maintaining eye contact is mandatory in establishing a positive relationship with your listeners. Having eye contact with the audience is one of the most, if not *the* most, important physical actions in public speaking. Eye contact maintains the quality of directness in speech delivery. It lets people know they are recognized, indicates acknowledgment and respect, and signals to audience members that the speaker sees them as unique human beings.

With an audience of a hundred to more than a thousand members, it's impossible to look at every listener. But in most speaking situations you are likely to experience, you should be able to look at most people in the audience by using a technique called **scanning**. When you scan an audience, you move your gaze from one listener to another and from one section to another, pausing to gaze at one person long enough to complete a full thought before removing your gaze and shifting it to another listener. One speaking professional suggests following the "rule of three": Pick three audience members to focus on—one in the middle, one on the right, and one on the left of the room; these audience members will be your anchors as you scan the room.[7]

Use Gestures That Feel Natural

Words alone seldom convey what we want to express. Physical gestures fill in the gaps, as in illustrating the size or shape of an object (e.g., by showing the size of it by extending two hands, palms facing each other), or expressing the depth of an emotion (e.g., by pounding a fist on a podium).[8] Gestures should be natural and spontaneous, arising from genuine emotions and conforming to your personality (see the Checklist below for tips on gesturing effectively).[9]

TIPS FOR EFFECTIVE GESTURING

_____ 1. Use natural, spontaneous gestures.

_____ 2. Avoid exaggerated gestures, but use gestures that are broad enough to be seen by each audience member.

_____ 3. Eliminate distracting gestures, such as fidgeting with pens or pencils or brushing back hair from your eyes.

_____ 4. Analyze your gestures for effectiveness in practice sessions.

_____ 5. Practice movements that feel natural to you.

CHECKLIST

Be Aware of General Body Movement

General body movement is also important in maintaining audience attention and processing of your message. Audience members soon tire of listening to a **talking head** who remains steadily positioned in one place behind a microphone or a podium. As space and time allow, try to get out from behind the podium and stand with the audience. As you do, move around at a comfortable, natural pace.

A speaker's posture sends a definite message to the audience. Listeners perceive speakers who slouch as being sloppy, unfocused, and even weak. Strive to stand erect, but not ramrod straight. The goal is to appear authoritative, not rigid.

BROAD DRESS CODE GUIDELINES

_____ 1. For a "power" look, wear a dark-colored suit.

_____ 2. Medium-blue or navy paired with white can enhance your credibility.

_____ 3. Yellow and orange color tones convey friendliness.

_____ 4. The color red focuses attention on you.

_____ 5. Flashy jewelry distracts listeners.

CHECKLIST

Dress Appropriately

As superficial as it may sound, the first thing an audience is likely to notice as you approach the speaker's position is your clothing. The critical criteria in determining appropriate dress for a speech are audience expectations and the nature of the speech occasion. If you are speaking as a representative of your business, for example, you will want to complement your company's image.[10] Consider Apple cofounder Steve Jobs, who invariably wears jeans and a black shirt when he rolls out a new product line. Jobs's attire conveys a signature style that is casual and "cool," personifying the Apple products he represents.

A CULTURAL PERSPECTIVE

Nonverbal Communication Patterns in Different Cultures

As a speaker, it's important to remember that, like verbal communication, nonverbal communication is also profoundly influenced by culture. Gestures, for example, have entirely different meanings in different cultures, and many an unsuspecting speaker has inadvertently made a rude gesture in his or her host's culture. In the late 1950s, for instance, Vice President Richard Nixon made a goodwill tour of Latin America, where there were feelings of hostility toward the United States. On one of his stops, Nixon stepped off his plane and, smiling, gestured with the A-OK sign to the waiting crowd. The crowd booed. In that culture, Nixon's gesture meant "Screw you." Days of delicate diplomacy were undone by two seconds of nonverbal behavior.[1] This same gesture, incidentally, means "zero" in French and "money" in Japan. Roger Axtell catalogs a variety of gestures in his book *Gestures: The Do's and Taboos of Body Language around the World*. This eye-opening account demonstrates how something in one culture can mean literally the opposite in another (e.g., nodding means "yes" in the United States but can mean "no" in the former Yugoslavia and Iran).

The display of emotions is also guided by the social rules of the culture. The Japanese are conditioned to mask emotion, whereas Americans express emotion more freely. Speakers in different cultures thus use different facial expressions to convey emotions. Eye behavior also takes quite different forms; people in the United States and Canada use eye contact as a form of acknowledgment or politeness in greeting, but in other cultures, such as in Southeast Asia, Nigeria, and Puerto Rico, among other countries, this is often considered disrespectful. Finally, appearance preferences also change from one culture to another.

No speaker should feel obliged to adopt nonverbal behaviors that are not his or her own. At the same time, a successful speech depends on shared meaning. As such, a thorough audience analysis is needed to anticipate potential misunderstandings that might occur nonverbally.

1. Roger Axtell, *Gestures: The Do's and Taboos of Body Language around the World* (New York: Wiley, 1991).

Source: Adapted from Dan O'Hair and Mary Wiemann, *Real Communication: An Introduction* (Boston: Bedford/St.Martin's, 2009), 122–23.

Although some speaking occasions permit casual dress, take care not to confuse casual with sloppy or unkempt.[11] Even casual attire should be professional in the sense that it conveys a responsible, credible, and confident image. Your attire reveals an attitude about what you are doing and the amount of effort you seem willing to put into it. The more professional you look, the more professional you will feel, and the more positive the attitude you will convey to audience members. This advice is no less important for your classroom speeches than it is for speeches given elsewhere. You should dress for your speeches in class just as you would if you were delivering them to a business or professional group that you want to impress. At the very least, it's good practice, and it's likely to benefit your speech by showing your respect for both the occasion and the audience.

An extension of dress is having various objects on or around your person while giving a speech—pencil and pen, a briefcase, a glass of water, or papers with notes on them. Always ask yourself if these objects are really necessary. A sure way to distract an audience from what you're saying is to drag a briefcase or backpack to the speaker's stand and open it while speaking, or to fumble with a pen or other object.

Practice the Delivery

WEB Video quizzes

Apple cofounder Steve Jobs is such an effective speaker that whole books are devoted to his techniques. Jobs delivers his presentations without notes and speaks in a conversational style, making emotional connections with his audience. But while Jobs projects an image of casualness, the time he devotes to preparation and practice is legendary.[12]

Practice is essential to effective delivery. The more you practice, the greater your comfort level will be when you actually deliver the speech. More than anything, it is uncertainty that breeds anxiety. By practicing your speech using a fully developed speaking outline (see Chapter 14), you will know what to expect when you actually stand in front of the audience.

Focus on the Message

The purpose of your speech is to get a message across, not to display extraordinary delivery skills. Keep this goal foremost in your mind. Psychologically, too, focusing on your message is likely to make your delivery more natural and more confident.

Record the Speech

Once you've practiced your speech several times, talk it out into an audio recorder. At a later stage in the practice process, you can place the recorder across the room from you and practice projecting your voice to the back row of the audience. To accurately gauge how you sound, use a good-quality recording device.

Videorecording two practice sessions can provide valuable feedback. As you watch your initial recording, make notes of the things you'd like to change.

Before rerecording, practice several more times until you are comfortable with the changes you've incorporated. Note that no one is ever entirely thrilled with his or her image on video, so try to avoid unnecessary self-criticism. Video-record your speech a second time, paying close attention to the areas of speech delivery that you want to improve.

Be Prepared to Revise Your Speaking Notes

As you practice, be prepared to revise your speech as needed. If your introduction or conclusion isn't as effective as you would like, rework it. Make other adjustments as necessary to improve your speech and make the outline easier to follow.

Practice under Realistic Conditions

Try to simulate the actual speech setting as you practice. Keep the seating arrangement in mind as you speak, picturing the audience as you go along. Turn various objects in the room into imaginary audience members, and project your voice in their direction. Practice scanning for eye contact. Practice with a podium of some kind (unless you know that you won't be using one). Stack some boxes to form a makeshift podium if you have to. Practice working with your speaking notes until you are confident that you can refer to them without overly relying on them. Practice placing your notes on a podium and moving around the podium for effective delivery.

At some point practice your speech in front of at least one other person. Ask your volunteer(s) to identify the purpose and key points of your speech. Question them about what they did or did not understand. Seek detailed feedback about the quality of your delivery.

Time Your Speech

As you practice, time each part of the speech (introduction, body, and conclusion) so that if you exceed your time limit you can adjust these sections accordingly. Recall that, as a general rule, the introduction and the conclusion should make up no more than 10 or 15 percent of your entire speech (see Chapters 15 and 16). If the speech is too long, look for extraneous material that can be cut. Consider your rate of speech. If it is too slow, practice speaking more concisely. If the speech is too short, review your evidence and make certain that you adequately support your main points. If your rate of speech is too fast, practice slowing your tempo.

Plan Ahead and Practice Often

Begin practicing your speech a couple of days before you are scheduled to deliver it. Many expert speakers recommend practicing your speech about five times in its final form. Since few speeches are longer than twenty minutes, and most are shorter, this represents a maximum of two hours of practice time—two hours well spent.

PRACTICING YOUR SPEECH

_____ 1. Practice with your speaking notes.

_____ 2. Revise those parts of your speech that aren't satisfactory, altering your speaking notes as you go.

_____ 3. Focus on your speech ideas rather than on yourself.

_____ 4. Time each part of your speech—introduction, body, and conclusion.

_____ 5. Practice with any presentation aids you plan to use.

_____ 6. Practice your speech several times, and then record it with an audio recorder.

_____ 7. If possible, video-record yourself twice—once after several practice sessions and again after you've incorporated changes into your speech.

_____ 8. Visualize the setting in which you will speak as you practice, projecting your words to different parts of the space to reach audience members.

_____ 9. Practice in front of at least one volunteer, and seek constructive criticism.

_____ 10. Schedule your practice sessions early in the process so that you have adequate time to prepare.

_____ 11. Practice your speech at least five times.

PRESENTATION AIDS

PRESENTATION AIDS

SPEAKER'S REFERENCE

CHAPTER **21** Using Presentation Aids in the Speech 284

    Functions of Presentation Aids 284

    Types of Presentation Aids 285

        ▶ **CHECKLIST** Tips for Using Props and Models Effectively 287

        ▶ **CHECKLIST** Tips for Creating Effective Pictograms 290

        ▶ **CHECKLIST** Tips for Creating Effective Line, Bar, and Pie Graphs 291

        ▶ **CHECKLIST** Tips on Incorporating Audio and Video into Your Presentation 292

    Options for Displaying the Presentation Aid 292

        ▶ **CHECKLIST** Incorporating Presentation Aids into Your Speech 292

        ▶ **FROM IDEA TO IMAGE** Using Presentation Aids 294

CHAPTER **22** Designing Presentation Aids 298

    Focus on the Message 298

    Strive for Simplicity 298

    Focus on Continuity 299

        ▶ **CHECKLIST** Applying the Principles of Simplicity and Continuity 300

    Select Appropriate Typeface Styles and Fonts 300

        ▶ **CHECKLIST** Tips for Using Typefaces, Fonts, and Sizes Effectively 301

    Use Color Carefully 302

CHAPTER **23** Using Presentation Software 304

    It's a Speech, Not a Slide Show 304

    A Brief Guide to Using PowerPoint 305

        ▶ **CHECKLIST** Preventive Maintenance: Avoiding PowerPoint Technical Glitches 305

        ▶ **CHECKLIST** Selecting Slide Layouts and Themes in PowerPoint 307

        ▶ **CHECKLIST** Inserting Tables and Worksheets into PowerPoint 312

    Finding Media for PowerPoint Slides 313

        ▶ **FROM SLIDE SHOW TO PRESENTATION** Getting Ready to Deliver a PowerPoint Presentation 314

    Developing PowerPoint Slides for a Speech 316

        ▶ **CHECKLIST** Tips for Successfully Using PowerPoint Presentations in Your Speech 316

PRESENTATION AIDS

CHAPTER **21** Using Presentation Aids in the Speech

Use Presentation Aids to Increase Understanding and Retention

- Presentation aids can concisely express complex ideas. (p. 285)
- Statistical relationships can be made clear through graphs and charts. (p. 285)
- Well-prepared presentation aids can boost your credibility. (p. 285)

Consider Using Props and Models

- Inanimate or live *props* can solidify your descriptions. (p. 285)
- In many areas of study, *models* are a central component of presentations. (p. 285)

Consider Illustrating Key Points with Pictures

- Look for visually arresting *photographs*. (p. 286)
- Create a *diagram* to demonstrate how something is constructed or used. (p. 286)
- Use a *map* to pinpoint an area or illustrate proportions. (p. 286)
- Use a *poster* to convey a brief message forcefully. (p. 286)

Use Graphs and Charts to Show Trends and Demonstrate Relationships

- Select a *line graph* to represent trends and other information that changes over time. (p. 287)
- Choose a *bar graph* to compare quantities or magnitudes. (p. 288)
- Use a *pie graph* to show proportions. (p. 288)
- Use a *pictogram* to characterize comparisons in picture form. (p. 288)
- Use a *flowchart* to diagram a procedure or process. (p. 288)
- Use an *organizational chart* to illustrate hierarchical relationships. (p. 289)
- Use a *table* to summarize large amounts of information. (p. 289)

Use Audio and Video to Add Interest

- Choose clips that illustrate ideas or bring humor to the mix. (p. 291)
- Consider incorporating clips into PowerPoint presentations. (p. 291)

Consider Using Multimedia to Enhance Key Speech Points

- Be familiar with software programs that produce multimedia. (p. 292)

Determine Options for Displaying Presentation Aids

- Choose the most appropriate graphics and display devices for the occasion. (p. 292)

CHAPTER **22** Designing Presentation Aids

Present One Major Idea Per Aid

- Limit the amount of information in any single visual. (p. 298)
- Use phrases or short sentences rather than complicated full sentences. (p. 298)
- Limit words to no more than six per line. (p. 298)
- Limit lines to no more than six per aid. (p. 298)
- Use parallel sentence structure. (p. 298)

Apply the Same Design Decisions to Each Aid

- Apply consistent colors, fonts, capitalization, and styling. (p. 300)

Use Type Large Enough to Be Read Comfortably

- For slides, use a sans serif typeface for titles and major headings. (p. 300)
- Experiment with a serif typeface for the body of the text. (p. 300)
- Experiment with 36-point type for major headings, 24-point type for subheadings, and 18-point type for the body of the text. (p. 300)
- Use upper- and lower-case type rather than all capitals. (p. 300)

Use Color Wisely

- Use bold, bright colors (yellow, orange, red) to highlight text or objects. (p. 302)
- For typeface and graphics, use colors that contrast with the background color. (p. 302)
- Restrict the number of colors to two, three, or four, and use the same colors consistently. (p. 302)

CHAPTER 23 Using Presentation Software

Remember That You're Giving a Speech, Not a Slide Show

- Use slides sparingly. (p. 304)
- Focus on your message and audience rather than the pizzazz of a slide show. (p. 304)
- Help your audience listen to you by not hiding behind your electronic presentation. (p. 304)

Refer to Chapter Text for Tips on Using Microsoft PowerPoint

- Become familiar with tools and features on the various PowerPoint screens. (p. 305)
- Use the Slide Layout features for the best assistance in developing your aid. (p. 305)

Practice Using Presentation Slides Until They Flow Smoothly with the Speech

KEY TERMS

Chapter 21

presentation aids	line graph	audio clip
multimedia effect	bar graph	video
visual rhetoric	pie graph	multimedia
prop	pictogram	overhead transparency
model	chart	flip chart
pictures	flowchart	handout
diagram	organizational chart	
graph	table	

Chapter 22

six-by-six rule	font	sans serif typefaces
typeface	serif typefaces	

Using Presentation Aids in the Speech

An old cliché states, "A picture is worth a thousand words." To modernize the cliché we should say, "A picture plus sound plus motion and other special effects are worth a thousand words"—that is, of course, when they are used in a context that is appropriate to the topic, the audience, and the occasion (i.e., the rhetorical situation).

Presentation aids include objects, models, pictures, graphs, charts, video, audio, and multimedia. Each of these elements, used alone and in combination, helps the audience see relationships among concepts and elements. Aids also help audience members store and remember material and critically examine key ideas. As valuable as they can be, however, the strength of any particular presentation aid lies in the context in which it is used. No matter how powerful a photograph or chart or video may be, the audience will be less interested in merely gazing at it than in discovering how you will relate it to a specific point. If even superior-quality aids are poorly related to a speech, listeners will be turned off. Thus presentation aids should be integrated with the whole of the message, not peripheral to it.[1]

Functions of Presentation Aids

 WEB Chapter quizzes

Used judiciously, presentation aids can help listeners process and retain information, spark interest, convey information in a time-saving fashion, and enhance an image of professionalism.

Help Listeners Process and Retain Information

Most people process and retain information best when they receive it in more than one format. Audience members better understand and remember what is seen *and* heard than what is only seen or only heard.[2] Put another way, we learn better from words and pictures than from words alone, a phenomenon dubbed the **multimedia effect**.[3] Importantly, however, the multimedia effect does *not work* if the accompanying aid, whether a picture, video, a piece of music, or combination thereof, merely repeats the spoken information. In this event, audience members will actually learn *less* than if the speaker used no aid. To be beneficial, the aid must complement, or add to, the information rather than simply match the spoken point.[4]

Promote Interest and Motivation

Effective presentation aids draw audience members into a speech and stimulate their interest through **visual rhetoric**—the conveyance of meaning by integrating the visual with the verbal message.[5] Literally seeing the facts of an argument laid out in front of them, for example, can make a significant difference in how listeners respond to a persuasive appeal. In a call for donations for the homeless, for instance, a good argument coupled with a photograph that portrays homeless conditions, or a chart that illustrates high rates of homelessness, can more eloquently convey the speaker's message than can the verbal argument alone.[6]

Convey Information Concisely

Presentation aids can concisely communicate ideas that might otherwise be difficult or time-consuming to express. Visual images, such as a child hugging her mother in uniform and just back from service in Iraq, can vividly represent an idea or a feeling instantaneously. Complex ideas and abstract or difficult concepts can also be more clearly explained with presentation aids. For example, graphs and charts efficiently summarize statistical relationships, enabling audience members to quickly apprehend the difference between the information represented by two elements of a bar graph or the dips and rises on a line graph.

Lend a Professional Image

By using quality visual aids, you show your listeners that you are approaching the presentation professionally and motivate them to approach it in the same way. This increases your credibility, which further helps get your message across. But moderation is important. Emphasis should be on using the aids to fulfill the speech purpose and not on the aids themselves.[7]

Types of Presentation Aids

WEB Video quizzes

A variety of presentation aids are at your disposal. Base your choices on which aid will most effectively convey the information visually (or aurally, or both). Here we move from least to most high-tech. (See Chapter 23 for a discussion of using presentation software.)

Props and Models

A **prop** can be any live or inanimate object—a snake or striated stone, for instance. Sometimes, the prop *is* the subject of the speech, as when a student brings a snake to class for a speech about snakes. (See the checklist on using props effectively on p. 287.)

In addition to props, models are an important and sometimes necessary presentation aid. A **model** is a three-dimensional, scale-size representation of something. Presentations in engineering, architecture, medicine, the visual arts, and many other disciplines often make use of models.

Pictures

Pictures are two-dimensional representations of people, places, ideas, or objects, including photographs, line drawings, diagrams, maps, and posters.

A **diagram** or *schematic drawing* explains how something works or how it is constructed or operated. Diagrams are best suited to clarifying complicated procedures and operations. They are the aid of choice when you need to explain how to construct or use something. Figure 21.1 is a diagram that shows how to connect a computer and other elements of a home media center.

Maps help audience members visualize geographic areas and understand various relationships among them. Thus if your speech is about becoming familiar with a company's various offices worldwide, you could incorporate a map depicting the locations of the offices in your talk. Maps also illustrate the proportion of one thing to something else in different areas of a region. You could create a map to illustrate the proportion of NCAA Division I colleges to Division II schools. For a speech on sightseeing in New York City, you could create a slide with an embedded map of the New York City subway system.

A *poster* is a large, bold, two-dimensional design incorporating words, shapes, and, if desired, color, placed on an opaque backing. Speakers can use posters to briefly convey a point forcefully and attractively. Because posters are economical and easy to use, they are a good choice for speakers who give the same presentation many times. Display posters on easels or chalkboard railings if you have several to show successively. Posters are featured in one form of presentation called the *poster session* (see Chapter 31).

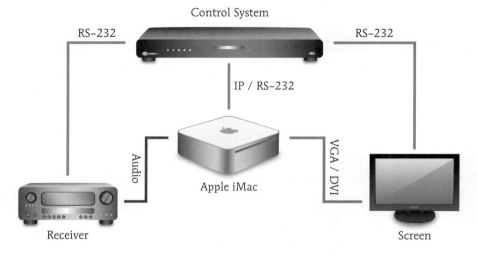

FIGURE 21.1 Diagram or Schematic Drawing of Media Center Connections *Source:* "Inline Control: Control Solutions for the Mac," accessed July 10, 2010, http://www.inlinecontrol.com.

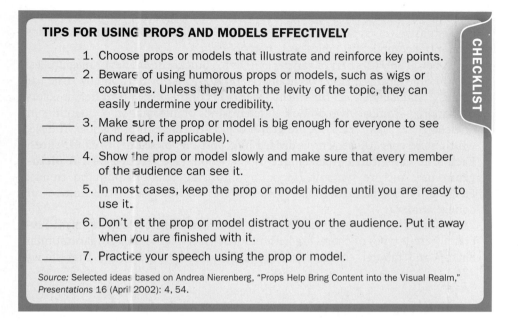

Source: Selected ideas based on Andrea Nierenberg, "Props Help Bring Content into the Visual Realm," *Presentations* 16 (April 2002): 4, 54.

Graphs and Charts

A **graph** represents numerical data in pictorial form. Graphs neatly depict relationships among components or units and show trends. Four major types of graphs are line graphs, bar graphs, pie graphs, and pictograms. A **line graph** uses points connected by lines to demonstrate how something changes or fluctuates in value. For example, Figure 21.2 represents fluctuations in the U.S.

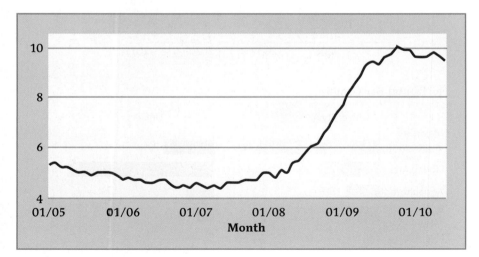

FIGURE 21.2 Percentage Rate of Unemployment in the United States, 2005–2010

Source: United States Department of Labor, Bureau of Labor Statistics, accessed July 10, 2010, http://www.bls.gov.

unemployment rate for the years 2005–2010. Line graphs are the most versatile and extensively used family of graphs[8] because they are easier to read at a glance than more complicated tables and charts of data.

A **bar graph** uses bars of varying lengths to compare quantities or magnitudes. Bars may be arranged either vertically (column graphs) or horizontally (true bar graphs). *Multidimensional bar graphs*—bar graphs distinguished by different colors or markings—compare two or more different kinds of information or quantities in one chart (see Figure 21.3). A **pie graph** depicts the division of a whole. The pie, which represents 100 percent, is divided into portions or segments called slices. Each slice constitutes a percentage of the whole (see Figure 21.4). A **pictogram** uses picture symbols (icons) to illustrate relationships and trends. Figure 21.5 is a pictogram that demonstrates an increase in the number of college students.

A **chart** visually organizes complex information into compact form. Several different types of charts are helpful for speakers: flowcharts; organizational charts; and tabular charts or tables. A **flowchart** is a diagram that shows

Vertical Bar Graph

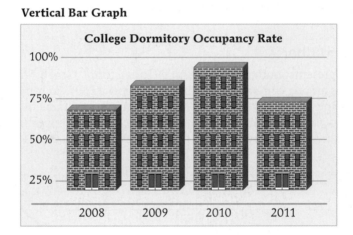

Horizontal Bar Graph

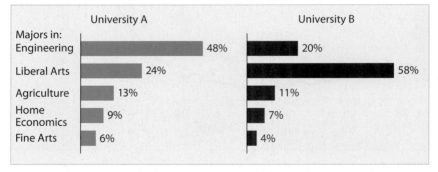

FIGURE 21.3 Bar Graphs of Quantities and Magnitudes

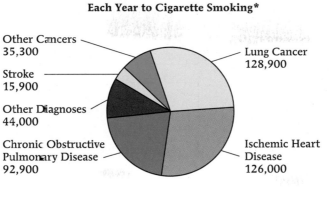

**About 443,000 U.S. Deaths Attributable
Each Year to Cigarette Smoking***

Other Cancers
35,300

Lung Cancer
128,900

Stroke
15,900

Other Diagnoses
44,000

Chronic Obstructive
Pulmonary Disease
92,900

Ischemic Heart
Disease
126,000

*Average annual number of deaths, 2000–2004.
Source: MMWR 2008;57(45):1226–1228.

FIGURE 21.4 Pie Graph Showing the Causes of Yearly Deaths Attributable to Cigarette
Smoking   *Source:* Centers for Disease Control and Prevention, accessed December 16, 2010,
http://www.cdc.gov.

step-by-step progression through a procedure, a relationship, or a process. Usually the flow of a procedure or a process is drawn horizontally or vertically and describes how key components fit into a whole. A flowchart is the visual aid of choice to show a sequence of activities or the directional flow in a process (see Figure 21.6).

An **organizational chart** illustrates the organizational structure or chain of command in an organization. It shows the interrelationship of the different positions, divisions, departments, and personnel (see Figure 21.7).

A tabular chart, or **table**, is a succinct display of comparative information or numerical data in rows and columns. Tables may lack some of the visual appeal of other visual aids, but they present data in a form that the viewer can examine and interpret quickly. Table 21.1 (see p. 291), for example, summarizes the best uses of different types of graphs and charts.

New College Students

FIGURE 21.5 Pictogram Showing Increase in College Students

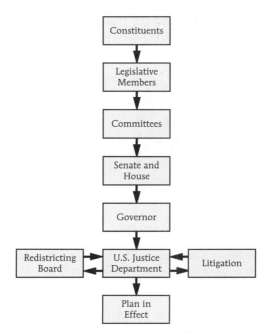

FIGURE 21.6 Flowchart Showing Decision Process for a State's Political Redistricting
Source: ESRI, accessed July 10, 2010, http://proceedings.esri.com/library/userconf/.

TIPS FOR CREATING EFFECTIVE PICTOGRAMS

_____ 1. When creating pictograms, choose pictures that symbolize the subject being represented to a broad spectrum of viewers.

_____ 2. To avoid confusing the eye, make all pictograms the same size.

_____ 3. Clearly label what the pictogram symbolizes.

_____ 4. Clearly label the axes of the pictogram graph.

CHECKLIST

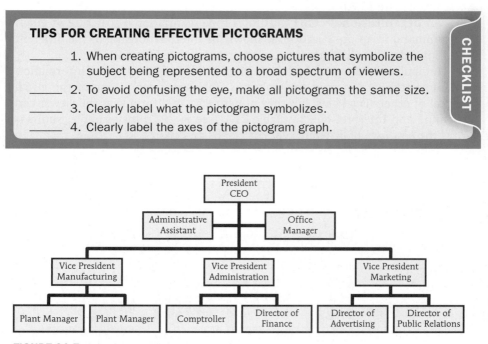

FIGURE 21.7 Organizational Chart Showing Personnel Hierarchy

TABLE 21.1	Best Use of Different Types of Graphs and Charts
Type of Graph or Chart	**Best Use**
Line graph	To represent trends or information that changes over time
Bar and column graph	To compare magnitude or volume among categories
Pie graph	To show proportions of the total
Pictogram	To depict comparisons in picture form
Flowchart	To diagram processes
Organizational chart	To show lines and direction of reporting in a hierarchy
Table	To summarize information or data in an easily viewable form

TIPS FOR CREATING EFFECTIVE LINE, BAR, AND PIE GRAPHS

_____ 1. Label both axes of the line or bar graph appropriately.

_____ 2. Start the numerical axis of the line or bar graph at zero.

_____ 3. Compare only like variables.

_____ 4. Put no more than two lines of data on one graph.

_____ 5. Assign a clear title to the graph.

_____ 6. Clearly label all relevant points of information in the graph.

_____ 7. When creating multidimensional bar graphs, do not compare more than three kinds of information.

_____ 8. When creating a pie graph, restrict the number of pie slices to seven.

_____ 9. When creating a pie graph, identify the value or percentage of each pie slice, and check that each slice of the pie accurately represents the value or percentage (e.g., use half of the pie to show 50 percent).

_____ 10. When creating a pie graph, consider using color or background markings to distinguish the different slices of the pie.

CHECKLIST

Audio and Video

Introducing an **audio clip**—a short recording of sounds, music, or speech—can add interest, illustrate ideas, and even bring humor to the mix. **Video**—including clips from movies, television, and other recording instruments—can also motivate listener attention by helping to introduce, transition into, and clarify points in a speech.[9] Because audio and video clips can be linked to PowerPoint slides, are easily stored on personal digital devices, and are transportable to a variety of playback devices, both are generally a safe choice as presentation aids.

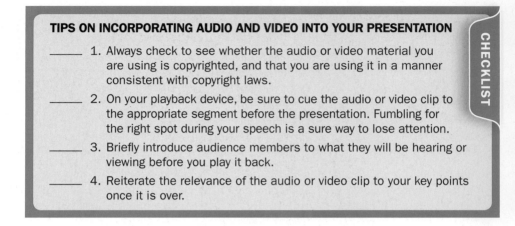

TIPS ON INCORPORATING AUDIO AND VIDEO INTO YOUR PRESENTATION

_____ 1. Always check to see whether the audio or video material you are using is copyrighted, and that you are using it in a manner consistent with copyright laws.

_____ 2. On your playback device, be sure to cue the audio or video clip to the appropriate segment before the presentation. Fumbling for the right spot during your speech is a sure way to lose attention.

_____ 3. Briefly introduce audience members to what they will be hearing or viewing before you play it back.

_____ 4. Reiterate the relevance of the audio or video clip to your key points once it is over.

Multimedia

Multimedia combines several media (stills, sound, video, text, and data) into a single production. The idea behind multimedia is that the richer the variety of information cues, the better for audience attention, comprehension, and retention.[10] But even though it's an increasingly popular option, multimedia does require more planning and is more time-consuming than other forms of presentation aids. To produce multimedia, you need to become familiar with presentation software programs such as Windows Live Movie Maker and Apple iMovie (see Chapter 23).

Options for Displaying the Presentation Aid

Once you've selected the types of aids that are best suited for communicating your ideas (e.g., chart or graph and so forth), you can choose from a variety of options for displaying them during your speech. Many presenters create computer-generated graphics for display with digital projectors or LCD displays (see Chapter 23). Traditional approaches include overhead transparencies, flip charts, chalkboards, and handouts.

Computer-Generated Graphics and Displays

With software programs such as Microsoft PowerPoint and Apple Keynote, many speakers create slides, transparencies, and other presentation aids on the computer. You can project these *computer-generated graphics* directly from a computer using LCD (liquid crystal display) panels and projectors or the newer DLP (digital light processing) projectors, or you can transfer the images to overhead transparencies. (See Chapter 23 for a discussion of how to use presentation software.) You can also use dual screens when available and appropriate to the audience context. Dual screens are useful when presenting comparative information, with one set of information on one screen and the other set on the other screen, because they help listeners retain information.[11]

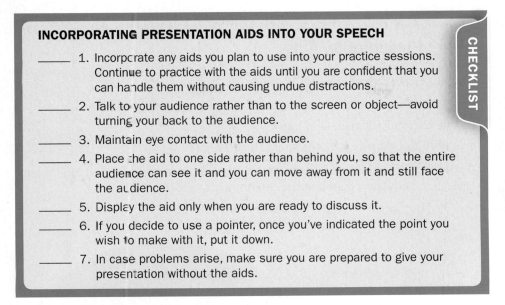

INCORPORATING PRESENTATION AIDS INTO YOUR SPEECH

_____ 1. Incorporate any aids you plan to use into your practice sessions. Continue to practice with the aids until you are confident that you can handle them without causing undue distractions.

_____ 2. Talk to your audience rather than to the screen or object—avoid turning your back to the audience.

_____ 3. Maintain eye contact with the audience.

_____ 4. Place the aid to one side rather than behind you, so that the entire audience can see it and you can move away from it and still face the audience.

_____ 5. Display the aid only when you are ready to discuss it.

_____ 6. If you decide to use a pointer, once you've indicated the point you wish to make with it, put it down.

_____ 7. In case problems arise, make sure you are prepared to give your presentation without the aids.

Overhead Transparencies

Sometimes portable computers and digital projectors don't function properly or simply are not available. For such times, it pays to have a contingency plan in your briefcase, such as a set of transparencies. An **overhead transparency** is an image printed on a clear sheet of acetate that can be viewed by projection, either onto a large film screen or a wall. If a transparency is handwritten during the presentation, it can be used much like a chalkboard (see p. 297). You can also create transparencies in advance using PowerPoint.

Transparencies have several advantages. First, most facilities that host presentations have overhead projectors. Second, transparencies are inexpensive, and overhead projectors are portable and simple to operate. Third, overhead projection is flexible. Material may be added to or taken away from the projector during the presentation, making the overhead a good choice for presentations that require multiple visual aids. Fourth, projection allows you to interact with the audience easily. Unlike writing on a chalkboard or handing out other visual aids, you can face the audience when using overhead projection. Also, you can keep lights on while using overhead transparencies. When using overhead transparencies:

- Check that the projector is in good order before the speech.
- Stand to the *side* of the projector and face the *audience,* not the projected image.
- Use a pointer to indicate specific sections of a transparency—point to the transparency, not the screen.

Using Presentation Aids

As you select each aid for your presentation, ask yourself:

- Is the *type* of aid the *best choice* to convey the information?
- Is my *timing* of the aid optimal?
- Will the aid help me achieve my *desired effect?*

Following are examples of one student's effective use of presentation aids in her speech about plastic bags and the environment.

The Plastic Bag Plague

Introduction

I.   Picture a swirling, plastic-laden gyre of ocean waters, twice the size of Texas . . . *(Attention getter)*

The notion of a plastic-laden gyre twice as large as Texas is difficult to fathom without a visual, so to build credibility, the student decides to show a map.

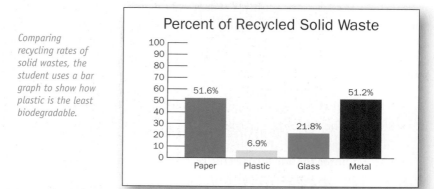

Body

I.   Plastic bags choke the land and water . . .

    A.   Americans throw out 30 million tons of plastic annually, or nearly 12 percent of all solid waste, and recycle only 6 percent of it.

Comparing recycling rates of solid wastes, the student uses a bar graph to show how plastic is the least biodegradable.

Percent of Recycled Solid Waste

Paper 51.6% · Plastic 6.9% · Glass 21.8% · Metal 51.2%

B. 100,000 marine animals are killed annually . . .

To appeal to the audience's emotions, or pathos, the student shows a video of marine life suffering the consequences of plastic bag pollution. She hyperlinks the image to the video URL. On the day of her presentation, she makes sure the presentation room has an Internet connection and that her hyperlinked video works.

C. 200,000 plastic bags get deposited in landfills every hour and take 1,000 years to decompose . . .

The student illustrates this dramatic statistic with a photograph of a landfill teeming with plastic.

Conclusion

I.   Prevent major impact on our world . . .

Stop Plastic Bag Waste

> Take plastic bags to recycle bin at local grocery store.
> Use reusable bags when shopping.
> Encourage stores to offer paper bags instead of plastic bags.
> Email your senator or representative in support of government regulation on plastics.

Stressing the need to act, the student concludes with a text slide listing actions students can take. Note that she keeps the background color consistent throughout the presentation and selects a font color that contrasts well with it.

II.   Use environmentally friendly bags . . .

The student shows this reusable bag from Whole Foods as a prop to demonstrate her point.

III.   Hold up your reusable bag and say, "No thank you, I brought my own . . ."
Once again, the student holds up a reusable shopping bag to reiterate one of her speech's primary points: Decrease plastic bag consumption.

- If creating transparencies by writing or drawing during the presentation, use a water-soluble transparency pen, and be sure to write clearly.
- Cover the transparencies when you are finished using them.
- Practice using your transparencies before your presentation.

Flip Charts

A **flip chart** is simply a large (27–34 inches) pad of paper on which a speaker can draw visual aids. They are often prepared in advance, although you can also write and draw on the paper as you speak. As you progress through the speech, you simply flip through the pad to the next sheet. The flip chart is one of the least expensive ways to display aids. In terms of equipment, colored markers and an easel are all that are required.

Chalkboards and Whiteboards

On the lowest-tech end of the spectrum lies the *writing board* on which you can write with chalk (on a *chalkboard*) or with nonpermanent markers (on a *whiteboard*). Writing boards are useful for impromptu explanations, as when someone asks a question for which you do not have an aid but feel you can clarify with words or drawings. In general, try to reserve the writing board for quick explanations, such as presenting simple processes that are done in steps, or for engaging the audience in short brainstorming sessions. If you have the time to prepare a speech properly, however, don't rely on a writing board. They force the speaker to turn his or her back to the audience; they make listeners wait while you write on the board; and they require legible handwriting that will be clear to all viewers.

Handouts

An ever-present option among presentation aids is the **handout**—page-size items of information that is either impractical to give to the audience in another format or intended for audience members to keep after the presentation. Handouts can effectively and inexpensively give an audience more information than can be covered in the presentation. They can also be useful when it is best to have audience members follow along with you while you go over information. Sometimes handouts have blanks to be filled in by the listeners as the speaker covers key points. This approach has been shown to enhance recall and retention, especially when the handouts contain relevant graphics.[12]

To avoid distracting listeners, unless you specifically want listeners to read the information or fill in blanks as you speak, *wait until you are done before you distribute the handout.* If you do want the audience to view a handout during the speech, distribute it only when you are ready to talk about it. Finally, avoid having too many or too lengthy handouts because audience members will find them tiresome and may lose interest.

CHAPTER 22

Designing Presentation Aids

Once you select the types of presentation aids you will use in your speech and decide on the method of displaying them (see Chapter 21), you can begin design and construction. Whether you fashion the aids with pen and paper or generate them on a computer, certain principles of rhetorical communication and graphic design apply.

Focus on the Message

Research and practice alike suggest that the use of presentation aids, particularly computer-generated slides such as PowerPoint, can hurt your effectiveness as a speaker if the audience's attention is drawn more to the aids than to the message itself.[1] Keep in mind that the purpose of a presentation aid is to support, summarize, or add to your ideas, not to repeat verbatim what you are saying in your speech. Thus you should focus on creating aids that will truly clarify information, taking care not to overweight the speech with slides.

Strive for Simplicity

Slides, posters, and other visual displays that try to communicate too many messages or that appear overly complex will quickly overwhelm the audience. On average, audience members have thirty seconds or less to view an aid, so focus on designing the aids simply and using text sparingly.

Assign Each Point a Separate Slide

Plan on presenting one major idea per aid. If you want to cover a series of points or ideas, use a sequential layout of separate aids. Wherever possible, use short phrases in place of full sentences. Consider the **six-by-six rule**—using no more than six words in a line and six lines on one slide—to minimize the number of words you use in each presentation aid. This lessens the likelihood that the audience will spend too much time reading the aid rather than listening to you.

Use Active Construction

Word your text in active verb form and parallel grammatical structure (see Chapter 17 on language); this too will keep it simple. For example, an informative speech on the process of looking for a new car could include a PowerPoint

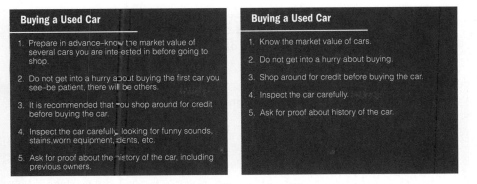

FIGURE 22.1 Cluttered versus Easy-to-Read Presentation Aid

slide labeled "Buying a Used Car." Note in Figure 22.1 the differences between a first draft and a final slide.

In the first-draft slide, observe the lack of parallel structure, with dissimilar grammatical and stylistic construction, the wordy use of full sentences, and the passive construction in point 3 ("It is recommended that . . .").

In the final slide, the speaker poses each point in the active rather than passive form ("Shop around" instead of "It is recommended that . . ."). All points are short, crisp phrases containing no more than six lines on a slide.

Avoid Clutter

Avoid cluttering your slides with unnecessary graphics and text. Certain kinds of information—especially statistical data and sequences of action—are best understood through visual reasoning. However, try to avoid what design expert Edward Tufte coined "chartjunk"—slides jammed with too many graphs, charts, and other meaningless design elements that obscure rather than illuminate information. Tufte counsels using as few slides as possible and only those design elements that truly enhance meaning.[2]

Focus on Continuity

The principle of continuity dictates that you apply the same design decisions you make for one aid to all of the aids you display in a speech. Businesses, agencies, and your college or university apply this principle to their Web sites and publications. Doing so maintains their consistent professional image and ensures that viewers don't become distracted (and irritated) by a jumble of unrelated visual elements.

To help maintain continuity, carry your choice of any key design elements—colors, fonts, upper- and lowercase letters, and styling (boldface, underlining, italics) through to each aid. If you select a certain color background for one aid, for instance, use it for each subsequent aid. Follow the same general page layout throughout, placing repeating elements, such as titles, in the same place and in the same style and typeface. Use the same symbols in every aid, whether they are colors, pictograms, or logos of one sort or another. For example, if in an aid comparing the computer-buying habits of men and women you illustrated the buying habits of men in red and those of women in green, you would continue using these colors in subsequent aids.

APPLYING THE PRINCIPLES OF SIMPLICITY AND CONTINUITY

✔ Restrict your coverage to one idea per aid.

✔ Create concise titles that reinforce your message.

✔ Use phrases or single words to display the points clearly.

✔ Use the six-by-six rule—no more than six words per line and six lines per aid.

✔ Apply design decisions consistently to each aid. Use the same combinations of fonts, upper- and lowercase lettering, styling (use of boldface, underlining, and italics), and spacing.

✔ Use colors consistently across all slides to highlight key ideas and enhance readability.

✔ Carry through any repeating elements such as logos or pictograms, across all aids.

CHECKLIST

Select Appropriate Typeface Styles and Fonts

A **typeface** is a specific style of lettering, such as Arial, Times Roman, or Courier. Typefaces come in a variety of **fonts**, or sets of sizes (called the point size) and upper- and lowercases.

Designers divide the thousands of typefaces available today into two categories: serif and sans serif. **Serif typefaces** include small flourishes, or strokes, at the tops and bottoms of each letter. **Sans serif typefaces** are more blocklike and linear; they are designed without the tiny strokes. Some studies show that small amounts of text, such as headings, are best viewed in sans serif type (see Figure 22.2). For a body of text, serif typefaces are easier on the eye. More recent studies[3] indicate that varying common typefaces and fonts for the body of a text, such as Helvetica and Times Roman, does not reduce audience recall or comprehension, so your choice of any of these is the safest option as long as you consistently apply them throughout. If you include only a few lines of text, however, consider using sans serif type throughout.

Following are a few key points to observe when selecting type styles for presentations:

1. Whether you are using a hand-drawn poster board or a computer-generated graphic, check your lettering for legibility, taking into consideration the audience's distance from the presentation. Most text for on-screen projection should be 18 points or larger. Generally, major headings should be displayed in 36-point type, subheadings in 24-point type, and regular text in 18-point type (see Figure 22.3).

2. Check that your lettering stands apart from your background, either light lettering on dark background (more commonly), or vice versa.

3. Use a familiar typeface that is simple and easy to read, not distracting.

4. Don't overuse boldface, underlining, or *italics*. Use them sparingly to emphasize a special or very important point.

5. Use standard upper- and lowercase type rather than all capitals.

TIPS FOR USING TYPEFACES, FONTS, AND SIZES EFFECTIVELY

✓ For on-screen projection, use a minimum 18-point font for body text, perhaps 24-point in large rooms.

✓ Avoid ornate typefaces—they are difficult to read.

✓ Use a sans serif typeface for titles and major headings.

✓ Consider a serif typeface when the body of the text is only a few lines.

✓ Experiment with 36-point type for major headings and 24-point type for subheads.

✓ As a rule, use no more than two different typefaces in a single visual aid.

✓ Use upper- and lowercase type rather than all capitals.

✓ Use boldface, underlining, or italics sparingly.

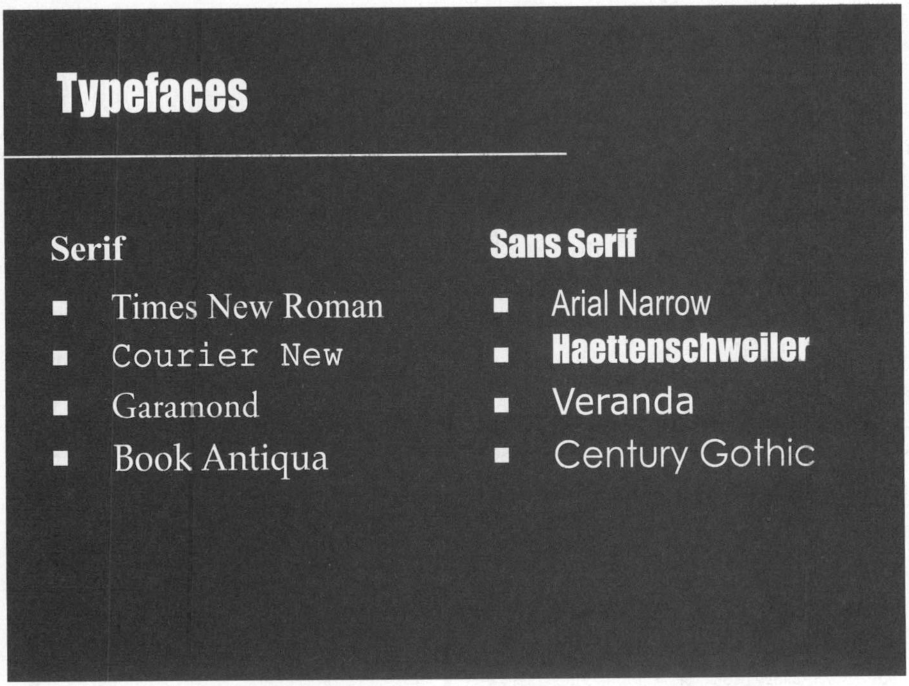

CHECKLIST

Typefaces

Serif

- Times New Roman
- Courier New
- Garamond
- Book Antiqua

Sans Serif

- Arial Narrow
- **Haettenschweiler**
- Veranda
- Century Gothic

FIGURE 22.2 Serif and Sans Serif Typefaces

Use Appropriate Font Sizes

- Use font sizes that can be seen by the entire audience.

- Use larger font sizes for headings; smaller sizes for subheads and body

- **54 point**
- **48 point**
- **36 point**
- **24 point**
- 18 point

FIGURE 22.3 Use Appropriate Font Sizes

Use Color Carefully

Skillful use of color can draw attention to key points, set the mood of a presentation, and make things easier to see. Conversely, poor color combinations will set the wrong mood, render an image unattractive, or make it just plain unreadable. Table 22.1 describes the effects of several color combinations.

Because colors evoke distinct associations in people, take care not to summon an unintended meaning or mood. For example, studies suggest that red evokes associations with failure, while green elicits those of success.[4] Table 22.2

TABLE 22.1 Effect of Color Combinations	
Color	Effect in Combination
Yellow	Warm on white, harsh on black, fiery on red, soothing on light blue
Blue	Warm on white, hard to see on black
Red	Bright on white, warm or difficult to see on black

Source: Cheryl Currid, *Make Your Point: The Complete Guide to Successful Business Presentations Using Today's Technology* (Rocklin, CA: Prima Publishing, 1995), 75.

TABLE 22.2	Subjective Interpretations of Color	
Cool Colors	**Mood, Emotion**	**Meanings**
Blue	calm, cool	reassurance, mystery, peace, importance, confidence, intelligence, stability
Green	life, renewal	restfulness, calmness, balance, harmony, stability
Gray	elegant, neutral	conservative, mourning, formality, strength, mystery
White	light, brilliance	purity, cleanliness, innocence, softness
Neutral Colors	**Mood, Emotion**	**Meanings**
Ivory	relaxation, quiet	earthiness, pleasantness, purity, elegance
Brown	down-to-earth	wholesomeness, earthiness, dullness, steadfastness, friendliness
Beige	dependable, flexible	calmness, crispness, conventionality, simplicity
Warm Colors	**Mood, Emotion**	**Meanings**
Red	love, hot	conflict, anger, exertion, power, danger, war
Yellow	warm, happiness	conflict, caution, hope, cowardice
Orange	flamboyant, energetic	vibrancy, energy, autumn, citrus
Black	dark, absence	conservative, seriousness, conventionality, mystery, sophistication

Source: Adapted from J. H. Bear, *The Meaning of Color*, About.com, accessed July 17, 2010, http://desktoppub.about.ccm/od/choosingcolors/p/color_meanings.htm.

describes some of the subjective interpretations attached to several colors. Following are some tips for using color effectively in your presentation aids:

- Keep the *background color* of your presentation constant, using colors consistently across all slides.
- Use *bold, bright colors* to emphasize important points. Warm colors such as yellow, red, and orange rank highest in visibility, so use these colors to highlight text or objects within a frame. But be careful: These colors can be difficult to see from a distance.
- For typeface and graphics, use colors that contrast rather than clash with or blend into the background color. Audiences will remember information just as easily if white text appears on dark background or dark text on light background, so long as the design is appealing.[5]
- Limit the number of colors you use in a graphic to two or three (or four at the most). More color choices can be used in complex and detailed aids.
- Consider that meanings associated with certain colors may differ across cultures.
- Stay within the same family of hues.

CHAPTER 23

Using Presentation Software

Public speakers have a variety of powerful software tools available for creating and displaying high quality visual aids. The best known and most available of these programs is Microsoft PowerPoint, the one we refer to throughout this chapter. Several Web-based presentation development tools provide some of the same basic features as PowerPoint but far fewer specialized elements. Examples include Google Docs (docs.google.com), Prezi (prezi.com), and Zoho Show (show.zoho.com). Each of these tools can display visuals directly from a computer via an LCD monitor or a projector, or they can be converted into handouts or overhead transparencies. Preloaded *templates* provide expert guidelines for font, color, and background combinations, but you can also design your own visual aids. In addition, you may use these programs to produce multimedia displays by importing audio and video into electronic slides.

It's a Speech, Not a Slide Show

 WEB Using PowerPoint

For all its promise, the use of presentation software can be fraught with peril. It takes time to learn PowerPoint, but the time is well worth it to avoid what some speech coaches call "death by PowerPoint."[1] As with any electronic device, technical errors are always a hazard with PowerPoint slides. Common risks include incompatibility of a PowerPoint file with an operating system, projector bulb burnout, or a computer drive freezing when a media file is clicked to play. (The checklist on preventive maintenance on p. 305 describes steps you can take to avoid these problems.) Arguably worse than any of these kinds of potential mishaps is the mistaken notion that the PowerPoint display itself is the presentation, or that it will somehow save an otherwise poorly planned speech.[2]

Frequently we hear someone say, "I'm giving a PowerPoint today," instead of "I'm giving a speech today." Some speakers become so enamored of generating graphics or creating glitzy multimedia presentations that they forget their primary mission: to communicate through the spoken word and through their physical presence.[3] Other speakers are tempted to hide behind their visual displays, focusing their attention on the slide show rather than on the audience. These problems usually signal poor preparation on the speaker's part.[4] Careful consideration and a good rationale are needed when you decide to use PowerPoint slides to complement your speeches.

A Brief Guide to Using PowerPoint

WEB Links

Students are so widely exposed to PowerPoint today that you doubtless know that it can be used to display text, artwork, photos, charts, graphs, tables, clip art, video, and sound. You can upload PowerPoint presentations onto the Web for viewing elsewhere, and with additional software you can stream your PowerPoint presentation online in real time. This section offers a brief overview of PowerPoint's primary features, with reference to PowerPoint 2010. (For more detailed guidance on using PowerPoint, consult Microsoft's PowerPoint online support site.)

To begin, after opening PowerPoint on your computer, familiarize yourself with the toolbars and icons at the top of the main screen (see Figure 23.1).

PREVENTIVE MAINTENANCE: AVOIDING POWERPOINT TECHNICAL GLITCHES

✓ Check that the operating system of the computer you will use during your speech (e.g., Windows XP, Mac OS X) is compatible with the operating system used to create the aids.

✓ Confirm that the version of the presentation software used to create the aids corresponds to the software on the computer you will use in the presentation; this will prevent distortions in your graphics, sound, and video.

✓ Save all the files associated with your presentation (i.e., images, sound files, videos) into the same folder you will use in your presentation.

✓ Verify that you've saved the files to a source—a flash drive, CD, DVD, Web site, or e-mail—that will be recognized by the presentation computer.

✓ Familiarize yourself with the layout and functioning of the presentation computer *before the speech* to facilitate smooth operation during the presentation.

✓ Prepare a printed and a digital backup of your presentation in case of technical challenges.

CHECKLIST

Become Familiar with the Presentation Options

PowerPoint provides you three options for composing a set of presentation slides.

1. The *Home tab* is the view you are most likely to see when you first open PowerPoint. The Home tab presents menus for inserting new slides after

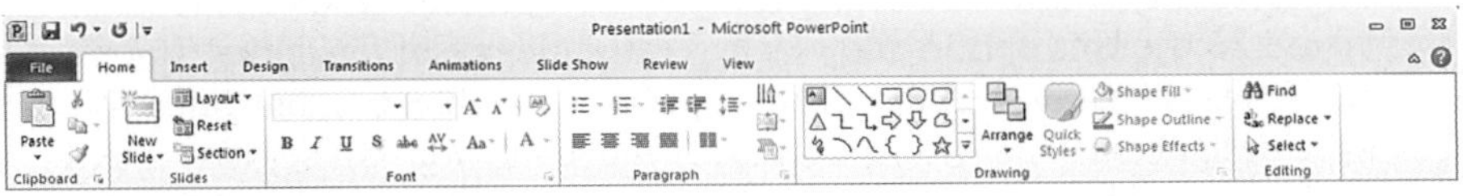

FIGURE 23.1 PowerPoint Toolbars

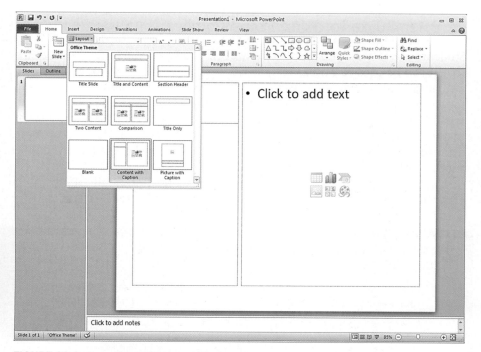

FIGURE 23.2 PowerPoint Slide Layout Options

the first one, choosing layouts and themes for your slides, and manipulating fonts and styles much as you do in Word. You can select *Slide Layout* to choose the format with which you want to display a title page and section pages, headings, body text, pictures, and captions (see Figure 23.2). Select the layout best suited to the information you have outlined in advance. This layout will apply to all slides. (You can change the layout for an individual slide in the New Slide drop-down menu.) In the left pane you can view slides in either thumbnail or outline form as you create them. You can enter text in either the individual slide in the center of the screen, or in the Outline view to the left.

2. The *Design tab* includes approximately forty-eight predesigned templates, called *Themes* (see Figure 23.3). Templates allow you to apply a consistent layout and color scheme to each slide in the presentation. Each template is designed to convey a certain look or feel.

3. With *Blank* slide layout, you customize every aspect of the presentation: color, font, type and size, organization of content, and graphics (see Figure 23.4). This option allows the greatest degree of flexibility. The challenge is that each slide essentially starts from scratch, but once you have designed a slide with the features you want, you can set it as a template so all slides share the same features.

SELECTING SLIDE LAYOUTS AND THEMES IN POWERPOINT

_____ 1. With PowerPoint open, choose File > New.

_____ 2. Click *Blank Presentation* and then, on the right side of the screen, click *Create*.

_____ 3. Now you see a title slide layout in Normal View. Create a draft title page by entering text where indicated.

_____ 4. In the tools ribbon select the *New Slide* pull-down menu and choose a layout for your next slide. It will appear in the large pane and as a thumbnail on the left. Give the slide a title and enter some bullet points in the body. Continue with more new slides.

_____ 5. To apply a consistent theme to your slides, click the *Design* tab. Click the pull-down arrow at the right end of the Themes ribbon to see all available themes. Click a theme to apply it to all your slides. For more topical themes, click File > New > Design Slides.

_____ 6. Review each slide in the chosen layout and theme by clicking its thumbnail in the left pane.

_____ 7. Save your draft presentation by clicking File > Save As.

FIGURE 23.3 PowerPoint Design Templates

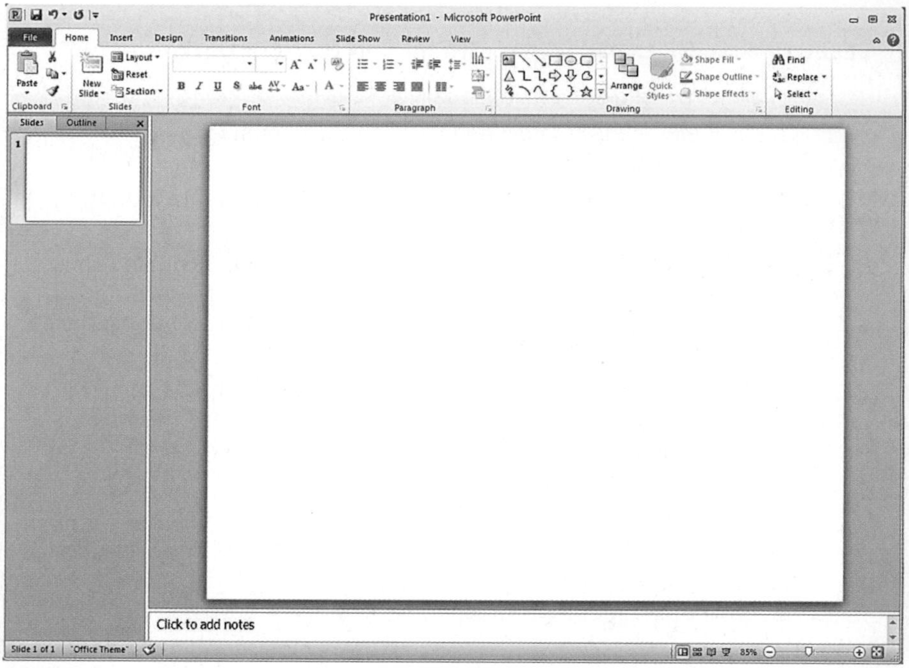

FIGURE 23.4 Blank Slide Layout

Become Familiar with View Options and Slide Masters

PowerPoint offers three different ways to view slides as you create them: normal view, slide-sorter view, and slide-show view.

1. *Normal view* allows you to view and edit the individual slides (see Figure 23.5). Below each slide is a space to add notes. The left pane of the normal view screen shows the thumbnail and outline views of the slides as they are created. You can enter and edit slide text in the outline pane.

2. *Slide-sorter view* provides a graphical representation of all the slides in the presentation, in the order they were created. In this view you can click and drag slides to reorganize the presentation sequence or to delete slides (see Figure 23.6).

3. *Slide-show view* is the actual view to use for projecting the presentation to an audience. Each slide appears in its proper sequence and fills the entire screen.

For each presentation you create using a design template, PowerPoint creates a *Slide Master*. Slide Masters contain any unique elements (font, background, colors, and so forth) that you want to appear on every slide. For example, if you want a logo, an image, or a line of text to appear on each slide, add that item to

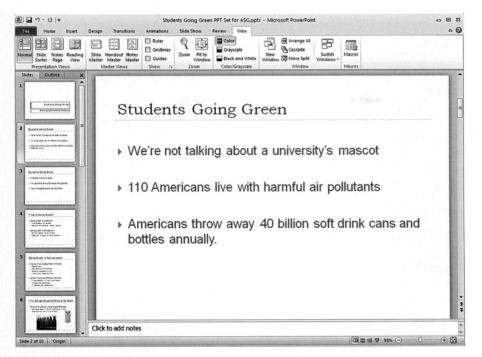

FIGURE 23.5 Normal View

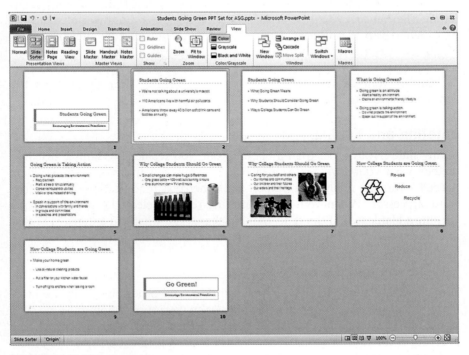

FIGURE 23.6 Slide-Sorter View

TABLE 23.1	Commands to Run a PowerPoint Slide Show
Function	Method
Show the next slide	Click the left mouse button or press the space bar, N, right arrow, down arrow, or Page Down
Show the preceding slide	Click the right mouse button or press Backspace, P, left arrow, up arrow, or Page Up
Show a specific slide	Type the number and press Enter
Access screen pointers	Click the right mouse button and select the appropriate option
Toggle the mouse pointer on or off (show or hide)	Type A or the equal sign
Toggle between a black screen and a current screen	Type B or a period
Toggle between a white screen and a current screen	Type W or a comma
End the show	Press ESC, hyphen, or CTRL-Break
Pause and resume an automatic slide show	Type an S or the plus sign

the Slide Master, and it will automatically appear on all the slides in your presentation. The *Handout Master* is a page-size view depicting a number of slides per page. When printed, this view may serve as a handout useful for audience members to have as a record of the presentation. To display a Master, click the View tab and select Slide Master.

During your actual presentation, you can control your slides using the commands listed in Table 23.1.

Entering and Editing Text

In any slide layout other than a blank layout, you replace the sample text in a textbox with your own text. (In a blank layout you insert a textbox where needed.) You can apply bold, italics, and other text modifications just as in a word processor. When you finish entering text, deselect the placeholder by clicking a blank area of the slide. Making changes to what you entered is as easy as clicking and retyping.

Using Slide Inserts

You can easily import photos, graphs, clip art, and other objects into Power-Point as *slide inserts* to supplement or illustrate your speech points. Some slide layouts display icons for each kind of object that, when clicked, activate the procedures for inserting that kind of object. Or you can use the same procedure as you would when inserting graphical elements into Microsoft Word documents and e-mail messages. With a slide open in normal view, select the

Insert menu at the top of your screen, and click on the type of object you want to insert: Picture, Clip Art, Shapes, Chart, WordArt, Equation, or even Sound or Video. Be careful not to overuse inserts; audience attention tends to lessen as slides appear more complex.[5]

- *Pictures.* Photos can be inserted from your own picture files, from a disk or portable drive, or from photo Web sites.

- *Clip Art.* You can select clip art from the PowerPoint Clip Art gallery. You can also import clip art from other programs or Web sites such as Microsoft's online Clip Art page (office.microsoft.com/images).

- *Charts.* Select Chart from your Insert menu to see a palette of different types of charts (see Figure 23.7). Select the type of chart you want to create (column, bar, line, pie, and so on) and input the appropriate data. The chart will automatically be inserted into the slide.

- *Tables and Worksheets.* To insert a table or a worksheet in PowerPoint, choose Insert Microsoft Table or Insert Microsoft Excel Worksheet in the standard toolbar.

- *Sound.* In PowerPoint you can also insert a playable music track from a file from your computer, an external device, or an audio clip art. To do so, select Audio from the Insert menu and then select the location to access the file.

PowerPoint presentations can include video clips and even portions of movies and television as supporting material for speeches. The growing availability

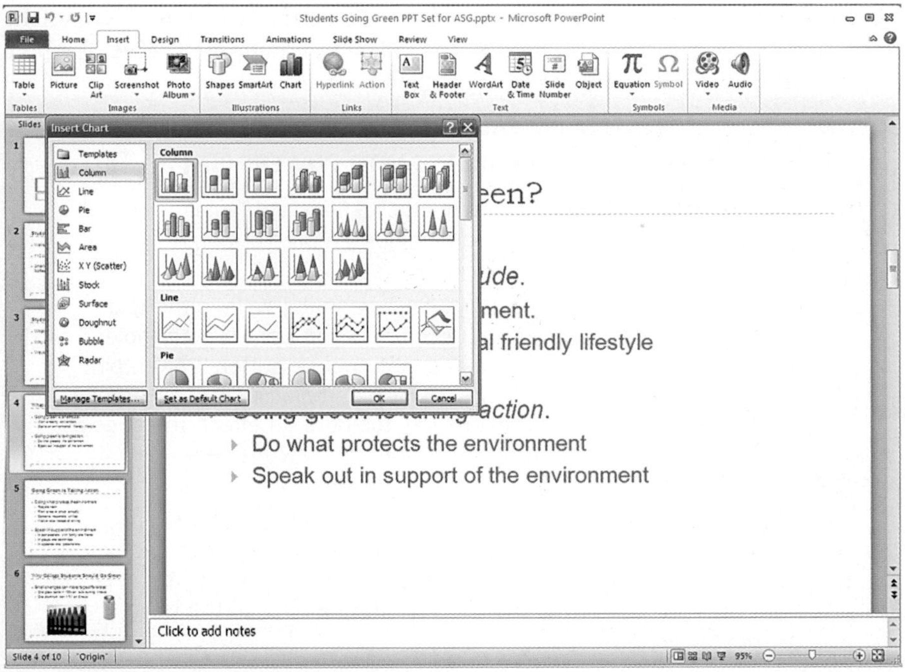

FIGURE 23.7 Using Charts in PowerPoint Slides

of amateur video on Web sites such as YouTube (www.youtube.com) and the increasing ease of transferring video to computers from portable digital devices make embedding video even simpler. It is not difficult to use video in a Power-Point presentation, but you may need to practice in order to get it right. To add video to a slide, follow these steps:

1. In Normal View, click the slide to which you want to add a video clip.

2. On the Insert menu, click the arrow under Video.

3. Do one of the following:

    • Click Video from File, locate the folder that contains the file, and then double-click the file that you want to add. You will have to include this file in the same folder with your PowerPoint file if you display the presentation from a different computer.

    • Click Video from Web site, paste the embed code from the Web site into the text box, then click Insert (an embed code is provided with each video on sites such as YouTube).

    • Click Clip Art Video, use the Clip Art task pane to find a suitable image, and then click it to add it to the slide.

You can also access PowerPoint Help (click the white question mark in the upper right corner of the PowerPoint screen) for instructions to add and play a video in a presentation.

Note that you cannot insert portions of a digital movie from a DVD to a PowerPoint slide, but you can use some third-party software to synchronize DVD video during a PowerPoint presentation. Be certain to abide by copyright restrictions when copying or downloading video and audio files. (See "Respect the Laws of Copyright and Fair Use" in Chapter 5.)

INSERTING TABLES AND WORKSHEETS INTO POWERPOINT

_____ 1. To create a table or a worksheet, click Insert > Table or Insert > Table > Excel Spreadsheet. A drop-down grid of cells appears.

_____ 2. Click and drag the mouse pointer across the cells in the grid to indicate how many rows or columns you want in your table or worksheet. When you release the mouse button, PowerPoint inserts a special object into your slide, replacing the PowerPoint toolbars with either Word or Excel toolbars. In effect, the special object allows you to use either Word or Excel inside a PowerPoint window.

_____ 3. To enter content into the table or worksheet, use the mouse, the tab key, or the arrow keys to move from cell to cell and type in the text. When you have entered all of the desired content, insert the object into the slide by clicking outside the table or worksheet.

CHECKLIST

Finding Media for PowerPoint Slides

With PowerPoint, you can import still images, clip art, video, or sound directly into your slides, either by downloading the files from the Internet or accessing them from a computer disk. Depending on your speech topic, you may be able to find clip art, video, picture, or sound files on the Internet that meet your needs.

For downloadable digital images, try the following Web sites:

- Corbis.com (www.corbisimages.com): Contains more than 2 million photographs, prints, and paintings, 35,000 of which you can download for your personal use (for a fee).
- Google (www.google.com), Yahoo! (www.yahoo.com), and Bing (www.bing.com): Popular search engines that offer extensive image searches.

The following sites contain free photographs and other still images:

- www.flickr.com/creativecommons: Access to thousands of photographs shared by amateur and hobbyist photographers.
- www.exalead.com/image: An innovative image search engine with over 2 billion images.
- memory.loc.gov/ammem: Free access to still and moving images depicting the history of the American experience.

The following sites offer downloadable music files and audio clips:

- www.mp3.com
- www.soundclick.com
- www.archive.org/ details/audio
- www.dailywav.com
- www.freeaudioclips.com

The following sites contain useful video clips:

- CNN Video (www.cnn.com/video) and ABC News Video (abcnews .go.com/video): Especially useful for speech topics on current events or timely social issues.
- video.search.yahoo.com
- www.bing.com/videos/ browse
- video.google.com

Getting Ready to Deliver a PowerPoint Presentation

PowerPoint slides can help listeners visually process information (especially complex statistical data; see From Idea to Image: Using Presentation Aids, p. 294). Following good preparation practices with PowerPoint can help you avoid distracting technical glitches and take full advantage of this powerful medium.

Check the Venue

Before your speech, take stock of the available presentation technology and the venue layout. It's worthwhile to perform this step even if the speech venue is your usual classroom—you may discover that you didn't know as much about the room as you thought, and familiarizing yourself with its layout and technology will also help you combat any speaking anxiety. See the annotated photo below for important considerations that can help you master a smooth delivery, especially if you are planning to use a computer and the Internet during your presentation.

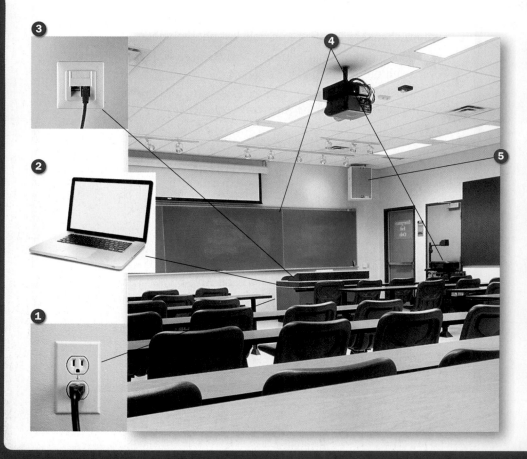

1. **Power sources.** Locate plugs and power strips and ensure that cords can reach the presentation equipment. Consider taping power cords to the floor to keep them from getting in the way.

2. **Computer needs and compatibility.** Figure out which computer you'll be using during the speech and check that all your files, from the slide show to audio and video clips, load successfully to this computer. If possible, you should practice at least once on the presentation computer.

3. **Internet access.** If any of your aids are online, test Internet access before the speech. Make sure you know any pertinent wireless log-in information or that you have a cable that reaches the Internet jack.

4. **Back-up plan.** Create a contingency plan that covers you in case of computer failure. If an overhead projector is available, you might print overhead transparencies from your slide show. Or you might be prepared to put pertinent information on the board. Paper handouts generated from the slide show are another solid backup plan.

5. **Audio.** Determine how you will broadcast any audio aids, and always make sure speaker volume is appropriate before your speech.

Pick Speaker Placement Carefully

Before your speech, choose a place to stand that gives the audience clear sight-lines to you and your slide show. When picking your placement, keep in mind that you should be able to face forward at all times, even when changing slides or gesturing toward your aids. This helps you connect with your audience, project clearly, and prevents you from reading off your slides.

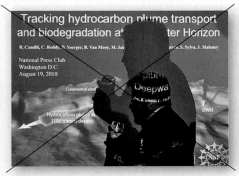

Needs improvement: As this speaker pauses to sip some water, he blocks the slide image with his shadow. His sideways stance discourages eye contact with the audience and indicates that he may be reading off his slides.

Good placement: This speaker's body placement leaves the audience with a clear view of the presentation screen. He can easily access the presentation computer and can also gesture toward the slides without blocking them.

Using Transitions and Animation Effects

When moving from one slide to the next in your presentation, or from one point to another within a single slide, you may wish to add special effects in the form of transitions and text animations. *Transition effects* add motion and sound as you click from one slide to another. For example, you can play a "swoosh" sound when the slide appears, or you can make the slides dissolve into black or red as you shift from one to another. *Animation effects*—sometimes referred to as *builds*—allow you to reveal text or graphics within a slide during a presentation. You can reveal one letter, word, or paragraph at a time as you discuss each item. Or you can make text or objects look dimmer or change color when you add another element.

Note that your PowerPoint presentation will be just as effective without transitions and animation effects. If you do decide to use them, however, use them sparingly and keep them consistent throughout the entire slide show or within different sections. Unnecessary effects can distract from your message and harm the presentation.

Developing PowerPoint Slides for a Speech

The fundamental principle for using PowerPoint slides for a speech is the same as for any visual support device: Make sure that the visuals will add value to your speech and will not distract from or become your speech. Like any visual support, PowerPoint slides are meant to supplement and not to supplant your speech. Often the best place to begin planning your slides is with your speaking outline.

Your speaking outline provides the content elements for your slides, and by thinking through which points in your speech might be better explained to your audience with some kind of visual, you can decide what the content of your slides will be, how many slides you'll need, and how to arrange your slides. A speaking outline may contain between three and five main points. Each main point has at least two subpoints. Are some points more suited for visual display than others? What features should be used for each slide? There is no fixed formula for answering these questions, so you must rely on your own creativity and critical thinking.

TIPS FOR SUCCESSFULLY USING POWERPOINT PRESENTATIONS IN YOUR SPEECH

✓ Don't let the technology get in the way of relating to your audience.

✓ Talk to your audience rather than to the screen. Maintain eye contact as much as possible.

✓ Have a backup plan in case of technical errors.

✓ If you use a pointer (laser or otherwise), turn it off and put it down as soon as you have made your point.

✓ Never shine a laser pointer into anyone's eyes. It will burn them!

✓ Incorporate the aids into your practice sessions until you are confident that they strengthen, rather than detract from, your core message.

CHECKLIST

FORMS OF
SPEECHES

FORMS OF SPEECHES

SPEAKER'S REFERENCE

CHAPTER **24** The Informative Speech 329

Focus on Sharing Knowledge 329
- ▶ **CHECKLIST** Help Listeners Follow Along 331

Categories of Informative Speeches 331

Decide How to Convey the Information 333

Take Steps to Reduce Confusion 336
- ▶ **CHECKLIST** Strategies for Explaining Complex Information 337

Arrange Speech Points in a Pattern 338
- ▶ **CHECKLIST** Guidelines for Clearly Communicating Your Informative Message 339
- ▶ **SAMPLE SPEECH OF DEMONSTRATION** An Ounce of Prevention Keeps the Germs Away, Christie Collins 340
- ▶ **SAMPLE VISUALLY ANNOTATED INFORMATIVE SPEECH** John Kanzius and the Quest to Cure Cancer, David Kruckenberg 344

CHAPTER **25** The Persuasive Speech 350

What Is a Persuasive Speech? 350
- ▶ **CHECKLIST** Conditions for Choosing a Persuasive Purpose 350
- ▶ **ETHICALLY SPEAKING** Persuasive Speeches Respect Audience Choices 351

The Process of Persuasion 352

Classical Persuasive Appeals: Using Proofs 353
- ▶ **ETHICALLY SPEAKING** Using Emotions Ethically 356

Contemporary Persuasive Appeals: Needs and Motivations 358
- ▶ **CHECKLIST** Displaying Ethos in the Persuasive Speech 358
- ▶ **SELF-ASSESSMENT CHECKLIST** Tips for Increasing Speaker Credibility 363

CHAPTER **26** Developing Arguments for the Persuasive Speech 365

What Is an Argument? 365
- ▶ **ETHICALLY SPEAKING** Engaging in Arguments in the Public Arena 366

Types of Claims, Evidence, and Warrants 368
- ▶ **A CULTURAL PERSPECTIVE** Addressing Culture in the Persuasive Speech 369
- ▶ **CHECKLIST** Testing the Strength of Your Evidence 372
- ▶ **CHECKLIST** Making Effective Use of Reasoning by Cause 375
- ▶ **CHECKLIST** Techniques for Addressing Competing Arguments 376

Fallacies in Reasoning 376

CHAPTER **27** Organizing the Persuasive Speech 379

Factors to Consider When Choosing an Organizational Pattern 379
Problem-Solution Pattern of Arrangement 381
▶ **CHECKLIST** Organizing a Claim of Policy 383
Monroe's Motivated Sequence 383
▶ **CHECKLIST** Steps in the Motivated Sequence 385
Comparative Advantage Pattern of Arrangement 386
Refutation Pattern of Arrangement 387
▶ **SAMPLE VISUALLY ANNOTATED PERSUASIVE SPEECH**
Emergency in the Emergency Room, Lisa Roth 388
▶ **SAMPLE VISUALLY ANNOTATED PERSUASIVE SPEECH** Preventing
Cyberbullying, Una Chua 393
▶ **SAMPLE VISUALLY ANNOTATED PERSUASIVE SPEECH**
The Importance of Community Engagement and
Volunteerism, Stephanie Poplin 401

CHAPTER **28** Special Occasion Speeches 406

Functions of Special Occasion Speeches 406
Types of Special Occasion Speeches 407
▶ **CHECKLIST** Guidelines for Introducing Other Speakers 409
▶ **CHECKLIST** Guidelines for Delivering Speeches of
Acceptance 410
▶ **CHECKLIST** Tips for Delivering Effective Eulogies 413
▶ **CHECKLIST** Delivering a Successful Speech of Inspiration 416
▶ **ETHICALLY SPEAKING** Tailor Your Message to the Audience
and Occasion 416
▶ **SAMPLE VISUALLY ANNOTATED SPECIAL OCCASION SPEECH**
"Love the Process": A Soccer Star's Philosophy of Life,
Yael Averbuch 417

FORMS OF SPEECHES

CHAPTER 24 The Informative Speech

Focus on Sharing Knowledge and Demonstrating Relevance

- Strive to enlighten (informative intent) rather than to advocate (persuasive intent). (p. 329)
- Use audience analysis to determine information needs. (p. 330)
- Show the audience why the topic is relevant to them. (p. 330)
- Present new and interesting information. (p. 330)
- Look for ways to increase understanding. (p. 330)

Consider the Types of Informative Speeches

- Speeches about objects or phenomena. (p. 331)
- Speeches about people. (p. 332)
- Speeches about events. (p. 332)
- Speeches about processes. (p. 332)
- Speeches about issues. (p. 333)
- Speeches about concepts. (p. 333)

Choose Strategies for Conveying Information

- Use *definition* to clarify. (p. 333)
- Provide *descriptions* to paint a picture. (p. 335)
- Provide a *demonstration*. (p. 335)
- Offer an in-depth *explanation*. (p. 335)

Clarify Complex Information

- Build on prior knowledge. (p. 336)
- Use analogies that link concepts to something familiar. (p. 336)
- Demonstrate underlying causes. (p. 337)
- Check for understanding. (p. 337)
- Use visual aids, including models and drawings. (p. 337)

Appeal to Different Learning Styles

- Consider listeners' learning styles as part of your audience analysis. (p. 337)

SPEAKER'S REFERENCE

- Plan on conveying and reinforcing information in a variety of modes—visually, aurally, with text, and with demonstrations. (p. 337)

Arrange Speech Points in an Organizational Pattern

CHAPTER 25 The Persuasive Speech

Select a Persuasive Purpose If Your Goal Is to:

- Influence an audience's attitudes, beliefs, or understanding of an issue. (p. 350)
- Influence an audience's behavior. (p. 350)
- Reinforce existing attitudes, beliefs, or behavior. (p. 350)

Increase the Odds of Achieving Your Persuasive Speech Goal by:

- Conducting a thorough audience analysis. (p. 352)
- Making your message relevant to the audience. (p. 352)
- Showing your listeners how the change you seek benefits them. (p. 352)
- Establishing credibility with your audience. (p. 352)
- Addressing topics that the audience feels strongly about. (p. 352)
- Seeking minor rather than major changes. (p. 352)

When Appealing to Emotion, Use Sound Reasoning

- Avoid deliberately arousing fear or otherwise manipulating listeners' emotions. (p. 356)

To Increase the Odds That Listeners Will Act on Your Message:

- Appeal to their needs. (p. 358)
- Appeal to the reasons they act as they do. (p. 359)
- Stress the message's relevance to listeners. (p. 361)
- Present the information at an appropriate level of understanding. (p. 361)
- Establish your credibility: Emphasize your expertise for speeches that stress facts and analysis; emphasize commonality with the audience for personal speeches. (p. 362)

CHAPTER **26** Developing Arguments for the Persuasive Speech

Structure the Claims According to the Issue You Are Addressing

- When addressing whether something is or is not true, or whether something will or will not happen, make a *claim of fact*. (p. 368)
- When addressing an issue that relies on individual judgment of right and wrong for its resolution, make a *claim of value*. (p. 368)
- When proposing a specific outcome or solution to an issue, make a *claim of policy*. (p. 368)

Consider the Kinds of Evidence That Best Support Your Claim

- When audience members are aware of the issue in question, consider using evidence with which they are already familiar, based on adequate audience analysis focusing on their opinions of your topic. (p. 371)
- If your knowledge and credentials are such that the audience will find your opinions credible and convincing, consider using your own expertise as evidence. (p. 371)
- If the audience lacks knowledge of the topic and you are not a known expert on the subject, consider using examples, stories, testimony, facts, and statistics from external sources. (p. 372)

Test Your Evidence

- Is it directly relevant to your claim? (p. 372)
- Is it timely? (p. 372)
- Will the audience find the evidence and its source credible? (p. 372)

Use Appropriate Lines of Reasoning to Validate Claims

- You can use the needs, desires, emotions, and values of audience members as the basis of their accepting some evidence *(motivational warrants)*. (p. 373)
- You can rely on audience members' beliefs about the credibility of a source as the basis of their accepting some evidence *(authoritative warrants)*. (p. 373)
- You can use audience members' beliefs about the reliability of factual evidence as the basis of their accepting some evidence *(substantive warrants)*. (p. 374)
- Use *warrants by cause* when offering a cause-effect relationship as proof of the claim. (p. 374)
- Use *warrants by sign* when the topic allows you to infer that such a close relationship exists between two variables that the presence or absence of one may be taken as an indication of the presence or absence of the other. (p. 375)

- Use *warrants by analogy* when the topic allows you to compare two similar cases and infer that what is true in one case is true in the other. (p. 375)

Anticipate and Plan on Addressing Counterarguments to Your Position

- If you ignore obvious counterclaims to your position, you may lose credibility. (p. 376)

Beware of Logical Fallacies That Will Weaken Your Arguments

- Avoid *begging the question*, or using circular reasoning to state an argument in such a way that it cannot help but be true. (p. 377)
- Do not rely on popular opinion as evidence that your claim is true *(bandwagoning)*. (p. 377)
- Avoid framing your argument as an either-or proposition *(either-or fallacy)*. (p. 377)
- Avoid *ad hominem arguments* that attack an opponent instead of attacking the opponent's arguments. (p. 377)
- Avoid relying on irrelevant information to argue your point *(red herring fallacy)*. (p. 377)
- Avoid using an isolated instance to make an unwarranted general conclusion *(hasty generalization)*. (p. 378)
- Avoid offering conclusions that do not connect to your reasoning *(non sequitur)*. (p. 378)
- Avoid claiming that something is true by stating that one example or case will inevitably lead to a series of events or actions *(slippery slope)*. (p. 378)
- Avoid *appeals to tradition*. (p. 378)

CHAPTER 27 Organizing the Persuasive Speech

Select an Organizational Pattern Based on Your Argument, Audience, and Speech Goal

- Choose a pattern that works with your particular argument and evidence. (p. 379)
- Choose a pattern that will help you appeal to the target audience. (p. 380)
- Consider the *refutation* or *problem-solution pattern* for a hostile or a critical and conflicted audience. (p. 380)
- Consider the *narrative pattern* for sympathetic listeners. (p. 380)

- For an uninformed, less educated, or apathetic audience, focus on gaining listeners' attention and establishing credibility. Consider arranging points logically in a *topical pattern*. (p. 380)
- Choose a pattern that will help you elicit the reaction you seek from your audience (your *specific speech purpose*). (p. 381)

Use the Problem-Solution Pattern to Demonstrate the Nature of a Problem and Provide Justification for a Solution

- Define the problem and offer a solution *(problem-solution)*. (p. 381)
- Define the problem, cite reasons for the problem, and offer a solution *(problem-cause-solution)*. (p. 381)

Consider the Motivated Sequence Pattern When Urging Action

- Step 1: *Attention*—address listeners' core concerns. (p. 384)
- Step 2: *Need*—show listeners they have a need or problem that must be satisfied or solved. (p. 384)
- Step 3: *Satisfaction*—introduce the solution to the problem. (p. 385)
- Step 4: *Visualization*—provide a vision of outcomes associated with the solution. (p. 385)
- Step 5: *Action*—make a direct request of listeners. (p. 386)

If the Audience Is Already Aware of an Issue and Agrees That It Should Be Addressed, Consider the Comparative Advantage Pattern

- Determine alternatives to the problem—both pro and con to your position—that the audience will be aware of. (p. 386)
- Organize points to favorably compare your position to alternatives. (p. 386)
- The summary should include brief but compelling evidence demonstrating the superiority or comparative advantage of your option over competing ones. (p. 386)

If Listeners Disagree with You or Are Conflicted, Consider the Refutation Pattern

- State the opposing claim. (p. 387)
- Explain the ramifications of the opposing claim. (p. 387)
- Present your argument and the evidence. (p. 387)
- Show the superiority of your claim through contrast. (p. 387)

CHAPTER 28 Special Occasion Speeches

Identify the Primary Purpose of Your Special Occasion Speech

- Is it to *entertain* the audience? (p. 406)
- Is it to *celebrate* or recognize a person, a place, or an event? (p. 406)
- Is it to *commemorate* a person, a place, or an event? (p. 407)
- Is it to *inspire* your listeners? (p. 407)
- Is it to establish or reinforce the goals and values of the group sponsoring the event *(setting a social agenda)*? (p. 407)

Focus Your Speech of Introduction on Motivating the Audience to Listen to the Speaker

- Establish the speaker's credibility by describing relevant facts about his or her background and qualifications for speaking. (p. 408)
- Briefly describe the speaker's topic and establish its relevance to the audience. (p. 408)
- Keep your remarks brief. (p. 408)

Focus Your Speech of Acceptance on Expressing Gratitude for the Honor Bestowed on You

- If you know that you are to receive an award or suspect that you may be honored, prepare the speech in advance. (p. 409)
- Let the audience know what the award means to you. (p. 409)
- Express yourself genuinely and with humility. (p. 409)
- Thank each of the individuals or organizations involved in giving you the award. (p. 410)
- Acknowledge others who helped you attain the achievement. (p. 410)

Focus Your Speech of Presentation on Explaining the Award and the Reason It Is Being Bestowed on the Recipient

- Explain what the award represents. (p. 411)
- Explain why the recipient is receiving the award. (p. 411)

Focus Remarks Made at Roasts and Toasts on the Person Being Honored

- For a roast, prepare a humorous tribute to the person. (p. 411)
- For a toast, pay brief tribute to the person or event. (p. 411)
- Prepare your remarks in advance. (p. 411)
- Rehearse any jokes in advance. (p. 411)
- Keep within your time limits. (p. 412)

When Delivering a Eulogy, Pay Tribute to the Life of the Deceased

- Stay in control of your emotions. (p. 412)
- Refer to each family member of the deceased by name. (p. 412)
- Focus on the person's life rather than on the circumstances of death. (p. 413)
- Emphasize the person's positive qualities. (p. 413)

When Delivering an After-Dinner Speech, Balance Insight and Entertainment

- Begin by recognizing the occasion and linking it to your theme. (p. 414)
- Avoid stand-up comedy. Use humor that is consistent with your personality. (p. 414)
- When addressing serious issues and causes, keep an eye on the audience's comfort level. (p. 414)

Focus Your Speech of Inspiration on Uplifting the Audience

- Seek to arouse the audience's better instincts. (p. 414)
- Focus on creating positive speaker ethos (see Chapter 5). (p. 414)
- Appeal to the audience's emotions through vivid descriptions and emotionally charged words. Consider the use of repetition, alliteration, and parallelism (see Chapter 17). (p. 414)
- Consider using real-life stories and examples. (p. 415)
- Strive for a dynamic delivery style. (p. 415)
- Clearly establish your speech goal. (p. 415)
- Consider using an acronym to organize your message. (p. 415)
- Make your conclusion strong. (p. 416)

KEY TERMS

Chapter 24

informative speech
preview statement
reportage
backstory

operational definition
definition by negation
definition by example
definition by synonym

definition by etymology (word origin)
analogy

Chapter 25

persuasion
persuasive speaking
rhetorical proofs
logos
reasoning
syllogism
general case
major premise
specific case

minor premise
deductive reasoning
inductive reasoning
hasty overgeneralization
enthymeme
pathos
demagogue
fear appeal
propaganda

ethos
Maslow's hierarchy of needs
expectancy-outcome values theory
elaboration likelihood model of persuasion (ELM)
central processing
peripheral processing
speaker credibility

Chapter 26

argument
claim
evidence
warrants
claims of fact
speculative claims
claims of value
cultural norms
cultural premises
claims of policy
motivational warrants

authoritative warrants
substantive warrants
warrants by cause (causal reasoning)
warrants by sign (reasoning by sign)
warrants by analogy (reasoning by analogy)
inoculation effect
logical fallacy
begging the question

bandwagoning
either-or fallacy
ad hominem argument
red herring fallacy
hasty generalization
non sequitur
slippery slope
appeal to tradition

Chapter 27

claim of policy
claim of value
claim of fact
target audience
hostile audience, or one that strongly disagrees
critical and conflicted audience
sympathetic audience

uninformed, less educated, or apathetic audience
specific speech purpose
problem-solution pattern of arrangement
problem-cause-solution pattern of arrangement

motivated sequence pattern of arrangement
comparative advantage pattern of arrangement
refutation pattern of arrangement

Chapter 28

special occasion speech
speech of introduction
speech of acceptance
speech of presentation

roast
toast
eulogy
after-dinner speech

canned speech
social agenda–setting
sermons
speech of inspiration

The Informative Speech

Ever wondered about the satellite technology behind Google Earth? Or which careers will be most financially rewarding in the next decade? How can you protect your reputation when using social networking sites? What does *Net neutrality* mean?

To *inform* is to communicate knowledge. The goal of informative speaking is to increase the audience's awareness of some phenomenon and/or deepen understanding of it by imparting knowledge.[1] **Informative speeches** bring new topics to light, offer new insights on subjects with which we are familiar, provide novel ways of thinking about a topic, or demonstrate how to do things. Some speeches do all of this in a single speech; others remain focused in one or another direction.

Focus on Sharing Knowledge

WEB Chapter quizzes

With information available today in so many forms, electronic and otherwise, it might appear that we have little need for informative speeches. Yet it is precisely because of this glut of gathered facts that we thirst for thoughtful perspectives, and informative speeches can answer this need. Your speech might be an in-depth analysis of a complex subject, a report of an event, or a physical demonstration of how something works. As long as your audience learns something, the options are nearly limitless.

Enlighten Rather Than Advocate

The goal of an informative speech stands in contrast to that of the persuasive speech, which explicitly attempts to influence people's attitudes, values, beliefs, or behavior about an issue. Whereas a persuasive speech would seek to modify attitudes or ask the audience to adopt a specific position, an informative speech stops short of this. Yet scholars of public speaking point out that there is no such thing as a purely informative or persuasive speech; that is, there are always elements of persuasion in an informative speech, and vice versa. Rarely are we entirely dispassionate about a subject, especially one that tends to elicit strong reactions. Nevertheless, if you keep in mind the general informative speaking goal, you will be able to deliver an informative speech whose primary function is to enlighten rather than to advocate.

Use Audience Analysis

Audience members must be able to identify with the informative topic and see how they can use and benefit from the information you give them. You therefore will need to gauge what your listeners already know about your informative topic as well as what they want and need to know about it. Then adapt your speech accordingly. If speaking about collecting violins to a general audience, for example, you might describe the parts of a violin, the sounds it produces, and the names of the Italian families who made the most prized instruments. Only a specialized audience of musicians will want or need to hear about staccato bowings, sforzandos, or other technical information.[2]

The importance of giving listeners a reason to care about your topic cannot be overstated. Early on in your speech (in your **preview statement**, for example) tell audience members why they should listen to you. Demonstrate the topic's relevance to the audience by pointing out how some aspect of it relates directly to listeners' lives.

Present New and Interesting Information

Audiences seek knowledge; they want to learn something new. To satisfy this drive, try to uncover information that is fresh and compelling. Seek out unusual sources (but make certain they are credible), novel (but sound) interpretations, startling facts, compelling examples, and moving stories. As professional speaker Vickie K. Sullivan notes:

> The first point that transforms an ordinary speaker into an industry beacon is a new perspective on a major problem. . . . If the speech does not convey provocative information, audience members feel their time has been wasted (and rightfully will feel offended). They expect their thinking to be challenged.[3]

As important as offering new information, however, is not overwhelming listeners with too much of it. Most people will recall less than half of the information you tell them, so focus on what you most want to convey and trim material that does not strongly support your central idea.[4]

Look for Ways to Increase Understanding

People are not simply empty vessels into which you can pour facts and figures and expect them to recognize and remember all that information. Before we can retain information, we must be motivated to listen to it and be able to recognize and comprehend it.[5] Incorporating the public speaking steps introduced in previous chapters will help you motivate the audience to listen and sustain their involvement as you move through the speech. For example, Chapter 8 discusses how to flesh out speech points with compelling supporting materials, such as examples, stories, opinions, and facts. Chapter 17 demonstrates ways you can use language to connect to your audience and help listeners to visualize ideas; it also demonstrates how rhetorical devices such as *repetition* and *parallelism* can reinforce information and drive home key themes. Other aspects of speechmaking covered in previous chapters that are necessary ingredients for an effective informative speech include:

- *A well-organized introduction that previews the main points* (see Chapter 15) and a conclusion that concisely summarizes them will help listeners anticipate and remember information (see Chapter 16).
- *Clear transitions.* Signal words, phrases, and sentences that tie speech ideas together are especially important when listeners are learning new information (see Chapter 12).
- *An appropriate organizational pattern* can help listeners mentally organize ideas and see relationships among them (see Chapters 12–14 and 27).[6]
- *Presentation aids.* People process and retain information best when they hear it *and* see related (but not duplicated) information, as, for instance, in charts and diagrams (see Chapters 21–23).

HELP LISTENERS FOLLOW ALONG

Audience members cannot put the speaker on "pause" in order to digest information, so help them stay on track:

✔ Preview main points in the introduction, and state what you hope listeners will gain from the speech.

✔ Use *internal previews* to forecast key points and *internal summaries* to reinforce them.

✔ Use transitions to help the audience follow the logical flow of ideas.

✔ Use repetition and parallel structure to help listeners grasp and retain key ideas and concepts.

✔ Choose an organizational pattern that suits the material.

✔ Reinforce your message with effective presentation aids.

CHECKLIST

Categories of Informative Speeches

 WEB Video

Informative speeches are sometimes categorized according to the types of subject matter they address. Thus an informative speech may be about objects or phenomena, people, events, processes, issues, or concepts. These are not hard-and-fast divisions—a speech can be about both the *process* of dance and the *people* who perform it, for example—but they show the range of informative subjects and can point to a logical organizational pattern. (See Chapter 13 and p. 338.)

Speeches about Objects or Phenomena

Speeches about objects or phenomena explore anything that isn't human; it can be animate, as in the animal kingdom, or inanimate, as in electronic devices or sports equipment. Topics for such speeches run the gamut from ribbons used to raise awareness about diseases to therapy dogs and the making of a musical score. Phenomena such as new inventions, the history of graphic novels, and the evolution of "Texas English" belong to this broad category.

Speeches about People

Speeches about people inform audiences about individuals and groups who have made contributions to society (both positive and negative) or those who for one reason or another we simply find compelling. For example, what led Rahul Singh, founder of GlobalMedic, to devote his life to providing disaster relief?

Speeches about people may also be autobiographical. Each of us has stories to tell, and if they express common themes—love, loss, growth, the overcoming of obstacles—audience members will be drawn in. The key to delivering an effective speech about yourself or another person is to provide a "lesson" that audience members can take away from the speech. How did the person face and overcome obstacles? What steps did the person take on the road to achievement? What human qualities harmed or helped the person?

Speeches about Events

Speeches about events focus on noteworthy occurrences, past and present. What was the timeline of the 2011 Egyptian opposition protests, and what is the state of freedom today in Egypt? Speeches about events rely on **reportage**—an account of the who, what, where, when, and why of the facts. The key to a speech about an event is to offer new insights and information about the event, and to shed light on its meaning. For example, what was the **backstory**—the story that leads up to the event that listeners might find interesting—that led to the online posting by Wikileaks of thousands of classified U.S. military intelligence documents? Giving audience members "behind the scenes" information is a surefire way of catching their attention.

Speeches about Processes

Speeches about processes refer to a series of steps that lead to a finished product or end result. In this type of speech, you can talk about how something is done, how it is made, or how it works. How do hybrid cars operate? What steps are involved in interviewing for a job?

When discussing a process, you can either explain how something works or develops (*How do baby penguins develop?*) or actually teach audience members to perform the process (*how to make a quilt*). When describing how to do something, speakers often perform the actual task during the speech, demonstrating each step as they describe it or using presentation aids to illustrate the steps involved. As a rule, presentation aids, from slides to models to the actual thing being demonstrated, assume importance in speeches of demonstration (see Chapter 21, "Using Presentation Aids in the Speech").

Speeches about Issues

An *issue* is a problem or a matter in dispute, one that people seek to bring to a conclusion. Informative *speeches about issues* provide an overview or a report of problems in order to raise awareness and deepen understanding. The French ban on wearing burkas in public spaces, and the obesity epidemic in the United States are examples of issues that might be addressed in an informative speech.

Of the various types of informative speeches, speeches about issues have the greatest potential of "crossing the line" into the persuasive realm. Yet as long as your goal is to inform rather than to advocate, you can legitimately address issues in an informative speech. Thus, in a speech on immigration law, you might describe current immigration laws at the state and federal level and discuss Supreme Court rulings. On the other hand, you would refrain from advocating for or against reforms to existing immigration policy.

Speeches about Concepts

Speeches about concepts focus on abstract or complex ideas, theories, or beliefs and attempt to make them concrete and understandable to an audience. What is chaos theory? What do Hindus believe? We've heard the term *hate speech,* but we're confused because it seems to encompass everything from racist expressions to racist actions.

Because they address abstract or complex ideas, speeches about concepts have the potential to confuse audience members. To ensure that this does not occur, follow the guidelines in "Take Steps to Reduce Confusion" later in this chapter (p. 336).

Decide How to Convey the Information

 Video quizzes

Whether in conversation, writing, or speeches, typically we communicate information by defining, describing, demonstrating, and/or explaining it. Some informative speeches rely almost exclusively on a single approach (e.g., their main purpose is to *demonstrate* how something works or to *explain* what something means). Many speeches, however, combine strategies within a presentation (see Table 24.1). As you prepare your speech, ask yourself, "How much emphasis should I give to defining my topic, demonstrating it, describing it, or explaining its meaning?"

Definition

Some informative topics clearly require more definition than others. When you define information, you identify the essential qualities and meaning of something. What is cholesterol? What does "equilibrium price" mean? What is the Americans with Disabilities Act?

When your speech focuses on something that is new to the audience or a complex concept (*"What is a fractal?"*), pay particular attention to using definition. Definition can also be necessary when clarifying a controversial idea or

TABLE 24.1 Types of Informative Speeches and Sample Topics	
Subject Matter	**Sample Topics**
Objects or phenomena Define and describe object or phenomenon Demonstrate properties and functions	• MRI-based lie detectors • eBook readers • Liquid-filled eyeglasses • El Niño wind patterns in the western United States
People Vividly describe person's compelling characteristics and explain person's significance Offer stories about overcoming obstacles and lessons to be drawn from person's actions	• Athletes • Authors • Inventors • Political leaders • Soldiers • War or hurricane refugees
Current or historical events Use description to paint a vivid picture Use reporting and analysis Tell the backstory	• General Motors' declaration of bankruptcy • National College Cheerleading Finals • Battle of Britain • Violence along U.S./Mexico border
Speeches about processes If physically showing a process, rely on demonstration Use presentation aids	• Isolation of DNA in cells • Visualization in sports • Production of algae-based biofuels • Power Yoga routine
Speeches about concepts Offer multiple definitions Use analogies Discuss underlying processes/causes	• Chaos theory • Free speech • Responsible knowledge • Nanotechnology
Speeches about issues Focus on explanation Avoid advocating for one position versus another	• Impact of long-term unemployment • Managing your reputation on social networking sites • Legalizing and taxing nonmedical marijuana

issue. For example, many of us are aware that prayer in the public schools has been ruled unconstitutional, but precisely how does the Constitution or its amendments define prayer?

Defining information may sound straightforward, but there are in fact a number of ways to define something, including the following:

- Defining the topic by explaining what it does (**operational definition**); for example, *A computer is something that processes information.*

- Defining the topic by describing what it is not (**definition by negation**); for example, *Courage is not the absence of fear.*

- Defining the topic by providing several concrete examples (**definition by example**); for example, *Health professionals include doctors, nurses, EMTs, and ambulance drivers.*

- Defining the topic by comparing it to something with which it is synonymous (**definition by synonym**); for example, *A friend is a comrade or a buddy.*
- Defining the topic by illustrating the root meaning of the word in question (**definition by etymology** [word origin]); for example, *The word* rival *derives from the Latin word* rivalis, *"one living near or using the same stream."*[7]

Description

Some speech topics, such as an overview of postwar architecture in Rotterdam, call for a good deal of description. When you *describe* information, you provide an array of details that paint a mental picture of your topic. Whether offering your audience a "virtual tour" of the top of Mount Everest, or describing the physical ravages wrought by drug abuse, the point of speeches, or sections of speeches, relying on description is to offer a vivid portrayal of the topic.

Demonstration

Yet another approach to presenting information is to explain how something works or to actually demonstrate it. The many "how to" television shows and podcasts on the Web, ranging from step-by-step guides to home remodeling to using software programs, rely on demonstration. A speech may not include an actual physical demonstration, but the speaker will nevertheless verbally demonstrate the steps involved. Speeches that rely on demonstration often work with the actual object, representations or models of it, or visual aids that diagram it. Table 24.2 contains sample topics for a speech of demonstration.

Explanation

Certain informative speech topics are built on explanation—providing reasons or causes, demonstrating relationships, and offering interpretation and analysis. The classroom lecture is a classic example of using explanation in an informative context (see Chapter 31). But many kinds of speeches rely on explanation, from those that address difficult or confusing theories and processes (*What is*

TABLE 24.2   Sample Topics for a Speech of Demonstration

- Treating a burn
- Posting videos on YouTube
- Stippling a wall
- Marbleizing furniture
- Programming an iPhone
- Performing the Heimlich maneuver on infants
- Performing an emergency tracheotomy
- Using Adobe Photoshop
- Doing genealogy on the Web

the relationship between the glycemic index and glycemic load?) to topics that challenge conventional thinking (*Why do researchers say that sometimes emotion makes us more rather than less logical?*)

See the checklist on p. 337 for strategies for explaining complex processes.

Take Steps to Reduce Confusion

New information can be hard to grasp, especially when it addresses a difficult concept or term (such as *equilibrium* in engineering), a difficult-to-envision process (such as *cash-flow management* in business), or a counterintuitive idea—one that challenges commonsense thinking (such as *drinking a glass of red wine a day can be healthy*).[8]

Useful for most any speech, the following strategies for communicating information are especially helpful when attempting to clarify complex ideas.

Use Analogies to Build on Prior Knowledge

Audience members will understand a new concept more easily if the speaker uses an **analogy** to relate it to something that they already know. Indeed, the process of learning itself is sometimes defined as constructing new knowledge from prior knowledge.[9] By linking the unfamiliar with the familiar through an analogy, you will give your listeners an easier way to venture into new territory. For example, to explain the unpredictable paths that satellites often take when they fall to Earth, you can liken the effect to dropping a penny into water: "Sometimes it goes straight down, and sometimes it turns end over end and changes direction. The same thing happens when an object hits the atmosphere."[10]

You can organize part or even all of a speech around an analogy. When explaining how the thyroid functions, for instance, you could liken it to a conductor directing a symphony (the body).[11] Bear in mind, however, that no analogy can exactly represent another concept; at a certain point, the similarities will end.[12] Therefore, you may need to alert listeners to the limits of the comparison. The statement "The heart is like a pump, *except that the heart actually changes size as it pushes blood out*" demonstrates that, though similar, a heart and a pump are not the same.[13]

In the following excerpt from a speech about nanotechnology, Wolfgang Porod explains the size of a nanometer by comparing it to the diameter of the moon. Note how he attempts to reduce confusion by first defining the root *nano* and then comparing it to the size of the moon:

> What is a nano and what is special about a nano? *Nano* is a prefix derived from the Greek word for dwarf and it means one billionth of something. So a nanosecond is a billionth of a second. A nanometer is a billionth of a meter. Now, just saying that doesn't really tell you that much. So what does it mean to have the length scale of a billionth of a meter? Well, imagine the diameter of the moon. It just happens to be, roughly . . . a billion meters. So take that and shrink it down to the length scale of a meter, which is what it means to go a billion size scales. So a nanometer is a billionth of a meter.[14]

Demonstrate Underlying Causes

Listeners may fail to understand a process because they believe that something "obviously" works a certain way when in fact it does not. To counter faulty assumptions, first acknowledge common misperceptions and then offer an accurate explanation of underlying causes.[15]

STRATEGIES FOR EXPLAINING COMPLEX INFORMATION

To explain a concept or term:

✔ Build on prior knowledge.

✔ Use analogies that link concepts to something familiar.

✔ Define terms in several ways (e.g., by example, by what it is not).

✔ Simplify terminology wherever possible.

✔ Check for understanding.

To explain a complex process or structure:

✔ All of the above, and:

✔ Make ample use of visual aids, including models and drawings.

To explain a counterintuitive idea:

✔ All of the above, and:

✔ Address the commonly held assumption first, acknowledge its plausibility, and then demonstrate its limitations using familiar examples.

CHECKLIST

Appeal to Different Learning Styles

Audience members are more likely to follow your points if you reinforce them with other media. The reason for this is that people have different learning styles, or preferred ways of processing information. One learning theory model suggests four such preferences: visual, aural, read/write, and kinesthetic.[16] *Visual learners* will most quickly grasp ideas by viewing visual explanations of them, either through pictures, diagrams, slides, or videos. Understanding for *aural learners* comes most easily through the spoken word, by hearing and speaking. *Read/write learners* are most comfortable processing information that is text-based. *Kinesthetic learners* learn best by experiencing information directly, through real-life demonstrations, simulations, and hands-on experience. Some of us are *multimodal learners,* in that we combine two or more preferences.

Audience analysis can sometimes give you a sense of the types of learners in an audience. For example, mechanics of all types have strong spatial visualization abilities and thus would be classified as visual learners; they may also be kinesthetic learners who want to "test" things for themselves. Often, however, you may not have enough information to determine your listeners' learning style, so *plan on conveying and reinforcing information in a variety of modes.* In your speech, use charts, diagrams, and other visual representations of ideas to

TABLE 24.3	Communicating Information to Different Types of Learners
Type	Advice for Communicating Information
Visual	Will most easily grasp ideas communicated through pictures, diagrams, charts, graphs, flowcharts, maps.
Aural	Will most easily grasp ideas communicated through the spoken word, whether in live lectures, tapes, group discussions, or podcasts.
Read/Write	Will most easily grasp ideas communicated through text-based delivery, handouts, PowerPoint with text-based slides.
Kinesthetic	Will most easily grasp ideas communicated through real-life demonstrations, simulations, movies, and through hands-on applications.

appeal to visual learners. Use colorful and concrete language and strong examples and stories that will engage aural listeners. Prepare text-based slides containing main ideas (but beware of crowding; see p. 299), and, if appropriate, consider distributing handouts at the end of your speech. Use demonstration to appeal to kinesthetic learners. Table 24.3 offers guidelines for presenting information to different types of learners.

Arrange Speech Points in a Pattern

Informative speeches can be organized using any of the patterns described in Chapters 13 and 27, including the topical, chronological, spatial, cause-effect, comparative advantage, circular, and narrative patterns. (Note that although the problem-solution pattern may be used in informative speeches, it often is a more logical candidate for persuasive speeches.)

There are any number of ways to organize the various types of informative speeches. A speech about the Impressionist movement in painting, for example, could be organized *chronologically*, in which main points are arranged in sequence from the movement's early period to its later falling out of favor (subpoints, as discussed in Chapter 13, can assume a different pattern than that of main points). It could be organized *causally* (cause-effect), by demonstrating that it came about as a reaction to the art movement that preceded it. It could also be organized *topically* (by categories), by focusing on the major figures associated with the movement, famous paintings linked to it, and notable contemporary artists who painted in the style.

Following are some possible pairings of speech types and organizational patterns:

Objects—spatial, topical

People—topical, narrative, chronological

Events—topical, chronological, causal, narrative

Processes—chronological, spatial, causal

Concepts—topical, causal, circular

Issues—topical, chronological, causal, circular

In a speech describing how to buy a guitar, Richard Garza organizes his main points chronologically:

THESIS STATEMENT: Buying and caring for a guitar involves knowing what to look for when purchasing it and understanding how to maintain it once you own it.

MAIN POINTS: I.   Decide what kind of guitar you need.

II.   Inspect the guitar for potential flaws.

III.   Maintain the guitar.

In a student speech on using radiofrequency waves to cure cancer, David Kruckenberg organizes his main points topically, dividing his points by categories:

THESIS STATEMENT: An engineer outside of the medical establishment discovers how to refine a medical procedure called radiofrequency ablation, potentially making it a critical tool in the fight against certain kinds of cancer.

MAIN POINTS: I.   Radiofrequency ablation, as currently practiced to treat cancer, poses risks to patients.

II.   Kanzius's invention uses nanoparticles to improve upon ablation.

III.   Kanzius's discovery is currently being tested in several large medical research centers.

GUIDELINES FOR CLEARLY COMMUNICATING YOUR INFORMATIVE MESSAGE

CHECKLIST

✔ In your introduction, tell audience members what you hope they will learn by listening to you.

✔ Stress the topic's relevance to your listeners.

✔ Use definition, description, explanation, and demonstration to convey your ideas.

✔ Use analogies to make your examples familiar to the audience.

✔ Choose an organizational pattern based on your communication goals, the nature of your topic, and the needs of your audience.

✔ Use presentation aids to reinforce your points.

SAMPLE SPEECH OF DEMONSTRATION

An Ounce of Prevention Keeps the Germs Away

CHRISTIE COLLINS

University of Oklahoma

In this speech of demonstration, student Christie Collins uses the chronological pattern of organization to take listeners step by step through the process of proper hand washing.

[PUT ON RUBBER GLOVES] Do you ever feel like you need to wear these when you go into the bathroom? I know I do! • According to a 2007 study commissioned by the American Society of Microbiology, researchers lurking in public restrooms discovered a nasty truth: Americans do not always wash up after using the toilet.

> • By putting on rubber gloves, the speaker effectively captures the audience's attention in the introduction.

The society's national survey found that 92 percent of a representative sample of 1,000 men and women surveyed by telephone claim to wash their hands after using the restroom. However, direct observation of more than 6,067 people (half males and half females) in four major U.S. cities revealed that only 77 percent really do so. Men are the worst culprits. Researchers said that only one-third of the males they observed washed their hands in public restrooms. Women fared better, with 88 percent hitting the sinks. •

> • The topic may be time-worn, but the speaker presents new and interesting information about it.

Hand washing is a critical factor in the spread of food-borne illnesses, colds, flu, and other diseases. • After extensive research and because I am somewhat of a cleaning freak, I have become a master at the art of hand washing. Today, I will be discussing the importance of hand washing, as well as the proper hand-washing technique. •

> • The speaker demonstrates the topic's relevance and previews the main points of the speech.

> • The speaker provides a transition into the body of the speech.

If you really think about it, we live in a very dirty world. Homes, offices, restaurants, classrooms, or just about anywhere you can think of, are all breeding grounds for those pesky little germs. Handle raw, uncooked food, shake someone's hand, take change from a clerk, or turn a doorknob and suddenly you have picked up a host of germs that can make you or others around you sick. For example, almost everyone has experienced a food-borne illness at some point in time.

According to the Centers for Disease Control and Prevention (CDC), each year food-borne illnesses kill up to 5,000 people. •

Annually, a whopping 76 million of us get some sort of food-borne sickness. Along with incomplete cooking and washing of foods, dirty hands are an important factor in spreading the bacteria that lead to food-borne illnesses.

Washing your hands is also an important step in preventing colds, flu, infectious diarrhea, and some pretty serious diseases like hepatitis A and meningitis. One of the most common ways people catch colds, for instance, is by rubbing their nose or eyes after their hands have been contaminated with a cold virus. You can lessen the odds of infection by avoiding touching your eyes, nose, and mouth with dirty fingers.

Failure to wash hands after handling money or using a pen or pencil picked up in a public place is common. According to the study sponsored by the American Society of Microbiologists, only 25 percent of us report washing our hands after touching money; fewer still even think about washing their hands after using someone else's writing implement. •

The most important thing that you can do to keep from getting a cold, as well as to keep from contracting more serious illnesses, is to wash your hands. • By frequently washing your hands, you wash away germs that you have picked up from other people, from contaminated surfaces, or from animals.

How do I wash my hands properly, you ask? The procedure, according to the Centers for Disease Control and Prevention, is as follows: •

[PICK UP SOAP AND MOVE NEAR BASIN] First, you wet your hands with warm running water.

Apply soap. Liquid or bar soap is OK, but liquid soap is easier, and the new antibacterial soaps may provide added protection in food preparation and during illness. If you do use a liquid soap, you'll need to disinfect the container each time before you refill it. If you are using a bar soap, it should be kept in a self-draining holder that is cleaned thoroughly to get rid of bacteria before new bars are put out.

• The speaker supports her points with a fact from the CDC.

• Again the speaker offers new information.

• The speaker shows how the information can benefit the audience (e.g., by allowing listeners to stay healthier).

• The speaker physically demonstrates proper procedures.

Using gentle friction, vigorously rub hands together, making a soapy lather. Do this away from the water for about twenty seconds, being careful not to wash the lather away. One common bit of advice is to lather as long as it takes to sing "Happy Birthday" to yourself twice. • Make sure you wash the front and back of your hands, as well as between your fingers, your knuckles, and under your fingernails.

> • The speaker offers memorable advice by suggesting listeners sing while hand washing.

Rinse your hands well under warm running water. Let the water run back into the sink, not down onto your elbows.

Turn off the faucet with a paper towel and dispose of it in a proper receptacle. Remember that you turned the water on with dirty hands, so a barrier such as a paper towel between your clean hands and the faucet prevents resoiling your hands. This is very important in public restrooms!

Dry hands thoroughly with a clean paper towel. To prevent chapping, pat rather than rub hands dry and apply lotion liberally and frequently.

[WALK TO DOOR AND HOLD DOORKNOB] • When exiting the restroom, use a paper towel to open the door. Remember the figures I cited earlier? If only one-third of men and women wash their hands in public restrooms, a lot of dirty hands are touching those knobs! Putting a barrier between your hands and the doorknob will prevent the recontamination of your hands.

> • The speaker again physically demonstrates her point.

If there is no soap or water available, there are other alternatives. For example, you can use an antibacterial, waterless hand sanitizer, such as Purel brand Instant Hand Sanitizer. You can use the larger bottle at home or maybe on your desk at work. The small bottles fit very nicely in a purse, pocket, tackle box, or glove compartment.

You can also use moist towelettes that contain an antibacterial agent, such as the Wet Ones brand. These can be conveniently kept in a purse or pocket. You can find these moderately priced hand sanitizers or towelettes in most supermarkets, drugstores, or department stores.

Washing your hands regularly can certainly save a lot of medical bills. • Because it costs less than a penny, you could say that this penny's worth of prevention could save you a $150 visit to the doctor.

> • The speaker points to another benefit to the audience, offering yet another new insight on a familiar process.

Now that you understand the importance of hand washing and how to properly wash your hands, practice and teach the proper hand-washing techniques to others, especially children, so that they too can form a good habit of hand washing. •

It's a simple fact. When hand washing is done correctly, it is the number-one means of preventing the spread of infection. • You don't have to take these rubber gloves into the public restroom with you. You just have to follow these simple steps. Doing so will make the world a healthier place for everyone.

• The speaker signals the close of the speech.

• The speaker concludes by reiterating the importance of hand washing.

Works Cited

American Society for Microbiology. "Harris Interactive 2007 Handwashing Survey Fact Sheet." Accessed November 8, 2007. www.asm.org.

Centers for Disease Control and Prevention. "Clean Hands Save Lives!" Accessed November 6, 2007. www.cdc.gov/cleanhands.

Division of Bacterial and Mycotic Diseases. Centers for Disease Control and Prevention. "Foodborne Illnesses Factsheet." Accessed November 6, 2007. www.cdc.gov/ncidod/dbmd/diseaseinfo/foodborneinfections_g.htm# howmanycases.

Lawhorn, Chad. "KU Prof Touts Hand Washing to Prevent Infectious Diseases." *Lawrence Journal-World,* September 25, 2007. www2.ljworld.com/news/2007/sep/25/ku_prof _touts_hand_washing_ prevent_infectious_dise/.

SAMPLE VISUALLY ANNOTATED INFORMATIVE SPEECH

John Kanzius and the Quest to Cure Cancer
DAVID KRUCKENBERG
Santiago Canyon College

The following speech by student David Kruckenberg describes a promising new way to treat cancer. David clarifies information with definitions and analogies and uses transitions and repetition to help listeners follow along. He also cites sources wherever he offers information gathered and reported by others.

David's topic could suggest a chronological pattern of arrangement. For example, he could have arranged his main points to trace the invention from inception to ongoing trials. Instead, he uses the topical pattern of arrangement (see Chapter 13) to move back and forth between describing the history of the new cancer treatment and explaining key concepts related to it.

One night in 2003, Marianne Kanzius awoke to a tremendous clamor coming from downstairs. She found her husband John sitting on the kitchen floor, cutting up her good aluminum pie pans with a pair of shears. •

> • Telling a story is an effective means of gaining the audience's attention.

As Peter Panepento describes the scene in an article titled "Sparks of Genius," published in the May 2006 edition of *Reader's Digest,* when Marianne asked John why he was wiring the pans to his ham radio, John told her to go back to bed. • So off she went, knowing that her singleminded husband wasn't the kind of person to quit until he was satisfied.

> • David artfully weaves a source citation into the narrative.

Making eye contact with every corner engages the whole room. Professional attire supports credibility.

Marianne soon learned that John's late-night experiment with pie pans was an attempt to use radio waves to kill cancer cells—and to rid himself of the rare form of leukemia threatening his life. In the next five years, John Kanzius would radically modify an existing cancer treatment technique called *radiofrequency ablation,* making it potentially far more effective than existing treatments. • Soon, the work of this retired TV and radio engineer might give additional hope to the 1.4 million Americans diagnosed with cancer

> • David draws listeners in with an unusual story.

every year, according to the 2008 American Cancer Society "Facts and Figures" section of its Web site. •

To understand John's discovery, we'll explore how the medical profession currently makes use of radio waves to treat cancer, learn about John's truly promising new approach, and consider the implications for the future. •

But first, to understand radiofrequency energy, we need a crash course in wave physics.

Energy moves in a wave and is measured in *frequency,* how quickly it moves up and down. *High frequency waves,* like Superman's X-ray vision—and real X-rays—move quickly and penetrate most matter, but can alter the chemical and genetic material in cells. • *Low frequency waves,* such as radio waves, move slowly and don't disturb the atomic balance of matter they pass through. Radio waves are harmless to healthy cells, making them a promising tool for ablation. •

Gestures effectively demonstrate the properties of waves.

Let me explain the term. *Ablation,* according to the National Cancer Institute's *Dictionary of Cancer Terms,* available on its Web site, is the medical term for "the removal or destruction of a body part or tissue or its function," using hormone therapy, conventional surgery, or radiofrequency. *Radiofrequency ablation,* or RFA, uses radiofrequency energy to "cook" and kill cancer cells, according to the Society of Interventional Radiology. The least invasive RFA technique practiced today is through the skin; it's also done laparoscopically.

David reveals photograph of RFA technique.

Here's how the Radiological Society of North America explains radiofrequency ablation on its Web site, last updated December 17, 2008. •

First, a doctor makes a small incision in the skin and inserts a needle electrode or a straight hollow needle containing retractable electrodes.

Combining hand gesture with visual aid helps David explain medical procedure.

The doctor guides the needle to the site of the tumor using an imaging technique such as ultrasound.

The needle in turn is connected to an electric generator, and once in place, electrodes extend out of it and into the tumor.

• Here David states his thesis.

• He previews the main points and then moves into a transition.

• David helps listeners understand the concept of frequency by offering an analogy.

• David defines terms that the audience may not know.

• This transition helps listeners focus on the ensuing explanation.

Covers the visual aid at end of discussion to minimize audience distraction.

Next, • contact pads, also wired to the generator, are placed on the patient's skin; this completes an electric circuit so that when the generator is turned on, electric energy in the form of radio waves passes through the body, going back and forth between the needles and the contact pads.

Here's the critical part: Every time that the radio waves meet the resistance of the electrodes at the treatment site, they create heat. It's kind of like an atomic mosh pit, with a crowd of atoms suddenly agitated by radio waves; the electrons begin to bounce around and collide, creating friction and thus heat. • This heat gets up to 212 degrees Fahrenheit, the temperature at which water boils. The heat destroys the cancerous cells in the tumor, essentially cooking them, but leaving noncancerous cells alone.

In many ways, it's a great treatment option right now. However, while it is called "minimally invasive" surgery, the needles required by this method can damage tissue and even organs near the tumor site, limiting its usefulness.

Enter John Kanzius. •

John was diagnosed with leukemia in 2002, and his ordeal with chemotherapy motivated him to find a better way to attack cancer cells.

Now John had no medical training, but he had worked in the radio industry for forty years, and he knew all about radio waves. He recalled that a colleague wearing wire-rimmed glasses got burned as he stood too close to a radio transmitter. As Peter Panepento describes it in *Reader's Digest,* this led Kanzius to theorize that if you could infuse cancer cells with a conductive substance, you could use a transmitter to heat them with radio waves, while avoiding invasive needles. • The cells marked with the substance would act like "tiny antennas," as Panepento put it.

It was this chain of thought which spurred John's late-night kitchen experiment with the pie pans and his ham radio.

Two things were amazing about John's initial experiment.

• Such signal words as *first* and *next* help listeners follow the procedure's chronologically organized steps.

• David's mosh-pit analogy helps listeners understand a complex concept.

• This transition adds drama.

• David is careful to credit direct quotations.

First, John was able to replicate RFA in his kitchen. Second, John made a huge improvement upon the technique, alone and at home. Instead of inserting needles into a tumor, he injected tiny metal minerals into a stand-in hotdog. He then placed the hotdog between the radio transmitter and receiver so that the radio waves would pass through the meat. When he cut the hotdog open, the area around the minerals was cooked, but the rest remained raw. Kanzius later repeated the experiment with liver, then steak, obtaining the same results.

Could there really be a way to use radiofrequency without side effects, and to treat more types of cancer with it? •

> • Here he uses a transition in the form of a rhetorical question.

As told by Charles Schmidt in the *Journal of the National Cancer Institute* on July 16, 2008, John shared his results with several leading oncologists, who immediately recognized the potential. He then filed for a patent for his RF machine.

Researchers at two prominent cancer centers decided to test John's theory, starting in August 2005 with the University of Pittsburgh's Liver Cancer Center. As detailed in the University of Pittsburgh Medical Center newsletter of March 22, 2006, instead of using a hotdog, the researchers placed a thin test tube between the radio transmitter and the receiver. Inside this tube was a solution of carbon nanoparticles— actually pieces of metal about 1/75,000 times smaller than the width of a human hair. A speck of dandruff is like a mountain to a nanoparticle. • When they turned on the electricity, the carbon nanoparticles successfully heated to 130 degrees Fahrenheit—the perfect temperature at which to kill cancer cells, according to Peter Panepento's *Reader's Digest* piece.

> • Because the size of a nanoparticle is hard to visualize, David compares it to something with which listeners are familiar—a strand of hair and dandruff.

Now that I've explained John's major improvement over current RFA procedures, let's consider the implications of his discovery. •

> • David alerts listeners to what he will discuss next.

John's noninvasive radiofrequency cancer treatment holds tremendous promise as an alternative to existing cancer therapies. First, because RFA uses electromagnetic energy in the form of radio waves, it's much safer than chemotherapy and traditional radiation treatment. As noted, radio waves are harmless to healthy cells, as compared to X-rays.

Second, as explained in the January 2008 issue of the *Journal of Nanobiotechnology* by Gannon et al., the current RFA procedure can only be used in cancers that are not difficult to reach, such as liver, breast, lung, and bone; John's new method potentially can target tumors anywhere in the body. •

Third, the current RFA procedure must be performed several times to target multiple tumors, but John's method could make it possible to target multiple tumors in just a single treatment.

Intensive research is now underway at the renowned M. D. Anderson Cancer Center in Houston. The goal is to find ways to make the nanoparticles target cancer cells exclusively. Success occurred in late 2007, when in a preclinical trial researchers at the M. D. Anderson Cancer Center used the technique to completely destroy liver cancer tumors in rabbits, as described in the October 2007 issue of the journal *Cancer*.

Another area they are trying to resolve, according to Schmidt, is the potential toxicity of nanoparticles in the bloodstream. Human trials may begin in two to three years, according to Dr. Steven Curley, lead investigator on the Kanzius project at M. D. Anderson, as reported in July 2008 by David Bruce in the *Erie Times-News*.

Today we learned how a man with vision discovered how to cook a hotdog with a ham radio. We explored first the current procedure, then John's new approach, and, finally, the implications of this new hope for treating cancer. •

John's cancer is in remission, and he's established the John Kanzius Cancer Research Foundation, which you can read about online. He is continuing to refine his technique and is working on clinical trials.

Marianne Kanzius was upset when she saw her husband destroying her good pie pans, but now it's clear that the loss of a few pie pans and a hotdog may soon save millions of lives. •

Works Cited

American Cancer Society. "Cancer Facts and Figures, 2008." www.cancer.org/docroot/STT/content/STT_1x_Cancer _Facts_and_Figures_2008.asp.

• Proper acknowledgment of each source increases David's credibility and allows the audience to seek further information on the topic.

• David signals the speech's conclusion with a summary of the main points.

• A return to David's opening story brings the speech full circle.

Bruce, David. "Community Unites Behind Kanzius, Human Trials." *Erie Times-News,* July 27, 2008. doc ID: 1222 E79CB5E00DA0.

Gannon, Christopher J., Chitta Ranjan Patra, Resham Bhattacharya, Priyabrata Mukherjee, and Steven A. Curley. "Intracellular Gold Nanoparticles Enhance Non-Invasive Radiofrequency Thermal Destruction of Human Gastrointestinal Cancer Cells," *Journal of Nanobiotechnology* 6, no. 2 (2008). doi:10.1186/1477- 3155-6-2.

Gannon, Christopher J., et al. "Carbon Nanotube-Enhanced Thermal Destruction of Cancer Cells in a Noninvasive Radiofrequency Field." *Cancer* (Wiley), October 24, 2007. doi: 10.1002/cncr.23155.

Match (a publication of the Thomas E. Starzl Transplantation Institute). University of Pittsburgh Medical Center Web Site. March 22, 2006.

National Cancer Institute. *Dictionary of Cancer Terms.* Accessed December 15, 2008. www.cancer.gov/templates/db_alpha.aspx?expand=A.

Panepento, Peter. "Sparks of Genius: Efforts Done by John Kanzius, a Cancer Patient, to Find a Better Cure for Cancer," *Reader's Digest* (May 2006): 132–36.

Radiological Society of North America. "Radiofrequency Ablation of Liver Tumors." Updated December 17, 2008. www.radiologyinfo.org/en/info.cfm?PG=rfa.

Schmidt, Charles. "A New Cancer Treatment from an Unexpected Source," *Journal of the National Cancer Institute* 100, no. 14 (July 16, 2008): 985–86. doi:10.1093/jnci/djn246.

Society of Interventional Radiology. "Radiofrequency Catheter Ablation." Accessed June 23, 2009. http://www.sirweb.org.

CHAPTER 25

The Persuasive Speech

Persuasive speaking is a type of public speaking you will practice frequently throughout your professional and personal life. To persuade is to influence, advocate, or ask others to accept your views. Whether you are bargaining for a raise, convincing a fellow classmate of the need to join a student group, or giving a formal speech advocating for a green policy, success or failure rests on how well or how poorly you understand the principles and practices of the art of persuasion.

Persuasive speaking skills are indispensable, especially if you want to make your voice count during public conversations about issues that are important to you. Knowledge of persuasive speaking not only helps you critically assess the persuasive messages of others but also contributes to the betterment of society and the world. As we saw in Chapter 1, the ability to speak persuasively ensures a healthy democracy. "In a Republican nation," Thomas Jefferson said during his term as the third president of the United States, "whose citizens are to be led by reason and persuasion and not by force, the art of reasoning becomes of first importance."

What Is a Persuasive Speech?

 WEB Chapter quizzes

Persuasive speeches are meant to appeal to the audience's attitudes, beliefs, and values about the issue in question and to sway listeners to the speaker's point of view. Derived from the Greek verb meaning "to believe,"[1] **persuasion** is the process of influencing attitudes, beliefs, values, and behavior. **Persuasive speaking** is a form of speech that is intended to influence the attitudes, beliefs, values, and actions of others.

CONDITIONS FOR CHOOSING A PERSUASIVE PURPOSE

You should select a persuasive purpose if:

_____ 1. Your goal is to influence an audience's beliefs or understanding about something.

_____ 2. Your goal is to influence an audience's behavior.

_____ 3. Your goal is to reinforce audience members' existing attitudes, beliefs, or behavior so the audience will continue to possess or practice them.

CHECKLIST

Persuasive Speeches Attempt to Influence Audience Choices

Similar to informative speeches, persuasive speeches also serve to increase understanding and awareness. They present an audience with new information, new insights, and new ways of thinking about an issue. In fact, persuasive speeches do all the things informative speeches do. But rather than seeking only to increase understanding and awareness, the explicit goal of the persuasive speech is to influence audience choices.[2] These choices may range from slight shifts in opinion to wholesale changes in behavior.

Persuasive Speeches Limit Alternatives

Any issue that would constitute the topic of a persuasive speech represents at least two viewpoints. For example, there are "pro-choice" advocates and "right-to-life" advocates; there are those who prefer a Droid over an iPhone. With any such issue, it is the objective of a persuasive speaker to limit the audience's alternatives to the side the speaker represents. This is done not by ignoring the unfavorable alternatives altogether but by contrasting them with the favorable alternative and showing it to be of greater value or usefulness to the audience than the other alternatives.

Persuasive Speeches Seek a Response

By showing an audience the best of several alternatives, the persuasive speaker asks listeners—sometimes explicitly and sometimes implicitly—to make a choice. If the speech is effective, the audience's choice will be limited; that is, listeners will understand that the alternative presented by the speaker is the "right" choice.

ETHICALLY SPEAKING

Persuasive Speeches Respect Audience Choices

Even though persuasive speeches present audiences with a choice, the ethical persuasive speaker recognizes that the choice is ultimately the audience members' to make—and he or she respects their right to do so. People take time to consider what they've heard and how it affects them. They make their own choices in light of or despite the best evidence. Your  role as a persuasive speaker is not to coerce or force your listeners to accept your viewpoint but to present as convincing a case as possible so that they might do so willingly. For instance, you might want to persuade members of your audience to become vegetarians, but you must also respect their choice not to adopt this path.

The Process of Persuasion

WEB Video quizzes

Persuasion is a complex psychological process of reasoning and emotion. When you speak persuasively, you try to guide the audience to adopt a particular attitude, belief, or behavior that you favor. But getting people to change their minds, even a little, is challenging and requires considerable skill. As in informative speeches, therefore, *audience analysis* is extremely important in persuasive speeches. The more "intelligence" you can gather about audience members, the better you can solve the puzzle of how best to reach them. Be aware, however, that regardless of how thoroughly you have conducted audience analysis or how skillfully you present your point of view, audiences may not respond immediately or completely to a persuasive appeal. An audience can be immediately "stirred," as the Roman orator Cicero put it, with relative ease. However, producing a lasting impact on listeners' attitudes, beliefs, and behavior is a more difficult matter. Changes tend to be small, even imperceptible, especially at first.

Research confirms that you can increase the odds of achieving your persuasive speech goal if you:

- Make your message personally relevant to the audience.[3]
- Clearly demonstrate how any change you propose will benefit the audience.[4]
- Establish your credibility. Audience members' feelings toward you strongly influence their receptivity towards the message.
- Set modest goals. Expect minor rather than major changes in your listeners' attitudes and behavior.
- Target issues that audience members feel strongly about.[5]
- Demonstrate how an attitude or a behavior might keep listeners from feeling satisfied and competent, thereby encouraging receptivity to change.
- Expect to be more successful when addressing an audience whose position differs only moderately from your own.[6]
- Try to convince your listeners that by taking the action you propose they will be rewarded in some way. For example, to persuade people to lose weight and keep it off, you must make them believe that they will be healthier and seem more attractive if they do so. Persuaders who achieve this are skilled at motivating their listeners to help themselves.[7]

Following is a brief overview of how the ancient scholars of rhetoric, and Aristotle in particular, viewed the process of persuasion. Much of classical theory on persuasion remains relevant today. Following that discussion is a review of how contemporary social scientists approach persuasion. Both classical and contemporary perspectives recognize that successful persuasion requires a balance of reason and emotion, and that audience members must be well-disposed toward the speaker.

Classical Persuasive Appeals: Using Proofs WEB Chapter quizzes

In his treatise on rhetoric, Aristotle explained that persuasion could be brought about by the speaker's use of three types of persuasive appeals, or forms of **rhetorical proofs**. The first concerns the nature of the message in a speech; the second, the nature of the audience's feelings; the third, the qualifications and personality of the speaker. According to Aristotle, and generations of scholars and practitioners who followed him, you can build an effective persuasive speech with any one or a combination of these proofs, termed *logos, pathos,* and *ethos.* The best speeches generally make use of all three proofs.

Logos: Proof by Reason

Many persuasive speeches focus on issues that require considerable thought. Should universities abolish tenure? Should the United States enact stricter immigration laws? When an audience needs to make an important decision or reach a conclusion regarding a complicated issue, appeals to reason and logic are necessary. Aristotle used the term **logos** to refer to persuasive appeals directed at the audience's **reasoning** on a topic. To reason is to draw conclusions based on evidence.

The Syllogism

Aristotle differentiated between two forms of reasoning in speeches. The first is the **syllogism**, a three-part argument consisting of a **general case** (also called a "**major premise**"), a **specific case** ("**minor premise**"), and a conclusion logically following from the first two steps. The classic example is this:

GENERAL CASE:	All men are mortal.
SPECIFIC CASE:	Socrates is a man.
CONCLUSION:	Therefore Socrates is mortal.

Syllogisms are a form of **deductive reasoning**, or reasoning from a general condition to a specific instance.[8] (Reversing direction, **inductive reasoning** moves from specific instances to a general condition; see p. 355.) A well-developed syllogism will lead listeners to a clearer understanding of an issue; one that is poorly thought through will lead them to unfounded conclusions. Here is an example of a contemporary syllogism that is effectively developed:

GENERAL CASE:	Regular exercise enhances your ability to study productively.
SPECIFIC CASE:	Swimming is good exercise.
CONCLUSION:	Swimming regularly will enhance your ability to study productively.

And here is one that is poorly developed:

GENERAL CASE: Rosslyn gets all A's even though she never attends class.

SPECIFIC CASE: Rosslyn is on the college softball team.

CONCLUSION: All college athletes get all A's even though they never attend class.

The preceding example shows how erroneous conclusions can be reached if you begin with a general case that is unfounded. Here, the general case is a **hasty overgeneralization**, or an attempt to support a claim by asserting that a particular piece of evidence (an isolated case) is true for all individuals or conditions concerned. (See the section on fallacies in reasoning in Chapter 26.) Although the specific instance may be true, the conclusion is based on an overgeneralization. In contrast, the first example is an effective syllogism. It reaches a sound conclusion from an accurate general case applied to a specific instance.

As you can see, appeals to reason using syllogism in a persuasive speech require accurate knowledge of the information that forms your general and specific cases. This is a key consideration as you build your arguments.

The Enthymeme

A second form of classical rational appeal, or use of logos, in a persuasive speech is the enthymeme. An **enthymeme** is a syllogism presented as a probability rather than as an absolute, and it states either a general case or a specific case but not both. The case not stated is implied and serves as a mental tool for connecting the speaker and audience.[9] For example, the syllogism about Socrates leads to the absolute conclusion that Socrates is mortal if both of the stated cases are accurate and true. The syllogism about swimming can be restated as an enthymeme so that the conclusion is probably true but not necessarily always true:

GENERAL CASE TO CONCLUSION: Regular exercise enhances your ability to study productively, so swimming regularly should enhance your studying.

Implied in this example is that swimming is a good form of exercise. Implied in the next example is that exercise will enhance your ability to study well:

SPECIFIC EXAMPLE TO CONCLUSION: Swimming is good exercise and should enhance your studying.

The use of *should* in each case makes the conclusion tentative instead of absolute. Why would you want to offer probable conclusions in a persuasive speech instead of certain conclusions? *Because most arguments are not based on certainty.* It is not absolutely certain, for example, that swimming regularly will enhance your studying because many other factors are involved in studying. The point is, if your argument is to hold sway, the conclusion has to be certain enough for the audience to accept the premise. The key for both syllogisms and enthymemes is that your premises—your general case and specific instance—be acceptable according to sound reasoning or logic. (See Chapter 26 for detailed advice on building arguments for the persuasive speech.)

Along with syllogisms and enthymemes—both forms of deductive reasoning, there are some other lines of classic reasoning. An argument using *inductive reasoning* moves from specific cases to a general conclusion supported by those cases. The speaker offers evidence that points to a conclusion that *appears to be,* but *is not necessarily,* true:

SPECIFIC CASE 1:   In one five-year period, the average daily temperature (ADT) on Continent X rose three degrees.

SPECIFIC CASE 2:   In that same period, ADT on Continent Y rose three degrees.

SPECIFIC CASE 3:   In that same period, ADT on Continent Z rose three degrees.

CONCLUSION: Globally, average daily temperatures appear to be rising by three degrees.

Arguments based on inductive reasoning can be *strong* or *weak*; that is, listeners may decide the claim is probably true, largely untrue, or somewhere in between. Arguments can follow other lines of reasoning, including reasoning by cause, by analogy, or by sign (see Chapter 26, pp. 374–76).

Pathos: Proof by Emotion

Another means of persuasion first described by classical theorists is appealing to listeners' emotions. The term Aristotle used for this is **pathos**. It requires "creating a certain disposition in the audience."[10] Aristotle taught that successful public speakers identify and appeal to four sets of emotions in their listeners.[11] He presented these sets in opposing pairs: anger and meekness, love and hatred, fear and boldness, shame and shamelessness. You can evoke these emotions in a speech by using *vivid descriptions* and *emotionally charged words.* Consider the following example from attorney Elpidio Villarreal, who spoke about the value of immigrants to the United States. In this excerpt, he refutes those who claim that this group does not want to assimilate into U.S. culture. Villarreal uses his uncle who died in combat during World War II as an example of the loyalty and sacrifice of Mexican Americans:

> On June 6, 1944, [my Uncle Lupe] landed at a place called Omaha Beach in Normandy, France. He was killed while leading an attack on an enemy bunker that was pinning down his platoon. He was nominated, but did not receive, the Congressional Medal of Honor. My grandparents received a photograph of a road my uncle's unit built in France. The road had been named Villarreal Road. Years ago, I was privileged to walk the battlefields of Normandy, including

Omaha Beach, and I visited the great American Cemetery there where lie 17,000 Americans who gave the "last full measure of devotion," as Lincoln so beautifully put it. Simple white marble crosses, interspersed with occasional Stars of David, stretch out for 70 acres. . . .

I thought about all the brave Americans buried there and of the meaning of their deaths, but I thought especially about my Uncle Lupe, the one who went to war knowing he would die for no other reason than that his country, the one that treated him as a second-class citizen, asked him to.[12]

Although emotion is a powerful means of moving an audience, relying solely on naked emotion to persuade will fail most of the time. As Aristotle stressed, *pathos functions as a means to persuasion not by any persuasive power inherent in emotions per se but by the interplay of emotions—or desire—and sound reasoning.* Emotion gets the audience's attention and stimulates a desire to act on the emotion; reason is then presented as justification for the action. Recent persuasion research confirms this effect.[13] For example, a popular television advertisement depicts a grandfatherly man in a series of activities with family members. An announcer makes the logical appeal that people with high blood pressure should maintain their prescribed regimen of medication; this is followed by the emotional appeal "If not for yourself, do it for them." The message invokes the desire to stay healthy as long as possible for the benefit of loved ones. The reasoning is sound enough: Blood pressure is controllable with medication, but one must take the medicine in order for it to work. In this case, as in many, emotion helps communicate the idea.

Appealing to an audience's emotions on the basis of sound reasoning ensures that your speech is ethical. However, as seen in the accompanying Ethically Speaking box, there are a host of ways in which emotions can be used unethically.

ETHICALLY SPEAKING

Using Emotions Ethically

The most successful persuaders are those who are able to understand the mind-set of others. With such insight comes the responsibility to use emotional appeals in speeches for ethical purposes. As history attests only too amply, not all speakers follow an ethical path in this regard. Demagogues, for example, clutter the historical landscape. A **demagogue** relies heavily on irrelevant emotional appeals to short-circuit the listeners' rational decision-making process.[1] Senator Joseph McCarthy, who conducted "witch hunts" against alleged Communists in the 1950s, was one such speaker. Adolf Hitler, who played on the fears and dreams of German citizens to urge them toward despicable ends, was another master manipulator.

Persuasive speakers can influence their listeners' emotions by arousing fear and anxiety and by using propaganda.

- *Fear and anxiety.* Some speakers deliberately arouse fear and anxiety in an audience so that listeners will follow their recommendations.[2] Sometimes this is done by offering a graphic description of what will happen if the audience doesn't comply (e.g., people will get hurt, children will starve). If used fairly and carefully, however, the **fear appeal** does have a legitimate place in public speaking. For example, it can be used to demonstrate to children the harm caused by smoking, or to show a group of drunken drivers graphic pictures of the results of their actions. It can also be used to encourage civic involvement to solve pressing social problems,[3] as Al Gore did for climate change with the film *An Inconvenient Truth*.

- *Propaganda.* Speakers who employ **propaganda** aim to manipulate an audience's emotions for the purpose of promoting a belief system or dogma. Propagandists tell audiences only what they want their listeners to know, deliberately hiding or distorting opposing viewpoints. For example, news commentator Bill O'Reilly has been accused of using propaganda techniques in his "Talking Points Memo" through his strategic language use.[4] Propagandists engage in name-calling and stereotyping to arouse their listeners' emotions.

Unlike the ethical persuader, the propagandist does not respect the audience's right to choose; nor does the speaker who irresponsibly uses fear appeals. Ethically, appeals to emotion in a persuasive speech should always be supported by sound reasoning.

1. Charles U. Larson, *Persuasion: Reception and Responsibility,* 6th ed. (Belmont, CA: Wadsworth, 1992), 37.
2. James Price Dillard and Michael Pfau, *The Persuasion Handbook: Developments in Theory and Practice* (Thousand Oaks, CA: Sage Publications, 2002); Paul A. Mongeau, "Another Look at Fear-Arousing Persuasive Appeals," in *Persuasion: Advances through Meta-Analysis,* ed. Mike Allen and Raymond W. Preiss (Cresskill, NJ: Hampton Press, 1998), 53–68; Kim Witte and Mike Allen, "A Meta-Analysis of Fear Appeals: Implications for Effective Public Health Campaigns," *Health Education and Behavior* 27, no. 5 (2000): 591–615.
3. Michael William Pfau, "Who's Afraid of Fear Appeals? Contingency, Courage, and Deliberation in Rhetorical Theory and Practice," *Philosophy and Rhetoric* 40 (2007): 216–37.
4. Grabe M. Conway, M. E. Grieves, and K. Grieves, "Villains, Victims and the Virtuous in Bill O Reilly's 'No-Spin Zone,'" *Journalism Studies* 8 (2007): 197–223.

Ethos: Proof through Speaker Character

No matter how well reasoned a message is or which strong emotions its words target, if audience members have little or no regard for the speaker they will not respond positively to his or her persuasive appeals. Aristotle recognized that the nature of the speaker's character and personality also plays an important role in how well the audience listens to and accepts the message. He referred to this effect of the speaker as **ethos**, or moral character.

Exactly which elements of a persuasive appeal are based on ethos? Let's briefly consider each element in turn, and how you as the speaker can demonstrate them. The first element is *good sense*. Another term for this element is *competence,* or the speaker's knowledge of and experience with the subject matter. Ethos-based appeals emphasize the speaker's grasp of the subject matter. Skillfully preparing the speech at all stages, from research to delivery, as well as emphasizing your own expertise, evokes this quality.

The second element of an ethos-based appeal is the speaker's *moral character.* This is reflected in the speaker's straightforward and honest presentation of the message. The speaker's own ethical standards are central to this element. Current research suggests, for example, that a brief disclosure of personal moral standards relevant to the speech or the occasion made in the introduction of a speech will boost audience regard for the speaker.[14] Indeed, you should prepare and present every aspect of your speeches with the utmost integrity so that your audiences will regard you as trustworthy.

The third element of an ethos-based appeal is *goodwill* toward the audience. A strong ethos-based appeal demonstrates an interest in and a concern for the welfare of your audience. Speakers who understand the concerns of their listeners and who address their needs and expectations relative to the speech exhibit this aspect of the ethos-based appeal.

DISPLAYING ETHOS IN THE PERSUASIVE SPEECH

✔ Demonstrate your competence as a speaker by knowing your subject well and by emphasizing your expertise.

✔ Be straightforward and honest in presenting the facts of your argument.

✔ Reveal early your personal moral standards vis-à-vis your topic.

✔ Demonstrate a genuine interest in and concern for your listeners' welfare.

CHECKLIST

Contemporary Persuasive Appeals: Needs and Motivations

 WEB Links

Classical theories of persuasion describe how appeals to reasoning (logos), emotion (pathos), and speaker credibility (ethos) can bring the audience to the speaker's point of view. Scientific research affirms the centrality of these elements in persuasive appeals,[15] while also investigating other factors that cause us to change or maintain our attitudes. These theories suggest that for persuasion to succeed, the message must effectively target (1) audience members' needs, (2) their underlying motivations for feeling and acting as they do, and (3) their likely approach to mentally processing the persuasive message.

Persuading Listeners by Appealing to Their Needs

Have you ever wondered why there are so many fast-food commercials during and after the evening news? Advertisers know that by this time of night many viewers are experiencing a strong need—to eat! Appealing to audience needs is one of the strategies most commonly used to motivate people, whether in advertising or in public speaking; thus, one way to persuade listeners is to point to some need they want fulfilled and then give them a way to fulfill it.

According to psychologist Abraham **Maslow's hierarchy of needs**, each person has a set of basic needs ranging from the essential, life-sustaining ones to the less critical, self-improvement ones. This set includes five categories arranged hierarchically (see Figure 25.1). An individual's needs at the lower, essential levels must be fulfilled before the higher levels become important and motivating. Using Maslow's hierarchy to persuade your listeners to wear seat belts, for example, you would appeal to their need for safety. Critics of this approach suggest that we may be driven as much by *wants* as by needs.[16] Nevertheless, the theory points to the fact that successful appeals depend on understanding what motivates the audience, and certainly appealing to the needs Maslow suggests cannot but help the persuader. Table 25.1 describes the five basic needs that Maslow identifies and suggests actions that you as a speaker can take to appeal to them.

Persuading Listeners by Appealing to the Reasons for Their Behavior

The audience is not merely a collection of empty vessels waiting to be filled with whatever wisdom and knowledge you have to offer. Members of an audience are rational, thinking, choice-making individuals. Their day-to-day behavior is directed mainly by their own volition, or will. According to **expectancy-outcome**

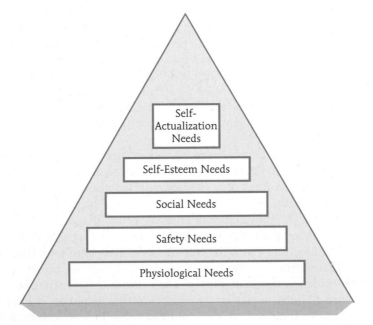

FIGURE 25.1 Maslow's Hierarchy of Needs

TABLE 25.1 Using Needs to Motivate Listeners	
Need	**Speech Action**
Physiological needs (to have access to basic sustenance, including food, water, and air)	• Plan for and accommodate the audience's physiological needs—are they likely to be hot, cold, hungry, or thirsty?
Safety needs (to feel protected and secure)	• Appeal to safety benefits—how wearing seat belts or voting for a bill to stop pollution will remove a threat or protect the audience from harm.
Social needs (to find acceptance; to have lasting, meaningful relationships)	• Appeal to social benefits—if you want teenagers to quit smoking, stress that if they quit they will appear more physically fit and attractive to their peers.
Self-esteem needs (to feel good about ourselves; to feel self-worth)	• Appeal to emotional benefits—stress that the proposed change will make listeners feel better about themselves.
Self-actualization needs (to achieve goals; to reach our highest potential)	• Appeal to your listeners' need to fulfill their potential—stress how adopting your position will help them "be all that they can be."

values theory, developed by Icek Ajzen and Martin Fishbein, each of us consciously evaluates the potential costs and benefits (or "value") associated with taking a particular action. As we weigh these costs and benefits, we consider our attitudes about the behavior in question (e.g., "Is this a good or a bad behavior?") as well as what other people who are important to us might think about the behavior (e.g., "My friend would approve of my taking this action"). On the basis of these assessments, we develop expectations about what will happen if we do or do not take a certain action (e.g., "My friend will think more highly of me if I do this"). These expected "outcomes" become our rationale for acting in a certain way. *Thus when you want to persuade listeners to change their behavior, you should try to identify these expected outcomes and use them to appeal to your audience.*[17] For instance, recent research has confirmed that when trying to motivate people to participate in physical activity, the most effective messages that actually move people to action are those that address the outcomes people want from exercise, such as losing weight, lowering blood pressure and blood sugar, and so forth.[18]

The principles of expectancy-outcome values theory can help you plan a persuasive speech in which the specific purpose is to target behavior. A thorough audience analysis (in the form of a questionnaire) is critical to this approach, however (see the section on surveys in Chapter 6). Putting the theory into practice, as you conduct your audience analysis, you will need to seek out (1) your listeners' attitudes about the behavior you are proposing that they change, as well as (2) their feelings about the consequences associated with that behavior. Knowing these attitudes, you have a good foundation for presenting your listeners with evidence that will support their attitudes and strengthen your argument. Third (3), try to determine what audience members believe other significant people in their lives think about the behavior in question, and the audience members' willingness to comply with those beliefs. You now have a basis for appealing to your audience's concerns. Figure 25.2 illustrates the steps to take when seeking to persuade an audience to adopt a course of action, based on the principles of expectancy-outcome values theory.

Persuading Listeners by Focusing on What's Most Relevant to Them

According to Richard Petty and John Cacioppo's **elaboration likelihood model of persuasion (ELM)**, listeners mentally process persuasive messages by one of two routes, depending on the degree of their involvement in the message.[19] When listeners are motivated and able to think critically about the content of a message, they engage in **central processing** of the message. That is, these audience members seriously consider what the speaker's message means to them and are the ones most likely to act on it. When listeners lack the motivation (or the ability) to pay close attention to the issues, they engage in **peripheral processing** of information. In this form of mental processing of the speaker's persuasive message, they respond to it as being irrelevant, too complex to follow, or just plain unimportant. Even though such listeners may "buy into" your message, they do so not on the strength of the arguments but on the basis of such superficial factors as reputation, entertainment value, or personal style. Listeners who use peripheral processing are unlikely to experience any meaningful changes in attitudes or behavior. Central processing produces the more long-lasting changes in audience perspective.

To encourage audience members to engage in central rather than peripheral processing during your speech, (1) make certain that your message is relevant to

1. Investigate listeners' attitudes toward the specific behavior you are targeting in your speech (e.g., taking vitamin supplements, purchasing a hybrid car, adopting a vegetarian diet, etc.).

↓

2. Identify listeners' beliefs about the consequences of their behavior (e.g., "I believe I will damage the environment if I don't buy a hybrid car" or "I believe hybrids aren't fun and are boring to look at").

↓

3. Investigate what the audience members believe *significant others in their lives* think about the behavior in question (e.g., my girlfriend is very environmentally conscious).

↓

4. Demonstrate the positive outcomes of adopting a course of action *favored by audience members' significant others* (e.g., "Choosing a hybrid car will lead to greater love and admiration from my girlfriend/boyfriend").

FIGURE 25.2 Steps in Persuading Listeners to Change Their Behavior

your listeners, (2) make certain that you present it at an appropriate level of understanding, and (3) establish your credibility with the audience (Figure 25.3). Establish a common bond with your listeners, and ensure that they see you as trustworthy. These steps will increase the odds that your persuasive appeal will produce lasting, rather than fleeting, changes in their attitudes and behavior.

Persuading Listeners through Speaker Credibility

Beyond the qualities of speaker knowledge, moral character, and goodwill toward the audience that ancient scholars such as Aristotle described in terms of ethos, modern behavioral science has identified four other speaker-based factors that affect the outcomes of persuasive messages: expertise, trustworthiness, speaker similarity, and physical attractiveness. Taken as a set, these factors are referred to as **speaker credibility**.

The audience's perceptions of a speaker's expertise and trustworthiness are critical contributors to persuasiveness.[20] Speaker *expertise* contributes to the persuasive outcomes of a speech under two conditions. First, when audience members are relatively unmotivated or unable to fully grasp a message, their responses to the speech will probably be in the speaker's favor if the speaker is perceived as an expert on the subject. Second, when audience members themselves are well informed about the message and perceive the speaker as someone who has expertise, he or she will be more apt to persuade them. Note that "expert" doesn't mean you're a world authority on the topic or issue of your speech. What it does mean is that you have enough knowledge and experience on the subject to be able to help the audience to better understand and accept it.

Link your argument to the practical concerns of your listeners
and emphasize direct consequences to them.

("Hybrid cars may not be the best-looking or fastest cars on the
market, but as gas prices continue to soar, they will save
you a great deal of money.")

↓

Present your message at an appropriate level of understanding.

(For a *general audience:* "The technology behind hybrid cars is
relatively simple." For an *expert audience:* "To save even
more gas, you can turn an EV into a PHEV with a generator
and additional batteries.")

↓

Demonstrate common bonds (i.e., foster identification).

("It took me a while to convince myself to buy a hybrid.")

↓

Stress your credibility to offer the claims.

("Once I selected the car, I found I saved nearly $1,000 this
year.")

FIGURE 25.3 Steps in Increasing Acceptance of Your Persuasive Message

If there is one speaker attribute that is more important than others, it is probably *trustworthiness*.[21] It's a matter of the "goodwill" that Aristotle taught—audiences want more than information and arguments; they want what's relevant to them from someone who cares. Indeed, audience members who perceive the speaker to be high in credibility will regard the communication as more truthful than a message delivered by someone who is seen to have low credibility.[22]

Speaker Similarity

Two additional critical elements in the speaker-audience relationship that influence the outcome of a persuasive message are speaker similarity and physical attractiveness. *Speaker similarity* involves listeners' perceptions of how similar the speaker is to themselves, especially in terms of attitudes and moral character. Generally, audience members are more likely to respond favorably to the persuasive appeals of a speaker whom they perceive to be a lot like them. However, in certain situations we actually attach more credibility to people who are actually dissimilar to us. For example, we are more likely to be persuaded by a dissimilar speaker, especially one viewed as an "expert," when the topic or issue emphasizes facts and analysis. This is why lawyers seek the expert testimony of psychiatrists or other specialists to provide insight into the personality of a suspect, the features of a crime scene, and the like. On the other hand, an audience is more likely to be persuaded by a similar speaker when the subject is personal or relational. For example, we prefer to watch *The Dr. Phil Show* instead of *60 Minutes* when the subject is fathers and daughters, or bosses and secretaries. We tend to perceive Dr. Phil as being more similar to us in relational concerns than we do Leslie Stahl. But if the issue involves new details in a political scandal or a foreign agreement, we would probably turn to Anderson Cooper as our preferred source. These facts point to an important lesson for the persuasive speaker: *For speeches that involve a lot of facts and analysis, play on whatever amount of expertise you can summon. For speeches that concern matters of a more personal nature, however, it's best to emphasize your commonality with the audience.*

TIPS FOR INCREASING SPEAKER CREDIBILITY

_____ 1. For speeches that involve a lot of facts and analysis, emphasize your expertise on the topic.

_____ 2. Enlighten your audience with new and relevant information.

_____ 3. Demonstrate your trustworthiness by presenting your topic honestly and in a way that shows concern for your listeners.

_____ 4. For speeches of a more personal nature, emphasize your commonality with the audience.

_____ 5. Be well groomed.

SELF-ASSESSMENT CHECKLIST

Speaker Attractiveness

Finally, the *physical attractiveness* of the speaker affects persuasive outcomes. In our culture, attractive people are perceived to be competent, in control of themselves, well organized, and confident. We tend to generalize these perceptions to public speakers as well. For example, Don Draper, the charismatic advertising executive on the TV series *Mad Men,* is an extremely effective persuasive speaker when giving presentations to clients. Though he is perceived to be the best in his field, a lot of his success with clients stems from the aura of attractiveness and confidence he projects. But there are limitations, even drawbacks, to physical attractiveness as a factor in persuasive speaking. First, highly attractive speakers can be a distraction to an audience, drawing their attention away from the message. Second, physical attractiveness can interfere with persuasive appeals when the speaker's appearance violates expectations for the occasion or the topic. Third, any positive outcomes of a persuasive speech that can be attributed to the speaker's attractiveness will probably be short-term gains at best. Our tendency is to respond positively to attractive speakers because we want to be like them or be associated with them. But responding primarily on that basis leads only to a superficial understanding of the message and fleeting attention to it.

Developing Arguments for the Persuasive Speech

The persuasive power of any speech is based on the arguments within it. Arguments themselves are comprised of three elements: claims, evidence, and reasoning (formally called *warrants*). A good argument uses sound reasoning to link claims to evidence.

In the broad sense, reasoning is the process of critical thinking that we try to engage in throughout our everyday lives and in our roles as public speakers and active listeners.[1] Another definition of *reasoning,* one we introduced in the previous chapter and that applies directly to creating a persuasive speech, is "the process of proving inferences or conclusions from evidence."[2] When you reason through a speech, you demonstrate to audience members why they should accept your claims and evidence—that is, why they should accept your arguments. This chapter describes how to use argument as a framework for making appeals in persuasive speeches. Most persuasive speeches consist of several arguments.

What Is an Argument?

WEB Chapter quizzes

An **argument** is a stated position, with support for or against an idea or issue. Persuasive speeches use arguments to present one alternative as superior to other alternatives. In an argument, you ask listeners to accept a conclusion about some state of affairs, support it with evidence, and provide reasons demonstrating that the evidence logically supports the claim. The core elements of an argument consist of a claim, evidence, and warrants:[3]

1. The *claim* states the speaker's conclusion about some state of affairs.
2. The *evidence* substantiates the claim.
3. The *warrants* provide reasons that the evidence is valid or supports the claim.

Stating a Claim

To state a **claim** (also called a *proposition*) is to declare a state of affairs. Claims answer the question "What are you trying to prove?"[4] If you want to convince audience members that they need to be more careful consumers of herbal supplements, you might make this claim: "Many herbal supplements contain powerful substances that may interact in harmful ways with over-the-counter (OTC) or prescription drugs." This claim asserts that taking herbal supplements together with certain OTC or prescription drugs potentially poses a health risk. But unless your listeners already agree with the claim, it's unlikely that they'll accept it at face value. To make the claim believable, the speaker must provide proof, or evidence, in support of the claim.

Providing Evidence

Every key claim you make in a speech must be supported with **evidence**, or supporting material that provides grounds for belief (see Chapter 8, "Developing Supporting Material"). In a speech about herbal supplements, for example, to support the claim that they can cause harm by interacting with OTC or prescription drugs, you might provide *statistics* showing the number of persons in a given year who were hospitalized as a result of such interactions. You might then couple these data with *testimony* from individuals who experienced health problems because of such drug interactions or from physicians who treated such patients.

The goal in using evidence is to make a claim more acceptable, or believable, to the audience. If the evidence itself is believable, then the claim is more likely to be found acceptable by the audience.

Warrants: Justifying the Link between the Claim and Evidence

Warrants, the third component of arguments, help to support a claim and to substantiate in the audience's mind the link between the claim and the evidence. A warrant is a line of reasoning. It shows why the link between the claim

ETHICALLY SPEAKING

Engaging in Arguments in the Public Arena

Because the potential to do harm is greater when more people are involved, public discourse carries a greater scope of responsibility and accountability than does private discourse. Consider the following guidelines when engaged in arguments in the public arena:

- Arguing is not "fighting."
- Arguing is reasoning about issues, not attacking personalities.
- Arguing is socially constructive and culturally sensitive.
- Arguing strives for accuracy.
- Arguing acknowledges value in alternative or opposing views.
- Arguing is ethical; the alternative is not.

and evidence is valid, or *warranted*. For listeners to accept the argument, the connection between the claim and the evidence must be made clear and justified in their minds. A warrant serves as a logical bridge between a claim and evidence. For example, the claim that "some herbal supplements, in conjunction with other drugs, can cause health problems" may not be clear to listeners. Some good warrants can make the link between claim and evidence clearer. Here the speaker offers evidence for the claim:

> According to the American Council on Science and Health, serious side effects have occurred in cases where people consumed prescription blood thinners such as warfarin (Coumadin®) with herbal supplements such as St. John's Wort, Kava, and Valerian. Further, drugs that suppress the immune system, such as corticosteroids or cyclosporine, have been shown to have harmful effects when interacting with supplements such as Echinacea, St. John's Wort, and Zinc.[5] [EVIDENCE]

The link between the claim and the evidence can be justified by the following warrant:

> Several leading medical journals and organizations, including the American Council on Science and Health, have reported cases documenting harmful interactions between a variety of supplements and medications. [WARRANT]

This provides a justification for accepting the link between the evidence and the claim. The claim is supported.

Diagramming the argument allows you to visualize how the evidence and warrants can be presented in support of your claim. Figure 26.1 illustrates the

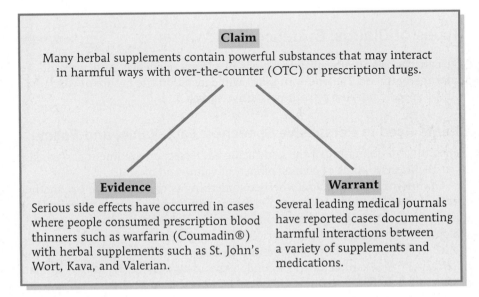

Claim

Many herbal supplements contain powerful substances that may interact in harmful ways with over-the-counter (OTC) or prescription drugs.

Evidence

Serious side effects have occurred in cases where people consumed prescription blood thinners such as warfarin (Coumadin®) with herbal supplements such as St. John's Wort, Kava, and Valerian.

Warrant

Several leading medical journals have reported cases documenting harmful interactions between a variety of supplements and medications.

FIGURE 26.1 Core Components of Argument

three components of the preceding argument about the dangers of drug and supplement interactions. As you consider formulating an argument, try to diagram it in a similar fashion:

1. Write down the claim.
2. List each possible piece of evidence you have in support of the claim.
3. Write down the corresponding warrants, or justifications, that link the evidence to the claim.

In the following excerpt from the 2010 State of the Union speech, President Barack Obama speaks about the recession and how his administration is already making changes that are having a positive impact on the American economy. Obama makes several claims and offers evidence and support for each of them. Excerpted here are several claims from the speech:

> Now, as we stabilized the financial system, we also took steps to get our economy growing again, save as many jobs as possible, and help Americans who had become unemployed. [CLAIM] That's why we extended or increased unemployment benefits for more than 18 million Americans, made health insurance 65 percent cheaper for families who get their coverage through COBRA, and passed 25 different tax cuts. . . . We cut taxes for 95 percent of working families. We cut taxes for small businesses. . . . [EVIDENCE] Now, because of the steps we took, there are about 2 million Americans working right now who would otherwise be unemployed. [WARRANT] Two hundred thousand work in construction and clean energy. Three hundred thousand are teachers and other education workers. . . . And we're on track to add another 1.5 million jobs to this total by the end of the year. [6] [WARRANT]

Types of Claims, Evidence, and Warrants

WEB Sample speeches

You can choose among different types of claims, evidence, and warrants to make an argument. The ones you select will depend on the nature of your topic and the specific purpose of your persuasive speech.

Claims Used in Persuasive Speeches: Fact, Value, and Policy

Depending on the nature of the issue being addressed, an argument can consist of three different kinds of claims: of fact, of value, and of policy.

Claims of fact focus on whether something is or is not true or whether something will or will not happen. They usually address one of two kinds of questions: those for which two or more competing answers exist, or those for which an answer does not yet exist (called a **speculative claim**). An example of the first is "Does affirmative action discriminate against nonminority job applicants?" An example of the second, a speculative claim, is "Will a woman president be elected in the next U.S. presidential election?"

Claims of value address issues of judgment. Rather than attempting to prove the truth of something, as in claims of fact, a speaker arguing a claim of value tries to show that something is right or wrong, good or bad, worthy or unworthy. Examples include "Is assisted suicide ethical?" and "Should late-term abortions be permitted when a woman's health is at stake?"

Like claims of fact, claims of value require evidence. However, the evidence in support of a value claim tends to be more subjective than factual. In defending assisted suicide, for example, a speaker might be able to show that in certain

A CULTURAL PERSPECTIVE

Addressing Culture in the Persuasive Speech

The audience members' cultural orientation will significantly affect their responses to persuasion.[1] Audience members of the same culture share core values, such as *self-reliance* and *individual achievement* (in individualist cultures) and *interdependence* and *group harmony* (in collectivist cultures) (see Chapter 6 on cultural differences). Usually, appeals that clash with core values are unsuccessful, although globalization may be leading to some cross-pollination of values.[2]

Cultural norms are a group's rules for behavior. Attempts to persuade listeners to think or do things contrary to important norms will usually fail.[3] The argument that intermarriage leads to happier couples, for example, will find greater acceptance among Reform rather than Orthodox Jews, since the latter group has strong prohibitions against the practice.

Listeners sharing a common culture usually hold culturally specific values about identity and relationships, called **cultural premises**. Prevalent among the Danes and Israelis, for example, is the premise of egalitarianism, the belief that everyone should be equal. An opposite premise exists in Korea, Japan, and other Asian societies, where status most often is aligned strictly with one's place in the social hierarchy. Bear in mind that it is difficult to challenge deeply held cultural premises.[4]

Culture also influences our responses to emotional appeals. Appeals that touch on *ego-focused* emotions such as pride, anger, happiness, and frustration, for example, tend to find more acceptance among members of individualist cultures;[5] those that use *other-focused* emotions such as empathy, indebtedness, and shame are more apt to encourage identification in collectivist cultures.[6] Usually, it is best to appeal to emotions that lie within the audience's "comfort zone."[7]

Persuasion depends on appeals to values; culture shapes these values. Eliciting a range of emotions may therefore help you appeal to diverse audience members.

1. Jennifer Aaker and Durairaj Maheswaran, "The Impact of Cultural Orientation on Persuasion," *Journal of Consumer Research* 24 (December 1997): 315–28.
2. Jennifer L. Aaker, "Accessibility or Diagnosticity? Disentangling the Influence of Culture on Persuasion Processes and Attitudes," *Journal of Consumer Research* 26 (March 2000): 340–57.
3. Kristine L. Fitch, "Cultural Persuadables," *Communication Theory* 13 (February 2003): 100–123.
4. Ibid.
5. Jennifer L. Aaker and Patti Williams, "Empathy versus Pride: The Influence of Emotional Appeals across Cultures," *Journal of Consumer Research* 25 (1998): 241–61.
6. Ibid.
7. Ibid.

situations compassion requires us to help terminally ill people take their own lives. Likewise, public opinion polls can be used to sway attitudes about a value ("after all, 83 percent of Americans support the death penalty").

Claims of policy recommend that a specific course of action be taken or approved. Legislators regularly construct arguments based on claims of policy: "Should we pass a law restricting the use of handguns/abortion/firecrackers?" Anyone can argue for a claim of policy as long as he or she advocates for or against a given plan. Such claims might include "Full-time students who commute to campus should be granted reduced parking fees" and "Property taxes should be increased to fund classroom expansions at the city's elementary schools."

Notice that in each claim the word *should* appears. A claim of policy speaks to an "ought" condition, proposing that better outcomes would be realized if the proposed condition was met.

To build a strong case for a claim of policy, you must provide the audience with a three-part justification consisting of (1) a need or a problem, (2) a solution, and (3) evidence of the solution's feasibility. (See Chapter 27 for more on the problem-solution pattern of arrangement.)

By nature, claims of policy involve claims of fact and often claims of value as well. Consider the following example:

POLICY CLAIM:	The city should provide walking paths in all municipal parks.
FACT:	Almost every park in the city is busy several times each day with recreational walkers. This activity is noticeably greater on weekends.
VALUE:	Walking on properly maintained paths is healthier both for walkers and for the park landscape.

The fact and value claims become, essentially, pieces of evidence in support of the policy claim. The fact statement provides objective evidence, and the value statement offers a more subjective justification of the policy. This suggests that successful speakers need to be quite familiar with all three kinds of argument (see Table 26.1).

As in different types of claims, you can choose among different types of evidence to support these claims.

Using Evidence to Support Your Claims

Every key claim must be supported with convincing evidence. In addition to the kinds of evidence described in Chapter 8 (examples, narratives, testimony, facts, and statistics), several other kinds of evidence exist that you can use to persuade audiences to believe your claims.[7] You might, for example, rely on audience members' existing knowledge and opinions—on what listeners already think and believe—as evidence for your claims. Or you might use *your own* knowledge and expertise as evidence.

TABLE 26.1   Sample Claims for Arguments of Fact, Value, and Policy

Type of Argument	Claim of fact	Claim of value	Claim of policy
	(Focuses on whether something is or is not true or whether something will or will not happen)	*(Addresses issues of judgment)*	*(Recommends that a specific course of action be taken, or approved of, by an audience)*
Sample Claim	• Demand for online college courses will be strong in the next decade. • Rising CO_2 levels are dangerously warming the earth. • Breastfeeding is healthier than bottle-feeding in the first year.	• The "three strikes" law is unfair. • The "ideal weight" chart is not ideal. • Title IX hurts male athletes.	• Cigarette prices should be lowered. • Airport security measures should be revamped. • The NBA draft should be changed to allow athletes to enter the draft after high school.

Audience Knowledge and Opinions

Research suggests that what your listeners already know or think about your topic ultimately determines their acceptance or rejection of claims you make about it.[8] Nothing is more persuasive to listeners than a reaffirmation of their own attitudes, beliefs, and values, especially when making claims of value and policy. For this reason, the *audience's preexisting knowledge and opinions* on the topic can often be the most persuasive evidence. Using the audience's existing knowledge as evidence for a claim works something like this:

CLAIM: Natural life support for human activity on the moon may come sooner than we think.

AUDIENCE KNOWLEDGE AS EVIDENCE: You've no doubt read or seen on the news that scientists recently discovered sources of water on the moon.

WARRANT: Water found on the moon can be used to produce oxygen for human life support.

Here the speaker uses the audience's knowledge of the discovery of water on the moon to support the claim that natural life support will eventually be possible there. The warrant that water on the moon could be converted into oxygen creates a bridge between the evidence and the claim.

Of course, if an audience lacks knowledge on the subject of your claims, you cannot use this kind of evidence. Another kind of evidence is required.

Speaker Expertise

When the audience will find your opinions credible and convincing, you may be able to use your own *speaker expertise,* or knowledge and opinions, as evidence. Doing so, however, will work only if the audience believes you have the authority or credibility to speak on the matter. This credibility may derive from your personal experience or from your original contribution to the topic. As support for a claim, speaker expertise might work like this:

CLAIM:	Natural life support for human activity on the moon may come sooner than we think.
SPEAKER EXPERTISE AS EVIDENCE:	My colleagues and I recently found signs of the existence of water on the moon.
WARRANT:	Water found on the moon can be used to produce oxygen for human life support.

In this case, the speaker is one of a group of scientists who discovered that reserves of water exist on the moon. The audience accepts the speaker's professional assertion as evidence.

Be aware, however, that few persuasive speeches can be convincingly built on speaker experience and knowledge alone. Offer your expertise in conjunction with other forms of evidence.

External Evidence

The most common form of evidence is *external* evidence—any information in support of a claim that originates with sources other than the audience's knowledge and opinions or the speaker's expertise. External evidence consists of the kind of supporting material discussed in Chapter 8—examples, narratives, testimony, facts, and statistics drawn from outside sources. External evidence is most powerful when it imparts new information that the audience has not previously used in forming an opinion,[9] so seek out supporting material that your audience is not likely to know but will find persuasive. Your audience must also believe the external evidence to be credible in order to accept it as successful support for your claim.

TESTING THE STRENGTH OF YOUR EVIDENCE

As you identify and apply evidence to a claim, keep in mind the three tests of evidence:

_____ 1. Is the evidence directly relevant to the claim?

_____ 2. Is it timely, or recent and up-to-date?

_____ 3. Will listeners find it credible, or from a source they can trust?

CHECKLIST

Types of Warrants Used to Link Claims with Evidence

As with claims and evidence, speakers use different types of warrants, or lines of reasoning linking claims with evidence, depending on the nature and goal of the persuasive speech. *Motivational warrants* appeal to the audience's needs and emotions. In Aristotle's terms, the motivational warrant makes use of *pathos*. *Authoritative warrants* appeal to the credibility the audience assigns to the source of the evidence; this appeal is based on *ethos*. *Substantive warrants*, based on *logos*, appeal to the audience's beliefs about the reliability of any factual evidence you offer. (See Chapter 25 for a review of these classical terms.)

Motivational Warrants: Appeals to Emotion

No doubt most readers have seen television and magazine advertisements asking viewers to give just pennies a day to sponsor a starving child in a distant land. The claim may say, "You can easily afford to join this organization dedicated to ending the hunger of thousands of children." The evidence may be stated as "For the price of one soft drink you can feed a child for a week." What's the warrant? "You don't want any child to starve or go without proper medical care." The speaker intends the warrant to motivate listeners by arousing their sympathy for those who lack basic human necessities. **Motivational warrants** use the needs, desires, emotions, and values of audience members as the basis for accepting some evidence as support for a claim, and thus accepting the claim itself. More often than not, motivational warrants are implied rather than stated outright. In terms of the ad to support a starving child, we don't have to be told that we don't want children to starve; if the value or desire is meaningful to us, we realize it while attending to other parts of the message.

Some other needs and values that can operate as motivational warrants in arguments include career success, physical attractiveness, financial security, and happy families.

Authoritative Warrants: Appeals to Credibility

Just as one form of evidence relies on the speaker's knowledge and opinions, some warrants rely on an audience's beliefs about the credibility or acceptability of a source of evidence. Such is the case with **authoritative warrants**. For example, in terms of sponsoring a hungry child, the speaker might make the claim that we should contribute financially to an agency that feeds hungry children. The speaker's evidence is that any amount we give, however small, will go far in meeting the agency's objectives. As a warrant, the speaker notes that the celebrity power couple Angelina Jolie and Brad Pitt work with the agency and its recipients; perhaps they are even the people delivering the message.

The success or failure of authoritative warrants rests on how highly the audience regards the authority figure. If listeners hold the person in high esteem, they are more likely to find the evidence and the claim acceptable. Thus authoritative warrants make the credibility of sources of evidence all the more important. In other words, it's possible that naming the source of evidence can also provide the authoritative warrant. For example, in support of the claim that "McDonald's Big Mac sandwiches are among the most popular fast-food sandwiches enjoyed by famous people," you could offer the evidence that "Celebrity X has said that Big Macs are his favorite fast food"; this gives both the evidence (a famous person who eats Big Macs) and the warrant (the specific famous person is Celebrity X) in the same sentence.

If you happen to be highly knowledgeable on a subject, an authoritative warrant can be made by reference to yourself. In this case, the warrant provides the speaker's knowledge and opinions as evidence. Your experience offers evidence for the claim, and you, having had the experience, give warrant to the evidence.

Substantive Warrants: Appeals to Reasoning

Substantive warrants operate on the basis of the audience's beliefs about the reliability of factual evidence. If you claim that your fellow college students should concern themselves more with learning from courses than with the grades they receive, you might offer as evidence the point that what is learned in a course is more applicable to future job responsibilities than the grade received in the course, and you might provide as the warrant a statement that "whereas better grades may lead to more job opportunities, better learning leads to better grades." The relationship between the claim and the evidence is that students will increase their chances for job opportunities if they concentrate on learning instead of on grades; for example, better grades follow from better learning.

There are several types of substantive warrants, or ways of factually linking evidence with a claim. Three that occur most commonly in speeches are *causation, sign,* and *analogy* (see also the discussion of deductive and inductive reasoning through an argument in Chapter 25, p. 353).

Warrants by cause (also called **causal reasoning**) offer a cause-and-effect relationship as proof of the claim. For example, welfare critics often reason by cause when they suggest that providing funds to people without making them work causes them to be lazy. Their opponents also reason by cause when they rebut this argument. Rather than suggesting a cause-to-effect relationship, however, they might suggest an effect-to-cause relationship, as in: "Welfare mothers don't work outside the home [EFFECT] because the welfare system does not help them with day care [CAUSE]." Similarly, a speaker might argue the following:

CLAIM: Candidate X lost his 2011 bid for the Senate largely because of his age.

EVIDENCE: Many available media reports refer to the age issue with which Candidate X had to contend.

WARRANT: Our society attributes less competence to people who are older versus those who are younger.

Older age is assumed to be a cause of Candidate X's loss in the senatorial campaign. The warrant substantiates the relationship of cause (age) to effect (loss of race) on the basis of society's negative stereotypes of older people.

As pointed out in the accompanying checklist, when using warrants by cause, it is essential to make relevant and accurate assertions about cause and effect.

MAKING EFFECTIVE USE OF REASONING BY CAUSE

_____ 1. Avoid making hasty assertions of cause or effect on the basis of stereotypes.

_____ 2. Avoid making hasty assertions of cause or effect based on hearsay or tradition.

_____ 3. Be certain that you don't offer a single cause or effect as the only possibility when others are known to exist.

_____ 4. When multiple causes or effects can be given, be sure to note their importance relative to one another.

Warrants by sign (also called **reasoning by sign**) imply that such a close relationship exists between two variables that the presence or absence of one may be taken as an indication of the presence or absence of the other.[10] For example, smoke is a sign of fire. Coughing and sneezing are signs of a cold. A claim and evidence are often associated by sign:

CLAIM: Summer job opportunities for college students will probably decline at resort locations in the southern Rocky Mountains.

EVIDENCE: Throughout the southern Rockies in the late winter and early spring, there was a record number of forest fires that destroyed many resorts.

WARRANT: Widespread natural disasters curtail employment in the affected areas.

In this example, negative effects on employment are an economic sign of natural disasters. The claim is supported by the evidence if the audience accepts the warrant that employment becomes unstable in the wake of natural disasters.

Finally, **warrants by analogy** (also called **reasoning by analogy**) compare two similar cases and imply that what is true in one case is true in the other. The assumption is that the characteristics of Case A and Case B are similar, if not the same, and that what is true for B must also be true for A.

Warrant by analogy or comparison occurs frequently in speeches. Consider this example:

CLAIM: Students will have a better feeling about Mr. Honnacker's communication class if he drops the absence policy.

EVIDENCE: Student satisfaction increased substantially in Ms. Orlander's math class when she dropped the absence policy.

WARRANT: Mr. Honnacker's communication class and Ms. Orlander's math class are equivalent with respect to other factors that satisfy students.

Here the speaker compares the communication class with the math class, assuming that both have in common students who are equally satisfied or dissatisfied depending on the nature of the absence policy. The analogy links the evidence from the math class example to the claim about the communication class.

Addressing the Other Side of the Argument

All attempts at persuasion are subject to counterpersuasion. Listeners may be persuaded to accept your claims, but once they are exposed to counterclaims they may change their minds. According to a theory called the **inoculation effect**, by anticipating counterarguments and then addressing or rebutting them, you can "inoculate" your listeners against the "virus" of these other viewpoints.[11] The theory rests on the biological principle of inducing resistance through exposure to small quantities of a harmful substance. Just as you can induce resistance to disease using a vaccine, the inoculation theory posits that you can induce resistance to counterclaims by acknowledging them.

If listeners are aware of counterclaims and you ignore them, you risk a loss of credibility. As described in the accompanying checklist on addressing competing arguments, however, this does not mean that you need to painstakingly acknowledge and refute all opposing claims.

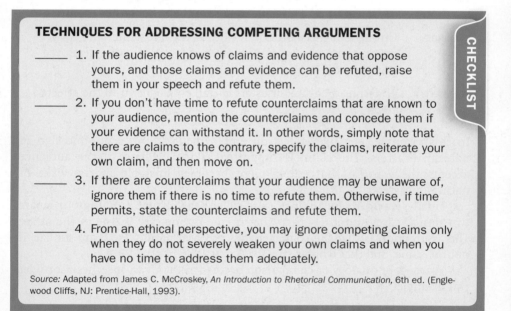

TECHNIQUES FOR ADDRESSING COMPETING ARGUMENTS

_____ 1. If the audience knows of claims and evidence that oppose yours, and those claims and evidence can be refuted, raise them in your speech and refute them.

_____ 2. If you don't have time to refute counterclaims that are known to your audience, mention the counterclaims and concede them if your evidence can withstand it. In other words, simply note that there are claims to the contrary, specify the claims, reiterate your own claim, and then move on.

_____ 3. If there are counterclaims that your audience may be unaware of, ignore them if there is no time to refute them. Otherwise, if time permits, state the counterclaims and refute them.

_____ 4. From an ethical perspective, you may ignore competing claims only when they do not severely weaken your own claims and when you have no time to address them adequately.

Source: Adapted from James C. McCroskey, _An Introduction to Rhetorical Communication_, 6th ed. (Englewood Cliffs, NJ: Prentice-Hall, 1993).

CHECKLIST

Fallacies in Reasoning

WEB Links

A **logical fallacy** is either a false or erroneous statement or an invalid or deceptive line of reasoning.[12] In either case, you need to be aware of fallacies in order to avoid making them in your own speeches and to be able to identify

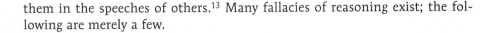

them in the speeches of others.[13] Many fallacies of reasoning exist; the following are merely a few.

Begging the Question

Begging the question is a fallacy in which an argument is stated in such a way that it cannot help but be true, even though no evidence has been presented. "Intelligent Design is the correct explanation for biological change over time because we can see godly evidence in our complex natural world" is an example of an argument that relies on the kind of circular thinking characteristic of the begging-the-question fallacy. "War kills" is another. In neither statement has the speaker offered any evidence for the conclusion.

Bandwagoning

Speakers who rely on **bandwagoning** pose arguments that use (unsubstantiated) general opinions as their (false) bases. "Nikes are superior to other brands of shoes because everyone wears Nikes" and "Everyone on campus is voting for her so you should, too" are examples of bandwagoning. The critical listener will ask, "Just who is 'everyone'?"

Either-Or Fallacy

The **either-or fallacy** poses an argument stated in terms of only two alternatives, even though there may be many additional alternatives. "If you don't send little Susie to private school this year, she will not gain admission to college" is an example of an argument posed as an either-or fallacy, as is "Either you're with us or against us."

Ad Hominem Argument

The **ad hominem argument** targets a person instead of the issue at hand in an attempt to incite an audience's dislike for that person. Examples include: "I'm a better candidate than X because, unlike X, I work for a living" and "How can you accept my opponent's position on education when he has been divorced?"

Red Herring

In the **red herring fallacy**, the speaker's argument relies on irrelevant premises for its conclusion. For example, "The previous speaker suggests that Medicare is in shambles. I disagree and recommend that we study why the young don't respect their elders." This argument makes no connection between the state of Medicare and the lack of respect for society's elders among the youth. Another example of a red herring fallacy is to say, "I fail to see why hunting should be considered cruel when it gives pleasure to so many people and employment to even more."[14] The speaker offers no statistics to support the truth of this statement.

Hasty Generalization

When a speaker uses a **hasty generalization**, the argument uses an isolated instance to make an unwarranted general conclusion, as in the following examples: "As shown by the example of a Labrador retriever biting my sister, this type of dog is dangerous and its breeding should be outlawed" and "My neighbor who works for Kmart is untrustworthy; therefore, Kmart is not a trustworthy company."

Non Sequitur

Non sequiturs "do not follow"; that is, the argument's conclusion does not connect to the reasoning. For example, "Because she lives in the richest country in the world" does not mean that "she must be extremely wealthy." Neither is it accurate to say, "If we can send a man to the moon, we should be able to cure cancer in five years."

Slippery Slope

When a speaker uses a **slippery slope** in his argument, he or she is making a faulty assumption that one case will lead to a series of events or actions. For example, "Helping refugees in the Sudan today will force us to help refugees across Africa and around the world" or "If we outsource jobs from the United States, then other companies will outsource jobs, and the U.S. economy will collapse again."

Appeal to Tradition

Speakers who use the **appeal to tradition** phrase arguments to suggest that the audience should agree with the claim because that is the way it has always been done. "A marriage should be between a man and a woman because that is how it has always been" is an example of an appeal to tradition, as is "The president of the United States must be a man because a woman has never been president."

CHAPTER 27

Organizing the Persuasive Speech

Once you've developed your speech claims, the next step in drafting a persuasive speech is to structure your speech points using one (or more) of the organizational patterns described in Chapter 13—topical, chronological, spatial, causal (cause-effect), problem-solution, narrative, and circular—and in this chapter. There is no one "best way" to organize a persuasive speech—or any kind of speech. Instead, individual speeches must be put together strategically in ways that will best achieve the goals you have set for them.

Factors to Consider When Choosing an Organizational Pattern

WEB Outliner

Three factors are critical to consider when selecting an organizational pattern: (1) the nature of your arguments and evidence, (2) the audience's attitudes toward the topic, and (3) the response you want to elicit from audience members. Note that these considerations should apply equally to your selection of types of evidence and persuasive appeals (see Chapter 26).

Do the Arguments and Evidence Suggest a Specific Pattern?

As described in Chapter 13, some speech topics or claims clearly suggest a specific design. A speech that argues for a reduction in the price of cigarettes, for example, implies that high cigarette prices represent a *problem* and that lower prices represent a *solution*. Thus one obvious way to arrange speech points is with the *problem-solution pattern* (see Chapter 13 and p. 381). Many such **claims of policy** (e.g., claims that address an "ought condition" and use the word "should") fit naturally into the problem-solution pattern.

Similarly, consider a speech in which it is argued that newborn children do best when their mothers stay home with them for at least the first six months. This **claim of value** (e.g., claims that address issues of judgment) implies that for at least a limited period, staying home is superior to working. One potentially effective way of ordering this claim is with the *comparative advantage pattern of arrangement* (see p. 386). Here, the speaker arranges main points to demonstrate a series of advantages associated with his or her claim versus an alternative position or positions—in this case, mothers who don't stay home.

Finally, consider the **claim of fact** (i.e., claims addressing whether something is or is not true or will or will not happen) that SUVs hurt the environment by releasing up to 30 percent more carbon monoxide and hydrocarbons and 75 percent more nitrogen oxide than passenger cars.[1] The claim implies that greater emissions of noxious gases (cause) lead to degradation of the environment (effect). Hence one way to arrange speech points for this claim is by using the *cause-effect pattern of organization* (see Chapter 13 for a description and sample outlines of this pattern). Alternatively, you could argue this claim in a *problem-solution* or *problem-cause-solution pattern,* so that the first point establishes the problem (SUVs hurt the environment) and subsequent points explain reasons for the problem (SUVs use too much fuel) and provide a solution (enact tougher fuel economy standards).

What Is the Disposition of the Audience?

Another factor to consider when deciding how to arrange your persuasive speech is where your **target audience** stands in relation to your topic (see Chapter 6). Are they likely to be receptive to your claims? Critical of them?

Persuasion scholar Herbert Simon describes four types of potential audiences, including the **hostile audience or one that strongly disagrees**; the **critical and conflicted audience**; the **sympathetic audience**; and the **uniformed, less educated, or apathetic audience**. Simon suggests various reasoning strategies and possible organizational patterns for each in Table 27.1.[2]

TABLE 27.1 Persuasive Strategies and Audience Type	
Audience	**Strategies**
Hostile audience or one that strongly disagrees	• Stress areas of agreement. • Address opposing views. • Don't expect major change in attitudes. • Wait until the end before asking audience to act, if at all. • Reason inductively, start with evidence, leaving conclusion until last ("tuition should be raised"). • Consider the *refutation* pattern (see p. 387).
Critical and conflicted audience	• Present strong arguments and audience evidence. • Address opposing views, perhaps by using the *refutation* pattern.
Sympathetic audience	• Use motivational stories and emotional appeals to reinforce positive attitudes. • Stress your commonality with listeners. • Clearly tell audience what you want them to think or do. • Consider the *narrative* (storytelling) pattern.
Uninformed, less-educated, or apathetic audience	• Focus on capturing their attention. • Stress personal credibility and "likability." • Stress the topic's relevance to listeners.

What Response Do You Seek?

A third consideration in choosing how you will order speech points is your **specific speech purpose**—how you want your audience to react to your message. What is the type and degree of change you seek? Some organizational patterns, such as Monroe's motivated sequence, explicitly call for audience members to act on the speaker's suggestions to, for example, donate to a cause or sign a petition. The other designs are appropriate when attempting to modify audience attitudes and behavior so that they move in the direction of your stance. Figure 27.1 illustrates the audience factors to consider when organizing a persuasive speech. Table 27.2 summarizes the patterns discussed in this chapter.

1. Review topic/argument/evidence for likely pattern.

   ↓

2. Determine where the audience stands in relation to the message. Are listeners hostile to it? Sympathetic? Critical? Informed or uninformed? Involved or apathetic?

   ↓

3. Identify the type and degree of change you seek from the audience. Modify attitudes and values? Change behavior? To what degree?

   ↓

4. Consider the cultural composition of the audience.

   ↓

5. Select an organizational pattern.

FIGURE 27.1 Factors to Consider When Organizing Your Persuasive Speech

Problem-Solution Pattern of Arrangement  WEB Chapter quizzes

One commonly used design for persuasive speeches, especially those based on claims of policy and claims of fact, is the **problem-solution pattern of arrangement** (see Chapter 13). Here you organize speech points to demonstrate the nature and significance of a problem and then to provide justification for a proposed solution:

   I.   Problem (define what it is)

  II.   Solution (offer a way to overcome the problem)

But many problem-solution speeches require more than two points to adequately explain the problem and to substantiate the recommended

TABLE 27.2 Organizational Formats	
Organizational Format	Description
Problem-Solution	Speech points arranged to demonstrate a problem and then to offer a solution.
Problem-Cause-Solution	Speech points arranged in order to demonstrate problem, reasons for problem, and solution to problem.
Monroe's Motivated Sequence	Speech points arranged to motivate listeners to act on something or to shift their attitudes in direction of speaker's.
Cause-Effect	Speech points arranged to demonstrate that a particular set of circumstances leads to a specific result (either desirable or undesirable) or, conversely, that various results (effects) follow from a particular set of circumstances. See Chapter 13 for the description of this pattern.
Comparative Advantage	Speech points arranged to demonstrate that your viewpoint or proposal contrasts favorably with (is superior to) one or more alternative positions.
Refutation	Speech points arranged to disprove opposing claims.

solution. Thus a **problem-cause-solution pattern of arrangement** may be in order:

I. The nature of the problem (define what it is)

II. Reasons for the problem (explain why it's a problem, for whom, etc.)

III. Unsatisfactory solutions (discuss those that have not worked) (*optional step*)

IV. Proposed solution (explain why it's expected to work, noting any unsatisfactory solutions)

When arguing a claim of policy, it may be important to demonstrate the proposal's feasibility. To do this, use a four-point *problem-cause-solution-feasibility* pattern: (1) a need or a problem, (2) reasons for the problem, (3) a solution to the need or problem, and (4) evidence of the solution's feasibility.

First comes a *need* or a *problem*. The policy must speak to a real issue that the audience would like to have resolved. If your claim is that "the NBA draft should be changed so that young athletes aren't tempted to throw away an opportunity to get an education," the need is for a revamping of the NBA draft policy to encourage athletes to complete their college education. Second, the justification for a policy must provide *reasons for the problem*. Some reasons that the NBA draft needs to be fixed might include the statement that its present policies lure young athletes to pursue unrealistic goals of superstardom and that immature players weaken the quality of the game. Next, you must provide a *solution to the problem,* a specific way to address the need. The policy claim that the NBA draft should be changed must then offer an alternative policy, such as "the NBA draft needs to adopt a minimum age of twenty." Fourth, the justification for the policy claim should offer *evidence of the solution's feasibility*. In this case, the speaker could provide evidence showing that sports organizations in other countries have successfully adopted a minimum age:

GENERAL PURPOSE: To persuade

SPECIFIC PURPOSE: To persuade my audience that the NBA draft should be changed so that young athletes are no longer tempted to throw away their chance to get an education.

THESIS STATED AS NEED OR PROBLEM: The NBA draft should be changed so that athletes like you aren't tempted to throw away an opportunity to get an education.

MAIN POINTS:

I.   The NBA draft should be revamped so that college-age athletes are not tempted to drop out of school. *(Need/ problem)*

II.   The NBA's present policies lure young athletes to pursue unrealistic goals of superstardom while weakening the quality of the game with immature players. *(Reasons for the problem)*

III.   The NBA draft needs to adopt a minimum age of twenty. *(Solution to the problem)*

IV.   National leagues in countries X and Y have done this successfully. *(Evidence of the solution's feasibility)*

ORGANIZING A CLAIM OF POLICY

✔ Describe the need or problem.

✔ Discuss reasons for the problem.

✔ Offer a solution to the need or problem.

✔ Offer evidence of the solution's feasibility.

CHECKLIST

Monroe's Motivated Sequence

WEB Links

The **motivated sequence pattern of arrangement**, developed in the mid-1930s by Alan Monroe,[3] is a five-step process that begins with arousing listeners' attention and ends with calling for action. This time-tested variant of the problem-solution pattern of arrangement is particularly effective when you want the audience to do something—buy a product, donate to a cause, and so forth. Yet it is equally useful when you want listeners to reconsider their present way of thinking about something or continue to believe as they do but with greater commitment.

Step 1: Attention

The *attention step* addresses listeners' core concerns, making the speech highly relevant to them. Here is an excerpt from a student speech by Ed Partlow on becoming an organ donor:

> Today I'm going to talk about a subject that can be both personal and emotional. I am going to talk about becoming an organ donor. Donating an organ is a simple step you can take that will literally give life to others—to your husband or wife, mother or father, son or daughter—or to a beautiful child whom you've never met.
>
> There is one thing I want to acknowledge from the start. Many of you may be uncomfortable with the idea of becoming an organ donor. I want to establish right off that it's OK if you don't want to become a donor.
>
> Many of us are willing to donate our organs, but because we haven't taken the action to properly become a donor, our organs go unused. As a result, an average of fifteen people die every day because of lack of available organs.

In this first step, the speaker makes the topic relevant to listeners by showing how their actions could help those closest to them. He further involves the audience by acknowledging the sensitive nature of his topic and assuring them that he respects their right to make up their own minds. The statistic he cites underscores the seriousness of his purpose.

Step 2: Need

The *need step* isolates and describes the issue to be addressed. If you can show the members of an audience that they have an important need that must be satisfied or a problem that must be solved, they will have a reason to listen to your propositions (see Chapter 25). Continuing with the organ donor speech, here the speaker establishes the need for organ donors:

> According to the U.S. Department of Health and Human Services, there are approximately 80,000 people on the waiting list for an organ transplant. Over 50,000 are waiting for kidney transplants alone, and the stakes are high: 90 percent of patients who receive a kidney from a living donor live at least ten years after the transplant. One of the people on the waiting list is Aidan Malony, who graduated from this college two years ago. Without a transplant, he will die. It is agonizing for his family and friends to see him in this condition. And it is deeply frustrating to them that more people don't sign and carry organ donor cards. I have always carried my organ donor card with me, but I didn't realize the extreme importance of doing so before talking to Aidan.
>
> Every sixteen minutes another name joins that of Aidan Malony and is added to the National Transplant Waiting List.

Step 3: Satisfaction

The *satisfaction step* identifies the solution. This step begins the crux of the speech, offering audience members a proposal to reinforce or change their attitudes, beliefs, and values regarding the need at hand. Here is an example from the speech on organ donation:

> It takes only two steps to become an organ donor.
>
> First, fill out an organ donor card and carry it with you. You may also choose to have a note added to your driver's license the next time you renew it.
>
> Second and most important, tell your family that you want to become an organ donor and ask them to honor your wishes when the time arrives. Otherwise, they may discourage the use of your organs should something happen to you. Check with your local hospital to find out about signing a family pledge—a contract where family members share their wishes about organ and tissue donation. This is an absolutely essential step in making sure the necessary individuals will honor your wish to become an organ donor.

STEPS IN THE MOTIVATED SEQUENCE

✔ Step 1: *Attention*   Address listeners' core concerns, making the speech highly relevant to them.

✔ Step 2: *Need*   Show listeners that they have an important need that must be satisfied or a problem that must be solved.

✔ Step 3: *Satisfaction*   Introduce your proposed solution.

✔ Step 4: *Visualization*   Provide listeners with a vision of anticipated outcomes associated with the solution.

✔ Step 5: *Action*   Make a direct request of listeners that involves changing or strengthening their present way of thinking or acting.

CHECKLIST

Step 4: Visualization

The *visualization step* provides the audience with a vision of anticipated outcomes associated with the solution. The purpose of the step is to carry audience members beyond accepting the feasibility of your proposal to seeing how it will actually benefit them:

> There are so many organs and such a variety of tissue that may be transplanted. One organ donor can help up to fifty people. Who can forget the story of 7-year-old American Nicholas Green, the innocent victim of a highway robbery in Italy that cost him his life? Stricken with unfathomable grief, Nicholas's parents, Reg and Maggie Green, nevertheless immediately decided to donate Nicholas's organs. As a direct result of the donation, seven Italians thrive today, grateful recipients of Nicholas's heart, corneas, liver, pancreas cells, and kidneys. Today, organ donations in Italy are twice as high as they were in 1993, the year preceding Nicholas's death. The Italians called this phenomenon "The Nicholas Effect."

Step 5: Action

Finally, in the *action step* the speaker asks audience members to act according to their acceptance of the message. This may involve reconsidering their present way of thinking about something, continuing to believe as they do but with greater commitment, or implementing a new set of behaviors. Here, the speaker makes an explicit call to action:

> It takes courage to become an organ donor.
> You have the courage to become an organ donor.
> All you need to do is say yes to organ and tissue donation on your donor card and/or driver's license and discuss your decision with your family.
> Be part of "The Nicholas Effect."

Comparative Advantage Pattern of Arrangement

WEB Chapter quizzes

Another way to organize speech points is to show how your viewpoint or proposal is superior to one or more alternative viewpoints or proposals. This design, called the **comparative advantage pattern of arrangement**, is most effective when your audience is already aware of the issue or problem and agrees that a need for a solution (or an alternative view) exists. Because listeners are alert to the issue, you don't have to spend time establishing its existence. Instead, you can proceed directly to favorably comparing your position with the alternatives.

In order to maintain your credibility, make sure to identify alternatives that your audience is familiar with and ones supported by opposing interests. If you omit familiar alternatives, your listeners will wonder if you are fully informed on the topic and become skeptical of your comparative alternative as well as your credibility. The final step in a comparative advantage speech is to drive home the unique advantages of your option relative to competing options with brief but compelling evidence.

Using the comparative advantage pattern, the main points in a speech addressing the best way to control the deer population might look like this:

THESIS: Rather than hunting, fencing, or contraception alone, the best way to reduce the deer population is by a dual strategy of hunting and contraception.

MAIN POINT I: A combination strategy is superior to hunting alone because many areas are too densely populated by humans to permit hunting; in such cases contraceptive darts and vaccines can address the problem. (*Advantage over alternative No. 1*)

MAIN POINT II: A combination strategy is superior to relying solely on fencing because fencing is far too expensive for widespread use. (*Advantage over alternative No. 2*)

MAIN POINT III: A dual strategy is superior to relying only on contraception because only a limited number of deer are candidates for contraceptive darts and vaccines. *(Advantage over alternative No. 3)*

Refutation Pattern of Arrangement

 WEB Chapter quizzes

Similar to debate, the **refutation pattern of arrangement** addresses each main point and then refutes (disproves) an opposing claim to your position. The aim here is to bolster your own position by disproving the opposing claim. This type of organizational pattern is often used in political campaigns in order to strengthen one candidate's position on an issue and debunk the position taken by the opposing candidate.[4] Note that it is important to refute strong rather than weak objections to the claim, since refuting weak objections won't sway the audience.[5] Further, it is probably best to use this pattern when you are confident that the opposing argument is weak and vulnerable to attack. If done well, refutation may influence audience members who either disagree with you or are conflicted about where they stand.

Main points arranged in a refutation pattern follow a format similar to this:

MAIN POINT I: State the opposing position.

MAIN POINT II: Describe the implications or ramifications of the opposing claim.

MAIN POINT III: Offer arguments and evidence for your position.

MAIN POINT IV: Contrast your position with the opposing claim to drive home the superiority of your position.

Consider the speaker who argues for increased energy conservation versus a policy of drilling for oil in protected land in Alaska:

THESIS: Rather than drilling for oil in Alaska's Arctic National Wildlife Refuge (ANWR), we should focus on energy conservation measures as a way of lessening our dependence on foreign oil.

MAIN POINT I: Proponents claim that drilling in the Arctic refuge is necessary to decrease dependence on foreign oil sources and hold down fuel costs while adding jobs, and that modern drilling techniques along with certain environmental restrictions will result in little negative impact on the environment. *(Describes opposing claims)*

MAIN POINT II: By calling for drilling, these proponents sidestep our need for stricter energy conservation policies, overlook the need to protect one of the last great pristine lands, and ignore the fact that the oil would make a negligible dent in oil imports—from 68 percent to 65 percent by 2025. *(Describes implications and ramifications of opposing claims)*

MAIN POINT III: The massive construction needed to access the tundra will disturb the habitat of caribou, polar bear, and thousands of species of birds and shift the focus from energy conservation to increased energy consumption, when the focus should be the reverse. *(Offers arguments and evidence for the speaker's position, as developed in subpoints)*

MAIN POINT IV: The proponents' plan would encourage consumption and endanger the environment; my plan would encourage energy conservation and protect one of the world's few remaining wildernesses. *(Contrasts the speaker's position with the opposition's to drive home the former's superiority)*

SAMPLE VISUALLY ANNOTATED PERSUASIVE SPEECH

WEB Video

Emergency in the Emergency Room
LISA ROTH
Illinois Central College

The following speech by college student Lisa Roth investigates the crisis in emergency room care and advocates a claim of policy—that our emergency room system should be overhauled. Note that the speech is organized in a problem-cause-solution pattern. Lisa offers a variety of types of claims, evidence, and reasoning to build her argument.

Last year, forty-nine-year-old Beatrice Vance began experiencing some alarming symptoms—nausea, shortness of breath, and chest pain. She called her daughter, Monique, and asked to be driven to the emergency room at Vista Medical Center in Lake County, Illinois. Upon arrival, a nurse briefly met with her. She asked Ms. Vance to wait until she could be seen by a doctor, as patients are treated in order of severity. •

• This dramatic incident serves as an effective attention getter.

Fully two hours later, when her name was finally called, Beatrice didn't respond. In fact, hospital officials found her slumped over in her chair, ten feet or so from the admitting station, unconscious and without a pulse. According to an ABC *Nightly News* report on September 17, 2007, Beatrice had already died from a massive heart attack while waiting to be seen by a doctor. •

• Lisa's vivid description appeals to listeners' emotions (pathos) and indicates that a problem exists.

Effective hand gesture emphasizes gravity of crisis

Sadly, Beatrice is not the only one who suffers at the hands of an overwhelmed, sometimes inconsistent, and sometimes incompetent emergency room staff. Hospitals across the country are wrought with discord. According to experts on the frontline, such as Dr. Brent Eastman, Chief Medical Advisor at Scripps Health Hospital in San Diego, America's emergency rooms are in a crisis that could jeopardize everyone in this room and all their loved ones. •

• Lisa states her thesis and backs it up with an expert's opinion; to ensure her source's credibility, she names his title and affiliation.

Uses body language and facial expression to add emphasis

Today, we'll uncover the catastrophic conditions existing in America's emergency rooms, discover what is causing these conditions, and look at how to restore our faith in a system that has—to quote from an editorial in the June 21, 2006, edition of the *New York Times*—"reached a breaking point." •

• Lisa's preview statement indicates a problem-cause-solution pattern.

To begin, emergency rooms are desperately overcrowded. • According to a landmark series of three reports on the breakdown of our emergency room system conducted by the Institute of Medicine, the need for emergency rooms has increased by 26 percent since 1993; during the same period, 425 emergency departments closed their doors. The average emergency room wait is now almost four hours, according to a report broadcast on *Good Morning America* on September 18, 2006, but patients could be asked to wait up to forty-eight hours before they are allowed into an inpatient bed. •

• Lisa introduces the first problem plaguing the ER system.

• Lisa cites recent statistics from a credible source about the ER system, emphasizing the gravity of the situation.

The United States emergency care system is also seriously understaffed, especially with regard to specialists. • As reported in the *New York Times* editorial, emergency rooms find it very difficult to get specialists to take emergency room and trauma center calls. Furthermore, specialists such as neurosurgeons shy

• Lisa introduces the second problem—understaffing.

away from emergency room procedures because of the lack of compensation associated with treating so many uninsured patients, as well as the risk of seeing their malpractice premiums rise.

Not only are emergency rooms understaffed; existing staff often are unprepared for disasters. An investigation in the July 6, 2006, edition of the *Columbus Dispatch* found that EMTs received only one hour of training for major disaster preparation. What's even scarier, says a team of reporters at the *Fort Worth Star Telegram* of June 15, 2006, is that with one major disaster our emergency care service could fall apart completely.

The third problem with our current system is not surprising. There is simply not enough money to adequately fund our emergency rooms. •

The *New York Times* reports that emergency rooms are notorious money losers. While most emergency rooms have operating budgets well in the millions, they receive only a fraction of that amount even while being asked to operate securely and safely. Additionally, as reported in the June 15, 2006, edition of the *Pittsburgh Tribune Review,* because of the lack of money, there are now 200,000 fewer hospital beds in the United States than there were in 1993, even as the need for them has increased tremendously.

So, our emergency rooms are broke, overcrowded, and understaffed. Don't you feel secure? •

We can pinpoint three specific causes for the emergency room crisis. These include the highly fragmented emergency medical care system, the uninsured patients, and the lack of money. •

Fragmentation occurs on all levels because there are no standardized procedures and no clear chain of command. On the regional level, emergency vehicles fail to communicate effectively with ER and trauma care centers, causing poorly managed patient flow. On the national level, there are no standardized procedures for the training and certification of emergency room personnel.

To complicate matters even more, there is no lead agency to control emergency room and trauma care centers.

So, as you can see, this lack of organization, from poorly managed patient flow to the absences of standardized training and certifying personnel, causes

> • Lisa introduces the third problem plaguing the ER system.

> • Lisa makes effective use of transitions here and throughout; here, she briefly summarizes the nature of the problem.

> • Lisa now turns to the causes of the crisis.

chaos and confusion in what should be a streamlined and secure service industry.

Consider the second cause of the crisis. •

● Lisa transitions into the second cause.

Uninsured patients cause about as much chaos in the emergency room as does fragmentation. According to the July 6, 2006, *Columbus Dispatch,* through no fault of their own, there are now 46 million uninsured in the United States. This of course leads to more unpaid ER bills, which leads to more financial problems for the emergency rooms.

But please understand, I am not blaming the patients who simply cannot afford or are not offered health insurance. They are merely the effect of a larger cause: a society that doesn't place a premium on affordable health care. A lack of affordable health care only perpetuates the cycle in which no affordable health care means no insurance, which in turn leads to unpaid ER bills.

The vast numbers of uninsured lead us to the third and final cause of the emergency room breakdown. Emergency rooms are plagued by insufficient reimbursements from insurers and insufficient funding by the government. •

● Lisa transitions from the second to the third cause of the crisis.

Lack of money is a major cause of the shortage of capacity and staffing stability in the emergency rooms. The June 15, 2006, *Fort Worth Star Telegram* tells us that emergency rooms received only 4 percent of the $3.38 billion that was allotted to them by the Homeland Security Department in 2002 and 2003 for emergency medical preparation. As government budgets continue to be slashed, the quality of our health care will continue to deteriorate.

So, how can we renovate a cycle that seems beyond control? Well, we can look to solutions on a national level and then on a personal level. •

● Lisa turns to solutions to the problem.

The first step to defeating the chaos in the emergency rooms is to create a coordinated, regionalized system with national standards and a lead agency. Everyone—from 911, to ambulances, to emergency care services—needs to coordinate their operations effectively and efficiently in order to ensure each patient a safe and secure emergency room visit. Additionally, the Institute of Medicine suggests that a lead agency be started in

Lisa uses the entire presentation space and connects with audience in all corners of the room

the Department of Health and Human Services in order to control emergency room and trauma care centers.

On a personal level, the National Association of Emergency Physicians asks us to be responsible before going to the emergency room. Before going to the emergency room, ask yourself, do I really need to go to the emergency room, or can my primary care physician take care of my needs? Take steps to lessen the impact of the uninsured on emergency rooms by following the lead of the people of Columbus, Ohio, who, according to the July 6, 2006, edition of the *Columbus Dispatch,* are building affordable primary care clinics in some of the poor neighborhoods. •

Lisa's professional dress fits her serious topic

Today we have uncovered some of the catastrophic conditions existing in America's emergency rooms. Armed with a greater understanding of what is causing these issues—overcrowding, lack of specialization and training, and funding—we can now look to the future and focus our energy on solving this national crisis. •

• Lisa offers listeners a concrete solution; this also serves as a call to action.

• Lisa's summary of the main points signals a close to the speech.

Unfortunately, while it is too late for Beatrice Vance, because she was not given an EKG within ten minutes of admission to the emergency room, authorities recently ruled that her death was a homicide. This paves the way for criminal prosecution of the Vista Medical Center and puts emergency rooms across the country on notice that they too could be found liable should they be found similarly negligent.

Perhaps this terrible tragedy will turn out to be the wake-up call that the United States has needed in order to restore safety and stability to our emergency care system.

Works Cited

Amen, Rob. "Emergency Rooms Turn Away More Patients." *Pittsburgh Tribune Review,* June 16, 2006.

Campo-Flores, Arian. "How to Stop the Bleeding." *Newsweek,* May 8, 2007. www.newsweek.com/id/34803.

"Code Blue." Editorial. *Columbus Dispatch,* July 6, 2006, 18A. www.dispatch.com.

Committee on the Future of Emergency Care in the United States Health System. *Emergency Medical Services: At the Crossroads.* Bethesda, MD: National Academies Press, 2007.

"Emergency in the Emergency Rooms." Opinion. *New York Times*, June 21, 2006. www.nytimes.com/2006/06/21/opinion/21Wed4.html?ex=1189137600&en=fdd466fef8f1534c&ei=5070.

"Illinois Woman's ER Wait Death Ruled a Homicide." *Good Morning America*. September 17, 2006. abcnews.go.com/GMA/Health/story?id=2454685&page=1.

"Inexcusable Death." *ABC Nightly News*. September 18, 2006. abcnews.go.com/Video/playerIndex?id=2457808.

National Association of EMS Physicians. Summary of "Future of Emergency Care: Hospital-Based Emergency Care at the Breaking Point" Recommendations. www.naemsp.org.

Perotin, Maria M. "Serious Condition." *Fort Worth Star Telegram*, June 15, 2006, C1.

SAMPLE VISUALLY ANNOTATED PERSUASIVE SPEECH

Preventing Cyberbullying
UNA CHUA
Tufts University

In this speech, college student Una Chua helps the audience recognize how problematic cyberbullying is and lets them know how they can address and prevent it. Organizationally, the speech is arranged along the lines of the problem-cause-solution pattern. Note that Una uses a variety of sources, from books to scholarly articles to publications posted on reputable Web sites, to support her arguments.

Appropriate attire and a sincere facial expression suit Una's serious topic

On the evening of September 22, 2010, Rutgers University freshman Tyler Clementi updated his Facebook status: "Jumping off the gw [George Washington] Bridge sorry." A few hours later, he did just that. But what would cause Clementi, recognized as a bright student and talented musician with a promising future, to take his own life? The answer, unhappily, involves two bullies and a Web cam.

According to a September 29, 2010, *New York Times* article, Clementi's roommate and a female acquaintance stand accused of invasion of privacy. The charge? Using a Web cam to view and transmit private images of Clementi in an intimate encounter with another young man. Tyler Clementi's story is tragic, but it's not an isolated event. You may recall an *ABC News* report on March 29, 2010, regarding the January 2010 suicide of Phoebe Prince. She was a 15-year-old high school student from Massachusetts who hanged herself after months of torment from other teens via text messages and social networking sites. •

• Una begins her speech with several dramatic examples that capture the audience's attention.

What is going on here? • In a word—and a new one at that—it's *cyberbullying*. According to the Merriam-Webster Dictionary, the first use of this term can be traced to the year 2000.

• Una introduces her topic with a rhetorical question and offers a little-known fact.

My name is Una Chua, and I'm here today to confront the growing problem of electronic harassment. I also want to offer steps you can take so that you and your loved ones don't have to endure the kind of pain and humiliation experienced by Tyler Clementi, Phoebe Prince, and so many others. • I'll start with a look at the various forms cyberbullying takes and describe the scope of the problem. • Next, I'll consider what causes cyberbullies to act as they do and explore the conditions that make this alarming crime so easy to commit. But I'm not here just to talk about one more social ill. I want to show you how you and your loved ones can stay safe—both by scrupulously guarding your personal information and by actively thwarting cyberbullies and taking a stand against them. Finally, should you or someone you know become a victim, I want you to be able to respond constructively. All of these steps will make the Internet a safer place for all the members of your community to enjoy.

• Here, Una sets up the organizational pattern of the speech, indicating that she will describe a problem, review its causes, and offer solutions.

• She previews her main points.

As you can imagine from the heartbreaking stories I've shared about Tyler Clementi and Phoebe Prince, cyberbullying poses serious mental health risks to the nation's children, teens, and young adults. The Cyberbullying Research Center, a leading resource on the topic, • defines *cyberbullying* as "willful and repeated harm inflicted through the use of computers, cell phones, and other electronic devices." • Cyberbullying can take many forms, including the following: posting

• Una qualifies her source and demonstrates its credibility.

• Una begins the body of her speech by ensuring that her audience knows what cyberbullying means.

or sending harassing messages via Web sites, blogs, or text messages; posting embarrassing or private photos of someone without their permission; recording or video taping someone and sharing it without permission; and creating fake Web sites or social networking profiles in someone else's name to humiliate them. Often these acts are done anonymously. School Psychologists Ted Feinberg and Nicole Robey, writing in the March 2009 edition of *Education Digest,* further explain that cyberbullying can involve stalking, threats, harassment, impersonation, humiliation, trickery, and exclusion.

Cyberbullying is a fairly recent social problem, but a substantial body of research has already formed around it. •

The research paints a chilling picture. According to the Cyberbullying Research Center, about 20 percent of the over 4,400 randomly selected 11-to-18-year-old students in 2010 said that they were repeatedly picked on by another person or persons online, on e-mail, or through text messages. About 10 percent said that in addition to being a victim, they had been cyberbullies themselves. Similarly, a 2010 study published in the *American Journal of Orthopsychiatry* found that of the more than 2,000 teenagers questioned, 49.5 percent indicated that they had been the victims of cyberbullying and 33.7 percent confessed to bullying others online.

A brief glance at her notes helps Una present these statistics accurately

Whether as victims, victimizers, or both, many young people are touched by the problem of cyberbullying. What does the research say about the causes of cyberbullying? What motivates the cyberbully, and under what conditions is cyberbullying most likely to occur? •

Sadly enough, one explanation for the motivation behind cyberbullying is that the bully wishes merely to "joke around." The National Crime Prevention Council, a leading anti-crime public service organization, • reports on its Web site that 81 percent of a nationally representative sample of youths said that others cyberbully because they think it's funny. In other words, despite their potentially disastrous consequences for victims, the cyberbully's harassing text messages and cruel Facebook wall postings are meant simply as a "joke."

- This transition effectively alerts the audience to what's coming next.

- Una now moves from describing the problem to exploring its causes.

- Note how Una lends credibility and context to this source by stating that it is a "leading anti-crime public service organization."

In a lot of cases, underlying this drive to amuse oneself at another's expense is an insecure sense of self. This, combined with a tendency towards aggressiveness, appears to characterize many cyberbullies, according to researchers Sameer Hinduja and Justin Patchin of the Cyberbully Research Center. For the bully, the act of harassing another person serves as an outlet for aggression and makes him or her feel at least momentarily powerful.

Eye contact and natural movement around the presentation area sustain audience interest

For many bullies, then, wanting to feel powerful and superior to someone else appears to be a prime motivation to bully. But what are the conditions that allow cyberbullies to act on this drive? •

According to the research, a lack of parental supervision and the ability to be anonymous provide especially fertile ground. As television talk show host Dr. Phil McGraw notes in his June 24, 2010, congressional testimony—and as many of us have experienced in our own lives—children and teens often know more about texting and social networking than parents and adult guardians. This makes their Internet and cell phone activities difficult for parents to regulate. One study by the National Crime Prevention Council found that a nationally representative sample of 80 percent of youth in the United States do not have enforced rules about Internet use at home, or the rules are easy to get around. •

Put another way, children and teens are left unchecked and, therefore, have the opportunity to either bully other teens directly or to inadvertently support such behavior. They do the latter by passing along bullying messages and contributing to damaging gossip.

A second, particularly powerful, condition enabling cyberbullying is anonymity. Cyberbullies feel emboldened by their ability to do nasty things with impunity, because no one need know that they are the culprits. In his book *Girls on the Edge: The Four Factors Driving the New Crisis for Girls,* psychologist and pediatrician Leonard Sax describes it this way: •

Twenty years ago, if a girl wanted to spread rumors about another girl, everybody would know who was doing it. That knowledge constrained what the bully

• This transition internally summarizes the previous point and previews the next one.

• Una cites a credible source, which helps to build her argument.

• Una clearly indicates that she is quoting a source.

might say. If you got too nasty, your nastiness could reflect badly on you. But now, you can pretend to be a boy who's just received sexual services from Leeanne, then post something about Leeanne online, and nobody will ever know that you are actually a girl who invented the whole story to make Leeanne look bad.

In essence, the anonymity of the Internet makes cyberbullying easy and, in many circumstances, difficult to catch and stop.

By now, you may be feeling that we Internet users are doomed to be victims of cruel torment at the hands of anonymous bullies who will never suffer the consequences of their actions. This is hardly the case, however. You can take steps to protect yourself. •

• Una moves on to the solution part of the organizational pattern.

A simple but effective sequence of gestures highlights the speech content

For one, you can be vigilant about safeguarding your personal information. Our school's Information Technology office lists the following advice on its Web site. First, never, ever, leave your laptops unattended. Second, keep your account passwords and Social Security numbers totally private. Third, use the highest privacy settings on your social networking sites. Finally, think carefully about the types of pictures of yourself and your friends that you post online, and restrict views of them to "friends" only. • Each of these steps can dissuade bullies from having the ability to pose as you in order to harm or embarrass you in some way.

• Una helps listeners follow along by using the signal words *first, second, third,* and *finally.*

In addition to zealously guarding your personal information, you can help combat cyberbullying by being a voice against it whenever you see it happening.

The Group "Don't Stand By, Stand Up!" is a student-led organization formed soon after Tyler Clementi's suicide and featured on Facebook. The group urges Internet users to take a stand against cyberbullying by recognizing that bullies—in all forms—rarely succeed in their harassment without the support and attention of bystanders. The National Crime Prevention Council Web site gives more specific tips on how to thwart the bully's attempts. The first is to refuse to pass bullying messages along to others—whether via text or photo messaging, social networking, or e-mail—and to let the original sender know that you find the message offensive or stupid. Remember, if bullies bully because they think their behavior is harmless and funny, then it makes sense to tell them that you find their messages to be quite the opposite.

Despite your best efforts to keep your personal information private and speak out against cyberbullying, you may still become a victim. I don't say this to scare you, but rather to advise you on what to do if it does happen to you or to someone you know. In this event, consider the "Stop, Block, and Tell" method of combating cyberbullying.

Una reveals her visual aid at the right moment

Online safety expert Parry Aflab, in a July 28, 2009, interview for PBS's *Frontline,* advises victims to use the "Stop, Block, and Tell" method to respond to bullying behaviors directed against them. While often directed at younger children, this method proves to be useful for victims of any age, as explained on the "Don't Stand By, Stand Up!" Web site. They advise that after receiving a bullying message you should first "Stop." In other words, do nothing. Take five minutes to cool down, take a walk, breathe deeply, or do whatever helps to calm down the understandable anger you are feeling. Then, "Block": Prevent the cyberbully from having any future communication with you. This may mean anything from removing him or her from your social networking sites' "friends" list to having your cell phone service provider block the bully from being able to call or text you. The third step is to "Tell" someone about the abuse without embarrassment or shame. For example, you might call campus security or confide in a counselor at the Health and Counseling Center—particularly if the abuse has been going on for a long time and you feel that your self-esteem or relationships have been affected. Similarly, parents should encourage their

Una gestures towards a clear presentation aid designed to help the audience remember an important part of her speech

Panning to all corners of the room helps Una's conclusion hit home

children to report any bullying to a trusted adult, whether a parent, teacher, principal, or guidance counselor.

Today we've ventured into the very real—and very dangerous—world of cyberbullying. • We've seen cyberbullying's negative impact on children, teens, and young adults. We've analyzed the insecure and aggressive personality traits that characterize cyberbullies and looked at two key conditions that make it easier for the cyberbully to operate: lack of parental supervision and the ability to be anonymous. We've also seen how you can counter this potentially deadly problem.

Be vigilant about protecting your personal information. Speak out against cyberbullying. And if you or someone you know experiences cyberbullying, react constructively with the "Stop, Block, and Tell" method.

Cyberbullying isn't just someone else's problem. It's very likely something you need to guard against, now or in the future, as a student today or as a parent tomorrow. I urge each of you to make a personal commitment to do your part to combat the problem. Refuse to stay silent in the face of cyberbullying. Resolve that you will never send nor pass along cyberbullying messages of any kind, no matter how harmless doing so might seem. This act alone can make a world of difference in the life of the intended victim. After all, wouldn't you want someone to take this simple step for you? • In addition, voice your concerns at the campus and community level. For example, students from our university recently attended a candlelight vigil to remember those who fell victim to bullying and discrimination. Even if you're not interested in becoming a member, you can support events that bring cyberbullying—and its serious consequences—to light.

We must never forget Tyler Clementi, Phoebe Prince, and the other young lives cut short by unnecessary bullying. Who knows? Your best friend, your younger brother, or your future son could just have easily been on that bridge that fateful September evening. •

• Una signals the conclusion of her speech with a summary of her main points.

• Una issues a call to action.

• By stressing the personal relevance of her topic to her audience, Una leaves them with something to think about.

Works Cited

Aflab, Parry. "Stop, Block, and Tell." *Frontline.* PBS Web site. July 28, 2009. http://www.pbs.org/wgbh/pages/frontline/digitalnation/relationships/predators-bullies/stop-block-and-tell.html?play.

"Don't Stand By, Stand Up!" Web site. Accessed February 9, 2011. http://www.stopcyberbullying.org/take_action/stop_block_and_tell.html.

Feinberg, Ted, and Nicole Robey. "Cyberbullying." *Education Digest* 74, no. 7 (March 2009): 26–31.

Foderaro, Lisa W. "Private Moment Made Public, Then a Fatal Jump." *New York Times,* September 29, 2010. http://www.nytimes.com/2010/09/30/nyregion/30suicide.html?_r=1.

Goldman, Russell. "Teens Indicted after Allegedly Taunting Girl Who Hanged Herself." *ABC News* Web site. March 29, 2010. http://abcnews.go.com/Technology/TheLaw/teens-charged-bullying-mass-girl-kill/story?id=10231357.

Hinduja, Sameer, and Justin Patchin. "Cyberbullying and Self-esteem." Fact Sheet. Cyberbully Research Center Web site. 2009. http://www.cyberbullying.us/cyberbullying_and_self_esteem_research_fact_sheet.pdf.

Hinduja, Sameer, and Justin W. Patchin. "Cyberbullying: Identification, Prevention, and Response." Fact Sheet. Cyberbullying Research Center Web site. 2010. http://www.cyberbullying.us/Cyberbullying_Identification_Prevention_Response_Fact_Sheet.pdf.

Mishna, Faye, Charlene Cook, Tahany Gadalla, Joanne Daciuk, and Steven Solomon. "Cyber Bullying Behaviors among Middle and High School Students," *American Journal of Orthopsychiatry* 80, no. 3 (July 2010): 362–74.

Sax, Leonard. *Girls on the Edge: The Four Factors Driving the New Crisis for Girls.* New York: Basic Books, 57–61.

"Stop Cyberbullying before It Starts." National Crime Prevention Council Web site. Accessed February 9, 2011. http://www.ncpc.org/resources/files/pdf/bullying/cyberbullying.pdf.

U.S. House of Representatives Education and Labor Committee Hearing on "Ensuring Student Cyber Safety." Testimony by Phillip C. McGraw, Ph.D. June 24, 2010. http://republicans.edlabor.house.gov/UploadedFiles/06.24.10_mcgraw.pdf.

SAMPLE VISUALLY ANNOTATED PERSUASIVE SPEECH

The Importance of Community Engagement and Volunteerism

STEPHANIE POPLIN

University of Oklahoma

In this speech, Stephanie Poplin argues that by volunteering we can enrich our lives (a claim of value). Stephanie organizes the speech using Monroe's five-step motivated sequence pattern. She begins with the attention step, making the speech relevant to listeners. She next points to audience members' innate thirst for fulfillment in life (the need step) and suggests that volunteering can satisfy or solve this need (the satisfaction step). She concludes by directly asking the audience to get involved (the action step).

Stands at attention before the speech

"Great social forces are the mere accumulation of individual actions." Think about that—*"Great social forces are the mere accumulation of individual actions."* This was said by noted economist and antipoverty activist Jeffrey Sachs in a March 2005 *Time* magazine essay about helping the world's poor. And it's true, right? Every great volunteer organization and every great social movement, from the Red Cross to the Peace Corps to the Civil Rights Movement achieved what it did through individual actions, yet all those actions were history changing. •

• Stephanie establishes the *attention step* by stating that listeners have the power to make profound changes in the world.

Appropriate dress—casual but respectful

I'm Stephanie Poplin, and I would like to speak to you today about why it is imperative that you give yourself the opportunity to live a more successful and meaningful life. One way of achieving this is by contributing—by putting yourself into the community that surrounds you. I'm referring to community service and civic engagement. Today, I will talk to you about what you can personally gain from your involvement and participation in your community.

Volunteering may seem like it requires too much time and energy. In truth, it's a requirement for happiness. • Marian Wright Edelman, founder of the Children's Defense Fund, made this observation: "We

• Stephanie introduces the *need step* by claiming that volunteering is a "requirement for happiness."

make a living by what we get, we make a life by what we give." Echoing this, Helen Keller, who was both blind and deaf, yet devoted her life to others, said, "The unselfish effort to bring cheer to others will be the beginning of a happier life for ourselves." •

Now, traditionally, when you hear the words *community service* and *volunteer,* what do you think of? Some of us become confused by "community service," since it can refer to both an alternative to jail time and to an altruistic act of giving to the community. Here I am speaking about the latter. And what about the term *volunteer?* Here, we think of someone who wants to do good—someone who wants to improve the lives of those who are less fortunate. • And while this remains true, attitudes towards volunteering are changing. Volunteers are realizing that in addition to satisfying altruistic goals, community service offers some major personal benefits.

Warm smile connects with audience

In today's job market, for example, it's becoming evident that college graduates need more than just paper qualifications. We'll need to be able to stand out from the crowd, to be resourceful, to be initiators, to be team players, and to possess a get-up-and-go attitude. These are now the desired skills of employers, and volunteering can provide all of this. •

Research bears this out. Student Volunteering UK conducted large-scale research into the benefits of volunteering. Results show that volunteering can enhance employability and develop and strengthen new and different job skills. • In our own country, the Corporation for National and Community Service has found that volunteering makes us better problem solvers, a key trait employers look for. • I think we'd all agree this is a necessity for us, especially given the stages our lives are in right now.

Virtually every paid job can be mirrored by a volunteering opportunity, according to both the Corporation for National and Community Service and Student Volunteering UK. Taking part in community service is a new and pioneering form of work experience. Not only is it seen as work experience, but employers view job applicants who have volunteered as having greater

• Stephanie quotes two credible sources to illustrate her point.

• Stephanie clarifies potentially unclear terms, which is important regardless of speech type.

• She establishes the *need step* by appealing to her listeners' core concerns and self-actualization needs.

• Demonstrating how volunteering can solve our innate need for fulfillment, Stephanie transitions into the *satisfaction step*.

• Stephanie uses sources that her college audience is likely to find credible.

initiative and commitment than applicants without volunteer experience.

Research from Student Volunteering UK and the Corporation for National and Community Service also lists outcomes, other than résumé building, that students felt they had gained through their participation in volunteering. Here's some of what they found: •

- Volunteering built confidence.
- It helped them decide on a career path.
- Making a difference gave them a feeling of exhilaration.
- Their service opened up unexpected opportunities and challenges.

• Stephanie demonstrates the *visualization step,* which reinforces outcomes associated with the solution (volunteering).

Effective hand gesture

Volunteering also benefits physical and emotional health. The Corporation for National and Community Service did a review of recent research on the health benefits of volunteering. It found that volunteering builds social support networks and enhances a sense of achievement and meaning, which in turn leads to lowered rates of depression and even lowered mortality rates.

Just as volunteering can help individuals become happier and healthier, it helps strengthen communities. *Community building* is an incredibly important social outcome of volunteering. According to the Corporation for National and Community Service, volunteers are absolutely crucial to creating and sustaining healthy communities.

Quick pause to check notecard

Fortunately, since the tragedy of 9/11 now nearly a decade ago, as well as the election of President Barack Obama and his call to national service, there has been a surge in student volunteers. • Volunteering has increased so much since 2001 that today's student volunteers are sometimes called the "9/11 generation" by leaders of charitable organizations. The Corporation reports, for example, that each year since 2001, 3.3 million college students—over 30 percent of the college population—gave their time, up from 27 percent before 9/11. Tutoring and mentoring

• Knowing that people tend to adopt a behavior if they know that people like themselves have done so, Stephanie mentions examples of student volunteers.

are the most popular volunteer activities, with 44 percent of students spending at least 12 hours a week on these activities. Students who take service learning courses and who work part-time volunteer more often than those who don't have jobs.

I have experienced the benefits of community service firsthand through my involvement in Habitat for Humanity. • Habitat for Humanity is an international organization fueled by hundreds of thousands of volunteers who join with future homeowners to build simple and affordable houses.

• Still in the *visualization step*, Stephanie offers personal testimony to demonstrate how volunteering can make a real impact.

It wasn't until my first experience building a home, here in Norman, that I realized the impact this organization has on its volunteers and the families involved. I've always had a bedroom of my own to escape to, and I've always had a kitchen to make breakfast in the morning, but there are two little boys who now have this for the first time, thanks to the University of Oklahoma's chapter of Habitat for Humanity. I have always taken my home for granted, but now I can be a part of giving these little boys a home of their own.

Sometimes big changes follow from small events, such as my sheetrocking an empty space that will eventually become a living room that these little boys and their mom and dad can enjoy together. •

• These words link back to the speech's central idea and promote thematic unity.

Brief pause adds emphasis

Someone once told me, "You don't find yourself; you create yourself." As college students, we have every opportunity in the world to create a life that is successful and meaningful. Use your good fortune, and choose to create a life that is service-oriented. • Walk over to OU's Volunteer Programs office on West California, or go to their Web page. You'll find great ways to combine volunteering with earning your degree. You can also go to *Step Up*'s community volunteer network—just Google "Step Up!"—to find volunteer opportunities in your area. Visit the *Habitat for Humanity* Web site and click on "Local Affiliates" to find the branch nearest you. • These are just a few ways to find volunteer opportunities. Many others exist, from countless nonprofits, to houses of worship, to local, state, and federal government programs.

• Here Stephanie transitions to the fifth and final step, the *action step.*

• To encourage action, Stephanie offers contact information for volunteer organizations.

We have seen how you can personally benefit from contributing to your community. • Whether you want to make new friends, improve your job prospects, test a potential career, or build confidence, help build communities, beat depression, and even live longer, volunteering can be the answer. • People who have spent time volunteering report they get back in personal fulfillment and satisfaction more than they ever expend in inconvenience and effort.

We all have the power to make an impact one way or another. After all, "Great social forces are the mere accumulation of individual actions." •

• Stephanie signals the conclusion.

• Stephanie briefly reiterates the main points.

• Stephanie concludes by repeating the quote from the introduction, bringing the speech full circle.

Works Cited

Corporation for National and Community Service. *College Students Helping America*. October 2006. www.nationalservice.gov/pdf/06_1016_RPD_college_full.pdf.

Motivational Quotes. Quotes on Volunteering Page. www.motivationalquotes.com/pages/volunteer-quotes.html.

Sachs, Jeffrey D. "The End of Poverty." *Time*, March 6, 2005.

Student Volunteering UK. *The Art of Crazy Paving: Volunteering for Enhanced Employability*. Accessed January 8, 2008. www.studentvolunteering.org.uk/.

CHAPTER 28

Special Occasion Speeches

Special occasions stand out from the ordinary rhythm of life, marking passages, celebrating life's highlights, and commemorating events. Such occasions often include the observance of important ceremonies and rituals as well as speeches. When it is delivered well, a special occasion speech forges a bond among audience members and helps them put the significance of the occasion in perspective.

Functions of Special Occasion Speeches

WEB Links

There are many kinds of occasions that call for speeches, some serious and some lighthearted. As is evidenced by its name, a **special occasion speech** is one that is prepared for a specific occasion and for a purpose dictated by that occasion. In the special occasion speech, the rhetorical situation truly gives rise to the speech content. Dedication ceremonies call for speeches that pay tribute. Awards ceremonies call for presentation speeches that acknowledge accomplishments, and acceptance speeches that display gratitude.

Special occasion speeches can be informative or persuasive or a mix of both. However, neither of these functions is the main goal; the underlying function of a special occasion speech is to entertain, celebrate, commemorate, inspire, or set a social agenda.

Entertainment

Many kinds of special occasions call for a speech that entertains. Banquets, awards dinners, and roasts, for example, frequently feature speakers whose main purpose is to entertain those in attendance. In such cases, listeners expect a lighthearted speech that amuses them. Depending on the event, they may also expect the speaker to offer a certain degree of insight into the topic at hand.

Celebration

Often a special occasion speech will celebrate a person, a place, or an event. Weddings, anniversaries, retirement parties, and awards banquets all call for speeches that recognize the person(s) or event being celebrated. The audience expects the speaker to praise the subject of the celebration and to cast him or her in a positive light. The listeners also expect a certain degree of ceremony in accordance with the norms of the occasion.

Commemoration

Certain special occasion speeches, called *commemorative speeches,* focus on remembrance and tribute. Commemorative speeches mark important anniversaries, such as the fiftieth anniversary of the landing of Allied troops in Normandy or the anniversary of the shootings at Virginia Tech. Speakers deliver commemorative speeches about events or people of note at memorials dedicated to them or at gatherings otherwise held in their honor.

Inspiration

Inaugural addresses, keynote speeches at conventions, and commencement speeches all have inspiration as their main function. With their examples of achievement and heroism, many commemorative speeches also inspire audiences as well as pay homage to the person or event being commemorated.

Social Agenda–Setting

Yet another function of the special occasion speech is social agenda–setting—establishing or reinforcing the goals and values of the group sponsoring the event. Occasions that call for agenda-setting speeches include gatherings of issues or cause-oriented organizations, fundraisers, campaign banquets, conferences, and conventions. Speakers asked to deliver keynote addresses at conferences or conventions are charged with establishing the theme of the meeting and with offering a plan of action related to that theme. Similarly, politically oriented organizations also routinely hold meetings at which invited speakers perform the function of agenda-setting.

Types of Special Occasion Speeches Video

Special occasion speeches include (but are not limited to) speeches of introduction, speeches of acceptance, award presentations, roasts and toasts, eulogies and other speeches of tribute, after-dinner speeches, and speeches of inspiration.

Speeches of Introduction

A **speech of introduction** is a short speech with two goals: to prepare or "warm up" the audience for the speaker, and to motivate audience members to listen to what the main speaker has to say. Many occasions call for speeches of introduction. You might be asked to introduce a guest speaker at a monthly meeting of a social organization to which you belong, to introduce an award presenter at your company's annual banquet, or to introduce an outside expert at a quarterly sales meeting. A good speech of introduction balances four elements: the speaker's background, the subject of the speaker's message, the occasion, and the audience.

Describe the Speaker's Background

A key part of the introducer's task is to tell the audience something about the speaker's background and qualifications for speaking. The object is to heighten audience interest and build the speaker's credibility. If you don't know the speaker personally, ask the speaker to describe important achievements, offices held, and other activities that will show audience members what kind of speaker they are about to hear and why they should listen.

Briefly Preview the Speaker's Topic

Part of the introducer's job is to give audience members a sense of why the speaker's subject is of interest to them. Is the subject timely? What significance does it have for the audience? What special connections exist between the subject or the speaker and the occasion? Is he or she an expert on the topic? Why was the speaker invited? Keep in mind, however, that it is not the introducer's job to evaluate the speech or otherwise offer critical commentary on it. *The rule is: Get in and out quickly with a few well-chosen remarks.* Introducers who linger on their own thoughts run the risk of stealing the speaker's thunder.

Ask the Audience to Welcome the Speaker

A final part of the introducer's task is to cue the audience to welcome the speaker. This can be done very simply by saying something like "Please welcome Anthony Svetlana." Hearing this, the audience will provide applause, thereby paving the way for the speaker to take his or her place at the podium.

In the following excerpt from a speech by Frank D. Stella, of F. D. Stella Products Company, Stella introduces Richard A. Grasso, former chairman and chief executive officer of the New York Stock Exchange, to the Economic Club of Detroit. Notice how Stella makes use of the date of the occasion—April 15, or income tax day—to engage the audience. Stella also provides a quick overview of who the speaker is and a reference to why he was a good choice for this occasion.

> Happy April 15! This may be only a quirk of history, but do you realize that not only is today Tax Day, it is also the anniversary of the sinking of the *Titanic*! Talk about double jeopardy!
>
> It's interesting, therefore, that we have scheduled today's speaker for April 15: If your company or individual stock did well and was listed on the New York Stock Exchange, you can, in part, thank Dick Grasso for keeping the Exchange so strong and competitive; but if your taxes went up because your stocks did so well, you can thank Dick for capital gains, the market upsurge, and profitability.
>
> It is a distinct honor for me to introduce Richard A. Grasso, chairman and chief executive officer of the New York Stock Exchange. He has enjoyed a remarkable 28-year-career at the Exchange. [Mr. Stella goes on to provide a more detailed background on Mr. Grasso.][1]

Respond to Introductions

Speakers who have been introduced should respond to the introduction in some way. Acknowledging and thanking the introducer is the most common method. For example:

- I appreciate those kind words.
- Thank you for making me feel welcome today.
- This is a wonderful event, and I appreciate being a part of it.

Most of us are not used to being publicly honored, and accepting praise and accolades from a speaker who introduces us can be awkward. One of the ways to show your humility toward a gracious introduction is through humor:

- That introduction was so gracious; you were more than halfway through it before I realized you were talking about me.[2]
- Thank you, Mr. Secretary, for that incredible introduction. If I had known you were going to eulogize me, I would have done the only decent thing and died.[3]
- I'm really not as good as she said, but neither am I as bad as my mother-in-law thinks. So I guess it averages out.[4]

GUIDELINES FOR INTRODUCING OTHER SPEAKERS

_____ 1. Identify the speaker correctly. Assign him or her the proper title, such as "vice president for public relations" or "professor emeritus."

_____ 2. Practice difficult-to-pronounce names several times before actually introducing the speaker.

_____ 3. Contact the speaker ahead of time to verify the accuracy of any facts about him or her that you plan to cite.

_____ 4. Consider devices that will capture the audience's attention, such as quotes, short anecdotes, and startling statements (see Chapter 15).

CHECKLIST

Speeches of Acceptance

A **speech of acceptance** is made in response to receiving an award of some sort. Its purpose is to express gratitude for the honor bestowed on the speaker. The speech should reflect that gratitude.

Prepare

If you know that you will be given an award, be sure to prepare an acceptance speech. Because the award is not a surprise, the audience will probably expect a fairly sophisticated acceptance speech. If you think it is at all likely that you will receive an award, prepare in advance so that your acceptance will go smoothly and you can avoid using standard responses such as "I really just don't know what to say."

React Genuinely and with Humility

Genuineness and humility are possibly the most important parts of expressing gratitude. Offering a sincere response shows your audience how much the award means to you. If you are surprised to receive the award, show it. If you are not surprised, don't try to feign excitement. Explain why the award is important to you and describe the value you place on it. Tell your listeners how it will affect your future and how it gives meaning to whatever you did in the past that led to its receipt. Express your gratitude with humility, acknowledging your good fortune in having received it.

Thank Those Giving the Award

Even though the attention is focused on you, don't forget to express your gratitude to the people who are giving you the award. If the award is given by an organization, specifically thank that organization. If it is given by a combination of organizations, remember to mention all of them. If there is a sponsor of the award, such as a donor that makes the award possible, remember to acknowledge the donor as well.

Thank Others Who Helped You

If the reason for your award represents a team effort, be sure to thank all members. If there are people who gave you the inspiration that helped you achieve the award, thank them.

Speeches of Presentation

The job of presenting an award can be an honor in itself. Whether you are presenting a bowling trophy or a Grammy music award, your goal in the **speech of presentation** is twofold: to communicate the meaning of the award and to explain why the recipient is receiving it.

GUIDELINES FOR DELIVERING SPEECHES OF ACCEPTANCE

_____ 1. Prepare an acceptance speech in advance of the event.

_____ 2. Explain why the award is important to you.

_____ 3. Express your gratitude to the people who are giving you the award.

_____ 4. Thank those who helped you attain the achievement.

_____ 5. Do not belabor your acknowledgments.

_____ 6. Accept the award gracefully by showing that you value it.

_____ 7. End your speech with an explicit expression of gratitude.

CHECKLIST

Convey the Meaning of the Award

It is the presenter's task to explain the meaning of the award to the audience. What is the award for? What kind of achievement does it celebrate? Who or what does the award represent? What is the significance of its special name or title? You might offer a brief history of the award, such as when it was founded and the names of some of its previous recipients. Because you are a presenter, it is also your job to identify the sponsors or organizations that made the award possible and to describe the link between the sponsor's goals and values and the award.

The following excerpt is a common way of communicating to the audience the significance of an award:

> It is an honor and a privilege to be the one making this presentation today. This plaque is only a token of our appreciation for Seamus's achievements, but we hope that this symbol will serve as a daily reminder of our admiration for his great work. Let me read the inscription. "Seamus O'Leary, in appreciation for the outstanding work. . . ."

Talk about the Recipient of the Award

The second part of the presenter's task is to explain why the recipient is receiving the award. Tell the audience why the recipient has been singled out for special recognition. Describe this person's achievements, the kind of work he or she does, and special attributes that qualify him or her as deserving of the award. Explain how the recipient was selected. What kind of selection process was used? The following example illustrates how this can be done:

> And, I might add, these were just some of the accomplishments of Carol Prodnya. When the selection committee reviewed all the nominees (some eighty-four of them), it became clear that Carol would be our choice. The committee met four times to narrow the list of nominees, and at each meeting it was clear who our winner would be. The other nominees were outstanding in their own right, but Carol stood apart in many ways.

Roasts and Toasts

A **roast** is a humorous tribute to a person, one in which a series of speakers jokingly poke fun at him or her. A **toast** is a brief tribute to a person or an event being celebrated. Both roasts and toasts call for short speeches whose goal is to celebrate an individual and his or her achievements. Should you be asked to speak at such events, it will be helpful to follow these guidelines.

Prepare

Remember that the audience is looking to you to set the tone and to express the purpose of the gathering. Being caught off guard and stammering for something to say can really let the air out of your speech and make it less than meaningful. Also, remember that others who speak before you may use material you had planned to use. Don't be alarmed. Make reference to this fact and put a different spin on it.

Before delivering a roast or a toast, many speakers rehearse in front of a trusted friend or friends. This is especially helpful if you are considering telling a joke that you are unsure about. Practicing with friends also allows them to time your speech. People often speak much longer than they realize.

Highlight Remarkable Traits of the Person Being Honored

Because these speeches are usually short, try to restrict your remarks to one or two of the most unique or recognizable attributes of the person. Convey what sets this person apart—the qualities that have made him or her worthy of celebrating. In other words, what would you want said about you if you were being honored?

Be Positive and Be Brief

Even if the speech pokes fun at someone, as in a roast, keep the tone good natured and positive. Remember, the overall purpose of your speech is to pay tribute to the honoree. It's great to have fun, but avoid saying anything that might embarrass the person being honored. Doing so could turn what should be a festive atmosphere into an uncomfortable situation. Also, be considerate of the other speakers by refraining from taking up too much time. This is particularly important for toasts, which are expected to be very short.

Eulogies and Other Tributes

The word **eulogy** derives from the Greek word meaning "to praise." Those delivering eulogies, usually close friends or family members of the deceased, are charged with celebrating and commemorating the life of someone while consoling those who have been left behind. Given these goals, the eulogy can be one of the most difficult and challenging special occasion speeches to deliver. At the same time, probably more people with little or no experience in public speaking deliver a eulogy at one time or another than any other type of special occasion speech.

Should you be called upon to give a eulogy, the following guidelines will help to ensure an effective speech.

Balance Delivery and Emotions

Many speakers fight the tendency to become overly emotional in a eulogy. Despite the sense of grief the speaker may be feeling, his or her job is to help others feel better. The audience looks to the speaker for guidance in dealing with the loss, and for a sense of closure. Therefore, it is essential to stay in control. Showing intense grief will probably make the audience feel worse. If you do feel that you are about to break down, pause, take a breath, and focus on your next thought.

Refer to the Family of the Deceased

Families suffer the greatest loss, and a funeral is primarily for their benefit. Make sure your presentation shows respect for the family; mention each family member by name. Make it clear that the deceased was an important part of a family by humanizing that family.

inspirational in nature. In the business world, occasions for inspirational speeches are so frequent that some people earn their living as inspirational speakers. A **speech of inspiration** seeks to uplift the members of the audience and to help them see things in a positive light. Effective speeches of inspiration touch on deep feelings in the audience. Their emotional force is such that our better instincts are aroused. They urge us toward purer motives and harder effort and remind us of a common good.

Thus, as in a persuasive speech, to create an effective inspirational speech you'll need to appeal to the audience's emotions (pathos) and display positive ethos. Two means of evoking emotion, or pathos, are *vivid description* and *emotionally charged words* (see Chapter 25). These and other techniques of language, such as repetition, alliteration, and parallelism, can help transport the audience from the mundane to a loftier level (see Chapter 17).

Use Real-Life Stories

Another way to inspire listeners is through real-life examples and stories. Few things move us as much as the example of the ordinary person who achieves the extraordinary, whose struggles result in triumph over adversity and the realization of a dream. Recognizing this, in their State of the Union addresses several recent U.S. presidents have taken to weaving stories about "ordinary American heroes" into their remarks.

Be Dynamic

If it fits your personality, use a dynamic speaking style to inspire not only through content but through delivery as well. An energetic style can do a great deal to motivate the audience; when it is combined with a powerful message, this can be one of the most successful strategies for inspirational speaking.

Make Your Goal Clear

Inspirational speeches run the risk of being vague, leaving the audience unsure about what the message was. Make sure that the audience cannot mistake your message for something else. Whatever you are trying to motivate your listeners to do, let them know. If you are speaking about a general goal, such as remaining positive in life, let your listeners know that. If you are trying to motivate your listeners to perform a specific action, such as donating money to a particular charity, clearly tell them so.

Consider a Distinctive Organizing Device

Many successful inspirational speakers, especially those in the business world, use devices such as *acronyms* or steps to organize their speeches. This clarifies the organizational pattern of the speech and helps the audience to remember the message. For example, a football coach speaking at a practice session might organize a short inspirational speech around the word *win*. His main points might be Work, Intensity, and No excuses, forming the acronym WIN. This device emphasizes the goal of the constituent elements of the speech. All three are aimed at winning games.

Here is an example of using steps. Giving an inspirational speech titled "Give Your Life a Dream with Design" to a graduating high school class, David Magill organized his presentation around three steps: "1. Design Your Vision," "2. Just Do It," and "3. Dig Deeper." Magill introduced his main points by saying, "My advice is simple, has three steps, and is easy to remember because the operative word in each step begins with the same letter with which *dream* begins—the letter *D*."[6]

Close with a Dramatic Ending

Using a dramatic ending is one of the best means of inspiring your audience to feel or act in the ways suggested by the theme of your speech. Recall from Chapter 16 the various methods of concluding a speech, including with a quotation, story, rhetorical question, or call to action.

DELIVERING A SUCCESSFUL SPEECH OF INSPIRATION

_____ 1. Focus the speech on uplifting the audience.

_____ 2. Seek to arouse the audience's better instincts.

_____ 3. Use emotional appeals.

_____ 4. Concentrate on creating positive speaker ethos (see Chapter 25).

_____ 5. Appeal to the audience's emotions through vivid description and emotionally charged words.

_____ 6. Consider the use of repetition, alliteration, and parallelism (see Chapter 17).

_____ 7. Consider using real-life stories and examples.

_____ 8. Strive for a dynamic style of delivery.

_____ 9. Clearly establish your speech goal.

_____ 10. Consider using an acronym to organize your inspirational message.

_____ 11. Make your conclusion strong.

CHECKLIST

ETHICALLY SPEAKING

Tailor Your Message to the Audience and Occasion

More so than in other kinds of speeches, audience expectation that the speaker will fulfill a specific need is quite high in the special occasion speech. People listening to a eulogy, for example, will be very sensitive to what they perceive to be inappropriate use of humor or a lack of respect shown to the deceased. Those attending a dedication ceremony for a war memorial will expect the speaker to offer words of inspiration. When a speaker violates audience expectations in situations like these, audience reaction is usually pronounced. When giving a special occasion speech, it is therefore critical to plan your speech with audience expectations firmly in mind.

SAMPLE VISUALLY ANNOTATED SPECIAL OCCASION SPEECH

"Love the Process": A Soccer Star's Philosophy of Life

YAEL AVERBUCH

U.S. Women's National Soccer Team

In this special occasion speech, soccer player Yael Averbuch addresses a gathering of women's soccer coaches at the National Soccer Coaches Association of America Soccer Breakfast in Philadelphia, Pennsylvania, on January 21, 2010. Averbuch's speech, which is inspirational in nature, describes her realization that she values the long-term process of playing the sport more than winning a particular game or championship. Averbuch is a member of the U.S. Women's National Soccer team, a player in the Women's Professional Soccer (WPS) league, and a member of the 2009 WPS Championship team, Sky Blue FC. She was a two-time NCAA Championship team member at the University of North Carolina, and recipient of the 2008 NCAA VIII, a top honor recognizing eight college seniors nationwide for athletic/academic/community achievement.

Good morning everyone. I'd like to start by thanking the women's committee for inviting me here today and to congratulate Louise Waxler on the Award of Excellence. . . . ●

When I was first asked to speak in front of this group, I have to be honest, I was slightly overwhelmed. Many of you in this room are the ones to whom I look for wisdom, and who have provided life-changing guidance to me over the years. ●

As I started to jot down some ideas, I realized that the person I am today is the result of so many different elements—elements I've picked up from some of the very people who I am standing in front of right now. ● These elements form the essence of what has become my passion.

Briefly reviews notes before taking the podium

Ever since I was a 9-year-old, attempting to get 10 thigh juggles on my front lawn, it has been my dream to be a professional soccer player. As a little girl, in my Mia Hamm jersey, I had no concept of exactly

● In a special occasion speech, it is important to acknowledge persons who are being honored.

● Averbuch offers respect to her audience of coaches.

● Averbuch again acknowledges her debt to the coaches of her sport.

what that meant. There was no way I could have imagined what lay ahead, what it would take, or how I would get there.

But I knew what I wanted, and my goals have never wavered. Roughly a year ago, my childhood dream became reality when I signed my first professional contract with Sky Blue FC.

As a 23-year-old professional player, and current member of the Women's National Team, I still see my journey as far from complete. Some people may look at my résumé and think I've "arrived," but I see my career as just beginning. It's a strange feeling to finally accomplish a goal for which you have sweat, bled, and cried for nearly 15 years to achieve. I would have expected to feel overjoyed—even just simply content.

But while I am very proud of what I have achieved to this point, none of those emotions are fitting. As I embarked on my first professional season, at times I almost felt a sense of disappointment. I found myself thinking, "Is this really IT?" It was in uncovering the answer to this question that I came to truly realize why I do what I do. . . . ●

● Averbuch segues into her thesis.

Since the summer of 2000, when I was 12 years old and away from home at the UNC summer camp, I've kept a journal . . . which has since then expanded into five written books . . . filled with my thoughts, worries, goals, disappointments, and successes. . . . There is an entry from December of 1999 in which I recorded parts of a conversation I had with my first real mentor, and coach at the time, Ashley Hammond. Under his name, I have the following quote: "People in the world need and love experts. In soccer, you must be an expert in many skills." I was 13 when I wrote that down.

A well-placed pause, with eye contact, helps Averbuch emphasize her central idea

Every month, I like to set myself 4 or 5 personal goals or ideas to keep in mind. I start off by choosing a quote or motto as a theme for the month, and then I pick a few simple goals to aim for. For example, . . . my December 2009 phrase captures what I have finally come to realize is most important in my quest for greatness in soccer. December's motto was: "love the process." ●

● Here Averbuch explicitly states her thesis, which is that she loves the process of being a soccer player most of all.

This concept has come to mean something very important to me. . . . [N]ow that soccer is my profession, I have found that

I need to put it in greater perspective within my life. The best way I have come to define my drive is this: I work TOWARDS a goal, but I do not work FOR it. . . .

I don't consider what I do as work, because every day that I train and compete, I find even greater joy in the process.

I believe that finding this joy, and loving the process itself, is essential. To truly be the best at what you do, the path will never be easy. The love of what we do is what provides the inspiration to see us through. My path to where I am today hasn't always been smooth. . . .

A glance down at her notes helps Averbuch jog her memory without interrupting the flow of the speech

And every time that I think I've reached smooth sailing, I am soon humbled. I was very confident going into this past WPS season. I was a first-round draft pick, felt well prepared after my college career at UNC, and had done everything that I could to be ready for pre-season. . . . Before our home opener against the LA Sol, I was shocked when we got the starting lineup and I wasn't in it. . . . I assumed I'd play the second half, considering that I thought I was going to start, but wasn't in the lineup. . . . I was honestly shocked, and devastated. There will never be another inaugural season Sky Blue FC home opener, and I hadn't even gotten the opportunity to step onto the field in front of my home crowd.

It's interesting to contemplate how our lives build to these special, pivotal moments—the moments we dream of, work towards, and emphasize so heavily. • But, in truth, the bulk of our life is in the in-between time, the waiting. The "off moments," so to speak. The special moments are only minor reference points along the way. After an extremely angry and disappointed drive home from that Sky Blue FC opener, that is what I came to realize. I don't play this sport for the moment of glory.

• Averbuch's inclusive language ("our") brings speaker and audience together in a common purpose.

And I think the people who DO are missing out. Yes, I love the roar of the crowd, the championship game, and the thrill of performing when it really matters—but I love the preparation—the process—equally as much.

I didn't always love the game the way I do now. I learned that love, just as I've learned numerous other skills. I feel very fortunate to have had great coaches and mentors along the way. . . .

I'm not trying to claim that I am always happy, smiling, and joyous when it comes to soccer. I take my goals and my career extremely seriously, and at times, it is very stressful, because I care SO much. I'm sure it's the same for most of you in this room. Sometimes, my entire life seems to revolve around soccer and my training. . . .

During the past WPS season, I read the book *Way of the Peaceful Warrior,* by Dan Millman. A major premise of the book is this line: "It's not about dedicating your life to training, but about dedicating your training to your life." •

This was an interesting new perspective for me. Yes, I dedicate an astounding number of my waking hours to soccer. Whether I'm training, watching soccer, or even just thinking about it, my life is consumed by the game. But what does this all mean in the bigger picture? I find that for what I put INTO the game . . . I get back tenfold. . . .

My training gives back to me in ways deeper than just success on the field. There is a sense of freedom, of peace, that I feel when I have a soccer ball at my feet. . . . We've all experienced it—the perfectly pure, uncompromised joy of being here, now. It is the moment of peace when all else fades away, and you are left fearless and energized. • It's often described as "flow" or being "in the zone," but whatever you call it, we are all familiar with that sensation—when you're doing something enjoyable, and it just comes so easily.

This feeling for me doesn't necessarily come in a moment of glory, in the last five minutes of a game, or in a winning play. It's born from the passion of what I do when it "doesn't matter," when no one is watching, when nothing is at stake.

I find this feeling in the process, more often than I do in the result. I was reminded of this the night my college soccer career ended. We had just won the 2008 National Championship, and I sat in my room in Chapel Hill, actually feeling depressed, rather than satisfied. The team was out celebrating, and all I could seem to think about was the fact that it was finished. That was it. All those Tuesdays of doing fitness, all the excruciating pre-game meetings, the effort, nerves,

> • Averbuch offers an inspirational quotation to emphasize her theme.

> • Averbuch's frequent use of the personal pronouns "we" and "you" fosters inclusiveness.

preparation to win a national championship, and it was over. Just like that. I felt like I would have given back my national championship to spend just one more week with the team. The more I thought about it, the more it dawned on me. It was the PROCESS of winning that I loved, not so much the actual win. •

And when I think back on my life since I began playing soccer, the seemingly unimportant moments are the ones that come to mind first. It's the videos I watched with my dad to learn about the game, and all our ridiculously naïve ideas on how things should be done.

Professional attire and upright posture show respect for the occasion and honorees

. . . It's the times playing on my own in the racquetball court, lost in the music of my iPod, when management would actually turn out the lights on me when my time was up.

. . . It's the time spent in parking garages, and basements of hotels, practicing tricks I had seen . . . or making up silly ways of training in the house when it was snowing outside.

. . . It's these moments that comprise the process, and that are most special to me. •

As I learned the night of the 2008 National Championship, if everything that you do, day in and day out, is solely building for a single moment—what becomes of it all when that moment has passed? It is this perspective that I have gained during the past year, and which I hope to carry with me throughout my life: Ideally, what we do in each moment should have value in and of itself. We should train just for the sake of training, play just for the sake of playing, and live just for the sake of living.

Winning is a process. Success is a process. Happiness is a process. And this point in my career is only one sliver of time within my process. . . . •

I have a tremendous amount of respect for everyone in this room, because you have the platform to shape players' journeys. You might never know the little things you do that will change a person's life. Maybe it's as simple as a smile at the right time. . . . Even on the days when you feel like your athletes or co-workers couldn't care less, and that no one is listening, there's

● Telling a story effectively engages the audience's attention.

● Beginning three successive sentences with the same or a similar phrase ("It's the time . . .") lends rhythm to the speech.

● The speaker reiterates her theme.

that one player in the group whose eyes light up when you speak, who is hanging on your every word, who will quote you in her journal. Coach for that player.

[Coach] Anson writes each senior a personal note before they're finished playing for him. I know my letter talks about soccer, national championships, and player of the year awards, but the following passage from the letter is what I have recorded in my journal, and what means more to me than anything else he could have said. Anson wrote:

> . . . Of all your wonderful achievements, what I cherish most is the lasting effect you have had on our culture here. You made sure everything was fun. Sometimes, in the fight for athletic success, many of us lose sight of what this is all about, and you never let us.

So, when I reflect back on the 15 years I've spent so far involved in this game, and the lifetime ahead I plan to, I hope to have an impressive list of accomplishments. I want to defend the WPS Championship, win a World Cup, and an Olympic gold medal. But when all is said and done, it is not only those accolades that I will cherish.

I will always smile when I think about the time at UNC when we were about to start our first of 10 cones (a dreaded fitness drill) and, as Anson yelled "GO!" we all fell to the ground as a joke.

I will always look forward to being home in New Jersey, where I can go kick the ball around at the local schoolyard with my sister.

I will always feel sentimental when I think about playing pickup on Fetzer Field (our UNC game field) in Chapel Hill at midnight, under the single light that's left on.

I will always laugh when I reminisce on the absurdity and turbulence of Sky Blue FC's first season, when, it seems, we had more coaches than are currently sitting in this room. •

These are the things that I love most about this game, because for me it's about the journey, not the destination.

Averbuch pans to all corners of the room to connect with the entire audience

• Averbuch once again uses the technique of anaphora—repeating the same phrase at the beginning of successive sentences—to make her conclusion memorable.

SPEAKING BEYOND THE SPEECH CLASSROOM

SPEAKING BEYOND THE SPEECH CLASSROOM

SPEAKER'S REFERENCE

CHAPTER **29** Preparing Online Presentations 435

Online and Face-to-Face Speaking: How Do They Compare? 435
▶ **CHECKLIST** Tools for Developing Online Presentations 437
Real-Time versus Recorded: Plan for the Delivery Mode 438
Online Presentation Formats: From Single Speaker to Panel 440
Online Presentation Platforms: From Podcast to Webinar 442
▶ **CHECKLIST** Creating a Podcast 443
Online Presentations Checklist: Planning Ahead 444
▶ **CHECKLIST** Steps in Preparing an Online Presentation 445

CHAPTER **30** Collaborating and Presenting in Groups 446

Becoming an Effective Group Participant 446
Adopting an Effective Leadership Style 448
▶ **CHECKLIST** Guidelines for Setting Group Goals 449
Making Presentations in Teams 450
▶ **CHECKLIST** Team Presentation Tips 452

CHAPTER **31** Speaking in Other College Courses 453

Presentational versus Public Speaking 453
Typical Speaking Assignments across the Curriculum 454
▶ **CHECKLIST** Tips for Winning a Debate 456
Presenting to Different Audiences 457
▶ **CHECKLIST** Tips on Presenting to a Mixed Audience 458
Speaking in Science and Mathematics Courses 458
▶ **SELF-ASSESSMENT CHECKLIST** Evaluating Your Original Research Presentation 460
▶ **CHECKLIST** Tips for Preparing Successful Scientific Presentations 461
Speaking in Technical Courses 462
Speaking in Social Science Courses 464
Speaking in Arts and Humanities Courses 466
Speaking in Education Courses 468
Speaking in Nursing and Allied Health Courses 469

CHAPTER **32** **Business and Professional Presentations** 472

The Case Study 472

Sales Presentations 472

▶ **ESL SPEAKER'S NOTES** Steps to Counteract Problems in Being Understood 473

▶ **CHECKLIST** Applying Monroe's Motivated Sequence in a Sales Presentation 474

Proposals 474

▶ **CHECKLIST** Preparing a Proposal 475

Staff Reports 475

Progress Reports 476

Crisis-Response Presentations 477

▶ **ETHICALLY SPEAKING** Code of Ethics for Professional Communicators 478

SPEAKING BEYOND THE SPEECH CLASSROOM

CHAPTER 29 Preparing Online Presentations

Recognize Similarities between Face-to-Face and Online Presentations

- Keep in mind your general speech purpose: to inform, persuade, or address a special occasion. (p. 435)
- Maintain an audience-centered approach. (p. 435)
- Provide credible supporting materials as well as a natural style of delivery. (p. 435)

Plan for the Unique Aspects of Online Speaking

- Anticipate the audience's technical ability to receive the presentation. (p. 436)
- Keep audience attention with clear pronunciation, variation in pitch and speaking rate, and meaningful "virtual body language." (p. 437)
- Provide engaging presentation aids that enhance the presentation. (p. 437)
- Get in plenty of practice time. (p. 437)

Understand the Advantages and Limitations of Real-Time and Recorded Presentations

- Real-time presentations allow for immediate feedback and a more personal delivery although they are best suited to use within the same or across proximate time zones. (p. 438)
- Recorded presentations can be recorded at any point and provide long-term availability; however, the speaker does not directly interact with the audience. (p. 439)

Choose a Meaningful Format for Structuring Your Presentation

- Select a single-speaker presentation format when you have a specific message to deliver, when you are sought out as a credible source, or when you serve as a spokesperson. (p. 440)
- Implement a speaker-audience interactive presentation when you wish to fully engage audience members via audio or video connectivity, perhaps using interactive tools to share ideas about a topic. (p. 440)

- Interview-style presentations may be used when the interviewer is a person already known and credible to the audience, who offers questions on behalf of the audience to the interviewee. (p. 441)
- A moderated panel presentation includes three or more people in a discussion, with one person serving as the moderator. (p. 441)

Choose among Several Different Online Technologies to Deliver Your Presentation

- Video is one of the most common ways people get their message out. (p. 442)
- Podcasts may be used when video recording is unnecessary or overly complex. (p. 442)
- Webinars connect presenters and audiences from their desktops regardless of where they are. (p. 444)
- Graphical presentations may often be used for training purposes. (p. 444)

CHAPTER 30 Collaborating and Presenting in Groups

Keep Your Focus on the Goal(s) of the Group

- Keep in mind that your purpose is to address a specific issue. (p. 446)
- Critically evaluate information in light of the group's goals. (p. 446)
- Create and follow an agenda. (p. 446)

Center Disagreements on Issues Rather Than Personalities

- Engage in issues-based conflict, not personal-based conflict. (p. 447)

Don't Accept Information and Ideas Uncritically Merely to Get Along

- Resist groupthink. (p. 448)
- Apply critical thinking skills to solve the problem at hand. (p. 448)
- Engage in devil's advocacy and dialectical inquiry. (p. 448)

As Leader, Set Goals and Identify the Problem

- Set a performance goal. (p. 448)
- Identify the resources necessary to achieving the goal. (p. 449)
- Recognize contingencies that may arise. (p. 449)
- Obtain feedback. (p. 449)

As Leader, Encourage Active Participation among Group Members

- Directly ask members to contribute. (p. 449)
- Redirect the discussion. (p. 449)
- Set a positive tone. (p. 449)

Adopt the Six-Step Framework for Making Decisions and Reaching Goals

- Identify the problem. (p. 449)
- Conduct research and analysis. (p. 449)
- Establish guidelines and criteria. (p. 449)
- Generate solutions. (p. 449)
- Select the best solution. (p. 449)
- Evaluate solutions. (p. 449)

Expect to Prepare and Deliver Team Presentations

CHAPTER 31 Speaking in Other College Courses

Expect to Prepare Oral Presentations in a Variety of Formats

- You will be asked to prepare both *individual* and *team presentations*. (p. 454)
- You may engage in *debates*. (p. 454)
- You may prepare *poster sessions*. (p. 456)

Expect to Adjust Your Presentations for Various On-the-Job Audiences

- Expert or insider audience. (p. 457)
- Colleagues within the field. (p. 457)
- Lay audience. (p. 457)
- Mixed audience. (p. 457)

In Science and Mathematics Courses, Expect to Present the Results of Experiments or Solutions to Problems

- The *research (oral scientific) presentation* describes original research you have done, either alone or as part of a team. (p. 458)

- The *methods/procedure presentation* describes and sometimes demonstrates an experimental or mathematical process, including the conditions under which the report can be applied. (p. 459)
- The *research overview presentation* provides context and background for a research question or hypothesis that will form the basis of an impending undertaking. (p. 460)
- The *field study presentation* describes an extended field study or research project. (p. 460)

Ground Scientific and Mathematical Presentations in the Scientific Method

- Provide detailed information about the methods used in gathering and analyzing data. (p. 461)
- Be prepared to use observations, proofs, and experiments as support for the presentation. (p. 461)
- Be selective in your choice of details. (p. 461)
- Use analogies to build on prior knowledge. (p. 461)
- Use presentation aids. (p. 461)

In Technical Courses such as Engineering, Computer Science, and Architecture, Expect to Describe Projects

- *Engineering* and *architecture design reviews* report on the results of a design project. (p. 462)
- The *request for funding presentation* provides evidence that a project is worth funding. (p. 463)
- Incorporate diagrams, prototypes, and other aids into the technical presentation. (p. 463)

In Social Science Courses, Expect to Focus on Qualitative and Quantitative Research

- Be prepared to describe experiments, naturalistic observations, case studies, and surveys. (p. 464)
- Expect to explain social or psychological phenomena by answering *what, how,* and *why* questions. (p. 464)

In Social Science Courses, Expect to Review and Evaluate the Research

- The *review of the literature presentation* examines the body of research related to a given topic or issue and offers conclusions about the topic based on this research. (p. 464)

- The *theoretical research presentation* reports on studies that attempt to analyze and explain a phenomenon, such as teen alcohol abuse or infant neglect. (p. 464)
- The *evaluation research presentation* examines the effectiveness of programs developed to address various issues. (p. 465)
- The *policy recommendation report* offers recommendations to solve a problem or address an issue. (p. 465)

In Arts and Humanities Courses, Focus on Interpreting and Analyzing the Topic

- Explain in an informative speech the relevance of a historical or contemporary person or event; a school of philosophical thought; or a piece of literature, music, or art. (p. 466)
- Compare and contrast events, stories, artifacts, or people in order to highlight the similarities or differences between them. (p. 466)
- Engage in debates. (p. 467)
- Research a topic and then lead a classroom discussion on it. (p. 467)

In Education Courses, Expect to Prepare Lectures and to Lead Group Activities and Classroom Discussions

- Pay careful attention to organizing and supporting presentations in education courses. (p. 469)
- Demonstrate how material in the lecture relates to the overall course content. (p. 469)
- Use student-friendly examples as evidence and support. (p. 469)

In Nursing and Allied Health Courses, Expect to Address a Range of Audiences on Health-Care Practices and Techniques

- You may be assigned a *community service learning project,* in which you report on the agency and its client base and your role in the project. (p. 470)
- You may prepare a *case conference,* in which you describe the patient's status, outline steps for treatment, review financial needs, and assess resources. (p. 470)
- You may be assigned a *shift report,* in which you give an oncoming caregiver a concise report of the patient's needs and status. (p. 470)
- You may prepare a *policy recommendation report,* in which you recommend a new or modified health plan or policy. (p. 470)

CHAPTER 32 Business and Professional Presentations

Prepare a *Sales Presentation* to Persuade Potential Buyers to Purchase a Service or Product

- Consider basing the organization of your sales presentation on Monroe's motivated sequence. (p. 474)

    Draw the potential buyer's attention to the product.

    Isolate and clarify the buyer's need for the product.

    Describe how the product will satisfy the buyer's need.

    Invite the buyer to purchase the product.

Prepare a *Proposal* When Promoting an Idea, a Product, or a Procedure

- Organize lengthy proposals as follows. (p. 475)

    Introduce and state the problem.

    Describe the method of inquiry.

    Describe the facts learned.

    Offer explanations and interpretations of the findings.

    Offer recommendations.

- Organize brief proposals as follows. (p. 475)

    State the recommendations.

    Offer a brief overview of the problem.

    Review the facts on which the recommendations are based.

    Offer 1–3 recommendations.

Prepare a *Staff Report* When Informing Personnel of Developments Affecting Them and When Reporting on the Completion of a Task

- Organize the staff report as follows. (p. 476)

    State the issue.

    Provide a description of procedures and facts used in addressing the issue.

    Discuss facts that are most pertinent to the issue.

    State the conclusions and the recommendations.

Prepare a *Progress Report* to Offer Updates on Developments in an Ongoing Project

- For long-term projects, prepare reports at designated intervals throughout the duration of the project. (p. 476)

- For short-term projects, prepare reports daily or as requested. (p. 476)
- Provide the following information in the progress report. (p. 477)

  Briefly review progress made up to the time of the previous report.

  Describe new developments since the previous report.

  Describe the personnel involved and their activities.

  Detail time spent on tasks.

  Describe supplies used and costs incurred.

  Explain any problems and their resolution.

  Provide an estimate of tasks to be completed for the next reporting period.

Prepare a *Crisis-Response Presentation* When Seeking to Reassure an Organization's Various Audiences and Restore Its Credibility

KEY TERMS

Chapter 29

online presentation
face-to-face (FtF) presentation
real-time presentation
synchronous communication

recorded presentation
asynchronous communication
single-speaker presentation
speaker-audience interactive presentation

interview-style presentation
moderated panel presentation
podcast
Webinar

Chapter 30

small group
virtual group
agenda
task roles
interpersonal roles

counterproductive roles
productive conflict
personal-based conflict
issues-based conflict
collective mind

groupthink
devil's advocacy
dialectical inquiry
participative leader
team presentations

Chapter 31

presentational speaking
review of academic article
debate
individual debate format
team debate format
claim
reasoning

evidence
poster session
expert or insider audience
colleagues within the field audience
lay audience
mixed audience

research presentation (oral scientific presentation)
methods/procedure presentation
research overview presentation
panel discussion

field study presentation
engineering design review
prototype
architecture design review
request for funding
presentation
qualitative research
quantitative research
review of the literature

presentation
theoretical research
presentation
evaluation research
presentation
policy recommendation
report
lecture
group activity presentation

classroom discussion
presentation
community service
learning project
case conference
shift report
evidence-based practice

Chapter 32

case study
sales presentation
proposal

staff report
progress report

crisis-response
presentation

Preparing Online Presentations

Recent developments in digital communication make it possible to extend the context of a speech or presentation far beyond its original time, place, and audience, and today, speaking online is an established part of the communications toolkit. Increasingly, employees are tasked with preparing presentations for delivery in virtual meetings and seminars ("Webinars"), as businesses seek to save on travel costs and reach a wider audience. Many students enroll in online education courses and deliver presentations online to classmates and instructors. Even applicants to colleges and graduate schools may now supplement their written applications with digital video presentations that highlight their talents.

As a speaker, you can prepare and deliver speeches for distribution online, to specific targeted audiences, such as fellow students, colleagues, clients, or to broader publics. Online speeches and presentations can be "streamed" live in real time, or recorded for distribution later whenever an audience (individual or group) wants to access them. All this is made possible by the increasing availability and affordability of tools such as Webinars, voice and video Internet conferencing, and free-to-the-consumer video storage sites such as YouTube.

Online and Face-to-Face Speaking: How Do They Compare?

Online presentations or speeches require the same elements of planning and delivery as **face-to-face (FtF)** presentations, yet important differences exist, primarily in the means of delivery and nature of the audience. These distinctive qualities pose some unique considerations in presenting an online speech.

Recognize Shared Features

As seen in Table 29.1, both online speeches and FtF speeches address the same general speech purposes: to inform, persuade, or address a special occasion. Both treat topics with the audience's interests and needs squarely in mind, making audience analysis a requirement. In addition, both online and FtF presentations call for credible supporting materials. Whether distributed electronically or delivered in person, a speaker should aim for a natural style of delivery, enhanced by sufficient rehearsal. Finally, all speakers must continually engage their audience; when speaker and audience are separated physically, this focus becomes all the more imperative.

TABLE 29.1	Comparison of Traditional Face-to-Face Speeches and Online Speeches	
	Face-to-Face Speeches	**Online Speeches**
General Purposes	To inform, persuade, entertain	To inform, persuade, entertain
Topic Selection	Assigned or speaker-selected	Assigned or speaker-selected
Audience Location	Same place, same time	Distant; same time or later
Audience Analysis	Audience demographics and psychology, including interests and topic knowledge	Audience demographics and psychology, including interests and topic knowledge, plus computer savvy, computer quality, Internet connectivity, software compatibility
Support Materials	Fewer media resources	Can be more graphics-oriented
Physical and Vocal Delivery	Emphasis on speaker nonverbal behavior and vocal qualities	Greater emphasis on vocal qualities than on nonverbal behavior
Delivery Method	Extemporaneous preferred with natural style	Natural style important but technology increases opportunities for manuscript delivery
Rehearsal	Practice entire speech at least six times, considering location	Practice entire speech at least six times, including sessions using equipment that will be used during delivery
Recording and Archiving	Not necessarily the intent but more easily doable with current technologies	Often recorded and stored as part of the planning and delivery of the speech by virtue of the technology used

Anticipate and Plan for Differences

Compared to FtF speeches, online presentations obviously rely more on technology for their delivery, and they can be played back and seen forever (as on YouTube). Depending on the format used to deliver them, online speeches can either be more or less interactive than a FtF speech. These qualities affect considerations of audience, delivery, presentation aids, and rehearsal.

Audience/Technical Considerations

Audience analysis is every bit as critical in online speeches as in FtF speeches. However, as well as investigating demographic and psychological variables (see Chapter 6), as an online presenter, you must also anticipate the audience's technical ability to receive the presentation. For example, audience members may need a broadband connection for seamless video transfer, processor speeds sufficient to download audio and video files timely, and the skills necessary to operate these utilities without distraction.

Delivery Considerations

Physical delivery, particularly facial expressions, is important in online presentations, but because the audience cannot interact with your physical presence, your voice becomes an even more crucial conduit of communication. Studies show that, in place of body movement, ample volume, clear pronunciation, variation in pitch, and speaking rate must hold audience interest. Nevertheless, in online presentations your "virtual body language" remains critical:

> The audience might not see you in person, but they still have an audiovisual experience based on what you deliver. The solution—and your opportunity to increase your impact—is not only to avoid a monotone delivery, but also to give the audience a connection with visual movement.[1]

As noted below, you can provide visual movement and variety with presentation aids.

Presentation Aids

Online presentations often use more presentation aids, such as PowerPoint slides or animations, than FtF presentations. Few online audience members want to watch "a talking head," preferring instead to see visual representations of the speaker's points, whether in attractive text form or with photos, animations, and video clips. You can use slides, for example, prior to the start of a presentation to inform the audience about the presentation's start time, speaker, and objectives.[2] During the presentation, whether live or recorded, you can alternate displays of presentation aids with views of yourself or, in some cases, yourself side-by-side with the aids.

Practice

Because so much can go wrong when you incorporate presentation aids into a speech and make use of multiple technologies, ample practice is essential. Not only is it necessary to rehearse the message itself, as with FtF speeches, but also to practice with any presentation technology you will be using, such as a Webcam, microphone, and video capture software. In fact, you should familiarize yourself with and practice using these utilities prior to planning any online presentation. See the accompanying checklist for a list of typical equipment and materials needed for online presentations.

TOOLS FOR DEVELOPING ONLINE PRESENTATIONS

✔ Standard desktop or laptop computer
✔ At least 10 GB of free hard-disk space
✔ 2–4 GB of RAM
✔ Broadband connection to the Internet (Your campus network speeds probably exceed those of home cable. Cable likely exceeds DSL.)

(continued on next page)

CHECKLIST

✔ Software for recording and editing audio and video
✔ Video capture software
✔ Podcasting software
✔ Graphical recording software
✔ Web-based presentation utilities (e.g., Prezi)
✔ Hardware for recording audio and video
✔ Microphones
✔ Webcams or video cameras
✔ Web site or intranet for distribution of presentation to audience
✔ Popular commercial Web sites such as YouTube or Vimeo
✔ Corporate or enterprise platforms such as Blackboard or Sharepoint

Real-Time versus Recorded: Plan for the Delivery Mode

A key consideration in planning for an online presentation is whether it will be delivered live, in real-time (or streamed) or recorded for later delivery. **Real-time presentations** connect the presenter and the audience live and at the same time, in **synchronous communication**. In **recorded presentations**, speaker and audience are separated by space and time, in **asynchronous communication**.[3]

Understanding the key advantages and limitations of both delivery modes can help you plan effectively.

Advantages of Real-Time Presentations

Real-time online presentations share some of the same advantages of live, FtF speech situations. Through interactive connectivity tools such as video, audio, chat, and e-mail, the speaker and audience can share in and benefit from relatively immediate feedback. The speaker can adapt the topic coverage and personal delivery according to real-time audience input and questions, for example, or adjust technical components depending on an audience's computer capabilities and connectivity. In fact, because of the ability to get instant feedback from a live, connected audience, real-time presentations lend themselves to a more natural, conversational style of speaker delivery.

Limitations of Real-Time Presentations

The biggest disadvantage of real-time presentations is the time constraints they can impose. Keep the audience's time zone in mind when planning a real-time presentation. The more geographically dispersed the audience, the more that start times and time zones become a factor in giving real-time presentations. Consider a presentation originating at 9:00 A.M. Central Daylight Time in the United States with audience members in Europe, the Middle East, and Indonesia. With time constraints in mind, real-time presentations often are reserved for occasions when speaker and audience are in proximate time zones of each other.

Advantages of Recorded Presentations

Online presentations developed and delivered for digital recording offer some unique advantages over real-time presentations. For one, start times and time zones are not a factor. Audience members can access recorded online presentations whenever convenient to them. Another is the long-term availability of the presentation, and thus the message, to current and future audience members. Audiences have the opportunity to return to the presentation whenever the information is needed, much like a book in a library or a consistently reliable Web site (see Figure 29.1).

Another advantage of recorded presentations is that you can build on and add to stored digital presentations. Perhaps one presentation covers only certain aspects of a topic such as how to use one feature of Adobe Photoshop. Subsequent presentations can cover other aspects. All the relevant presentations can be filed and cataloged as parts of a sequence of presentations, useful to audiences wanting to learn more about the topic over a period of time.

Presentations stored online also provide the speaker a portfolio of speaking experiences to share with prospective employers and clients—a potentially big advantage over competitors whose speaking experiences might only be listed on their résumés.

FIGURE 29.1 Example of a Video-Recorded Presentation Distributed Online

Limitations of Recorded Presentations

As a speaker, one of the most significant limitations of recorded presentations you may experience is the lack of direct interaction with the audience. You won't have the benefit of immediate feedback and must try harder and think of more creative ways to keep the presentation as a whole engaging. Additionally, recorded presentations eventually become outdated. The trick is to keep them current for as long as possible. The better the overall quality of the presentation in content and delivery, the more lasting its value over time.

Technical limitations also present challenges with recorded online presentations. For example, a moderate-quality digital video camera generally will produce a clearer picture than a simple Web camera. The better the quality of the computer system or Web service that is hosting the online presentation, the more fluid and smooth the video playback will be. Operating the technology for digitally recording and storing presentations can introduce limitations. If not the presenter, then someone else must be competent to properly use the recording device and to transfer the recording to its storage media, such as a DVD, a hard drive, or a Web streaming service.

Online Presentation Formats: From Single Speaker to Panel

Beyond the option of selecting real-time and recorded delivery modes, online presentations may be structured as single-speaker, speaker-audience interactive, interview-style, or moderated panel presentations.

Single-Speaker Presentations

Most online presentations, like FtF speeches, are delivered by one speaker. A speaker may select the **single-speaker presentation** format when the individual has his or her own message to deliver, is sought out as a credible source by an audience, or serves as a spokesperson for an organization, a group, or a cause. Persons who use this format might include experts who offer online training and officials who address far-flung employees.

A potential drawback to the single-person online presentation is the difficulty of keeping audience attention. For this reason, plan on using this format only for relatively brief presentations of less than seven minutes, and utilize a strong, enthusiastic delivery.

Speaker-Audience Interactive Presentations

One noteworthy advantage of online presentations and the sophisticated technology they are based on is the opportunity for interactive presentations even though the speaker and audience are not in the same location. **Speaker-audience interactive presentations** fully engage audience members with the speaker via audio or even video connectivity, and perhaps use collaborative, real-time textual or graphical utilities to share ideas about the topic. The speaker's role may range from providing a monologue to the audience, to which they respond with questions or comments at relevant times, to facilitating discussion and summing up conclusions at the end of the presentation.

The interactive presentation style is common to some distance education courses that your college or university probably offers, and to Webinars and Internet-based videoconferences that serve as virtual meetings (see p. 444). Chat rooms are an example of this type of presentation in its simplest form. Add video capability software, such as PowerPoint or Prezi, and collaborative writing tools, such as Google Docs, and you can fairly easily develop an interactive presentation for an audience scattered across the globe. In addition, depending on the nature of the interactive software built into the presentation program, the speaker can monitor audience reactions and invite feedback via a question-and-answer board, a polling feature, or chat. For greatest benefit, the number of participants in this type of presentation should be rather small, probably fewer than ten, in order to assure efficiency of participation and clarity of message.

Interview-Style Presentations

An interview is another useful format for an online presentation. In an **interview-style presentation**, one speaker serves as interviewer, who poses a series of questions to the other person, who is the interviewee.[4] Interview presentations work well when the interviewer is a person already known and credible to the audience, who offers questions on behalf of the audience to the interviewee, and whose experience or expertise is the basis for eliciting answers that will benefit the audience.

Interviews are most effective when the presenters use a conversational style of delivery and ask questions that touch upon the key points of a speech; that is, the questions and answers help meet a specific purpose and thesis of the presentation. Essentially, the interviewer's questions pose the main points, and the interviewee's responses offer support material. See Appendix B for some tips about radio interviews that can be applied to online interviews.

Moderated Panel Presentations

A **moderated panel presentation** involves three or more people in a discussion. One person serves as a moderator or facilitator of the discussion, which is contributed by the other people, the panelists. The discussion among the panelists follows a predetermined topic and set of points arranged to meet a specific purpose for the audience and occasion. The moderator's responsibility includes keeping the panelists on topic and moving through key points to fulfill the specific purpose. Panel presentations are helpful when the panelists bring different perspectives to the topic,[5] enabling the moderator to approach the topic from each perspective using comments from each panelist. See Appendix C for tips on panel discussions generally.

Online Presentation Platforms: From Podcast to Webinar

Depending on your communication goal, you may choose from among several different online platforms to deliver your presentation, including videos, podcasts, Webinars, and graphical presentations.

Video

Many people get their message out by presenting it visually via video. One of the fastest growing segments of the Internet in the past few years has been video-sharing sites such as YouTube. Among the millions of videos shared on these sites are thousands of presentations and speeches—from people who are just recording these themselves with their personal Flip camera or Web cam, to professional companies sending out messages using high definition digital video cameras.

Online video presentations run the gamut from personal introductions to how-to demonstrations, to political and civic speeches, to memorials and tributes. Video works equally well for single-speaker, interview, and panel presentation formats. But note that the more people involved in a video presentation, the more complex the camera and audio setups needed to produce a quality recording.

Podcast

Single-speaker, interview, and panel presentations can also be done entirely via audio alone, in the format known as podcasting. A **podcast** is simply a digital audio recording of a speech or presentation captured and stored in a form that is accessible via the Web. News sites, government information repositories such as the Library of Congress (www.loc.gov/podcasts/), and academic institutions offer myriad examples of podcasts (see Figure 29.2). Commercial recording outlets such as iTunes also provide a wide selection of podcasts.

A speaker might prefer podcasts for online delivery when video recording is unnecessary, overly complex, or expensive for the purpose of the presentation. Whereas online video presentations can be downloaded and transferred to portable viewing devices, podcasts are even more portable, requiring less digital memory and more hands-free listening than video players.

To record, store, and deliver a speech via podcast, you will need a microphone attached to your computer, simple, cost-free digital audio recording software (e.g., Audacity), and a Web site to host your podcast and provide its access to your audience. If you are familiar with PowerPoint, you can use the "Record Narration" feature in the slide creation function to produce a podcast-like presentation file. The presentation file can be used and distributed as you would any PowerPoint file, even via e-mail.

Once you have learned the procedures for creating a podcast, you may find podcasting an excellent way to practice your speeches and obtain feedback on them from family and friends.

FIGURE 29.2 Podcast Offerings from Tunxis Community College

CREATING A PODCAST

CHECKLIST

Most current models of desktop, laptop, and tablet computers include the basic equipment and software needed to create a podcast. The only other pieces you may need are a microphone to plug into your computer (if your computer monitor doesn't already have one built in) and audio recording software such as Audacity (http://audacity.sourceforge.net/). Then try these steps:

✓ Plan what you want to say.

✓ Seat yourself in an upright, direct position facing your computer, with the microphone no more than eight inches from your mouth.

✓ Make sure that your external microphone is plugged into your computer, or that your built-in microphone is operational.

✓ Open your audio recording software. Be familiar with how to start, pause, and stop a recording.

✓ Activate the recording software and begin speaking into the microphone. You're now making your presentation.

✓ At the conclusion of your presentation, stop the recording.

✓ Save the new recording as an audio file, such as .mp3.

✓ Close your audio recording software and disengage the microphone.

✓ Go to the new audio file saved to your computer, and open and play it. Now you are listening to your recorded presentation.

✓ Transfer the saved file to a Web site, blog, or podcast hosting site.

Webinar

Sometimes referred to as Web conferences, **Webinars** are real-time seminars, meetings, training sessions, or other presentations that connect presenters and audiences from their desktops, regardless of where they are in the world.[6] In many respects, Webinars function like other formats of online presentations, with one speaker presenting to an audience of many. However, the technologies that enable Webinars are specifically designed to facilitate actual meeting contexts, or many-to-many presenters.

Graphical/Multimedia-Intensive Presentation

In any given online presentation—single-speaker, interview-style, or panel—you may use graphical displays as part of your support material. But some online presentations are wholly graphics-driven and have no video or audio of a speaker. The speaker presents the message entirely via text and associated graphics; however, some audio or video clips of information, other than the presenter, might be embedded as support material. This format is especially useful for training purposes. For example, a presentation relying on screen captures can be used to demonstrate how to proceed through the series of steps necessary to conduct a Web search for available rental properties near your college or university. Graphics-driven presentations should be just that—more graphics than anything else, including text; and what text is used should be brief and visually engaging without being flamboyant.[7] The Web-based presentation utility Prezi (http://prezi.com/) is one example of a free, easy-to-use, highly dynamic tool for creating graphics-driven online presentations.

Online Presentations Checklist: Planning Ahead

Online presentations can both give you more flexibility to reach a wider audience and provide you with the opportunity to use a variety of creative technologies. In this way, delivering an online presentation brings unique characteristics to the traditional speech situation. One can only imagine what Aristotle's reaction to a persuasive speech on YouTube would be! Keeping in mind both the traditional guidelines for preparing and presenting a speech as well as those unique qualities of online presentations, here are some additional tips to follow.[8]

- *Be well organized.* Provide your audience with a clear statement of purpose and a preview of main points. Proceed with a solid structure that your audience can easily follow. Conclude by restating your purpose, reviewing the main points, and closing with a comment that encourages your audience to watch or listen for more.

- *Have reasonable expectations.* Fit the amount of content to the amount of time you have. Don't pack too much into too little time.

- *Design powerful presentation aids.* For video and Webcasts, plan for graphics and images that properly convey your ideas and have meaning to your audience. Use the capabilities of your computer and software to provide stunning visuals.

- *Keep your audience engaged.* Encourage audience interaction in real-time presentations by incorporating chat, instant messaging, or polling features. In recorded presentations, offer an e-mail address, Weblog comment, URL, or Twitter address where audience members can submit comments and questions. Use these tools to acquire feedback from your audience, much like you would use eye contact in a face-to-face speech or presentation.

- *Prepare a contingency plan in case of technology glitches.* For example, have a backup computer running simultaneously with the one used to deliver the presentation. Provide a list of FAQs or a Web page with instructions for audience members to manage technology problems.

- *Maintain ethical standards.* Be sure to carry out the same degree of decorum as you would in a FtF speech, with a keen eye to the idea that online presentations have the potential to go viral. Don't do anything that you wouldn't want your future boss, significant other, or instructor to see.

- *Get in plenty of practice time.* Rehearse, record, and listen to yourself as many times as needed. In online presentations, the audience still has an audio-visual experience, so it's important to give them good delivery and visual movement.[9]

STEPS IN PREPARING AN ONLINE PRESENTATION

✔ Keep in mind the similarities and differences between online and FtF speeches.

✔ Decide whether your speech or presentation will be in real time or recorded.

✔ Choose the format for speaker delivery: single-speaker, speaker-audience interactive interview-style, or moderated panel.

✔ Plan for specific online technologies: video, podcast, Webinar, or graphical.

CHECKLIST

CHAPTER 30

Collaborating and Presenting in Groups

Most of us will spend a substantial portion of our educational and professional lives communicating in **small groups** or teams (usually between three and twenty people) as opposed to a large public audience,[1] and many of the experiences we have as speakers, in the classroom, workforce, or in virtual groups online, occur in a group setting. In a **virtual group**, members who are geographically dispersed interact and exchange ideas through mediated communication such as e-mail, chat rooms, and video conferencing.[2] Whether they are virtual or face-to-face, groups often report on the results they've achieved, and some groups form solely for the purposes of coordinating oral presentations. Thus clear communication is vital to working cooperatively in groups and to getting to the point where you have something worthwhile to report.

Becoming an Effective Group Participant   WEB Chapter quizzes

How well or poorly you meet the objectives of the group—whether it is to coordinate a team presentation or to meet some other purpose—is largely a function of how you keep sight of the group's goals and avoid behaviors that detract from these goals. The more you use the group's goals as a steadying guide, the less likely you are to be diverted from your real responsibilities as a participant. Setting an **agenda** can help participants stay on track by identifying the items to be accomplished during a meeting; often it will specify time limits for each item of business.[3] Figure 30.1 offers an example of an agenda.

Plan on Assuming Dual Roles

In a group, you will generally assume dual roles: a task role and an interpersonal role. **Task roles** are the hands-on roles that directly relate to the group's accomplishment of its objectives. Examples include "recording secretary" (takes notes), "moderator" (facilitates discussion), "initiator" (helps the group get moving by generating new ideas, offering solutions), and "information seeker" (seeks clarification and input from the group).[4] Members also adopt various **interpersonal roles**, or styles of interacting in the group. These "relational" roles facilitate group interaction and include, for example, "harmonizer" (reduces tension) and "gatekeeper" (keeps the discussion moving and gets everyone moving).[5]

AGENDA

Staff meeting, June 4, 2012
Creative Communication Innovations
9 to 11 A.M.
Third Floor Conference Room

Participants: Lisa Gomez, Jonathan Halberstat, Juliann Chen,
Georgianna Walker, Carol Ludlow, Jerry Freely

1. Welcome and call to order
2. Opening remarks
3. Introduction of guests
4. Approval of minutes from previous meeting
5. Briefing from product line managers
6. Update from auditors
7. Report from consultants on new product line rollouts
8. Report on architecture designs for new assembly plant in Mexico
9. Summary
10. Adjournment

FIGURE 30.1 Sample Meeting Agenda   *Source:* Adapted from Dan O'Hair, Gustav Friedrich, and Lynda Dixon, *Strategic Communication in Business and the Professions,* 7th ed. (Boston: Allyn Bacon, 2011).

Task roles and interpersonal roles help the group maintain cohesion and achieve its mission. Sometimes, however, group members focus on individual versus group needs. These needs are usually irrelevant to the task at hand and are not oriented toward maintenance of the group as a team. **Counterproductive roles**, such as "floor hogger" (not allowing others to speak), "blocker" (being overly negative about group ideas; raising issues that have been settled), and "recognition seeker" (acts to call attention to oneself rather than to group tasks) do not further the group's goals and should be avoided.

Center Disagreement around Issues

Whenever people come together to consider an important issue, conflict is inevitable. But conflict doesn't have to be destructive. In fact, the best decisions are usually those that emerge from productive conflict.[6] In **productive conflict**, group members clarify questions, challenge ideas, present counterexamples, consider worst-case scenarios, and reformulate proposals. After a process like this, the group can be confident that its decision has been put to a good test. Productive conflict centers disagreements around issues rather than personalities. In **personal-based conflict**, members argue about one another instead of about the issues, wasting time and impairing motivation. In contrast, **issues-based conflict** allows members to test and debate ideas and potential solutions. It requires each member to ask tough questions, press for clarification, and present alternative views.[7]

Resist Groupthink

For groups to be truly effective, members eventually need to form a **collective mind**,[8] that is, engage in communication that is critical, careful, consistent, and conscientious.[9] Maintaining a collective mind obviously requires the careful management of issues-based and personal-based conflict, but at the same time group members must avoid the tendency to think too much alike. **Groupthink** is the tendency to accept information and ideas without subjecting them to critical analysis.[10]

Groups prone to groupthink typically exhibit these behaviors:

- Participants reach a consensus and avoid conflict in order not to hurt others' feelings, but without genuinely agreeing.
- Members who do not agree with the majority of the group feel pressured to conform.
- Disagreement, tough questions, and counterproposals are discouraged.
- More effort is spent justifying the decision than testing it.

Research suggests that groups can reach the best decisions by adopting two methods of argument: **devil's advocacy** (arguing for the sake of raising issues or concerns about the idea under discussion) or **dialectical inquiry** (devil's advocacy that goes a step further by proposing a countersolution to the idea).[11] Both approaches help expose underlying assumptions that may be preventing participants from making the best decision. As you lead a group, consider how you can encourage both methods of argument.

Adopting an Effective Leadership Style

Capable leadership is critical to the success of any group effort. It is the group leader's task to set goals, to encourage active participation among group participants, and to assess a group's productivity and adapt accordingly.[12] Four broad styles of leadership are possible within groups: *autocratic* (leaders make decisions and announce them to the group), *consultative* (leaders make decisions after discussing them with the group), *participative* (leaders make decisions with the group), and *delegative* (leaders ask the group to make the decision). Research suggests that of these four types of leaders, often the most effective is the **participative leader**—that is, one who facilitates a group's activities and interaction in ways that lead to a desired outcome. Following the steps below will help you become an effective participative leader.

Set Goals

Most negative experiences in groups result from a lack of a clear goal. Each member of a group should be able to clearly identify the purpose(s) of the group and the goals it is charged with reaching. The group leader should be a catalyst in setting these goals and ensuring that they are reached, either independently or in collaboration with other group members. The latter option is preferable because group members are likely to be more committed and excited about goals that they have helped create. The accompanying checklist contains guidelines for setting group goals.

GUIDELINES FOR SETTING GROUP GOALS

_____ 1. Identify the problem.

_____ 2. Map out a strategy.

_____ 3. Set a performance goal.

_____ 4. Identify the resources necessary to achieving the goal.

_____ 5. Recognize contingencies that may arise.

_____ 6. Obtain feedback.

CHECKLIST

Encourage Active Participation

Group members tend to adopt solutions that receive the largest number of favorable comments, whether these comments emanate from one individual or many. If only one or two members participate, it is their input that sets the agenda, whether or not their solution is optimal.[13] When you lead a group, take these steps to encourage active participation:

- *Directly ask members to contribute.* Sometimes one person, or a few people, dominates the discussion. Encourage the others to contribute by redirecting the discussion in their direction ("Patrice, we haven't heard from you yet" or "Juan, what do you think about this?").

- *Set a positive tone.* Some people are reluctant to express their views because they fear ridicule or attack. Minimize such fears by setting a positive tone, stressing fairness, and encouraging politeness and active listening.

- *Make use of devil's advocacy and dialectical inquiry.* Raise pertinent issues or concerns, and entertain solutions other than the one under consideration.

Use Reflective Thinking

WEB Links

To reach a decision or solution that all participants understand and are committed to, guide participants through a six-step process of reflective thinking shown in Figure 30.2, which is based on the work of the educator John Dewey.[14] Dewey suggested that this sequence of steps encourages group members to "think reflectively" about their task. In this way, all the relevant facts and opinions can be discussed and evaluated, thereby ensuring a better decision.

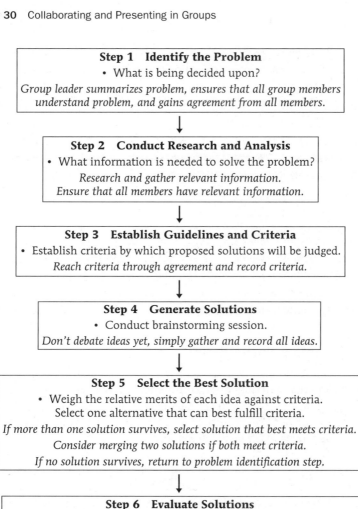

Step 1   Identify the Problem
• What is being decided upon?
Group leader summarizes problem, ensures that all group members understand problem, and gains agreement from all members.

↓

Step 2   Conduct Research and Analysis
• What information is needed to solve the problem?
Research and gather relevant information.
Ensure that all members have relevant information.

↓

Step 3   Establish Guidelines and Criteria
• Establish criteria by which proposed solutions will be judged.
Reach criteria through agreement and record criteria.

↓

Step 4   Generate Solutions
• Conduct brainstorming session.
Don't debate ideas yet, simply gather and record all ideas.

↓

Step 5   Select the Best Solution
• Weigh the relative merits of each idea against criteria.
Select one alternative that can best fulfill criteria.
If more than one solution survives, select solution that best meets criteria.
Consider merging two solutions if both meet criteria.
If no solution survives, return to problem identification step.

↓

Step 6   Evaluate Solutions
• Does the solution have any weaknesses or disadvantages?
• Does the solution resemble the criteria that were developed?
• What other criteria would have been helpful in arriving at a better solution?

FIGURE 30.2 Making Decisions in Groups: John Dewey's Six-Step Process of Reflective Thinking

Making Presentations in Teams

Once a group has achieved its goal or selected a solution, members face the task of communicating their results to others in the form of a written report, an oral presentation, or a combination of the two. Group presentations, or **team presentations**, have many of the same characteristics as presentations done individually, but there are differences; while in an individual presentation one person assumes all responsibility for presenting a topic, in a team presentation some or all of the group members share responsibility. Regularly assigned in the classroom and frequently delivered in the workplace, successful team presentations require close cooperation and planning.

Analyze the Audience and Set Goals

Even if the topic is assigned and the audience consists solely of the instructor and classmates (perhaps virtually), consider their interests and needs with respect to the topic and how you can meet them. Then, just as you would do during group work, establish goals for the presentation that you can all agree upon.

Assign Roles and Tasks

Similar to collaborating in a group, one of the first steps in delivering a team presentation is designating a *team leader* to help guide coordination among members, beginning with the selection of roles and tasks. Next, assign team members to various aspects of the research, perhaps selecting different team members to present the introduction, body of the presentation, and conclusion, or other responsibilities. Set firm time limits for each portion of the presentation.

Establish Transitions between Speakers

Work out transitions between speakers ahead of time—for example, whether one team member will introduce every speaker or whether each speaker will introduce the next speaker upon the close of his or her presentation. The quality of the presentation will depend in great part on smooth transitions between speakers.

Be Mindful of Your Nonverbal Behavior

During a team presentation, the audience's eyes will fall on everyone involved, not just the person speaking. Thus any signs of disinterest or boredom by a team member will be easily noticed. Give your full attention to the other speakers and project an attitude of interest toward audience members.

For Maximum Impact, Consider the Presenters' Strengths

Audiences become distracted by marked disparities in style, such as hearing a captivating speaker followed by an extremely dull one. If you are concerned about an uneven delivery, consider choosing the person with the strongest presentation style and credibility level for the opening. Put the more cautious presenters in the middle of the presentation. Select another strong speaker to conclude the presentation.[15]

Coordinate the Presentation Aids

Consider assigning one person the job of coordinating templates for slides or other visuals. Doing so will ensure each presentation aid is consistent in color, font size, and overall style. The team can also decide to assign a single individual the task of presenting the aids as another team member speaks. If this is the case, be sure that the team member presenting the aids or showing the slides remains unobtrusive so as not to distract the audience from the speaker. If the presentation will include a video and/or an audio component, assign one person the job of presenting them.

Rehearse the Presentation Several Times

Together with the whole group, members should practice their portions of the presentation, with any presentation aids they will use, in the order they will be given in the final form. Rehearse several times, until the presentation proceeds smoothly, using the techniques for rehearsal described in Chapter 20.

TEAM PRESENTATION TIPS

✓ Establish in writing each team member's responsibilities regarding content and presentation aids.

✓ Determine how introductions will be made—all at once at the beginning or by having each speaker introduce the next one.

✓ Practice introductions and transitions to create a seamless presentation.

✓ Establish an agreed-upon set of hand signals to indicate when a speaker is speaking too loud or soft, too slow or fast.

✓ Assign someone to manage the question-and-answer session.

✓ Rehearse the presentation with presentation aids several times from start to finish.

CHECKLIST

Speaking in Other College Courses

Your opportunities to speak publicly at college won't end once you complete the introductory public speaking course. Often, you will be called on to prepare oral presentations in your major classes and in other general-education courses. No matter which major you select or what profession you choose, oral presentations will be part of the mix. As an engineering major, for example, you might prepare a design review of your major project. A student of history might deliver a presentation linking a historical event with a contemporary issue. Nursing majors might be asked to communicate a treatment plan to a medical team.

Presentational versus Public Speaking

Rather than being formal public speeches, oral presentations in the classroom are a form of **presentational speaking**—reports delivered by individuals or teams addressing classmates or persons in the workplace. Presentational speaking has much in common with formal public speaking, yet important differences exist:

- *Degree of formality.* Presentational speaking is *less formal* than public speaking; on a continuum, it would lie midway between public speaking at one end and conversational speaking at the other.[1]

- *Audience factors.* Public speaking audiences tend to be self-selected or voluntary participants, and they regard the speech as a one-time event. Attendees of oral presentations are more likely to be part of a "captive" audience, as in a classroom, and may be required to attend frequent presentations. Due to the ongoing nature among participants, the attendees also share more information with one another than those who attend a public speech and thus can be considered more homogeneous.

- *Speaker expertise.* Listeners generally assume that a public speaker has more expertise or firsthand knowledge than they do on a topic. Presentational speakers, by contrast, are more properly thought of as "first among equals." No doubt your classmates will regard you in this manner.

Apart from these differences, the rules of public speaking described in this handbook apply equally to presentations in the classroom (and workplace; see Chapter 32, "Business and Professional Presentations") as to public speeches.

Typical Speaking Assignments across the Curriculum

Before familiarizing yourself with the various course-specific types of oral presentations assigned in different disciplines, beginning on p. 458, consider the following kinds of presentations that are frequently assigned across the curriculum: *academic articles, team presentations, debates, poster sessions,* and *community service learning project reports* (see p. 470 for this last type of presentation). Whatever your major, you will be asked to prepare one or more of these.

Review of Academic Articles

WEB Exercises and quizzes

A commonly assigned speaking task in many courses is the **review of academic articles**. A biology instructor might ask you to review a study on cell regulation published in *Cell Biology,* for example, or a psychology teacher may require that you talk about a study on fetal alcohol syndrome published in the journal *Neuro-Toxicology.* Typically, when you are assigned an academic article, your instructor will expect you to:

- Identify the author's thesis or hypothesis.
- Explain the methods by which the author arrived at his or her conclusions.
- Explain the author's findings.
- Identify the author's theoretical perspective, if applicable.
- Evaluate the study's validity, if applicable.
- Describe the author's sources and evaluate their credibility.
- Show how the findings of the study might be applied to other circumstances, and make suggestions for how the study might lead to further research.[2]

Team Presentations

Frequently assigned in many courses, a *team presentation* is an oral presentation prepared and delivered by a group of three or more individuals. Successful team presentations require close cooperation and planning. Chapter 30, "Collaborating and Presenting in Groups," contains detailed guidelines for preparing and delivering a team presentation.

Debates

WEB Exercises and quizzes

Debates are another popular presentation format in many college courses. Debates call upon skill in persuasion (especially the reasoned use of evidence), in delivery, and in the ability to think quickly and critically. Much like a political debate, in an *academic debate* two individuals or groups consider or argue an issue from opposing viewpoints. Generally there will be a winner and a loser, lending this form of speaking a competitive edge.

Take a Side

Opposing sides in a debate are taken by speakers in one of two formats. In the **individual debate format**, one person takes a side against another person. In the **team debate format**, multiple people (usually two) take a side against another team, with each person on the team assuming a speaking role.

The *pro* side (also called "affirmative") in the debate supports the topic with a *resolution*—a statement asking for change or consideration of a controversial issue. "Resolved, that the United States Congress should pass the Flag Desecration Amendment" is a resolution that the affirmative side must support and defend. The pro side tries to convince the audience (or judges) to address, support, or agree with the topic under consideration. The *con* side (also called "negative") in the debate attempts to defeat the resolution by dissuading the audience from accepting the pro side's arguments.

Advance Strong Arguments

Whether you take the affirmative or negative side, your primary responsibility is to advance strong arguments in support of your position. Arguments usually consist of the following three parts (see also Chapter 26):

- **Claim:** A **claim** makes an assertion or declaration about an issue. "Females are discriminated against in the workplace." Depending on your debate topic, your claim may be one of fact, value, or policy (see Chapter 26).
- **Reasoning: Reasoning** (e.g., warrants; see Chapter 26) is a logical link or explanation of why the evidence supports the claim. "Females make less money and get promoted less frequently than males."
- **Evidence: Evidence** is the support offered for the claim. "According to a recent report by the U.S. Department of Labor, women make 28 percent less than men in comparable jobs and are promoted 34 percent less frequently."

Debates are characterized by *refutation,* in which each side attacks the arguments of the other. Refutation can be made against an opponent's claim, evidence, or reasoning, or some combination of these elements. In the previous argument, an opponent might refute the evidence by arguing "The report used by my opponent is ten years old, and a new study indicates that we are making substantial progress in equalizing the pay among males and females; thus we are reducing discrimination in the workplace."

Refutation also involves rebuilding arguments that have been refuted or attacked by the opponent. This is done by adding new evidence or attacking the opponent's reasoning or evidence.

"Flow" the Debate

In formal debates (in which judges take notes and keep track of arguments), debaters must attack and defend each argument. "Dropping" or ignoring an argument can seriously compromise the credibility of the debater and her or his side. To ensure that you respond to each of your opponent's arguments, try using

Affirmative → Negative		Affirmative → Negative		Affirmative → Negative	
Nonviolent prisoners should be paroled more often.	Nonviolent prisoners can become violent when they are paroled.	Studies show nonviolent prisoners commit fewer crimes upon their release.	Those studies are outdated and involve only a few states.	My studies are recent and include big states like New York and California.	The studies from New York and California were flawed owing to poor statistics.

FIGURE 31.1 Flowchart of the Arguments for the Resolution "Resolved That Nonviolent Prisoners Should Be Paroled More Often"

a simple technique adopted by formal debaters called "flowing the debate" (see Figure 31.1). Write down each of your opponent's arguments, and then draw a line or arrow to indicate that you (or another team member) have refuted it.

TIPS FOR WINNING A DEBATE

✓ Present the most credible and convincing evidence you can find.

✓ Before you begin, describe your position and tell the audience what they must decide.

✓ If you feel that your side is not popular among the audience, ask them to suspend their own personal opinion and judge the debate on the merits of the argument.

✓ Don't be timid. Ask the audience to specifically decide in your favor, and be explicit about your desire for their approval.

✓ Emphasize the strong points from your arguments. Remind the audience that the opponent's arguments were weak or irrelevant.

✓ Be prepared to think on your feet (see Chapter 18 on impromptu speaking).

✓ Don't hide your passion for your position. Debate audiences appreciate enthusiasm and zeal.

CHECKLIST

Poster Sessions

A **poster session** presents information about a study, an issue, or a concept concisely and visually on a large (usually 3'8" by 5'8") poster. Presenters display their key findings on posters, which are hung on freestanding boards; on hand are copies of the written report, with full details of the study. A good poster presenter considers his or her audience, understanding that with so much competing information, the poster must be concise, visually appealing, and restricted to the most important points of the study. Different disciplines (e.g., geology vs. sociology) require unique poster formats, so be sure that you follow the guidelines specific to the discipline.

When preparing the poster:

• Select a concise and informative title.

• Include an abstract (a brief summary of the study) describing the essence of the report and how it relates to other research in the field. Offer compelling and "must know" points to hook viewers and summarize information for those who will only read the abstract.

- Ensure a logical and easy-to-follow flow from one part of the poster to another.
- Ruthlessly edit text to a minimum, using clear graphics wherever possible.
- Select a muted color for the poster itself, such as gray, beige, light blue, or white and use a contrasting, clear font color (usually black).
- Make sure your font size is large enough to be read comfortably from at least three feet away.
- Design figures and diagrams to be viewed from a distance, and label each one.
- Include a concise summary of each figure in a legend below each one.
- Be prepared to provide brief descriptions of your poster and to answer questions; keep your explanations short.

Presenting to Different Audiences

WEB Quizzes

In the workplace, oral presentations may be delivered to fellow workers, colleagues, managers, or clients, among others. Knowing this, instructors may ask that you tailor your talk to a mock (practice) on-the-job audience, with your classmates serving as stand-ins. Typical audiences include the **expert or insider audience**, the **colleagues within the field audience**, the **lay audience**, and the **mixed audience**; Table 31.1 describes each type of audience. The nearby Checklist: Tips on Presenting to a Mixed Audience offers guidelines on addressing one of the most common types of audiences.

TABLE 31.1 Types of Audiences in the Working World	
Type of Audience	**Characteristics**
Expert or insider audience	People who have intimate knowledge of the topic, issue, product, or idea being discussed (e.g., an investment analyst presents a financial plan to a group of portfolio managers).
Colleagues within the field audience	People who share the speaker's knowledge of the general field under question (e.g., psychology or computer science) but who may not be familiar with the specific topic under discussion (e.g., short-term memory or voice-recognition systems, respectively).
Lay audience	People who have no specialized knowledge of the field related to the speaker's topic or of the topic itself (e.g., a physical education teacher discusses a proper diet and exercise regimen with a group of teenagers).
Mixed audience	An audience composed of a combination of people—some with expert knowledge of the field and topic and others with no specialized knowledge. This is perhaps the most difficult audience to satisfy (e.g., an attending surgeon describes experimental cancer treatment to a hospital board comprising medical professionals, financial supporters, and administrative personnel).

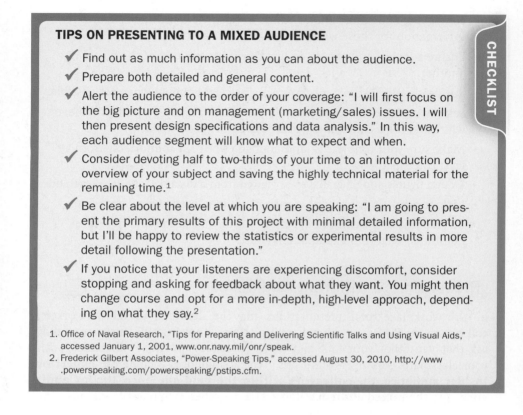

TIPS ON PRESENTING TO A MIXED AUDIENCE

✓ Find out as much information as you can about the audience.

✓ Prepare both detailed and general content.

✓ Alert the audience to the order of your coverage: "I will first focus on the big picture and on management (marketing/sales) issues. I will then present design specifications and data analysis." In this way, each audience segment will know what to expect and when.

✓ Consider devoting half to two-thirds of your time to an introduction or overview of your subject and saving the highly technical material for the remaining time.[1]

✓ Be clear about the level at which you are speaking: "I am going to present the primary results of this project with minimal detailed information, but I'll be happy to review the statistics or experimental results in more detail following the presentation."

✓ If you notice that your listeners are experiencing discomfort, consider stopping and asking for feedback about what they want. You might then change course and opt for a more in-depth, high-level approach, depending on what they say.[2]

1. Office of Naval Research, "Tips for Preparing and Delivering Scientific Talks and Using Visual Aids," accessed January 1, 2001, www.onr.navy.mil/onr/speak.
2. Frederick Gilbert Associates, "Power-Speaking Tips," accessed August 30, 2010, http://www.powerspeaking.com/powerspeaking/pstips.cfm.

Speaking in Science and Mathematics Courses

Known for their focus on exacting processes, *science-related disciplines* include the physical sciences (e.g., chemistry and physics), the natural sciences (e.g., biology and medicine), and the earth sciences (e.g., geology, meteorology, and oceanography). Fields related to mathematics include accounting, statistics, and applied math.

The focus of many presentations in science-related disciplines is reporting the results of original or replicated research. Instructors will want you to inform the class of the processes by which you arrived at your experimental results. Persuasion may also be required, as when an engineering student must convince classmates of a design. Commonly assigned types of these presentations include the *oral scientific, methods/procedure, research overview,* and *field study* presentations.

Research (Oral Scientific) Presentation

In the **research presentation** (also called **oral scientific presentation** or "scientific talk") you describe original research you have done, either alone or as part of a team. The research presentation usually follows the standard

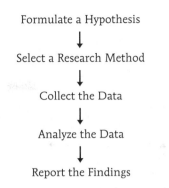

Formulate a Hypothesis

↓

Select a Research Method

↓

Collect the Data

↓

Analyze the Data

↓

Report the Findings

FIGURE 31.2 Steps in a Scientific Investigation

model used in scientific investigation (see Figure 31.2) and includes the following elements:

1. An *introduction* describing the research question and the scope and objective of the study

2. A *description of methods* used to investigate the research question, including where it took place and the conditions under which it was carried out

3. The *results of the study* summarizing key findings and highlighting insights to the questions/hypotheses investigated; this is the "body" of the presentation

4. A *conclusion* (also called "Discussion"), in which the speaker interprets the data or results and discusses their significance. As in any speech, the conclusion should link back to the introduction, reiterating the research question and highlighting the key findings

Methods/Procedure Presentation

The **methods/procedure presentation** describes how an experimental or mathematical process works and under what conditions it can be used. This is generally a ten- to fifteen-minute individual presentation. In a theoretical math class, for example, your assignment might be to describe an approach to solving a problem, such as the Baum–Welch algorithm, including examples of how this approach has been used, either inappropriately or appropriately. This type of methods/procedure presentation generally does the following:

1. Identifies the conditions under which this particular process should be used

2. Offers a detailed description of the process (at times including an actual demonstration)

3. Discusses the benefits and shortcomings of the process

Research Overview Presentation

The **research overview presentation** provides background for a research question that will form the basis of an impending experiment or investigation. Instructors often ask students to organize research overviews with the following sections:

1. Overview of research relevant to the question at hand
2. Discussion of key studies that are central to the question
3. Analysis of the strengths and weaknesses of research in light of the current hypothesis or question

The format for the research overview may be an individual presentation or a **panel discussion**, in which a group of people (usually between three and nine) explores specific lines of research that contribute to a general hypothesis or question. (See Appendix C for more on panel discussions.)

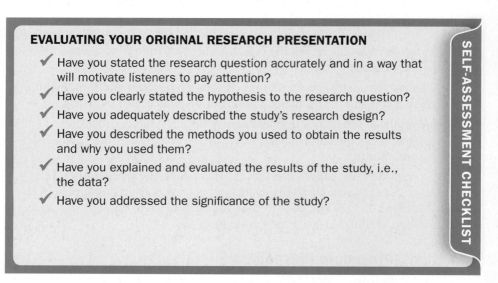

EVALUATING YOUR ORIGINAL RESEARCH PRESENTATION

✔ Have you stated the research question accurately and in a way that will motivate listeners to pay attention?

✔ Have you clearly stated the hypothesis to the research question?

✔ Have you adequately described the study's research design?

✔ Have you described the methods you used to obtain the results and why you used them?

✔ Have you explained and evaluated the results of the study, i.e., the data?

✔ Have you addressed the significance of the study?

SELF-ASSESSMENT CHECKLIST

Field Study Presentation

A **field study presentation** describes research conducted in naturalistic surroundings. An environmental studies major might describe animal behavior in an oil spill, for example, or a geology major may report on a dig. Field study presentations can be delivered individually, in teams, or in poster session format. Whatever the nature of the observations, field study presentations address the following:

- Overview and scope of the field research
- Description of the site
- Methods used in the research (e.g., participant observation, type of sample collection, measurement techniques)
- Interpretation/analysis of the data
- Future directions for the research

TIPS FOR PREPARING SUCCESSFUL SCIENTIFIC PRESENTATIONS

✔ Create an informative title that describes the research.

✔ Place your presentation in the context of a major scientific principle.

✔ Focus on a single issue and adjust it to the interests of your audience.

✔ Identify the underlying question you will address, divide it into sub-questions, and answer each question.

✔ Follow a logical line of thought.

✔ Explain scientific concepts unambiguously, with a minimum of professional jargon.

✔ Use appropriate analogies and metaphors to associate the unknown with familiar knowledge.

✔ End with a concise, clearly formulated conclusion in the context of your chosen scientific principle.

Source: Based on Robert Anholt, *Dazzle 'Em with Style: The Art of Oral Scientific Presentation* (New York: W. H. Freeman, 1994), 89–90.

Preparing Successful Presentations in Science and Mathematics

Science and mathematics instructors, and employers and colleagues on the job, will expect your presentations to be grounded in the scientific method. Credible presentations must clearly illustrate the nature of the research question, ideally in a way that audience members will find compelling and relevant, describe the methods used in gathering and analyzing data, and explain the results.

Clearly executed presentation aids often are critical to these kinds of reports, and instructors generally require them. Aids can range from data tables and graphs to equations drawn on a chalkboard.

Typically, instructors will expect you to do the following:

- *Use observation, proofs, and experiments as support for your points.*

- *Be selective in your focus on details,* highlighting critical information but not overwhelming listeners with details they can learn about by referring to the written paper and the cited sources.

- *Use analogies to build on prior knowledge and demonstrate underlying causes.* (See Chapter 24 for detailed guidelines on explaining difficult concepts.)

- *Use graphics to visually illustrate* important processes and concepts. Remember when preparing aids: Condense data in tables to essential information and clearly label each axis and variable in graphs. The more simply you can render the complex information visually (without distorting findings), the more likely it is that audience members will grasp your points.

Speaking in Technical Courses

Technical disciplines include the range of engineering fields (mechanical, electrical, chemical, civil, aerospace, industrial, nuclear), computer-science fields (computer and software engineering), and design-oriented fields (industrial design, architecture, graphic design). Oral presentations in technical courses often focus on a project, whether it is a set of plans for a building, a prototype robot, or an innovative computer-circuit design. Rather than addressing research, as is often the case in scientific and social scientific reports, the focus of technical presentations usually rests on the product or design itself.

Of the various types of presentations assigned in technical courses, the *design review* is perhaps the most common. Other types of presentations in technical courses include the *request for funding* and the *progress report* (see Chapter 32, p. 476 for information on progress reports).

Engineering Design Review

The **engineering design review** provides information on the results of a design project. Many capstone-engineering courses require that students prepare design reviews, which are generally informative in nature, although their purpose may include convincing the audience that the design decisions are sound. Design reviews often incorporate a **prototype** (model) demonstration and are delivered as team presentations or in poster sessions. Design reviews typically include the following:

1. Overview of the design concept
2. Description of the design specifications
3. Discussion of any experimental testing that has been completed on the design
4. Discussion of future plans and unresolved problems
5. Discussion of schedule, budget, and marketing issues

Architecture Design Review

The **architecture design review** combines two functions: it enables the audience to visualize the design, and it sells it. A narrative approach, in which you tell the "story" of the design, combined with a *spatial organizational pattern,* in which you arrange main points in order of physical proximity of the design (see Chapter 13), can help you do this. At a minimum, architecture design reviews typically cover:

1. Background on the site
2. Discussion of the design concept
3. Description and interpretation of the design

Request for Funding

In the **request for funding presentation**, a team member or the entire team provides evidence that a project, proposal, or design idea is worth funding. As such, this kind of presentation is persuasive in nature. Requests for funding usually cover the following ground:

1. Overview of customer specifications and needs
2. Analysis of the market and its needs
3. Overview of the design idea or project and how it meets those needs
4. Projected costs for the project
5. Specific reasons why the project or idea should be funded

The request for funding may be delivered as an individual or team presentation. On the job, the audience for the request for funding is made up of people who are concerned with the marketing, economic, and customer aspects of the idea or project (e.g., colleagues within the field; see Table 31.1).

Preparing Successful Technical Presentations

Technical presentations sell ideas, provide hard data, rely on visual aids, and are results oriented.[3] As you prepare, pay attention to the following:

- *Sell your ideas.* The technical presenter must persuade clients, managers, or classmates that a design, an idea, or a product is a good one. As one instructor notes, "You can never assume that your product or design will just sell—you have to do that."[4]
- *Provide hard data.* Good technical presentations are detailed and specific and use numbers as evidence. Instead of general, sweeping statements, provide hard data and clearly stated experimental results.
- *Use ample presentation aids.* Use diagrams, prototypes, and drawings, including design specifications, computer simulations, physical models, and spreadsheets. Construct aids early in the process, and practice the presentation with the presentation aids in place.
- *Use concrete imagery* to help listeners visualize how your design will function and appear.
- *Lead with the results.* Technical disciplines such as engineering are about results—the end product. When organizing your presentation, consider telling the audience the most important result first. Then fill in the details.[5]
- *Gear the information to the appropriate level.* Typically, people who attend technical presentations possess a range of technical knowledge, from little or none to an expert understanding of the topic at hand. See the checklist on p. 458 for tips on presenting to a mixed audience.

Speaking in Social Science Courses

Students in the social sciences (including psychology, sociology, political science, and communication) learn to evaluate and conduct **qualitative research** (in which the emphasis is on observing, describing, and interpreting behavior) as well as **quantitative research** (in which the emphasis is on statistical measurement).[6] Research methods and areas of investigation can be far-ranging, from experiments on biological bases of behavior to participant observation studies of homelessness.

For students in the social sciences, the focus of investigation is often on explaining or predicting human behavior or social forces, answering such questions as "What," "How," and "Why?"[7] Instructors may ask you to evaluate a theory or body of research, debate an issue, review the relevant literature, or make policy recommendations. Additionally, as in science and mathematics courses, you might prepare a research, field study, or methods/procedure presentation (see p. 458).

Debate Controversial Topics

Students taking social science courses often prepare for *debates* on controversial issues (see p. 454 for guidelines on preparing for a debate). Sometimes an assignment involves advocating a position that you do not support. For example, a sociology instructor may require students who oppose euthanasia to defend the practice. Whichever side of an issue you address, you will need to prepare a well-composed argument with strong supporting evidence (see Chapter 26, "Developing Arguments for the Persuasive Speech").

Review the Literature

Frequently, instructors ask students to review the body of research related to a given topic or issue and offer conclusions about the topic based on this research. A communications student, for example, might review the literature on gender bias in the hiring of journalists. In addition to describing the available research, the student would offer conclusions uncovered by the research and suggest directions for future research. A **review of the literature presentation** typically includes the following:

1. Statement of the topic under review
2. Description of the available research, including specific points of agreement and disagreement among sources
3. Evaluation of the usefulness of the research
4. Conclusions that can be drawn from the research
5. Suggested directions for future study

Explain Social Phenomena

Social scientists attempt to analyze and explain social or psychological phenomena such as "Why do some college students abuse alcohol?" "What leads to infant neglect?" This type of **theoretical research presentation** typically addresses the following:

1. Description of the phenomenon under discussion (e.g., "*What* is taking place?")
2. Theories of *how* and *why* it occurs, as described by research
3. Explanation of and suggestions for future research

Evaluate Policies and Programs

In addition to explaining phenomena, social scientists often measure the effectiveness of programs developed to address these issues. Instructors may ask you to evaluate a program or policy, perhaps one you observed in a service learning project. Typically, a policy/program **evaluation research presentation** includes the following:

1. Explanation of the program's mission
2. Description of the program's accomplishments
3. Discussion of how the accomplishments were measured, including any problems in evaluation
4. Conclusions regarding how well or poorly the program has met its stated objectives

Recommend Policies

As well as evaluating programs and policies, you may be asked to recommend a course of action on a current issue or problem. This mirrors what is sometimes required of psychologists, sociologists, communications specialists, and others who investigate an issue and then present their findings to the person or body commissioning the report. A **policy recommendation report** typically includes the following:

1. Definition and brief discussion of the problem
2. Recommendations to solve the problem or address the issue
3. Application of forecasting methods to show likely results of the recommended policy
4. Plan for implementation of the recommendations
5. Discussion of future needs or parameters to monitor and evaluate the recommendations

Preparing Successful Presentations in the Social Sciences

Good social scientific presentations clearly explain the research question, refer to current research, and use timely data.

- *Illustrate the research question.* Pay attention to clearly illustrating the nature of the research question and the means by which the results were achieved.

- *Refer to current research.* Credible social scientific presentations refer to recent findings in the field. Instructors are more likely to accept experimental evidence if it is replicated over time and supported by current research.
- *Use timely data.* Instructors expect student presentations to include timely data and examples. A report on poverty rates for a sociology course must provide up-to-date data, because poverty rates change yearly. A research presentation on treatments for the mentally ill, for example, should accurately reflect current treatments.

Since most of your social scientific and literature review presentations will be relatively brief, make sure to sufficiently narrow your topic research question and scale your findings to the time allotted. To ensure that you report the research accurately, maintain a working bibliography of your sources.

Speaking in Arts and Humanities Courses

Speaking assignments in arts and humanities courses (including English, history, religion, philosophy, foreign languages, art history, theater, and music) often require that you interpret the meaning of a particular idea, event, person, story, or artifact. Your art history professor, for example, might ask you to identify the various artistic and historical influences on a sculpture or painting. An instructor of literature may ask you to explain the theme of a novel or a poem. A theater instructor might ask you to offer your interpretation of a new play.

Rather than focusing on quantitative research, presentations in the arts and humanities often rely on your analysis and interpretation of the topic at hand. These interpretations are nonetheless grounded in the conventions of the field and build on the research within it.

Oral presentation assignments in arts and humanities courses can range from informative speeches of explanation to individual and team debates. Some presentations may be performative in nature, with students expressing artistic content.

Informative Talks of Description and Analysis

Often in the arts and humanities, students prepare informative (see Chapter 24) presentations in which they explain the relevance of a historical or contemporary person or event; a genre or school of philosophical thought; or a piece of literature, music, or art. For example, an art history professor may require students to discuss the artist Bernini's contribution to St. Peter's Cathedral in Rome. Visual aids are often a key part of such presentations; in this case, audiences would expect to see relevant reproductions and photographs.

Presentations That Compare and Contrast

Another common assignment in arts and humanities courses is to compare and contrast events, stories, people, or artifacts in order to highlight their similarities or differences. For example, you might compare two works of literature from different time periods, or two historical figures or works of art. These presentations may be informative or persuasive in nature. Presentations that compare and contrast include the following:

1. *Thesis statement* outlining the connection between the events, stories, people, or artifacts
2. *Discussion of main points,* including several examples that highlight the similarities and differences
3. *Concluding evaluative statement* about the comparison (e.g., if the presentation is persuasive, why one piece of literature was more effective than another; if informative, a restatement of similarities and differences)

Debates

Often students will engage in debates on opposing ideas, historical figures, or philosophical positions. In a history class, for example, students might argue whether sixteenth-century women in Western Europe experienced a Renaissance. The speaker must present a brief assertion (two to three minutes) about the topic; the opposing speaker then responds with a position. Whatever side of an issue you address, prepare a well-composed argument with strong supporting evidence.

Classroom Discussions

Many students taking arts and humanities courses must research a question and then lead a classroom discussion on it. For example, a literature student may lead a discussion on Anton Chekov's *The Cherry Orchard*. The speaker would be expected to provide a synopsis of the plot, theme, and characters and offer an analysis of the play's meaning. For directions on leading a discussion, see "Facilitating a Classroom Discussion" on p. 468.

Preparing Successful Arts and Humanities Presentations

Good presentations in the arts and humanities help the audience think of the topic in a new way by providing an original interpretation of it. A presentation on the historical significance of Reconstruction after the Civil War of 1861–1865, for example, will be more effective if you offer a new way of viewing the topic rather than reiterating what other people have said or what is already generally accepted knowledge. A debate on two philosophical ideas will be most effective when you assert issues and arguments that are different from those that the audience has thought of before. Because many speaking events in the arts and humanities call for interpretation, the more original the interpretation (while remaining logical and supported by evidence), the more compelling the presentation will be for the audience.

Speaking in Education Courses

In education courses (including subfields such as curriculum and instruction, physical education, secondary and elementary education, and educational administration), the most common speaking assignments focus on teaching and related instructional tasks, such as giving a lecture or demonstrating an activity. In a mathematics education course, you may prepare a mini-lecture on a particular geometric theorem. In a learning-styles course, you may tailor an activity to a variety of different learners.

Delivering a Lecture

A **lecture** is an informational speech for an audience of student learners. Standard lectures range from fifty minutes to an hour and a half; *a mini-lecture presentation,* designed to give students an opportunity to synthesize information in a shorter form, generally lasts about fifteen to twenty minutes. Effective lectures tend to be interactive, incorporating frequent questions designed to assess student understanding and encourage students to engage in the material. Typically, lectures include the following:

1. A clear introduction of the topic to be covered (see Chapter 15)
2. Statement of the central idea/thesis
3. Statement of the connection to previous topics covered
4. Clearly stated learning objectives
5. Discussion of the main points
6. Summary of the lecture and preview of the next assigned topic

Facilitating a Group Activity

In the **group activity presentation**, the speaker describes an activity to be completed following a lecture. Typically this short presentation includes the following:

1. A brief review of the main idea of the lecture
2. An explanation of the goal of the activity
3. Directions on carrying out the activity
4. A preview of what students will gain from the activity and what the discussion following it will cover

Facilitating a Classroom Discussion

In the **classroom discussion presentation**, the speaker facilitates a discussion following a lecture or class activity, offering brief remarks and then guiding the discussion as it proceeds.

1. Begin by outlining critical points to be covered.
2. Prepare several general guiding questions to launch the discussion.
3. Prepare relevant questions and examples to use during the discussion.

Preparing Successful Presentations in Education

Good presentations in education are marked by clear organization, integration of the material into the broader course content, and student-friendly supporting material.

- *Invite participation.* Engage students in the learning process by posing frequent questions and eliciting answers. Begin a lecture by posing a question about the topic, for example, and allow time for discussion. Avoid delivering monologues and focus instead on encouraging class participation.

- *Organize material logically.* Presentations in education must be tightly organized so that the audience can easily access information. The simpler the organizational structure, the better (see Chapters 13 and 27). Use organizing devices such as preview statements and transitions to help listeners follow ideas in a lecture, for example.

- *Integrate discussion to overall course content.* Describe how the lecture relates to the previous day's lecture. In a discussion or group activity, make clear connections between students' comments and other topics that have been raised or will be raised later in the course.

- *Tailor examples and evidence to the audience.* Use familiar examples and evidence that the audience can grasp easily. The successful instructor will not support an idea with a statistical proof, for example, unless students are trained in statistics. Use familiar examples that will enhance learning (see the section on analogies in Chapter 24); try to choose examples that are close to students' experiences.

Speaking in Nursing and Allied Health Courses

Speaking assignments in nursing and allied health courses—physical therapy, occupational therapy, radiology, and other areas of health care—range from *reviews of research articles* in professional journals to *reports on community service projects* in a clinical setting. Students are assigned a mix of individual and team presentations that do the following:

1. Instruct clients on health care practices and techniques
2. Describe plans of care to medical teams
3. Communicate patient status at changes of shifts
4. Make policy recommendations to managers

Visual aids such as PowerPoint slides may be required; certain courses also entail preparation of individual or team poster sessions.

Community Service Learning Project

In a **community service learning project**, students learn about and help address a need or problem in a community agency, such as may exist in an adult daycare center, a mental health facility, or a burn center. Typically, presentations about your participation in these projects should include the following:

1. Description of the community agency and its client base
2. Overview of the service project and your role in it
3. Description of your accomplishments
4. Report of any problems encountered
5. Relationship of service learning to course content
6. Summary of what you learned

Treatment Plan Report

The ability to communicate information about patients or clients is important for all health care providers. Either individually or as part of a health care team, persons in the helping professions often evaluate patients' conditions and outline plans of treatment. One form of treatment plan, called the **case conference**, includes the following:

1. Description of patient status
2. Explanation of the disease process
3. Steps in the treatment regimen
4. Goals for the patient and family
5. Plans for the patient's care at home
6. Review of financial needs
7. Assessment of available resources

The **shift report** is a concise report of the patient's status and needs, which is delivered to the oncoming caregiver. It includes the following information:

1. Patient's name, location, and reason for care
2. Current physical status
3. Days on clinical pathway for particular diagnosis
4. Pertinent psychosocial data, including plans for discharge and involvement of family
5. Care needs (physical, hygiene, activity, medication, nutritional)

Policy Recommendation Report

In the policy recommendation report, the speaker recommends the adoption of a new (or modified) health practice or policy, such as introducing a new treatment regimen at a burn center. This report, sometimes assigned as part of a capstone course, includes the following:

1. Review of the existing policy or practice
2. Description of the proposed policy recommendation
3. Review of the existing scientific literature on the policy recommendation
4. Plan of action for implementing the policy or practice

Preparing Successful Presentations in Nursing and Allied Health

Good presentations in health-related courses accurately communicate scientific information while simultaneously assessing practical conditions. Depending on the audience (e.g., patient or staff), the communication will shift in tone from therapeutic/empathetic to more matter-of-fact, and instructors will expect to see these shifts in tone reflected in your presentations. They will also want you to support any assertions and recommendations with relevant scientific literature and other reports containing evidence of effective clinical practice. Instructors will expect you to do the following:

- Use **evidence-based practice** (EBP) supported by current research findings for all assignments. Evidence-based practice is an approach to treatment in which caregivers make decisions based on current research and "best practices."
- Apply concepts in the literature to your work with patients
- Evaluate the results of your interventions

CHAPTER 32

Business and Professional Presentations

In many sectors of the workplace, various types of business and professional presentations serve as a primary medium for communicating vital company information. Delivering effective business presentations is therefore one of the most important ways that business professionals gain visibility in their organization.[1] As with other presentations given in the classroom, business and professional presentations are forms of *presentational speaking*—in this case, reports delivered by individuals or teams addressing colleagues, managers, clients, or customers.

The curriculum of most business courses mimics the demands and challenges of the business world, and instructors typically require students to deliver the same types of presentations that they will later deliver on the job. Five of the most common of these presentations are *sales presentations, proposals, staff reports, progress reports,* and *crisis-response presentations.* The case study, described below, is unique to the classroom environment.

The Case Study

To help students understand the potential complexities of real-world business situations, instructors often require them to report orally on case studies, either alone or in teams. A **case study** is a detailed analysis of a real (or realistic) business situation. Students are typically expected to consider the case study carefully and then report on the following:

1. Description/overview of the major issues involved in the case
2. Statement of the major problems and issues involved
3. Identification of any relevant alternatives to the case
4. Presentation of the best solutions to the case, with a brief explanation of the logic behind them
5. Recommendations for implementing the solutions, along with acknowledgment of any impediments

Sales Presentations

A **sales presentation** attempts to lead a potential buyer to purchase a service or a product. The general purpose of sales presentations is to persuade.

Audience Considerations

The audience for a sales presentation depends on who has the authority to make the purchase under consideration. Some sales presentations are invited by the potential buyer. Others are "cold sales" in which the presenter/seller approaches a first-time potential buyer with a product or a service. In some cases, the audience might be an intermediary—a community agency's office manager, for example, who then makes a recommendation to the agency director

Sales presentations are most successful when you clearly show how the product or service meets the needs of the potential buyer, and you demonstrate how it surpasses other options available.

ESL SPEAKER'S NOTES

Steps to Counteract Problems in Being Understood

With the exception of young children, virtually everyone who learns to speak another language will speak that language with an accent. This issue is especially important in business and professional settings, where being understood can have a direct impact on your career. What steps can you take when your accent will make your oral presentation difficult for the audience to understand?

In the long term, interacting with native speakers in everyday life will help enormously. Engaging in dialogue with cross-cultural partners is an excellent way to adjust to native communication styles.[1] With immersion, non-native speakers can begin to stop translating word for word and start thinking in English. Using a tape recorder and practicing your speech in front of others is also very important.

But what if, although your experience with English is limited, you must nonetheless give an oral presentation? Robert Anholt, a scientist and author, suggests the following:

1. Practice the presentation often, preferably with a friend who is a native English speaker.

2. Learn the presentation almost by heart.

3. Create strong presentation aids that will convey most of the story by themselves, even if your speech is hard to understand.

By practicing often and ensuring that your presentation aids convey the bulk of your meaning, you can be confident that you will get your message across. And with time and effort, be assured that even the most difficult accent can be tamed to the point where speech is clearly understood.

1. Yuxia Z., "Using Authentic Cross-Cultural Dialogues to Encourage International Students' Participation in Tutorial Activities," *Business Communication Quarterly* 70 (2007): 43–47.

Source: Robert Anholt, *Dazzle 'Em with Style: The Art of Oral Scientific Presentation* (New York: W. H. Freeman, 1994), 156.

Organizing the Sales Presentation

Due to its inherently persuasive nature, plan on organizing a sales presentation as you would a persuasive speech. Suitable patterns include the motivated sequence, comparative advantage, and problem-solution or problem-cause-solution models (see Chapter 27). The comparative advantage pattern works well when the buyer must choose between competing products and seeks reassurance that the product being presented is indeed superior. The problem-solution or problem-cause-solution pattern is especially effective when selling to a buyer who needs a product to solve a problem.

With its focus on audience needs, the motivated sequence (sometimes called the *basic sales technique*), offers an excellent means of appealing to buyer psychology. To use it to organize a sales presentation, do the following:

1. Draw the potential buyer's attention to the product.
2. Isolate and clarify the buyer's need for the product.
3. Describe how the product will satisfy the buyer's need.
4. Invite the buyer to purchase the product.

The extent to which you focus on each step depends on the nature of the selling situation. In cold-call sales situations, consider spending more time discovering the potential buyer's needs. Being a good listener is critical in these situations.[2] For invited sales presentations, in which you will probably know the buyer's needs in advance, spend more time detailing the characteristics of the product and showing how it will satisfy the buyer's needs.

APPLYING MONROE'S MOTIVATED SEQUENCE IN A SALES PRESENTATION

✓ Identify the potential buyer's needs and wants and appeal to them.

✓ Using the product's features, match its benefits to the customer's needs and wants.

✓ Stress what the product can do for the customer.

✓ Engage the customer's senses, using sight, sound, smell, and touch.

CHECKLIST

Proposals

Organizations must constantly make decisions based on whether to modify or adopt a product, procedure, or policy. Should Armen Construction purchase new drill bits? Should Kmart stores implement a new employee-grievance procedure? Such information is routinely delivered as a **proposal**. For example, the Giant Lollipop Company wants to upgrade its telephone system. The facilities manager consults with the system provider to learn about the recommended equipment for making the upgrade. The manager then prepares a presentation that will provide the necessary information to assist the company in making its decision.

Proposals may be strictly informative, as when a facilities manager provides information to his or her superiors. Often, proposals are persuasive in nature, with the presenter arguing in favor of one course of action over another.

Audience Considerations

The audience for a proposal can vary from a single individual to a large group; the individual or individuals have primary or sole decision-making responsibility. Because many proposals seek to persuade listeners, careful adaptation to the audience is critical to an effective presentation.

PREPARING A PROPOSAL

Organize lengthy proposals as follows:

_____ 1. Introduce the issue.

_____ 2. State the problem.

_____ 3. Describe the method by which the problem was investigated.

_____ 4. Describe the facts learned.

_____ 5. Offer explanations and an interpretation of the findings.

_____ 6. Offer recommendations.

Organize brief proposals as follows:

_____ 1. State your recommendations.

_____ 2. Offer a brief overview of the problem.

_____ 3. Review the facts on which the recommendations are based.

_____ 4. Offer 1–3 recommendations.

CHECKLIST

Organizing the Proposal

A proposal can be quite lengthy and formally organized or relatively brief and loosely structured. More formal reports include a full introduction, statement of the problem, method of inquiry, summary of the facts learned, explanation, conclusion, and recommendation. If the facilities manager of the aforementioned telephone system must interview several people and read several sources of information pertaining to the upgrade, a formal plan may be appropriate. If the information is relatively straightforward and limited in scope, the presenter can begin with a statement of recommendation (or offer a list of 1–3 prioritized recommendations), provide a brief overview of the problem, and conclude with a review of the facts on which he or she has based the recommendation.

Staff Reports

A **staff report** informs managers and other employees of new developments that affect them and their work. A company's personnel division might implement a new plan for subscribers to the company's health insurance program.

To explain the changes, the personnel director will present the plan at a meeting of the sales division, review the reasons for the plan, explain how it works, and describe its ramifications. Another function of staff reports is to provide information on the completion of a project or task. A district manager of a restaurant chain might assign three local restaurant managers the task of devising a plan for expanding the seating capacity at each location. The managers will present their designs at the next district meeting.

Audience Considerations

The audience for a staff report is usually a group, but it can be an individual. The managers of the chain restaurant will make their report in a meeting attended only by the district manager, or in a meeting at which managers from the entire district are present. The recipients of a staff report then use the information to implement new policy, to coordinate other plans, or to make other reports to other groups.

Organizing the Staff Report

Organize a formal staff report as follows:

1. State the problem or question under consideration (sometimes called a "charge" to a committee or a subcommittee).
2. Provide a description of procedures and facts used to address the issue.
3. Discuss the facts that are most pertinent to the issue.
4. Provide a concluding statement.
5. Offer recommendations.

Progress Reports

A **progress report** is similar to a staff report, with the exception that the audience can include people *outside* the organization as well as within it. A progress report updates clients or principals on developments in an ongoing project. On long-term projects, these reports may be scheduled at designated intervals or at the time of specific task completions. For example, subcontractors on a housing-construction project meet weekly with the project developers. On short-term projects, reports can occur daily. For example, medical personnel in the intensive-care unit of a hospital meet each morning to review the treatment protocol and progress of each patient.

Audience Considerations

The audiences for progress reports might be a group of clients or customers, developers and investors, next-line supervisors, company officers, media representatives, or same-level co-workers assigned to the same project. For example, a work team consisting of workers from various departments (engineering, marketing, and cost analysis) may be assigned to the development of a new product. Once a week, members of the team present the rest of the division with a progress report, especially during the early stages. Once the project is well under way and activity is focused on one particular segment, such as marketing, those representatives may be the only personnel to make progress reports, and the audience may extend to potential buyers, corporate officers, and other staff in the various departments.

Progress reports are commonplace in staff and committee meetings where subcommittees report on the development of their designated tasks. Audience questions are common at the end of progress reports. (See Appendix A, "Handling Question-and-Answer Sessions," and Chapter 4, "Listeners and Speakers.")

Organizing the Progress Report

There is no set pattern of organization for a progress report. In many instances, the report begins with a brief statement to review progress made up to the time of the previous report, followed by a more thorough statement of new developments since the previous report was made. This statement may include descriptions of personnel involved and their activities, time spent on tasks, supplies used and costs incurred, problems encountered and how they were handled, and an estimate of tasks to be completed for the next reporting period.

You may wish to organize a progress report as follows:

1. Briefly review progress made up to the time of the previous report.
2. Describe new developments since the previous report.
3. Describe the personnel involved and their activities.
4. Detail time spent on tasks.
5. Describe supplies used and costs incurred.
6. Explain any problems and their resolution.
7. Provide an estimate of tasks to be completed for the next reporting period.

Crisis-Response Presentations

Crisis-response presentations (also called *crisis communication*) are meant to reassure an organization's various audiences (its "publics") and restore its credibility in the face of an array of threats, such as contaminated products, layoffs, chemical spills, or bankruptcy. Perhaps as a result of an increase in natural disasters, terrorism, and societal violence, the need for crisis communication arises often in both the profit and the nonprofit sectors.

Audience Considerations

Crisis-response presentations may target one, several, or multiple audiences, both inside and outside of an organization. A personnel manager may address a group of disgruntled employees unhappy over a new policy. Seeking to allay fears of ruin and shore up stockholder confidence, the CEO of an embattled corporation may target anxious employees and shareholders alike.

Organizing the Crisis-Response Presentation

A variety of strategies exist for organizing crisis communication, from simple denial to admitting responsibility for a crisis and asking forgiveness.[3] Familiarity with a range of *image-restoration strategies* will allow the speaker to select the techniques that best apply to the situation at hand.[4] In essence, the crisis-response presentation is based on persuasion and argument. Sound reasoning and evidence are essential to its effectiveness. Depending on the issue and the audience(s) involved, consider one or another of the four organizational patterns described in Chapter 27.

ETHICALLY SPEAKING

Code of Ethics for Professional Communicators

Because hundreds of thousands of business communicators worldwide engage in activities that affect the lives of millions of people and because this power carries with it significant social responsibilities, the International Association of Business Communicators developed the Code of Ethics for Professional Communicators.

Articles

1. Professional communicators uphold the credibility and dignity of their profession by practicing honest, candid, and timely communication and by fostering the free flow of essential information in accord with the public interest.

2. Professional communicators disseminate accurate information and promptly correct any erroneous communication for which they may be responsible.

3. Professional communicators understand and support the principles of free speech, freedom of assembly, and access to an open marketplace of ideas, and act accordingly.

4. Professional communicators are sensitive to cultural values and beliefs and engage in fair and balanced communication practices that foster and encourage mutual understanding.

5. Professional communicators refrain from taking part in any undertaking that the communicator considers to be unethical.

6. Professional communicators obey laws and public policies governing their professional activities and are sensitive to the spirit of all laws and regulations. Should any law or public policy be violated, for whatever reason, they act promptly to correct the situation.

7. Professional communicators give credit for unique expressions borrowed from others and identify the sources and purposes of all information disseminated to the public.

8. Professional communicators protect confidential information and, at the same time, comply with all legal requirements for the disclosure of information that affects the welfare of others.

9. Professional communicators do not use confidential information gained as a result of professional activities for personal benefit and do not represent conflicting or competing interests without the written consent of those involved.

10. Professional communicators do not accept undisclosed gifts or payments for professional services from anyone other than a client or an employer.

11. Professional communicators do not guarantee results that are beyond the power of the practitioner to deliver.

12. Professional communicators are honest not only with others but also, and most important, with themselves as individuals; for a professional communicator seeks the truth and speaks that truth first to the self.

Source: International Association of Business Communicators (IABC) Web site, accessed September 20, 2002, www.iabc.com/members/joining/code.htm.

SAMPLE SPEECHES

SAMPLE SPEECHES

SAMPLE VISUALLY ANNOTATED INFORMATIVE SPEECH

The History and Sport of Mountain Biking, Zachary Dominque 483

SAMPLE PERSUASIVE SPEECH

Remarks at a Human Trafficking Symposium, Washington, D.C.,
W. Ralph Basham 489

SAMPLE SPECIAL OCCASION SPEECH

2008 Harvard University Commencement Address, J. K. Rowling 495

SAMPLE SPEECHES
(481–502)

Sample Speeches

SAMPLE VISUALLY ANNOTATED INFORMATIVE SPEECH

The History and Sport of Mountain Biking
ZACHARY DOMINQUE

St. Edwards University

The following speech by student Zachary Dominque describes the sport of mountain biking. Zachary reveals the colorful background of the sport, explains how it differs from road biking, and describes the various types of mountain biking. Zachary himself is a championship cyclist, and his own experience partially informs the speech.

Zachary organizes the speech in a topical pattern, in which each of the main points is a subtopic or category of the overall speech topic of mountain biking. This is one of the most frequently used patterns for informative speeches.

Before I begin, if you'd like, close your eyes for a moment and picture this. You're on a bike, plunging down a steep, rock-strewn mountain, yet fully in control. Adrenaline courses through your body as you hurtle through the air, touch down on pebbled creeks and tangled grasses, and rocket upward again at breakneck speed. You should be scared, but you're not. In fact, you're having the time of your life. •

To help the audience recognize their familiarity with his topic, Zachary poses a question and uses a show of hands to informally poll the response

How many of you like to bike? Perhaps you ride to campus, bike for fitness, or cycle just for fun. Some of you might own bikes with lightweight frames and thin wheels, and use them to log some serious mileage. Or possibly you ride a comfort bike, with a cushy seat and bigger tires.

Good morning, ladies and gentlemen. My name is Zachary Dominque, and I'm a

• By asking the audience to visualize racing down a mountain, Zachary effectively captures the audience's attention.

mountain biker. Today, I'm going to take you on a tour of this exciting sport. Our stops along the way will include an overview of mountain biking, followed by a brief history of the sport. We'll also investigate the forms and functions of mountain bikes and road bikes, the different types of mountain biking, and we'll explore some noteworthy bike courses. • I've been racing since I was eight years old and won state champion three years ago, so this topic is close to my heart. •

To start, let me briefly define mountain biking. •

To accompany a definition of his topic, Zachary shows a simple but compelling image

Mountain biking is a sport that can be extreme, recreational, or somewhere in-between. The Web site ABC of Mountain Biking offers a good basic definition: "Mountain biking is a form of cycling on off-road or unpaved surfaces such as mountain trails and dirt roads; the biker uses a bicycle with a sturdy frame and fat tires." •

Mountain bikes are built to tackle rough ground. They feature wide tires with tough tread. They have straight, wide handlebars and rugged but light frames. These bikes have 18 to 24 or more specialized gears. The idea behind mountain biking is to go where other bikes won't take you, because those other bikes aren't equipped to handle the terrain. Mountain bikers ride on backcountry roads and on single-track trails winding through fields or forest. They climb up steep hills and race down them. The focus is on self-reliance, because these bikers often venture miles from help.

According to the National Bicycle Dealers Association Web site, in 2009 mountain bikes accounted for 28 percent of all bikes sold in the United States. If you factor in sales of the comfort bike, which is actually a mountain bike modified for purely recreational riders, sales jump to nearly 40 percent of all bikes sold. •

A photo of one of the founders of the sport. Zachary could trim the text on this slide even further for better legibility

So you see that mountain biking is popular with a lot of people. But the sport itself is fairly new. •

The man in this picture is Gary Fisher, one of the founders of mountain biking. According to *The Original Mountain Bike Book,* written by pioneering mountain

• Zachary previews the speech using metaphoric language in which the speech becomes a tour with courses.

• Pointing to his lengthy experience with the sport lends Zachary credibility to address the topic.

• Zachary transitions into the speech body.

• Zachary is careful to define his topic for the audience.

• Zachary uses reputable sources and informs the audience of where the information can be located.

• Zachary uses a transition to signal a change in focus.

bikers Rob van der Plas and Charles Kelly, they, along with Fisher and others from the Marin County, California, area, founded the modern sport of mountain biking in the early 1970s.

Early on, these guys decided to take on the adventure of racing downhill on the slopes of Mount Tamalpais, or Mt. Tam, in Corte Madera, California. Back then, they didn't have mountain bikes as we know them, so as you can see, Fisher's riding a modified one-speed Schwinn cruiser. • Cruisers aren't made to go off road at all; they're just supposed to ferry people around town on their so-called balloon tires. They have hard shocks, and the brakes aren't remotely equipped to handle stops on steep descents. But this is how Fisher and others started out.

> • To add interest and involvement, Zachary supplements his description with photographs.

Very quickly, however, Kelly, Fisher, and other founding cyclists like Charles Cunningham began to adapt the bikes to their needs. By the mid-1970s, they, along with a growing number of bikers in California, took to racing down the rough slopes of mountains on "fat tire" bikes. This activity led to the famed Repack Downhill Race on Mt. Tam, held from 1976 to 1979. According to the brief history of mountain biking on the 2012 Olympics Web site, the Repack race attracted many participants and helped put the sport on the map. Bit by bit, Fisher, Cunningham, Kelly, and others modified their bikes, added gearing, drum brakes, and a suspension system to the frames. As van der Plas and Kelly write in *The Original Mountain Bike Book,* it wasn't until 1982 that standardized production of these machines began. •

To get a better sense of what the mountain bike can and cannot do today, consider how they compare to road bikes. This is the class of bikes cyclists such as Tour de France winners Alberto Contador and Lance Armstrong use. •

> • Rather than relying solely on Internet sources, a practice that lessens speaker credibility, Zachary cites a key book on the topic, written by two founders of the sport.

The speaker contrasts his own bike with a photograph of a road bike

Whereas mountain bikes are built to tackle rough ground, road bikes stay on paved, smooth surfaces. And while mountain bikes feature wide tires with tough tread, road bike tires are very thin and the frames are extremely lightweight. This configuration lets the cyclist race hard and fast on a road course. This is fine for road bikes, because they're

> • To help foster understanding, Zachary compares and contrasts the mountain bike with the more familiar road bike.

all about productivity. If you take the road bike off-road, however, chances are you'll destroy it. The thinner tires can't provide the stability required, and without the knobby tread found on mountain bike tires, road bike tires can't grip onto the rocks, roots, and other obstacles that cover off-road courses.

The seats, or saddle as we call it, on road and mountain bikes also differ, as do the gearing, suspension systems, and handlebar configuration.

Road bike seats are thin and hard to sit on. This suits road cyclists well because they tackle flat, relatively smooth courses. We mountain bikers need a bit more cushion, and as you can see, our seats have a split in the middle so it bends with our gluteus maximus. •

Choosing an object for his visual aid, his own bike, allows him to point out all the important details, from the seat to the gears and shocks

Road bikes are geared to go faster than mountain bikes, with higher, or harder gears than those on mountain bikes. With mountain bikes, riders can rapidly adjust the gears to match conditions, using lower gears to overcome higher resistance, such as when climbing hills, and higher gears when the cycling is easier. The big gear on a road bike is probably twice the size of my big gear on this mountain bike.

The suspension systems on the two bikes also differ. Many mountain bikes have at least a great front shock-absorbing suspension system; some have rear-suspension systems, and some bikes have dual suspension systems. Road bikes generally don't have shock absorbers because they're not supposed to hit anything. •

A final feature distinguishing mountain from road bikes is the handlebars. Mountain bikes have flat handlebars. These promote an upright stance, so that the cyclist doesn't flip over when he or she hits something. The drop handlebars on road bikes require the cyclist to lean far forward to hold onto them. This position suits this type of cycling, which prizes speed.

I hope by now you have a sense of the overall form and functions of the mountain bike. The exact configurations of these bikes vary according to the type of riding they're designed to handle—downhill, trails, and cross-country. Let's begin with downhill. •

• Zachary again supplements his verbal description with a visual aid.

• Zachary could use more signal words such as *first* and *next* to help listeners follow along.

• Zachary internally summarizes the speech points he's covered thus far and signals a shift in gears.

As he discusses each type of mountain biking, Zachary reveals a photo of that type

Downhill biking is a daredevil sport—these bikers are crazy! They slide down hills at insane speeds, and they go off jumps. As described on the Web site Trails.com, downhill racers catch a shuttle going up the mountain, then speed downhill while "chewing up" obstacles. Downhill racing has been compared to skiing with a bike, and in fact in the summer many downhill racers do race on ski slopes.

As far as bikes go, downhill racers need a special downhill bike; one with fewer gears, and one that is heavier than other types of mountain bikes.

Now let's ride over to trails biking. •

Revealing one photo at a time keeps the audience focused on the subject at hand

Trails bikers hop and jump their bikes over obstacles—cars, rocks, and large logs. Their goal is to not put a foot down on the ground. In trails biking, the course is set right there in front of you. This is one of the few types of biking where you can watch the entire race, and it's done by time, not all at a mass start.

Trails bikes look quite different than other mountain bikes. They have very small wheels, measuring either 20, 24, or 26 inches, and they have smaller frames.

A third type of mountain biking, cross-country, is my sport.

• In this transition, Zachary extends the metaphor of his speech as a tour.

The photos clearly represent each type of mountain biking, aiding audience comprehension and retention

Cross-country biking—also called XC cycling—is the most common type of mountain biking. It's also the type of mountain biking sponsored by the Olympics. That's right. In 1996, mountain biking became an Olympic sport—just two decades after its inception.

With cross-country, you get the best of all worlds. The courses are creative, incorporating hills and valleys and rough to not-so-rough terrain. If done competitively, cross-country biking is like competing in a marathon. Done recreationally, it offers you the chance to see the great outdoors while getting, or staying, in great shape.

Cross-country bikes come in two forms: XC bikes are very lightweight, with either full or partial suspension. The Trails/Marathon XC bikes are a bit heavier, with full suspension. These latter bikes are designed for the seriously long rides.

Now that you're familiar with the main types of mountain biking, let's cruise through some notable cross-country courses. •

There are many great cross-country courses throughout the United States, some geared to entry-level cyclists and others for the pros. Depending on what state you're in, you may find very technical or very rocky courses. The McKenzie River Trail in Eugene, Oregon, goes on for hours through gorgeous, old-growth forest. In Utah you'll find awesome biking meccas among the incredible canyons and mesas of Moab.

Our own state of Texas draws a lot of riders to the state, with courses running through the desert in the south and flats and mountains in the west and north.

My personal favorite is Colorado. Breckenridge, a ski town in the Rockies, has some of the best courses I've ever ridden. Although I haven't been to Fruita in Colorado, its courses are legendary.

You can find great courses in New York, Vermont, North Carolina, Puerto Rico; Ketchum, Idaho; Downieville, California; and many other states nationwide. You'll find a good resource for exploring the variety of trails that exist on the Web site Trails.com.

Well, it has been quite a tour. Our course began with an overview of mountain biking and a brief history of the sport. We also learned about the forms and functions of mountain bikes compared to road bikes, the different types of mountain biking, as well as noteworthy courses. •

To me, mountain biking is the perfect sport—fulfilling physical, spiritual, and social needs. It's a great sport to take up recreationally. And if you decide to mountain bike competitively, just remember: ride fast, drive hard, and leave your blood on every trail. •

Works Cited

"Cycling, Mountain Biking." London 2012 Olympics Web site. Accessed November 9, 2010. http://www .london2012.com/games/olympic-sports/cycling -mountain-bike.php.

• Here Zachary uses the "cast-recast" form of transition, in which he states what he has just discussed and previews what he will describe next.

• Zachary signals the close of the speech by reiterating his opening analogy in which he compared the speech to a tour.

• Zachary's use of vivid language makes the conclusion memorable and leaves the audience with something to think about.

National Bicycle Dealers Association. "A Look at the Bicycle Industry's Vital Statistics." Accessed November 19, 2010. http://nbda.com/articles/industry-overview-2009-pg34.htm.

"Types of Mountain Bikes," Trails.com.

Van der Plas, Rob, and Charles Kelly. *The Original Mountain Bike Book*. Minneapolis: Motorbooks, 1998.

"What Is Mountain Biking." ABC of Mountain Biking Web site. Accessed November 23, 2010. http://www.abc-of -mountainbiking.com/mountain-biking-basics/whatis -mountain-biking.asp.

SAMPLE PERSUASIVE SPEECH

Remarks at a Human Trafficking Symposium, Washington, D.C.

W. RALPH BASHAM

W. Ralph Basham, Commissioner of U.S. Customs and Border Protection (CBP) from 2006 to 2008, delivered the following remarks on September 9, 2009, at a daylong symposium—a meeting in which various speakers deliver short speeches on different aspects of the same topic (see Appendix C, p. 509). One of several dozen speakers representing various government and nongovernmental agencies, Basham addresses the CBP's activities to combat human trafficking. His speech, available at www.cbp.gov, follows a problem-solution pattern, in which he lays out the problem of human trafficking and then describes the steps his department is taking to combat it. At various junctures in the speech, Basham appeals to the audience's logic (logos), emotions (pathos), and his own speaker credibility (ethos) to persuade the audience of the gravity of his subject.

It's a pleasure to have so many experts here at this symposium to address a serious global problem and a tragic crime—the trafficking and enslavement of human beings against their will—and against the law.

You have already heard some of the experts talk about the problem and what is being done. What I hope to add are the steps CBP is taking to address this issue, and why we all have a moral obligation to end these hideous crimes against humanity by working together in every way we can. •

We Americans • are a privileged people who live in a country whose very founding is based on respect for individual rights and liberty for all people. When this country was founded, our wise Founding Fathers created astounding documents outlining principles of freedom that have endured for over two centuries. And, for centuries, we have consistently fought and died to protect those freedoms and continue to fight for the rights of others to enjoy those same freedoms—in Europe . . . in Korea and Vietnam . . . and now in the Middle East. Freedom is not for sale. Human dignity can't be bought or sold. •

Our nation and our laws are built on this foundation of freedom, but we know there are those who—for money and power—will trample these laws and the rights of others.

CBP officers and Border Patrol Agents come across these atrocities every day. • An example: in Riverside, California, CBP responded to a request for assistance from the Riverside County Sheriff's Department for what they thought was a routine call for translation assistance. Instead, what they found was astounding. Sixty-four illegal aliens—men, women, and young people from Mexico, Ecuador, Honduras, and El Salvador— held captive in a 1,000 square foot house that was in deplorable condition. Some of these people needed medical attention—and all were held against their will.

Unfortunately, this occurs all too often across our country—and around the world. The United Nations indicates that after guns and drugs, trafficking of human beings is the third largest source of money for organized crime. Trafficking generates billions of dollars in profit each year and is one of the world's fastest growing criminal activities.

The State Department estimates are no doubt familiar to those in this room: between 600,000 and 800,000 people are trafficked across borders each year— with as many as 17,000 right here in the U.S. •

• Because speakers preceded him at the symposium, Basham doesn't need to spend much time previewing the topic of human trafficking.

• Note the speaker's frequent use here and elsewhere of the inclusive pronouns "we" and "our." These words make the audience feel directly included in his remarks.

• The speaker appeals to the audience's values (sacrifice, patriotism) to strengthen their involvement in the message.

• The speaker begins laying out the problem of human trafficking, as experienced by the CBP.

• Basham frames the problem with facts, but he knows that facts alone, or appeals to logic (logos), won't be enough to make people care about the problem. For that he needs to portray the plight of the people behind the figures, as he does in the following paragraphs.

The majority are female. Most still children. Most are trafficked for sexual purposes. Men, women, and children from Eastern Europe, Latin America, Asia, and Africa, too, are trafficked for forced prostitution, forced labor and domestic servitude.

In some countries, government corruption drives the trade. The marginalized status of women in many societies puts them at a higher risk of being targeted by traffickers. Many times they are promised jobs or educational opportunities. Desperate conditions, poverty, and political repression drive these victims to seek a better life, only to become trapped against their will, in even more desperate conditions. They set out with high hopes, but all too often, those hopes are crushed, • and what they experience is modern day slavery.

• Basham's use of descriptive words such as "desperate" and "crushed" adds emotional power to the plight of those who are trafficked.

Traffickers isolate them, take away their travel documents, and force the victims to rely on them. Most can't speak the language and are fearful of their captors—not only what they will do to them, but what they threaten to do to their family members. Victims are often beaten and brutalized. They face diseases, tuberculosis, rape, disfigurement, and even murder.

Children are the most vulnerable. Street kids and runaways are defenseless and have no choice but to do what they are told. Many are forced into begging rings and beaten if they don't bring in enough money. Others are forced to work in sweatshops, working from sunup until sundown—and sleeping on the floor. •

• The plight of these victims of trafficking is sure to arouse the audience's sympathy.

As we all know, there is no end to what criminals will do to attain power and money—and the trafficking in fellow human beings is one of the most insidious of crimes. It's an offense not just against the individual, but against humanity as a whole.

Law enforcement officers certainly have a part to play in stopping these atrocities of human trafficking. CBP—its officers and agents—are guardians of our nation's borders. Vigilance is one of our core values. CBP has the widest authority of any law enforcement agency in our government, especially the authority to detain people or products at the border. •

• Here, Basham turns to how his agency is helping to solve the problem of human trafficking.

On any given day, the mass humanity that CBP encounters and processes through our ports of entry is staggering. Over 1 million a day — and over 400 million a year—at our official ports of entry. And, our Border

Patrol agents and air and marine interdiction agents encounter hundreds a day in between the ports of entry.

We are uniquely positioned to intercept victims of traffickers—and the traffickers themselves. Our officers are frequently the first people these victims will see and there is a small window of opportunity to detect those who are being trafficked. Once that window closes, it may be too late to intervene and save them.

It's sometimes difficult to detect human trafficking, but one of the most important ways we can fight against this heinous crime is to educate—both our officers and the general population. • We can train our officers so they know what to look for and how best to identify these situations. Last year, we launched a campaign to educate our officers and the public. All of our officers and agents have been trained to detect traffickers and victims of trafficking. •

We have posted signs at airports and ports of entry in many languages besides English—among them, Spanish, Russian, and Chinese—to help reach out to potential victims of trafficking. We distribute information in these different languages to arriving visitors. This information lets potential victims know that we will help if they suspect they are a victim of trafficking. . . .

When we encounter situations where we suspect trafficking, our officers refer them for secondary inspection. We have provided them training to ask questions creatively and be alert to signs that their freedoms are restricted. They ask how they arrived in the U.S. and whether they have control over their documents.

But, unfortunately, victims of human trafficking are much like victims of domestic violence. They may mistrust law enforcement because they are illegally in the country . . . or because they fear they will be punished for the criminal acts they were forced into. They may fear retribution on other family members. Or they may feel shame for what they have been forced to do. And, they may believe they have no rights.

One trafficking victim revealed: "I didn't believe in police. I really believed what my trafficker said. My trafficker said they will put you in jail; they will send you back. . . . She said in this country, dogs have more

• Basham suggests that raising awareness about trafficking is one part of the solution to the problem.

• He provides examples of educational efforts that have been made.

rights. And I believe. I believe everything she said because she's been living here for a long time, she knows, she speaks English, she has money, everything . . . and I didn't have anything." •

But victims of trafficking do have rights. Much like refugees, they may be allowed to stay in the country temporarily during an investigation or prosecution. Some speakers today have mentioned the special "T-visas" and "U-visas" that allow victims of trafficking to apply for legal permanent residence status. You will hear a presentation on these rights and protections later today.

Other laws protect the rights of victims, too. In 2003, President Bush signed into law the Trafficking Victims Protection Reauthorization Act—and the PRO-TECT Act, which is the acronym for Prosecutorial Remedies and Other Tools to End the Exploitation of Children Today. Both of these laws strengthen the tools law enforcement use to combat trafficking. •

And programs, such as OASISS—the Operation Against Smugglers and Traffickers Initiative on Safety and Security—have been created to protect trafficking victims. OASISS is a bilateral agreement between Mexico and the U.S. to help identify and prosecute violent human traffickers.

The Border Enforcement Security Task Forces—or BEST units—work cooperatively with domestic and foreign law enforcement to dismantle criminal organizers operating near the border. There are now ten BEST teams located along the borders, including new teams in Phoenix, Yuma, and Imperial Valley.

CBP also works closely with other federal agencies—with the Department of Health and Human Services, the Department of Justice, and our sister agency, Immigration and Customs Enforcement (ICE). We share information and provide assistance to victims—and help to ensure prosecution of criminals in this illegal trade. •

I applaud all of you here today for raising awareness and forming partnerships to combat the barbaric practice of human trafficking. As compassionate protectors of the rights of human beings, the world must unite to fight this heinous crime. Human trafficking is a great moral test of our times—as much as AIDS . . . as much

• By putting the crime of human trafficking into the victim's own words, Basham evokes powerful emotions.

• Laws protecting trafficking victims are another aspect of the solution.

• Programs that encourage cooperation between the U.S. and other nations, as well as local and federal agencies within the U.S., form another part of the solution.

as ethnic cleansing . . . and as much as terrorist attacks against innocents. •

I grew up in a time when we were expected to follow the Golden Rule—"do unto others as you would have others do unto you." It wasn't considered a political or religious statement. It was just a good rule for living. It was a guide for being a responsible citizen and a good neighbor.

And I grew up in a time when children were allowed to be children—to be innocent and hopeful—and full of dreams for a bright future. Where adults were protectors—not exploiters. Where adults could be trusted and believed—not feared.

I believe that is one of the reasons I chose law enforcement as a career. Law enforcement officers protect the most vulnerable in our society from those who prey on innocence and goodness.

If you have ever heard me speak, you know that I am the grandfather of twelve, and those little children influence me in many ways. • Those twelve children make me want to work even harder to create a world that is safe and just for all the children of the world. Freedom and protection are their rights—and you and I must fight for all those who can't fight for themselves.

Thank you again for coming together today to address this important issue. On behalf of Customs and Border Protection, I can assure you that you have my support as you work to save lives and preserve freedoms.

• Framing the problem as a "great moral test of our times" adds persuasive punch.

• The speaker uses his ethos—his personal credibility—to appeal to the audience's involvement.

SAMPLE SPECIAL OCCASION SPEECH

2008 Harvard University Commencement Address

J. K. ROWLING

This commencement speech by J. K. Rowling, author of the Harry Potter series of books, does what any good speech of inspiration must do: It focuses on uplifting audience members and arousing their better instincts. Rowling achieves this by sharing her hard-won life lessons with the graduates. Rhetorically, Rowling uses rhythmic language, emotional appeals, and a dynamic style of delivery, all key components of speeches of inspiration.

President Faust, members of the Harvard Corporation and the Board of Overseers, members of the faculty, proud parents, and, above all, graduates. •

    The first thing I would like to say is "thank you." Not only has Harvard given me an extraordinary honor, but the weeks of fear and nausea I have endured at the thought of giving this commencement address have made me lose weight. A win-win situation! Now all I have to do is take deep breaths, squint at the red banners and convince myself that I am at the world's largest Gryffindor reunion. •

    I have wracked my mind and heart for what I ought to say to you today. I have asked myself what I wish I had known at my own graduation, and what important lessons I have learned in the 21 years that have expired between that day and this. •

    I have come up with two answers. On this wonderful day when we are gathered together to celebrate your academic success, I have decided to talk to you about the benefits of failure. And as you stand on the threshold of what is sometimes called "real life," I want to extol the crucial importance of imagination. •

    These may seem quixotic or paradoxical choices, but please bear with me.

    Looking back at the 21-year-old that I was at graduation is a slightly uncomfortable experience for the 42-year-old that she has become. Half my lifetime ago, I was striking an uneasy balance between the ambition I had for myself, and what those closest to me expected of me. •

• When delivering a special occasion speech, it is especially important to acknowledge members of the audience, as Rowling does here.

• Rowling's use of humor draws the audience in.

• The function of a commencement speech is to inspire and to arouse the audience's better instincts, so it is appropriate that Rowling considers what lessons she can share with graduates.

• Because inspirational speeches run the risk of being vague, it is important to tell audience members what your message will be about, as Rowling does here.

• Recalling how she felt as a 21-year-old establishes a common bond with listeners, encouraging identification with Rowling and receptivity to her message.

I was convinced that the only thing I wanted to do, ever, was to write novels. However, my parents, both of whom came from impoverished backgrounds and neither of whom had been to college, took the view that my overactive imagination was an amusing personal quirk that would never pay a mortgage, or secure a pension. I know that the irony strikes with the force of a cartoon anvil, now.

So they hoped that I would take a vocational degree; I wanted to study English Literature. A compromise was reached that in retrospect satisfied nobody, and I went up to study Modern Languages. Hardly had my parents' car rounded the corner at the end of the road than I ditched German and scuttled off down the Classics corridor. •

Of all the subjects on this planet, I think they would have been hard put to name one less useful than Greek mythology when it came to securing the keys to an executive bathroom.

I would like to make it clear, in parenthesis, that I do not blame my parents for their point of view. There is an expiry date on blaming your parents for steering you in the wrong direction; the moment you are old enough to take the wheel, responsibility lies with you. • What is more, I cannot criticize my parents for hoping that I would never experience poverty. They had been poor themselves, and I have since been poor, and I quite agree with them that it is not an ennobling experience. Poverty entails fear, and stress, and sometimes depression; it means a thousand petty humiliations and hardships. Climbing out of poverty by your own efforts, that is indeed something on which to pride yourself, but poverty itself is romanticized only by fools.

What I feared most for myself at your age was not poverty, but failure.

At your age, in spite of a distinct lack of motivation at university, where I had spent far too long in the coffee bar writing stories, and far too little time at lectures, I had a knack for passing examinations, and that, for years, had been the measure of success in my life and that of my peers. •

Ultimately, we all have to decide for ourselves what constitutes failure, but the world is quite eager to give you a set of criteria if you let it. So I think it fair to say

• Many audience members will likely identify with the struggle between the lure of creativity and the pull of practicality.

• Rowling offers guidance here.

• Frequent references to her audience encourage audience involvement.

that by any conventional measure, a mere seven years after my graduation day, I had failed on an epic scale. An exceptionally short-lived marriage had imploded, and I was jobless, a lone parent, and as poor as it is possible to be in modern Britain, without being homeless. The fears that my parents had had for me, and that I had had for myself, had both come to pass, and by every usual standard, I was the biggest failure I knew. ●

● Everyone can identify with fears of failure.

Now, I am not going to stand here and tell you that failure is fun. That period of my life was a dark one, and I had no idea that there was going to be what the press has since represented as a kind of fairy tale resolution. I had no idea then how far the tunnel extended, and for a long time, any light at the end of it was a hope rather than a reality.

So why do I talk about the benefits of failure? ● Simply because failure meant a stripping away of the inessential. I stopped pretending to myself that I was anything other than what I was, and began to direct all my energy into finishing the only work that mattered to me. Had I really succeeded at anything else, I might never have found the determination to succeed in the one arena I believed I truly belonged. I was set free, because my greatest fear had been realized, and I was still alive, and I still had a daughter whom I adored, and I had an old typewriter and a big idea. And so rock bottom became the solid foundation on which I rebuilt my life.

● An effective use of a rhetorical question.

Failure gave me an inner security that I had never attained by passing examinations. Failure taught me things about myself that I could have learned no other way. ● I discovered that I had a strong will, and more discipline than I had suspected; I also found out that I had friends whose value was truly above the price of rubies.

The knowledge that you have emerged wiser and stronger from setbacks means that you are, ever after, secure in your ability to survive. You will never truly know yourself, or the strength of your relationships, until both have been tested by adversity. Such knowledge is a true gift, for all that it is painfully won, and it has been worth more than any qualification I ever earned.

● Repeating the word "failure" several times in succession—a rhetorical device called anaphora—creates rhythm and thereby implants ideas in listeners' minds.

So given a Time Turner, I would tell my 21-year-old self that personal happiness lies in knowing that life is not a checklist of acquisition or achievement. Your qualifications, your CV, are not your life, though you will meet many people of my age and older who confuse the two. Life is difficult, and complicated, and beyond anyone's total control, and the humility to know that will enable you to survive its vicissitudes.

Now you might think that I chose my second theme, the importance of imagination, because of the part it played in rebuilding my life, but that is not wholly so. • Though I personally will defend the value of bedtime stories to my last gasp, I have learned to value imagination in a much broader sense. Imagination is not only the uniquely human capacity to envision that which is not, and therefore the fount of all invention and innovation. In its arguably most transformative and revelatory capacity, it is the power that enables us to empathize with humans whose experiences we have never shared.

• Rowling clearly states her second theme.

One of the greatest formative experiences of my life preceded Harry Potter, though it informed much of what I subsequently wrote in those books. This revelation came in the form of one of my earliest day jobs. Though I was sloping off to write stories during my lunch hours, I paid the rent in my early 20s by working at the African research department at Amnesty International's headquarters in London.

There in my little office I read hastily scribbled letters smuggled out of totalitarian regimes by men and women who were risking imprisonment to inform the outside world of what was happening to them. I saw photographs of those who had disappeared without trace, sent to Amnesty by their desperate families and friends. I read the testimony of torture victims and saw pictures of their injuries. I opened handwritten, eye-witness accounts of summary trials and executions, of kidnappings and rapes.

Many of my co-workers were ex-political prisoners, people who had been displaced from their homes, or fled into exile, because they had the temerity to speak against their governments. Visitors to our offices included those who had come to give information, or to try and find out what had happened to those they had left behind.

And as long as I live I shall remember walking along an empty corridor and suddenly hearing, from behind a closed door, a scream of pain and horror such as I have never heard since. The door opened, and the researcher poked out her head and told me to run and make a hot drink for the young man sitting with her. She had just had to give him the news that in retaliation for his own outspokenness against his country's regime, his mother had been seized and executed. •

Every day of my working week in my early 20s I was reminded how incredibly fortunate I was, to live in a country with a democratically elected government, where legal representation and a public trial were the rights of everyone.

Every day, I saw more evidence about the evils humankind will inflict on their fellow humans, to gain or maintain power. I began to have nightmares, literal nightmares, about some of the things I saw, heard, and read.

And yet I also learned more about human goodness at Amnesty International than I had ever known before.

Amnesty mobilizes thousands of people who have never been tortured or imprisoned for their beliefs to act on behalf of those who have. The power of human empathy, leading to collective action, saves lives, and frees prisoners. Ordinary people, whose personal well-being and security are assured, join together in huge numbers to save people they do not know, and will never meet. My small participation in that process was one of the most humbling and inspiring experiences of my life. •

Unlike any other creature on this planet, humans can learn and understand, without having experienced. They can think themselves into other people's places.

Of course, this is a power, like my brand of fictional magic, that is morally neutral. One might use such an ability to manipulate, or control, just as much as to understand or sympathize.

And many prefer not to exercise their imaginations at all. They choose to remain comfortably within the bounds of their own experience, never troubling to wonder how it would feel to have been born other than they are. They can refuse to hear screams or to peer inside cages; they can close their minds and hearts to

> • Relating real-life stories is a very effective way to inspire audience members.

> • Effective speeches of inspiration make frequent use of emotional appeals. Here Rowling appeals to the human impulse to fight against evil.

any suffering that does not touch them personally; they can refuse to know.

I might be tempted to envy people who can live that way, except that I do not think they have any fewer nightmares than I do. Choosing to live in narrow spaces leads to a form of mental agoraphobia, and that brings its own terrors. I think the willfully unimaginative see more monsters. They are often more afraid.

What is more, those who choose not to empathize enable real monsters. For without ever committing an act of outright evil ourselves, we collude with it, through our own apathy.

One of the many things I learned at the end of that Classics corridor down which I ventured at the age of 18, in search of something I could not then define, was this, written by the Greek author Plutarch: What we achieve inwardly will change outer reality. •

• Rowling shares a profound and timeless lesson.

That is an astonishing statement and yet proven a thousand times every day of our lives. It expresses, in part, our inescapable connection with the outside world, the fact that we touch other people's lives simply by existing.

But how much more are you, Harvard graduates of 2008, likely to touch other people's lives? Your intelligence, your capacity for hard work, the education you have earned and received, give you unique status, and unique responsibilities. Even your nationality sets you apart. The great majority of you belong to the world's only remaining superpower. The way you vote, the way you live, the way you protest, the pressure you bring to bear on your government, has an impact way beyond your borders. That is your privilege, and your burden.

If you choose to use your status and influence to raise your voice on behalf of those who have no voice; if you choose to identify not only with the powerful, but with the powerless; •if you retain the ability to imagine yourself into the lives of those who do not have your advantages, then it will not only be your proud families who celebrate your existence, but thousands and millions of people whose reality you have helped change. We do not need magic to change the world; we carry all the power we need inside ourselves already: we have the power to imagine better.

• Again, Rowling begins successive sentences with the same phrase ("If you choose . . ."), creating a rhythm that sustains attention.

I am nearly finished. • I have one last hope for you, which is something that I already had at 21. The friends with whom I sat on graduation day have been my friends for life. They are my children's godparents, the people to whom I've been able to turn in times of trouble, people who have been kind enough not to sue me when I took their names for Death Eaters. At our graduation we were bound by enormous affection, by our shared experience of a time that could never come again, and, of course, by the knowledge that we held certain photographic evidence that would be exceptionally valuable if any of us ran for Prime Minister.

So today, I wish you nothing better than similar friendships. And tomorrow, I hope that even if you remember not a single word of mine, you remember those of Seneca, another of those old Romans I met when I fled down the Classics corridor, in retreat from career ladders, in search of ancient wisdom:

> As is a tale, so is life: not how long it is, but how good it is, is what matters. •

I wish you all very good lives. Thank you very much.

• Rowling very directly signals the conclusion of her speech.

• As she does throughout her speech, Rowling turns to classical sources for inspiration. This final quotation by Seneca encapsulates Rowling's theme of taking risks in pursuit of a meaningful life and leaves the audience with a powerful message to ponder.

REFERENCE AND RESEARCH APPENDICES

A Handling Question-and-Answer Sessions

B Preparing for Mediated Communication

C Public Discussions: Panels, Symposiums, and Forums

D Commonly Mispronounced Words

E Chicago Documentation

F APA Documentation

G MLA Documentation

H CBE/CSE Documentation

I IEEE Documentation

J Glossary

REFERENCE AND RESEARCH APPENDICES

A   HANDLING QUESTION-AND-ANSWER SESSIONS   505

B   PREPARING FOR MEDIATED COMMUNICATION   507

C   PUBLIC DISCUSSIONS: PANELS, SYMPOSIUMS, AND FORUMS   509

D   COMMONLY MISPRONOUNCED WORDS   511

E   CHICAGO DOCUMENTATION   513

F   APA DOCUMENTATION   517

G   MLA DOCUMENTATION   521

H   CBE/CSE DOCUMENTATION   526

I   IEEE DOCUMENTATION   529

J   GLOSSARY   530

Handling Question- and-Answer Sessions

Deftly fielding questions is a final critical component of making a speech or a presentation. As the last step in preparing your speech, anticipate and prepare for questions the audience is likely to pose to you. Write these questions down, and practice answering them. Spend time preparing an answer to the most difficult question that you are likely to face. The confidence you will gain from smoothly handling a difficult question should spill over to other questions.[1]

Protocol during the Session

As a matter of courtesy, call upon audience members in the order in which they raise their hands. Consider these guidelines:

- *Repeat or paraphrase the question* ("The question is, 'Did the student council really vote against . . .'"). This will ensure that you've heard it correctly, that others in the audience know what you are responding to, and that you have time to reflect on and formulate an answer. Note that there are a few exceptions to repeating the question, especially when the question is hostile. One expert suggests that you should always repeat the question when speaking to a large group; when you're in a small group or a training seminar, however, doing so isn't necessary.[2]

- *Initially make eye contact with the questioner, then move your gaze to other audience members.* This makes all audience members feel as though you are responding not only to the questioner but to them as well.

- *Remember your listening skills.* Give questioners your full attention and don't interrupt them.

- *Don't be afraid to pause while formulating an answer.* Many speakers feel they must feed the audience instantaneous responses; this belief sometimes causes them to say things they later regret. This is especially the case in media interviews (see Appendix B). Pauses that seem long to you may not appear lengthy to listeners.

- *Keep answers concise.* The question-and-answer session is not the time to launch into a lengthy treatise on your favorite aspect of a topic.

Handling Hostile and Otherwise Troubling Questions

When handling hostile questions, do not get defensive. Doing so will damage your credibility and only encourage the other person. Maintain an attitude of respect, and stay cool and in control. Attempt to defuse the hostile questioner with respect and goodwill. Similarly, never give the impression that you think a question is stupid or irrelevant, even if it clearly is.

- *Do not repeat or paraphrase a hostile question.* This only lends the question more credibility than it is worth. Instead, try to rephrase it more positively[3] (e.g., in response to the question "Didn't your department botch the handling of product X," you might respond, "The question was, 'Why did product X experience a difficult market entry?' To that I would say that . . .").
- *If someone asks you a seemingly stupid question, do not point that out.* Instead, respond graciously.[4]

Ending the Session

Never end a question-and-answer session abruptly. As time runs out, alert the audience that you will take one or two more questions and then must end. The session represents one final opportunity to reinforce your message, so take the opportunity to do so. As you summarize your message, thank your listeners for their time. Leave an air of goodwill behind you.

Preparing for Mediated Communication

The underlying principles described throughout this guide will stand you in good stead as you prepare to communicate online, as discussed in Chapter 29, or on television or radio. These speaking situations do present some unique challenges, however.

Speaking on Television

On television, you are at the mercy of reporters and producers who will edit your remarks to fit their time frame. Therefore, before your televised appearance, find out as much as you can about the speech situation—for example, how long you will be on camera and whether the show will be aired live or taped. You may need to convey your message in sound bite form—succinct statements that summarize your key points in twenty seconds or less.

Eye Contact, Body Movements, and Voice

The question of where to direct your gaze is critical on televised appearances, as is controlling body movement and voice. The following are some guidelines:

- Don't play to the camera. In a one-on-one interview, focus on the interviewer. Do not look up or down or tilt your head sideways; these movements will make you look uncertain or evasive.[1]

- If there is an audience, treat the camera as just another audience member, glancing at it only as often as you would at any other individual during your remarks.

- If there is only you and the camera, direct your gaze at it as you speak.

- Keep your posture erect.

- Exaggerate your gestures slightly.

- Project your voice, and avoid speaking in a monotone.

Dress and Makeup

To compensate for the glare of studio lights and distortions caused by the camera, give careful consideration to dress and grooming:

- Choose dark rather than light-colored clothing. Dark colors such as blue, gray, green, and brown photograph better than lighter shades.
- Avoid stark white, because it produces glare.
- Avoid plaids, dots, and other busy patterns, as they tend to jump around on the screen.
- Wear a little more makeup than usual because bright studio lights tend to make you look washed out.

Speaking on Radio: The Media Interview

The following are guidelines for preparing for media interviews on the radio. These same guidelines can also be applied to the television interview.

- Know the audience and the focus of the program. What subjects does the broadcast cover? How long will the interview be? Will it be taped or live?
- Brush up on background information, and have your facts ready. Assume that the audience knows little or nothing about the subject matter.
- Use the interviewer's name during the interview.
- Prepare a speaking outline for the interview. Remember that the microphone will pick up the sound of papers being shuffled.
- Remember that taped interviews may be edited. Make key points in short sentences, and repeat them using different words.[2] Think in terms of sound bites.
- Anticipate questions that might arise, and decide how you will answer them.
- Use transition points to acknowledge the interviewer's questions and to bridge your key message points, such as "I am not familiar with that, but what I can tell you is . . ."; "You raise an interesting question, but I think the more important matter is. . . ."[3]
- Avoid the phrase "No comment." It will only exaggerate a point you are trying to minimize. Instead, say "I am not at liberty to comment/discuss. . . ."

Public Discussions: Panels, Symposiums, and Forums

The Panel Discussion

In a **panel discussion**, a group of people (at least three, and generally not more than nine) discusses a topic in the presence of an audience. Panel discussions do not feature formally prepared speeches. Usually the participants are arranged in a semicircle or behind a table placed in front of the audience; participants address their remarks to each other. The purpose of a panel discussion can be either to inform or to persuade audience members on the issue being addressed.

Panels require the presence of a skilled chairperson or moderator to direct the discussion. The moderator begins by describing the purpose and topic, or agenda, of the presentation and introduces the panel members. He or she then launches the discussion by directing a question to one or more of the participants. At the conclusion of the panel, the moderator summarizes the discussion and directs questions from the audience.

When preparing remarks for a panel discussion, or when preparing to serve as moderator, consider the following:

- What is the agenda for the discussion? (Generally, the moderator will deliver one to you.)
- Who is your audience? What do audience members know about the topic?
- What do they need to know about it?
- What are the ground rules? (Generally, the moderator will prepare a list and distribute it to each participant.)
- What aspects of the topic are the other participants likely to address?
- What are their areas of expertise?
- Will questions from the audience be permitted during the discussion or deferred until the panel has ended?
- How much time is allotted for the question-and-answer session? You will need to plan accordingly.

The Symposium

A **symposium** is a formal meeting at which various speakers deliver short speeches on different aspects of the same topic. Symposiums are organized to provide audiences with a detailed look at a topic by providing multiple perspectives on it. Sometimes the symposium concludes with a question-and-answer period; at other times, it is followed by a panel discussion among some or all members of the symposium.

When preparing a presentation for a symposium, consider the following:

- What aspects of the topic will the other participants address?
- In what order will the speakers address the audience?
- What are your time constraints?
- Who is your audience?
- Will you engage in questions and answers with the other speakers, or just with the audience?
- How much time is allotted for the question-and-answer session? You will need to plan accordingly.

The Forum

A **forum** is an assembly for the discussion of issues of public interest. Forums are often convened to help policymakers and voters alike deliberate about key policy issues. Forums can take place in a physical space, such as a town hall, or online, in moderated Web chats and other forms of virtual forums.

Forums may feature a panel or a symposium, followed by an extensive question-and-answer period by the audience. One well-known forum is the *town hall meeting*, in which citizens deliberate on issues of importance to the community. Often, city and state governments will sponsor town hall meetings in order to gather citizen input about issues that affect them, using this input to formulate policy. Sometimes the media will gather citizens together for a town hall meeting and will televise the event.

When participating in public forums (not as a featured speaker, but as a member of the audience), consider the following:

- Organize your thoughts as much as possible in advance by jotting down your question or comment on a piece of paper. Use the guidelines for impromptu speaking described in Chapter 18, p. 261
- Do not duplicate someone else's questions or comments unless it adds to the discussion.
- Be conscious of not wasting the audience's time. Use no more time than necessary to make your points.
- If appropriate, include a call to action at the conclusion of your comments.

Commonly Mispronounced Words

The following lists of errors in pronunciation are from *Basic Public Speaking*, Third Edition, by Paul L. Soper (Oxford University Press, 1968), with gratitude. The correct pronunciation or proper spelling is given in parentheses.

Misplacing the Accent

admir'able (ad'mirable)

applic'able (ap'plicable)

ce'ment (cement')

compar'able (com'parable)

exemplar'y (exemp'lary)

exig'ency (ex'igency)

finan'cier (financier')

formid'able (for'midable)

hor'izon (hori'zon)

i'dea (ide'a)

impi'ous (im'pious)

impot'ent (im'potent)

incompar'able (incom'parable)

incongru'ous (incon'gruous)

infam'ous (in'famous)

in'terest'ed (in'terested)

irrepar'able (irrep'arable)

municip'al (munic'ipal)

prefer'able (pref'erable)

proj'ectile (projec'tile)

reg'ime (regime')

respite' (res'pite)

superflu'ous (super'fluous)

u'nited (unit'ed)

vehe'ment (ve'hement)

vehi'cle (ve'hicle)

Addition of Sounds

athaletics (athletics)

attack-ted (attacked)

barbarious (barbarous)

colyum (column)

corpse (corps)

drawr (draw)

drownded (drowned)

elum (elm)

enterance (entrance)

ekscape (escape)

filum (film)

grievious (grievous)

height-th (height)

hinderance (hindrance)

idear (idea)

lightening (lightning)

mischievious (mischievous)

of-ten (of[t]en)

rememberance (remembrance)

sing-ger (singer)

stastistics (statistics)

sub-tle (su[b]tle)

sufferage (suffrage)

umberella (umbrella)

warsh (wash)

Omission of Sounds

accerate (accurate)

actully (actually)

assessory (accessory)

blong (belong)

canidate (candidate)

defnite (definite)

guarntee (guarantee)

ineffecshal (ineffectual)

jography (geography)

nuclus (nucleus)

particlar (particular)

plice (police)

pome (poem)

quite (quiet)

reconize (recognize)

resume (résumé)

sedimentry (sedimentary)

simlar (similar)

superntenent (superintendent)

sussinct (succinct)

temperture (temperature)

vilent (violent)

uzhal (usual)

Sound Substitutions

agin (again)

blaytant (blatant)

boquet (bouquet)

brochr (brochure)

capsl (capsule)

calvary (cavalry)

tshasm (chasm)

click (clique)

conscious (conscience)

crooks (crux)

cullinary (culinary)

dictionury (dictionary)

diptheria (diphtheria)

dipthong (diphthong)

dis-hevel (dishevel)

fewtyle (futile)

genuwine (genuine)

gesture (*g* is soft)

gigantic (first *g* is soft)

hiccough (hiccup)

homidge (homage)

ullusion (illusion)

interduce (introduce)

irrevelent (irrelevant)

jist (just)

larnyx (larynx)

lenth (length)

longgevity (longevity)

loose (lose)

memor (memoir)

miradge (mirage)

preform (perform)

prespiration (perspiration)

preelude (prelude)

prestidge (prestige)

rench (rinse)

saloon (salon)

statue (stature)

strenth (strength)

substantuate (substantiate)

tedjius (tedious)

theayter (theater)

Chicago Documentation

Two widely used systems of documentation are outlined in *The Chicago Manual of Style,* Sixteenth Edition (2010). The first, typically used by public speakers, provides for bibliographic citations in endnotes or footnotes. This method, which is also frequently used by journalists and scholars in the humanities, is illustrated in this appendix. The second system, often used by writers in the physical and natural sciences, employs an author-date system: sources are cited in the text with full bibliographic information given in a concluding list of references.

For information about the author-date system—and more information generally about Chicago-style documentation—consult the *Chicago Manual,* 16th ed., Chapters 14 and 15.

1. Book by a Single Author   Give the author's full name followed by a comma. Then italicize the book's title. In parentheses, give the city of publication followed by a colon, the publisher's name followed by a comma, and the publication date. Place a comma after the parentheses, and then give the page numbers from which your paraphrase or quotation is taken.

1. Eric Alterman, *What Liberal Media? The Truth about Bias and the News* (New York: Basic Books, 2003), 180–85.

2. Book by Multiple Authors   Give all the authors' full names, the book's title in italics, the publication information in parentheses, and the pages from which your paraphrase or quotation is taken.

2. Bill Kovach and Tom Rosenstiel, *The Elements of Journalism: What Newspeople Should Know and the Public Should Expect* (New York: Three Rivers Press, 2001), 57–58.

2. Bill Kovach and Tom Rosenstiel, *The Elements of Journalism: What Newspeople Should Know and the Public Should Expect,* rev. ed. (New York: Three Rivers Press, 2007), 61–62.

2. Leonard Downie Jr. and Robert G. Kaiser, *The News about the News: American Journalism in Peril* (New York: Knopf, 2002), 72–75.

3. Edited Work without an Author   Give the editor's full name followed by a comma, "ed." for *editor,* and another comma. Then give the title in italics, publication information in parentheses, and the pages you're citing.

3. Joseph B. Atkins, ed., *The Mission: Journalism, Ethics, and the World* (Ames: Iowa State University Press, 2002), 150–57.

4.   Encyclopedia or Dictionary   Give the title of the work in italics followed by a comma, the edition (if any), the letters "s.v." (from the Latin *sub verbo*, "under the word"), and then the term you looked up, in quotation marks, and a period. If the citation is from an online reference work, add the publication date or date of last revision; if neither is available, add your date of access. Conclude with the URL (Internet address).

4. *Routledge Encyclopedia of Philosophy*, s.v. "Ethics of journalism."

4. *Encyclopaedia Britannica Online*, s.v. "Yellow Journalism," accessed October 17, 2010, http://www.britannica.com/EBchecked/topic/652632/yellow-journalism.

5.   Article in a Magazine   Include the author's full name, the title of the article in quotation marks, the title of the magazine in italics, and the publication date. If you use a quotation, give the page number of the quotation. Otherwise, there is no need to cite the page numbers of the article.

5. John Leo, "With Bias toward All," *U.S. News & World Report*, March 18, 2002, 8.

6.   Article in a Journal   Give the author's full name, the title of the article in quotation marks, the title of the journal in italics, the volume number, the issue number (if available), the year of publication in parentheses followed by a colon, and the pages used. If the journal article was found online, list the URL of the article or use the DOI (digital object identifier) instead of the URL if one is available. It is not necessary to include page numbers for articles accessed online.

6. Tom Goldstein, "Wanted: More Outspoken Views; Coverage of the Press Is Up, but Criticism Is Down," *Columbia Journalism Review* 40, no. 4 (2001): 144–45.

6. Bree Nordenson, "Vanity Fire," *Columbia Journalism Review* 45, no. 5 (2007), http://www.cjr.org/profile/vanity_fire.php.

7.   Article in a Newspaper   Include the author's full name, the title of the article in quotation marks, the title of the newspaper in italics, the date of publication, the edition (such as "national edition") if relevant, and the section of the paper in which the article appeared. Omit page numbers, even for a citation to a quotation. If the article was found online, give the URL to the article itself (or to the newspaper's home page, if the article is archived).

7. Felicity Barringer, "Sports Reporting: Rules on Rumors," *New York Times*, February 18, 2002, sec. C.

7. Peter M. Shane, "Repair the Electoral College: Four Steps Would Help Balance Majority Rule with Minority Rights," *Washington Post*, October 31, 2004, final edition, http://www.washingtonpost.com.

8. Web Site   Give the name of the author (if available), the title or description of the site, the name of any sponsoring organization, the date of publication or modification, and an address (URL) that links directly to the site or site section. If there is no author, give the owner of the site as the author. Italicize the title of the Web site only if it is an online book, periodical, or blog. Use quotation marks for titles of articles, pages, or sections of a Web site. Include the access date only if there is no publication date or date of modification.

8. FAIR (Fairness & Accuracy in Reporting), "Challenging Hate Radio: A Guide for Activists," accessed September 21, 2010, http://www.fair.org/index.php?page=112.

9. E-mail Message   Treat e-mail messages like personal communications. Give the sender's full name, the phrase "e-mail message to author," and the date of the message.

9. Grace Talusan, e-mail message to author, March 20, 2010.

10. Discussion Lists, Newsgroups, or Online Postings   Give the author's full name, followed by the name of the discussion list, the date of the posting, and the URL of the posting.

10. Ola Seifert to Society of Professional Journalists discussion list, August 23, 2011, http://f05n16.cac.psu.edu.

11. Blog Posts   Include the author's full name, the title of the blog entry (in quotation marks) followed by the name of the blog (in italics). Include "(blog)" after the name if it is not part of the name. If the blog is part of a larger publication, include the name of the publication as well. End with the date of the blog post and the URL.

11. Brian Stetler. "Study: Some Viewers Were Misinformed by TV News," *Media Decoder* (blog), *New York Times*, December 17, 2010, http://mediadecoder.blogs.nytimes.com.

12. Article in an Electronic Database   Give the author's full name, the title of the article (in quotation marks), the title of the periodical (in italics), publication information for the periodical, and the pages you are citing. Then cite the DOI (if available) or the name of the database and the document number.

12. Mark J. Miller, "Tough Calls: Deciding When a Suicide Is Newsworthy and What Details to Include Are among Journalism's More Sensitive Decisions," *American Journalism Review* 24, no. 10 (2002): 43, Expanded Academic ASAP (A95153129).

13. Government Document   Use the governmental body or office as the author. Give the governmental body's name ("U.S. Congress," "U.S. House," "Senate Committee on Foreign Relations"), the title of the article (in quotation marks) or publication (italicized), the usual publication information, and the page numbers you are citing.

13. U.S. Congress, *Electronic Freedom of Information Amendments of 1996* (Washington, D.C.: GPO, 1996), 22.

14. Personal Communication   Give the author's name, the type of communication (e.g., "letter to author," "e-mail message to author," "conversation with author," "telephone conversation with author"), and the date.

14. Soo Jin Oh, letter to author, August 13, 2010.

15. Interview   Give the name of the interviewee, the interviewer, the name of the program or forum, the publication or network, and the date. Interviews that have not been published or broadcast should be cited with a description of the type of interview (e.g., "audio recording") and the place the interview was conducted.

15. Walter Cronkite, interview by Daniel Schorr, *Frontline*, PBS, April 2, 1996.

16. Video Recording   Give the title of the video, film, or other work, the director, the date of the original release, the place and name of the distribution company, the date of the recording, and the medium (VHS, DVD).

16. *All the President's Men*, directed by Alan J. Pakula (1976; Burbank, Calif.: Warner Home Video, 1997), DVD.

17. Sound Recording   List the composer or writer, the title of the work, the performer or conductor, the recording company or publisher, the recording number or date of release, and the medium.

17. Noam Chomsky, *The Emerging Framework of World Power*, read by the author (AK Press, 2003), compact disc.

17. Antonio Vivaldi, *The Four Seasons*, Boston Symphony Orchestra, conducted by Seiji Ozawa, Telarc 80070, compact disc.

APA Documentation

Most disciplines in the social sciences—psychology, anthropology, sociology, political science, education, and economics—use the author-date system of documentation established by the American Psychological Association (APA). This citation style highlights dates of publication because the currency of published material is of primary importance in these fields. For more information about APA format, see the *Publication Manual of the American Psychological Association*, Sixth Edition (2010).

This new edition now advises users to omit retrieval dates for content that is unlikely to change, such as published journal articles, and to omit the database from which material is retrieved as long as an identifier such as a URL (Internet address) or DOI (digital object identifier) is included.

The numbered entries that follow introduce and explain some conventions of this citation style using examples relating to the topic of stress management. Note that in the titles of books and articles only the first word of the title and subtitle and proper nouns are capitalized.

1. Book by a Single Author Begin with the author's last name and initials followed by the date of publication in parentheses. Next, italicize the book's title and end with the place of publication and the publisher.

> Nakazawa, D. J. (2009). *The autoimmune epidemic*. New York, NY: Simon & Schuster.

2. Book by Multiple Authors or Editors Begin with the authors' last names and initials followed by the date of publication in parentheses. Next, italicize the book's title and end with the place of publication and the publisher. Invert all authors' names and use an ampersand before the last name.

> Williams, S., & Cooper, L. (2002). *Managing workplace stress: A best practice blueprint*. New York, NY: Wiley.

3. Article in a Reference Work List the author of the article, the publication date, and the article title. This information is followed by the word *In* and the italicized title of the reference work. Include the volume number and inclusive page numbers of the article in parentheses, followed by the place of publication and the publisher. If an online edition of the reference work is cited, give the retrieval date and the URL. Omit end punctuation after the URL.

> Beins, B. C. (2010). Barnum effect. In I. B. Weiner & W. E. Craighead (Eds.), *The Corsini encyclopedia of psychology* (4th ed., Vol. 4, pp. 203–204). Hoboken, NJ: Wiley.

Biofeedback. (2007). In *Encyclopaedia Britannica online*. Retrieved from http://www

.britannica.com/EBchecked/topic/65856/biofeedback

4. Government Document   Use the office or governmental department as the author followed by the publication date. Italicize the title of the document and end with the place of publication and the publisher (usually "Washington, DC," and "Government Printing Office").

U.S. Department of Health and Human Services. (1997). *Violence in the workplace: Guide-*

lines for understanding and response. Washington, DC: Government Printing Office.

5. Journal Article   Begin with the author's last name and initials followed by the date of publication in parentheses. Next, list the title of the article, and italicize the title of the journal in which it is printed. Then give the volume number, italicized, and the issue number in parentheses if the journal is paginated by issue. End with the inclusive page numbers of the article.

Dollard, M. F., & Metzer, J. C. (1999). Psychological research, practice, and production:

The occupational stress problem. *International Journal of Stress Management, 6*(4),

241–253.

6. Journal Article Online   If a DOI number is given, add "doi:" and the number after the publication information. If there is no DOI, add "Retrieved from" and the URL for the journal home page. It is no longer necessary to include the database from which an article is retrieved or the date of retrieval for a published article. Omit the end period after a DOI or URL.

Christian, M. S., Bradley, J. C., Wallace, J. C., & Burke, M. J. (2009, September).

Workplace safety: A meta-analysis of the roles of person and situation factors.

Journal of Applied Psychology, 94, 1103-1127. doi:10.1037/a0016172

7. Magazine Article   Begin with the author's last name and initials followed by the date of publication, including the month or the month and day, in parentheses. Next, list the title of the article and the title of the magazine, italicized. Give the volume number, italicized, followed by the inclusive page numbers of the article.

Cobb, K. (2002, July 20). Sleepy heads: Low fuel may drive brain's need to sleep. *Science*

News, 162, 38.

8. Newspaper Article   Begin with the author's last name and initials followed by the date of publication, including the month and day, in parentheses. Next, list the title of the article and, in italics, the newspaper in which it is printed. End with the section and page or pages on which the article appears. Note that the abbreviation *p.* or *pp.* is used for newspaper page numbers. If the article was found online, omit page numbers, give the URL for the home page, and do not add end punctuation.

Zimmerman, E. (2010, December 19). Learning to tame your office anxiety. *The New York Times*, p. BU8.

Zimmerman, E. (2010, December 19). Learning to tame your office anxiety. *The New York Times*. Retrieved from http://www.nytimes.com

9. Unsigned Newspaper Article   If a newspaper article does not list an author, give the title, the publication date in parentheses, the name of the newspaper in italics, and the page on which the article appears.

Stress less: It's time to wrap it up. (2002, December 18). *Houston Chronicle*, p. A1.

10. Document from a Web Site   List the author, the date of publication (use "n.d." if there is no date), the title of the document, italicized, the words "Retrieved from" and the URL for the document. If there is no author, begin the entry with the document title followed by the date. Do not include a retrieval date unless the content is likely to change. Do not add punctuation at the end of the URL.

Centers for Disease Control and Prevention. (1999). *Stress . . . at work* (NIOSH Publication No. 99-101). Retrieved from http://www.cdc.gov/niosh/docs/99-101

11. Entire Web Site   To cite an entire Web site, including personal Web sites, it is usually sufficient to simply note the site in your speech. For example,

Dr. Wesley Sime's stress management page is an excellent resource (http://www.unl.edu/stress/mgmt).

It is not necessary to include a citation in the reference list.

12. Electronic Mailing List, Newsgroup, Online Forum, or Discussion Group Message   Cite the author's name, the posting date in parentheses, the subject line, and a description of the message in brackets, followed by "Retrieved from" and the URL for the list or an archived copy of the message. Include the name of the list if this is not part of the URL.

Lippin, R. (2008, November 2). Re: The relation between work-related psychosocial factors and the development of depression [Electronic mailing list message]. Retrieved from Occupational & Environmental Medicine Mailing List, http://lists.unc.edu/read/archive?id=4872034

Dimitrakov, J. (2001, February 21). Re: Immune effects of psychological stress [Online discussion group message]. Retrieved from http://groups.google.com/group/sci.med.prostate.prostatitis/browse_thread/thread/5cd921bc1b52688b/b28274accd8aec0f?lnk=gst&q=immune+effects+of+psychological+stress#b28274accd8aec0f

13. Blog post or comment   Cite the author's name, the date of the post, the title of the post and the description "Web log post" in brackets, and then give

the URL for the post. For a comment to a blog post, add "Re:" before the title and use "Web log comment" for the description.

> Lippin, R. (2007, July 31). US corporate EAP programs: Oversight, Orwellian or Soviet
>
> psychiatry redux? [Web log post]. Retrieved from http://medicalcrises.blogspot
>
> .com/2007/07/us-corporate-eap-programs-oversight.html

14. E-mail Message   To cite personal e-mail correspondence, it's sufficient to simply note the message in your speech. For example,

> An e-mail message from the staff of AltaVista clarifies this point (D. Emanuel, per-
>
> sonal communication, May 12, 2005).

The APA manual states that e-mail correspondence, like other personal communications, should not be included in the reference list; check with your instructor to see what his or her expectations are for your APA reference list.

15. Abstract from an Information Service or Online Database   Begin the entry with the publication information as for a print article. End the entry with "Abstract retrieved" followed by the URL of the database or the name of the database and any identifying number.

> Viswesvaran, C., Sanchez, J., & Fisher, J. (1999). The role of social support in the
>
> process of work stress: A meta-analysis. *Journal of Vocational Behavior, 54,*
>
> 314–334. Abstract retrieved from ERIC database. (EJ581024)

16. Personal Interview   To cite a personal, unpublished interview, it's usually sufficient to note the interview in your speech. For example,

> During her interview, Senator Cole revealed her enthusiasm for the new state-funded
>
> stress management center (M. Cole, personal communication, October 7, 2005).

The APA manual states that personal interviews, like other personal communications, should not be included in a bibliography; check with your instructor to see what his or her expectations are for your APA bibliography.

MLA Documentation

Created by the Modern Language Association, MLA documentation style is fully outlined in the *MLA Handbook for Writers of Research Papers,* Seventh Edition (2009). Disciplines that use MLA style include English literature, the humanities, and various foreign languages. The sample citations below all relate to a single topic: film appreciation and criticism.

1. Book by a Single Author Citations for most books are arranged as follows: (1) the author's name, last name first; (2) the title and subtitle, italicized; and (3) the city of publication, an abbreviated form of the publisher's name, and the date. Each of these three pieces of information is followed by a period and one space. End the citation with the medium of publication (Print) and a period.

> Berg, Charles Ramírez. *Latino Images in Film: Stereotypes, Subversion, and Resis-*
>
> > *tance*. Austin: U of Texas P, 2002. Print.

2. Book by Multiple Authors or Editors Give the first author's name, last name first; then list the name(s) of the other author(s) in regular order with a comma between authors and the word *and* before the last one. The final name in a list of editors is followed by a comma and "ed." or "eds."

> Grieveson, Lee, and Haidee Wasson, eds. *Inventing Film Studies*. Durham: Duke UP,
>
> > 2008. Print.

3. Article in a Reference Work Begin with the author of the article; if none is provided, begin with the title of the article in quotation marks. Cite the name of the reference work, followed by the edition (if provided) and the date of publication. If the work is arranged alphabetically, no volume or page numbers are required. If the citation is to an online version of the work, give the author, article title, and Web site. Then add the publisher or sponsor of the site, the date of publication or last update, the medium (Web), and the date you accessed the work (day, month, year). End with a period.

> Katz, Ephraim. "Film Noir." *The Film Encyclopedia*. 6th ed. 2008. Print.
>
> "Auteur Theory." *Encyclopaedia Britannica Online*. Encyclopaedia Britannica, 2007.
>
> > Web. 22 Oct. 2007.

4. Government Document In most cases, give the name of the governmental body or office followed by the agency and any subdivision as the author, using standard abbreviations. Italicize the title of the document. Congressional documents should include the congressional number and session, house, and type of document (report, resolution, etc.) in abbreviated form, and the number of the material. Add the publication information (the publisher is often the Government Printing Office [GPO]). Then end with the medium (Print). For an online government document, after the title of the document, give any additional print information, the database you accessed, the medium (Web), and your date of access.

> United States. Cong. House. Committee on the Judiciary. *National Film Preservation Act of 1996*. 104th Cong., 2nd sess., H. Rept. 104–558. Washington: GPO, 1996. Print.

> United States. Cong. House. Committee on House Administration. *Library of Congress Sound Recording and Film Preservation Programs Reauthorization Act of 2008*. 110th Cong., 2nd sess., H. Rept. 110–683. *GPOAccess, Congressional Reports*. Web. 15 Jan. 2010.

5. Magazine Article Along with the author's name, the title of the article in quotation marks, and the title of the magazine in italics, include the full date of publication and inclusive page numbers of the article. The date of publication should be listed as day, month, year, with no commas between them. For monthly magazines, list the month and year only. Use three-letter abbreviations for all months except May, June, and July. End with the medium (Print).

If you are citing the article from an online edition of the magazine, after the title of the article, add the name of the Web site in italics, followed by a period. Then add the publisher or sponsor of the site, the date of publication, the medium (Web), and the date you accessed the article.

> Ansen, David. "Shock and Yawn." *Newsweek* 26 Oct. 2009: 48. Print.

> Horn, Robert. "From Bangkok to Cannes, Thai Political Tensions Remain." *Time*. Time, 24 May 2010. Web. 3 Nov. 2010.

6. Journal Article Follow the format for magazine articles, but include the journal's volume number and the issue number (if any), with a period between them. Give the year in parentheses followed by a colon and the page numbers. End with the medium (Print).

If an article is accessed online through a database service, after the publication information, add the name of the database in italics, followed by a period. Then give the medium (Web) and your date of access. End with a period.

> Skrebels, Paul. "*All Night Long*: Jazzing around with Othello." *Literature/Film Quarterly* 36.2 (2008): 147–56. Print.

> Holcomb, Mark. "A Classic Revisited: *To Kill a Mockingbird*." *Film Quarterly* 55.4 (2002): 34–40. *Academic OneFile*. Web. 22 Oct. 2010.

7. Newspaper Article   Documenting a newspaper article is similar to documenting a magazine article. In citing the name of the newspaper, do not include any initial *A*, *An*, or *The*. Add the city in brackets after the name if the newspaper is not well known and the city's name is not part of the newspaper's title. Give the date, the edition (if any), a colon, a space, the section number or letter (if any), and the page number(s). If the article appears on discontinuous pages, give the first page followed by a plus sign (+) to indicate that the article continues on other pages. End with the medium (Print).

If you are citing an article found online, after the title of the article, give the name of the newspaper's Web site followed by a period. Then specify the publisher or sponsor of the site, the date of publication, the medium consulted (Web), and the date you accessed the article.

> Peers, Martin. "HBO Could Draw True Blood Online." *Wall Street Journal* 23 Oct. 2010:
>
> B16+. Print.
>
> Dargis, Manohla. "Unblinking Eye, Visual Diary: Warhol's Films." *New York Times* 21
>
> Oct. 2007. Web. 22 Jan. 2010.

8. Newspaper Editorial   Document an editorial as a standard newspaper article, but add the word "Editorial" after the title. If the editorial is signed, list the author's name first; otherwise, begin with the title.

> "Avatars Don't Smoke." Editorial. *New York Times* 8 Jan. 2010: A26. Print.

9. Single-Issue CD-ROM, Diskette, or Magnetic Tape   Cite these electronic sources as you would books, with the title of the source in italics. Add the number of the electronic edition, release, or version (if applicable), the city and publisher of the source, and the year of publication. End with the medium (CD-ROM, Diskette, etc.).

> "Pulp Fiction." *Blockbuster Movie Trivia*. 3rd ed. New York: Random, 1998. CD-ROM.

10. Online Scholarly Project or Reference Database   Begin with the author if one is listed. Then give the title of the work you are citing, in quotation marks, followed by the title of the site, in italics. If the site has an editor, give the abbreviation "Ed." followed by the editor's name. Then cite the name of the sponsoring organization, the date of electronic publication or of the latest update, the date on which you accessed the site, and the medium (Web).

> "Origins of American Animation." *American Memory*. Lib. of Cong., 31 Mar. 1999. Web.
>
> 26 June 2010.

11. Commercial Web Site   Include the creator of the Web site (if known); the title of the work you are citing, in quotation marks; the site's title, in italics; the name of any sponsoring organization or publisher (if none is found, use "N.p."). Then give the date the site was last updated (if none is listed, use "n.d."), the medium (Web), and your date of access.

> "American Beauty." *Crazy for Cinema*. N.p., n.d. Web. 24 Oct. 2010.

12. Personal Web Site   The guidelines for citing a personal Web site are similar to those for a commercial site. Include the name of the person who created the site and the title of the site in italics. If there is no title, include a description such as "Home page." Then give the publisher or sponsor of the site, the date of the last update, the medium, and your date of access.

> Last, Kimberly. *007*. Kimberly Last, n.d. Web. 18 Oct. 2007.

13. Article in an Online Periodical   Begin with the author, the title of the article in quotation marks, and the name of the Web site in italics, followed by a period. Then add the publisher or sponsor of the site, the date of publication, the medium (Web), and the date you accessed the article.

> Williams, Mary Elizabeth. "The NC-17 Rating's Perverse Failure." *Salon*. Salon Media
>
> Group, 8 Dec. 2010. Web. 3 Jan. 2011.

14. Posting to a Discussion Group   Begin with the author's name; the title of the posting in quotation marks (if there is no title, use "Online posting"). Then give the name of the Web site, e-mail discussion list, or newsgroup, in italics; the sponsor or publisher of the site (if none, use "N.p."); and the date of the posting. Add the medium (Web) and your date of access.

> Granger, Susan. "Review of *The Cider House Rules*." *Rotten Tomatoes*. IGN Entertain-
>
> ment, 30 Mar. 2000. Web. 2 Oct. 2010.

15. E-mail Message   Give the writer's name, the subject of the message in quotation marks, and then the phrase "Message to" and the name of the recipient (if the message was addressed to the author of the work in which the message is being cited, use "Message to the author"). Include the date of the message. End with the medium (E-mail).

> Boothe, Jeanna. "Re: Top 100 Movies." Message to the author. 16 Feb. 2010. E-mail.

16. Work of Art or Photograph   The basic citation for artwork includes the name of the artist, the work's title, the date of composition (if unknown, use "n.d."), the medium of composition (Oil on Canvas, Bronze, Photograph), the museum or other location, and the city. For artwork cited in a book, use the basic citation followed by the publication information for the book, and end with the medium consulted (Print). For artwork cited online, omit the medium of composition from the basic citation, and then after the city, add the Web site or database, the medium consulted (Web), and your date of access.

Christenberry, William. *Coleman's Café*. 1971. Ektacolor Brownie Print. Hunter Museum of Art, Chattanooga.

Christenberry, William. *Signs Near Greensboro, Alabama*. 1973. Smithsonian American Art Museum, Washington. *Smithsonian American Art Museum*. Web. 14 Jan. 2003.

Vermeer, Jan. *A Woman Weighing Gold*. 1664? Oil on Canvas. Natl. Gallery of Art, Washington. Ed. Gerald F. Brommer. *Discovering Art History*. 2nd ed. Worcester: Davis, 1983. 308. Print.

17. Personal Interview   Begin with the name of the person interviewed. Then specify the type of interview (Personal, Telephone, or Internet interview) and the date on which it was conducted.

Sanderson, Andrew. Telephone interview. 12 June 2010.

CBE/CSE Documentation

The CSE (Council of Science Editors, formerly the Council of Biology Editors) style is most frequently used in the fields of biology and environmental science.

The current CBE/CSE style guide is *Scientific Style and Format: The CSE Manual for Authors, Editors, and Publishers,* Seventh Edition (2006). Publishers and instructors who require the CBE/CSE style do so in three possible formats: a citation-sequence superscript format, a name-year format, or a citation-name format, which combines aspects of the other two systems.

- Citation-sequence superscript format: Use superscript numbers for in-text references. In the references list, number and arrange the references in the sequence in which they are first cited in the speech.
- Name-year format: Use the name and year, in parentheses, for the in-text reference. In the references list, give the references, unnumbered, in alphabetical order.
- Citation-name format: Use superscript numbers for in-text references. In the references list, arrange the references in alphabetical order and number the list sequentially.

In the following examples, all of which refer to environmental issues, you will see that the citation-sequence format calls for listing the date after the publisher's name in references for books and after the name of the periodical in references for articles. The name-year format calls for listing the date immediately after the author's name in any kind of reference. Notice also the absence of a comma after the author's last name, the absence of a period after an initial, and the absence of italics for titles of books or journals.

1. Book by One Author   Be sure to list the total number of pages in the book.

CITATION-SEQUENCE AND CITATION-NAME

1. Houghton JT. Global warming: the complete briefing. 4th ed. Cambridge (UK): Cambridge University Press; 2009. 456 p.

NAME-YEAR

Houghton JT. 2009. Global warming: the complete briefing. 4th ed. Cambridge (UK): Cambridge University Press. 456 p.

2. Book by Two or More Authors

CITATION-SEQUENCE AND CITATION-NAME

2. Harf JE, Lombardi MO. Taking sides: clashing views on global issues. 6th ed. New York: McGraw-Hill; 2010. 432 p.

NAME-YEAR

Harf JE, Lombardi MO. 2010. Taking sides: clashing views on global issues. 6th ed. New York: McGraw-Hill. 432 p.

3. Journal Article   CBE/CSE style uses standard scientific abbreviations for titles of journals (*Am Sci* for *American Scientist* and *J Am Med Assoc* for *Journal of the American Medical Association*, for instance). One-word titles are never abbreviated.

To cite a journal article on the Internet, add the medium ([Internet]) after the journal title, the date cited after the publication date (in brackets), and end the entry with the words "Available from:" and the URL (Internet address). Also give the DOI (digital object identifier) code, if available. Omit end punctuation after a URL or DOI.

CITATION-SEQUENCE AND CITATION-NAME

3. Brussard PF, Tull JC. Conservation biology and four types of advocacy. Conserv Biol. 2007;21(1):21–24.

3. Brussard PF, Tull JC. Conservation biology and four types of advocacy. Conserv Biol [Internet]. 2007 [cited 2010 Oct 22];21(1):21–24. Available from: http://www.blackwell-synergy.com/toc/cbi/21/1 doi:10.1111/j.1523–1739 .2006.00640.x

NAME-YEAR

Brussard PF, Tull JC. 2007. Conservation biology and four types of advocacy. Conserv Biol. 21(1):21–24.

Brussard PF, Tull JC. 2007. Conservation biology and four types of advocacy. Conserv Biol [Internet]. [cited 2010 Oct 22];21(1):21–24. Available from: http://www.blackwell-synergy .com/toc/cbi/21/1 doi:10.1111/j.1523-1739.2006.00640.x

4. Magazine Article

CITATION-SEQUENCE AND CITATION-NAME

4. Sheppard K. Bad breakup: why BP doesn't have to tell the EPA—or the public—what's in its toxic dispersants. Mother Jones. 2010 Sep-Oct:41.

NAME-YEAR

Sheppard K. 2010 Sep-Oct. Bad breakup: why BP doesn't have to tell the EPA—or the public—what's in its toxic dispersants. Mother Jones. 41.

5. Newspaper Article

CITATION-SEQUENCE AND CITATION-NAME

5. Zeller T Jr. Negotiators at climate talks face deep set of fault lines. New York Times. 2009 Dec 6;Sect. WK:3 (col. 1).

NAME-YEAR

Zeller T Jr. 2009 Dec 6. Negotiators at climate talks face deep set of fault lines. New York Times. Sect. WK:3 (col. 1).

6. Web Site   For material found on a Web site, give the author's name (if any) and the title of the material, followed by "Internet" in brackets. Add the place of publication, the publisher, and the date of publication (usually found at the bottom of the Web page), followed by the date of update and the date of citation in brackets. Add "Available from:" and the URL.

CITATION-SEQUENCE AND CITATION-NAME

6. Coastal Programs: The Barnegat Bay Estuary Program [Internet]. Trenton (NJ): Department of Environmental Protection, Division of Watershed Management. c1996–2004 [updated 2010 Feb 18; cited 2010 Oct 23]. Available from: http://www.nj.gov/dep/watershedmgt/bbep.htm

NAME-YEAR

Coastal Programs: The Barnegat Bay Estuary Program [Internet]. c1996-2004. Trenton (NJ): Department of Environmental Protection, Division of Watershed Management. [updated 2010 Feb 18; cited 2010 Oct 23]. Available from: http://www.nj.gov/dep/watershedmgt/bbep.htm

7. E-mail Message   CBE/CSE style recommends mentioning personal communications, such as letters and e-mails, in text but not listing them in the list of references. An explanation of the material should go in a separate "Notes" section. . . . (2010 e-mail from Maura O'Brien to me; unreferenced, see "Notes") . . .

8. E-mail Discussion List Message or Newsgroup Message

8. Affleck-Asch W. Lawncare methods causing heavy damage to environment [discussion list on the Internet]. 2004 Aug 17, 2:30 pm [cited 2010 Dec 2]. [about 10 paragraphs]. Available from: http://www.mail-archive.com/ecofem%40csf.colorado.edu

IEEE Documentation

The Institute of Electrical and Electronics Engineers (IEEE) style requires that references appear at the end of the text, not in alphabetical order but in the order in which the sources are cited in the text. A bracketed reference number beginning with *B* precedes each entry. For speakers, this means creating a bibliography of sources listed in the order in which they are cited in the speech. For more information on IEEE documentation, check the *IEEE Standards Style Manual* online at https://development.standards.ieee.org/myproject/Public/mytools/draft/styleman.pdf.

1. Book List the author by last name and first initial followed by a comma. Then list the book's title in italics and the edition (if applicable). Finally, list the place of publication, the publisher, the date of publication, and the pages cited.

[B1] Thomas, R. E., Albert, R. J., and Toussaint, G. J., *The Analysis and Design of Linear Circuits*, 6th ed. Hoboken, NJ: Wiley, 2009, p. 652.

2. Periodical List the author, the title of the article in quotation marks, the title of the periodical in italics, the volume number, the issue number, the pages cited, and the date. Only the first word of the article title and subtitle and proper nouns are capitalized.

[B2] Melfi, M., Evon, S., and McElveen, R., "Induction versus permanent magnet motors," *IEEE Industry Applications Magazine*, vol. 15, no. 6, pp. 28–35, Nov./Dec. 2009. doi: 10.1109/MIAS.2009.934443

3. Web Page List the author, the title of the Web page, volume and issue number (for an online journal), page number (if relevant or given), and the year and the month of publication. This information should be followed by a footnote to the Internet location. The footnote should begin with "Available at" and then list the URL of the most stable location possible (an index to the page rather than the page itself).

[B3] National Academy of Engineering, "Lasers and fiber optics timeline," *Greatest Engineering Achievements of the 20th Century*, 2010.*

*Available at www.greatachievements.org.

Glossary

abstract language   Language that is general or nonspecific. See also *concrete language*.

active listening   A multistep, focused, and purposeful process of gathering and evaluating information.

ad hominem argument   A form of fallacious argument that targets people instead of issues and attempts to incite an audience's dislike for an opponent.

advanced search   (often called *field searching*) A search tool in most Internet search engines that targets specific search parameters to narrow search results.

after-dinner speech   A speech that is likely to occur before, after, or during a formal dinner, a breakfast or lunch seminar, or other type of business, professional, or civic meeting.

agenda   A document identifying the items to be accomplished during a meeting.

agora   In ancient Greece, a public square or marketplace. See also *forum*.

alliteration   The repetition of the same sounds, usually initial consonants, in two or more neighboring words or syllables.

allusion   A figure of speech in which the speaker makes vague or indirect reference to people, historical events, or concepts to give deeper meaning to the message.

almanac   A reference work that contains facts and statistics in many categories, including those that are related to historical, social, political, and religious subjects.

analogy   An extended metaphor or simile that compares an unfamiliar concept or process with a more familiar one in order to help the listener understand the one that is unfamiliar.

anaphora   A rhetorical device in which the speaker repeats a word or phrase at the beginning of successive phrases, clauses, or sentences.

anecdote   A brief story of an interesting, humorous, or real-life incident that links back to the speaker's theme.

antithesis   Setting off two ideas in balanced (parallel) opposition to each other to create a powerful effect.

anxiety stop-time   A strategy for managing pre-performance anxiety by allowing the anxiety to build up for a few minutes without resistance so that it diffuses itself as you declare it time to overtake the anxiety and get on with preparing your speech.

appeal to tradition   A fallacy of reasoning in which the speaker argues for the truth of a claim based solely on common practices in the past.

architecture design review   Oral presentation with the dual goal of helping listeners visualize the design concept while also selling it.

argument   A stated position, with support, for or against an idea or issue; contains the core elements of claim, evidence, and warrants.

arrangement   The strategic process of deciding how to order speech points into a coherent and convincing pattern for your topic and audience; also refers to one of the five parts of the classical canons of rhetoric.

articulation   The clarity or forcefulness with which sounds are made, regardless of whether they are pronounced correctly.

asynchronous communication   Communication in which interaction between speaker and receiver does not occur simultaneously; recorded (offline) presentations rely on asynchronous communication.

atlas   A collection of maps, text, and accompanying charts and tables.

attitudes   A predisposition to respond to people, ideas, objects, or events in evaluative ways.

audience analysis   The process of gathering and analyzing demographic and psychological information about audience members with the explicit aim of adapting your message to the information you uncover.

audience-centered approach   An approach to speech preparation in which each phase of the speech preparation process—from selection and treatment of the speech topic to making decisions about organization, language, and method of delivery—is geared toward communicating a meaningful message to the audience.

audience segmentation   Dividing a general audience into smaller groups, called *target audiences,* with similar characteristics, wants, and needs.

audio clip   A short recording of sounds, music, or speech. Introducing sound into a speech can add interest, illustrate ideas, and even bring humor to the mix.

aural channel   A nonverbal channel of communication made up of the vocalizations that form and accompany spoken words. These vocalizations, also called *paralanguage,* include the qualities of volume, pitch, rate, variety, and articulation and pronunciation.

authoritative warrant   A warrant that appeals to the credibility the audience assigns to the source of the evidence; also called an *ethos-based appeal.*

average   A summary of a set of data according to its typical or average characteristics; may refer to the *mean, median,* or *mode.*

backstory   The story that leads up to an event that listeners might find interesting; offering a backstory can enliven an informative speech, especially those about events.

bandwagoning   A fallacious argument that presents itself as true because "general opinion" supports it.

bar graph   A type of graph used to compare quantities or magnitudes with the use of bars of varying lengths.

begging the question   A fallacious argument presented in such a way that it is necessarily true, even though no evidence has been presented.

beliefs   The ways in which people perceive reality or determine the very existence or validity of something.

blog   Short for "Weblog"; an online personal journal.

body (of speech)   The part of the speech in which the speaker develops the main points intended to fulfill the speech purpose.

brainstorming   A problem-solving technique, useful for developing speech topics, that involves the spontaneous generation of ideas. You can brainstorm by making lists, using word association, and mapping a topic, among other techniques.

brief example   A single illustration of a point.

call to action   A challenge to audience members to act in response to a speech, see the problem in a new way, change their beliefs about the problem, or change both their actions and their beliefs with respect to the problem; placed at the conclusion of a speech.

canned speech   A speech used repeatedly and without sufficient adaptation to the rhetorical speech situation.

canons of rhetoric   A classical approach to speechmaking in which the speaker divides a speech into five parts: invention, arrangement, style, memory, and delivery.

captive audience   An audience in attendance not because they necessarily freely choose to listen to a speech but because they must.

case conference   An oral report prepared by health-care professionals evaluating a patient's condition and outlining a treatment plan.

case study   A detailed illustration of a real or hypothetical business situation.

causal (cause-effect) pattern of arrangement   A pattern of organizing speech points in order, first of causes and then of effects or vice versa; it is used when the cause-effect relationship is well established.

central processing   A mode of processing a persuasive message that involves thinking critically about the contents of the message and the strength and quality of the speaker's arguments. People who seriously consider what the speaker's message means to them are most likely to experience a relatively enduring change in thinking.

channel   The medium through which the speaker sends a message (e.g., sound waves, air waves, electronic transmission, and so forth).

chart   A method of visually organizing complex information into compact form. Several different types of charts are helpful for speakers: flowcharts, organization charts, and tabular charts or tables.

cherry-picking   To selectively present only those facts and statistics that buttress your point of view while ignoring competing data.

chronological pattern of arrangement   (also called *temporal pattern*) A pattern of organizing speech points in a natural sequential order; it is used when describing a series of events in time or when the topic develops in line with a set pattern of actions or tasks.

circular pattern of arrangement   A pattern of organizing speech points so that one idea leads to another, which leads to a third, and so forth until the speaker arrives back at the speech thesis.

claim   The declaration of a state of affairs, in which a speaker attempts to prove something.

claim of fact   An argument that focuses on whether something is or is not true or whether something will or will not happen.

claim of policy   A claim that recommends that a specific course of action be taken, or approved, by an audience.

claim of value   A claim that addresses issues of judgment.

classroom discussion presentation   A type of oral presentation in which the speaker presents a brief overview of the topic under discussion and introduces a series of questions to guide students through the topic.

cliché   An expression that is predictable and stale.

closed-ended question   A question designed to elicit a small range of specific answers supplied by the interviewer. See also *scale question* and *open-ended question*.

co-culture   A community of people whose perceptions and beliefs differ significantly from those of other groups within the larger culture.

code-switching   The selective use of dialect within a speech.

colleagues within the field audience   An audience of individuals who share a speaker's knowledge of the general field under question but who may not be familiar with the specific topic under discussion.

collective mind   A state of mind adopted by group members in which they determine that the group communication will be careful, consistent, and conscientious.

collectivist culture   A culture that tends to emphasize the needs and desires of the larger group rather than those of the individual.

colloquial expression   An informal expression, often with regional variations of speech.

common knowledge   Information that is likely to be known by many people and is therefore in the public domain; the source of such information need not be cited in a speech.

community service learning project   Oral report in which the speaker describes a community agency and its client base, his or her role and accomplishments in working with the agency, any problems encountered, and what was learned.

comparative advantage pattern of arrangement   A pattern of organizing speech points so that the speaker's viewpoint or proposal is shown to be superior to one or more alternative viewpoints or proposals.

conclusion   The part of the speech in which the speaker reiterates the speech purpose, summarizes main points, and leaves the audience with something to think about or act upon.

concrete language   Specific, tangible, and definite language (nouns or verbs). See also *abstract language.*

connotative meaning   The individual associations that different people bring to bear on a word.

conversation stopper   Speech designed to discredit, demean, and belittle those with whom one disagrees.

coordinate points   The alignment of points in a speech outline according to their equal importance to the topic and purpose.

coordination and subordination   The logical placement of ideas relative to their importance to one another. Ideas that are coordinate are given equal weight. An idea that is subordinate to another is given relatively less weight.

copyright   A legal protection afforded original creators of literary or artistic works, including works classified as literary, musical, dramatic, choreographic, pictorial, graphic, sculptural, audiovisual, sound recording, or architectural.

counterproductive roles   Negative interpersonal roles of group members who focus on individual versus group needs. These needs are usually irrelevant to the task at hand and are not oriented toward maintenance of the group as a team.

crisis-response presentation   Oral presentation in which the speaker seeks to reassure an organization's various audiences ("publics") and restore its credibility in the face of potentially reputation-damaging situations.

critical and conflicted audience   Audience members whose attitudes are critical of or conflicted with the speaker's topic.

critical thinking   The ability to evaluate claims on the basis of well-supported reasons.

cultural intelligence   The willingness to learn about other cultures and gradually reshape your thinking and behavior in response to what you've learned.

cultural norms   A group's rules for behavior; attempts to persuade people to do things contrary to their cultural norms will usually fail.

cultural premises   A group's shared beliefs and values about personal identity and relationships; persuasive attempts that challenge cultural premises will usually fail.

culture   The language, beliefs, values, norms, behaviors, and even material objects that are passed from one generation to the next.

database   A searchable place, or "base," in which information is stored and from which it can be retrieved.

debate   An oral presentation in which two individuals or groups consider or argue an issue from opposing viewpoints.

decoding   The process of interpreting a message.

deductive reasoning   Reasoning from a general condition to a specific instance. See also *inductive reasoning; syllogism*.

defensive listening   A poor listening behavior in which the listener reacts defensively to a speaker's message.

definition by etymology (word origin)   Defining something by providing an account of a word's history.

definition by example   Defining something by providing an example of it.

definition by negation   Defining something by explaining what it is not.

definition by synonym   Defining something by comparing it with another term that has an equivalent meaning. For example: A friend is a comrade or a buddy.

deliberative oratory   In ancient Greece, speech addressing legislative or political policy issues.

delivery   The vocal and nonverbal behavior that a speaker uses in a public speech; one of the five canons of rhetoric.

delivery cues   Brief reminder notes or prompts placed in the speaking outline; can refer to transitions, timing, speaking rate and volume, presentation aids, quotations, statistics, and difficult-to-pronounce or -remember names or words.

demagogue   An unethical speaker who relies heavily on irrelevant emotional appeals to short-circuit listeners' rational decision-making process.

demographics   Statistical characteristics of a given population. Characteristics typically considered in the analysis of audience members include age, gender, ethnic or cultural background, socioeconomic status (including income, occupation, and education), and religious and political affiliation.

denotative meaning   The literal or dictionary definition of a word.

devil's advocacy   Arguing for the sake of raising issues or concerns about the idea under discussion.

Dewey decimal number   An identifying number that allows the user to retrieve library books and other works that have been classified according to the Dewey decimal system.

diagram   A schematic drawing that explains how something works or how it is constructed or operated; used to simplify and clarify complicated procedures, explanations, and operations.

dialectical inquiry   Devil's advocacy (see above) that goes a step further by proposing a countersolution to an idea.

dialects   Subcultural variations of the mainstream pronunciation and articulation of a language.

dialogic communication   The sharing of ideas and open discussion through words.

dignity   The feeling that one is worthy, honored, or respected as a person.

direct quotation   A statement quoted verbatim, or word for word, from a source. Direct quotations should always be acknowledged in a speech. See also *paraphrase*.

disinformation   The deliberate falsification of information.

domain   The suffix at the end of a Web address that tells you the nature of the Web site: educational (.edu), government (.gov), military (.mil), nonprofit organization (.org), business/commercial (.com), or network (.net). A tilde (~) in the address usually indicates that it is a personal page rather than part of an institutional Web site. Understanding the domain can help you assess the credibility of a site.

dyadic communication   Communication between two people, as in a conversation.

effective delivery   The skillful application of natural conversational behavior to a speech in a way that is relaxed, enthusiastic, and direct.

either-or fallacy   A fallacious argument that is stated in terms of two alternatives only, even though there may be multiple ways of viewing the issue.

elaboration likelihood model of persuasion (ELM)   A model of persuasion that states that people process persuasive messages by one of two routes—either central processing or peripheral processing—depending on their degree of involvement in the message.

elocutionary movement   An approach to public speaking in which speechmaking is regarded as a type of performance, much like acting.

encoding   The process of organizing a message, choosing words and sentence structure, and verbalizing the message.

encyclopedia   A reference work that summarizes knowledge found in original form elsewhere and provides an overview of subjects.

engineering design review   An oral presentation providing information on the results of a design project.

enthymeme   A syllogism stated as a probability rather than as an absolute. Because the enthymeme states either a major or a minor premise, but not both, the premise not stated remains implied.

epideictic oratory   In ancient Greece, speech addressing special occasions, such as celebrations and funerals.

epiphora   A rhetorical device in which the speaker repeats a word or phrase at the end of successive statements.

ethical appeal   An attempt to persuade audience members by appealing to speaker credibility.

ethics   The rules or standards of moral conduct, or how people should act toward one another. In terms of public speaking, *ethics* refers to the responsibilities speakers have toward both their audience and themselves. It also encompasses the responsibilities that listeners have toward speakers.

ethnocentrism   The belief that the ways of one's own culture are superior to those of other cultures. Ethnocentric speakers act as though everyone shares their point of view and points of reference, whether or not this is in fact the case.

ethos   The Greek word for "character." According to the ancient Greek rhetorician Aristotle, audiences listen to and trust speakers if they exhibit competence (as demonstrated by the speaker's grasp of the subject matter) and good moral character.

eulogy   A speech whose purpose is to celebrate and commemorate the life of someone while consoling those who are left behind; typically delivered by close friends and family members.

evaluation research presentation   An oral presentation reporting on the effectiveness of programs developed to address various issues; frequently delivered in social scientific fields.

evidence   Supporting material that provides grounds for belief.

evidence-based practice An approach to medical treatment in which caregivers make decisions based on current research and "best practices."

example An illustration whose purpose is to aid understanding by making ideas, items, or events more concrete and by clarifying and amplifying meaning.

expectancy-outcome values theory A theory of persuasion developed by Icek Aizen and Martin Fishbein positing that audience members act according to the perceived costs and benefits ("value") associated with a particular action; useful when developing a persuasive speech targeting behavior.

expert or insider audience An audience composed of individuals who have an intimate knowledge of the topic, issue, product, or idea being discussed.

expert testimony Any findings, eyewitness accounts, or opinions by professionals who are trained to evaluate or report on a given topic; a form of supporting material.

extended example Multifaceted illustrations of the idea, item, or event being described, thereby getting the point across and reiterating it effectively.

external listening distraction Anything in the environment that distracts listeners from receiving the speaker's message.

fabrication The making up of information, such as falsifying data or experiments or claiming a source where none exists.

face-to-face (FtF) presentation A presentation delivered in the physical presence of others; an "offline" presentation.

fact book A reference work that includes key information on a given topic (e.g., facts about the geography, government, economy, and transportation of a given country).

facts Documented occurrences, including actual events, dates, times, places, and people involved.

fairness One of four "ground rules" of ethical speaking, fairness is the act of making a genuine effort to see all sides of an issue and to be open-minded.

fair use Legal guidelines permitting the limited use of copyrighted works without permission for the purposes of scholarship, criticism, comment, news reporting, teaching, and research.

faulty analogy An inaccurate or misleading comparison suggesting that because two things are similar in some ways, they are necessarily similar in others.

fear appeal A persuasive appeal to audience members that deliberately arouses their fear and anxiety.

feedback Audience response to a message, which can be conveyed both verbally and nonverbally through gestures. Feedback from the audience often indicates whether a speaker's message has been understood.

feedback loop The continual flow of feedback between speaker and listener. A situation in which successful speakers adjust their message based on their listeners' reactions, and vice versa (also known as *circular response*).

field study presentation An oral presentation, typically delivered in the context of science-related disciplines, in which the speaker provides (1) an overview of field research, (2) the methods used in the research, (3) an analysis of research results, and (4) a time line indicating how the research results will be used to go forward.

"fighting words" A speech that uses language that provokes people to violence.

"fight or flight response" These are automatic physiological reactions that result from the body's automatic response to a threatening or fear-inducing event, including public speaking.

figures of speech Expressions, such as metaphors, similes, analogies, and hyperbole, in which words are used in a nonliteral fashion.

First Amendment   The amendment to the U.S. Constitution that guarantees freedom of speech ("Congress shall make no law . . . abridging the freedom of speech . . .").

fixed alternative question   A closed-ended question that contains a limited choice of answers, such as "Yes," "No," or "Sometimes."

flip chart   A large (27–34 inches) pad of paper on which a speaker can illustrate speech points.

flowchart   A diagram that shows step-by-step progression through a procedure, relationship, or process. Usually the flow of a procedure or process is drawn horizontally or vertically and describes how key components fit into a whole.

font   A set of type of one size and face.

forensic oratory   In ancient Greece, speech addressing legal matters, such as the settlement of disputes.

forum   In ancient Rome, a public space in which people gathered to deliberate about the issues of the day; see also *agora, public forum.*

free speech   The right to be free from unreasonable constraints on expression.

frequency   A count of the number of times something occurs or appears.

full-sentence transitions   Signals to listeners, in the form of declarative sentences, that the speaker is turning to another topic.

gender   Our social and psychological sense of ourselves as males or females.

gender-neutral language   Language that avoids the use of third-person generic masculine pronouns (*his, he*) in favor of inclusive pronouns such as *his or her, he or she, we, ours, you, your,* or other gender-neutral terms.

gender stereotypes   Oversimplified and often severely distorted ideas about the innate nature of men or women.

general case   See *major premise.*

general encyclopedia   A reference work that attempts to cover all important subject areas of knowledge.

general speech purpose   A declarative statement that answers the question "Why am I speaking on this topic for this particular audience and occasion?" Usually the general speech goal is to inform, to persuade, or to mark a special occasion. See also *specific speech purpose.*

generational identity   The collective cultural identity of a generation or a cohort.

graph   A graphical representation of numerical data. Graphs neatly illustrate relationships among components or units and demonstrate trends. Four major types of graphs are line graphs, bar graphs, pie graphs, and pictograms.

group activity presentation   An oral presentation that introduces students to an activity and provides them with clear directions for its completion.

groupthink   The tendency of a group to accept information and ideas without subjecting them to critical analysis. Groupthink results from strong feelings of loyalty and unity within a group and can lead to a decline in the quality of the group's decisions.

hackneyed language   Language that is poorly crafted and lacking in freshness.

handheld (or fixed) microphone   A microphone that is attached by a cord to an electrical power source.

handout   Page-size items that convey information that is either impractical to give to the audience in another manner or is intended to be kept by audience members after a presentation.

hasty generalization   A fallacy of reasoning in which the speaker attempts to support a claim by asserting that a particular piece of evidence (an isolated case) is true for all individuals or conditions concerned.

hate speech   Any offensive communication—verbal or nonverbal—directed against people's racial, ethnic, religious, gender, or other characteristics. Racist, sexist, or ageist slurs, gay bashing, and cross burnings are all forms of hate speech.

heckler's veto   Speech meant to drown out a speaker's message; such speech silences freedom of expression.

hedges   Unnecessary words and phrases that qualify or introduce doubt into statements that should be straightforward.

high-uncertainty avoidance culture   One of five "value dimensions," or major cultural patterns, that are significant across all cultures to varying degrees; identified by Geert Hofstede.

hostile audience or one that strongly disagrees   One of four potential types of audiences the persuasive speaker may encounter.

hyperbole   A figure of speech in which the speaker uses obvious exaggeration to drive home a point.

hypothetical example   An illustration of something that could happen in the future if certain things occurred.

identification   A feeling of commonality with another; when appropriate, effective speakers attempt to foster a sense of identification between themselves and audience members.

imagery   Colorful and concrete words that appeal to the senses. See also *analogy, metaphor,* and *simile.*

indentation   In an outline, the plotting of speech points to indicate their weight relative to one another; subordinate points are placed underneath and to the right of higher-order points.

individual debate format   A debate in which one person takes a side against another person.

individualistic culture   A culture that tends to emphasize personal identity and the needs of the individual rather than those of the group, upholding such values as individual achievement and decision making.

individual search engine   A search engine that compiles its own database of Web pages, such as Google or AltaVista. See also *meta-search engine.*

inductive reasoning   Reasoning from specific instances to a general condition; see also *deductive reasoning.*

information   Data set in a context for relevance.

informative speech   Public speaking that is intended to increase an audience's understanding and awareness by imparting knowledge. Informative speeches provide an audience with new information, new insights, or new ways of thinking about a topic.

inoculation effect   A theory of persuasive speaking in which a speaker anticipates and addresses counterarguments. The theory is modeled on the biological principle of inducing resistance through exposure to small quantities of a harmful substance.

integrity   The quality of being incorruptible, or able to avoid compromise for the sake of personal expediency.

intellectual property   The ownership of an individual's creative expression.

internal listening distraction   Thoughts and feelings, both positive and negative, that intrude on our attention as we attempt to listen to a speaker.

internal preview   An extended transition used within the body of a speech that alerts audience members to ensuing speech content.

internal summary An extended transition that draws together important ideas before proceeding to another speech point.

interpersonal roles Types of roles or styles of interacting in a group that facilitate group interaction.

interview A type of communication conducted for the purpose of gathering information. Interviews can be conducted one-on-one or in a group.

interview-style presentation An online presentation in which one speaker interviews an interviewee.

intonation The rising and falling of voice pitch across phrases and sentences. Intonation is what distinguishes a question from a statement.

introduction The first part of a speech, in which the speaker establishes the speech purpose and its relevance to the audience and previews the topic and the main points.

invective Abusive speech; accusatory and attacking speech.

invention The classical rhetorical term for the process of selecting information to illustrate or prove speech points.

invisible (deep) Web The portion of the Web that includes pass-protected sites, documents behind firewalls, and the contents of proprietary databases.

irony A figure of speech in which the speaker uses humor, satire, or sarcasm to suggest a meaning other than the one that is actually being expressed.

issues-based conflict Conflict that allows group members to test and debate ideas and potential solutions. It requires each member to ask tough questions, press for clarification, and present alternative views.

jargon Specialized terminology developed within a given endeavor or field of study.

key-word outline The briefest of the three forms of outlines, the key-word outline uses the smallest possible units of understanding associated with a specific point to outline the main and supporting points. See also *phrase outline* and *sentence outline*.

lavalier microphone A microphone that attaches to a lapel or a collar.

lay audience An audience of individuals who have no specialized knowledge of the general field related to a speaker's topic or of the topic itself.

lay testimony Testimony by a nonexpert; a form of supporting material.

lazy speech A poor speech habit in which the speaker fails to properly articulate words.

lecture An informative speech prepared for an audience of student learners.

Library of Congress call number An identifying number that allows the user to retrieve books and other works that have been classified according to the Library of Congress classification system.

library portal An entry point into a large collection of research and reference information that has been selected and reviewed by librarians.

linear-active culture A culture in which members approach tasks systematically, preferring to do things one at a time and in an orderly fashion; one of three cultural types identified by Richard D. Lewis. See also *multi-active culture* and *reactive culture*.

line graph A type of graph used to represent trends and other information that changes over time. A line graph displays one measurement on the horizontal axis and other units of measurement or values on the vertical axis. The values or points are connected with a line.

listening The conscious act of recognizing, understanding, and accurately interpreting the messages communicated by others.

listening distraction   Anything that competes for a listener's attention; the source of the distraction may be internal or external.

logical fallacy   A statement that is based on an invalid or deceptive line of reasoning.

logos   An appeal to the audience's reason and logic.

low-uncertainty avoidance culture   One of five "value dimensions" or major cultural patterns that are significant across all cultures to varying degrees; identified by Geert Hofstede.

main points   The key ideas or primary points intended to fulfill the speech purpose. Their function is to make claims in support of the thesis. See also *subordinate points.*

major premise   A general case; used in syllogisms and enthymemes. See also *minor premise.*

malapropism   The inadvertent use of a word or phrase in place of one that sounds like it.

Maslow's hierarchy of needs   A model of human action based on the principle that people are motivated to act on the basis of their needs.

mass communication   Communication that occurs between a speaker and a large audience of unknown people. In mass communication the receivers of the message are not present with the speaker, or they are part of such an immense crowd that there can be little or no interaction between speaker and listeners. Communication that occurs via a television or radio news broadcast or a mass rally is an example of mass communication.

mean   The sum of the scores divided by the number of scores; the arithmetic (or computed) average.

median   A type of average that represents the center-most score in a distribution; the point above and below which 50 percent of the scores fall.

memory   One of five parts of the classical canons of rhetoric; refers to the practice of the speech until it can be artfully delivered.

message   The content of the communication process—thoughts and ideas put into meaningful expressions. A message can be expressed both verbally (through the sentences and points of a speech) and nonverbally (through eye contact and gestures).

metaphor   A figure of speech used to make an implicit comparison without the use of *like* or *as* (e.g., "Love is a rose"). See also *simile.*

meta-search engine   A search engine that searches several search engines simultaneously. Examples include MetaCrawler and Dogpile. See also *individual search engine.*

methods/procedure presentation   An oral presentation describing and sometimes demonstrating an experimental or mathematical process, including the conditions under which that process can be applied; frequently delivered in scientific and mathematical fields.

minor premise   A specific case; used in syllogisms and enthymemes. See also *major premise.*

misinformation   Information that is false.

mixed audience   An audience composed of a combination of individuals, some of whom have expert knowledge of the field and topic while others have no specialized knowledge.

mixed metaphor   A metaphor that juxtaposes or compares unlike images or expressions ("Before plunging into the pool, let's walk through these steps").

mode   A type of average that represents the most frequently occurring score(s) in a distribution.

model   A three-dimensional, scale-size representation of an object such as a building.

moderated panel presentation   An online presentation in which three or more people engage in discussion, with a moderator as facilitator.

Monroe's motivated sequence   See *motivated sequence pattern of arrangement.*

motivated sequence pattern of arrangement   A five-step process of persuasion developed by Alan Monroe.

motivational warrant   A warrant that uses the needs, desires, emotions, and values of audience members as the basis for accepting evidence in support of a claim.

multi-active culture   A culture in which members do many things at once, are people oriented, and extroverted; one of three cultural types identified by Richard D. Lewis. See also *linear-active culture* and *reactive culture.*

multimedia   A single production that combines several types of media (stills, sound, video, text, and data).

multimedia effect   A learning principle that suggests that we learn better from words and pictures than from words alone, provided that the aids complement, or add to, the information rather than simply match the spoken point.

mumbling   Slurring words together at a very low level of volume and pitch so that they are barely audible.

narrative   A story; it can be based on personal experiences or imaginary incidents.

narrative pattern of arrangement   A pattern of organizing speech points so that the speech unfolds as a story, with characters, plot, setting, and vivid imagery. In practice, this pattern often is combined with other organizational patterns.

noise   Anything that interferes with the communication process between a speaker and an audience, so that the message cannot be understood; noise can derive from external sources in the environment or from internal psychological factors.

non sequitur   An argument in which the conclusion is not connected to the reasoning.

online presentation   A presentation delivered over any distance via the Internet; can include both real-time and recorded presentations.

onomatopoeia   A figure of speech in which the speaker imitates natural sounds in word form in order to add vividness to a speech (e.g., "The rain dripped a steady plop, plop, plop").

open-ended question   A question designed to allow respondents to elaborate as much as possible. Open-ended questions are particularly useful for probing beliefs and opinions. They elicit more individual or personal information about audience members' thoughts and feelings. See also *closed-ended question.*

operational definition   Defining something by describing what it does (e.g., "A computer is something that processes information").

oral citation   An oral acknowledgment by a speaker of the source of speech material that is derived from other people's ideas.

oratory   In classical terms, the art of public speaking.

organizational chart   A chart that illustrates the structure or chain of command in an organization, plotting the interrelationships among different positions, divisions, departments, and personnel.

organizational pattern   The arrangement of speech content into a specific organizational model, such as the chronological or cause-effect pattern. Different patterns produce different outcomes, depending upon the type of information contained in the speech, as well as the speaker's goals.

outlining   The physical process of plotting speech points on the page in hierarchical order of importance.

overgeneralization   An attempt to support a claim by asserting that a particular piece of evidence is true for everyone concerned.

overhead transparency   An image on a transparent background that can be viewed by transmitted light, either directly or through projection onto a screen or wall. The images may be written or printed directly onto the transparency or handwritten during the presentation.

paid inclusion   The practice of paying a fee to a search engine company for inclusion in its index of possible results, without a guarantee of ranking.

paid placement   The practice of paying a fee to a search engine company for inclusion in its search results and a guaranteed higher ranking within those results.

pandering   To identify with values that are not your own in order to win approval from an audience.

panel discussion   An oral presentation in which a group of three to nine people discuss a topic in the presence of an audience and under the direction of a moderator.

paralanguage   See *aural channel*.

parallel form   The statement of equivalent speech points in similar grammatical form and style.

parallelism   The arrangement of words, phrases, or sentences in similar grammatical and stylistic form. Parallel structure can help speakers emphasize important ideas in a speech.

paraphrase   A restatement of someone else's statements or written work that alters the form or phrasing but not the substance of that person's ideas. See also *direct quotation*.

participative leader   A leader who facilitates a group's activities and interactions in ways that will lead to a desired outcome.

patchwrite plagiarism   A form of plagiarism in which you copy material from a source and then change and rearrange occasional words and sentence structures to make it appear as if the material were your own. See also *plagiarism*.

pathos   The appeal to an audience's emotions.

pauses   Strategic elements of a speech used to enhance meaning by providing a type of punctuation emphasizing a point, drawing attention to a key thought, or allowing listeners a moment to contemplate.

percentage   The quantified portion of a whole, or 100 percent.

performance anxiety   A form of *public speaking anxiety* (*PSA*) that occurs the moment a speaker begins to deliver a speech. See also *preparation anxiety*.

periodical   A regularly published magazine, journal, or newspaper.

peripheral processing   A mode of processing a persuasive message that does not consider the quality of the speaker's message but is influenced by such noncontent issues as the speaker's appearance or reputation, certain slogans or one-liners, or obvious attempts to manipulate emotions. Peripheral processing of messages occurs when people lack the motivation or the ability to pay close attention to the issues.

personal-based conflict   Conflict in which group members personalize disagreements over issues, thereby wasting time, distracting the group from its mission, and impairing motivation.

personification   A figure of speech in which the speaker endows an abstract idea or inanimate object with human qualities (e.g., "Computers have become important members of our family").

persons with disabilities (PWD)   A person whose physical or mental impairment substantially limits his or her major life activities.

persuasion   The process of influencing others' attitudes, beliefs, values, and behavior.

persuasive speaking   Speech whose general purpose is to effect some degree of change in the audience's beliefs, attitudes, values, or behavior.

phrase outline   A delivery outline that uses a partial construction of the sentence form of each point instead of using complete sentences that present precise wording for each point. See also *key-word outline* and *sentence outline*.

pictogram   A type of graph that illustrates comparisons in picture form. The pictures represent numerical units and are drawn to relate to the items being compared.

picture   A two-dimensional representation of people, places, ideas, or objects produced on an opaque backing; types of pictures commonly used by speakers include photographs, line drawings, diagrams, maps, and posters.

pie graph   A type of graph used to depict the division of a whole. The pie, which represents 100 percent, is divided into portions or segments called "slices." Each slice constitutes a percentage of the whole.

pitch   The range of sounds from high to low (or vice versa). Pitch is determined by the number of vibrations per unit of time; the more vibrations per unit (also called frequency), the higher the pitch, and vice versa.

plagiarism   The act of using other people's ideas or words without acknowledging the source. See also *patchwrite plagiarism* and *wholesale plagiarism*.

podcast   A digital audio recording of a presentation captured and stored in a form accessible via the Internet.

policy recommendation report   An oral presentation that offers recommendations for solving a problem or addressing an issue.

poster session   A format for the visual presentation of posters, arranged on freestanding boards, that contains the concise display of a study or an issue for viewing by participants at professional conferences. The speaker prepares brief remarks and remains on hand to answer questions as needed.

power distance   As developed by Geert Hofstede, a measure of the extent to which a culture values social equality versus tradition and authority.

preparation anxiety   A form of *public speaking anxiety* (*PSA*) that arises when the speaker begins to prepare for a speech, at which point he or she might feel overwhelmed at the amount of time and planning required. See also *performance anxiety*.

pre-performance anxiety   A form of *public speaking anxiety* (*PSA*) that occurs when the speaker begins to rehearse a speech.

pre-preparation anxiety   A form of *public speaking anxiety* (*PSA*) that occurs the moment speakers learn they must give a speech.

presentation aids   Objects, models, pictures, graphs, charts, video, audio, and multimedia, used alone or in combination within the context of a speech; such aids help listeners see relationships among concepts and elements, store and remember material, and critically examine key ideas.

presentational speaking   Reports delivered by individuals or groups within a business or professional environment.

preview statement   A statement included in the introduction of a speech in which the speaker identifies the main speech points that will be covered in the body of the speech.

primacy effect   Psychological principle in which listeners have a better recall of the main points made at the beginning of a speech than of those made later (unless the ideas made later are far more striking than the others).

primary source   Original or firsthand research, such as an interview or survey conducted by the speaker. See also *secondary source*.

problem-cause-solution pattern of arrangement   A pattern of organizing speech points so that they demonstrate (1) the nature of the problem, (2) reasons for the problem, (3) unsatisfactory solutions, and (4) proposed solutions.

problem-solution pattern of arrangement   A pattern of organizing speech points so that they demonstrate the nature and significance of a problem first, and then provide justification for a proposed solution.

productive conflict   A form of group conflict in which questions are clarified, ideas are challenged, counterexamples are presented, worst-case scenarios are considered, and proposals are reformulated.

progress report   A report that updates clients or principals on developments in an ongoing project.

pronunciation   The formation of word sounds.

prop   Any live or inanimate object used by a speaker as a presentation aid.

propaganda   Information represented in such a way as to provoke a desired response.

proposal   A type of business or professional presentation in which the speaker provides information needed for decisions related to modifying or adopting a product, procedure, or policy.

prototype   A physical model of a design.

public discourse   Open conversation or discussion in a public forum.

public domain   Bodies of work, including publications and processes, available for public use without permission; not protected by copyright or patent.

public forum   Any physical or virtual space in which people gather to voice their ideas about public issues.

public speaking   A type of communication in which the speaker delivers a message with a specific purpose to an audience of people who are physically present during the delivery of the speech. Public speaking always includes a speaker who has a reason for speaking, an audience that gives the speaker its attention, and a message that is meant to accomplish a purpose.

public speaking anxiety (PSA)   Fear or anxiety associated with a speaker's actual or anticipated communication to an audience.

qualitative research   Research with an emphasis on observing, describing, and interpreting behavior.

quantitative research   Research with an emphasis on statistical measurement.

questionnaire   A written survey designed to gather information from a large pool of respondents. Questionnaires consist of a mix of *open-* and *closed-ended questions* designed to elicit information.

reactive culture   A culture in which members rarely initiate discussions or actions, preferring to listen to what others have to say first; one of three cultural types identified by Richard D. Lewis. See also *linear-active culture* and *multi-active culture*.

real-time presentation   A presentation broadcast at the time of delivery via the Internet; real-time presentations connect the presenter and audience live and at the same time.

reasoning   Drawing inferences or conclusions from the evidence the speaker presents.

receiver   The recipient (an individual or a group) of a source's message.

recency effect   Psychological principle in which listeners have a better recall of the most recent points in the speech (unless the ideas made earlier are far more striking than the others).

reckless disregard for the truth   A quality of defamatory speech that is legally liable. See also *slander.*

recorded presentation   Presentation in which speaker and audience are separated by time and space and the presentation is stored and played back from a digital medium.

red herring fallacy   A fallacy of reasoning in which the speaker relies on irrelevant information to support an argument.

reference librarian   A librarian trained to help library users locate information resources.

refutation pattern of arrangement   A pattern of organizing speech points in which each main point addresses and then refutes (disproves) an opposing claim to the speaker's position.

reportage   An account of the who, what, where, when, and why of the facts; informative speeches about events may rely on reportage.

request for funding presentation   An oral presentation that provides evidence that a project, proposal, or design idea is worth funding; it is frequently delivered in such technical fields as engineering, computer science, and architecture.

research overview presentation   A type of oral presentation in which the speaker provides the context and the background for a research question or hypothesis that will form the basis of an impending undertaking; it is typically delivered within the context of scientific and mathematical disciplines.

research presentation (oral scientific presentation)   An oral presentation describing original research undertaken by the speaker, either alone or as part of a team; it is frequently delivered in scientific and social scientific fields.

respect   To feel or show deferential regard. For the ethical speaker, respect ranges from addressing audience members as unique human beings to refraining from rudeness and other forms of personal attack.

responsibility   A charge, trust, or duty for which one is accountable.

"restate-forecast" form   A type of transition in which the speaker restates the point just covered and previews the point to be covered next.

review of academic article   Oral presentation in which the speaker reports on an article or a study published in a scholarly journal.

review of the literature presentation   An oral presentation in which the speaker reviews the body of research related to a given topic or issue and offers conclusions about the topic based on this research; it is frequently delivered in social scientific fields.

rhetoric   The practice of oratory, or public speaking.

rhetorical device   A technique of language to achieve a desired effect.

rhetorical proof   In classical terms, a means of persuasion (*ethos, pathos, logos*).

rhetorical question   A question that does not invite an actual response but is used to make the audience think.

rhetorical situation   The circumstances that call for a public response; in broadest terms, consideration of the audience, occasion, and overall speech situation when planning a speech.

roast   A humorous tribute to a person, one in which a series of speakers jokingly poke fun at the individual being honored.

roman numeral outline   An outline format in which main points are enumerated with roman numerals (I, II, III), supporting points with capital letters (A, B, C), third-level points with arabic numerals (1, 2, 3), and fourth-level points with lowercase letters (a, b, c).

rules of engagement   Standard of conduct for communicating with others in the public arena, including speaking the truth, listening, and responding civilly.

sales presentation   A presentation that attempts to persuade a potential buyer to purchase a service or product described by the presenter.

sans serif typeface   Typefaces that are blocklike and linear and are designed without tiny strokes or flourishes at the top or bottom of each letter. See also *serif typeface.*

scale question   Also called an "attitude scale," a closed-ended question that measures the respondent's level of agreement or disagreement with specific issues.

scanning   A technique for creating eye contact with large audiences; speakers move their gaze across the audience from one listener to another and from one section to another, pausing as they do so to gaze briefly at individual listeners.

search engine   Using powerful software programs, a search engine scans millions of Web documents that contain the keywords and phrases you command it to search. A program then creates a huge index from the Web pages that have been read, compares it with your search request, and returns matching results to you, usually in order of relevance.

secondary source   Information gathered by others; can include published facts and statistics, texts, documents, and any other information not originally collected and generated by the researcher. See also *primary source.*

selective perception   A psychological principle that posits that listeners pay attention selectively to certain messages and ignore others.

sentence outline   An outline in which each main and supporting point is stated in sentence form and in precisely the way the speaker wants to express the idea. Generally, sentence outlines are used for working outlines. See also *key-word outline* and *phrase outline.*

serif typeface   Typefaces that include small flourishes, or strokes, at the top and bottom of each letter. See also *sans serif typeface.*

sermon   A speech of inspiration given in a religious context.

sexist language   Language that oversimplifies or distorts ideas about the innate nature of what it means to be male or female. An example is the generic use of the pronoun *he* or *she.*

shared meaning   The mutual understanding of a message between speaker and audience. Shared meaning occurs in varying degrees. The lowest level of shared meaning exists when the speaker has merely caught the audience's attention. As the message develops, depending on the encoding choices made by the source, a higher degree of shared meaning is possible.

shift report   An oral report prepared by health-care workers that concisely relays patient status and needs to incoming caregivers.

signposts   Conjunctions or phrases (such as "Next," "First," "Second," and so forth) that indicate *transitions* between supporting points.

simile   A figure of speech used to compare one thing with another by using the word *like* or *as* (e.g., "He works *like* a dog"). See also *metaphor.*

single-speaker presentation   An online presentation delivered by a single speaker.

six-by-six rule   Rule of design suggesting having no more than six words in a line and six lines or bullet points per slide or other kind of visual aid.

slander   Defamatory speech.

slippery slope   An argument based on a faulty assumption that one case will necessarily lead to a series of events or actions.

small group   A group that consists of between three and twenty people as opposed to a large public audience.

small group communication   Communication involving a small number of people who can see and speak directly with one another, as in a business meeting.

social agenda–setting   In a special occasion speech, a type of speech purpose whose goal is to focus on a social/political issue and reinforce a message that relates to it.

social news site(s)   Web sites dedicated to specific kinds of news or entertainment in which users can share stories, articles, and video (e.g., Digg, Propeller, Reddit).

socioeconomic status (SES)   A cluster of demographic characteristics of audience members, including income, occupation, and education.

source   The source, or sender, is the person who creates a message. The speaker transforms ideas and thoughts into messages and sends them to a receiver, or an audience.

source qualifier   A brief description of the source's qualifications to address the topic (e.g., "Pulitzer-Prize–winning author," "researcher at the Mayo Clinic").

source reliability   The qualities that determine the value of a source, such as the author's background and reputation, the reputation of the publication, the source of the data, and how recent the reference is.

spatial pattern of arrangement   A pattern of organizing main points in order of their physical proximity or direction relative to each other; it is used when the purpose of a speech is to describe or explain the physical arrangement of a place, a scene, or an object.

speaker-audience interactive presentation   A real-time, multimedia presentation linking speaker and audience via audio, video, and collaborative tools such as instant messaging and synchronous document creation. Examples include Webex.com and GoToMeeting.com.

speaker credibility   The quality that reveals that a speaker has a good grasp of the subject, displays sound reasoning skills, is honest and unmanipulative, and is genuinely interested in the welfare of audience members; a modern version of *ethos*.

speaking extemporaneously   A type of delivery that falls somewhere between impromptu and written or memorized deliveries. Speakers delivering an extemporaneous speech prepare well and practice in advance, giving full attention to all facets of the speech—content, arrangement, and delivery. Instead of memorizing or writing the speech word for word, they speak from a *key-word outline* or *phrase outline.*

speaking from manuscript   A style of delivery in which the speaker reads the speech verbatim—that is, from a prepared written text (either on paper or on a Tele-PrompTer) containing the entire speech.

speaking from memory   A type of delivery in which the speaker puts the entire speech, word for word, into writing and then commits it to memory.

speaking impromptu   A type of delivery that is unpracticed, spontaneous, or improvised.

speaking outline   A delivery outline to be used when practicing and actually presenting a speech.

speaking rate   The pace at which a speech is delivered. The typical public speech occurs at a rate slightly below 120 words per minute.

specialized encyclopedia   A reference work that delves deeply into one subject area, such as religion, science, art, sports, or engineering.

specialized search engine   A search engine that searches for information only on specific topics.

special occasion speech   A speech whose general purpose is to entertain, celebrate, commemorate, inspire, or set a social agenda.

specific case   See *minor premise.*

specific speech purpose   A refined statement of purpose that zeroes in more closely than the general purpose on the goal of the speech. See also *general speech purpose.*

speculative claim   A type of *claim of fact* that addresses questions for which answers are not yet available.

speech of acceptance   A speech made in response to receiving an award. Its purpose is to express gratitude for the honor bestowed on the speaker.

speech of inspiration   A speech whose purpose is to inspire or motivate the audience to positively consider, reflect on, and sometimes even act on the speaker's words.

speech of introduction   A short speech defined by two goals: to prepare or "warm up" audience members for the main speaker and to motivate them to listen to what that speaker has to say.

speech of presentation   A speech whose purpose is twofold: to communicate the meaning of an award and to explain why the recipient is receiving it.

staff report   A report that informs managers and other employees of new developments relating to personnel that affect them and their work.

statistic   Quantified evidence; data that measures the size or magnitude of something, demonstrates trends, or shows relationships with the purpose of summarizing information, demonstrating proof, and making points memorable.

stereotype   A generalization about an apparent characteristic of a group, culture, or ethnicity that falsely claims to define all of its members.

story   See *narrative.*

style   The speaker's choice of words and sentence structure.

subject (Web) directory   A searchable database of Web sites organized by categories (e.g., Yahoo! Directory).

subordinate points   The alignment of points within a speech outline that have somewhat lesser weight than main points; they provide support for or extend the more central ideas or *main points.*

substantive warrant   A warrant that relies on factual evidence to link a claim to evidence. See also *warrant by analogy, warrant by cause,* and *warrant by sign.*

supporting material   Examples, narratives, testimony, facts, and statistics that support the speech thesis and form the speech.

supporting points   Information (examples, narratives, testimony, and facts and statistics) that clarifies, elaborates, and verifies the speaker's assertions.

syllogism   A form of rational appeal defined as a three-part argument consisting of a major premise or general case, a minor premise or specific case, and a conclusion. See also *deductive reasoning.*

sympathetic audience   An audience that already shares much agreement with the speaker; one of four types of potential audiences that persuasive speakers may encounter.

symposium   A formal meeting at which various speakers deliver short speeches on different aspects of the same topic.

synchronous communication   Communication in which people exchange messages simultaneously, in real time; real-time presentations rely on synchronous communication.

table A systematic grouping of data or numerical information in column format.

tag questions Unnecessary questions appended to statements or commands; the use of such weak language undermines a speaker's authority.

talking head A speaker who remains static, standing stiffly behind a podium, and so resembles a televised shot of a speaker's head and shoulders.

target audience Those individuals within the broader audience who are most likely to be influenced in the direction the speaker seeks.

task roles Types of roles that directly relate to the accomplishment of the objectives and missions of a group. Recording secretary and moderator are examples of task roles.

team debate format A debate in which multiple people take sides against another team, with each person on the team assuming a speaking role.

team presentation An oral presentation prepared and delivered by a group of three or more people.

TelePrompTer A device that contains a magnified script of a speech; it is commonly used when a speaker's remarks are televised.

testimony Firsthand findings, eyewitness accounts, and opinions by people, both lay (nonexpert) and expert.

theoretical research presentation An oral presentation focusing on studies that attempt to analyze and explain a phenomenon; frequently delivered in social scientific fields.

thesis statement The theme, or central idea, of a speech that serves to connect all the parts of the speech. The main points, the supporting material, and the conclusion all relate to the thesis.

tilde (~) A symbol that appears in the domain of a Web address; it usually indicates a personal page rather than an institutional Web site.

toast A brief tribute to a person or an event being celebrated.

topic What the speech is about; a topic may be assigned to the speaker, or the speaker may have to choose one based on personal interests, experience, and knowledge.

topical pattern of arrangement (also called *categorical pattern*) A pattern of organizing main points as subtopics or categories of the speech topic; of all organizational patterns, this one offers the most freedom to structure speech points as desired.

topic map A brainstorming technique in which you lay out the words in diagram form to show categorical relationships among them; it is useful for selecting and narrowing a speech topic.

trait anxiety A person's general baseline level of anxiety. People with high trait anxiety are naturally anxious much of the time, whereas people with low trait anxiety will usually experience nervousness only in novel situations.

transitions (connectives) Words, phrases, or sentences that tie speech ideas together and enable a speaker to move smoothly from one point to the next.

triad A rhetorical device that makes use of three parallel elements.

trustworthiness The quality of displaying both honesty and dependability.

typeface An assortment or set of type or characters (fonts) all of one style and sometimes one size (called the "point size"). Typefaces come in a variety of lettering styles, such as Arial, Times Roman, or Courier.

uncertainty avoidance The extent to which people feel threatened by ambiguity.

understatement A figure of speech in which a speaker draws attention to an idea by minimizing its importance (e.g., "Flunking out of college might be a problem").

uninformed, less educated, or **apathetic audience** An audience that knows or cares little about a specific topic.

U.S. Government Printing Office (GPO) Responsible for publishing and distributing all information collected and produced by federal agencies, from the Census Bureau to the Department of Education and the Environmental Protection Agency. GPO publications also include all congressional reports and hearings.

valid generalization A generalization that is supported by different types of evidence from different sources and that does not make claims beyond a reasonable point.

values Our most enduring judgments or standards of what's important to us (e.g., equal opportunity, democracy, change and progress, or perseverance).

videoconference Synchronized visual and audio communication between two or more remote locations.

virtual group A group in which members who are physically dispersed interact and exchange ideas through mediated communication such as e-mail and *videoconferencing*.

virtual library A collection of library holdings available online.

visual channel A nonverbal channel of communication that includes the speaker's physical actions and appearance—facial expressions, gestures, general body movement, physical appearance, dress, and objects held.

visualization An exercise for building confidence in which the speaker closes his or her eyes and envisions a series of positive feelings and reactions that will occur on the day of the speech.

visual rhetoric Meaning conveyed by the images or graphics in visual aids beyond merely clarifying the verbal message.

vocal fillers Unnecessary and undesirable phrases or utterances that are used to cover pauses, such as "uh," "hmm," "you know," "I mean," and "it's like."

vocal variety The variation of volume, pitch, rate, and pauses to create an effective delivery.

voice The feature of verbs in written and spoken text that indicates the subject's relationship to the action; verbs can be either active or passive.

volume The relative loudness of a speaker's voice while giving a speech.

warrant A core component of an argument that serves to justify the link made between the claim and the evidence.

warrant by analogy A statement, based on the comparison of two similar cases, that infers that what is true in one case is true in the other. The assumption is that the characteristics of case A and case B are so similar, if not the same, that what is true for B must also be true for A.

warrant by cause The provision of a cause-effect relationship as proof of a claim.

warrant by sign A statement based on an inference that such a close relationship exists between two variables that the presence or absence of one may be taken as an indication of the presence or absence of the other (e.g., smoke is a sign of fire).

Webinar Real-time presentations, including training sessions, seminars, and other presentations that connect presenters and audiences from their desktop, regardless of where they are in the world. Tend to be more speaker-centered than interactive.

wholesale plagiarism   A form of plagiarism in which you "cut and paste" material from print or online sources into your speech and represent that material as your own. See also *plagiarism.*

word association   A *brainstorming* technique in which you write down ideas as they occur to you, beginning with a single word, in order to generate and narrow speech topics.

working bibliography   An in-process list of source materials used to support the claims made in a speech.

working outline   A preparation or rough outline that refines and finalizes the *specific speech purpose,* firms up and organizes *main points,* and develops *supporting material.*

Notes

Chapter 1

1. Vickie K. Sullivan, "Public Speaking: The Secret Weapon in Career Development," *USA Today* 133 (May 2005): 24.
2. Peter D. Hart Research Associates, "How Should Colleges Prepare Students to Succeed in Today's Global Economy?" (survey conducted on behalf of the Association of American Colleges and Universities, 2006); D. Uchida, M. J. Cetron, and F. McKenzie, "What Students Must Know to Succeed in the Twenty-First Century" (special report by the World Future Society based on "Preparing Students for the Twenty-First Century," a report on a project by the American Association of School Administrators, 1996).
3. Ronald Alsop, "Poor Writing Skills Top M.B.A. Recruiter Gripes," *Wall Street Journal*, January 17, 2006.
4. "Who Votes, Who Doesn't, and Why," Pew Research Center for the People & the Press Web site, October 18, 2006, http://people-press.org/reports/display .php3?ReportID=292.
5. Rebecca Rimel, "Policy and the Partisan Divide: The Price of Gridlock" (speech given at the Commonwealth Club in San Francisco, November 2004), Pew Charitable Trusts Web site, accessed May 10, 2007, www.pewtrusts.org/news_room_detail.aspx?id=23012.
6. For a discussion of Daniel Yankelovich's three-step process by which public judgments occur, see Yankelovich, *Coming to Public Judgment: Making Democracy Work in a Complex World* (Syracuse, NY: Syracuse University Press, 1991).
7. For a discussion of conversation stoppers and rules of engagement, see W. Barnett Pearce, "Toward a National Conversation about Public Issues," in *The Changing Conversation in America: Lectures from the Smithsonian*, ed. William F. Eadie and Paul E. Nelson (Thousand Oaks, CA: Sage, 2002), 16.
8. James L. Golden, Goodwin F. Berquist, William E. Coleman, and J. Michael Sproule, *The Rhetoric of Western Thought: From the Mediterranean World to the Global Setting*, 8th ed. (Dubuque, IA: Kendall/Hunt, 2003), 37–43.
9. The scholarly basis for this model is an integration of rhetorical theory (Aristotle), information theory (Shannon and Weaver), semantics (Ogden and Richards), and systems theory (Bertalonffy). Taken together, these important concepts allow us to view communication as a highly interactive yet holistic process.
10. Lloyd F. Bitzer, "The Rhetorical Situation," *Philosophy and Rhetoric* 1 (Winter 1968): 1–14.
11. Robert Perrin, "The Speaking-Writing Connection: Enhancing the Symbiotic Relationship," *Contemporary Education* 65 (1994): 62–64.
12. David C. Thomas and Kerr Inkson, *Cultural Intelligence: People Skills for a Global Business* (San Francisco: Berrett-Koehler Publishers, 2004), 14.
13. Ibid., 14.

Chapter 3

1. See, for example, M. J. Beatty, "Situational and Predispositional Correlates of Public Speaking Anxiety," *Communication Education* 37 (1988): 28–39.
2. Adapted from James C. McCroskey, "Oral Communication Apprehension: A Summary of Recent Theory and Research," *Human Communication Research* 4 (1977): 79–96.
3. "Etiology of Anxiety Disorders," Chapter 4, "Adults and Mental Health," *Mental Health: A Report of the Surgeon General*, accessed May 30, 2010, http://www.surgeongeneral.gov/ library/mentalhealth/chapter4/sec2_1.html.

4. R. Behnke, C. R. Sawyer, and R. Chris, "Milestones of Anticipatory Public Speaking Anxiety," *Communication Education* 48 (April 1999): 165–72.
5. C. Kane, "Overcoming Stage Fright—Here's What to Do," *Christinekane* (blog), April 24, 2007, http://christinekane.com/blog/overcoming-stage-fright-heres-what-to-do/.
6. Behnke, Sawyer, and Chris, "Milestones of Anticipatory Public Speaking Anxiety."
7. David-Paul Pertaub, Mel Slater, and Chris Barker, "An Experiment on Public Speaking Anxiety in Response to Three Different Types of Virtual Audience," *Presence: Teleoperators and Virtual Environments* 11 (2002): 670–78.
8. P. L. Witt, Kennaria C. Brown, J. B. Roberts, J. Weisel, C. R. Sawyer, and R. R. Behnke, "Somatic Anxiety Patterns before, during, and after Giving a Public Speech," *Southern Communication Journal* 71 (2006): 87–100.
9. Lenny Laskowski, "Overcoming Speaking Anxiety in Meetings and Presentations," Speakers Platform Web site, accessed July 26, 2007, http://www.speaking.com/articles_html/LennyLaskowski_532.html.
10. John Robert Colombo, "Speech Anxiety: Overcoming the Fear of Public Speaking," SpeechCoachforExecutives.com, accessed July 25, 2007, http://www.speechcoachforexecutives.com/speech_anxiety.html.
11. Ibid.
12. Joe Ayres, "Coping with Speech Anxiety: The Power of Positive Thinking," *Communication Education* 37 (1988): 289–96; Joe Ayres, "An Examination of the Impact of Anticipated Communication and Communication Apprehension on Negative Thinking, Task-Relevant Thinking, and Recall," *Communication Research Reports* 9 (1992): 3–11.
13. Pamela J. Feldman, Sheldon Cohen, Natalie Hamrick, and Stephen J. Lepore, "Psychological Stress, Appraisal, Emotion, and Cardiovascular Response in a Public Speaking Task," *Psychology and Health* 19 (2004): 353–68; S. Hus, S. Romans-Kroll, and Joung-Min, "Effects of Positive Attitude toward Giving a Speech on Cardiovascular and Subjective Fear Responses during Speech on Anxious Subjects," *Perceptual and Motor Skills* 81 (1995): 609–10.
14. M. T. Motley, "Public Speaking Anxiety qua Performance Anxiety: A Revised Model and Alternative Therapy," *Journal of Social Behavior and Personality* 5 (1990): 85–104.
15. Joe Ayres, C. S. Hsu, and Tim Hopf, "Does Exposure to Visualization Alter Speech Preparation Processes?" *Communication Research Reports* 17 (2000): 366–74.
16. Elizabeth Quinn, "Visualization in Sport: Imagery Can Improve Performance," About.com: SportsMedicine, accessed August 29, 2007, http://sportsmedicine.about.com/cs/sport_psych/a/aa091700a.htm; Joe Ayres and Tim Hopf, "Visualization: Is It More Than Extra Attention?" *Communication Education* 38 (1989): 1–5; Joe Ayers and Tim Hopf, *Coping with Speech Anxiety* (Norwood, NJ: Ablex, 1993).
17. Ayres and Hopf, "Visualization," 2–3.
18. "Etiology of Anxiety Disorders."
19. H. Benson and M. Z. Klipper, *The Relaxation Response* (New York: HarperCollins, 2000).
20. Mayo Clinic Staff, "Relaxation Techniques: Learn Ways to Calm Your Stress," MayoClinic.com, accessed May 30, 2010, http://www.mayoclinic.com/health/relaxation-technique/SR00007.
21. Kane, "Overcoming Stage Fright."
22. Lars-Gunnar Lundh, Britta Berg, Helena Johansson, Linda Kjellén Nilsson, Jenny Sandberg, and Anna Segerstedt, "Social Anxiety Is Associated with a Negatively Distorted Perception of One's Own Voice," *Cognitive Behavior Therapy* 31 (2002): 25–30.

Chapter 4

1. Dirk Heylen, "Understanding Speaker-Listener Interactions." Paper presented at the Interspeech 2009 International Speech Communication Association Conference. http://www.interspeech2009.org/conference.
2. F. E. Gray, "Specific Oral Communication Skills Desired in New Accountancy Graduates," *Journal of Business Communication* 73 (2010): 40–67; J. Maes, T. Weldy, and M. Icenogle, "A Managerial Perspective: Oral Communication Competency Is Most

Important for Business Students in the Workplace," *Journal of Business Communication* 34 (1999): 67–80.

3. Graduate Management Admissions Council (GMAC), "Corporate Recruiters Survey, 2011," http://www.gmac.com

4. Kathy Thompson, Pamela Leintz, Barbara Nevers, and Susan Witkowski, "The Integrative Listening Model: An Approach for Teaching and Learning Listening," *Journal of Education* 53 (2004): 225–46.

5. Andrew Wolvin and C. Coakley, *Listening,* 4th ed. (Dubuque, IA: Brown, 1992).

6. Philip Vassallo, "Dialogue: Speaking to Listen: Listening to Speak," *ETC* (Fall 2000): 306–13.

7. Ronald D. Gordon, "Communication, Dialogue, and Transformation," *Human Communication 9,* no. 1 (2006): 17–30.

8. S. Golen, "A Factor Analysis of Barriers to Effective Listening," *Journal of Business Communication* 27 (1990): 25–36.

9. G. D. Bodie, "Evaluating Listening Theory: Development and Illustration of Five Criteria," *International Journal of Listening* 23 (2009): 81–103; S. Fraser, J. Gagne, M. Alepins, and P. Dubois, "Evaluating the Effort Expended to Understand Speech in Noise Using a Dual-Task Paradigm: The Effects of Providing Visual Speech Cues," *Journal of Speech, Language, and Hearing Research* 53 (2010): 18–33.

10. Thomas E. Anastasi, Jr., *Listen! Techniques for Improving Communication Skills* (Boston: CBI Publishing, 1982); thanks to Barry Antokoletz of New York City College of Technology for suggesting the inclusion of these strategies.

11. W. Mathews, "Just Like Starting Over," *Communication World* 27 (2010): 16–21.

12. Anastasi, *Listen!*

13. M. Cueva, "A Living Spiral of Understanding: Community-Based Adult Education," *New Directions for Adult and Continuing Education* 125 (2010): 79–90.

14. Fraser, Gagne, Alepins, and Dubois, "Evaluating the Effort."

15. H. Weger, G. R. Castle, and M. C. Emmett, "Active Listening in Peer Interviews: The Influence of Message Paraphrasing on Perceptions of Listening Skill," *International Journal of Listening* 24 (2010): 34–49.

16. Carole Wade and Carol Tavris, *Psychology,* 4th ed. (New York: HarperCollins, 1996), 31–35.

17. Ron Hoff, *I Can See You Naked,* rev. ed. (Kansas City, MO: Andrews McMeel, 1992), 300–301.

Chapter 5

1. Michael Josephson, interview by author, May 10, 1996.

2. *The Compact Edition of the Oxford English Dictionary,* 1971 ed., 2514.

3. Cited in Edward P. J. Corbett, *Classical Rhetoric for the Modern Student* (New York: Oxford University Press, 1990).

4. Dominic A. Infante, Andrew S. Rancer, and Deanna F. Womack, *Building Communication Theory,* 3rd ed. (Prospect Heights, IL: Waveland Press, 1997).

5. Rebecca Rimel, "Policy and the Partisan Divide: The Price of Gridlock" (speech given at the Commonwealth Club in San Francisco, November 2004), Pew Charitable Trusts Web site, accessed May 10, 2007, www.pewtrusts.org/news_room_detail.aspx?id=23012.

6. For an excellent discussion of the tension between these two rights, see Douglas M. Fraleigh and Joseph S. Tuman, *Freedom of Speech in the Marketplace of Ideas* (New York: Bedford/St. Martin's, 1997).

7. David L. Hudson, "Fighting Words," First Amendment Center Web site, accessed April 8, 2010, firstamendmentcenter.org/Speech/arts/topic.aspx?topic=fighting_words.

8. Ann Coulter, *Godless: The Church of Liberalism* (New York: Crown Forum, 2006).

9. W. Barnett Pearce, "Toward a National Conversation about Public Issues," in *The Changing Conversation in America: Lectures from the Smithsonian,* eds. William F. Eadie and Paul E. Nelson (Thousand Oaks, CA: Sage, 2002), 16.

10. W. Gudykunst, S. Ting-Toomey, S. Suweeks, and L. Stewart, *Building Bridges: Interpersonal Skills for a Changing World* (Boston: Houghton Mifflin, 1995), 92.

11. Ibid.
12. Josephson, interview.
13. Louis A. Day, *Ethics in Media Communications: Cases and Controversies,* 2nd ed. (Belmont, CA: Wadsworth, 1997).
14. Rebecca Moore Howard, "A Plagiarism Pentimento," *Journal of Teaching Writing* 11 (1993): 233.
15. With thanks to Keith Perry, Department of Humanities, Abraham Baldwin Agricultural College.
16. Skyscraper Museum Web site, accessed June 26, 2002, http://www.skyscraper.org.
17. U.S. Copyright Office Web site, accessed January 11, 2006, www.copyright.gov.
18. Steven E. Gillen, "Rights Clearance and Permissions Guidelines" (paper prepared by the law firm Greenbaum, Doll, and McDonald, Cincinnati, 2002).
19. U.S. Copyright Office Web site, section on fair use, accessed February 19, 2005, http://www.copyright.gov/fls/fl102.html.
20. Gillen, "Rights Clearance."

Chapter 6

1. James C. McCroskey, Virginia P. Richmond, and Robert A. Stewart, *One-on-One: The Foundations of Interpersonal Communication* (Englewood Cliffs, NJ: Prentice-Hall, 1986).
2. Daniel O'Keefe notes that while attitudes and behavior are "generally consistent," there are "a large number of possible moderating variables," including the relative demands of the behavior, whether there is a vested position, and others. Daniel J. O'Keefe, *Persuasion: Theory and Research,* 2nd ed. (Thousand Oaks, CA: Sage, 2002), 17.
3. McCroskey, Richmond, and Stewart, *One-on-One.*
4. E. D. Steele and W. C. Redding, "The American Value System: Premises for Persuasion," *Western Speech* 26 (1962): 83–91; Robin M. Williams Jr., *American Society: A Sociological Interpretation,* 3rd ed. (New York: Alfred A. Knopf, 1970).
5. Inter-University Consortium for Political and Social Research, *World Values Survey, 1981–1984 and 1990–1993* (Irvine: Social Science Data Archives, University Libraries, University of California, 1997). The 1990 World Values Survey (1990) covers four Asian countries (China, India, Japan, and South Korea) and eighteen Western countries.
6. "Tip Sheet: Communicating about Biodiversity," Biodiversity Project Web site, accessed May 20, 2010, http://www.biodiversityproject.org/docs/publicationsandtipsheets/communicatingaboutbiodiversity_tipsheet.pdf.
7. "Human Values and Nature's Future: Americans' Attitudes on Biological Diversity," Biodiversity Project Web site, accessed May 20, 2010, http://www.biodiversityproject.org/html/resources/publicopinionresearch.htm.
8. Ibid.
9. McCroskey, Richmond, and Stewart, *One-on-One,* 76.
10. Herbert Simon, *Persuasion in Society* (Thousand Oaks, CA: Sage, 2001), 385–87.
11. McCroskey, Richmond, and Stewart, *One-on-One,* 76.
12. Hillary Rodham Clinton, "Abortion Is a Tragedy," *Vital Speeches of the Day* 71, no. 9 (2005): 266–70.
13. J. Gordon Melton, *Encyclopedia of American Religions,* 8th ed. (Detroit: Gale, 2009).
14. Daniel Canary and K. Dindia, eds., *Sex Differences and Similarities in Communication* (Mahwah, NJ: Lawrence Erlbaum, 1998).
15. "Frequently Asked Questions," Office of Disability Employment Policy Web site, April 23, 2010, http://www.dol.gov/odep/faqs/people.htm.
16. *American FactFinder,* U.S. Census Bureau Web site, accessed April 25, 2010, factfinder.census.gov.
17. *American FactFinder.*
18. Richard D. Lewis, *When Cultures Collide: Leading across Cultures,* 3rd ed. (Boston: Intercultural Press-Nicholas Brealey International, 2005), 27.
19. Geert Hofstede, *Culture's Consequences: International Differences in Work-Related Values* (Beverly Hills, CA: Sage, 1980). Adapted from a discussion in Larry A. Samovar,

Richard E. Porter, and Lisa A. Stefani, *Communication between Cultures* (Belmont, CA: Wadsworth, 1998).

20. Lewis, *When Cultures Collide*, 27.
21. "Human Values and Nature's Future."
22. Rushworth M. Kidder, *Shared Values for a Troubled World: Conversations with Men and Women of Conscience* (San Francisco: Jossey-Bass Publishers, 1994).

Chapter 8

1. Rodney Reynolds and Michael Burgoon, "Evidence," in *The Persuasion Handbook: Developments in Theory and Practice,* eds. J. P. Dillard and M. Pfau (Thousand Oaks, CA: Sage, 2002), 427–44.
2. Barrington D. Parker, "International Exodus: Visa Delays and Denials," *Vital Speeches of the Day* 70, no. 19 (2004): 583–87.
3. Jonathan Drori, "Every Pollen Grain Has a Story," speech posted on TED Web site, April 2010, http://www.ted.com/talks/lang/eng/jonathan_drori_every_pollen_grain_has_a_story.html.
4. Quoted in K. Q. Seelye, "Congressman Offers Bill to Ban Cloning of Humans," *New York Times,* March 6, 1997, sec. A.
5. Mark Turner, *The Literary Mind* (New York: Oxford University Press, 1996).
6. Ibid.
7. Melinda French Gates, "Raising the Bar on College Completion," Keynote address, American Association of Community Colleges, April 20, 2010, http://www.gatesfoundation.org/speeches-commentary/Pages/melinda-gates-2010-american-association-of-community-colleges.aspx#.
8. Brock Evans, "A Gift for All of America" (address delivered to the biennial session of the Wyoming Conservation Congress, Casper, WY, July 10, 1999), http://www.votd.com/evans.htm.
9. Testimony of Derek P. Ellerman to Subcommittee on Human Rights and Wellness, Committee on Government Reform, U.S. House of Representatives, July 8, 2004, Polaris Project, http://www.polarisproject.org/polarisproject/news_p3/DPETestimony_p3.htm.
10. See for example R. S. Zaharna, "Understanding Cultural Preferences of Arab Communication Patterns," *Public Relations Review* 21, no. 3 (Autumn 1995): 241–55.
11. J. C. Reinard, *Foundations of Argument* (Dubuque, IA: William C. Brown, 1991).
12. Steve Jobs (keynote address delivered at Worldwide Developers Conference, San Francisco's Moscone West, June 11, 2007).
13. *Profile of General Demographic Characteristics 2000, Geographic Area Colorado, American FactFinder*, U.S. Census Bureau Web site, http://factfinder.census.gov/servlet/QTTable?_bm=n&_lang=en&qr_name=DEC_2000_SF1_U_DP1&ds_name=DEC_2000_SF1_U&geo_id=04000US08.
14. Sara Kehaulani Goo, "Airbus Hopes Big Plane Will Take Off, Beat Boeing," *Washington Post,* December 19, 2004, http://www.washingtonpost.com/wp-dyn/articles/A9900-2004Dec18.html (accessed May 13, 2005).
15. Centers for Disease Control and Prevention, "Births to Youngest Teens at Lowest Levels in Almost 60 Years," http://www.cdc.gov/od/oc/media/pressrel/r041115.htm (accessed May 13, 2005).
16. April Airline On-Time Performance Higher Than Last Year and March, Bureau of Transportation Statistics Web site, June 3, 2010, http://www.bts.gov/press_releases/2010/dot111_10/html/dot111_10.html.
17. Center on Budget and Policy Priorities, "Behind the Numbers: An Examination of the Tax Foundation's Tax Day Report," April 14, 1997, http://www.cbpp.org/taxday.htm.
18. "Binge Drinking Among High School Students and Adults—United States, 2009." Morbidity and Mortality Weekly Report (*MMWR*), October 5, 2010, http://www.cdc.gov/mmwr.

19. Roger Pielke Jr., "The Cherry Pick," *Ogmius: Newsletter for the Center for Science and Technology Research* 8 (May 2004), http://sciencepolicy.colorado.edu/ogmius/archives/issue_8/index.html.

20. Ibid.

Chapter 9

1. James C. McCroskey, *An Introduction to Rhetorical Communication,* 9th ed. (Boston: Allyn and Bacon, 2006), makes this point throughout his text.

2. "Identifying Primary and Secondary Sources," Indiana University, Bloomington, Libraries page, accessed May 9, 2010, www.libraries.iub.edu/index.php?pageId=1483.

3. Jennifer Keohane, reference librarian, Simsbury Public Library, conversation with author, Simsbury, CT, May 10, 2010.

4. Robert G. Torricelli, *Quotations for Public Speakers: A Historical, Literary, and Political Anthology* (New Brunswick, NJ: Rutgers University Press, 2002).

5. Robert J. Morgan, *Nelson's Complete Book of Stories, Illustrations, and Quotes: The Ultimate Contemporary Resource for Speakers* (Nashville, TN: Thomas Nelson, 2000).

Chapter 10

1. Barbara Burg et al., "Writing with Internet Sources," Lamont Library of the Harvard College Library Web site, accessed June 28, 2010, http://isites.harvard.edu/fs/docs/icb.topic500638.files/Writing_with_Internet_Sources.pdf.

2. Elizabeth E. Kirk, "Information and Its Counterfeits," Sheridan Libraries of Johns Hopkins University, 2001, www.library.jhu.edu/researchhelp/general/evaluating/counterfeit.html.

3. Richard A. Nelson, *A Chronology and Glossary of Propaganda in the United States* (Westport, CT, and London: Greenwood Press, 1996).

4. Jorgen J. Wouters, "Searching for Disclosure: How Search Engines Alert Consumers to the Presence of Advertising in Search Results," *Consumer Reports WebWatch,* November 8, 2004, http://www.consumerwebwatch.org/dynamic/search-report-disclosureabstract.cfm.

5. "Meta-search Engines," University of California, Berkeley Library Tutorial, accessed July 1, 2010, http://www.lib.berkeley.edu/TeachingLib/Guides/Internet/MetaSearch.html.

6. Wouters, "Searching for Disclosure."

Chapter 11

1. Ralph Underwager and Hollida Wakefield, "The Taint Hearing," *IPT* 10 (1998). Originally presented at the 13th Annual Symposium in Forensic Psychology, Vancouver, BC (April 17, 1997). Retrieved September 1, 2007, from www.ipt-forensics.com/journal/volume10/j10_7.htm#en0.

Chapter 12

1. E. Thompson, "An Experimental Investigation of the Relative Effectiveness of Organization Structure in Oral Communication," *Southern Speech Journal* 26 (1960): 59–69.

2. R. G. Smith, "Effects of Speech Organization upon Attitudes of College Students," *Speech Monographs* 18 (1951): 292–301.

3. H. Sharp Jr. and T. McClung, "Effects of Organization on the Speaker's Ethos," *Speech Monographs* 33 (1966): 182ff.

4. "Communication Skills, Honesty/Integrity Top Employers' Wish List for Job Candidates," *Job Outlook 2005 Survey,* January 20, 2005, National Association of Colleges and Employers, accessed June 12, 2005, http://www.naceweb.org/products/jo2005report.htm.

5. G. H. Bower, "Organizational Factors in Memory," *Cognitive Psychology* 1 (1970): 18–46.

6. Murray Glanzer and Anita R. Cunitz, "Two Storage Mechanisms in Free Recall," *Journal of Verbal Learning and Verbal Behavior* 5 (1966): 351–60.

7. Rodney Reynolds and Michael Burgoon, "Evidence," in *The Persuasion Handbook: Developments in Theory and Practice,* eds. J. P. Dillard and M. Pfau (Thousand Oaks, CA: Sage, 2002), 427–44.

Chapter 13

1. R. G. Smith, "Effects of Speech Organization upon Attitudes of College Students," *Speech Monographs* 18 (1951): 547–49; E. Thompson, "An Experimental Investigation of the Relative Effectiveness of Organizational Structure in Oral Communication," *Southern Speech Journal* 26 (1960): 59–69.
2. PBS, "Life on the Internet Timeline," accessed April 3, 2000, http://www.pbs.org/internet/timeline/index.html.
3. Anita Taylor, "Tales of the Grandmothers: Women and Work," *Vital Speeches of the Day* 71, no. 7 (2005): 209–12.
4. Sonja K. Foss and Karen A. Foss, *Inviting Transformation: Presentational Speaking for a Changing World* (Prospect Heights, IL: Waveland Press, 1994).

Chapter 14

1. For an enlightening review of the history of outlining from Cicero to electronic software, see Jonathan Price, "STOP: Light on the History of Outlining," *Journal of Computer Documentation* 23, no. 3 (August 1999): 69–78.
2. Mark B. McClellan (speech presented at the fifth annual David A. Winston lecture, Washington, DC, October 20, 2003), http://www.fda.gov/oc/speeches/2003/winston1020.html.
3. Gratitude goes to Carolyn Clark, Ph.D., of Salt Lake Community College, for sharing this assignment with us.

Chapter 15

1. Ron Hoff, *I Can See You Naked,* rev. ed. (Kansas City, MO: Andrews McMeel, 1992), 41.
2. William Safire, *Lend Me Your Ears: Great Speeches in History* (New York: Norton, 1992), 676.
3. For a rich discussion of the role of stories and narratives in communication, see Walter Fisher, "Narration as a Human Communication Paradigm: The Case of Public Moral Argument," *Communication Monographs* 51, no. 1 (1984): 1–22.
4. Edward P. J. Corbett, *Classical Rhetoric for the Modern Student,* 3rd ed. (New York: Oxford University Press, 1990).
5. Bas Andeweg and Jap de Jong, "May I Have Your Attention? Exordial Techniques in Informative Oral Presentations," *Technical Communication Quarterly* 7, no. 3 (1998): 271–84.
6. National Center for Victims of Crime, "Statistics on Domestic Violence," compiled from data reported by the Bureau of Justice Statistics (2007) and the Federal Bureau of Investigation (2008), accessed July 26, 2010, http://www.ncvc.org/ncvc/main.aspx?dbName=DocumentViewer&DocumentID=38711.
7. As quoted in M. A. Guffey and D. Loewy, *Essentials of Business Communication,* 8th ed. (Mason, OH: South-Western/Cengage Learning, 2010), 339.
8. Nelson Mandela, "Our March to Freedom Is Irreversible," in *The Penguin Book of Twentieth-Century Speeches,* ed. B. MacArthur (New York: Penguin, 1992).
9. Vance Coffman, "Help Wanted: 'Busineers,'" *Vital Speeches of the Day* 66, no. 16 (2000): 488–92.
10. C. A. Kiesler and S. B. Kiesler, "Role of Forewarning in Persuasive Communication," *Journal of Abnormal and Social Psychology* 68 (1964): 547–69, cited in James C. McCroskey, *An Introduction to Rhetorical Communication,* 8th ed. (Boston: Allyn & Bacon, 2001), 253.
11. Marvin Runyon, "No One Moves the Mail Like the U.S. Postal Service," *Vital Speeches of the Day* 61, no. 2 (1994): 52–55.
12. Andeweg and de Jong, "May I Have Your Attention?"
13. Robert L. Darbelnet, "U.S. Roads and Bridges: Highway Funding at a Crossroads," *Vital Speeches of the Day* 63, no. 12 (1997): 379.

Chapter 16

1. R. O. Skovgard, interview by author, June 10, 1995.
2. Holger Kluge, "Reflections on Diversity," *Vital Speeches of the Day* 63, no. 6 (1997): 171–72.
3. Elpidio Villarreal, "Choosing the Right Path" (speech delivered to the Puerto Rican Legal Defense and Education Fund Gala in New York City, October 26, 2006), *Vital Speeches of the Day* 72, no. 26 (2007): 784–86.
4. Queen Gorga, "300," accessed May 30, 2010, http://www.americanrhetoric.com/MovieSpeeches/moviespeech300queengorgo.html.
5. Sue Suter, "Adapting to Change, While Holding on to Values: *Star Trek*'s Lessons for the Disability Community" (speech delivered to the Annual Conference of the Association for the Severely Handicapped, Springfield, IL, September 22, 1999).
6. Oprah Winfrey (speech delivered at Wellesley College commencement, Wellesley, MA, May 30, 1997), http://www.wellesley.edu/PublicAffairs/Commencement/1997/winfrey.html.
7. James C. May, president and CEO, Air Transport Association of America (address delivered to the European Aviation Club, Brussels, Belgium, October 30, 2008), http://www.airlines.org/News/Speeches/Pages/speech_10-30-08May.aspx.

Chapter 17

1. Robert Harris, "A Handbook of Rhetorical Devices," *Virtual Salt,* July 26, 2002, http://www.virtualsalt.com/rhetoric.htm.
2. Michael J. Lewis, "When Presidents Speak," *Commentary* 111, no. 6 (2001): 48–51.
3. Peggy Noonan, *Simply Speaking: How to Communicate Your Ideas with Style, Substance, and Clarity* (New York: Regan Books, 1998), 51.
4. William Safire, *Lend Me Your Ears: Great Speeches in History* (New York: Norton, 1992), 26.
5. Dan Hooley, "The Lessons of the Ring," *Vital Speeches of the Day* 70, no. 20 (2004): 660–63.
6. James E. Lukaszewski, "You Can Become a Verbal Visionary" (speech delivered to the Public Relations Society of America, Cleveland, OH, April 8, 1997), Executive Speaker Library, http://www.executive-speaker.com/lib_moti.html.
7. Catherine H. Zizik, "Powerspeak: Avoiding Ambiguous Language," *Speech Communication Teacher* (Summer 1995): 8–9.
8. Loren J. Naidoo and Robert G. Lord, "Speech Imagery and Perceptions of Charisma: The Mediating Role of Positive Affect," *Leadership Quarterly* 19, no. 3 (2008): 283–96.
9. Ibid; phrase taken from President Franklin Delano Roosevelt's 1933 inaugural address.
10. L. Clemetson and J. Gordon-Thomas, "Our House Is on Fire," *Newsweek,* June 11, 2001, 50.
11. Andrew C. Billings, "Beyond the Ebonics Debate: Attitudes about Black and Standard American English," *Journal of Black Studies* 36 (2005): 68–81.
12. Sylvie Dubois, "Sounding Cajun: The Rhetorical Use of Dialect in Speech and Writing," *American Speech* 77, no. 3 (2002): 264–87.
13. Gloria Anzaldúa, "Entering into the Serpent," in *The St. Martin's Handbook,* eds. Andrea Lunsford and Robert Connors, 3rd ed. (New York: St. Martin's Press, 1995), 25.
14. P. H. Matthews, *The Concise Oxford Dictionary of Linguistics* (New York: Oxford University Press, 1997).
15. Howard K. Battles and Charles Packard, *Words and Sentences,* bk. 6 (Lexington, MA: Ginn & Company, 1984), 110.
16. Robin Lakoff, *Language and Woman's Place* (New York: Harper & Row, 1975); Deborah Tannen, *You Just Don't Understand: Women and Men in Conversation* (New York: William Morrow, 1990); Deborah Tannen, *Talking from 9 to 5* (New York: William Morrow, 1994); Anthony Mulac, "The Gender-Linked Language Effect: Do Language Differences Really Make a Difference?" in D. Canary and K. Dindia (eds.), *Sex Differences and Similarities in Communication* (Mahwah, NJ: Lawrence Erlbaum, 1998); Phyllis Mindell,

A Woman's Guide to the Language of Success: Communicating with Confidence and Power (Englewood Cliffs, NJ: Prentice Hall, 1995).

17. "Frequently Asked Questions," Office of Disability Employment Policy Web site, April 23, 2010, http://www.dol.gov/odep/faqs/people.htm; "American FactFinder," U.S. Census Bureau Web site, accessed April 25, 2010, http://factfinder.census.gov.

18. Remarks of President-Elect Barack Obama, Election Night, Chicago, IL, November 04, 2008, www.barackobama.com/2008/11/04/remarks_of_presidentelect_bara.php.

19. Cited in William Safire, *Lend Me Your Ears: Great Speeches in History* (New York: Norton, 1992), 22.

20. Remarks of Senator Barack Obama, New Hampshire Primary, Nashua, NH, January 8, 2008, www.barackobama.com.

Chapter 18

1. James A. Winans, *Public Speaking* (New York: Century, 1925). Professor Winans was among the first Americans to contribute significantly to the study of rhetoric. His explanation of delivery is considered by many to be the best coverage of the topic in the English language. His perspective infuses this chapter.

2. Judee K. Burgoon, Thomas Birk, and Michael Pfau, "Nonverbal Behaviors, Persuasion, and Credibility," *Human Communication Research* 17, no.1 (1990): 140+. *Academic OneFile.*

3. Winans, *Public Speaking,* 17.

4. Thomas M. Conley, *Rhetoric in the European Tradition* (New York: Longman, 1990).

5. William Safire, PBS *NewsHour,* August 15, 1996, http://www.pbs.org/newshour/gergen/july-dec96/safire_8-15.html.

6. Robbin Crabtree and Robert Weissberg, *ESL Students in the Public Speaking Classroom: A Guide for Teachers* (Boston: Bedford/St. Martin's, 2000), 24.

Chapter 19

1. Kyle James Tusing and James Price Dillard, "The Sounds of Dominance: Vocal Precursors of Perceived Dominance during Interpersonal Influence," *Human Communication Research* 26 (2000): 148–71.

2. Caryl Raye Krannich, *101 Secrets of Highly Effective Speakers* (Manassas Park, VA: Impact Publications, 1998), 121–22.

3. Kenneth C. Crannell, *Voice and Articulation,* 4th ed. (Belmont, CA: Wadsworth, 2000), 41.

4. MaryAnn Cunningham Florez, *Improving Adult ESL Learners' Pronunciation Skills,* National Clearinghouse for ESL Literacy Education (1998), accessed July 16, 2005, http://www.cal.org/caela/digests/Pronun.htm.

5. Tusing and Dillard, "Sounds of Dominance."

6. The digitized audio of King's "I Have a Dream" speech can be accessed at http://www.americanrhetoric.com/speeches/Ihaveadream.htm.

Chapter 20

1. Robert Rivlin and Karen Gravelle, *Deciphering the Senses: The Expanding World of Human Perception* (New York: Simon & Schuster, 1998), 98; see also A. Warfield, "Do You Speak Body Language?" *Training & Development* 55, no. 4 (2001): 60.

2. Dan O'Hair and Mary Wiemann, *Real Communication: An Introduction* (Boston: Bedford/St. Martin's, 2009), 105.

3. C. F. Bond and the Global Deception Research Team, "A World of Lies," *Journal of Cross-Cultural Psychology* 37 (2006): 60–74; T. R. Levine, J. K. Asada, and H. S. Park, "The Lying Chicken and the Gaze Avoidant Egg: Eye Contact, Deception, and Causal Order," *Southern Communication Journal* 71 (2006): 401–11.

4. Ibid.

5. D. Canary, M. J. Cody, and V. Manusov, *Interpersonal Communication: A Goals Approach,* 4th ed. (New York: Bedford/St. Martin's, 2008).

6. E. Krumburger, "Effects of Dynamic Attributes of Smiles in Human and Synthetic Faces: A Simulated Job Interview Setting," *Journal of Nonverbal Behavior* 33 (2009): 1–15.

7. Laurie Schloff and Marcia Yudkin, *Smart Speaking* (New York: Plume, 1991), 108.
8. A. Melinger and W. M. Levelt, "Gesture and the Communicative Intention of the Speaker," *Gesture* 4 (2004): 119–41.
9. Reid Buckley, *Strictly Speaking: Reid Buckley's Indispensable Handbook on Public Speaking* (New York: McGraw-Hill, 1999), 209.
10. J. P. Davidson, "Shaping an Image That Boosts Your Career," *Marketing Communications* 13 (1988): 55–56.
11. See speaking consultant Rick Segel's witty comments on the problems of dressing down in the workplace, accessed July 18, 2005, http://www.ricksegel.com/reprints8.html.
12. Carmine Gallo, *The Presentation Secrets of Steve Jobs* (New York: McGraw-Hill, 2009), 181.

Chapter 21

1. D. Cyphert, "Presentation Technology in the Age of Electronic Eloquence: From Visual Aid to Visual Rhetoric," *Communication Education* 56, no. 2 (2007): 168–92.
2. K. Wing, "Simple Secrets of Power Presenters," *Strategic Finance* 90, no. 12 (2009): 21–22.
3. Richard E. Mayer, *The Multimedia Principle* (New York: Cambridge University Press, 2001).
4. See discussion of the redundancy effect in Richard E. Mayer, ed., *The Cambridge Handbook of Multimedia Learning* (New York: Cambridge University Press, 2005).
5. D. Cyphert, "Presentation Technology."
6. D. Cyphert, "The Problem of PowerPoint: Visual Aid or Visual Rhetoric?" *Business Communication Quarterly* 67, no. 1 (2004): 80–84.
7. J. Doumont, "The Cognitive Style of PowerPoint: Slides Are Not All Evil," *Technical Communication* 52, no. 1 (2005): 64–70.
8. "Line Graph," BusinessDictionary.com, accessed July 10, 2010, http://www.businessdictionary.com/definition/line-graph.html.
9. G. Jones, "Message First: Using Films to Power the Point," *Business Communication Quarterly* 67, no 1 (2004): 88–91.
10. K. M. Axtell, "The Effect of Presentation Software on Classroom Verbal Interaction and on Student Retention of Higher Education Lecture Content," *Journal of Technology in Teaching and Learning* 4, no. 1 (2008): 21–23.
11. J. B. Lanir, "The Benefits of More Electronic Screen Space on Students' Retention of Material in Classroom Lectures," *Computers & Education* 55, no. 2 (2010): 892–903.
12. R. Larson, "Enhancing the Recall of Presented Material," *Computers & Education* 53, no. 4 (2009): 1278–84.

Chapter 22

1. R. Worley, "Presentations and the PowerPoint Problem," *Business Communication Quarterly* 67, no. 1 (2004): 78–80.
2. Edward Tufte, "PowerPoint Is Evil," *Wired* 11 (2003), www.wired.com/archive/11.09/ppt2_pr.html.
3. R. Larson, "Enhancing the Recall of Presented Material," *Computers & Education* 53, no. 4 (2009): 1278–84.
4. A. C. Moller, A. J. Elliot, and M. A. Maier, *Red Is for Failure and Green for Success: Achievement-Related Implicit Associations to Color* (poster presented at the Society for Personality and Social Psychology Conference, Tampa, FL, February 2009).
5. R. Larson, "Slide Composition for Electronic Presentations," *Journal of Educational Computing Research,* 31, no. 1 (2004): 61–76.

Chapter 23

1. Angela Garber, "Death by PowerPoint," SmallBusinessComputing.com, April 1, 2001, http://www.smallbusinesscomputing.com/biztools/article.php/684871/Death-By-PowerPoint. htm; Dave Pavadi, "How to Avoid 'Death by PowerPoint,'" ThinkOutside TheSlide.com, accessed July 17, 2010, http://thinkoutsidetheslide.com/articles/avoid_death_by_ppt.htm.

2. R. Worley, "Presentations and the PowerPoint Problem," *Business Communication Quarterly* 67, no. 1 (2004): 78–80.
3. D. Cyphert, "Presentation Technology in the Age of Electronic Eloquence: From Visual Aid to Visual Rhetoric," *Communication Education* 56, no. 2 (2007): 168–92; D. Cyphert, "The Problem of PowerPoint: Visual Aid or Visual Rhetoric?" *Business Communication Quarterly* 67, no. 1 (2004): 80–84.
4. J. Thomas, "PowerPoint Is Not the Problem with Presentations Today," March 21, 2010, *Presentation Advisors,* http://blog.presentationadvisors.com/presentationadvisors/2010/03/powerpoint-is-not-the-problem-with-presentations.html.
5. R. Larson, "Slide Composition for Electronic Presentations," *Journal of Educational Computing Research* 31, no. 1 (2004) 61–76.

Chapter 24

1. Katherine E. Rowan subdivides informative communication into *informatory discourse,* in which the primary aim is to represent reality by increasing an audience's awareness of some phenomenon; and *explanatory discourse,* with the aim to represent reality by deepening understanding. See Katherine E. Rowan, "Informing and Explaining Skills: Theory and Research on Informative Communication," in *Handbook of Communication and Social Interaction Skills,* eds. J. O. Greene and B. R. Burleson (Mahwah, NJ: Erlbaum, 2003), 403–38.
2. With thanks to Barry Antokoletz, NYC College of Technology, for these comments.
3. Vickie K. Sullivan, "Public Speaking: The Secret Weapon in Career Development," *USA Today*, May 2005, 24.
4. Nick Morgan, "Two Rules for a Successful Presentation," *Harvard Business Review Blog* ("The Conversation"), May 14, 2010, http://blogs.hbr.org/cs/2010/05/two_rules_for_a_successful_pre.html; H. E. Chambers, *Effective Communication Skills for Scientific and Technical Professionals* (Cambridge, MA: Perseus Publishing, 2001).
5. Tina Blythe et al., *The Teaching for Understanding Guide* (Hoboken, NJ: Jossey-Bass, 1997); Kenneth D. Frandsen and Donald A. Clement, "The Functions of Human Communication in Informing: Communicating and Processing Information," in *Handbook of Rhetorical and Communication Theory,* eds. Carroll C. Arnold and John Waite Bowers (Needham, MA: Allyn & Bacon, 1984), 334.
6. E. Thompson, "An Experimental Investigation of the Relative Effectiveness of Organization Structure in Oral Communication," *Southern Speech Journal* 26 (1966): 59–69.
7. Howard K. Battles and Charles Packard, *Words and Sentences,* bk. 6 (Lexington, MA: Ginn & Company, 1984), 459.
8. Katherine E. Rowan, "A New Pedagogy for Explanatory Public Speaking: Why Arrangement Should Not Substitute for Invention," *Communication Education* 44 (1995): 236–50.
9. S. Kujawa and L. Huske, *The Strategic Teaching and Reading Project Guidebook,* rev. ed. (Oak Brook, IL: North Central Regional Educational Laboratory, 1995).
10. Shawn M. Glynn et al., "Teaching Science with Analogies: A Resource for Teachers and Textbook Authors," *National Reading Research Center, Instructional Resource,* no. 7 (Fall 1994).
11. Altoona List of Medical Analogies, "How to Use Analogies," Altoona Family Physicians Residency Web site, accessed August 5, 2010, http://www.altoonafp.org/analogies.htm.
12. Glynn et al., "Teaching Science," 19.
13. Altoona List of Medical Analogies, "How to Use Analogies."
14. Wolfgang Porod, "Nanotechnology," *Vital Speeches of the Day* 71, no. 4 (2004): 125–28.
15. Tina A. Grotzer, "How Conceptual Leaps in Understanding the Nature of Causality Can Limit Learning: An Example from Electrical Circuits" (paper presented at the annual conference of the American Educational Research Association, New Orleans, April 2000), http://pzweb.harvard.edu/Research/UnderCon.htm.
16. Neil D. Fleming and C. Mills, "Helping Students Understand How They Learn," *Teaching Professor* 7, no. 4 (1992).

Chapter 25

1. Edward P. J. Corbett, *Classical Rhetoric for the Modern Student,* 3rd ed. (New York: Oxford University Press, 1990).
2. Communications scholars Winston Brembeck and William Howell define the goal in this way: "Persuasion is communication intended to influence choice." See Winston L. Brembeck and William S. Howell, *Persuasion: A Means of Social Influence,* 2nd ed. (Englewood Cliffs, NJ: Prentice Hall, 1976).
3. Richard E. Petty and John T. Cacioppo, *Communication and Persuasion: Central and Peripheral Routes to Attitude Change* (New York: Springer-Verlag, 1986).
4. Kathleen K. Reardon, *Persuasion in Practice* (Newbury Park, CA: Sage, 1991), 210.
5. Russel H. Fazio, "How Do Attitudes Guide Behavior?" in *The Handbook of Motivation and Cognition: Foundations of Social Behavior,* eds. Richard M. Sorrentino and E. Tory Higgins (New York: Guilford, 1986).
6. Joseph R. Priester and Richard E. Petty, "Source Attributions and Persuasion: Perceived Honesty as a Determinant of Message Scrutiny," *Personality and Social Psychology Bulletin* 21 (1995): 637–54. See also Kenneth G. DeBono and Richard J. Harnish, "Source Expertise, Source Attractiveness, and the Processing of Persuasive Information: A Functional Approach," *Journal of Personality and Social Psychology* 55 (1987): 541.
7. Priester and Petty, *Personality,* 11.
8. Eveline Feteris, "A Pragma-Dialectical Approach of the Analysis and Evaluation of Pragmatic Argumentation in a Legal Context," *Argumentation* 16 (2002): 349–67.
9. Nathan Crick, "Conquering Our Imagination: Thought Experiments and Enthymemes in Scientific Argument," *Philosophy and Rhetoric* 37 (2004): 21–41.
10. Corbett, *Classical Rhetoric for the Modern Student,* 1356a, 1377b.
11. Ibid.
12. Elpidio Villarreal, "Choosing the Right Path" (speech delivered to the Puerto Rican Legal Defense and Education Fund Gala in New York City, October 26, 2006), *Vital Speeches of the Day* 72, no. 26 (2007): 784–86.
13. Kim Witte and Mike Allen, "A Meta-Analysis of Fear Appeals: Implications for Effective Public Health Campaigns," *Health Education and Behavior* 27, no. 5 (2000): 591–615.
14. Robert A. Stewart, "Perceptions of a Speaker's Initial Credibility as a Function of Religious Involvement and Religious Disclosiveness," *Communication Research Reports* 11 (1994): 169–76.
15. For an extensive review of the history of the field of communication from the classical period to the present era, see Dominic A. Infante, Andrew S. Rancer, and Deanna F. Womack, *Building Communication Theory,* 4th ed. (Prospect Heights, IL: Waveland Press, 2003).
16. B. Soper, G. E. Milford, and G. T. Rosenthal, "Belief When Evidence Does Not Support the Theory," *Psychology and Marketing* 12 (1995): 415–22, cited in Stephen M. Kosslyn and Robin S. Rosenberg, *Psychology: The Brain, the Person, the World* (Boston: Allyn & Bacon, 2004), 330.
17. Icek Ajzen and Martin Fishbein, *Understanding Attitudes and Predicting Social Behavior* (Englewood Cliffs, NJ: Prentice Hall, 1980).
18. A. E. Latimer, T. A. Rench, S. E. Rivers, N. A. Katulak, S. A. Materese, L. Cadmus, A. Hicks, J. Keamy-Hodorowski, and P. Salovey, "Promoting Participation in Physical Activity Using Framed Messages: An Application of Prospect Theory," *British Journal of Health Psychology* 13, no. 4 (2008): 659–81.
19. Richard Petty and John T. Cacioppo, "The Elaboration Likelihood Model of Persuasion," in *Advances in Experimental Social Psychology,* vol. 19, ed. L. Berkowitz (San Diego, CA: Academic Press, 1986), 123–205; Richard Petty and Duane T. Wegener, "Matching versus Mismatching Attitude Functions: Implications for Scrutiny of Persuasive Messages," *Personality and Social Psychology Bulletin* 24 (1998): 227–40.
20. For good reviews of the literature on source credibility in general, see Richard M. Perloff, *The Dynamics of Persuasion* (Hillsdale, NJ: Lawrence Erlbaum, 1993), and Infante, Rancer, and Womack, *Building Communication Theory.*

21. K. K. Sereno and G. I. Hawkins, "The Effects of Variations in Speakers' Nonfluency upon Audience Ratings of Attitude toward the Speech Topic and Speakers' Credibility," *Speech Monographs* 34 (1967): 58–64.
22. Priester and Petty, "Source Attributions and Persuasion."

Chapter 26

1. *Merriam-Webster's Collegiate Dictionary,* 10th ed. (Springfield, MA: Merriam-Webster, 1993).
2. Austin J. Freeley, *Argumentation and Debate,* 8th ed. (Belmont, CA: Wadsworth, 1993), 158.
3. Thomas A. Hollihan and Kevin T. Baaske, *Arguments and Arguing* (New York: St. Martin's Press, 1994), 27.
4. The model of argument presented here follows Stephen Toulmin, *The Uses of Argument* (New York: Cambridge University Press, 1958), as described in James C. McCroskey, *An Introduction to Rhetorical Communication,* 6th ed. (Englewood Cliffs, NJ: Prentice Hall, 1993).
5. Annette Rottenberg, *Elements of Argument,* 4th ed. (Boston: Bedford/St. Martin's, 1994), 10.
6. American Council on Science and Health, "What's the Story? Drug-Supplement Interaction," November 2000, http://www.acsh.org/publications/story/index.html.
7. "State of the Union: President Obama's Speech: President Obama Delivers State of the Union at US Capitol in Washington, D.C.," January 27, 2010, http://abcnews.go.com/Politics/State_of_the_Union/state-of-the-union-2010-president-obama-speech -transcript/story?id=9678572/.
8. Based on McCroskey, *An Introduction to Rhetorical Communication.*
9. See the discussion of the relationship between attitudes and behavior in Daniel J. O'Keefe, *Persuasion: Theory and Research,* 2nd ed. (Thousand Oaks, CA: Sage, 2002), 16–17.
10. Dennis S. Gouran, "Attitude Change and Listeners' Understanding of a Persuasive Communication," *Speech Teacher* 15 (1966): 289–94; J. P. Dillard, "Persuasion Past and Present: Attitudes Aren't What They Used to Be," *Communication Monographs* 60 (1966): 94.
11. Freeley, *Argumentation and Debate,* 175.
12. M. Pfau, S. M. Semmler, L. Deatrick, A. Mason, G. Nisbett, L. Lane, et al., "Nuances about the Role and Impact of Affect in Inoculation," *Communication Monographs* 76, no. 1 (2009): 73–98.
13. Edward P. J. Corbett, *Classical Rhetoric for the Modern Student,* 3rd ed. (New York: Oxford University Press, 1990).
14. T. Edward Damer, *Attaching Faulty Reasoning: A Practical Guide to Fallacy-Free Arguments* (Belmont, CA: Cengage, 2009).
15. Herbert Simon, *Persuasion in Society* (Thousand Oaks, CA: Sage, 2001), 385–87.

Chapter 27

1. *Motor Vehicle Facts and Figures* (American Automobile Manufacturers Association, 1997), 84.
2. Herbert Simon, *Persuasion in Society* (Thousand Oaks, CA: Sage, 2001), 385–87.
3. A. H. Monroe, *Principles and Types of Speeches* (Chicago: Scott, Foresman, 1935).
4. C. Ilie, "Strategies of Refutation by Definition: A Pragma-Rhetorical Approach to Refutations in a Public Speech," in *Pondering on Problems of Argumentation: Twenty Essays on Theoretical Issues,* eds. F. H. van Eemeren and B. Garssen (Springer Science + Business Media, 2009), DOI: 10.1007/978-1-4020-9165-0_4.
5. James R. DiSanza and Nancy J. Legge, *Business and Professional Communication: Plans, Processes, and Performance,* 2nd ed. (Boston: Allyn & Bacon, 2002), 236.

Chapter 28

1. Frank D. Stella, "Introductory Remarks Delivered to the Economic Club of Detroit, Detroit, Michigan," *Executive Speaker* 17 (April 15, 1996): 3.
2. G. Parret, *I Love My Boss and 969 Other Business Jokes* (New York: Sterling Publishing, 1993).

3. H. H. Shelton, "Victory, Honor, Sacrifice," *Vital Speeches of the Day* 66, no. 20 (2000): 627.
4. Ibid.
5. Paul Fatout, ed., *Mark Twain Speaks for Himself* (West Lafayette, IN: Purdue University Press, 1978).
6. David Magill, "Give Your Life a Dream with Design," *Vital Speeches of the Day* 62, no. 21 (1996): 671–72.

Chapter 29

1. 1080 Group, LLC, *Engage! How to Avoid the Seven Sins of Live, Online Presentations,* July 27, 2009, http://bit.ly/4s0wjO.
2. P. Fripp, "15 Tips for Webinars: How to Add Impact When You Present Online," *eLearn Magazine,* July 7, 2009, http://elearnmag.org/subpage.cfm?section=best _practices&article=56-1.
3. K. Callahan, "Online Learning Comes into Its Own at SNHU," *New Hampshire Business Review,* March 26, 2010, http://www.nhbr.com/business/education/683779-272/online-learning-comes-into-its-own-at.html.
4. K. Griffiths and C. Peters, *10 Steps for Planning a Successful Webinar,* TechSoup, January 27, 2009, http://www.techsoup.org/learningcenter/training.
5. Ibid.
6. 1080 Group, LLC, *Engage!*
7. K. Molay, *Webinar Basics,* Webinar Success, June 4, 2007, http://www.brainshark.com/brainshark/vu/view.asp?pi=675863777.
8. Fripp, "15 Tips for Webinars."
9. 1080 Group, LLC, *Engage!*

Chapter 30

1. Dan O'Hair and Mary Wiemann, *Real Communication,* 2nd ed. (New York: Bedford/St. Martin's, 2012).
2. Feng-yang Kuo and Chia-ping Yu, "An Exploratory Study of Trust Dynamics in Work-Oriented Virtual Teams," *Journal of Computer-Mediated Communication* 14 (2009): 823–54; O'Hair and Wiemann, *Real Communication;* W. L. Tullar and P. R. Kaiser, "The Effect of Process Training on Process and Outcomes in Virtual Groups," *Journal of Business Communication* 37 (2000): 408–27.
3. Dan O'Hair, Gustav Friedrich, and Lynda Dixon, *Strategic Communication for Business and the Professions,* 7th ed. (Boston: Allyn Bacon, 2011); O'Hair and Wiemann, *Real Communication.*
4. K. D. Benne and P. Sheats, "Functional Roles of Group Members," *Journal of Social Issues* 4 (1948): 41–49.
5. Ibid.
6. Amy Edmondson and Ingrid Nembhard, "Product Development and Learning in Project Teams: The Challenges Are the Benefits," *Journal of Product Innovation Management* 26 (2009): 123–38; M. S. Poole and J. T. Garner, "Perspectives on Workgroup Conflict and Communication," in *The SAGE Handbook of Conflict Communication,* eds. J. Oetzel and S. Ting-Toomey (Thousand Oaks, CA: Sage, 2002), 267–92.
7. O'Hair and Wiemann, *Real Communication.*
8. Robert McPhee, Karen Myers, and Angela Trethewey, "On Collective Mind and Conversational Analysis," *Management Communication Quarterly* 19 (2006): 311–26.
9. Geoffrey A. Cross, "Collective Form: An Exploration of Large-Group Writing," *Journal of Business Communication* 37 (2000): 77–100.
10. Claire Ferrais, "Investigating NASA's Intergroup Decision-Making: Groupthink and Intergroup Social Dynamics," paper presented at the Annual Meeting of the International Communication Association, 2004; Irving Lester Janis, *Groupthink: Psychological Studies of Policy Decisions and Fiascoes* (Berkeley: University of California Press, 1982).

11. S. Schulz-Hardt, F. C. Bordbeck, A. Mojzisch, R. Kerschreiter, and D. Frey, "Group Decision Making as a Facilitator for Decision Quality," *Journal of Personality and Social Psychology* 91 (1080–93): O'Hair, Friedrich, and Dixon, *Strategic Communication for Business and the Professions.*
12. Gloria J. Galanes, "Dialectical Tensions of Small Group Leadership," *Communication Studies* 60, no. 5 (2009): 409–25.
13. L. Richard Hoffman and Norman R. F. Maier, "Valence in the Adoption of Solutions by Problem-Solving Groups: Concept, Method, and Results," *Journal of Abnormal and Social Psychology* 69 (1964): 264–71.
14. John Dewey, *How We Think* (Boston: D.C. Heath Co., 1950).
15. Lin Kroeger, *The Complete Idiot's Guide to Successful Business Presentation* (New York: Alpha Books, 1997), 113.

Chapter 31

1. For a review, see Priscilla S. Rogers, "Distinguishing Public and Presentational Speaking," *Management Communication Quarterly* 2 (1988): 102–15; Frank E. X. Dance, "What Do You Mean 'Presentational' Speaking?" *Management Communication Quarterly* 1 (1987): 270–81.
2. With thanks to Michal Dale of Southwest Missouri State University's Department of Communication.
3. Deanna P. Daniels, "Communicating across the Curriculum and in the Disciplines: Speaking in Engineering," *Communication Education* 51 (July 2002): 3.
4. Ibid.
5. Ibid.
6. James M. Henslin, *Sociology: A Down-to-Earth Approach,* 8th ed. (Boston: Allyn & Bacon, 2007), 138.
7. William E. Thompson and James V. Hickey, *Society in Focus: An Introduction to Sociology,* 2nd ed. (New York: HarperCollins, 1996), 39.

Chapter 32

1. Rick Weinholdt, "Taking the Trauma Out of the Talk," *Information Management Journal* (November/December 2006): 62.
2. Mark Hunter, "Shut Up, Listen and Sell," *B to B* 92 (2007): 11.
3. Dan O' Hair and R. L. Heath, eds., *Handbook of Risk and Crisis Communication: A Framework for Success* (Cincinnati: Southwestern, 2001).
4. William L. Benoit, *Accounts, Excuses, and Apologies: A Theory of Image Restoration Strategies* (Albany: State University of New York Press, 1995).
5. Ibid.

Appendix A

1. Patricia Nelson, "Handling Questions and Answers," Toastmasters International, Edmonton and Area, revised November 3, 1999, http://www.ecn.ab.ca/toast/qa.html.
2. Diane DiResta, *Knockout Presentations: How to Deliver Your Message with Power, Punch, and Pizzazz* (Worcester, MA: Chandler House Press, 1998), 236.
3. Ibid., 237.
4. Lilyan Wilder, *Talk Your Way to Success* (New York: Eastside Publishing, 1986), 279.

Appendix B

1. Patricia Nelson, "Handling Questions and Answers," Toastmasters International, Edmonton and Area, revised November 3, 1999, http://www.ecn.ab.ca/toast/qa.html.
2. Daria Price Bowman, *Presentations: Proven Techniques for Creating Presentations That Get Results* (Holbrook, MA: Adams Media, 1998), 177.
3. Oklahoma Society of CPAs (OSCPA), "Tips for Successful Media Interviewing," accessed June 10, 2006, http://www.oscpa.com/?757.

Acknowledgments

Text Credits

Page 42: "Visualization: Is It More Than Extra Attention?" by Joe Ayres and Theodore Hopf, *Communication Education*, vol. 38:1 (1989) pp. 1–5. Copyright © National Communication Association. Reprinted by permission of Taylor & Francis Ltd. http://www.tandf.co.uk/journals on behalf of The National Communication Association.

Pages 59–60: From *The Nature of Human Values* by Milton Rokeach. Reprinted with the permission of Free Press, a Division of Simon & Schuster, Inc. Copyright © 1973 by The Free Press. Copyright renewed © 2001 by Sandra Ball-Rokeach. All rights reserved.

Page 235: "Speech to Puerto Rican Legal Defense and Education Fund Gala," October 26, 2006. Elpidio Villarreal. Reprinted by permission of the author. Photos reprinted by permission of the Puerto Rican Legal Defense and Education Fund.

Page 236: Adapted from "Phenomenal Woman," copyright © 1978 by Maya Angelou, from *And Still I Rise* by Maya Angelou. Used by permission of Random House, Inc.

Page 270: Lilyan Wilder, "Thirteen Commonly Mispronounced Words," from *Seven Steps to Fearless Speaking*, pp. 210–211. Copyright © 1999 by Lilyan Wilder. Reproduced with permission of John Wiley & Sons, Inc.

Pages 417–422: From "'Love the Process': A Soccer Star's Philosophy of Life." Yael Averbuch, U.S. Women's National Soccer Team. Reprinted with permission of Yael Averbuch.

Pages 495–501: J. K. Rowling, Commencement Speech, Harvard University, 2008. Used by permission of Harvard University Public Affairs and Communications.

Pages 511–512: Paul L. Soper, Commonly Mispronounced Words. From *Basic Public Speaking*. Published by Oxford University Press (1968). All rights reserved. Reproduced by Permission.

Photo Credits

1: Jason Kempin/WireImage/Getty Images; **29:** Matthew Steigbigel/Getty Images; **71:** Junko Kimura/Getty Images; **103:** © Google; **105:** (top-bot) Andersen Ross/Getty Images, Manfred Rutz/Getty Images, Anne Ackermann/Getty Images; **106:** (L-R) Screenshots courtesy of Brooklyn Public Library; Isabella Golmier, abstract of article "Can Cigarette Warnings Counterbalance Effects of Smoking Scenes in Movies?" From *Psychological Reports*, February 2007, copyright 2007 by Ammons Scientific, Ltd., reproduced with permission of Ammons Scientific, Ltd., in the format Textbook via Copyright Clearance Center; **107:** Screenshots courtesy of Brooklyn Public Library; **115:** Inti St. Clair/Getty Images; **148:** (L) Copyright © 2008 by Dan Ariely. Reprinted by permission of HarperCollins Publishers, (R) Copyright © 2008 by Dan Ariely. Reprinted by permission of HarperCollins Publishers; **150:** Reproduced with permission. Copyright © 2010 Scientific American, a division of Nature America, Inc. All rights reserved; **154:** Library of Congress; **157:** NASA; **159:** © 2010 Netscape Communications Corporation. Used with permission; **162:** © Google; **164:** The Nobel Foundation. Screenshot of Anders Cullhed homepage, nobelprize.org/nobel_prizes/literature/articles/cullhed/index.html. © Nobel Web AB. Reprinted by permission; **171:** Reprinted with permission from the Institute of Medicine of the National Academy of Sciences, courtesy of the National Academies Press, Washington, D.C.; **175:** Rubberball/Mike Kemp/Getty Images; **219:** Bryan Bedder/Getty Images for The Miami Project; **251:** AFP PHOTO/CESAR RANGEL/Getty Images; **279:** Justin Sullivan/Getty Images; **294:** Used with permission of San Jose Mercury News. Copyright © 2010. All rights reserved; **295:** Sami Sarkis/Getty Images; **296:** David McNew/Getty Images; **314:** (clockwise) Caspar Benson/Getty Images, Purestock/Getty

Images, Jeff Presnail/Getty Images, iStockphoto; **315:** Mark Wilson/Getty Images; **317:** © Ocean/Corbis; **417:** Robyn W. McNeil; **418:** Robyn W. McNeil; **419:** Robyn W. McNeil; **421:** Craig Bohnert/NSCAA; **422:** (top) Craig Bohnert/NSCAA, (bot) Craig Bohnert/NSCAA; **423:** Jose Luis Pelaez, Inc./Getty Images; **439:** Power Presentations, Inc. www.youtube.com/powerpresentation; **443:** Podcasts from Tunxis Community College, Farmington, CT; **481:** Photo by Brendan Smialowski/Bloomberg via Getty Images.

Index

A

abstract language, 241–42
abstracts, online, APA documentation, 520
academic article review, 454
academic setting. *See* college course
    presentations
acceptance speeches, 409–11
acronyms, as organizing device, 415
action, in motivated sequence pattern, 386
active listening
    defined, 48
    See also listening
active voice, 245
ad hominem argument, 377
after-dinner speeches, 413–14
age
    audience analysis for, 82–83
    generational identity, 83
agenda
    -setting speeches, 407, 414
    small groups, 446–47
Agnew, Spiro, 250
agora, 9
Ajzen, Icck, 360
alliteration, 250
allusion, 244
almanacs, 139
American Psychological Association (APA)
    documentation, 145, 517–20
analogy
    faulty, 243
    as figure of speech, 243
    in informative speech, 336
    warrants by, 375–76
anaphora, 249
anecdotes
    in conclusion, 236
    in introduction, 226–27
    as supporting material, 127
Angelou, Maya, 236
Anholt, Robert, 473
antithesis, 250
anxiety. *See* public speaking anxiety
appeals
    to tradition, 378
    See also persuasive appeals
architecture design review, 462

argument, 365–78
    claims in, 365–66, 368–72
    defined, 365
    evidence in, 366, 370–73
    inoculation effect, 376
    warrants, 366–68
Aristotle, 6, 10, 57, 134, 166, 352–53, 355,
    373, 444
Armstrong, Neil, 250
arrangement, in canons of rhetoric, 10,
    11, 181
articles
    citation, recording, 150
    note taking, 151
    See also database articles; journal articles;
        newspaper articles; reference work
        articles
articulation, 268–69
    defined, 22
    problems, overcoming, 269
arts and humanities course presentations
    effective, guidelines for, 467
    types of, 466
art works, MLA documentation, 524–25
asynchronous communication, 438
atlases, 140
attention, in motivated sequence pattern,
    384
attire of speaker, 275–76, 508
attitudes
    audience analysis for, 78
    defined, 78
audience (listeners)
    active listening. *See* listening
    analysis of. *See* audience analysis
    apathetic/uniformed, 380
    captive audience, 82
    cultural factors. *See* cultural differences;
        cultural sensitivity
    delivery, effective, 257–58
    disruptive, 49–50, 63
    ethos of speaker, 57–58
    goodwill toward, 358, 363
    heckler's veto, 63
    hostile/critical/conflicted, 380
    on-the-job audiences, 457
    learning styles of, 337–38

audience (listeners) *(continued)*
  nonverbal cues from, 12, 81, 272
  pandering to, 77–78
  perspective, speaker awareness of, 14
  polling, 227
  public speaking audiences, 457–58
  speaker's style, adjusting to, 54–55
  supporting material, choosing for, 124–25
  sympathetic, 380
audience analysis, 82–85
  age of audience, 82–83
  for attitudes/beliefs/values, 78–79
  audience segmentation, 81
  common bonds, identifying, 80–81
  culture/ethnicity. *See* cultural differences;
    cultural sensitivity
  defined, 17, 77
  gender, 84–85
  interviews, 90
  and occasion for speaking, 81–82
  for online presentations, 436
  persons with disabilities (PWD), 85
  and persuasive speech, 351
  political affiliation, 84
  and presentational speaking, 453, 457–58
  perspective taking of speaker, 77–82
  for progress reports, 476–77
  proposals, 475
  from published sources, 92–93
  religion, 84
  setting for speech, 93
  size of audience, 93
  small group presentations, 451
  socioeconomic status (SES), 83
  for staff reports, 476
  surveys, 90–92
  target audience, identifying, 82–85
  transitions as guide to, 192–93
audience-centered approach, 14, 16
audio clips. *See* sound recordings
audio recorder
  for interviews, 143
  for practicing speaking, 22, 276
aural channel, 271
aural learners, 337–38
authoritative warrants, 373–74
averages, as supporting material, 130–31
awards
  acceptance speeches, 409–11
  presentation speeches, 410–11
Axtell, Roger, 275

B

backstory, 332
balance of speech, 188–89

bandwagoning, 377
bar graphs, 288
begging the question, 377
behavior of listeners, persuasive appeal to,
  359–61
beliefs, audience analysis for, 78
Berners-Lee, Tim, 153
biased language, avoiding, 246
bibliography, working, 145
biographical resources, 139
Blair, Jayson, 147
blogs
  APA documentation, 519–20
  oral citation for, 172
  as research source, 137
body language, 51, 53
body movement
  and online presentations, 435–36
  small group presentations, 451
  See also nonverbal communication
body of speech, 19–20, 182
  of research presentation, 459
  in speaking outline, 213–15
  in working outline, 207–9
books, as research source, 135
books, documenting
  APA style, 517
  CBE/CSE style, 526–27
  Chicago style, 513–14
  citation, recording, 148
  IEEE style, 529
  MLA style, 521
  oral citation for, 169
Boolean operators, 161–62
brainstorming
  on the Internet, 102–3
  narrowing topic by, 108
  topic selection, 101
breathing, stress management by, 43–44
brief examples, 125–26
bullets, in notes, 52
business presentations, 472–79
  case study, 472
  crisis-response situation, 477–78
  progress reports, 476–77
  proposals, 474–75
  sales presentations, 472–75
  staff reports, 475–76

C

Cacioppo, John, 361
call to action, 235
canned speeches, 414
canons of rhetoric, 3, 10–11
captive audience, 82

case conferences, 470
case study, 472
catalog, library, 135
cause, warrants by, 374–75
cause and effect, transitions for, 189, 193
cause-effect arrangement pattern
    features of, 196–97, 382
    informative speech, 338–39
    persuasive speech, 380
CD-ROMs, documentation, MLA style, 523
celebratory speeches, 406–7
central processing of messages, 361
chalkboard, 297
channel, 14
charts
    flowchart, 288–90
    organizational chart, 289–90
    in PowerPoint, 311
    science and math presentations, 461
chat rooms, 441, 446
cherry-picking, 133
Chicago Manual of Style, The, 145, 513–16
chronological arrangement pattern
    features of, 195
    informative speech, 338–39
Cicero, 6, 352
circular arrangement pattern, 200
citizens
    engagement, Web sites, 9
    grassroots issues, 101
    speaking up, importance of, 8–9
civil liberties, 59
civil rights, 59
claims, 368–72
    counterclaims, addressing, 376
    in debate, 455
    defined, 365
    of fact, 368, 380
    of policy, 370, 379
    supporting evidence for, 370–73
    of value, 368–69, 379
classroom discussions, 467–69
classroom presentations. *See* college course
        presentations
clichés, 243
Clinton, Hillary, 81
clip art, PowerPoint, 311, 313
closed-ended questions, 90
co-culture listeners, 83, 247
Code of Ethics for Professional Communi-
        cators, 478–79
code-switching, 245
Coffman, Vance, 229
coherence of speech, 183
colleagues, as audience, 457

collective mind, 448
collectivist cultures, 89
college campuses, speech codes on, 64–65
college course presentations, 453–71
    academic articles, review of, 454
    architecture design review, 462
    case conferences, 470
    classroom discussions, 467–69
    community service learning project, 470
    compare/contrast presentations, 466–67
    debates, 454–56, 467
    engineering design review, 462
    evaluation research presentation, 465
    field study presentation, 460
    group activity presentation, 468
    lectures, 468
    literature review, 464
    methods/procedures presentation, 459
    nursing shift report, 470
    panel discussions, 460
    policy recommendation report, 465,
        470–71
    poster sessions, 456–57
    request for funding, 463
    research overview presentation, 460
    research presentation, 458–59
    team presentations, 454
colloquial expressions, 247
Colombo, John Robert, 40
color, for presentation aids, 302–3
column method, note taking, 52
commemorative speeches, 407
common ground, in introduction, 229
common knowledge, 173
communication
    categories of, 11
    components of. *See* communication
        process
    dialogic communication, 48
    in public arena. *See* public speaking
communication process, 13–15
    channel, 14
    context, 14
    feedback loop, 14
    goals in, 14–15
    message, 14
    outcome, 15
    receiver, 14
    rhetorical situation, 14
    shared meaning, 14
    source, 13
community service learning project, 470
comparative advantage pattern
    features of, 382
    persuasive speech, 379, 386–87

compare/contrast presentations, 466–67
comparisons, transitions for, 189
computer-generated graphics, 292
concepts, speeches about, 333, 334, 337
conciseness, language use, 239–40
conclusion of speech, 233–37
    anecdote in, 236
    concluding challenge in, 235
    defined, 19
    functions of, 233
    listening for, 51
    main points, restatement in, 19, 234
    quotation in, 236
    of research presentation, 459
    rhetorical questions in, 237
    signals to audience, 234
    in speaking outline, 215
    thesis restatement in, 19
    topic/purpose restatement in, 234–35
    transitions for, 193
    in working outline, 210
concrete language, versus abstract, 241–42
confidentiality of sources, 147
conflict, small groups, 447
conjunctions, transitional, 190–91
connectives. See transitions
connotative meaning, 245
context of speech, 14
continuity principle, 299–300
contractions, ESL speakers, 240
contrast, transitions for, 189
controversial topics, 101
conversation
    defined, 3
    compared to public speaking, 15
conversation stoppers, 61
Cooper, Anderson, 363
coordinate points, in speech outline, 20
coordination and subordination, 186–88
copyright, protections, 68–69
Corbett, Edward, 226
core values, 78–79, 369
Coulter, Ann, 61
Council of Science Editors (CSE) documen-
        tation, 145, 526–28
counterintuitive ideas, 336–37
counterproductive roles, 447
Crabtree, Robin, 260
credibility
    assessing, guidelines for, 144
    and ethical appeals, 230
    of interviewer, 142
    and language use, 244–47
    library database sources, 103
    listener trust, factors in, 58

moral character of speaker, 357–58
and nonverbal communication, 272
of oral citations, 167–68, 170–71
and physical attractiveness of speaker,
        364
and presentation aids, 285
and presentational speaking, 453
and speaker similarity, 363
of statistical information, 131–32, 144
of testimony, 128
of Web site information, 137, 156–57
crisis-response presentation, 477–78
critical thinking, 53–54
    defined, 53
    and public speaking training, 7
    steps in, 53–54
    thought/speech differential, 54
criticism. See feedback
cross-national surveys, 89
cultural differences, 85–89
    cross-national surveys for, 89
    cultural norms, 369
    cultural premises, 369
    cultural types model, 88–89
    emotional appeals, 369
    high versus low uncertainty, 87
    linear-active cultures, 88
    masculine/feminine dimension, 87
    multi-active cultures, 88
    nonverbal communication, 275
    and persuasive speech, 369
    power distance, 87
    reactive cultures, 88–89
    time orientation, 87
    value-dimensions model, 86–87
    values, 78–79, 369
cultural sensitivity, 85–89
    co-culture listeners, 83
    components of, 16
    cultural barriers, minimizing, 50–51
    cultural intelligence, 16
    dialects, 269
    humor, use/misuse, 231
    language use, 246–48
    multicultural reference works, 139
    nonverbal communication, 51
    and organizational patterns, 201
    respect of speaker, 63–64
    values-related, 58, 62, 89, 369
culture, defined, 16
current events, and topic selection, 101

D

Darbelnet, Robert L., 230
database articles, documenting

APA style, 520
Chicago style, 515
MLA style, 523
databases, 135–37
    functions of, 135
    for newspapers/periodicals, 136
    specialized, listing of, 137
    of speeches, 140
debates, 454–56
    academic, 454–56, 467
    arguments, parts of, 455
    flowing the debate, 455–56
    individual/team formats, 455
    social science topics, 464
    winning, tips for, 456
decision making, group, 449–50
decoding, 14
deductive reasoning, 353–54
deep Web, 153
defamation, 60–61
defensive listening, 49
definition, methods for, 334–35
deliberative oratory, 9
delivery, 257–78
    in canons of rhetoric, 10, 11
    cues in speaking outline, 211
    effective, characteristics of, 257–58
    extemporaneous, 263
    impromptu speaking, 261–62
    from memory, 260–61
    online presentations, 437
    practicing. *See* practicing delivery
    speaking from manuscript, 259–60
    voice in, 264–70
demagogue, 356
demographics, 82–85
    age, 82–83
    defined, 82
    disability, 85
    gender, 84–85
    political affiliation, 84
    religion, 84
    socioeconomic status (SES), 83
    See also audience analysis
demonstration, 335
denotative meaning, 245
description, 335
devil's advocacy, 448, 449
Dewey, John, 449–50
Dewey decimal number, 135
diagrams, 286
dialectical inquiry, 448, 449
dialects
    of Americans, 269
    proper use of, 244–45

dialogic communication, defined, 48
dictionaries, *Chicago*-style documentation, 514
dignity of speaker, 62
direct quotations, citing, 144–51, 163–65
    Internet sources, 163–65
    note taking, 146
    plagiarism, avoiding, 66–67
    speech excerpt containing, 149, 165
discussion groups (online) documentation
    APA style, 519
    CBE/CSE style, 528
    Chicago style, 515
    MLA style, 524
disinformation, 155
disruptive behavior by audience, 49–50
distractions to listening, 48–49
documentation of sources, 144–51
    American Psychological Association
        (APA), 145, 517–20
    articles, 150–51
    bibliography, working, 145
    Chicago Manual of Style, The, 145,
        513–16
    Council of Science Editors (CSE), 145,
        526–28
    Institute of Electrical and Electronics
        Engineers (IEEE), 145, 529
    Internet sources, 163–65
    Modern Language Association (MLA),
        145, 521–25
    and note taking, 146–51
    orally in speech. *See* oral citations
    purposes of, 166
    for quotations/paraphrase/summary,
        146–47
    in working outline, 205, 210
    Works Cited/Works Consulted, 205
domain name, 156, 162
Draper, Don, 364
Drori, Jonathan, 126
dyadic communication, 11

E
editorials, MLA documentation, 523
educational level, audience analysis for, 84
education course presentations
    effective, guidelines for, 469
    types of, 468
Ehlers, Vernon, 126
either-or fallacy, 53, 377
elaborate likelihood model (ELM), persuasion, 361–62
electronic media, MLA documentation, 523
elocutionary movement, 257–58

e-mail, documenting
    APA style, 520
    CBE/CSE style, 528
    Chicago style, 515
    MLA style, 524
emotional appeals
    cultural differences, 369
    pathos, proof by emotion, 355–57
    unethical use of, 63–64, 356–57
encoding, 13
encyclopedias
    Chicago-style documentation, 514
    as library resource, 138
engineering design review, 462
English as a second language. *See* ESL
        speakers (notes)
enthusiasm of speaker, 258
enthymeme, 354–55
epideictic oratory, 9
epiphora, 249
ESL speakers (notes)
    contractions, using, 240
    linguistic issues, identifying, 22–23
    listening, learning by, 47
    manuscript delivery, avoiding, 260
    mispronounced words, common, 270,
        511–12
    personal experiences, sharing, 128
    practice, importance of, 473
    primary stress, 260
    public speaking anxiety management, 41
    sensitivity to. *See* cultural differences; cul-
        tural sensitivity
    vocal variety, 267
    word stress, 260
ethical appeals, in introduction, 230
ethical public speaking, 57–69
    argument, engaging in, 366
    audience expectations, violating, 416
    college campuses, 64–65
    copyright/fair use, 68–69
    credibility of speaker, 58
    emotional appeals, 356–57
    emotional appeals, misuse of, 63–64
    fairness, 65
    free speech rights, 59–61
    information versus disinformation/mis-
        information, 154–55
    by leaders, 262, 356–57
    and persuasive speech, 351, 366
    plagiarism, avoiding, 66–68, 147
    for professional communications, 478–79
    propaganda, 155
    and research process, 147
    respect, 63–64

responsibility for, 57–59
    rules of engagement, 61–62
    self-assessment checklist, 69
    speaker, positive contribution by, 61–62
    statistics, presenting, 131–32, 144
    and topic selection, 110
    and trustworthiness, 63
    values, 58–59
ethics, defined, 57
ethnocentrism
    defined, 63
    eliminating. *See* cultural sensitivity
ethos
    defined, 57
    and ethical public speaking, 57–58
    persuasive appeal through, 357–58
etymology, definition by, 335
eulogies, 412–13
evaluation research presentation, 465
Evans, Brock, 127
events, speeches about, 332, 334
evidence, 370–73
    audience knowledge/opinions as, 371
    external, 372
    speaker expertise as, 371–72
evidence-based practice (EBP), 471
examples
    definition by, 334
    oral citation for, 173
    as supporting material, 125–26
    transitions for, 189, 193
expert audience, 457
expertise of speaker
    and credibility, 362
    as evidence, 371–72
    of public speaker, 453
expert testimony
    oral citation for, 172
    as supporting material, 128
explanation, 335–36
    transitions for, 189
extemporaneous speaking, 263
extended examples, 126
external evidence, 372
external listening distraction, 48
eye contact, 273–74
    cultural differences, 275
    direct and shifting gaze, 52
    scanning, 273–74
    speaker and audience, 52, 258

F
fabrication, 147
face-to-face (FtF) delivery, compared to
        online presentation, 435–36

facial expressions, 53, 273
cultural differences, 275
of speaker, 53, 258
facts
claims of, 368
fact books, 139
oral citation for, 172–73
as supporting material, 129
fairness of speaker, 65
fair use rules, 69
faulty analogy, 243
fear appeal, 357
feedback
in communication process, 14
loop, 46
about speech. *See* speech evaluations
feminine dimension of culture, 87
field searching, 162
field study presentation, 460
fighting words, 60
fight or flight response, 43
figures of speech, types of, 242–44
First Amendment, 59–61, 64
first speech. *See* speech preparation
Fishbein, Martin, 360
fixed alternative questions, 90
fixed microphone, 265
flip charts, 297
flowcharts, 288–90
font size, 300–302
forensic oratory, 9
formality, degree of, and public speaking,
12–13, 453
forums, 510
online. *See* online forums, documenting
free speech
versus campus speech codes, 64–65
and responsibility of speaker, 59–61
full-sentence transitions, 190

G

Garvey, Marcus, 250
Gates, Melinda French, 127
gender
in audience analysis, 84–85
defined, 84
stereotypes, 84–85
gender-neutral language
inclusive pronouns, list of, 247
neutral terms, examples of, 247
General American (GA) English, 244
general case, 353–54
general encyclopedia, 138
generalizations, 53
stereotyping, 63–64

general purpose speech, 97–99
for special occasions, 99
topic selection for, 97–98
generational identity, 83
Gillen, Steve, 66
goals
in communication process, 14–15
listening goals, 51
small group presentations, 448–49, 451
Google, topic selection tools, 102–3
Google Docs, 304
GoogleScholar, 159
Gore, Al, 228, 357
Gorga, Queen, 235
government publications, documenting
APA style, 518
Chicago style, 515–16
MLA style, 521–22
as research source, 137–38
government search engine, 159
graphs, 287–89
creating, guidelines for, 291
science and math presentations, 461
types of, 287–89
Grasso, Richard A., 408
grassroots issues, and topic selection, 101
Greece, ancient
and ethical public speaking, 57–58
persuasive appeals, 353–58
rhetoric, development of, 8–10
group activity presentation, 468
groups, small. *See* small group
presentations
groupthink, 448

H

hackneyed phrases, 250
Hager, Bradford, 66
Handout Master, 310
handouts, 297
hasty generalization, 378
hasty overgeneralization, 354
hate speech, 64
health courses. *See* nursing/allied health
course presentations
heckler's veto, 63
hedges, 246
hierarchy of needs, 359–61
high-uncertainty avoidance cultures, 87
Hitler, Adolf, 262, 356
Hofstede, Geert, 86–87
Hudson, David L., 60
humanities course presentations.
See arts and humanities course
presentations

humor
and cultural sensitivity, 231
inappropriate use of, 228, 414
in introduction, 228
Hussein, Saddam, 262
hyperbole, 244
hypothetical examples, 126

I

identification, speaker with audience, 80–81
idioms
avoiding, 51
defined, 51
"I" language, 246
image-restoration strategies, 478
imagery, 242
impromptu speaking, 261–62
income level, audience analysis for, 83
indentation, 185
individual debate format, 455
individualistic cultures, 86–87
inductive reasoning, 353–54
Infomine, 159
information
defined, 154
versus disinformation/misinformation,
154–55
information sources, plagiarism, avoiding,
66–68
Information You Can Trust, 159
informative speech, 97–98, 329–49
analogies in, 336
audience understanding, devices for,
330–31, 336–39
complex information in, 337
conclusion of, 235
definition in, 334–35
demonstration in, 335
examples of, 340–49, 483–89
goals of, 329–31
and learning styles, 337–38
organizational patterns, 338–39
versus persuasive speech, 329, 333
thesis statement, 111, 113
topic selection for, 97–98
types of, 331–33
in-group distinctions, 63–64
Inkson, Kerr, 16
inoculation effect, 376
insider audience, 457
inspiration, speeches of, 414–16
Institute of Electrical and Electronics Engineers (IEEE) documentation, 145, 529
instrumental values, 59–60
integrity of speaker, 62

intellectual property, copyright/fair use,
68–69
interactive presentations, online, 440–41
internal listening distraction, 48
internal previews, 191, 193
internal summary, 191, 193
International Social Survey Program (ISSP),
88, 89
Internet, 152–65
blogs, 137
brainstorming on, 102–3
credibility of sources, 137, 156–57
library portals, 103, 106–7, 152–54
newspaper/periodical databases, 136
search commands, 161–62
search engines, 158–59
search methods, 161–62
social news sites, 137
sources, evaluating, 153–58
topic selection resources, 102–3
virtual libraries, 152–54
See also Web sites
Internet Public Library, 168
interpersonal roles, 446–47
interviews, 141–43
audience analysis, 90
preparing for, 143
questions, types of, 141–42
recording, 143
for research purposes, 141–43
on TV/radio, 507–8
interviews, documenting
APA style, 520
Chicago style, 516
MLA style, 525
oral citation for, 172
interview-style presentations, online, 441
intonation, 265
introduction, 225–32
anecdote in, 226–27
common ground in, 229
functions of, 225
humor in, 228
listening for, 51
main points, previewing, 230–31, 330
motivating audience, 231–32
quotations in, 226
relevance, creating, 231
of research presentation, 459
rhetorical questions in, 227
in speaking outline, 212–13
special occasion in, 229
startling statement in, 227–28
topic and purpose in, 229–30
in working outline, 205, 206–7

introduction, speeches of, 407–9
invective, 61
invention, in canons of rhetoric, 10, 11, 134
invisible Web, 153
irony, 244
issues
    issues-based conflict, 447–48
    speeches about, 333–34

J

Jackson, Jesse, 250
jargon, avoiding, 239
Jesus Christ, 249
Jobs, Steve, 129, 275–76
Josephson, Michael, 57
journal articles, documenting
    APA style, 518
    CBE/CSE style, 527
    Chicago style, 514
    IEEE style, 529
    MLA style, 522, 524
    oral citation for, 169
journalists' questions, to check supporting points, 185
justification. *See* warrants

K

Kane, Christine, 39
key words
    Internet search, 161–62
    key-word outline, 203–4
kinesthetic learners, 337–38
King, Martin Luther Jr., 249, 262, 266–67
Kluge, Holger, 234

L

Lakoff, Robin, 246
language use, 238–50
    active voice, 245
    biased language, avoiding, 246–47
    colloquial expressions, avoiding, 247
    conciseness, 239–40
    concrete language, 241–42
    contractions, 240
    and credibility, 244–47
    cultural sensitivity, 51, 246–48
    denotative/connotative meaning, 245
    of dialects, 244–45
    figures of speech, 242–44
    gender-neutral language, 247
    idioms, avoiding, 51
    "I" language, 246
    imagery, 242
    jargon, avoiding, 239

oral versus written, 238–39
    parallelism, 250
    personal pronouns, 240–41
    persons with disabilities, sensitivity to, 247
    poetic language, 250
    powerless speech, avoiding, 246
    repetition, 240, 249–50
    sentence fragments, use of, 240
    sexist language, 84–85
    transitions, 189–93
lavaliere microphone, 265
lay audience, 457
lay testimony, as supporting material, 128
lazy speech, 269
LCD display, 292
leaders
    ethical public speaking, 262, 356–57, 478–79
    participative, 448
    small group presentations, 448–51
    styles of leadership, 448
leading questions, 141
learning styles, 337–38
lectures, 468
Leno, Jay, 272
Lewis, Richard D., 79, 86, 88–89
Library of Congress call number, 135
library resources, 135–40
    books, 136
    catalog, 135
    digital collections, 138
    government publications, 137–38
    Internet library portals, 103, 106–7
    library portals, 152–54
    newspapers/periodicals, 136
    reference desk, 135
    reference works, 138–40
    sources, evaluating, 154–55
    specialized databases, 137
Lincoln, Abraham, 129, 250, 262
linear-active cultures, 88–89
line graphs, 287–88
listeners. *See* audience (listeners)
listening
    active, defined, 48
    active listening strategies, 50–54
    barriers to, 48–49
    and critical thinking, 53–54
    defensive listening, 49
    defined, 46
    in dialogic communication, 48
    evaluating speech, 54–55
    goals, setting, 51
    as interviewer, 142–43

listening (continued)
  for main idea, 51–52
  nonverbal cues, 52–53
  and note taking, 52
  thought/speech differential, 54
literature review presentation, 464
loaded questions, 141
logic, faulty. See logical fallacies
logical fallacies, 376–78
  ad hominem argument, 377
  appeal to tradition, 378
  bandwagoning, 377
  begging the question, 377
  either-or fallacy, 377
  and evaluating speech, 53
  hasty generalization, 378
  non sequitur, 378
  red herring, 377
  slippery slope, 378
logos, proof by reason, 353–55
low-uncertainty avoidance cultures, 87

M
magazine articles, documenting
  APA style, 518
  CBE/CSE style, 527–28
  Chicago style, 514
  MLA style, 522
  online, oral citation for, 169
mailing list, APA documentation, 519
main points, 182–86
  developing, 19
  in introduction, 230–31, 330
  listener's recollection of, 184
  listening for, 51–52
  multiple, limiting, 183–85
  parallel form, 184–85, 188
  and position of speech, 183
  restated in conclusion, 234
  supporting points, position of, 187, 191
  and thesis statement, 183–85
  transitions among, 51–52, 190
malapropism, 245
Mandela, Nelson, 229
Mao Tse-tung, 262
maps, 286
masculine dimension, of culture, 87
Maslow, Abraham, 359
mass communication, defined, 3, 11
mathematics. See science-math
    presentations
May, James, 236
McCarthy, Joseph, 356
McClellan, Mark B., 203
McGraw, Dr. Phil, 363

mean, arithmetic, 131
median, 131
meditation, public speaking anxiety man-
    agement, 43–44
meetings, online. See online presentations
memory
  in canons of rhetoric, 10–11
  speaking from, 260–61
message
  in communication process, 14
  listener processing of, 361–62
metaphor, 243
meta-search engine, 158
methods/procedure presentation, 459
microphone, use of, 265
misinformation, 155
mixed audience, 457–58
mixed metaphors, 243
mode, 131
models, 285–87
moderated panel presentations, online, 441
Modern Language Association (MLA), 145,
    521–25
monologue, defined, 48
Monroe, Alan, 383
Monroe's motivated sequence pattern, 381–86
  features of, 382
  sales presentations, 474
  steps in, 384–86
motivational warrants, 373
multi-active cultures, 88
multimedia aids, 292
multimedia effect, 284
multimedia-intensive online presentations,
    444
multimodal learners, 337–38
mumbling, 269

N
narrative arrangement pattern, 199–200
narratives
  first-person/third-person, 127
  in introduction, 226–27
  in speeches of inspiration, 415
  as supporting material, 127–28
narrowing topic, 104–5, 108
needs
  in motivated sequence pattern, 384
  needs hierarchy, 359–61
negation, definition by, 334
neutral questions, 141
newsgroup messages, documenting
  APA style, 519
  CBE/CSE style, 546
  Chicago style, 515

newspaper articles, documenting
APA style, 519
CBE/CSE style, 546
Chicago style, 514
MLA style, 523
newspapers
online databases, 136
as research source, 136
Nicks, Stevie, 36
Nixon, Richard, 275
noise, 14
non sequitur, 378
nonverbal communication, 271–78
attire, 275–76
of audience, 12, 81, 272
body language, 53
cultural differences, 275
eye contact, 273–74
facial expressions, 53, 273
functions of, 271–72
gestures, relaxed, 274
posture, 274
See also body movement
Noonan, Peggy, 239
norms, cultural, 369
notecards, use during speech, 212
note taking
book citation, recording, 148
for direct quotations, 149
to document sources, 146–51, 165
from Internet sources, 165
methods for, 52
for paraphrase, 149, 151
for summary, 151
nursing/allied health course
presentations
effective, guidelines for, 471
types of, 469–71

O

Obama, Barack, 14, 249, 368
occupation, audience analysis for, 83
online forums, documenting
APA style, 519
MLA style, 524
online presentations, 435–45
audience analysis, 436
delivery, 437
compared to face-to-face, 435–36
interactive presentations, speaker-
audience, 440–41
interview-style, 441
moderated panel, 441
multimedia-intensive presentations,
444

planning checklist, 444–45
podcasts, 442–43
practicing delivery, 437
presentation aids, 437
real-time, 438–39
recorded presentations, 439–40, 440
single-speaker, 440
technical requirements, 436, 437–38
video presentations, 442
Webinars, 441, 444
onomatopoeia, 244
Open Directory Project (DMOZ), 159
open-ended questions, 91, 142
operational definition, 334
opinion polls, 93
oral citations, 166–74
for blogs, 172
for books, 169
delivery style for, 168
direct quotations, 149, 165
for journal articles, 169
for online magazine article, 169
paraphrase, 149, 151, 165
source information, form of delivery for,
166–67
source reliability, 166, 170–71
for supporting materials, 172–73
for testimony, 172
time for citing, 166
for TV/radio programs, 172
for Web sites, 169
oral scientific presentation, 458–59
oratory
ancient Greeks, 8–9
forms of, 9
See also rhetoric
O'Reilly, Bill, 357
organizational charts, 289–90
organizational patterns, 194–201
acronyms as device, 415
cause-effect pattern, 196–97
choosing, 20
chronological pattern, 195
circular pattern, 200
comparative advantage, 382
for informative speech, 338–39
listening for, 51
Monroe's motivated sequence pattern,
381–86
narrative pattern, 199–200
persuasive speech, 381–88
problem-solution pattern, 197–98
refutation, 382
spatial pattern, 195–96
topical pattern, 198–99

organization of speech, 181–93
  balance, 188–89
  body of speech, 21, 182
  coherence, 188
  conclusion, 182
  introduction, 19–20, 189–90
  main points, 182–86
  supporting points, 185–87
  transitions, 189–93
  unity, 188
outcome, in communication process, 15
out-group distinctions, 63–64
outline method, note taking, 52
outline of speech, 20, 202–18. *See also*
    speaking outline; working outline
  coordinate and subordinate patterns, 20
  and delivery, 204
  extended outline format, 182
  functions of, 181
  key-word outline, 203–4
  organizational patterns, 20
  and parts of speech, 20
  phrase outline, 203
  roman numeral outline, 185–86
  sentence outline, 202–3
  working and speaking outlines, 20
overgeneralizatons, 53
overhead transparencies, 293, 297

P
paid inclusion, 161
paid placement, Internet, 161
pandering, 77–78
panel discussions, 460, 509
panel presentations, online, 441
paralanguage, 271
parallel form
  antithesis, 250
  main points, 184–85, 188
  parallelism, 250
  triads, 250
paraphrase, citing, 146–51, 163–65
  Internet sources, 163–65
  note taking, 146, 151
  plagiarism, avoiding, 67
  speech excerpt containing, 149, 151, 165
participative leaders, 448
passive voice, versus active voice, 245
patchwrite plagiarism, 66
pathos, 355–57
Pausch, Randy, 15
pause in delivery, 266–67
Pearce, W. Barnett, 61–62
peer evaluation form, 56
people, speeches about, 332, 334

percentages, as supporting material, 130
performance anxiety. *See* public speaking
    anxiety
Pericles, 9–10
periodicals
  defined, 136
  as research source, 136
periodicals, documenting
  APA style, 518
  CBE/CSE style, 527–28
  Chicago style, 514
  IEEE style, 529
  online, MLA style, 524
  of sources, 150–51
peripheral processing of message, 361–62
Perry, Katy, 67
personal-based conflict, 447–48
personal communication
  Chicago-style documentation, 516
  See also e-mail, documenting; interviews
personal experiences, as supporting mate-
    rial, 136
personal interests, and topic selection,
    99–100
personal pronouns. *See* pronouns
personification, 244
persons with disabilities (PWD)
  in audience analysis, 85
  language sensitivity to, 247
perspective taking of speaker, 77–82
persuasive appeals, 353–78
  to behavior of listeners, 359–61
  character of speaker known by, 357–58
  claim/evidence/warrants in, 366–76
  debates as, 454–55
  elaboration likelihood model (ELM),
      361–62
  enthymeme, 354–55
  ethos/proof through speaker's character,
      357–58
  expectancy-outcome values theory,
      359–60
  logos/proof by reason, 353–55
  needs of listeners, use of, 359–61
  pathos/proof by emotion, 355–57
  reason, proof by, 353–55
  relevance, creating, 361–62
  syllogism, 353–54
persuasive speech, 98–99, 350–405
  argument, 365–78
  and audience analysis, 351
  call to action, 235
  cause-effect pattern, 380
  comparative advantage, 379, 386–87
  cultural factors, 369

effective, guidelines for, 352
examples of, 388–405, 489–94
features of, 365
goals of, 350–51
versus informative speech, 329, 333
inoculation effect, 376
logical fallacies, 376–78
Monroe's motivated sequence pattern, 381–86
opposing arguments, addressing, 376
persuasion, process of, 352. *See also* persuasive appeals
problem-cause-solution pattern, 382–83
problem-solution pattern, 379, 381–83
refutation pattern, 387–88
target audience, identifying, 380
thesis statement, 111, 113
topic selection for, 98
truth, importance of, 63
Petty, Richard, 361
Pew Global Attitudes Project, 88
phenomena, speeches about, 331–32, 334
photographs, documenting, MLA style, 524–25
phrase outline, 203
phrases
in speeches, 240
transitional, 189
physical attractiveness, and speaker credibility, 364
pictograms, 288–89
pie graphs, 288–89
pitch of voice, 264–65
plagiarism, 66–68
avoiding, rules for, 66–68
copyright/fair use, 68–69
defined, 66, 147
on Internet, 68
versus proper documentation. *See* documentation of sources
wholesale and patchwrite, 66
Plato, 262
podcasts, creating, 442–43
poetic language, 250
poetry, collections of, 140
policy, claim of, 370, 379
policy recommendation report, 465, 470–71
political affiliation, audience analysis for, 84
polling, audience, 227
Pope, Alexander, 250
poster sessions, 286, 456–57
posture of speaker, 274
power distance, and culture, 87
powerless speech, avoiding, 246
PowerPoint, 304–16
charts, 311

commands, 310
effective use, guidelines, 316
versus giving speech, 304
Handout Master, 310
media, downloads, 313
predesigned templates, 306–7
presentation, example of, 314–15
presentation options, 305–6
slide inserts, 310–12
slide layouts/themes, selecting, 307
Slide Master, 308, 310
technical glitches, avoiding, 305
text entering/editing, 310
transitions/animation, 316
video clips in, 311–13
view options, 308–10
practicing delivery, 276–78
audio recorder, use of, 22, 276
checklist for, 45, 278
and ESL speakers, 473
by group members, 452
for online presentations, 437
speaking notes, revising, 277
speech evaluations, 44
timing speech, 277
videotaping, 276–77
premises, cultural, 369
preparation anxiety, 39
pre-performance anxiety, 39
presentation, speeches of, 410–11
presentation aids, 284–316
audio/video clips, 291–92
chalkboards, 297
color, use of, 302–3
continuity principle, 299–300
flip charts, 297
functions of, 284–85
graphics, computer-generated, 292
graphs/charts, 287–91
handouts, 297
and learning styles, 338–39
multimedia, 292
for online presentations, 437
overhead transparencies, 293, 297
pictures, 286–87
posters, 286
for poster session, 456–57
presentation software. *See* PowerPoint
props/models, 285–87
science and math presentations, 461
simplicity principle, 298–99
technical presentations, 461
typeface/font size, 300–302
types of, 21
use in speech, examples of, 294–96

presentational speaking, 453–79
  audience analysis, 453, 457–58
  business presentations, 472–79
  college course presentations, 453–71
  defined, 453
  ethical factors, 478–79
  compared to public speaking, 453
previews
  main points, in introduction, 230–31
  preview statement, 191, 193, 330
  as transition, 191, 193
Prezi.com, 304
primacy effect, 184
primary questions, 142
primary research
  defined, 134, 141
  interviews, 141–43
  surveys, 143–44
problem-cause-solution pattern, 382–83
problem-solution pattern
  features of, 197–98
  persuasive speech, 379, 381–83
processes, speeches about, 332, 334, 337
productive conflict, 447
professional goals, and communication
    skills, 6–7
professional presentations. See presenta-
    tional speaking
progress reports, 476–77
  organizational pattern for, 477
pronunciation, 268–69
  defined, 22
  ESL speakers, 22, 41
  mispronounced words, list of, 270,
    511–12
  online aids, 47
pronouns
  gender-neutral language, 247
  in public speaking, 81, 240–41
proof, rhetorical. See persuasive appeals
propaganda, 155, 357
proposals, 474–75
  audience analysis, 475
  organizational patterns for, 475
props, 285–87
prototype, engineering design review, 462
public discourse
  rules of engagement, 61–62
  speaker contributions to, 61–62
public domain, 68
public forum, 9
public speaking
  audience-centered approach, 14, 16, 77
  college course presentations, 453–71
  cultural sensitivity. See cultural sensitivity

defined, 11
ethical, 57–69
formality, degree of in, 12–13
and nervousness. See public speaking
    anxiety
oral style, developing, 16
versus other forms of communication, 3,
    12–13, 15–16, 238–39
presentational speaking, 453, 453–79
presentations, length of, 93–94
public discussions, 509–10
question-and-answer sessions, 505–6
small group presentations, 446–52
speeches, preparing. See speech
    preparation
study, reasons for, 6–8
TV/radio appearances, 507–8
unique requirements of, 15–16
public speaking anxiety, 36–40
  defined, 36
  managing. See public speaking anxiety
    management
  natural events leading to, 36–38
  performance anxiety, 39–40
  preparation anxiety, 39
  pre-performance anxiety, 39
  pre-preparation anxiety, 38–39
  and trait anxiety, 40
public speaking anxiety management, 40–45
  anxiety stoptime, 39
  confidence building steps, 42
  for ESL speakers, 41
  moving during speech, 44
  positive attitude, maintaining, 41–42, 45
  practicing speaking, 41–42
  relaxation methods, 43–44
  visualization, 42
public speeches. See presentational speaking
purpose of speech
  general, 18, 97–99
  informative speech, 97–98
  in introduction, 229–30
  and main points, 183
  organizational pattern, choosing, 381
  persuasive speech, 98–99
  restated in conclusion, 234
  special occasions, 99
  specific purpose, 18, 108–9
  thesis statement, 18, 109–13
  and topic selection, 104–5

Q

qualitative research, 464
quantitative research, 464
question-and-answer sessions, 505–6

questionnaires
    audience analysis, 90–92
    types of questions, 90–92
quotation marks, in Internet search, 161
quotations
    books of, 139–40
    in conclusion, 236
    in introduction, 226

R

radio appearance, 508
radio programs, documenting, oral citation
        for, 172
rate of speaking, 266–67
reactive cultures, 88–89
read/write learners, 337–38
Reagan, Ronald, 238
real-time presentations, 438–39
reason, proof by, 353
reasoning
    in debate, 455
    deductive/inductive, 353–54
    fallacies of. See logical fallacies
    syllogism, 353–54
    See also warrants
receiver, in communication process, 14
recency effect, 184
recorded presentations, online, 439–40
red herring, 377
refereed journals, 135
reference desk, 135
reference librarians, 135
references
    documenting. See documentation of
        sources
    plagiarism, avoiding, 66–68
reference work articles, documenting
    APA style, 517–18
    Chicago style, 514
    MLA style, 521
reference works, types of, 138–40
reflective thinking, 449–50
refutation
    debates, 455
    defined, 455
refutation pattern
    features of, 382
    persuasive speech, 387–88
relaxation methods, 43–44
relevance
    in introduction, 231
    in persuasive speech, 361–62
reliability
    of sources, 131–33, 167–68, 170–71
    of statistics, 131

religion, audience analysis for, 84
repetition
    anaphora, 249
    effectiveness in speech, 240
reportage, 332
request for funding presentation, 463
research, 134–74
    documenting. See documentation of
        sources
    ethical factors, 147
    evaluating sources, 144
    interviews, 141–43
    library. See library resources
    most recent, using, 144
    needs, assessing, 134–35
    online. See Internet
    primary/secondary sources. See primary
        research; secondary sources
    qualitative/quantitative, 464
    sources, oral citation in speech, 149, 151,
        166–74
    surveys, 143–44
research overview presentation, 458–60
resolution, debates, 455
respect of speaker, toward audience, 63–64
responsibility
    defined, 57
    See also ethical public speaking
restate-forecast transitions, 190
review
    academic articles, 454
    of literature presentation, 464
rhetoric
    canons of, 3, 10–11
    classical, Web sites for, 10
    corrupt, 262
    historical view, 8–11
rhetorical devices
    defined, 238
    See also language use
rhetorical questions
    in conclusion, 237
    in introduction, 227
    as transitions, 190, 193
rhetorical situation
    audience analysis, 94
    in communication process, 14
    defined, 4, 94
Rimel, Rebecca, 8
roasts, 411–12
Rokeach, Milton, 59
roles, group, 446–47
roman numeral outline, 185–86
Romans, ancient, rhetoric, development of,
        6, 9–10

Roosevelt, Franklin D., 242
Rosen, Nir, 66
rules of engagement, 8, 61–62
Runyon, Marvin, 230

S

Safire, William, 239, 259
sales presentations, Monroe's motivated sequence, 474
sans serif typefaces, 300–301
satisfaction, in motivated sequence pattern, 385
scale questions, 90–91
scanning, 273–74
schematic drawings, 286
Schultz, George, 238
science-math presentations
    effective, guidelines for, 461
    types of, 458
search engines, 158–59
    defined, 158
    versus subject directories, 160
    and topic selection, 102–3
    types of, 158–59
secondary questions, 142
secondary sources, 135–41
    blogs, 137
    defined, 134
    Internet sources, 152–65
    library resources, 135–40
    most recent, using, 144, 156
    social news sites, 137
segmentation, audience analysis, 81
selective perception, and listening, 47
sensationalism, 63
senses, appeal to, 242, 244
sentence fragments, in speeches, 240
sentence outline, 202–3
sequence of events, transitions for, 189
serif typefaces, 300–301
sermons, 414–15
setting for speech, audience analysis, 93
sexist language
    avoiding. See gender-neutral language
    defined, 84
shared meaning, in communication process, 14
shift report, nurses, 470
sign, warrants by, 375
signposts, 190–91
similarity of speaker, and credibility, 363
simile, 242–43
Simon, Herbert, 380
Singh, Rahul, 332

single-speaker presentations, online, 440
six-by-six rule, 298
slander, 60–61
slides
    six-by-six rule, 298
    See also PowerPoint
slippery slope, 378
small group presentations, 446–52
    academic setting. See college course presentations
    agenda, 446–47
    collective mind, maintaining, 448
    conflicting personalities, 447
    decision making, 449–50
    defined, 3, 11
    delivery, practicing, 452
    group goals, setting, 448–49
    groupthink, 448
    interpersonal roles in, 446–47
    issues, conflict concerning, 447–48
    leadership, 448–51
    nonparticipating members, 449
    participation, encouraging, 449
    presentational speaking, 454
    reflective thinking, use of, 449–50
    task roles in, 446–47
    team presentations, 450–52
    transitions in, 451
    virtual groups, 446
smiling, 273
social news sites, 137
social science presentations
    effective, guidelines for, 465–66
    types of, 464–66
socioeconomic status (SES), audience analysis for, 83–84
sound recordings
    audio clips, 291–92
    Chicago-style documentation, 516
    in PowerPoint, 311, 313
source, in communication process, 13
sources
    research material. See research
    source qualifiers, 168
    source reliability, 167–68
    of support. See supporting materials
spatial organizational pattern, 195–96
speaker-audience interactive online presentations, 440–41
speaking outline, 211–18
    body of speech, 213–15
    conclusion, 215
    delivery cues, 211
    examples of, 212–15
    purpose of, 20, 202
specialized encyclopedias, 138

specialized search engines, 158–59
special occasion speeches, 406–22
    acceptance speech, 409–11
    after-dinner speech, 413–14
    agenda-setting speeches, 407, 414
    eulogies, 412–13
    examples of, 417–22, 495–501
    features of, 99
    functions of, 406–7
    inspiration, speeches of, 414–16
    introduction, speeches of, 407–9
    presentation, speeches of, 410–11
    toasts/roasts, 411–12
specific case, 353–54
specific purpose, of speech, 16, 108–9
speech codes, 64–65
speech(es)
    informative speech, 329–49
    online databases of, 140
    parts of, 19–20
    persuasive speech, 350–405
    special occasion speeches, 406–22
speech evaluations, 54–56
    benefits of, 12, 15, 44
    compassionate criticism, 55
    peer evaluation forms, 56
    during practice sessions, 44
speech preparation, 17–28
    audience analysis, 17, 77–95
    audience-centered approach, 58
    conclusion of speech, 233–37
    delivery, practicing, 22
    introduction, 225–32
    language use, 238–50
    main point, developing, 19
    organizational patterns, 194–201
    outline of speech, 20, 202–18
    presentation aids, choosing, 21
    purpose, determining, 18
    research, 134–74
    supporting materials, 19, 124–51
    thesis statement, 18, 109–13
    topic selection for, 17, 96–113
staff reports, 475–76
Stahl, Leslie, 363
Stalin, Joseph, 262
statistics, 139–44
    averages, 130–31
    credibility, assessing, 131–32, 144
    ethical factors, 131–32
    frequencies, 130
    in introduction, 228
    oral citation for, 172–73
    percentages, 130
    presenting in context, 131–32
    reliability/validity, 131–32

Stella, Frank D., 408
stereotypes
    avoiding in language use, 246–48
    defined, 63
    gender, 84–85
    versus respect of speaker, 63–64
stories
    in conclusion, 236
    in introduction, 226–27
    oral citation for, 173
    in speeches of inspiration, 415
    as supporting material, 127–28
students, and communication skills,
        7
style
    in canons of rhetoric, 10, 11
    language use, 238
subject directories, Internet, 159–60
subordinate points, in outline of
        speech, 20
subordination, and coherence, 188
substantive warrants, 374
summary
    internal, as transition, 191, 193
    transitions for, 189
summary, citing
    note taking, 147, 151
    speech excerpt containing, 151
supporting materials, 124–51
    examples, 125–26
    facts, 129
    functions of, 124
    oral citation for, 172–73
    oral descriptions, 134–35
    reliability/credibility of, 131–33
    statistics, 139–44
    stories/narratives, 127–28
    testimony, 128
    types of, 19
    variety of, using, 124
    See also research
supporting points, 185–87
    journalists' questions, checking with,
        185
    and purpose of speech, 185
    transitions among, 190–91
surveys
    audience analysis, 90–92
    research, 143–44
Suter, Sue, 236
syllogism, 353–54
symposium, 510
synchronous communication, 438
synonyms
    defined, 41
    definition by, 335

T

tables, 289
  in PowerPoint, 311, 312
tag questions, 246
talking heads, 274, 437
Tannen, Deborah, 246
target audience
  identifying, 82–85
  and persuasive speech, 380
task roles, 446–47
Taylor, Anita, 200
team presentations, 450–52, 454–55
technical presentations
  guidelines for, 462
  types of, 462–63
TelePromTer, 259
television appearances, 507–8
television programs, documenting, oral
    citation for, 172
terminal values, 59–60
testimony
  oral citation for, 172–73
  as supporting material, 128
text animations, PowerPoint, 316
thesaurus, 41
thesis statement, 109–13
  defined, 18
  functions of, 109–13
  and main points, 183–85
  and organizational patterns, 195–99
  and preparing speech, 111–12
  and purpose of speech, 111
  relevance, creating, 113
  restated in conclusion, 112
thinking, thought/speech differential, 54
Thomas, David C., 16
tilde (~), in Web address, 156
time factors
  length of presentation, examples of, 93
  time orientation of culture, 87
  timing speech, 96, 277
title, in working outline, 205
toasts, 411–12
topical arrangement pattern
  features of, 198–99
  informative speech, 338–39
topic map, 102
topic of speech
  choosing. *See* topic selection
  in conclusion, 234–35
  in introduction, 229–30
topic selection, 17, 96–113
  classroom speech, 104–5
  ethical factors, 110

Internet directories for, 102–3
  narrowing topic, 104–5, 108
  and purpose of speech, 99–101,
    104–5
  topic mapping, 102
  topics to avoid, 101
  word association, 101–2
town hall meetings, 510
trait anxiety, 40
transition effects, PowerPoint, 316
transitions, 189–93
  full-sentence, 190
  functions of, 189, 189–90
  as guide for listener, 192–93
  listening for, 51–52
  among main points, 51–52,
    190
  previews/summaries as, 191
  restate-forecast form, 190
  rhetorical questions as, 190, 193
  signposts as, 190–91
  small group presentations, 451
  in speaking outline, 213–14
  among supporting points, 190–91
  in working outline, 207–9
triads, 250
trivial topics, 101
trustworthiness of speaker, 63, 363
truth, reckless disregard for, 61
Tufte, Edward, 299
Turner, Mark, 127
Twain, Mark, 413
typeface, 300–302

U

uncertainty avoidance, 87
understatement, 244
unity of speech, 188
universal values, 89
U.S. Government Printing Office (GPO),
  137–38

V

validity
  of generalizations, 53
  of statistics, 132
values, 58–59
  audience analysis, 78–79
  claim of, 368–69, 379
  core values, 78–79, 369
  cultural differences, 78–79, 89, 369
  defined, 58, 78
  instrumental/terminal, 59–60
  sharing by speaker, 58–59

universal values, 89
value-dimensions model, 86–87
verbs, active versus passive voice, 245
video clips
   Chicago style documentation, 516
   in PowerPoint, 311–13
   as presentation aid, 291–92
video presentations, online, 442
videotaping, practice speeches, 276–77
Villarreal, Elpidio, 234–35, 355
virtual groups, 446
virtual libraries, 152–54
virtual meetings. *See* online presentations
visual aids. *See* presentation aids
visual channel, 271
visualization
   in motivated sequence pattern, 385
   and practicing speech, 45
   public speaking anxiety management, 42
visual learners, 337–38
vocal effectiveness. *See* voice
voice, 264–70
   articulation, 268–69
   pauses, 266–67
   pitch, 264–65
   pronunciation, 268–69
   rate of speaking, 266–67
   vocal fillers, 266
   vocal variety, 267–68
   volume, 264
voice (verbs), active versus passive, 245
volume, voice, 264

W

Wahlberg, John, 64–65
warrants, 372–76
   by analogy, 375–76
   authoritative, 373–74
   by cause, 374–75
   and claims/evidence, 366–68
   defined, 366
   and external evidence, 372
   motivational, 373
   by sign, 375
   substantive, 374
Webinars, 441, 444
Weblogs. *See* blogs
Web sites
   civic engagement sites, 9
   classical rhetoric sites, 10
   credibility, evaluating, 137, 156–57
   cross-national surveys, 88
   note taking from, 165

oral citation for, 169
   paid placement, 161
   pronunciation guide, 47
   See also Internet
Web sites, documenting
   APA style, 519
   CBE/CSE style, 546
   Chicago-style, 515
   IEEE style, 529
   information to include, 163–65
   MLA style, 523–24
   plagiarism, avoiding, 68
Weissberg, Robert, 260
wholesale plagiarism, 66
Wikileaks, 332
Wilders, Geert, 64
Wilson, Joe, 14
Wilson, Phil, 243
Winans, James Albert, 257
Winfrey, Oprah, 236
Wonder Wheel, Google, 103
word association, for speech topics, 101–2
word use. *See* language use
working outline, 204–10
   body of speech, 207–9
   conclusion, 210
   example of, 206–10
   introduction, 205, 206–7
   purpose of, 20, 202
   source credit, listing, 205
   title in, 205
   transitions in, 207–9
   Works Cited/Works Consulted, 210
Works Cited
   examples, 343, 348–49, 392–93, 400, 405
   in working outline, 210
Works Consulted, 205
worksheets, PowerPoint, 311–12
World Values Survey, 88
World Wide Web. *See* Internet
written language, compared to spoken language, 15, 238–39
WWW Virtual Library, 153

Y

Yahoo! Directory, 159
YouTube, 312, 442, 444

Z

Zoho Show, 304

ESL SPEAKER'S NOTES

Identifying Linguistic Issues as You Practice Your Speech   22
Confidence and Culture: When English Isn't Your First
    Language   41
Learning by Listening   47
Comparing Cultural Values   89
Broaden Your Listeners' Perspectives   128
Avoiding the Pitfalls of Manuscript Delivery   260
Vocal Variety and the Non-Native Speaker   267
Steps to Counteract Problems in Being Understood   473

ETHICALLY SPEAKING

The Responsibilities of Listening in the Public Arena   49
Speech Codes on Campus: Protection or Censorship?   64
Ethical Considerations in Selecting a Topic and Purpose   110
Evaluating the Validity of the Statistics You Cite   132
Researching Your Speech in an Ethical Manner   147
A Tool for Good and Evil   262
Persuasive Speeches Respect Audience Choices   351
Using Emotions Ethically   356
Engaging in Arguments in the Public Arena   366
Tailor Your Message to the Audience and Occasion   416
Code of Ethics for Professional Communicators   478

A CULTURAL PERSPECTIVE

Helping Diverse Audiences Understand You   51
Comparing Cultural Values   62
Cross-National Surveys   88
Discovering Diversity in Reference Works   139
Arrangement Formats and Audience Diversity   201
Humor and Culture: When the Jokes Fall Flat   231
Adapting Your Language to Diverse Audiences   247
Using Dialect (Language Variation) with Care   269
Nonverbal Communication Patterns in Different Cultures   275
Addressing Culture in the Persuasive Speech   369

CITING SOURCES

Chicago Documentation   513
APA Documentation   517
MLA Documentation   521
CBE/CSE Documentation   526
IEEE Documentation   529

CHECKLISTS

GETTING STARTED WITH CONFIDENCE

Record the Speech to Bolster Confidence 22
Self-Assessment: My First Speech 23

PUBLIC SPEAKING BASICS

Recognizing and Overcoming Your Underlying Fears about
Public Speaking 38
Preparing to Speak with Confidence 45
Dealing with Distractions during Delivery of a Speech 49
Use the Thought/Speech Differential to Listen Critically 54
Self-Assessment: Identifying Values 60
Steps to Avoid Plagiarism 68
Self-Assessment: An Ethical Inventory 69

AUDIENCE ANALYSIS AND TOPIC SELECTION

Respond to the Audience as You Speak 81
Analyzing the Speech Situation 94
Reviewing Your Speech in Light of Audience Demographics 95
Identifying Your General Speech Purpose 99
Criteria for Selecting a Topic 103
Narrowing Your Topic 108
Formulating the Thesis Statement 112

SUPPORTING THE SPEECH

Selecting the Right Example or Story 128
Evaluating the Credibility of Testimony 129
Self-Assessment: Using Statistics in Your Speech:
An Ethical Inventory 133
Making an Inventory of Your Research Needs 135
Finding Speeches Online 140
Preparing for the Interview 143
Creating a Bibliography 145
Is My Online Research Effective? 158
Choosing between a Subject (Web) Directory and a Search
Engine 160
Identifying Paid Listings in Search Results 161
Documenting Internet Sources 163
Offering Key Source Information 167

ORGANIZING AND OUTLINING

Self-Assessment: Do the Speech Points Illustrate or Prove
the Thesis? 183
Do the Speech Points Reflect Unity, Coherence, and
Balance? 189
Self-Assessment: Using Transitions 191
Choosing an Organizational Pattern 194
Evaluating Organizational Patterns 201
Steps in Creating a Working Outline 206
Tips on Using Notecards or Sheets of Paper 212
Steps in Creating a Speaking Outline 212

INTRODUCTIONS, CONCLUSIONS AND LANGUAGE

Guidelines for Preparing the Introduction 226
Self-Assessment: Using Humor Appropriately 228
Self-Assessment: How Effective Is Your Introduction? 232
Guidelines for Preparing the Conclusion 233
Self-Assessment: How Effective Is Your Conclusion? 237
Personalizing Your Speech with Personal Pronouns 241
Self-Assessment: Does Your Speech Incorporate Effective
Oral Style? 241
Is Your Speech Language Concrete? 242
Self-Assessment: Does Your Language Build Trust and
Credibility? 248

VOCAL AND NONVERBAL DELIVERY

Speaking Off-the-Cuff: Preparing for the Impromptu
Speech 261
Ready for the Call: Preparing for the Extemporaneous
Speech 263
Tips on Using a Microphone 265
Self-Assessment: Practice Check for Vocal
Effectiveness 268
Self-Assessment: Tips for Using Effective Facial
Expressions 273
Tips for Effective Gesturing 274
Broad Dress Code Guidelines 274
Practicing Your Speech 278

PRESENTATION AIDS

Tips for Using Props and Models Effectively 287
Tips for Creating Effective Pictograms 290
Tips for Creating Effective Line, Bar, and Pie Graphs 291
Tips on Incorporating Audio and Video into Your
Presentation 292
Incorporating Presentation Aids into Your Speech 293
Applying the Principles of Simplicity and Continuity 300
Tips for Using Typefaces, Fonts, and Sizes Effectively 301
Preventive Maintenance: Avoiding PowerPoint Technical
Glitches 305
Selecting Slide Layouts and Themes in PowerPoint 307
Inserting Tables and Worksheets into PowerPoint 312
Tips for Successfully Using PowerPoint Presentations in
Your Speech 316

FORMS OF SPEECHES

Help Listeners Follow Along 331
Strategies for Explaining Complex Information 337
Guidelines for Clearly Communicating Your Informative
Message 339
Conditions for Choosing a Persuasive Purpose 350
Displaying Ethos in the Persuasive Speech 358
Self-Assessment: Tips for Increasing Speaker
Credibility 363
Testing the Strength of Your Evidence 372
Making Effective Use of Reasoning by Cause 375
Techniques for Addressing Competing Arguments 376
Organizing a Claim of Policy 383
Steps in the Motivated Sequence 385
Guidelines for Introducing Other Speakers 409
Guidelines for Delivering Speeches of Acceptance 410
Tips for Delivering Effective Eulogies 413
Delivering a Successful Speech of Inspiration 416

SPEAKING BEYOND THE SPEECH CLASSROOM

Tools for Developing Online Presentations 437
Creating a Podcast 443
Steps in Preparing an Online Presentation 445
Guidelines for Setting Group Goals 449
Team Presentation Tips 452
Tips for Winning a Debate 456
Tips on Presenting to a Mixed Audience 458
Self-Assessment: Evaluating Your Original Research
Presentation 460
Tips for Preparing Successful Scientific Presentations 461
Applying Monroe's Motivated Sequence in a Sales
Presentation 474
Preparing a Proposal 475

Sample Speeches

SPEECHES OF INTRODUCTION

WEB The Dance of Life,* Ashley White 24

Past, Present, and Future, Lisa Tran 26

SPEECH OF DEMONSTRATION

An Ounce of Prevention Keeps the Germs Away,
Christie Collins 340

INFORMATIVE SPEECHES

Staying Ahead of Spyware, John Coulter 215

WEB John Kanzius and the Quest to Cure Cancer,*
David Kruckenberg 344

The History and Sport of Mountain Biking,*
Zachary Dominque 483

PERSUASIVE SPEECHES

WEB Emergency in the Emergency Room,* Lisa Roth 388

Preventing Cyberbullying,* Una Chua 393

WEB The Importance of Community Engagement and Volunteerism,*
Stephanie Poplin 401

Remarks at a Human Trafficking Symposium,
W. Ralph Basham 489

SPECIAL OCCASION SPEECHES

"Love the Process": A Soccer Star's Philosophy of Life,*
Yael Averbuch 417

2008 Harvard University Commencement Address,
J. K. Rowling 495

*In addition to traditional textual annotations, these speeches feature "visual annotations" — photographs of speakers delivering their presentations.